Perspectives from *Historical Archaeology*

Public Archaeology, From Outreach and Education to Critique and Global Justice

Compiled by
Christopher Matthews and Carol McDavid

No. 8

SOCIETY *for* HISTORICAL ARCHAEOLOGY

A Society for Historical Archaeology Publication

13017 Wisteria Drive #395
Germantown, MD 20874, U.S.A.

Compiled with an introduction by:

Christopher N. Matthews
Department of Anthropology
Montclair State University
1 Normal Avenue
Montclair, NJ 07043
matthewsc@montclair.edu

Carol McDavid, Ph.D.
Executive Director, Community Archaeology Research Institute, Inc.
1638 Branard
Houston, TX 77006
mcdavid@publicarchaeology.org

Cover: Mrs. Betty Welch, Corresponding Secretary of the Society for the Preservation of Weeksville and Bedford-Stuyvesant History sits with Project Weeksville staff member Larry Poole at outdoor annual exhibit of Bedford-Stuyvesant artists held at Fulton Park. — 1971 After the Report What? The Uses of Historical Archaeology, A Planner's View. *Historical Archaeology* 5:49-61

www.sha.org

Perspectives from Historical Archaeology is a reader series providing collected articles from the journal of the Society for Historical Archaeology (SHA). Published since 1967, <u>Historical Archaeology</u> is the oldest North American scholarly publication on the archaeology of sites and materials from the historic past, and one of the world's premier publications on this subject. Each volume in the *Perspectives* series is developed on either a subject or regional basis by a compiler, who selects the articles for inclusion and their order. The compilers also provide an introduction that presents an overview of the substantive work on that topic. *Perspectives* volumes offer non-archaeologists a convenient source for important publications on a subject or a region; an excellent resource for students interested in developing a specialization in a specific topic or area; as well as a convenient reference for archaeologists with an interest in the material.

The *Perspectives* series is managed by the SHA's Co-Publications Editor and is published through the SHA's Print-On-Demand Press. Individuals interested in compiling a volume for publication through this series are encouraged to contact the Series Editors:

Annalies Corbin, PhD
Co-Publications Editor, SHA
The PAST Foundation
1003 Kinnear Road
Columbus, OH 43212
annalies@pastfoundation.org

J. W. Joseph, PhD, RPA
Perspectives Series Co-Editor, SHA
New South Associates, Inc.
6150 East Ponce de Leon Avenue
Stone Mountain, GA 30083
jwjoseph@newsouthassoc.com

Formed in 1967, the SHA is the largest scholarly group concerned with the archaeology of the modern world (A.D. 1400-present). The main focus of the society is the era since the beginning of European exploration. SHA promotes scholarly research and the dissemination of knowledge concerning historical archaeology. The society is specifically concerned with the identification, excavation, interpretation, and conservation of sites and materials on land and underwater. Geographically the society emphasizes the New World, but also includes European exploration and settlement in Africa, Asia, and Oceania.

To learn more about the SHA and historical archaeology, visit www.sha.org.

Contents

Part III: African American Archaeology and the Public

Part IV: Archaeology, Heritage, and Justice

Carol McDavid
Christopher Matthews

Public Archaeology in the Society for Historical Archaeology: From Outreach and Education to Critique and Global Justice

We will do two things in this introductory essay. First, we describe the framework and methods that we used to select the papers for this reader. Second, using this same framework we review how public archaeology, as a subfield of archaeological practice, has evolved over the past few decades. This review focuses on the development of public archaeology within the publications of the Society for Historical Archaeology, in particular, the journal *Historical Archaeology* and the quarterly SHA Newsletter. It is outside our scope here to examine the trends, approaches, theories, research questions, and debates in public archaeology that have emerged in other discourses (for example, Americanist prehistoric archaeology or global heritage movements). However, we will do so to the extent that they have either appeared (or not) in the context of historical archaeology scholarship (see Little 2009b for a useful review).

To begin we offer a provisional definition for the term "public archaeology", which comes with an important caveat: a fixed, timeless definition of public archaeology is neither possible nor desirable. This is because public archaeology, as a contemporary social practice, is extremely context-dependent, especially when disciplinary, ideological, political, or other cleavages constrain what is desirable or possible. For example, the public archaeology that is possible in some areas of the Middle East is very different from what archaeologists should or could perform in the grassy villages of England, the communities of "disappeared" in South America, the urban centers of the United States, or anywhere else. Even so, the papers here demonstrate a remarkable heterogeneity of motivations and approaches within the limits of (mostly) Americanist historical archaeology. In this introduction, we describe how public archaeology has developed within that particular disciplinary context, using the following working definition:

Public archaeology is any endeavor in which archaeologists interact with the public, and any research (practical or theoretical) that examines or analyses the public dimensions of doing archaeology.

Viewed in this way, public archaeology includes practices described by individual archaeologists as outreach, archaeology education, tourism, engagement, Cultural Resource Management (CRM), collaboration, public memory, activist archaeology, heritage, co-creation, and the public aspects of "critical archaeology". Our use of the term here refers to this broad scope, although we will discuss other definitional trends that have emerged over the past several decades.

Public Archaeology and the SHA

To understand public archaeology practices within the SHA and its publications, we collected two types of data. First, we obtained input from several senior members of the field, using both email interviews and conversations. Although the collection process for this anecdotal data was non-systematic and limited, it helped to cover gaps in our own experience and provided important first-hand knowledge from people with long memories and rich insights. Second, we conducted a systematic survey of both journal and newsletter content, using the SHA's online "Publications Explorer" search engine. Our analysis of all this data drew on our individual experiences as active society members and formed the basis of this volume and this introduction.

Informal Email Interviews: Early Public Historical Archaeology

In our email interviews, we first told respondents what we meant by the term "public archaeology", framing it as described above. We then asked three primary questions and exchanged follow-up emails to explore further:

1. Did you see either the journal or the newsletter as a place to publish writing about your work with the public – that is, "public archaeology" in the broader sense? If so, or if not, why?
2. Do you recall the early discussions about public archaeology, within the society?
3. Would you be able to describe any discussions connected to public archaeology that have proven to be formative in how the SHA developed?

Detailed responses came in from 10 people, including several ex-presidents of SHA and at least one person who was present at the founding meeting in 1967 (Jelks

1993). Here we refer to the information they provided (with our thanks) as "personal communications". These responses made it clear that, from the beginning days of historical archaeology, many of the discipline's founders had a strong and active commitment to sharing their work with the public, and, in particular, to the value of archaeology education. Although education and outreach are not the only forms of public archaeology covered by the definition proposed above, they are still dominant and have been important for decades (Frost 2004).

For example, Stanley South worked regularly with the public, even as early as the 1950s while he was with the North Carolina Historic Sites program (J. Joseph pers. comm.). Likewise, John L. Cotter and J.C. ""Pinky" Harrington were also early advocates of sharing findings with the public. Cotter's work with the National Park Service (NPS) is well known, and much of it included leading tours, talking to public groups, and otherwise being "engaged" (J. Joseph pers. comm., E. Jelks pers. comm.). Cotter also wrote a booklet for the American Revolution Bicentennial Commission for use in public schools that the Commission and other partner organizations widely distributed to school boards across the country (Cotter 1974). Nan Rothschild (pers. comm.) noted that the Professional Archaeologists of New York City produced a public brochure on archaeology (probably in the mid-1980s), and did "an exhibit at the Museum of the City of New York which was meant as an educational/outreach device."

Ivor Noël Hume was also an active proponent of public engagement. His keynote address at the SHA meetings in 1973 focused specifically on the topic, and the journal published a transcript included here (Hume 1973). Other historical archaeologists who included substantive public engagement in their early projects were Pam Cressey at Alexandria Archaeology and Elizabeth Comer at the Baltimore Center for Urban Archaeology (J. Joseph pers. comm., P. Cressey pers. comm.). Doug Scott (pers. comm.) noted that public engagement was common in many early projects. He recalled that in the 1970s at Fort Larned in Kansas:

> We had a public entrance so the visitors could see the lab in operation and someone was designated to talk to the visitors and answer questions. The same was true with our excavations that were in publically accessible and safe areas. I continued doing this type of outreach in other places, and we had a very formal process for our work at Little Bighorn in the 1980s.

James Deetz provides another notable example, as several respondents mentioned. We learned that local schoolchildren helped to excavate the Parting Ways site, and that the project itself was initiated at the behest of a local African American community (M. Brown pers. comm.; E. Deetz pers. comm.). Deetz worked actively with various communities (including educators) throughout his career – for example, bringing Native groups into Plimoth Plantation programming, and running NEH-funded summer institutes for high school educators during his Flowerdew Hundred Plantation research (P. Jeppson pers. comm.). The Flowerdew research, funded by various sources, involved many summers of field research that was open to students as a field school and to the public as a field experience.

The projects that Bert Salwen and Sarah Bridges directed at the Weeksville site in New York City, as well as Robert Schuyler's work at Sandy Ground on Staten Island, also began at the request of African American communities (T. Singleton pers. comm.). We did find one publication that described the public aspects of the Weeksville work (Maynard 1992), and an SHA conference paper discussed it (Scott 2009). Another conference paper described Schuyler's work with the African American community at Sandy Ground (Schuyler 1974). Also of note is the Archaeology in Annapolis program, which began in 1981 as a partnership between Mark Leone at the University of Maryland and the Historic Annapolis Foundation, and provided tours of intentionally public-access investigations. We will consider the still-ongoing role of Leone's critical archaeology with respect to public archaeology later in this essay.

These are but a few examples of the mostly unheralded and unpublished public archaeology that was common in the field early on, which countless historical archaeologists over the decades since have continued to practice. Building upon these early foundations, "public archaeology" slowly emerged as a legitimate subfield of archaeology practice within the broad scope noted above. It is now analyzed and published as scholarship, in the pages of *Historical Archaeology* and elsewhere, including a number of specialty journals. Later we will draw further on these interviews to illustrate other points.

Survey of SHA Publications: Search Data

After collecting this anecdotal interview data, we examined the SHA's written output of public archaeology writing in order to select the articles that appear here and to create Appendix A (Newsletters) and Appendix B (Journals). We describe our search methods in more detail below.

Method Used: Newsletters and Underwater Proceedings (Appendix A)

We searched for individual occurrences of the terms "public", "public archaeology", or "public education" in all SHA newsletters and underwater proceedings prior to 1998. For each occurrence, we decided whether the term was being used in the sense we defined above, and did not tally irrelevant instances– for example, "publication" and "public accountant". We also culled instances where the search term was mentioned only briefly, used in an unrelated context (such as routine listings of projects underway), or mentioned only in the regular column of the Public Education (PEC) or Public Education and Interpretation Committee (PEIC). If column content went beyond routine announcements, however, we listed it. We then categorized entries as "Column/other", or "Conference Proceedings or Conference Symposium".

Method Used: The SHA Journal, Historical Archaeology (Appendix B)

We searched all past issues of Historical Archaeology using the following search terms: public, public archaeology, outreach, education, public education, heritage, tourism, collaboration, memory, and engagement. Our search was detailed and systematic; we did not rely only on keywords but also searched the texts themselves for instances of the above words. Early on we also included the term "public interpretation" in our searches, but we eliminated that term because the other terms located the same articles.

After examining each journal occurrence of the terms above for relevance (as we did for newsletters), we annotated the listing with key text excerpts. Often the excerpt is very brief because we listed any instance in which an author discussed his or her public work, or the public impacts of that work – again, using the broad definition noted above. We then assigned all entries to one of the following categories:

- Substantively about public archaeology.
- Mentions public archaeology in meaningful way, but as a small part of larger article.
- Mentions public archaeology very briefly.
- Closely related to public archaeology concerns, but not specifically about public archaeology.

We did not include papers including the term "public archaeology" when authors were reporting on archaeological data produced by CRM projects, unless the article discussed the public aspects of the work. Therefore, we only listed articles on CRM as a public policy funded (or driven) enterprise, or when it reported on the public aspects of the project (even if briefly).

This reader only includes papers that discussed public archaeology in a substantive way, or were representative of a general theme or idea related to public archaeology. However, each Appendix lists all of the articles identified in our systematic searches. Although there may be disagreements with our curatorial choices, we believe that these exhaustive Appendix listings will illustrate the scope of coverage and the broad trends we will describe shortly. Even with the systematic and rather painstaking methods and the large number of search terms we used, there may be inadvertent omissions.

Trends and Timelines: Analysis and Discussion

We first wanted to understand how public archaeology started to appear in SHA publications – that is, when were the public archaeology practices described above, already part of what many historical archaeologists were "doing", also seen as worthy of discussing in print? The following table notes the first time that each search term appeared in either the newsletter or the journal in any substantive way. Again, if the usage was outside the scope of our intended coverage we omitted it from consideration.

We then tallied the number of public archaeology papers (using the definition and search terms described above) that appeared in the journal, by decade.

As Table 2 makes clear, despite active participation in public archaeology as a practice, (and even considering the weighting of full versus truncated decades and the physical growth of the journal), historical archaeologists did not publish their public archaeology work with any regularity in *Historical Archaeology* until after 1997. This was true in part because for a long period, as several of our interview respondents mentioned, the journal's editorial policy discouraged public archaeology submissions – the newsletter was seen as the more appropriate venue. Even so, we found 15 articles in *Historical Archaeology* that discussed public archaeology in a substantive way prior to 1997, and several are included here (South 1969; Fleming 1971; Noël Hume 1973; Potter 1992). We would argue that Potter's 1992 article – and arguably the entire issue it was part of – was seminal in setting the stage for much of the public archaeology work that followed later in the decade. The text excerpts in both Appendices describe these pieces in more detail.

Ronald L. Fleming wrote another early public archaeology paper in 1971, which discussed, in some detail, how archaeologists (and historians) should

Search Term	First Mention
Public Archaeology	1980 (from 1967-1991)
Public Education (and Education)	1988 (most instances concerned the SHA committees, the Public Education Committee [PEC] and the Public Education and Interpretation Committee [PEIC]
Public (stand-alone term) Tourism Collaboration	1992 1992 1992
Engagement Public Outreach	1997 1997 (one occurrence)
Memory (as historical memory)	1998
Heritage	2003

TABLE 1: First mentions of search terms.

have "bolder" roles in public life (Fleming 1971). He also described how the local community initiated the aforementioned Weeksville project, which had a role in dismantling stereotypes about the Bedford-Stuyvesant community and its history. In addition, there was a short but widely-read (and cited) entry in the "research note" section of the journal by Parker B. Potter (Potter 1991b) entitled "What is the Use of Plantation Archaeology?", to which Larry McKee responded in another journal a few years later (McKee 1994).

After 1992, no more articles dealing substantively with public archaeology appeared until 1997, when the journal published a thematic issue devoted to public participation in the archaeology of African American sites (McDavid and Babson 1997; Joseph pers. comm., Leone pers. comm.) Although contributions to this issue appear often in literature of African American archaeology and public archaeology (several are in this collection), this issue exemplified another shift in SHA discourse as it concerned the public. For this particular issue, the editors asked for and received special permission for the "judicious" use of the first person

Time Span	Number of Articles
1967-1969	2
1970-1979	3
1980-1989	1
1990-1999	37 (post-1997: 28)
2000-2009	59
2010-2014	51
Total	**153**

TABLE 2: Newsletter and journal public archaeology publications by decade, all categories.

(McDavid pers. comm.), because the journal prohibited it at the time. This move reflected changes elsewhere in the Society (and, arguably, the larger discipline, but it is outside our scope here to explore those). Debate about the prohibition of first person pronouns had begun in the early 1990's in the society's newsletter (Potter 1991a:9-10; Beaudry 1992:17-18), as some scholars saw it as an antithesis to any serious consideration of archaeology as a publicly relevant practice. The disciplinary discussion continued in Spring 1993, when a panel, including Potter and others, discussed issues of voice, reflexivity, and objectivity at the "Radical Archaeologists Talking Shop" conference at the University of Massachusetts, Amherst (John McCarthy pers. comm.).

By the late 1990s public archaeology was starting to appear in the broader archaeology literature as edited volumes (e.g., Jameson 1997), but the journal literature was still scant. A few of our interview respondents noted that public archaeology was still seen as an ancillary (if desirable) activity that was outside the primary business (or reward system) of scholarly archaeological research. It simply did not occur to people to publish it as scholarship (Rothschild pers. comm., Little pers. comm.).

To be fair, the SHA journal was not the only professional journal with a reluctance to publish public archaeology as serious archaeological scholarship. In 1998, the editor of the flagship publication of the Society for American Archaeology, *American Antiquity*, published a passionate appeal for more submissions about public archaeology – in particular, archaeology education writing (Goldstein 1998:529). Even though her appeal clearly supported the value of public work (even arguing that academic departments should consider it when making tenure and promotion decisions), it was limited in some key respects, as is evident from the quotation below:

*I would like to see a series of articles focused on the theoretical and intellectual contributions of those who write for the general or specific publics ... a series of critical reviews and evaluations of the public education and archaeology literature. I think the key is, however, that **these reviews and evaluations should be done not by those who "do" public education but rather by more traditional, archaeological scholars, well-known within the discipline.** If American Antiquity began to publish such reviews and analyses on a semi-regular basis, the journal could incorporate the public education literature into a serious scholarly discussion and also provide a way for some of this literature to be evaluated in tenure and promotion considerations ... I am suggesting that unless the discipline begins to consider these contributions as important and serious contributions to knowledge, such work will never be taken seriously by the profession (Goldstein 1998:529, emphasis added).*

We do not criticize the limitation emphasized in Goldstein's plea -- it was aimed at those who were still "unconverted" (indeed, to have public archaeology reviewed by "traditional archaeological scholars" would have provided useful validation). It is clear, however, that although many archaeologists during that period supported the idea of doing public archaeology (especially when framed as archaeology education), few publications published it as archaeology scholarship.

Changing Definitions of Public Archaeology

We will now examine some broad definitional trends in public archaeology since the first SHA journal appeared in 1967. We realize that many readers will be aware of much of this disciplinary history (Little 2012), and accept that some will have a different opinion about it than we do. Although this summary focuses mainly on Americanist work, we reference work from broader contexts as needed.

"Public Archaeology" as CRM

For many years, the definition of public archaeology, especially in the United States, referred specifically to archaeology conducted as a response to public laws, regulations, or policies – many forms of which have been enacted at national, state, and local levels for over a century. These forms of archaeology are often referred to as Cultural Resource Management (CRM), although CRM also includes "cultural landscapes, archaeological sites, historical records, social institutions, expressive cultures, old buildings, religious beliefs and practices, industrial heritage, folklife, artifacts [and] spiritual places" (King 2002:1). One of the earliest appearances of the term "public archaeology" was in 1972 (McGimsey 1972) in an important early book about CRM. At that point the word "public" referred to both the rationale driving the work (that is, laws enacted in response to political initiatives with public support) and to the way that it was and is regulated and reviewed by public agencies funded by public dollars (see Dickens and Bowen 1980).

In our view, there are two major types of CRM archaeological practice, and the distinction is important in terms of how, and how much, "the public" is meaningfully involved in the work. One type is usually conducted by for-profit private firms – that is, "contract" or commercial archaeology, often referred to as "compliance" archaeology. This work began in earnest in the early to mid-1970s, driven largely by the National Historic Preservation Act of 1966 (Advisory Council on Historic Preservation 2002). Private-sector firms are hired by both commercial clients and public agencies (such as public transportation and utility authorities) to conduct archaeology before construction takes place on public land or with public funds or permits. Despite the widespread use of the term "public archaeology" to categorize it, "the public" at large is seldom directly involved in this type of work. Certain representatives of public agencies and entities, such as municipal and indigenous governments, do intersect with the process at various points. Their participation is, however, highly regulated and formalized, with certain people included as "interested parties" and others excluded from decision-making. Publics are also involved indirectly, in the sense that public funds pay for the work of state historic preservation officers and local preservation specialists who review commercial projects.

Despite these types of involvements, in this commercial realm there is typically little public engagement with the archaeological process itself – such as formulating research questions, participating in archaeological excavation, or helping to interpret archaeological findings (although exceptions are noted below). Commercial clients seldom fund public engagement (or must be convinced to do so) and reviewing agencies often do not require it. Indeed, some archaeological clients (property developers and some agencies) often discourage (or prohibit) contract archaeologists from engaging with "the public" at all, even when the work itself is a matter of public record or funded by the public purse.

Despite this, many commercial archaeology firms do conduct public outreach (site tours, public talks, and special publications for public readerships, as well as oral history and other forms of engagement), and this is often because they see such work as an ethical obligation (e.g., Roberts 1984; Roberts and McCarthy 1995; Maynard 1992; McCarthy 1996, 2001; Crist and Roberts 1996; Green et al. 1997; Stewart and Praetzellis 1997; Praetzellis et al. 2007; Boyd et al. 2011; Matternes and Coco 2012). In addition, some commercial firms have created non-profit "arms" that focus on engagement and outreach (SRI Foundation N.D.).

A second type of archaeological CRM is conducted by or at the behest of the public agencies – many of which are the same as those that oversee or review commercial projects. At the federal level, the National Park Service and Bureau of Land Management are two of the largest, and state-level agencies would include the State Historic Preservation Offices (SHPOs) that federal legislation mandates. These and other entities at various governmental levels conduct archaeology themselves, hire commercial firms to do archaeology for them on the public lands that they manage, and often sponsor archaeology projects with substantive public participation (see for example the President's House Project; Levin 2012). In this form of CRM, the public often has a larger role, especially with respect to site tours, outreach activities, and the like. The constellation of public agencies in the U.S. has been the locus for countless publicly engaged archaeology outreach projects for decades (a sampling includes Cressey 1980; Cressey et al. 2003; King 2006; Cressey and Vinton 2008; Bruseth et al. 2011; Wilson 2015). As noted earlier, several of those who helped to found the SHA were active in this arena (e.g. John L. Cotter). The role of the public with respect to sharing archaeological decision-making, however, is often limited.

By the 1980s, in some accounts as much as 80% of archaeology done worldwide was taking place in the for-profit CRM sector (Little 2009b:46, citing Roberts 2004:12) . Also by the mid-1980s, two new threads of public archaeology practice began to emerge. We will explore them below, noting that all still operate, along with some additional approaches that have emerged more recently. That is, the idea of "public archaeology as CRM" did not disappear, but gradually the term "public archaeology" expanded to include additional forms of practice. The development of these two new threads of public archaeology tracked alongside concurrent movements in anthropological and archaeological theory – that is, both can be seen as public archaeology versions of the varied disciplinary and epistemological critiques of processualism that were occurring during the same period. To elaborate on this point is outside the scope of this introduction, but in general we refer to the growth of post-processual, reflexive approaches as an alternative to the objectivism promoted in the so-called "new archaeology".

"Public Archaeology" as Archaeology Education and Outreach

The first new thread to emerge as "public archaeology" was archaeology education and outreach. Those who participated in this work (especially early on) tended to characterize archaeology as scientific and objective, with special tools and skills to enable a more accurate understanding of the past than other ways of knowing. Part of their effort was aimed at persuading the public of the value of scientific archaeology, while also convincing them that archaeological sites were worthy of preservation. Archaeology education was seen by many of its proponents as a way to promote or even save archaeology – or, at least, to save archaeological sites (for a recent history of archaeology education in North America, see Ellick 2016; for a longer view, see Kehoe 2012).

Theoretical biases aside, this work was quite necessary because the archaeological community, especially in the U.S., was becoming alarmed about the many archaeological sites being destroyed by widespread looting and "pot-hunting". Initially archaeology education initiatives were a response to damage at indigenous sites, but as the field of historical archaeology grew the looting of historic sites also became popular. Battlefield sites, for example, were (and are) particularly endangered, in part because of the growing popularity of amateur metal detecting (Thomas 2015). As a result, in the late 1980s archaeologists began focused, discipline-wide efforts to "educate" the non-archaeological public about the importance of saving archeological sites. This was seen as "a strategy to combat the rampant vandalism that was destroying the nation's archaeological resources" (Friedman 2000:13).

As this effort started to receive attention at the upper reaches of the discipline, archaeology education and outreach began to coalesce as a legitimate subfield of archaeology, and to be referred to as "public archaeology," although it was also referred to as "archaeology education" (e.g., Smith and Ehrenhard 1991; Smith and McManahon 1991; Smith et al. 1992; Kerber 1994). For histories, commentaries, reviews, and edited volumes see (Smardz and Smith 2000; Frost 2004; Jameson 2004 a, b; Jeppson 2012; Little 2012; Kehoe 2012; Ellick 2016).

Thus, even though the conflation of public archaeology with CRM was still common, a new definition of public archaeology as education and outreach began to take hold. Not all archaeologists participated, but many supported the idea. For example, as we searched the SHA Newsletters, we noticed that after the published slates for SHA elective positions started to include written campaign statements (about 1991), candidates often used these statements to state their support for archaeology education or public archaeology (see Scott 1991:4 for one example).

Professional archaeology societies began to institutionalize this approach to public archaeology as early as the mid-1980s by creating public education committees and other outreach initiatives. Scholars began to publish rationales to promote the effort (Gibb pers. comm.; see also McManamon 1991, 2000). Appendix A includes several items excerpted from Newsletter columns written by the public education committees that existed within the SHA. At the same time, archaeological conferences began to feature sessions on "public archaeology", most focusing on education and outreach, and three conferences focused on public concerns in the conference theme. Appendix A lists several examples of public archaeology sessions at SHA conferences from 1986-1989, and it is interesting to note the shifts in topics and terminology over time.

"Public archaeology as education" work continues to be productive and has evolved in some important ways. First, some archaeologists began to frame it as "public interpretation" instead of "public education". The interpretive profession (which informs, for example, the work of U. S. National Park Service interpreters) is a stand-alone profession with its own theory and practices, which these archaeologists drew on to forge new connections between the public and archaeology (L. Derry pers. comm.; see Jameson 1997, 2004a). The SHA recognized this in the early 1990s by changing the name of its "Public Education Committee" to the "Public Education and Interpretation Committee".

Second, archaeologists began to understand that to do educational work properly they needed to collaborate with professional educators, not just rely on archaeological training for the necessary skills (Jeppson 2000; Jeppson and Brauer 2003; Davis 2005; Franklin and Moe 2012). During this period the SHA also published a major electronic book and accompanying website devoted to archaeology outreach and education (Jameson and DuCunzo 2005).

A supportive link between archaeology education and science/social science education still exists, not least because it creates useful content that both educators and learners enjoy. Indeed, recent public and community archaeology work framed as "citizen science" have made this link even more explicit (Smith 2014; Grady et al. 2016). Citizen science enlists the public in collecting scientific data, but advocates for more active, mutually empowered contributions than are possible with simple "participation" (such as washing artifacts). It attempts to integrate non-archaeologists fully into the scientific processes of doing archaeology, and is possible when collaborations between members of the public and professional scientists are mutually empowered on some level. In any event, as discussed more below, as more reflexive, interpretive archaeological methods became more common, so did a willingness to incorporate multiple perspectives (both archaeological and public) into educational and outreach activities (Jameson 1997; McDavid and Babson 1997; Derry and Malloy 2003; Merriman 2004; Stottman 2010).

The ethos behind "public archaeology as education" work also found expression in the concept of "stewardship," which began to appear in the early 1990s (Lynott and Wylie 1995). Some archaeologists began to consciously promote the "stewardship principle" (that anyone can be an archaeological steward) as a way to encourage members of the public to join forces with them to protect and preserve sites. In one early example of this, the Texas State Historic Preservation Office (the Texas Historical Commission) created its "Texas Archaeological Stewards" program in 1984. It continues today as an active force in Texas archaeology, and similar examples exist elsewhere.

Because of its primary goals (promoting archaeology and preventing looting), it is arguable that archaeology education and outreach developed (mostly) to support archaeology's needs. This is not a bad thing, but it is why we distinguish it from a second thread of public archaeology that emerged during the same period – critical public archaeology.

"Public Archaeology" as Critical Archaeology

As noted above, most early archaeology educators promoted the value of scientific archaeology, and believed that sharing it with the public was one way to protect archaeological sites. We also noted that this view expanded through the 1990s to accept other ways of understanding (such as descendant knowledge) as legitimate. We will return to the subject of descendant engagement, but will first discuss another important thread in public archaeology that emerged concurrently with the growth of archaeology education. We refer to the public archaeology that emerged from "critical archaeology" as developed by Mark Leone, his students and others from the late 1980s onward (Leone, Potter and Shackel 1987). Based in both research and public engagement, critical archaeology embraced and expanded upon the idea that "publics" and "public interests" were an integral component of contemporary archaeological practice. An influential scholar in this movement was Parker Potter (Potter 1992, 1994). Even though Potter subsequently left the field, many of his contemporaries have come to wield considerable influence in public archaeology today. A few examples of their considerable output include Babiarz (2011), Leone et al. (2005), Little (2002, 2007b, 2009a, 2009b), Little and Shackel (2007), Matthews (2004, 2005), Mullins (2006, 2008), Palus (2001), Palus et al. (2006), Shackel (2001, 2003) and Shackel and Chambers (2004).

The premise of critical archaeology is that archaeologists cannot separate themselves from the contexts of their work in the present nor, in historical archaeology, from the fact that these present contexts descend from those they excavate and interpret. Therefore, critical archaeologists seek to understand the contemporary world by examining its origins (Handsman and Leone 1989). Embedded in this approach are the ideas that archaeology is not a politically neutral practice, and that public engagement is an essential part of successful archaeological research. Like their "archaeology education" colleagues, critical archaeologists want to share archaeological findings with the public, but for a different reason – to use those findings to understand the present (Leone et al. 1987, Davis and Gibb 1988, Gibb and Davis 1989).

In this way, they situate archaeological interpretations firmly in the present, which leads to key insight from critical archaeology: archaeologists and others can interpret any site in multiple ways, and differences in interpretations depend as much on interpreter bias as on "science" or "scientific results". Critical archaeologists

refer to these different biases (rooted in backgrounds, ideas, training, etc.) as "embedded ideologies", and everyone – even scientists – have them. The idea is to open discussions about how embedded ideologies operate in both past and present, and to challenge both publics and archaeologists to think about their own interests and biases when interpreting archeological sites or "consuming" archaeological interpretations (Potter 1989). Among other things, critical archaeologists were concerned with power, transparency, and reflection – they wanted archaeologists to consider, very carefully, their own "taken-for-granteds" and to ask their publics to do the same thing (Leone et al. 1987; Leone and Potter 1988; Palus et al. 2006).

Among the most prominent developments in critical archaeology was to connect this archaeological critique of the present with the social justice struggles of so many people and groups fighting for recognition and change in the contemporary world. This connection found especially strong footing in historical archaeology through the work of researchers in African Diaspora archaeology. Still, even in that area, the impact of public engagement was slow to develop. In our interviews, archaeologist Theresa Singleton noted that she had circulated a questionnaire on public outreach in African Diaspora archaeology projects as early as the mid-1980s. She recalled that

"...with a few notable exceptions, most archaeologists involved in African Diaspora projects had done little to communicate their results to African American communities. The most significant exception was the David Gradwohl and Nancy Osborn's study of Buxton, Iowa, a company town with a large African-American population [Gradwohl and Osborn 1990]. Through their research, they developed an ongoing relationship with the black community organizing public programs, exhibitions, teaching workshops, etc., both during the research and long after the research had been completed and published." (T. Singleton, pers. comm.).

She also noted that she "never shared the results of the survey with anyone because many of the respondents were embarrassed and apologetic that they had failed to work with black communities." Singleton also recalled a session organized for the 1991 SHA meetings by the late Carol Cowan-Ricks entitled "Is Historical Archaeology, White?" This session

"...was trying to get archaeologists to see that most of historical archaeology is a white, middle-class discourse in the way that it is written, the imagery used to illustrate African-American life or other people of color, and in its interpretations. She was trying to point out that these issues are what keep archaeology an exclusive, ivory tower discourse rather than a public discourse ... After that session there were roundtable luncheons on descendant communities, discussion in the newsletter, and the eventual publication in 1997 of Carol McDavid and David Babson's issue on the politics of African-American archaeology" (Singleton pers. comm.).

This work and that of others established a clear connection between the archaeological study of African Diaspora sites and contemporary anti-racist and vindicationist agendas addressing present injustices (Mullins 2008). They also led to several important discussions, projects, and publications on the public meaning of African Diaspora research, including McDavid and Babson's 1997 special issue of *Historical Archaeology* that Singleton mentions, which is part of the discourse explored below. We have selected some of its articles for this volume (Derry 1997; Franklin 1997; Jeppson 1997; McDavid 1997; LaRoche and Blakey 1997; Singleton 1997) and several others that further expand the discussion of public engagement with African Diaspora communities (Potter 1991b; Agbe-Davies 2010; Mullins and Jones 2011). Other examples appear in Appendix B. Most recently, some historical archaeologists have expanded these discussions (which heretofore revolved around race and racism as they related to particular archaeology projects) to initiatives designed to transform the discipline (and the SHA) to an overtly anti-racist stance (Nassaney and LaRoche 2011; Nassaney et al. 2015). We see these developments as, in part, an outcome of these earlier conversations with multiple racialized publics (LaRoche 2011, 2012).

Working with Descendants

Concurrent with these developments in historical archaeology – in both archaeology education and critical archaeology – a momentous early benchmark for discipline-wide change in the United States came with the 1990 passage of the Native American Graves Protection and Repatriation Act (NAGPRA). Another important development occurred at about the same time – the National Park Service published National Register Bulletin 38, which clarified regulations associated with

the 1966 National Historic Preservation Act (NHPA) to make it clear that "traditional cultural properties" (TCPs) were worthy of recognition on the National Register of Historic Places. Bulletin 38 defined these places as significant because of the ongoing practices of a living group or community (Parker and King 1990; King 1993).

The law and regulations were limited in many ways, but the key point is that during this period (in part because of these changes, and because of the movements described above) the meaning of the word "public" in "public archaeology" began to clearly include diverse living communities as publics. Archaeologists began to seek the opinions of living descendants, and archaeological methods and interpretations (both scientific and public) began, slowly, to reflect this inclusion, as noted above. These changes were part of a wider discipline-wide transformation in how archaeologists continued to redefine "public archaeology".

The most famous example of this transformation within Americanist historical archaeology was the New York African Burial Ground project (ABG), which took place in the early and mid-1990s. The public uproar over the treatment and interpretation of the human remains found at this site, and the public debate about how to excavate and interpret them, continued throughout the decade and established new understandings of the words "descendant", "community", and "client" within historical archaeology (Perry 1997; Perry, et al. 2006). As the cultural descendants of those buried at this New York African Burial Ground site successfully took control over how their ancestors' remains were excavated and interpreted, they also articulated the necessity of accepting descendant and other community interests as "ethical clients" (Mack and Blakey 2004:14). The ABG project had tremendous influence in archaeology, and the ethos that underpinned, drove, and emerged from these early-1990s developments is now commonplace in many historical archaeology projects across the United States.

It is worth noting that the ABG project emerged within commercial CRM archaeology, which, as noted earlier, is controlled largely by governmental, regulatory, and corporate entities, along with professional archaeologists. See LaRoche and Blakey (1997) for a description of how commercial and other agendas played out at the ABG, and LaRoche (2012) for an examination of similar developments with other projects.

By 2000, the definition of public archaeology embraced the direct relevance of the past in the present, especially regarding the interests of the varied and sometimes conflicting groups who seek to engage with archaeology. Although inequities continue to exist, by this time archaeology had begun to adopt a more proactive and purposeful willingness to support activist agendas, and much of the writing about this was situated as "public archaeology" (Little 2007a, b, 2009a; McDavid 2004, 2010; Stottman 2010; Little and Shackel 2014).

Community Archaeology and Heritage as Public Archaeology

The trends noted above emerged alongside and often overlapped two other identifiable trends, both of which were also influenced by critical archaeology and a growing willingness to bring descendant agendas into the practice of archaeology. One was referred to as "community-based" archaeology or simply community archaeology (Silverman 2011, this volume). While "communities" have long been a focus of research (with community engagement as one mechanism for archaeological education and outreach) (Cressey 1980; Derry and Malloy 2003), community archaeology more recently tends to refer to "bottom-up" collaborative process of defining and completing archaeological projects (Faulkner 2000). It rests on the premise that the interests of communities—descendent, local, or other— should influence and when possible drive the agendas of archaeological research and outreach (for examples and methodologies see Marshall 2002; Moser, et al. 2002). Community archaeology thus requires that archaeological "expertise" not be limited to scientific fieldwork and analysis, but to a broader understanding of the ways that communities are known by themselves and others (Matthews 2008). It also requires that archaeologists consider and act on their roles as defined by the community rather than by only their professionally ascribed status. In some cases an archaeologist can be asked (by a community) to be simply a researcher, whereas in others they are expected to advocate for community interests, or to deploy their access to powerful institutions on behalf of community collaborators (e.g. Castañeda and Matthews 2008; Atalay 2012; McGhee 2012; Keitumetse and Pampiri 2016).

Definitions of "community" are by no means static or easy to pin down, and they are frequently un-examined by those doing community archaeology (for one examination see Agbe-Davies 2010). Even so, a principal theme throughout community archaeology is the idea that power should be shared between archaeological professionals and community members, however defined (see Marshall 2002; Moshenska and Dhanjal 2012; Smith and Waterton 2009; Waterton and Smith 2010; Waterton and Watson 2011; McDavid et al. 2016). A common goal – although by no means a common reality – is to thread "community engagement" throughout the entire archaeological process.

In some parts of the world, a slightly different definition of community archaeology has also emerged – this is in the growth of avocational archaeology, or archaeology practiced by non-professional archaeologists, often by communities themselves. Although avocational archaeologists are very active across the United States, defining this work as "community archaeology" tends to be most prevalent in Great Britain (Thomas 2011). These projects are often field-directed by professional archaeologists, but the overall direction and work force is often community and/or amateur-driven.

One early U.S. example of community-based historical archaeology was Carol McDavid's work at Levi-Jordan Plantation in Brazoria, Texas (McDavid 1997, 2003). Through various collaborative strategies, project participants (from archaeology and outside it) built an interpretive community of descendants that represented both enslaved Africans and their owners. This inter-racial group decided together how to publicly interpret the site, and developed strategies to incorporate the contributions of all descendants – of both enslaver and enslaved. Their contributions enhanced the meaning of the rich archaeological discoveries already underway (Brown and Cooper 1990) while recognizing the multiple and sometimes bloodstained histories that community members had shared over the previous 100 years. It is worth noting that when this site's ownership shifted from a community-managed non-profit to a state agency, the nature of public/descendant involvement changed dramatically. Descendants and other community members now have limited input (formal or informal) into any aspect of site management or public interpretation (McDavid 2007).

Community archaeologists make increasing use of ethnographic methods in order to allow community interests to inform archaeological projects in new ways. In this sort of work, archaeologists attempt to understand and address community concerns such as gentrification and racial injustice, but also to understand how community members perceive and use archaeology for themselves. Chris Matthews (Matthews 2008) employed such an approach in New Orleans, Louisiana, where he undertook ethnographic research in the African American Tremé community. Community participation was varied and reflected diverse interests in the archaeology of the Tremé plantation, a site later used as a convent and a school for free girls of color. By examining distinct and conflicting historically formed racial standpoints, the project showed that that the city's "races" (white, creole, and black) each drew from and sought a distinct heritage. This discovery prompted a community-driven reminder, to project archaeologists and others, that archaeology happens now, and begins with the surface of the ground, not just those discoveries found below. Through these and other projects, the practice of community archaeology has matured in the last two decades as one important form of public archaeology, and has begun to contribute significant new interpretive avenues for historical archaeology, in both theory and practice. Some, though not all, of this work is framed as "ethnographic archaeology" or "archaeological ethnography" (Meskell 2005; Castañeda and Matthews 2008; Hamilakis and Anagnostopoulos 2009; Mortensen and Hollowell 2009).

A second development in public archaeology that can be traced to the influence of critical archaeology is a vital interest in heritage and counter narratives about the past – or put another way, the archaeologies of hidden heritage. Like communities, heritage has long been an avenue of interest and intersection for public engagement in archaeology. However, rather than working with public interests in their own and others' established heritages, recent work in this area has established forms of public engagement that elicit new or unknown histories from the spaces and people hidden by dominant narratives. This work is not necessarily "about" public archaeology, per se, but rather it is archaeology that fully engages with public concerns and interests. As noted, the heritage of African Diaspora communities has been one important focus in this work, but other work has recovered heritages of other ethnic groups (Voss 2008; Voss and Williams 2008; Brighton 2009; Cipolla 2013) and the heritage of labor and working class communities (Shackel 2004, 2013; Saitta 2007; Shackel 2004, 2013; Shackel and Roller 2013; Shackel and Westmont 2013). Research in historical memory is also part of this trend (Shackel 2004; see also Shackel 2001, 2008).

Beyond adding to the corpus of knowledge about the diversity of past people, heritage-based research is a form of public archaeology in two ways. First, many of these projects are community-based such as the Ludlow Coalfield War project's association with present-day United Mine Worker members (Saitta 2007) or the

Hampden Community Archaeology project's association with the working class of a gentrifying neighborhood in Baltimore (Gadsby and Chidester 2007, 2012). Another example is V. Camille Westmont's community-engaged dissertation work with the Latimer Archaeology Project (Lattimer Archaeology Project N.D.; Shackel and Westmont 2016).

Second, many heritage-based projects are also very interested in addressing the way public knowledge of history can itself be a form of exclusion and oppression. Thus, some archaeologists have considered the importance of their writing as well as their understanding and critique of dominant narratives. One path taken has explored the idea of archaeologists as storytellers. In this work, archaeologists have experimented with alternative forms for reporting, including archaeologically informed fiction (e.g., Gibb 2000, included here, and van Dyke and Bernbeck 2015). Another path has been to develop, especially with community input, counter-narratives about the past that not only recover but also write against what we think we know about the past. Examples include projects examining slavery in the American north (LaRoche and Blakey 1997; LaRoche 2011), the persistence of indigenous practices despite oppression (Gallivan 2000; Colwell-Chanthaphonh and Ferguson 2006; Colwell-Chanthaphonh 2007; Atalay 2008, 2010; Silliman 2008), or the sometimes contradictory meanings embraced by descendant communities and the larger communities within which they exist (Horning 2002; Byrne 2003; McDavid 2004; Gadsby and Chidester 2007, 2012; Shackel 2010; Matthews 2011).

It is also important to note that "heritage" does not necessarily refer to archaeology at all, although in our broad framework the two discourses often overlap or conflate (see Smith 2006; White and Carman 2006; Smith and Waterton 2009; Waterton and Smith 2010;). Although a detailed review of international heritage discourses is outside our scope, we touch on global movements briefly below.

Public Archaeology Now: Moving To The Present

While changes have occurred in the U.S., similar shifts also occurred elsewhere, and a variety of worldwide post-colonial and global justice movements have played important roles in how scholars and their publics frame archaeology and public archaeology today. A major milestone in the global arena was the 1986 founding of the World Archaeology Congress, in part as a response to apartheid in South Africa (Gero 1999; Ucko 1997).

Over the last two decades, there have been other key developments within global governmental, non-governmental, and scholarly arenas, all of which have been part of an ongoing global process of re-imagining how archaeological work (historical or otherwise) can, and should, intersect with public interests and needs (Hamilakis and Duke 2007, Lydon and Rizvi 2010, Shepherd 2007). Of note, with respect to social justice and public archaeology, is the work of Barbara Little and Paul Shackel (Little and Shackel 2007, 2014), Helaine Silverman and D. Fairchild Ruggles (Silverman and Ruggles 2007), and Anne Pyburn (Pyburn 2007, 2009). Examples in this volume (or Appendix A) include Chiccone (2011), Weik (2010), and Little (2009a, 2013).

As this has occurred, the term "public archaeology" has expanded in meaning, and it is fair to say that many more archaeologists, worldwide, now conceive of public archaeology as we suggested earlier – that is, very broadly, encompassing any aspect of the public dimensions of doing archaeology. In addition to those described here, other variants emerge from time to time. One is the recent "co-creative archaeology", which borrows from both the museum and business literature to frame a collaborative form of public archaeology that emphasizes the co (it has to share power in some way) and the creative (it has to do something new). Even though the ideas in this framework are not completely new, borrowing as they do from other disciplines, they build on the collaborative trends described earlier (Bollwerk and Connolly 2015).

Because this collection focuses on the particular discourses published by the Society for Historical Archaeology, before moving ahead we will mention three other publications that publish contemporary public archaeology. The first, the international journal Public Archaeology, began publication in 2000. Its masthead statement defines public archaeology much as we do:

> …an arena for the growing debate surrounding archaeological and heritage issues as they relate to the wider world of politics, ethics, government, social questions, education, management, economics, and philosophy. Key issues covered include: the sale of unprovenanced and frequently looted antiquities; the relationship between emerging modern nationalism and the profession of archaeology; privatization of the profession; human rights and, in particular, the rights of indigenous populations with respect to their sites and material relics; representation of archaeology in the media; the law on portable finds or treasure troves; [the] archaeologist

> as an instrument of state power, or catalyst to local resistance to the state.

Second, a newer online journal, *arqueologiapublica* (published in Spain, but for an international audience) defines public archaeology as "the study of the relations between this archaeology and society in every aspect of daily life (social, economical [sic], and political)", and provides a list of topics, including:

- The economic and political impact of archaeology
- Archaeology as popular culture
- The history and development of archaeology as a professional practice
- Theoretical issues around the publicity of archaeology
- The image of archaeology
- Legal issues on archaeological practice and the illicit trade of antiquities
- The presentation of archaeology to the public

Third, the *Journal of Community Archaeology and Heritage* narrows the focus to recognize "the growing interest in voluntary activism in archaeological research and interpretation" and to "create a platform for discussion about … both the diversity of community archaeology and its commonalities in process and associated theory". Unlike other journals, *JCAH* actively seeks contributions from avocational, voluntary, and professional sectors of archaeology.

In institutional terms, the SHA has also legitimized public archaeology within its formal award structure. Early in this century, Martha Williams received the SHA Award of Merit for her PEIC work in 2001 (Jim Gibb, pers. comm). At least three recipients of the SHA's Cotter Award, given to historical archaeologists as the start of their careers, were honored at least in part because of their focus on public engagement (Carol McDavid in 2007, Cheryl Janifer LaRoche in 2011, and Joseph M. Bagley in 2016). More recently, the society has created two major awards for "public" work. The Daniel G. Roberts Award for Excellence in Public Historical Archaeology began in 2011, and was first awarded to Pam Cressey in 2012. It recognizes public archaeology in the wider sense, particularly in the heritage management framework. The Mark E. Mack Community Engagement Award, first awarded in 2016 to Jun Sunseri, focuses specifically on engagement with stakeholder and descendant communities.

Preview Of The Collection

Of course, the most exciting part of our work for this volume was reviewing the history of SHA publications and selecting examples from this corpus several pieces that illustrate the practice of public archaeology to reprint here as a collection. The downside is that we cannot reprint every example we discovered. So, as noted earlier, we created two comprehensive annotated bibliographies of works published in *Historical Archaeology* and the SHA Newsletter, which include discussions of aspects of public archaeology. These are included here as Appendix A (Newsletter) and Appendix B (Journal).

We have divided this collection into four sections of previously published articles from *Historical Archaeology*. Part 1 includes five articles from the journal's first 25 years. These lay some of the key groundwork for later publications on public archaeology, and also make it clear that the topic was considered important early on, and by some the Society's founders. Stanley South and Ivor Noel-Hume both contributed early essays that included public outreach and engagement as essential to the field during its formative years. Ronald Fleming addressed how historical archaeology could be used to inform urban planning. Similarly, Dickens and Bowne's article includes the place of public outreach education in large urban projects in Atlanta. This section ends with an article by Parker Potter (1992) which, as noted earlier, illustrates how public archaeology had, by the late 1980s, begun to shift from "outreach" to internal and external critique.

The second section of articles all build on the transition away from the self-evident value attached to archaeology and public outreach to examine various issues and concerns about the way archaeological public engagements should be understood and put into practice. We see these articles as presenting methods that practitioners can adopt. Patrice Jeppson's article sets the stage by calling for archaeologists to consider the difference between public archaeology and a democratized "people's" archaeology. She illustrates this concept through a discussion of the practice of historical archaeology and public outreach in South Africa in the 1990s. James Gibb's article provides an overview of the use of storytelling devices employed by several archaeologists in the late 1990s and early 2000s. Storytelling was not exclusively promoted as a form of public archaeology, but the effort to craft semi-fictional, fleshed-out events and characters interacting with material culture provides a clear method for producing more publicly accessible texts than is possible with traditional scholarly articles and professional reports. Sharing a common concern with Gibb regarding the issue of archaeological writing, Stahl, Mann, and diPaolo published an important article on the struggle of writing as archaeologists for different sorts of audiences. They (2004:86) also review key aspects in critical theory and promote an "embedded model of writing" that "works against the separation of the 'politics of knowledge' from the end product."

Chris Matthews' article shares an interest in critical theory but focuses more closely on the conception of archaeological problems and subjects in closer alignment with the public interests and contexts that make these visible and important. He proposes a theory of Marxist reflexivity as a method to draw attention to how archaeology itself is always already a public endeavor as long as archaeologists actively and professionally participate in the social construction of the past. Timothy Baumann's article examines a far-reaching series of efforts to address the after effects of urban renewal in Old North St. Louis. These included an inclusive public archaeology program aimed to repair class tensions that emerged as the historic working class dealt with displacement while other, more affluent, persons did not. The final article in this section by Helaine Silverman provides an overview of the practice of community archaeology as of 2011, which served as a commentary for a thematic issue on Archaeologies of Engagement, Representation and Identity edited by Paul Shackel and David Gadsby (2011). The article provides useful insights on how archaeology can and should engage with public concerns. It also reviews the contributions to the thematic issue, which were excellent works, but could not all be included here.

The next section of this collection presents a range of studies focused on African American Archaeology and the public, and working with descendant African Diaspora communities has been a rich area for developing innovative theory and practice in public historical archaeology. We include in this section five articles that originally appeared in the thematic issue *In the Realm of Politics: Prospects for Participation in African-American and Plantation Archaeology*, edited by Carol McDavid and David Babson (1997). Among these, some have become seminal pieces for public archaeology throughout the discipline. We also include in this section Parker Potter's (1991) powerful statement, "What's the Use of Planation Archaeology?", which served as a call to action for archaeologists to consider the relevance of their work to descendant communities and contemporary anti-racist activism. Finally, articles by Anna Agbe-Davies, Paul Mullins, and Lewis Jones provide recent considerations of the intersection of the practice of engaged archaeologies and African American community interests.

The final section of the collection brings together a range of articles on archaeology, heritage, and justice. Articles by Tracey Ireland and Denis Byrne provide important observations on the impact of the dominant heritage discourse in Australia on Aboriginal and other marginal populations that are left out of the national narrative. Mark Walker examines how doing archaeology at the site of the Colorado's 1914 Ludlow Massacre brings to the fore a greater appreciation of working class struggle and resistance. Paul Shackel's article broadens this appreciation to consider multiple cases of the heritage of labor sites and working people. Another engagement with working class communities is presented in Gadsby and Chidester's article on their research in the Hampden community in Baltimore.

Barbara Little's forum article on "What can Archaeology do for Justice, Peace, Community, and the Earth?" explains the process by which historical archaeologists can build connections to national and global social justice movements. We have included the full forum here so that the dialogue between Little and her respondents may flesh out this area of interest. Gallivan et al.'s article provides an example of social justice archaeology as they examine their work with Native Americans in Virginia, who are not recognized as tribes by the federal government. Through the lens of strategic essentialism, community engagements with their research at Werowocomoco are supporting the decolonization of the heritage discourse on colonial Virginia. The last articles in the collection by Jamie Brandon and Barbara Little are two pieces from another important thematic collection on Reversing the Narrative, edited by Paul Shackel and Michael Roller (2013). This thematic issue includes several powerful pieces on the impact of popular historical narratives on the identity and lives of descendant communities. Brandon's article presents a case study of the "hillbilly" narrative in the Arkansas Ozarks and how archaeology counters the narrative of backward rural whiteness. We think Little's contribution to this thematic issue is a good way to close out this collection, as she presents a reflection on how historical archaeology is primed to work together with communities and engaged publics to reconsider the content and structure of historical narratives. She puts a special focus on why historical narratives so often emphasize moments of violence rather than efforts to create peace. We endorse this standpoint.

Conclusion

At this writing in mid-2016, it is clear that the range of practices known as public archaeology is extremely varied. Those who do public archaeology can be from academic archaeology, practice settings, heritage studies, or even "the public". They can self-identify as anthropologists (applied or otherwise), ethnographers, heritage professionals, tourism and museum workers, journalists and writers, or archaeologists. They do qualitative and quantitative research about the public perceptions of archaeology, they examine pasts that are created and used, and they explore the conflicts between academic and popular views of the past. They deal actively with the political, social, and economic contexts in which archaeology is undertaken, the attitudes of disempowered and indigenous peoples and archaeologists towards each other, and the educational and public roles of the discipline.

Within its narrower frame of reference, the articles in this Perspectives reader illustrate how these practices have emerged in one particular historical archaeology discourse since the founding of SHA in 1967. It has been, and will continue to be, constrained, defined, and (by now) "mainstreamed" as an accepted part of archaeology practice and scholarship – by its institutional policies, its members, and the larger discipline that surrounds it. What is clear, and what we find exciting, is that public historical archaeology is now, truly, an arena in which past and present merge, as contemporary people (however identified) use information about the past for contemporary agendas and needs.

1. *Matthews and McDavid have been active participants in SHA since 1996 and 1991, respectively, and both have published extensively on public archaeology topics.*

2. *According to the booklet, the Society for American Archaeology initiated this text, the American Association for Museums and the American Society for State and Local History reviewed it, and U S Government Printing Office printed it. Precise distribution details are unknown.*

3. *We use the word "public" in an everyday sense – that is, anyone who is not, themselves, an archaeology or heritage professional. We do not consider (here) the*

broader civic context of the word, e.g., "the public sphere", because the everyday definition is the one usually used by "the public", and because a critical examination of the word "public" is outside our scope here. Even so, it is important to acknowledge that members of "the public" often operate on the edges of archaeology/heritage as a formal discipline. Intersectionality can shape how they see themselves, and how archaeologists see them – and of course, archaeologists are a public too (Carman 2017 forthcoming).

4. *By 2010 at least 90% of US archaeologists were working in either commercial or agency CRM (Sebastian and Lipe 2010:7).*

5. *Public archaeology and/or archaeology education shared thematic top billing with immigration and ethnicity at the 1996 annual meeting of the SHA in Cincinnati, OH ("Forging Partnerships in Outreach and Education" was the co-theme). It was also the primary theme of two other meetings: 2001 ("Teach the Mind, Touch the Spirit", in Long Beach, CA) and 2008 ("The Public Benefits of Historical Archaeology", in Albuquerque, NM).*

6. *For example, NAGPRA recognized "descendants" as such only when they were both documented and lineal, and regulating agencies often do not recognize African American TCPs as worthy of protection under Bulletin 38.*

Acknowledgements

We thank our "senior" colleagues who spent considerable time replying to our queries about the beginnings of public historical archaeology. We hope we did justice to your recollections here. We also thank our reviewers, whose input certainly improved this volume (although mistakes are, of course, our own).

References

ADVISORY COUNCIL OF HISTORIC PRESERVATION (ACHP)
2002   The National Historic Preservation Program: Overview. Accessed on September 24,

2016   <http://www.achp.gov/overview.html> Last accessed 27 September 2016.

AGBE-DAVIES, ANNA S.
2010   Concepts of community in the pursuit of an inclusive archaeology. *International Journal of Heritage Studies* 16(6):371-387.

ATALAY, SONYA
2008   Multivocality and Indigenous Archaeologies. In *Evaluating Multiple Narratives: Beyond Natonalist, Colonialist, Imperialist Archaeologies*, edited by J. Habu, C. Fawcett and J. M. Matsunaga, pp. 29-44. Springer, New York, NY.

2010   "Diba Jimooyung" -Telling Our Story: Colonization and Decolonization of Archaeological Practice from an Anishinabe Perspective. In *Handbook of Postcolonial Archaeology*, edited by J. Lydon and U. Z. Rizvi, pp. 61-72. World Archaeological Congress Research Handbooks in Archaeology. Left Coast Press, Walnut Creek, CA.

2012   *Community-Based Archaeology: Research With, By, and For Indigenous and Local Communities.* University of California Press, Berkeley, CA.

BABIARZ, JENNIFER J.
2011   White Privilege and Silencing within the Heritage Landscape: Race and the Practice of Cultural Resource Management. In *The Materiality of Freedom: Archaeologies of Postemancipation Life*, edited by J. A. Barnes, pp. 47-57. University of South Carolina Press, Columbia, SC.

BEAUDRY, MARY C.
1992   First Person Pronouns and the Myth of Unmediated Truth: Response to Potter. *The Society for Historical Archaeology Newsletter* 25(1):17-18.

BOLLWERK, ELIZABETH, AND ROBERT CONNOLLY
2015   Special Issue on Co-Creation: Co-Creation and Public Archaeology. *Advances in Archaeological Practice* 3(3):178-187.

BOYD, DOUGLAS K., MARIA FRANKLIN, AND TERRI MYERS
2011   From Slave to Landowner: Historic Archeology at the Ransom and Sarah Williams Farmstead. *Current Archaeology in Texas* 13(1):8-14.

BRIGHTON, STEPHEN A.
2009   *Historical Archaeology of the Irish Diaspora: A Transnational Approach 2nd Edition Second ed.* University of Tennessee Press, Knoxville, TN.

BROWN, KENNETH L., AND DOREEN C. COOPER
1990   Structural Continuity in an African-American Slave and Tenant Community. In *Historical Archaeology on Southern Plantations and Farms*, C. E. Orser, Jr., editor. Thematic issue, *Historical Archaeology* 24(4):7-19.

BRUSETH, JIM, PAT MERCADO-ALLINGER, JAMES WOODRICK, TIFFANY OSBURN, JEFF DURST, BRAD JONES, BILL PIERSON, CHARLES GORDY, AND ROBERT MARCOM
2011   Remote Sensing and Archeological Testing at the Bernardo Plantation's Main House. *Bulletin of the Texas Archeological Society* 82:355-377.

CASTAÑEDA, QUETZIL E., AND CHRISTOPHER N. MATTHEWS (EDITORS)
2008   *Ethnographic Archaeologies: Reflections on Stakeholders and Archaeological Practices.* Altamira, Lanham, New York, Toronto, Plymouth, UK.

CARMAN, JOHN
(2017 forthcoming)   'Herding Cats': Building Archaeological Communities. *Journal of Community Archaeology and Heritage.*

CIPOLLA, CRAIG N.
2013   *Becoming Brothertown: Native American Ethnogenesis and Endurance in the Modern World.* Second edition. University of Arizona Press, Tuscon, AZ.

COLWELL-CHANTHAPHONH, CHIP
2007   History, Justice and Reconciliation. In *Archaeology as a Tool for Civic Engagement*, edited by B. J. Little and P. A. Shackel, pp. 23-46. Altamira Press, Lanham, MD.

COLWELL-CHANTHAPHONH, CHIP AND T.J. FERGUSON
2006   Memory Pieces and Footprints: Multivocality and the Meanings of Ancient Times and Ancestral Places among the Zuni and Hopi. *American Anthropologist* 108(1):148-162.

COTTER, JOHN L.
1974   *Above Ground Archaeology.* Booklet written for the American Revolution Bicentennial Commission, the American Association of Museums, the American Society for State and Local History, and the Society for American Archaeology American Quarterly, Vol. 26 (3): 266-280.

CRESSEY, PAMELA J.
1980   An Enduring Afro-American Neighborhood: An Archaeological Perspective from Alexandria, Virginia. *Black Heritage* 20(1):1-10.

CRESSEY, PAMELA J., RUTH REEDER, AND JARED BRYSON
2003   Held in Trust: Community Archaeology in Alexandria, Virginia. In *Archaeologists and Local Communities: Partners in Exploring the Past*, edited by L. Derry and M. Malloy, pp. 1-18. The Society for American Archaeology, Washington, D.C.

CRESSEY, PAMELA J, AND NATELIE VINTON
2008   Smart Planning and Innovative Public Outreach: The Quintessential Mix for the Future of Archaeology. In *Past Meets Present*, edited by J. H. Jameson and S. Baugher, pp. 393-410. Springer, New York, NY.

CRIST, THOMAS A. J. AND DANIEL G. ROBERTS
1996   Engaging the Public through Mortuary Archaeology: Philadelphia's First African Baptist Church Cemeteries. *CRM* 10(5-8).

DAVIS, KAREN LEE, AND JAMES G. GIBB
1988   Unpuzzling the Past: Critical Thinking in History Museums. *Museum Studies Journal* 3:41-45.

DAVIS, M. ELAINE
2005   *How Students Understand the Past: From Theory to Practice.* Altamira Press, New York, NY.

DERRY, LINDA
1997   Pre-Emancipation Archaeology: Does it Play in Selma, Alabama? In *In the Realm of Politics: Prospects for Public Participation in African-American Archaeology*, special issue of *Historical Archaeology*, edited by C. McDavid and D. Babson, 31(3): 18-26.

DERRY, LINDA AND MAUREEN MALLOY (EDITORS)
2003   *Archaeologists and Local Communities: Partners in Exploring the Past.* The Society for American Archaeology, Washington, D.C.

DICKENS, ROY S., JR. AND WILLIAM R. BOWEN
1980   Problems and Promises in Urban Historical Archaeology: The MARTA Project. *Historical Archaeology* 14:41-57.

ELLICK, CAROL J.
2016 in press   A Cultural History of Archaeological Education. In *Advances in Archaeological Practice*, edited by E. King. Society for American Archaeology, Washington, D.C. (page numbers pending).

FAULKNER, NEIL
2000   Archaeology from Below. *Public Archaeology* 1(1):21-34.

FLEMING, RONALD L.
1971   After the Report What? The Uses of Historical Archaeology, A Planner's View. *Historical Archaeology* 5:49-61.

FRANKLIN, MARIA
1997   "Power to the People": Sociopolitics and the Archaeology of Black Americans. In *In the Realm of Politics: Prospects for Public Participation in African-American Archaeology*, special issue of *Historical Archaeology*, edited by C. McDavid and D. Babson, 31(3): 36-50.

FRANKLIN, M. ELAINE, AND JEANNE M. MOE
2012   A Vision for Archaeological Literacy. In *The Oxford Handbook of Public Archaeology*, edited by R. Skeates, C. McDavid and J. Carman, pp. 566-580. Oxford University Press Inc., New York, NY.

FRIEDMAN, ED
2000   Preface. In *The Archaeology Education Handbook: Sharing the Past with Kids*, edited by K. Smardz and S. J. Smith, pp. 13-16. Altamira Press, Walnut Creek, CA.

FROST, KAROLINE E. SMARDZ
2004   Archaeology and Public Education in North America: View from the Beginning of the Millennium. In *Public Archaeology*, edited by N. Merriman, pp. 59-84. Routledge, London, England.

Perspectives from the Society for Historical Archaeology:

GADSBY, DAVID A., AND ROBERT C. CHIDESTER
2007   Heritage in Hampden: A Participatory Research Design for Public Archaeology in a Working-Class Neighborhood, Baltimore, Maryland. In *Archaeology as a Tool of Civic Engagement*, edited by B. Little and P. Shackel, pp. 223-242. Altamira, Lanham, MD.

2012   Class, Labour, and the Public. In *The Oxford Handbook of Public Archaeology*, edited by R. Skeates, C. McDavid and J. Carman, pp. 513-536. Oxford University Press Inc., New York, NY.

GERO, JOAN
1999   The History of World Archaeological Congress. Paper presented at the 1999 Annual Meetings of the American Anthropological Association. Published online by the World Archeology Conference <http://www.worldarchaeologicalcongress.org/about-wac/history/146-history-wac> Last accessed 27 September 2016.

GIBB, JAMES G.
2000   Imaginary, But By No Means Unimaginable: Storytelling, Science, and Historical Archaeology. Lead Paper, Thematic Forum, *Historical Archaeology* 34(2)1-6

GIBB JAMES G., AND KAREN LEE DAVIS
1989   History Exhibits and Theories of Material Culture. *Journal of Material Culture* 12:27-35.

GOLDSTEIN, LYNNE
1998   Editor's Corner. *American Antiquity* 63(4):529-530.

GRADY, SARAH A., VALERIE M. J. HALL, AND SARAH N. JANESKO
2016   Engagement, Agency, and Activism through Environmental Archaeology: A Citizen Science Program at the Smithsonian Environmental Research Center. *Practicing Anthropology* 38(3):46-47.

GRADWOHL, DAVID M., AND NANCY M. OSBORN
1990   *Exploring Buried Buxton: Archaeology of an Abandoned Iowa Coal Mining Town with a Large Black Population.* University of Iowa Press, Iowa City, IA.

GREEN, MELISSA M., DUANE E. PETER, AND DONNA K. SHEPHERD
1997   *Friendship: An African American Community of the Prairie Margin of Northeast Texas. Volume VI, Delta County.* Geo Marine, Inc., Plano, TX.

HAMILAKIS, YANNIS AND ARIS ANAGNOSTOPOULOS (EDITORS)
2009   *Archaeological ethnographies: a special double issue of* Public Archaeology 8:2/3.

HAMILAKIS, YANNIS, AND PHILLIP DUKE (EDITORS)
2007   *Archaeology and Capitalism: From Ethics to Politics.* University of Arizona Press, Tucson, AZ.

HANDSMAN, RUSSELL G., AND MARK LEONE
1989   Living History and Critical Archaeology and the Reconstruction of the Past. In *Critical Traditions in Contemporary Archaeology*, edited by V. Pinsky and A. Wylie, pp. 117-35, Cambridge University Press, Cambridge, UK.

HORNING, AUDREY J.
2002   Myth, Migration, and Material Culture: Archaeology and the Ulster Influence on Appalachia. *Historical Archaeology* 34(4):129-149.

HUME, IVOR NOËL
1973   Historical Archaeology: Who Needs It? *Historical Archaeology* 7:3-10.

JAMESON, JOHN H., JR. (EDITOR)
1997   *Presenting Archaeology to the Public: Digging for Truths.* Altamira Press, Walnut Creek, London, New Delhi.

2004a   *The Reconstructed Past: Reconstructions in the Public Interpretation of Archaeology and History.* Rowman Altamira, Lanham, MD.

2004b   Public Archaeology In the United States. In *Public Archaeology*, edited by N. Merriman, pp. 21-58. Routledge, London, England.

JAMESON, JOHN H. JR. AND LU ANN DU CUNZO
2005   Unlocking the Past: Celebrating Historical Archaeology in North. Society for Historical Archaeology. <https://sha.org/unlockingthepast/index.htm> Last accessed on September 24, 2016.

JELKS, EDWARD B.
1993   The Founding Meeting of the Society for Historical Archaeology. *Historical Archaeology* 27(1):10-11.

JEPPSON, PATRICE L.
1997   "Leveling the Playing Field" in the Contested Territory of the South African Past: A "Public" versus a "People's" Form of Historical Archaeology Outreach. In *In the Realm of Politics: Prospects for Public Participation in African-American Archaeology*, special issue of Historical Archaeology, edited by Carol McDavid and David Babson, 31(3): 65-83.

2000   An Archaeologist/Educator Collaboration: Lessons Learned During a Year of Archaeology in the Baltimore County Public Schools. *Proceedings of the Annual Meetings of the Society for Historical and Underwater Archaeology.* Quebec City, Canada.

2012   Public Archaeology and the US Culture Wars. In *The Oxford Handbook of Public Archaeology*, edited by R. Skeates, C. McDavid, and J. Carman. vol. 581-604. Oxford University Press, Oxford, UK.

JEPPSON, PATRICE L., AND GEORGE BRAUER
2003   Hey, Did You Hear about the Teacher Who Took the Class Out to Dig a Site? Some Common Misconceptions about Archaeology in Schools. In *Archaeologists and Local Communities: Partners in Exploring the Past,* edited by L. Derry and M. Malloy, pp. 77-96. The Society for American Archaeology, Washington, D.C.

KEHOE, ALICE BECK
2012   Public Education in Archaeology in North America: The Long View. In *The Oxford Handbook of Public Archaeology,* edited by R. Skeates, C. McDavid, and J. Carman, pp. 537-551. Oxford University Press, Oxford, UK.

KEITUMETSE, SUSAN OSIREDITSE, AND MICHELLE GENEVIEVE PAMPIRI
2016   Community Cultural Identity in Nature-Tourism Gateway Areas: Maun Village, Okavango Delta World Heritage Site, Botswana. *Journal of Community Archaeology and Heritage* 3(2):99-117.

KERBER, JORDAN E.
1994   *Cultural Resource Management: Archaeological Research, Preservation Planning, and Public Education in the Northeastern United States.* Bergin & Garvey, Westport, CT.

KING, ELEANOR M.
2006   Archaeology and the Warriors Project: Exploring a Buffalo Soldier Campsite in the Guadalupe Mountains of Texas. In *People, Places, and Parks,* edited by D. Harmon, pp. 475-481. The George Wright Society, Hancock, MI.

KING, THOMAS F.
1993   Beyond Bulletin 38: Comments on the Traditional Cultural Properties Symposium. In thematic issue, *Traditional Cultural Properties: What You Do and How We Think,* P. L.Parker, editor. CRM 16:60-64. National Park Service, Washington, D.C.

2002   *Thinking About Cultural Resource Management: Essays from the Edge.* Rowman & Littlefield Publishing, Lanham, MD.

LATTIMER ARCHAEOLOGY PROJECT
N.D.   Blog on Latimer project. Accessed on September 24, 2016; entries date from January 2012 to July 2015. *https://lattimerarchaeology.wordpress.com/*

LAROCHE, CHERYL J. AND MICHAEL BLAKEY
1997   Seizing Intellectual Power: The Dialogue at the New York African Burial Ground. *In the Realm of Politics: Prospects for Public Participation in African-American Archaeology,* thematic issue, *Historical Archaeology,* edited by Carol McDavid and David Babson, 31(3):84-106.

LAROCHE, CHERYL JANIFER
2011   Archaeology, the Activist Community, and the Redistribution of Power in New York City. In *Archaeologies:* Special Issue, The Dynamics of Inclusion, edited by C. N. Matthews, C. McDavid, and P. L. Jeppson. vol. 7/3. World Archaeology Congress.

2012   The Anthropology of Archaeology: The Benefits of Public Intervention at African-American Archaeological Sites. In *The Oxford Handbook of Public Archaeology,* edited by R. Skeates, C. McDavid, and J. Carman, pp. 629-658. Oxford University Press Inc., New York, NY.

LEONE, MARK P. AND PARKER B. JR. POTTER (EDITORS)
1988   *The Recovery of Meaning.* Smithsonian Institution Press, Washington, D.C..

LEONE, MARK P., PARKER B. POTTER, JR., AND PAUL A. SHACKEL
1987   Toward a Critical Archaeology. *Current Anthropology* 28(3):283-302.

LEONE, MARK P., CHERYL JANIFER LAROCHE, AND JENNIFER J. BABIARZ
2005   The Archaeology of Black Americans in Recent Times. *Annual Review of Anthropology* 34:575-598.

LEVIN, JED
2012   Activism leads to Excavation: The Power of Place and the Power of the People at the President's House in Philadelphia. Special Issue of *Archaeologies,* edited by Christopher N. Matthews, Carol McDavid, and Patrice L. Jeppson 7(3):596-618.

LITTLE, BARBARA J.
2002   Archaeology as a Shared Vision. In *Public Benefits of Archaeology,* edited by B. J. Little. University Press of Florida, Gainesville, FL.

2007a   Archaeology and Civic Engagement. In *Archaeology as a Tool of Civic Engagement,* edited by B. J. Little and P. A. Shackel, pp. 1-22. Alta Mira Press, Lanham, MD.

2007b   *Historical Archaeology: Why the Past Matters.* Left Coast Press, Walnut Creek, CA.

2009a   Forum: What Can Archaeology Do for Justice, Peace, Community and the Earth? *Historical Archaeology* 43(4):115-129.

2009b   Public Archaeology in the United States in the Early Twenty-first Century. In *Heritage Studies: Methods and Approaches,* edited by M.-L. S. Sorensen and J. Carman, pp. 29-51. Routledge, London, UK.

2012   Public Benefits of Public Archaeology. In *The Oxford Handbook of Public Archaeology,* edited by R. Skeates, C. McDavid, and J. Carman, pp. 395-413. Oxford University Press Inc., New York, NY.

LITTLE, BARBARA J., AND PAUL A. SHACKEL (EDITORS)
2007   *Archaeology as a Tool of Civic Engagement.* Alta Mira Press, Lanham, MD.

LITTLE, BARBARA J., AND PAUL A. SHACKEL
2014   *Archaeology, Heritage and Civic Engagement: Working Toward the Public Good.* Left Coast Press, Walnut Creek, CA.

LYDON, JANE, AND UZMA Z. RIZVI (EDITORS)
2010   *WAC Handbook of Postcolonialism and Archaeology.* Left Coast Press and World Archaeology Congress, Walnut Creek, CA.

LYNOTT, MARK J., AND ALISON WYLIE
1995   Stewardship: The Central Principle of Archaeological Ethics. In *Ethics in American Archaeology,* pp. 28-32. Society for American Archaeology, Washington, D.C.

MACK, MARK E., AND MICHAEL L. BLAKEY
2004   The New York African Burial Ground Project: Past Biases, Current Dilemmas, and Future Research Opportunities. *Historical Archaeology* 38(1):10-17.

MARSHALL, YVONNE
2002   What is Community Archaeology? *World Archaeology,* Special Issue on *Community Archaeology* 34(2):211-219.

MATTERNES, HUGH B., AND JULIE COCO
2012   Hold Your Light on Canaan's Shore: Views of Past and Present: African American Heritage at the Avondale Burial Place, Bibb County, Georgia. Paper presented at the Symposium held at the 45th Annual Meeting of the Society of Historical Archaeology, Baltimore, MD.

MATTHEWS, CHRISTOPHER N.
2004   Public Significance and Imagined Archaeologists: Authoring pasts in Context. *International Journal of Historical Archaeology* 8(1):1-25.

2005   Public Dialectics: Marxist Reflection in Archaeology. *Historical Archaeology* 39(4):18-36.

2008   The Location of Archaeology. In E*thnographic Archaeologies: Reflections on Stakeholders and Archaeological Practices,* edited by Q. Castañeda and C. N. Matthews, pp. 157-182. AltaMira Press., Lanham, MD.

2011   Lonely Islands: Culture, Community, and Poverty in Archaeological Perspective. *Archaeologies of Poverty,* in *Archaeologies of Poverty,* edited by Christopher N. Matthews and Suzanne Spencer-Wood, special issue of *Historical Archaeology* 45(3):41-54.

MAYNARD, JOAN
1992   The Weeksville Project. *CRM Online* 15(7).

McCARTHY, JOHN P.
1996   Who Owns These Bones?: Descendant Community Rights and Partnerships in the Excavation and Analysis of Historic Cemetery Sites in New York and Philadelphia. *Public Archaeology Review* 4(2):3-12.

2001   From African-American Cemeteries in New York And Philadelphia toward a Community-Based Paradigm for the Excavation and Analysis of Human Remains In *Human Remains: Conservation, Retrieval, and Analysis,* edited by E. Williams, pp. 11-15. BAR International Series, Oxford, UK.

McDAVID, CAROL
1997   Descendants, Decisions, and Power: The Public Interpretation of the Archaeology of the Levi Jordan Plantation. In *In the Realm of Politics: Prospects for Public Participation in African-American Archaeology,* special issue of *Historical Archaeology* 31(3):114-131.

2003   Collaboration, Power, and the Internet: The Public Archaeology of the Levi Jordan Plantation. In *Archaeologists and Local Communities: Partners in Exploring the Past,* edited by L. Derry and M. Malloy, pp. 45-66. The Society for American Archaeology, Washington, D.C.

2004   From "Traditional" Archaeology to Public Archaeology to Community Action. In *Places in Mind: Public Archaeology as Applied Anthropology,* edited by P. A. Shackel and E. Chambers, pp. 35-56. Routledge, New York, NY.

2007   The Death of a Community Archaeology Project? Ensuring 'Consultation' in a Non-mandated Bureaucratic Environment. In *World Heritage: Global Challenges, Local Solutions: Proceedings of a Conference at Coalbrookdale, 4-7 May 2006, hosted by the Ironbridge Institute,* edited by R. White & J. Carman, pp. 107-111. British Archaeological Reports (BAR) International Series 1698. Archaeopress, Oxford, UK.

2010   Public Archaeology, Activism, and Racism: Rethinking the heritage "product". In *Archaeologists as Activists: Can Archaeologists Change the World?,* edited by M. J. Stottman, pp. 36-47. University of Alabama Press, Tuscaloosa, AL.

2011   When is "Gone" Gone? Archaeology, Gentrification, and Competing Narratives about Freedmen's Town, Houston. In *Archaeologies of Poverty, C. N. Matthews and S. M. Spencer-Wood,* editors. Thematic Issue, Historical Archaeology 45(3):74-88.

McDAVID, CAROL AND DAVID BABSON (EDITORS)
1997   *In the Realm of Politics: Prospects for Public Participation in African-American Archaeology,* special issue of *Historical Archaeology.* 31:3.

McDavid, Carol, Uzma Rizvi, and Laurajane Smith
2016   Community Archaeology and Heritage in Africa: Conversations inspired by a workshop. In *Community Archaeology and Heritage in Africa: Decolonizing Practice,* edited by P. R. Schmidt and I. Pikirayi. Routledge, pp. 250-269. New York, NY.

McGhee, Fred L.
2012   Participatory Action Research and Archaeology. In *The Oxford Handbook of Public Archaeology,* edited by R. Skeates, C. McDavid, and J. Carman, pp. 213-229. Oxford University Press Inc., New York, NY.

McGimsey, Charles R. III (editor)
1972   *Public Archaeology.* Seminar Press, New York, NY.

McKee, Larry
1994   Commentary: Is It Futile to Try and Be Useful? Historical Archaeology and the African-American Experience. *Northeast Historical Archeaology* 23:1 - 7.

McManamon, Francis P.
1991   Forum: The Many Publics for Archaeology. In *American Antiquity,* pp. 121-130. vol. 56.

2000   Public Education: A Part of Archaeological Professionalism. In *The Archaeology Education Handbook: Sharing the Past with Kids,* edited by K. Smardz and S. J. Smith, pp. 17-24. Altamira Press, Walnut Creek, CA.

Merriman, Nick (editor)
2004   *Public Archaeology.* Routledge, London, UK.

Meskell, Lynn
2005   Archaeological ethnography: Conversations around Kruger National Park. *Archaeologies* 1(1):81-100.

Mortensen, Lena, and Julie Hollowell (editors)
2009   *Ethnographies and Archaeologies: Iterations of the Past.* University Press of Florida, Gainesville, FL.

Moser, Stephanie, Darren Glazier, James E. Phillips, Lamya Nasser el Nemr, Susan Richardson, Andrew Conner, and Michael Seymour
2002   Transforming Archaeology Through Practice: Strategies for Collaborative Archaeology and the Community Archaeology Project at Quseir, Egypt. *Community Archaeology,* special issue edited by Y. Marshall, *World Archaeology* 34(2):220-248.

Moshenska, Gabriel, and Sarah Dhanjal (editors)
2012   *Community Archaeology: Themes, Methods and Practices.* Oxford University Press, Oxford, UK.

Mullins, Paul R.
2006   Racializing the Commonplace Landscape: An Archaeology of Urban Renewal Along the Color Line. *World Archaeology* 38(1):60-71.

2008   Excavating America's Metaphor: Race, Diaspora, and Vindicationist Archaeologies. *Historical Archaeology* 42(2):104-122.

Nassaney, Michael S., Whitney Battle-Baptiste, Florie Bugarin, Kathy Ehrhardt, Lewis Jones, Cheryl LaRoche, Carol McDavid, and Paula Saunders
2015   Statement of Purpose of the Anti-Racism (A-R) Sub-committee. Report submitted to the Gender and Minority Affairs Committee and Board of Directors, Society for Historical Archaeology, January 2015.

Nassaney, Michael S., and Cheryl J. LaRoche
2011   Race and the Society for Historical Archaeology: Steps Towards Claiming an Anti-Racist Institutional Identity. *Society for Historical Archaeology Newsletter* 44(4):4-6.

Palus, Matthew M
2001   Authenticity, Legitimation, and the Twentieth-Century Tourism: The John D Reckefeller, Jr., Carriage Roads, Acadia National Park, Maine. In *Myth, Memory, and the Making of the American Landscape,* edited by P. A. Shackel, pp. 179-196. University Press of Florida, Gainesville, FL.

Palus, Matthew M., Mark P. Leone, and Matthew D. Cochran
2006   Critical Archaeology: Politics Past and Present. In *Historical Archaeology,* edited by M. Hall and S. Silliman, pp. 84-104. Wiley-Blackwell, Oxford, UK.

Parker, Patricia L., and Thomas F. King
1990   Guidelines for Evaluating and Documenting Traditional Cultural Properties. National Register Bulletin 38., edited by N. P. Service, Washington, D.C.

Perry, Warren R.
1997   Archaeology as Community Service: The African Burial Ground Project in New York City. *North American Dialogue: Newsletter for the Society for the Anthropology of North America* 2(1):1-5.

Perry, Warren R., Jean Howson, and Barbara A. Bianco
2006   *Chapter 15: Summary and Conclusions. Howard University.* Final Report available at http://core.tdar.org/project/4859/the-archaeology-of-african-burial-ground-national-monument-new-york.

Potter, Parker B., Jr.
1989   Archaeology in Public in Annapolis: An Experiment in the Application of Critical Theory to Historical Archaeology. Doctoral dissertation, Department of Anthropology, Brown University, University Microfilms, Ann Arbor, MI.

1991a   Opinion: Stick a Needle in My I: Whither the (Withered?) First Person? *The Society for Historical Archaeology Newsletter* 24(3):9-10.

1991b   What is the use of Plantation archaeology? *Historical Archaeology* 25(3):94-107.

1992   Critical Archaeology: In the Ground and on the Street. *Historical Archaeology* 6(3).

1994   *Public Archaeology in Annapolis: A Critical Approach to History in Maryland's Ancient City.* Smithsonian Institution Press, Washington.

PRAETZELLIS, MARY, ADRIAN PRAETZELLIS, AND THAD VAN BUEREN
2007   Remaking Connections: Archaeology and Community after the Loma Prieta Earthquake. In *Archaeology as a Tool of Civic Engagement,* edited by B. J. Little and P. A. Shackel, pp. 109-130. Alta Mira Press, Lanham, MD.

PYBURN, K. ANNE
2007   Archeology as Activism. *Cultural Heritage and Human Rights* 2:172-183.

2009   Practising Archaeology -- As if it Really Matters. *Public Archaeology* 8(2/3):161-175.

ROBERTS, DANIEL G.
1984   Management and Community Aspects of the Excavation of a Sensitive Urban Archeological Resource: An Example from Philadelphia. *American Archaeology* 4:235-340.

ROBERTS, DANIEL G., AND JOHN P. MCCARTHY
1995   Descendant Community Partnering in the Archaeological and Bioanthropological Investigation of African-American Skeletal Populations: Two Interrelated Cases from Philadelphia. In *Bodies of Evidence: Reconstructing History Through Skeletal Analysis,* edited by A. L. Grauer, pp. 19-36. John Wiley and Sons, New York, NY.

ROBERTS, HEIDI, RICHARD V. N. ALSTROM, AND BARBARA ROTH ROBERTS (EDITORS)
2004   *From Campus to Corporation: the Emergence of Contract Archaeology in the Southwestern United States.* The Society for American Archaeology, Washington, D.C.

SAITTA, DEAN J.
2007   *The Archaeology of Collective Action.* The American Experience in Archaeological Perspective. University Press of Florida, Gainesville, FL.

SCHUYLER, ROBERT L.
1974   Sandy Ground: Archaeological Sampling in a Black Community in Metropolitan New York. *Proceedings of the Papers of the Conference on Historic Site Archaeology* 7:13-51.

SCOTT, DOUGLAS D.
1991   Campaign Statement. *SHA Newsletter* 24(2):4.

SCOTT, JENNIFER
2009   Placing Weeksville in the Past and Present: Documenting and Interpreting the Stories of Brooklyn's Forgotten 19th-Century African American Community. Paper presented at electronic symposium. Paper presented at the Conference on Historical and Underwater Archaeology, Toronto, Ontario.

SEBASTIAN, LYNNE, AND WILLIAM P. LIPE
2010   *Archaeology & Cultural Resource Management: Visions for the Future.* SAR Press, Santa Fe, NM.

SHACKEL, PAUL A (EDITOR)
2001   *Myth, Memory, and the Making of the American Landscape.* University Press of Florida, Gainesville, FL.

2003   *Memory in Black and White: Race Commemoration, and the Post-Bellum Landscape.* Altamira, Walnut Creek, CA.

SHACKEL, PAUL A.
2004   Introduction: Working with Communities: Heritage Development and Applied Archaeology. In *Places in Mind: Public Archaeology as Applied Anthropology,* edited by P. A. Shackel and E. J. Chambers, pp. 1-18. Routledge, New York, NY.

2008   Memory Studies in Historical Archaeology: Introduction. *The SAA Archaeological Record (Special Issue: Archaeology and Historical Memory)* 8(1):10-12.

2010   *New Philadelphia: An Archaeology of Race in the Heartland.* University of California Press, Berkeley, and Los Angeles, CA.

2013   An Historical Archaeology of Labor and Social Justice. *American Anthropologist* 115(2):212-215.

SHACKEL, PAUL A. AND ERVE J. CHAMBERS (EDITORS)
2004   *Places in Mind: Public Archaeology as Applied Anthropology.* Routledge, New York.

SHACKEL, PAUL A., AND MICHAEL P. ROLLER
2013   Archaeology of Anthracite Coal Patch Towns in Northeastern Pennsylvania. *The International Committee for the Conservation of the Industrial Heritage Bulletin* 62(4):2-4.

SHACKEL, PAUL A., AND V. CAMILLE WESTMONT (EDITORS)
2016   When the Mines Closed: Heritage Building in Northeastern Pennsylvania. *General Anthropology: A Bulletin of the General Anthropology Division* 23(1):1, 7-10.

SHEPHERD, NICK
2007   What Does It Mean 'To Give the Past Back to the People'? Archaeology and Ethics in the Postcolony. In *Archaeology and Capitalism,* edited by Y. Hamilakis and P. Duke, pp. 99-114. Left Coast Press, Walnut Creek, CA.

SILLIMAN, STEPHEN W. (EDITOR)
2008   *Collaborating at the Trowel's Edge: Teaching and Learning in Indigenous Archaeology.* The University of Arizona Press, Tucson, AZ.

SILVERMAN, HELAINE
2011   Epilogue: Perspectives on Community Archaeology. In *Archaeologies of Engagement, Representation, and Identity, special issue of Historical Archaeology,* edited by Paul A. Shackel and David Gadsby, 45(1):152-166

SILVERMAN, HELAINE AND D. FAIRCHILD RUGGLES (EDITORS)
2007   *Cultural Heritage and Human Rights.* Springer, New York.

SINGLETON, THERESA A.
1997   Facing the Challenges of a Public African-American Archaeology. In *In the Realm of Politics: Prospects for Public Participation in African-American Archaeology, Historical Archaeology,* edited by Carol McDavid and David Babson, 31(3):146-152.

SMARDZ, KAROLYN AND SHELLEY J. SMITH (EDITORS)
2000   *The Archaeology Education Handbook.* Altamira Press, Walnut Creek, CA.

SMITH, GEORGE S., AND JOHN E. EHRENHARD (EDITORS)
1991 (2001)   *Protecting the Past.* CRC Press, Boca Raton, FL.

SMITH, KC AND FRANCIS P. MCMANAHON (EDITORS)
1991   *Archeology and Education: The Classroom and Beyond.* U. S. Department of the Interior, National Park Service, Washington, D.C.

SMITH, LAURAJANE
2006   *The Uses Of Heritage.* Routledge, Oxford, UK.

SMITH, LAURAJANE AND EMMA WATERTON (EDITORS)
2009   *Heritage, Communities and Archaeology.* Bloomsbury, London, UK.

SMITH, MONICA L.
2014   *Citizen Science in Archaeology.* American Antiquity 79(4):749-762.

SMITH, SHELLEY, JEANNE MOE, KELLY LETTS, AND DANIELLE PATERSON
1992   *Intrigue of the Past: Investigating Archaeology.* Bureau of Land Management, Salt Lake City, UT.

SOUTH, STANLEY
1969   Wanted! A Historic Archaeologist. *Historical Archaeology* 3:75-84.

SRI FOUNDATION
N.D.   Accessed on September 26, 2016. http://www.srifoundation.org/

STEWART, SUZANNE, AND MARY PRAETZELLIS
1997   Connecting the Sources: Archaeology, Material Culture, Memory and Archives. In *Sights and Sounds: Essays in Celebration of West Oakland -- Cypress Replacement Project Report No. 1,* edited by S. Stewart and M. Praetzellis. California Department of Transportation, CA.

STOTTMAN, JAY (EDITOR)
2010   *Archaeologists as Activists: Can Archaeologists Change the World?.* University of Alabama Press, Tuscaloosa, AL.

THOMAS, SUZIE
2011   The Values of Community Archaeology: A Comparative Assessment between the UK and US. *Public Archaeology* 10(1):59-62.

2015   Collaborate, Condemn, or Ignore? Responding to Non-Archaeological Approaches to Archaeological Heritage. *European Journal of Archaeology* 18(2):312-335.

UCKO, PETER J.
1987   *Academic Freedom and Apartheid: The story of the World Archaeological Congress.* Gerald Duckworth & Co., London, UK.

VAN DYKE, R. M., AND R. BERNBECK
2015   *Subjects and Narratives in Archaeology.* University of Colorado Press, Boulder, CO.

VOSS, BARBARA L.
2008   *The Archaeology of Ethnogenesis: Race and Sexuality in Colonial San Francisco.* University of California Press, Berkeley, CA.

VOSS, BARBARA L., AND BRYN WILLIAMS (EDITORS)
2008   *The Archaeology of Chinese Immigrant and Chinese American Communities.* Thematic issue, *Historical Archaeology* 42(3).

WATERTON, EMMA, AND LAURAJANE SMITH
2010   The Recognition and Misrecognition of Community Heritage. *International Journal of Heritage Studies* 16(1):4-15.

WATERTON, EMMA, AND STEVE WATSON
2011   Heritage and Community Engagement: Finding a new Agenda. In *Heritage and Community Engagement: Collaboration or Contestation?,* edited by E. Waterton and S. Watson, pp. 1-11. Routledge, Abingdon, UK.

WHITE, ROGER, AND JOHN CARMAN (EDITORS)
2007   *World Heritage: Global Challenges, Local Solutions.* Irongbridge Institute and IGMT, in co-operation with English Heritage and ICOMOS, Ironbridge Institute, Birmingham, UK.

WILSON, DOUGLAS C.
2015   A Mongrel Crowd of Canadians, Kanakas and Indians: The United States National Park Service Public Archaeology Program and Fort Vancouver's Village. *Journal of Community Archaeology and Heritage* 3(3):221-337.

CAROL MCDAVID, PH.D.
EXECUTIVE DIRECTOR, COMMUNITY ARCHAEOLOGY RESEARCH
INSTITUTE, INC.
1638 BRANARD
HOUSTON, TX 77006
MCDAVID@PUBLICARCHAEOLOGY.ORG

CHRISTOPHER N. MATTHEWS
DEPARTMENT OF ANTHROPOLOGY
MONTCLAIR STATE UNIVERSITY
1 NORMAL AVENUE
MONTCLAIR, NJ 07043
MATTHEWSC@MONTCLAIR.EDU

Part I:
Foundations

1969 Wanted! A Historic Archaeologist. *Historical Archaeology* 3:75-84

WANTED!

An Historic Archaeologist

STANLEY SOUTH

Recently a colleague remarked that although he was prepared to pay $12,000 for an historical archaeologist, he was having difficulty filling the position. The requirements did not appear to be prohibitively restrictive. He wanted a man who was familiar with the nature of archaeological data as seen in the ground, as well as having some familiarity with the associated artifacts. He should have a master's degree or above, and some field experience, and should be able to see that the archaeological process was carried out. This latter requirement presented the problem, the execution of the archaeological process as required on a typical historic site. A similar search for a qualified man was made at the Charles Towne project in recent months by the Institute of Archaeology and Anthropology.

Instances have been brought to my attention where agencies have employed individuals to carry out archaeology, with disappointing results. For instance, problems arose from a lack of familiarity with the use of the transit, a light meter, a film pack, triangulation, a protractor and scale, the management of the excavating crew, etc., all of which might be expected from a student trainee, but not from an individual holding an advanced degree. Such cases are apparently not unique, which reflects a need in the training of historical archaeologists. The blame may lie, therefore, with the institutions awarding advanced degrees in anthropology and history without having exposed the recipients to surveying, photography, geometry, drafting, cartography, or the business end of a shovel. Yet, archaeologists have emerged in spite of this lack of formalized training, having picked up the necessary skills along the way. This facility with the archaeological process is not a product that can be education-machine produced. Therefore, agencies searching for historical archaeologists often find that the product they seek is a relatively rare commodity in a time of need for such men.

This expanding need for competent field or "dirt archaeologists" and the sometimes frustrating search for the men to carry out the archaeological process with competence, confidence, and skill, has prompted this paper which will attempt to examine the minimum requirements necessary for adequately filling the role of historical archaeologist as seen from this corner of the field.

I like the term "dirt archaeologist" for it implies that archaeology is by necessity involved with the earth. The term "field archaeology" is more proper, perhaps, but both denote a concern with the process of archaeology in the earth. This does not mean to imply that the archaeologist who does not dig does not make a contribution. Many make a far greater contribution out of the field than they would in it. However, this paper is primarily aimed at clarifying and outlining the role of the historical archaeologist in the field. What does he do to carry out the daily process of archaeology on his site? Although there are specific and important differences between the historical archaeologist and his colleagues not involved in historic site work, this paper will not attempt to weigh these differences, rather it will concentrate on the process of archaeology as required on historic sites.

A research institute advertises for a man to carry out the process of archaeology on historic sites, "Wanted! Historical Archaeologist". What should the applicant bring to the institute in order to answer the call? Surprisingly, applicants often state that they think the job will offer a good opportunity for them to broaden their range of experience, or would prove challenging, or would prove of value in a study they are doing. Their concern should not be what they can derive from the position, but what they can bring to it. That is the important question! Perhaps a summary of requirements would be of use to those who anticipate becoming historical archaeologists, and if their own training and experience has left them unprepared to carry out certain of the tasks on the list, then the serious archaeological student will take it *upon himself* to correct the lacunae before attempting to sell himself as an historical archaeologist This may sound harsh to aspiring archaeologists, but holders of advanced degrees are very often deficient in a number of basic requirements for archaeological work, and yet are confident they can do it "once they get the hang of it." As a result, employers are forced to train their own personnel, with varying degrees of success. The apprenticeship method is a very fine approach, but is quite time consuming when the need is for an archaeologist *now.*

Field schools are often the answer to this problem, but some are not set up so that each trainee obtains a maximum of experience on any phase of the archaeological process except, perhaps, the shovel. However, many institutions have no field schools for their archaeologically oriented majors. Again, the answer lies with the individual and his devotion to the goal of becoming an archaeologist. It requires a particular type of individual.

A Digging Archaeologist

The archaeologist should first be an individual with an uncommon amount of common sense; a tool user, a chain saw user, an ax man, a carpenter, a mechanic, a tractor driver; an action man — an engineer. He should be an observer, a searcher, a doer, a craftsman — an artist. He should also be aware of the broad questions requiring broad answers, and he should be able to see the reflection of these questions in relation to the few answers he has been able to arrive at from the examination of his particular site. The theme of cultural, social and historical interpretation is an ever-present background highlighted and interwoven by the accented melody of specifics as he probes the site for meaning.

The historical archaeologist should also be familiar with the use of deed records, land grants, maps, drawings and verbal accounts as they apply to historic sites and the archaeological data. The blending of the document with the ruin is the pivot and challenge of historical archaeology.

Site Survey

The technique of surface survey is essential in the process of historical archaeology. The recovery of surface artifacts is only one facet of this technique. The use of resistivity methods, topographical features, documents and tradition are important factors in a competent surface survey of an area.

Surface survey often involves preliminary testing or trenching. Test squares have traditionally been used to determine stratigraphic relationships, but such exploration of sites is too often the only examination the site ever receives. Questions as to the location of features such as ditches, walls, wells, privy holes, palisade lines, and horizontal differences in artifact concentrations can also be examined in an exploratory survey through a series of parallel and cross trenches dug to the subsoil level. Such survey trenching is important in the early stages of the exploration of an historic site when questions relating to the future extent of archaeology on the site are being asked.

In traditional site survey the emphasis is usually oriented toward the determination of archaeological sites not known through documentary sources. Site survey in historic archaeology, however, more often involves a specific search for a particular ruin whose general location is known from documentary sources. In this respect historic site survey is usually more locally focused than the broader blanket survey approach to locate and record prehistoric Indian sites.

Once the site is located, the establishment of a base·line or grid system for controlling the horizontal provenience is basic to the archaeological process. The grid system is the standard and most used method, but may prove cumbersome when used over an area of some thirty or forty acres when broad testing is carried out, and where thick woods are involved. Under such conditions the base line method which does not require the use of the 90° angle, and which has proven to be a fast and accurate method, is a most useful means of data recording.

Plow Zone

On sites where plowing has taken place one of the first decisions an archaeologist must make is how to handle the plowed zone; whether to remove it by hand with shovels or by machine. If the artifacts are abundant in the plowed soil zone sifting would be desirable, and if they are not, perhaps stripping with a front-loader would be the best solution. If this is the case would such a machine damage the ruin or the features such as burials lying just beneath the topsoil? How much time is involved in the project and is it a salvage job? Will contractors move in and totally destroy any evidence lying beneath the plowed soil zone within a matter of weeks or

FIGURE 1. *Gang schnitting the area of the west fortification ditch of the 1670 settlement of Charles Towne, South Carolina. The plowed soil was first removed by using a front loader. Two days were required to remove the topsoil from the area shown here.*

days? Are the features that lie beneath the plowed soil zone more pregnant with data than the plowed soil blanket? Is it better to locate one burial with a shovel crew and have it undamaged by machine pressure on a salvage project, or is it better to recover a dozen slightly crushed burials by using the machine? In other words, what is the most efficient method of removing the plowed soil zone to obtain the greatest amount of data? This is the question the archaeologist must answer as he approaches such a site, and the answer will hardly ever be the same, for conditions will vary with each site. Historical archaeologists are constantly having to make such judgments for the sake of maximum data recovery in the minimum amount of time, though time in itself, when no danger of destruction of the site is involved, should not be used as an excuse for using salvage archaeology methods. Again, judgment must be used.

There are sites, of course, that have no plowed soil blanket, such as untouched historic ruins or Indian structures or camp sites, as well as shelter and cave sites. In such cases detailed examination with trowels often begins with the surface of the ground, and stripping of a top blanket of disturbed soil is not a consideration.

In order to reveal the features that lie beneath the blanket of plowed soil on many sites it is necessary that the subsoil surface be cleanly cut or "schnitted",* just below the bottom of the plow zone but deep enough to remove most of the plow scars. Through this

---

* A term picked up some years ago from Martin Biddle when he visited Brunswick Town. It comes from a German noun *schnitt*, meaning cut, and seems quite appropriate to the process, and has proved most useful. Bob Stephenson informs me that in the Plains and other areas the same process is referred to as "skimming".

process subsoil intrusions are revealed for plotting and photographing. On any archaeological site, historic or Indian, postholes will most likely be found, representing previous activity. It is unlikely that on an occupied site, postholes and tree holes, recent holes, and ancient holes, would not be revealed through the schnitting process. For this reason a drawing of an historic ruin which shows no postholes, tree holes, etc., would appear to be cause for suspicion as to the degree of selectivity of the data by the archaeologist, or of his failure to cleanly schnitt the area.

The schnitting process can be carried out to some degree by the use of a front-loader with a sharp cutting blade in the *hands of a good operator*. The result must still be hand schnitted to completely reveal all features intruding into the subsoil.

Reading the Dirt

Once the features are located the archaeologist must be alert at all times to "read the dirt" in both the plan and profile examination During excavation he must take care that the shape of the excavated feature corresponds to the original shape, and is not influenced by the shape of the excavating tool. He must be familiar with the various types of subsoil as well as the visual appearance and texture of disturbances, some of which are extremely difficult to distinguish from undisturbed subsoil. Familiarity with the meaning and importance of stratigraphic data as revealed in profiles is a must, and the determination as to whether a layer of earth is a result of intentional filling to level a depression, filling to dispose of the fill material such as a midden deposit, deposition resulting naturally from movement of soil by wind or water, faulting and cave-in resulting from pressure and freezing, deposits associated with architectural features such as earth embanked around an open hearth, the surfacing of a walk, etc., are constant challenges to the archaeologist in the examination of features.

The importance of "reading the dirt" relates, of course, to the recovery of artifacts from the various layers deposited on the site. The presence or absence of artifact types within the stratigraphic layers and features and the recording of these through drawings, verbal notes, and particularly photographs, is of utmost importance to the proper understanding of the cultural relationships that existed on a site. Needless to say, careful excavating technique is a significant factor as to the amount of *in situ* data that is recovered

through the association of artifacts in layers or in horizontal position in relation to features. The photographing of artifacts *in situ* showing their position in relation to archaeological features and stratigraphic layers is an important means of data recording that cannot be over emphasized.

In examining the layers and features of a site the question as to whether to sift or not *to sift must be answered early in the process of examining such data*. The argument has been presented that when proper troweling is done no sifting is warranted, however, this rule cannot always be applied, for instance in the removal of the contents of a ditch six hundred feet long and six feet deep while recovering small lead shot and seed beads. Such features must be shifted through window screen in order to recover these small artifacts. If a feature or layer does not produce enough cultural material to warrant sifting, then it should not be sifted merely to satisfy the demands of a technique.

Record Keeping

Throughout the recovery process the pinpointing of objects in relation to the matrix in which they are found is, of course, of particular importance because it is through these relationships that meaningful analysis of artifacts can be undertaken. Using the grid system, designation as to the vertical and horizontal position of objects is given in terms of the coordinates of the grid. The base line method requires a provenience card numbering system which allows for control of these relationships, but carries the disadvantage of not immediately providing reference to the provenience in terms of the number itself as does the grid system designation. It has an advantage, however, in that it allows the relatively small provenience number to be directly utilized as a field catalog number, without the necessity of subsequently assigning a field catalog number, such as is necessary when the grid system is used. The saving in time through dealing with only a single provenience number is considerable. Whatever method is used by the archaeologist, the important fact is that the materials in the field be accurately and conveniently recorded as to their provenience, without so much as a single sherd becoming misplaced, misnumbered, or loosing its contextual association.

Besides the provenience data record, scaled profile drawings, detailed feature drawings, etc., the archaeologist should keep a daily log of events as they unfold. This account should be as complete as possible, and should include human interest events, public relations events, contacts with individuals and groups, etc. A pocket notebook kept during the course of the day aids in making notations to make the recording of the archaeological process more complete.

Photography

Photography, as has been mentioned, is a primary means of recording features, profiles, artifacts *in situ*, and the various stages of the archaeological process. The archaeologist should have more than a passing acquaintance with the camera, both press type and roll film cameras, as well as 35mm and movie equipment, all of which should be used to record the various aspects of the examination of a site. Exposure meters should be used to take the guess work out of picture taking and insure good results. As far as possible, each picture should be a publishable photograph, and if this fact is kept in mind, more competent photographs will result. Photography should never be looked on as only an incidental tool which can be periodically used. Rather, it should assume a major data-collecting position in the archaeologist's plan of site examination and recording.

Master Site Plan

Throughout the data-collecting process the surveyed points for any feature, wall, excavated area, etc., recorded on data sheets are transferred by protractor and scale to the master site plan which is kept up to date each day as the site is excavated. Thus a plan drawing of all the pertinent features of the site is available for easy reference so that judgment of areas yet to be examined can be made daily as related features are revealed on the master plan.

For greatest understanding, the entire area of a site should be shown in one drawing, and a scale of more than four feet to the inch produces postholes and features that are often too small to be comfortably handled. A scale of four feet to the inch allows such features to be accurately shown, but has the disadvantage of producing drawings too large to be easily handled. This problem is solved, however, when the ink drawing on drafting film is made over the master plan, complete with appropriate titling and labeling. This drawing can then be reduced when the master negative is made through photogrammetry for

use in printing the final drawings for publication. This master site plan, along with the profile drawings and the photographs, constitute the major graphic data the site has produced, and is a primary document. The drafting of the master map after the field work is completed is unwise for there is a constant interaction between the features being revealed in the field, the archaeologist, and the drawing. This interaction, with each day's decisions predicated on the previous day's discoveries as seen on the master site plan, is one of the most stimulating and challenging aspects of the archaeological process.

Directing A Crew

With the archaeologist's efforts in the field centered on the process of data recording with the instrument, feature recording, provenience control, public relations, etc., it is imperative that a crew chief be present to immediately direct the activities of the crew. The function of the crew, of course, is to reveal and recover the data under the direction of the crew chief and the archaeologist. The size may vary from two or three individuals to large gangs. Both the archaeologist and crew chief must be able to manage the efforts of the crew so that the maximum effort is exerted. In order to do this the archaeologist and crew chief must clearly know what they are doing, what goals they wish to achieve, and proceed to positively direct the crew toward these ends. A crew will respond positively to a positive, competent, and confident crew chief, and morale will break down and chaos may result when indecisiveness is revealed by their leader. The crew chief must be something of a drill instructor combined with a knowledge of personality so that he can appeal to the crew at whatever level they can be reached, and this varies considerably as to whether the crew is composed of college students, high school students, professional laborers or a combination.

The ideal size of a crew for maximum production from each individual is around ten. At Charles Towne a crew of fifty was used, and is the maximum that can be effectively handled by a single crew chief, who must be an exceptional leader to continue to produce maximum energy from so large a crew. There are advantages to breaking down such a group into smaller units with several crew chiefs, but this fragments authority, which may result in a loss of energy for achieving the goals of the archaeologist. On the other hand, if several strong crew chiefs are available smaller units may be warranted, with a consequent increase in efficiency. Again, the archaeologist must use judgment to evaluate how the most energy can be produced from the group.

An important factor in successful communication with the crew is consideration of the generation gap. If the archaeologist is over 30 he will likely find that a younger crew chief can achieve more positive results with less resentment from the younger crew. The archaeologist can deal with such a crew chief and transmit goals into action through him more effectively than attempting to carry out this function himself. In this time of nonconformity to tradition, this archaeologist has found in dealing with a large crew composed almost entirely of individuals resenting Establishment authority, a young crew chief was a crucial bridge for communication and action. As important as this point is, perhaps a more significant factor which can override the generation gap is that the archaeologist can instill respect, not through a show of authority, but through his archaeological competence, and devotion to achieving the goals of the project. For such a man, there is no generation gap.

Artifacts

Once the data is recovered from the field the process of washing, cataloging, preservation and restoration of artifacts in the laboratory begins. Much of this work may be carried out during the course of the excavation. Ideally, day by day washing and cataloging will keep just behind the recovery of artifacts from the field, so that by the end of the season the artifacts will be ready for study by the archaeologist. This procedure is something not possible, and as a result the analysis of the data must await the completion of the laboratory process. The laboratory work must be handled by a competent, intelligent person who has an interest in, and an inclination toward order. One sherd in the wrong bag with the wrong provenience number can change the entire interpretation of a feature, so it is imperative that the laboratory personnel be aware of the importance of exactness and error-free operation. The archaeologist must be aware of the properties of all types of objects recovered from the field so that this information can be passed on to the laboratory personnel, and proper steps for preservation and storage of artifacts be carried out.

Analysis and Report

Once the artifacts are cataloged and processed, the archaeologist must be able to take the materials and through typology and comparative research, establish meaningful groupings of artifacts that hopefully have cultural significance for the period from which the artifacts originated. Historical archaeologists are at an advantage in that written sources often reveal a great deal of information as to form, function and cultural significance of certain artifacts. On the other hand, this information is not always easily available, or may be completely lacking, leaving the archaeologist with the traditional tools of typology, archaeological context, stratigraphy, association, and his knowledge of the evolution of forms. If his knowledge of the forms is lacking, specialists in the study of glass, buttons, ceramics, buckles, military hardware, etc., are primary sources for information for the historical archaeologist in his analysis of the materials he has recovered. He may be a specialist in one type of artifact, but he must call on others to milk the most from his archaeological data.

Whether his analysis consists of statistical relationships, hopefully representing a cultural relationship, during the period represented by his site, or whether he treats the artifacts individually as reflective of a historical period as revealed in documents, the archaeologist is favored with the responsibility of putting into print the accumulation of knowledge and insight that has resulted from the challenging archaeological process.

Public Relations

In his observation, description and explanation of the site the archaeologist is still an interacting unit within the society of which he is a part, and therefore cannot isolate himself in the ivory tower of his archaeological investigation. From the moment he sets foot on a site the archaeologist is often in the spotlight of the local news. Statements he makes will reflect directly on the institution who is sponsoring his work, and his comments should represent the views of the field of archaeology and not the personal opinions of the archaeologist. When questions are asked with the view of drawing out the personal feelings of the archaeologist, his response should always be in terms of the professional archaeologist, the scientist involved in the collection of data.

Upon occasion the archaeologist may find himself the pivot of a controversy due to the nature of his findings which may disturb traditional assumptions. In such cases he should point out what he has found, its significance in relation to other similar discoveries, its significance in terms of potential development as an historic monument, and its historical and scientific significance. In this regard he must be extremely careful not to overstate his case, for to do so will undermine anything he says in the future. If the discovery is thought to be unique, he should verify his position by conferring with colleagues to obtain their evaluation, and so armed with a broad professional base, he can present his position in the strongest and most effective manner. He may find that others are willing to stake their political and personal reputations on the archaeologist's evaluation of the significance of the historic site. If he has improperly judged and weighed the situation, if he cannot support his scientific position in the brilliant spotlight of the world's press, radio and television media, then his misjudgment will mean that those who based their actions on his evaluation will suffer. Therefore, although the archaeologist should never take a political stand, he may find that those in political position will rely on his judgment, so it behooves him to stand firmly on the base provided for him

by his archaeological, historical, and scientific research, and in so doing the battle may rage around him and he will not be hit in the cross-fire.

Archaeology and Site Development

The field of historical archaeology, perhaps more so than the field of Indian site archaeology, frequently becomes involved with site development for public education and entertainment. The historical archaeologist should be well aware of the attitudes and concepts of the general public as well as his colleagues in regard to the development of historic sites as compared to the purely observational and descriptive aspects of his undertaking. His explanation of the meaning of his site may be immediately translated into three-dimensional reality through rebuilding of houses, forts and other features based on information revealed through research and archaeology. In this regard there are two questions that present themselves: "Should the archaeologist engage in archaeology only, or should he become involved in site development?" and "Is historical archaeology with a problem oriented base more 'high-level' than that originating from a sponsor's desire for site development?"

FIGURE 2. *The junction of the excavated and re-shaped east fortification ditch and embankment with the west fortification ditch not yet excavated. This fortification was dug in 1670 to protect against possible Indian attack, and the east ditch was shown on a 1671 map.*

The sponsors of archaeological projects usually have some goal in mind, usually this is other than purely scientific in nature. The development of historic sites associated with historical people and events has assumed a major role in the interest of groups devoted to history and archaeology. Therefore, before the archaeologist sets foot on many sites his approach has been dictated by the interests of the sponsoring agencies. The interest may be as general as determining what was on the site, to excavation for the purpose of locating specific foundations for the purpose of rebuilding. In either case the archaeologist must not compromise his method for the sponsors. He may know that the sponsors are primarily interested in the foundation wall, but this should not prevent him from examining in all detail necessary the stratigraphic picture he finds, or of locating and excavating every possible feature associated with the foundation wall. It should go without saying that the archaeological method and scientific approach and recovery of data will not be altered merely because the sponsors have the limited interest of the foundation alone. Yet, some have assumed that because the sponsor's goals are limited that the archaeologists who carry out such investigation also are limited by the same goals. Now if the recording of the foundation walls is all the archaeologist comes up with in his report, then he is surely to be criticized, but archaeology on historic ruins need not be classified as low-level by nature merely because sponsors have limited

objectives. The archaeologist's objectives and methods must remain consistent with scientific exploration and recording regardless of the specific questions asked by sponsors.

The view has been stated that historical archaeology should remain a purely investigative process and that the archaeologist should not involve himself in the problems of site development. However, an alternative position sees the archaeologist as the most qualified person to recommend and direct the execution of certain phases of historic site development. This view sees the role of the archaeologist as going beyond the strictly data gathering and reporting level. If the site is to be developed for public use as an historic site the archaeologist has different considerations than if the site is to be backfilled. For instance, stone or brick walls must be stabilized and protected from the damaging effects of freezing and exposure, fortification ditches may very well be left open after they are excavated and the accompanying parapet mound placed back in its original position, based on archaeological and historical data. Palisade ditches and postholes may very well again be supplied with posts to mark the position where others once stood. This activity, it is agreed, is not archaeological except in the interpretive sense, yet interpretive explanation is a basic facet of the archaeological process.

Interpretive explanation through site development can proceed along with the archaeological examination of the site in many

FIGURE 3. *The stabilized fortification ditch under irrigation. A palisade ditch line was found paralleling the ditch at a point just beneath the center of the embankment in several places where the plow had not completely erased the ditch. Palisade poles will be placed throughout the length of the embankment as an interpretive exhibit.*

instances, while a time for analysis and research is required in other cases before site development can begin. There are times when interpretive explanation becomes more than that, and takes on a political aspect. In erecting a sample of parapet and palisade in the position indicated by archaeological data the archaeologist has merely expressed what the archaeology and his research have dictated was present. Yet, who can deny that such a step is an overtly political move in that it is significantly impressive and effective, and is likely to bring results in terms of funds for archaeology and development when lesser efforts may fail. Should the archaeologist not use the data and skills at his command to present the interpretation based on his archaeology? Should he only find and record evidence and write his report and turn this over to the developers to do the reconstruction and development for interpretive explanation? If he does this he can remain aloof and point out the errors committed by the developers, but this seems to be the easy way out. It seems that the archaeologist's responsibility *does* extend into the area of site development for interpretive explanation. Whether he goes beyond the level dictated by archaeology and research is, of course, a matter to be judged. Drawings, models and full scale reconstructions are a basic feature of Classical archaeology, and should be a basic feature of American historical archaeology as well. Once in the field of historical archaeology the archaeologist will find that most of the sites he examines will be development oriented in terms of interpretive explanation and not problem oriented in terms of answering specific questions such as, "What was the protein consumption of the eighteenth century colonist as reflected in their midden deposits?" It would be ideal if such problems could be posed, a site selected to examine, and the answer conveniently brought forth, but the site just might not answer the questions we had asked, and would likely yield answers to questions we had not thought of asking. This does not mean that I am against problem oriented excavations, rather I am only saying that a problem oriented site is not necessarily more "pure", "noble", "scientific", or "high-level" than a development oriented site. Just because funds are available to dig a seventeenth century fort, and you happen to be interested in nineteenth century ceramics, we do not disdain the fort project because it is not problem oriented to suit our questions. The fort just might have some answers to questions

the archaeologist never thought of posing as a problem.

The prime problem on most historic sites is: What was there? Why was it there? When was it there? Who put it there? What does it mean? These are by no means all the questions asked routinely by the historical archaeologist, but they are a good start, and the answering of them takes some doing. Historical archaeology needs both development and problem oriented approaches to historic sites explored more fully, but one cannot say that one is a more exalted pursuit than the other.

Conclusion

As the title of this paper suggests, historical archaeologists are wanted by institutions throughout America, and this want-ad has attempted to outline the process the institutions have a right to expect the historical archaeologist to be able to carry out. It was stimulated by the fact that some individuals entering the field of historical archaeology are seen to be unfamiliar with many of the facets of the process as outlined in the summary presented here. Specialization has been so emphasized as a necessity for historical archaeologists that an involvement in the broad fabric of the endeavor has taken a secondary role. The ironic result is that in a time of great national need for historical archaeologists to handle the growing demand for competent historic site examination, there is a shortage of historical archaeologists capable of effectively carrying out the archaeological process on historic sites.

If the applicant for the position of historical archaeologist is a specialist instead of a generalist, if he cannot competently handle the various aspects of the position, then he should consider himself as a technician, an engineer, a craftsman, a digger, a specialist, but not an historical archaeologist. A specialist in the excavation of burials is a technician, a surveyor is a technician, a draftsman is a technician, a researcher is a researcher (or a scholar), a photographer is a technician (or an artist), a ceramics expert is a specialist, a developer is an engineer, a public relations man is a politician, a laboratory chief may be a scientist, a crew chief is a drill instructor and a psychologist, a shovel man is a ditch digger, a writer is a scholar. Combine these talents in one individual and you may have a catastrophe; and then again, you may have an historical archaeologist.

THE HISTORICAL ARCHAEOLOGIST

The Job	The Man	Related Field	Personality Characteristic and Aptitude Requirements
Theory	Theoretician	Anthropology, History	Scholar
Research	Researcher	History	Scholar
Crew Chief	Crew Chief	Drill Instructor, Engineer	Leadership, Intelligent, Archaeologically Informed
Survey	Site Surveyor	Crew Chief	Athletic
Data Recovery	Field Technician	Geology	Competent and Exacting
Feature Excavation	Field Technician	Geology	Patience
Transit Surveying	Surveyor	Surveying	Competent and Exacting
Photography	Photographer	Graphics	Familiarity with Equipment
Shoveling	Laborer	Ditch Digging	Strong Back, Willing
Schnitting	Shovel Craftsman	Specialized Labor	Not Afraid of Work
Machine Use	Machine Operator	Engineering, Contracting, Construction	Grasp of Archaeological Needs and Approach
Note Taking	Descriptive Writer	Writing, Secretarial	Literacy with a Facility for Letters and Numbers
Drawing Profiles	Drawing, Draftsman	Drafting, Art, Geometry, Architecture	Exacting, Competent, Accurate, Observant
Drafting Maps and Plans	Draftsman	Drafting, Art, Geometry, Architecture	Precise, Accurate, Neat, Exacting
Provenience Control	File Clerk	Secretarial	Exacting, Neat, Sense of Order
Recognition of Soils	Technician	Geology, Art	Accurate Observer
Data Preservation	Technician	Technician	Craftsman, Artist, Tool User
Cataloging, Restoration of Artifacts, Preservation	Laboratory Technician	American Civilization, Ceramics, Glass, Material Culture	Craftsmanship, Accuracy, Patience
Analysis, Typology, Comparative Study, Wedding of Archaeological and Historical Data Writing Report	Specialist in Glass, Ceramics, Material Culture Synthesist, Typist	American Civilization, Anthropology, History	Systematic Data Organization, Insight, Judgment, Comprehensive
Public Exhibition of Archaeological Features, Ruins, Exhibits, Ruin Stabilization, Construction of Palisades, Parapets, etc.	Historic Site Developer	Contractor, Engineer, Artist, Exhibits Designer, Craftsman	Craftsmanship, Condenser of Data for Public Use to Bridge the Gap Between History, Archaeology, Science, and the Level of Public Understanding

AFTER THE REPORT, WHAT?:
The Uses Of Historical Archaeology, A Planner's View

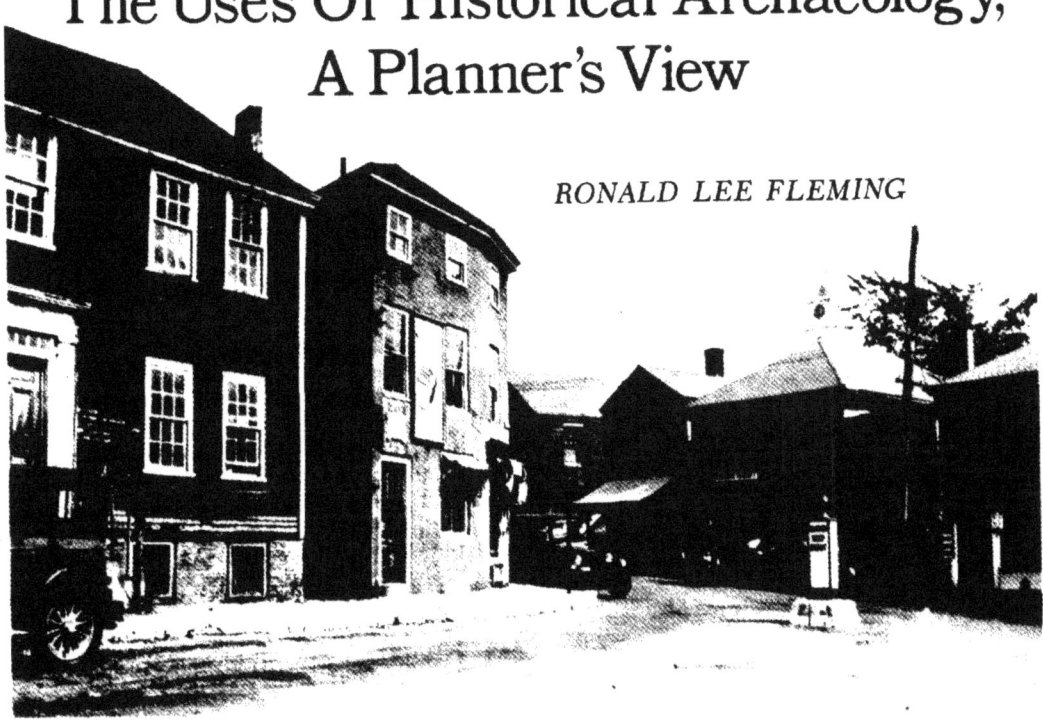

RONALD LEE FLEMING

INTRODUCTION

At a time when the American past is rapidly being swept away in the name of progress—whether it be called a plethora of freshly minted parking lots, a curtain wall of commercial office space or the roaring sprawl of a regional shopping center over the site or across the ruin of some olden structure, the views of a planner might be suspect. Certainly the planning profession has largely failed to curtail the destruction of evidence and artifacts which archaeologists study, interpret, and attempt to preserve. Urban growth and change has levied a heavy toll on the number of historic sites recognized in the WPA Historic Buildings Survey in the thirties. Admittedly, planners who carry out urban renewal and redevelopment are partially responsible for this loss.

I would submit, however, that archaeologists and historians are also responsible. I do not mean directly responsible for the destruction. That would be an anathema. Rather, they are responsible for not being creative enough about their own roles and not being resourceful enough about the areas of public life where they could assert these roles. Like planners who make reports that are often totally divorced from implimentation strategies, historians and archaeologists have sometimes preferred to maintain a scholarly detachment while producing voluminous reports and precise studies. The loss we have all suffered is not merely a loss of artifacts and buildings. It is a loss of the meaning of our society. It is a removal of the physical fabric of our culture and with it the set of associations which inform us where we are—that tell us what we have come from.

This task of restoring the significance of our environment is the very real responsibility of archaeologist, historian, and planner, and it cannot wait until all of the reports are in. This task of interpretation, of making the reports relevant to the people, demands that the scholar develop a new role. Scholarly detachment, a dubious virtue in my judgement, might be superceded by the skills of cultural impressarios who will bring the exhibits of this historical significance to the people where they live—not into the storage rooms of museums or the pages of another arcane report. Consequently I have chosen to speculate about some of the uses of historical archaeology which can make the archaeologists efforts more meaningful to the communities around them. I would suspect that these uses might well increase public support for archaeological work.

This is a more optimistic task than boring you with a dreary recital of the larger problems with which planners, archaeologists and historians must continually cope—these problems include; a short-sighted view of the profit motive which frustrates effective land use planning; preservation and archaeological work which get short shrift before the barren coffers of nearly bankrupt city and state government; and the hodge-podge of jurisdictional lines which makes comprehensive planning for historic preservation a more difficult task. Nevertheless, even these perimeters may be scaled if a sufficient public awareness is generated. This requires a look, first, at role development, which I have provisionally titled, "getting a piece of the action."

"GETTING A PIECE OF THE ACTION:" SOME BOLDER ROLES

I have chosen to discuss roles for the archaeologist and historian because it seems one of the blunt facts of American life that historic preservation, archaeological investigation and interpretation remain near the bottom of priorities for most funding agencies. Unless archaeologists can make their work meaningful to other funding agencies, they will remain in the role of a crippled mendicant-poor and handicapped. According to Ivor Nöel Hume in his excellent address, "Archaeology: Doorway to the American Past," delivered at the annual meeting of the Athenaeum of Philadelphia; the actual appropriation available under the Historic Preservation Act of 1966, (which states that the Department of Interior will provide up to 50% of the funds for preservation work on listed sites and properties) is "little more than a gesture." Mr. Noel Hume went on to say that "the monies last year were insufficient to cover half the costs of restoring more than two medium sized houses, or digging and reporting on more than a dozen archaeological sites of any size or complexity."

For Fiscal 1971, there is a record $5.9 million appropriation which represents a quantum jump in potential expenditures: however, the act's importance to archaeologists will probably remain its protection of unexcavated sites. Presumably archaeologists should lobby the state review boards to assure that they are registering these sites now, with the proviso that they may be dropped upon excavation. This would inhibit the ravaging of sites by other arms of government. It would be necessary to minimize the publicity attendant on legislation to discourage private vandalism. Much of the new money will go into the planning process—more reports, more state surveys, more state preservation plans and conferences. This is laudable, but the onus for seed money for the projects that follow remains with the states, which are usually financially strapped.

As a planner, used to producing reports, I remain skeptical of their impact. Far too often they are merely inventories without priorities attached to them. Surveys should provide the basis for evaluation which leads to a strategy for action. Do archaeologists and historians have quantified lists of sites needing the protection of eminent domain legislation? Have they plotted future urban renewal areas? Have they determined sites needed by future renewal clearance?

I think that in order to make real progress, archaeologists and historians will have to adopt an aggressive, "What can we do for you?" role when looking for funding sources, and they will have to broaden the range of agencies to which they speak. Federal urban renewal funds, 701 planning grants, residential rehabilitation monies, and model cities supplemental funds to city and private agencies all represent funding sources, which can, and in limited cases, are being utilized by archaeologists and historians. It is true of course that sometimes the ponderous and public process of utilizing federal monies so escalates the cost of preservation that social objectives such as low income rehabilitation are more difficult to fulfill. It is also true that the grantees of these funds might have a limited view of what the monies can be used for.

Both to acquire federal funds and to insure that their utilization increasingly benefits the larger community will involve coordination with public bodies who may be regarded with some hostility or suspicion by archaeologists — i.e., urban renewal and housing authorities, and city planning commissions. In the past, historians and archaeologists have often worked with such public authorities only when the bulldozers were on the street preparing to wipe out the last old house on the block. There has been much public hand wringing but little coordination.

Incidentally, there is also very little publicity in many cases. With a nation of emerging film makers and a new public service demand for documentaries, how many film documentaries on preservation have you seen recently? A HUD film on profitable rehabilitations of old structures in different parts of America might prove more convincing to small town bankers than all the preservationist rhetoric on the values of the past. There have been some examples of cooperation. Most notably, funds were provided in the urban renewal planning budget for the Fort Stanwix Central Business District project in Rome, New York. Here, at this fort in August, 1777, historians believe the Stars and Stripes were first flown in battle. In Sante Fe, the Museum of the University of New Mexico is currently requesting funds from the Model Cities Agency to do an archaeological dig on the site of an urban renewal clearance and housing project in the model neighborhood. Archaeological investigations of Puddle Dock are also a part of Strawberry Bank, Inc., the private, non profit organization which contracted with the Portsmouth Housing Authority to use urban renewal funds for the preservation of a waterfront section in this New Hampshire city.

The Department of Housing and Urban Development cites other cities where there is apparent cooperation between historians, preservationists, and archaeologists on the one side and the local public authorities on the other, but in perusing these examples it is apparent that in most cases the preservationists conceived a very limited role for themselves. In Strawberry Bank, where urban renewal funds preserved 30 old houses and relocated 90 families, the population leaves at 5 o'clock. Portsmouth has a housing shortage, but Strawberry Bank contains only two apartments — which are used for caretakers. As an in-town house museum, it has largely ignored the potential of a trade off with the housing authority, which could mean more houses saved in exchange for rehabilitation and accommodation of low income people.

Such a trade off could stand preservationists in good stead when negotiating with the very reluctant housing authority in the North Portsmouth Urban Renewal Project. The 40 historic houses there were scheduled for clearance. Strawberry Bank only offered to move five. It did not see the social role in making the housing a viable asset to the city-integrating the texture of the old housing in the homeowner's relationship to new development. With large blocks of tax exempt museum houses in the downtown area and no plan to provide some social utility to the city, is it any wonder that the city council was unenthusiastic?

Fortunately, Portsmouth Preservation Inc., after some initial collisions over land use plans, appears ready to present a scheme for the on-site rehabilitation of these houses in the private market. They are learning (with the help of a public relations firm) how to work with the housing authority. Still, I am informed that there is a long waiting list for public housing in Portsmouth which might provide the preservationists with an opportunity to do some scattered site low income housing. A more socially conscious role could also mean archaeological outreach services to the schools, work with various employment programs to train people in rehabilitation work — perhaps even of the dislocatees from urban renewal projects where preservation was scheduled to take place. Such a role would place archaeologists, preservationists, and historians in a much better position to negotiate with city governments because they would be meeting the agendas of these agencies — which are often as hostile and apathetic as the local population.

A Case Study: Salem and Plymouth

It is useful to look briefly at two cities, Salem and Plymouth, where archaeologists and historians have not carved out a role which would enable them to greatly influence the urban planning or prevent the destruction that took place under their noses, or, more appropriately, beyond their enclaves. Given the minimal role of archaeologists and historians in the policy making, it is little wonder that the uses of historic archaeology have been so limited here.

Both cities are cited glowingly in the HUD booklet, *Preserving Historic America*, as cases where there was cooperation between preservationists and planners. Although I have no more than a cursory knowledge of either city,

FIGURE 1. *Recent urban dig at Plymouth.*

after first examination this laudatory text has the rhetorical ring of an Orwellian Big Lie. In my view, both represent real failures for the preservation community, and sources of frustration to the archaeologists contemplating what is left. These cities are interesting because their architectural quality was well and early recognized and because they both contain institutions of varying degrees of wealth which could have played an aggressive role in compelling the respective urban renewal authorities to do justice to their sites. Instead, much of downtown Salem has been demolished, and most of Summer Street in Plymouth now contains Howard Johnson Mt. Vernon moderns. I understand that neither urban renewal site received archaeological attention.

The preservationists in Salem obtained some 701 planning assistance funds to do an historic district study as part of the city comprehensive planning program. Their study, massive in bulk and apparently read by very few, noted that there should be a firm public policy with respect to the use and renewal of historic areas. It also blocked off large sections of the city for historic districting, including the city hall, which was politically tactless. Meanwhile, the city moved ahead on Heritage Plaza, an urban renewal project in the heart of the old city, perhaps the nation's greatest repository of federal period ar-

chitecture. Preservationists did not at this stage demand that they serve on an advisory committee.

I have read the renewal plan and it does not talk about historic preservation. Only as it became apparent that the plan involved widespread demolition of some eighty historic structures were a few voices raised. Private citizens led by Mrs. Frothingham of Historic Salem, Inc. rather than the professionals on the staffs of the institutions, the Essex and Peabody Museums, carried the battle. The institutions with their resources, their expertise, and their prestige-ridden boards did not lead the fight. They refused to commit funds to buy land so that four buildings could be moved which even the authority said it wished to save, and failed to testify for the historic districting proposals which the city council now has tabled. Even with the mailed tramp of the bulldozers, they did not take remedial actions. There were no archaeological excavations on the freshly demolished sites and no interpretive programs or displays in the urban renewal area which might have roused public opinion. Apparently the agitation of historic Salem resulted in the saving of only a few brick buildings around the old town hall which was originally slated to become a parking lot. The institutions never took an advocacy role; little about the dispute appeared in the press, and

FIGURE 2. *Plymouth before renewal.*

the buildings and even the potential of urban archaeological digs on the site, have largely disappeared.

In Plymouth too, only a few private citizens were involved and were ultimately unsuccessful in saving the High-Summer Street urban renewal area from demolition. This area is more interesting for archaeologists, who were notably quiet at the time, because it contained the original town square, part of the historic Burial Hill, and the town brook where most of the early colonial settlement stood. A few 17th and 18th century houses were preserved and one building, the

FIGURE 3. *After renewal.*

FIGURE 4. *Plymouth before renewal.*

Bishop House, was moved. It was about the last house left, and was saved at the insistence of an irate summer resident. She managed to get the precedent setting Kennedy-Tower amendment to the urban renewal law which allows federal funds to be used for relocating historic buildings. Consequently it cost about $60,000 to move and restore a minor build-ing, and by the admission of the urban renewal authority, it was a bad restoration job. Meanwhile the Plymouth Plantation, with its ersatz village enclave, remained silent. Although the plantation had excellent research facilities, at this time the professional staff appeared not to have ventured from their park-like grounds.

FIGURE 5. *After renewal.*

Before the demolition began, the Redevelopment Authority wrote about 25 foundations, societies, and trusts which they thought might be interested in coming to Plymouth to preserve the better buildings. All replies were negative. They then ran adds in the local weekly newspaper saying that the houses were for sale for moving within the project area or out of it. There were still no responses. The urban renewal authority then began demolition of 125 buildings—half were built between 1683 and 1850; fifteen were 17th century houses. Only the houses on the south side of Summer Street were saved as conservation properties.

According to the urban redevelopment director, Allen Batista, the authority asked the Plymouth Plantation, which has a research staff and facilities, to undertake some archaeological work, but in his words "no one has ever come to this office." Sites included Jenny Pond, where the first grist mill was installed in 1630. This was dredged eventually by the renewal authority as a beautification project, with outsiders scavanging for the artifacts in this oldest part of Plymouth. Similarly, the authority eventually got a housing developer to reconstruct a grist mill and in the process dug mill stones from the site of the original mill. They could have benefited from the advice of a historical archaeologist. Other 17th century cellars as well as the pilgrim spring area offered possibilities for archaeologists. Now much of the area has been repaved and the lots covered with psuedo colonial housing.

Not only did the local organizations fail to play an aggressive role in coordinating with the urban redevelopment authority, but they failed to provide leadership in developing environmental programs in Plymouth. When HUD and the redevelopment authority proposed a systematic code enforcement program, the best method of preventing slums, the Plymouth Plantation took no stand on the issue, and it was defeated in the Town Meeting. Although there now are some urban renewal funds that could be available for identification and interpretation programs in the historic area, no historical organization has advocated that funds be utilized for this purpose. Houses could be labelled, sites marked in a spot that saw so many firsts in America (first saw mill, etc.), and there could be some programs in the local schools that dealt with the artifacts from these sites. Maybe this situation has changed with the arrival of Dr. James Deetz who has begun some digs (Figure 1) and has storefront displays of his work in downtown Plymouth.

Perhaps it is too harsh to infer from these examples that archaeologists and historians sometimes become affected with a certain preciousness about the limits of their responsibilities or that their position as technical staff excuses them from policy making roles.

Figure 6. *Plymouth renewed.*

I am suggesting though that there is an important connection between a more aggressive expansion of their roles and the more community-related uses for historical archaeology which I have alluded to and will now discuss specifically.

NEW USES FOR
HISTORICAL ARCHAEOLOGY

I have suggested that a new aggressiveness in making archaeological programs relevant to the agenda of other institutions might originally stem from a desire merely to tap their funding sources. But it is my contention that the basic impact involves archaeologists and historians in new uses for their respective disciplines. As they learn to merge agendas, there will be a greater public benefit. Certainly, in an age when the young are increasingly demanding "relevance" from their institutions, historical archaeology should not remain something confined to museums or to historical village ghettos. A policy relevant role involving merged agendas and funding sources suggests a number of, as yet, undeveloped uses:

1. Archaeological excavations can be employed as a tool to weld community consciousness by telling the people about their historic role in a place. Displays can clear up myths and cliches which are injurious to the pride of a community.

2. Archaeological exhibits and descriptions can enhance physical neighborhood identity and definition. Working with physical planners, archaeologists can interpret and use their skills to spark neighborhood conservation programs.

3. Archaeological work can serve as a dramatic focal point for community organization with spin offs into block clubs for preservation efforts.

4. Archaeological projects can be utilized to encourage changes in local school curriculum. School children can be involved in exhibits and sometimes even in aspects of the project work.

5. Archaeologists can utilize work to foster environmental education programs in the community at large.

A Prototype for New Uses

The recent urban archaeological project in the Weeksville section of Bedford Stuyvesant probably most epitomizes both a new role for archaeologists *and* broader utilization of

their work in the community. James Hurley, a local historian and amateur archaeologist, initiated the project. For some years Mr. Hurley wrote articles about local phenomena, such as old ice cream parlors, and took people on neighborhood walking tours sponsored by the Museum of the City of New York.

In 1968 he read an article in the *New York Times* stating that the Model Cities program in Brooklyn would begin slum clearance in what he theorized as the heart of the original settlement of Weeksville. He thought that an investigation of the old buildings and the sites might uncover clues leading to a clear picture of life in the original community. He knew Weeksville was supposed to have been settled by ex-slaves from the neighboring village of Bedford. Probably after World War II it became a largely black residential area again. Little was known about the area except some stereotyped notions in the *Brooklyn Eagle* of July 30, 1873, which depicted the black community as a sordid slum occupied by shiftless people.

Working through the New York City Landmarks Commission, Mr. Hurley contacted city hall and was given permission to investigate the site as the buildings were being demolished. He requested funds from the Model Cities program, but conflicts between different groups within the program and a low project priority from the city council caused him to turn to other sponsors, while his application lay pending.

The first two years of the project were financed by the Youth in Action Community Corporation and then a $25,000 grant from the City University of New York in 1969 replenished funds. Under the aegis of the project, a local association was established, the Society for the Preservation of Weeksville and Bedford Stuyvesant History. Several hundred neighborhood people including students from a nearby community school, boy scouts, and neighborhood youth corps people became involved in the excavation work during the summers. The Community Council for the Bedford Stuyvesant part of the model cities program officially endorsed the project; the community school asked to display the artifacts uncovered in the dig.

The survey of written materials and the discoveries so far indicate that the cliches about the black community were false. Hurley discovered that Weeksville had existed as a black entity between 1825 and 1875 and that it contained at least seven institutions including a black womens' organization for self

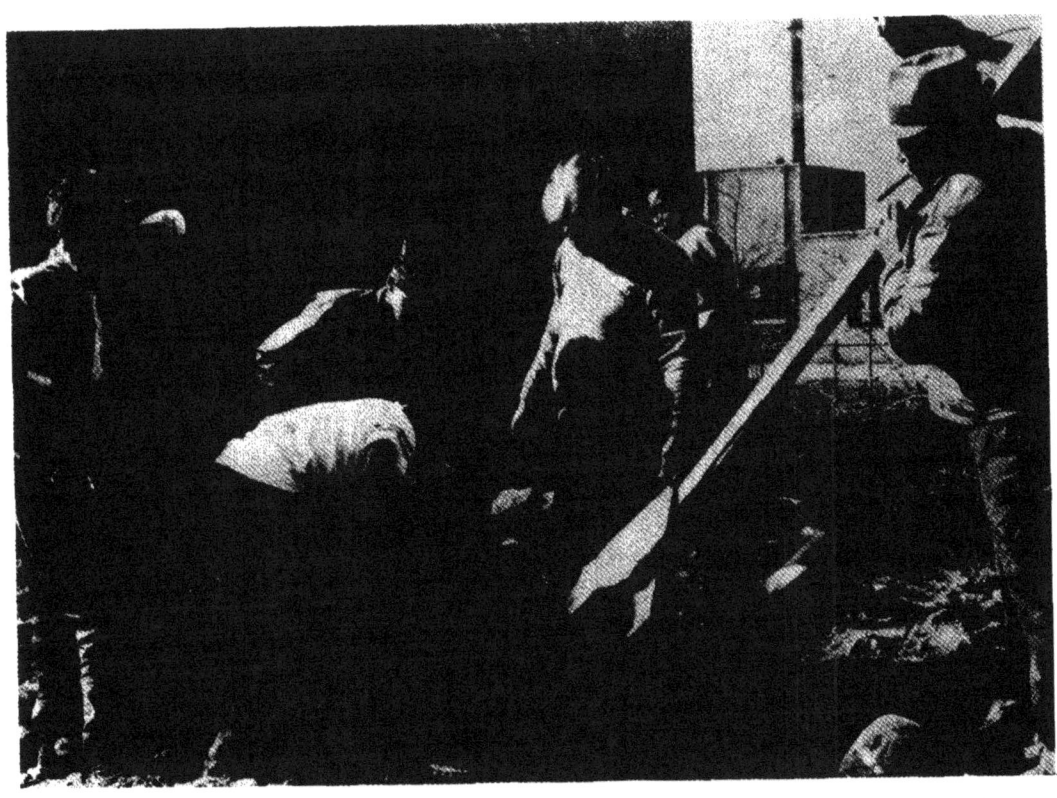

FIGURE 7. *Scoutmaster Wilson A. Williams, Sr. (center) directs Scouts of Troop 342 in excavation of old well site remembered by septuagenarian William T. Harley (right), Assistant Director of Project Weeksville, who was born across street in 1899.*

help and insurance coverage denied them by white companies. Although not wealthy, the research indicated that there was a wide range of occupations and that the community did not resemble the sordid picture depicted in the *Brooklyn Eagle* article.

With most of the excavation complete, the project is now quartered at the New York City Community College where it has received active support from the Brothers and Sisters of Afro-American Unity. Recently, the local preservation organization was able to secure landmark designation for three old buildings adjacent to the site. The project hopes now to encourage graduate research, particularly by black historians. Attention will also focus on an oral project to tape the reminiscenses of the older residents of Bedford Stuyvesant. Once a sufficient body of information is accumulated on the true history of Weeksville, the plan is to utilize the materials in a new curriculum design for the community schools.

FIGURE 8. *Boy Scout Daryl Ford marking artifact bag.*

FIGURE 9. *William Permanand (left) and Ronald Weathers (right) of Bedford-Stuyvesant Youth In Action's Neighborhood Youth Corps team working with Project Weeksville measure strata of large deposit of oyster shells found near 1599 Dean Street. Both are high school students.*

Now the Weeksville project has a new black directress and a new $36,000 grant from the National Endowment for the Humanities which will implement this curriculum design study and pay for a professional archaeologist to classify the excavated materials. During the excavation period the Boston educational TV station, WGBH, filmed a kind of socratic dialogue between some young black school boys and Mr. Hurley, the project director. This is probably the best film in the innovational TV series on urban conservation which WGBH produced under a HUD grant.

The Weeksville urban archaeology project can be labeled a rather didactic effort to support a black sense of identity and pride in community, and by the admission of its first director, there were many mistakes made in the actual excavation due to an abundance of volunteers and the often conflicting opinions of amateur archaeologists. Nevertheless, the project represents an interesting prototype for the uses of archaeology which I outlined above.

Mr. Hurley fully utilized the resources of the local community, and he broadened the uses of his project to fit the agendas of local

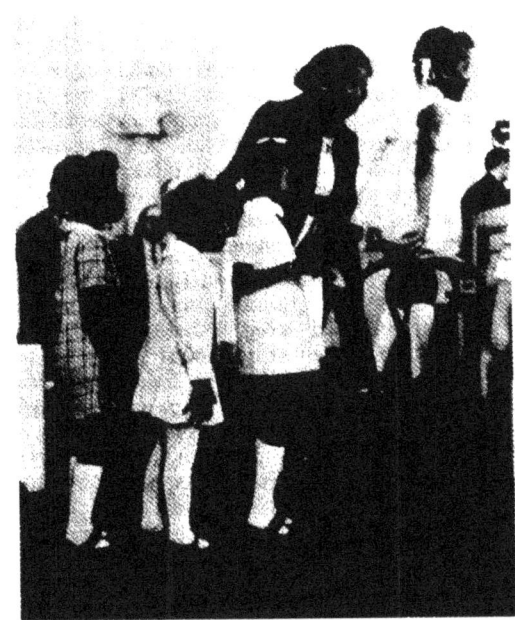

FIGURE 10. *Pupils of Public School 243 (successor to 19th century Colored School No. 2) testifying before Landmarks Commission at City Hall on behalf of Hunterfly Road buildings, June 1970. Accompanied by teacher Mrs. Marguerite Thompson who is presently writing a lower-grades curriculum based on Weeksville findings.*

institutions, including schools and the community college. He acted aggressively and untiringly to affect the policy of these organizations. Coordination with governmental bodies was not accomplished without much painful effort, which perhaps, only an amateur would undertake. Mr. Hurley estimated that he made some ninety phone calls, on just the proposal to utilize model cities funds, which, only now, two years after the first request, appears likely to be funded with $1000. In effect, the Weeksville project encouraged neighborhood identification, aided the preservation of surrounding buildings, generated the development of a community organization, caused funds to be spent for curriculum design, and stimulated environmental awareness in the community.

Environmental Education: Some Thoughts

Perhaps the sum total of the specific uses of archaeology in the Weeksville example demonstrate a kind of course in the uses of environmental education. I think environmental education programming is of particular interest to planners because it offers the possibility for some teamwork in which the archaeologists and historians feed the planners information of neighborhood origins for a more comprehensive identification system in a designated conservation area. A system of clear enamel markers identifying landmarks, ar-

FIGURE 11. *Mrs. Betty Welch, Corresponding Secretary of the Society for the Preservation of Weeksville and Bedford-Stuyvesant History sits with Project Weeksville staff member Larry Poole at outdoor annual exhibit of Bedford-Stuyvesant artists held at Fulton Park. Mr. Poole, a college student, wrote an article on Weeksville which appeared in the national periodical,* Negro Heritage.

chitectural and historical features of a neighborhood, periods of development, and outlines of former buildings would help to nurture a sense of place that so many Americans try to obtain by osmosis in Europe. Exhibits in subway stations, artifacts sunk in plastic cases embedded in sidewalks, window space in commercial buildings, displays in public buildings like the Post Office, representations of neighborhood architectural motifs on community bulletin boards are all rather simple physical elements in such an identification process. I would speculate, however, that such a comprehensive system could have more impact than a building survey by the Pilgrim Society in making the public aware of a heritage, even if their ancestors were not the builders. I feel that such an awareness would support historians and planners involved in preservation battles or seeking funding sources in the local community.

Admittedly with some great artifactual props, planners in other societies have launched notable interpretive efforts. The new Mexico City subway stations, for example, include Aztec design elements in the station motifs and even retain some of the artifacts found in the excavations. A pyramid shaped alter serves as the centerpiece in one station. Similarly, the vast housing project on the outskirts of the city includes a Spanish colonial church and acres of restored Aztec ruins in the grid of dramatic twentieth century architecture. Obviously, there is interpretive material to go with these built-in exhibits. In the old Arab city of Acre, in Israel, there are several buildings with wall phones where one can listen to a tape in five languages which records the history of the structure. UNESCO is now funding a cultural planning program which involves interpretive displays in Isfahan, Katmandu, Cartagina, and Cuzco as well as plans to preserve the unique quality of these cities. Here in America, I should like to see some archaeologists and historians design an identification system for a HUD demonstration grant. Our meagre efforts, usually involving unreadable bronze tablets, seem geared to those who already know and want confirmation, rather than for those who could be incidentally interested.

Curriculum Reform

Another educational use for archaeologists is the development of materials for school children. On October 30, the Congress approved an environmental education law #91-516 which authorizes the United States Com-

missioner of Education to establish education programs to encourage an understanding of policies and support of activities designed to enhance environmental quality. Under section 5 of that law small grants are available to citizen groups, private non-profit agencies and organizations to develop proposals for innovative approaches toward environmental education. Will archaeologists and historians respond to this challenge?

Last year, before the passage of this act, an architect and planner, named C. Richard Hatch, developed what I believe to be the first archaeological educational game. Under a grant from the Office of Education, Mr. Hatch produced a series of game-size cardboard pieces which depict excavated layers of an Indian dwelling mound in the southwest. As one takes away the layers, it is possible to uncover earlier walls as well as numbered depictions of artifacts. These drawings are then related to a series of numbered photographs which the children must identify. The Museum of Natural History supplied the photographs of actual Indian relics from a site in Arizona.

The children have to construct chronologies of events in the pueblo complex which relate to the discovery of the artifacts at different strata. They must also describe the role of different types of people in this Indian society which they have uncovered. Later they have to ask questions about the artifacts in their own society—and what they feel future archaeologists will say about this society. Finally they have to choose what artifacts they would like to see in a time capsule for the year 2000.

Mr. Hatch's game involves children in the potentially subversive concept of making choices about their environment, as they decide what artifacts they want for the time capsule. This game reflected Mr. Hatch's experience in Harlem where he founded an organization that provided advocate planning services to local people and tried to involve them in the decision-making for their community. In that instance, he designed games for children which allowed them to restructure their city blocks and thus consider the alternatives to their present environment.

Just as I feel archaeologists should be involved in the curriculum changes that produce games like these, so I think they must relate to the larger community issues of environmental education and reform. In the broadest sense, archaeologists in American cities have an opportunity to interpret a community to itself, and with that task should go a reverence for preserving its quality. In effect, I should like to see archaeologists as advocates of good design. Often they work in carefully zoned historic districts or in reconstructed historical villages which portray yesteryear in bucolic hues. Often too these preserves are the magnates of a considerable tourist horde which in turn is badgered by a neon blur lining the byways and arteries around the historic attraction. There you sit beautifully juxtaposed against the commercial squalor you have helped attract. How many organizations have boldly sponsored model sign codes or beautification measures for the surrounding areas. If, indeed, one of the inadvertent uses of the past (including historical archaeology) is to generate tourist dollars which support roadside blight, then it should be the obligation of the curators and interpreters of the past to bear some responsibility for safeguarding the future from the excesses of that commercialism.

SUMMARY

In this paper I have examined some situations which demonstrate a need for a more socially responsive role. Implicit in this discussion was the very pragmatic assumption that a larger public role involving shared agenda with other public agencies would be in the self interest of archaeologists because it would provide money for their work. I also stated that it would broaden the frame of the work program and find uses for it that were community related. Then I discussed some of these uses including community development, environmental education and curriculum reform. Uses like the neighborhood identification program and environmental advocacy should involve a closer coordination with members of my own planning profession. In conclusion, my concept is to use historical archaeology as a means to help a community develop its own sense of worth and to help it to define its past values. The definition of such values ultimately becomes a political act because it asks that the community make choices based on an emerging environmental awareness. Such uses of historic archaeology then, are not merely concerned with uncovering the past, but rather in developing a wider process of interpreting it, which, I submit, is supportive of a better environment in the present.

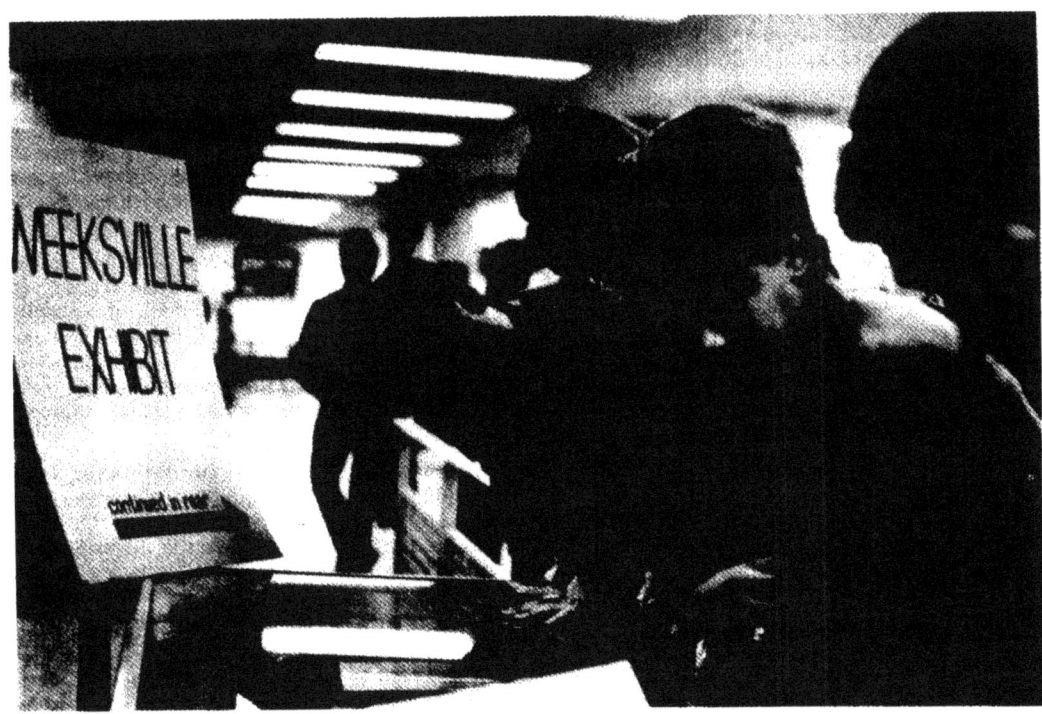

FIGURE 12. *High School students view Weeksville artifacts on exhibit at New York City Community College.*

Historical Archaeology: Who Needs It?

IVOR NOËL HUME

This article was presented as the keynote address at The Sixth Annual Conference of The Society for Historical Archaeology meeting concurrently with the Fourth International Conference on Underwater Archaeology in St. Paul, Minnesota, January 11, 1973.

Anyone called upon to give what is billed as a "keynote address" immediately following an election year, can expect to be dismissed as obsolete before he begins. Furthermore, it is in the nature of such addresses that they should be in step with the platform of the party leadership, and say what they say in rhetoric designed to excite and inspire the faithful. For these reasons, therefore, my presence up here is just about as appropriate as was Governor Wallace's at George McGovern's convention. Even Wallace was slightly better off in that he knew what the leadership had in mind, even if he didn't like it. I haven't the first idea where your joint directors want you to go, or what lies ahead for this society. I realize that I have already goofed by addressing myself to "this society" when we are, in fact, privileged to be sharing the meeting with the conferees on Underwater Archaeology.

ARCHAEOLOGICAL GOALS

I would add that I see this joint conference as one of the most valuable steps yet taken in the field of historical archaeology. It would be tragic, indeed, if underwater archaeologists should ever feel that their goals are any different from those of the rest of us who don't like to get our sites wet. It would

be sad, too, if we should underestimate the importance of underwater sites, or fail to recognize the difference between the competent underwater archaeologist and the treasure hunter who gives him a bad name — essentially the same distinction that we find so easy to draw on land. I think it is unlikely that any such doubts linger in your minds — or you would not be here.

It would be foolish to pretend that misunderstandings do not exist between the wet and dry people, or that the public's impression of both leaves much to be desired, and I can but hope that in painting the picture with an overly large brush, you will forgive me if now and then I let the paint fly too freely. I can assure you, however, that it is water soluble.

I doubt whether any of you will take issue with me, if I say that both the underwater and the terrestrial archaeologist are primarily seekers of knowledge about the past, whether it is derived from the ocean bed or from the basement of a burned brothel. Only the methods of retrieval differ. You will note that in my definition I have made no reference to objects, only to knowledge. It is, of course, a foolishly idealistic and naive assumption, for it is a safe bet that if the material remains of the past evaporated into the air within a half an hour of retrieval leaving nothing but knowledge in their wake, the ranks of alleged archaeologists would be decimated. We glibly condemn the amateur "pot-hunter", but forget that were it not for the lure of the artifact, the world's great archaeologically-fed museums from Cairo to New York would be a haven only for custodians and their cats. Having "something to show for it", has been the yardstick that has guided archaeological endeavours for literally thousands of years, and it can be argued that from a pragmatic point of view, it is not an entirely deprecable criterion.

This joint meeting is here to address itself to the dramatic prospect of a "Crisis in American Archaeology," and by the time you are through we should know whether it really exists, what it looks like, and if we are lucky, what to do about it. For my part, I would agree that there *is* a crisis, but I would argue that there always has been one, ever since Man first did anything lasting — and then discovered that it didn't. Furthermore, it is the threats and crises that make us get things done; without them we put off to somebody else's tomorrow the things that we should be doing today. I suggest, too, that while we readily see the bulldozer and the horny-handed land-developer as the architects of our crises, we are less inclined to recognize the enemy within. Yet, there is an indictment that rolls out through the centuries, charging the archaeological champions of the past with having inflicted the deepest wounds, for they have driven their spades to the heart, plucking it out, and leaving behind those parts that were damaged or mundane. By archaeologists bringing home only the best, and curators accepting only the finest of everything, the museum-visiting public and the history-reading school child have been given a markedly false impression of life as it was lived, were it in 18th century England or 1st century Rome. It is both a misconception and a danger that lives on today as far as shipwrecks are concerned, at least in the popular mind, for each year we hear of the recovery of specie and bullion and the prices that it commands at auction, but rarely do we hear about the wrecks that contained nothing of monetary value. Where are the reports describing in full the information derived even from the treasure-bearing wrecks? Is an article in the *National Geo-*

graphic, or a Parke-Bernet auction catalogue to be the sole contributions to knowledge that we can expect from some of the Western Hemisphere's most important wreck sites? Is a registered salvage company an acceptable archaeological organization: if not, why do states and nations grant them licenses to disturb archaeological sites? If you want a simplistic answer, it is that licensing officials have a hard enough time learning to spell the word archaeology, let alone understanding what it is all about.

Let me say, quickly, if belatedly, that I have singled out the underwater salvor only as a dramatically visible example of a popular misconception. Terrestrial archaeology, particularly in the historical period, tends to be strong on garbage and weak on treasure, and therefore does not suffer as much from the pot hunters and grave robbers who do such damage to earlier, and non-Christian sites. I am not lightly dismissing the blight of the bottle hunter; my point is only that the archaeologically motivated assaults on land sites are more likely to be undertaken for educational purposes than for profit — and that frequently cannot be said of underwater sites. Yet wreck sites are potentially equally, if not more historically informative, and valuable as educational resources, than are archaeological sites of comparable periods on land.

It is hard to deny that Man needs to know more about his origins and about those evolutionary and cultural periods about which he is ignorant. To that extent, therefore, it is easier to justify the preservation of American aboriginal sites than it is to defend the remains of the historical period — particularly when many distinguished political, economic, and cultural historians still deny that the evidence of archaeology has anything useful to contribute. Of course I think they are wrong, — as I am sure you do; but I believe that if it came to the crunch, I would man the prehistorians' stockade rather than do battle in defense of the average historical site. This brings me again to the question: Historical archaeology, who needs it? Here, I believe, is the very vortex of the crisis, for our future depends upon defining the need, and then seeking the people who will serve it.

LEVELS OF NEED

Needs come in various forms and at various levels, beginning with your all-purpose, all embracing national need, and diminishing all the way down to the local interest group, such as happy bands of descendants getting together to preserve the home of someone they think was worthy of such a memorial. As a rule, the national "biggies" are not archaeological sites, and if they are, they have already been at least partially explored by professional, Park Service archaeologists. I am thinking of such places as the Yorktown battlefield, Jamestown, and St. Augustine. Then there are scores of lesser sites that have either aspired to national protection through circumstances that stemmed from availability and political clout, or which, by accident, happen to be on land owned by the Federal Government. Many of these, too, have already been dug into with archaeology in mind, by such diverse diggers as W.P.A. teams and keen colonels with time and men on their hands. In theory, such sites are protected and should be able to obtain Federal funds for preservation and study without too much trouble.

There are infinitely more historical sites that are of importance at the State level, but one still may have trouble getting anyone sufficiently powerful to substitute money for lip service, for here we are asking to give archaeological sites a budgetary priority. It is now much easier to ensure the preservation of historical sites on state lands, particularly since the needs of the National Register and the establishing of state landmarks commissions have made historic preservation official business. It does not follow, however, that registered sites not on state land enjoy similar protection. As a rule they don't, nor are public funds readily available for their archaeological exploration. When we get to the local level, strictly archaeological sites must take their chances between the Scylla of the developer's bulldozers and the Charybdis of the amateur archaeologist.

Historical sites are more obviously worthy of protection if there is something visible upon them, an historic house (preferably with shrine potential), a picturesque ruin, or even a large sign letting everybody know that something "meaningful" happened there. Of course, "meaningful" is another of those gaseous words, like "relevant" and "significant" whose validity and interpretation runs a gamut from everything to nothing, depending on the points of view of the speaker and the listener. Nevertheless, if it cannot be said that a site was "meaningful" in history to a sufficient degree that people will pay to have that meaning studied and enshrined, the site stands little chance of riding out the crisis — and why should it?

Ironically, existing historic buildings do not readily cry their need for archaeological study, yet in truth they can frequently benefit most from it; first by enabling their evolutionary story to be more accurately told, then by making it possible for their surroundings to be reconstructed; next by providing information needed by curators responsible for furnishing the places, and finally by providing data on what happened there and how the inhabitants lived, — not to mention the desirability of being able to exhibit the actual artifacts from the past which can be of such help in making history come alive in a world that looks much more readily than it listens.

The need for historical archaeology can be much better expressed to the people who hold the purse strings if we can show that the houses, the sites, the artifacts, have a practical and specific use. In essence, the results of what we do should be something that the public will want to see, enjoy, and learn from — *if* we are hoping to use public money to do it. By extension, I am voicing the heretical view that digging up another 18th-century tavern site, and another, and another, or fighting to preserve every 19th-century farmstead, quickly becomes repetitious, adds too little to general knowledge to justify the time and money involved, and eventually leads to the self-defeating crying of "Wolf".

ARCHAEOLOGICAL STRATEGY

I have long contended that inventorying is an essential precurser to digging, and that every state should do what it can to list its historical and archaeological holdings, determine what it would like to do with them, and then decide what it actually *can* do. As far as archaeological sites are concerned, I see four categories; Those that must be preserved at all costs and which, if not already state protected, should be acquired for permanent preservation; secondly, those sites that need to be archaeologically explored, but have no lasting practical value, but which should be leased and excavated as soon as possible; next, those that might be interesting but are not of major importance and so call for careful salvage archaeology alongside whatever development their future may bring; and finally, those sites which have no obvious potential and, for lack of staff and funds, must be written off. This last group, coupled with those that are not known at all until it is too late, represent perhaps seventy-five percent of any state's historical archaeological sites. As even the recovery of unstratified artifacts from them can be better than nothing, I would urge that they be earmarked for amateur salvage projects, school training programs in archaeological discipline and reasoning — anything that will enable those otherwise wasted sites to educate, give healthful exercise, or give pleasure to people who care about the past.

Of course we are all destroyers; that's the name of the game, but along with the competent professional, can we not draw a distinction between the amateur who behaves in a professional way without being paid for it, and the looter, the grave robber, and the bad professional who is paid for his vandalism. If that distinction cannot be validly drawn, then surely it is up to us to devote every effort to make it possible. Because nine-tenths of the nation's historical sites will never re-

ceive the attentions of a first rate, professional archaeological historian, it seems to me that our most pressing need is to educate at the grass roots so that we have willing hands and, eventually, knowledgeable heads, to fight the brush fires that the professionals will always be too few to handle. But if the armies are to be marshalled and effectively used, the battlegrounds must be carefully chosen, and the troops trained.

ARCHAEOLOGICAL PUBLISHING

This is easier said than done, for as you well know, the digging is the simple part and no matter how professionally *it* is done, all is wasted if the excavated facts and artifacts are not properly treated, analyzed, and reported on. We generally claim that three months digging generates nine months of lab and library work, but as your know, it can take much longer than that if the professional archaeologist has a digging crew of ten, and a lab, drafting, research, and curatorial staff of two, or even only one (himself), to see the project to its end. All too often this is the case, and it is particularly true of contract archaeology when the contractor lacks the back-up facilities to do the project justice. What, too, is to become of the artifacts after they have been preserved? How will they be made available for others to study? What provisions have been made for publishing the report — always supposing, of course, that the project yielded information worth publishing.

THE NEED FOR HISTORICAL ARCHAEOLOGY

I have titled these key-note observations "Historical archaeology, who needs it?" and I have already tried to intimate that there are all sorts of *who's*, and I'll come back to be more specific anon. But right now I want to say something about the *need*. Why is there a need for historical archaeology, or *is* there a need for it? What does it offer to the world that the world absolutely has to have? Is it something that the United States can afford?

Would we put it on a par, say, with the need to solve the urban crises? If you were on a state's budget committee, would you give it funding before the needs of the environment had been served? Is digging up another colonial plantation more important than cleaning up a river or remodeling an antique sewage disposal plant? But then, how can one compare such totally different things? It's like weighing apples against rocks. Nevertheless, budget directors have to do just that.

There was a time, ten or fifteen years ago, when preservation and conservation were terms that belonged almost exclusively to antiquaries and bird-watchers. Today they have been commandeered by the environmentalists who have also gone off with the funding. If challenged, they will have the gall to suggest that potsherd patriotism will be of little use to a population poisoning itself and choking for breath. Can we make a good enough case to prove them wrong? How would the public vote on such a proposition? Ever since it chose Barrabas, it has preferred the ideas it best understands, and I suggest that right now it would take the future over the past, and do it laughing. If that is true, then the investigation and preservation of the past is the concern of a minority, a vocal minority as all minorities must be, but a minority, just the same — and history has demonstrated again and again that until that minority makes enough noise to con the majority into thinking that their numbers are reversed, the fervent few must live off their own resources.

When it comes to publishing, we tend to mouth the same credos that have been parroted for years, regardless of the fact that they may be totally out of touch with the cold wind of contemporary reality. "No excavation is complete until the report is published." The dictum is still valid, *if* we strike the work "published", for I suggest that the publishing of report describing, inch by inch, the progress of an excavation, with innumerable profiles, and plans of unexplained post holes, is a waste of money. Nobody gives a damn whether one's building is

two inches out of true at the south-east corner — unless that fact has something useful to say. Similarly, the illustration of a few rim sherds of common 18th-century ceramic forms that are already on record as having been found from southern Australia to northern Canada, contributes virtually nothing — unless they happen to be incorrectly described, and so warn the reader to beware of the whole report. I am not saying that this material should not be recorded or that any detail should be omitted from the final manuscript. But I am saying that a small number of copies of that report, cheaply duplicated, and housed in safe, known repositories, is all that is needed. Much more valuable to fellow archaeologists, curators, and social historians, are research studies on specific topics stemming from excavations and which have something new and useful to say. When money and publishing outlets are scarce, it is these studies that will be of the greatest practical value.

ARCHAEOLOGICAL LICENSES

It has been suggested that by backing away from the obligation to publish everything, we open the door to writing nothing. I don't believe this to be true; if it was, few of us would be here today. Nevertheless, I would like to see every archaeological excavation licensed by the state, with such licenses being granted only when the state (through whatever agency seems appropriate) is satisfied that the group or individual requesting the license is deemed properly equipped and competent to do the proposed job. I would like to see this apply equally to professionals as to amateurs, on land and underwater, without regard for whether all the expertise rests in the heads and hands of a single individual or of a group, — although I would expect the license to be issued to a specific "principal investigator" or whatever jargon one chooses to use to describe him. The calibre of the experience and expert knowledge required, would vary depending on the category of site to be explored. Thus, licenses to excavate on my grade four, "written-off" sites would be more easily obtained than would permits to work on grade one or two sites of primary importance and obvious complexity. Licenses would be withdrawn if adequate procedural standards were not maintained, and no further permits would be issued to any individual or group until an acceptable report on the previous project had been delivered. At the same time, I would hope to see the states do their part by involving themselves in archaeological education, through accredited summer school courses.

THE ARCHAEOLOGICAL PROFESSION

What about the professionals? Or let me put it another way: What about the profession? By which I mean, what is the future for historical archaeology as a profession? Fifteen, or even ten years ago, it was hard to find anyone with a desire to make a career in historical archaeology. It was generally looked upon as a slightly unworthy undertaking to be ripped off by any prehistorian who had failed to secure a summer contract to do what he was trained to do. I contended then, that America's historical past was deserving of something better, calling for special training in the use and marriage of artifactual and documentary evidence, as well as for field and laboratory techniques designed to meet its special needs. This was looked upon as a denunciation of the anthropologist's training and credentials; but it was nothing of the sort. It was just that I would rather not entrust my kidneys to an "ear-nose-and-throat man", even if he was the only doctor in town. Again, one has only to look to the people here for this meeting to see that all this has changed; the ear-nose-and-throat specialists are still here, but now they are ear-nose-throat and kidney men, and doing very nicely at it. But what about all their students anxious to follow in their footsteps? Where are the professional opportunities for them, and what about the high school graduates with archaeological star-dust in their eyes, who want advice on what university to attend?

I suggest that here is another arm of the crisis. We desperately need a new generation of trained personnel from field directors to draftsmen, conservators, and researchers. But where are the jobs for them? I get two or three letters a week from young people either asking for jobs or wanting to know what training they need to make them eligible for careers in historical archaeology. I don't know what to tell them, for it is unfair to encourage them to direct their education towards a relatively narrow goal that may not provide them with an adequate living. My friend Bob Stephenson, who will be chairing the discussion on contract archaeology, seems much more optimistic, and I believe he feels that that area offers adequate opportunities. Personally, I would not want to have to make a living as a contract archaeologist, for I am convinced that the costs involved in major ventures in historical archaeology are such that very soon the needs of the site would be at odds with the necessity to make a profit on the contract. On the other hand, the small job that can be fairly easily handled would have to be so numerous or so highly priced that the pursuit of them could be more time-consuming than fulfilling the contracts. There is a big difference between private contracting, and institutions with a permanent salaried staff taking on contractual jobs, and it is unlikely that there will be enough of those to employ any but a handful of the people wanting to enter the profession. Save for a few fortunate individuals, historical archaeology is a tool to be used by people in education, in museums, by administrators of historical places, restoration architects, anybody with a question to ask that the examination of the material remains of the past can answer. If this is true, then we must look to a future wherein the needs of historical archaeology will continue to be served more by part-time than full-time professionals — as it is today. It is unrealistic to suggest that the crisis can be met by enlarging the profession sufficiently to cope with all the problems and to take advantage of every opportunity that may present itself. Instead, there will always be ample room for the training of competent amateurs willing to give the time for which professionals, of necessity, must be paid.

Meanwhile we must look to our own professional standards which can best be improved through a closer relationship between university departments of anthropology and history, and an increased willingness to see merit in each other's contributions. At the moment, it seems to me that trained archaeologists are making more use of historical sources than historians are making of archaeological evidence. To this end we must provide the historian with our information set out in a way that is acceptable to him and which promotes his confidence.

Furthermore, when we borrow his tools, we must show him that we know how to use and respect them. If we fail to do so, and we let the historian see that our historiography is shallow, he will assume that our archaeological credibility is equally poorly rooted. I suggest, too, that while displays of expertise may impress one's peers, they serve to deter readers who may be unwilling to delve through the methodology in search of the matter. It might be nice to be able to be so independent as to be able to say that if the non-archaeologist reader isn't able to understand what we're talking about, that's his tough luck. I put it to you that in the long run, the tough luck is ours. For in this application, archaeology is the servant of history, and if historians decline to accept, believe, or use what we discover, then we have been wasting our time. Unbelievable as it may sound, I have seen professional historians write studies on colonial gunsmithing, on silversmithing, even on the colonial apothecary without making any use of archaeological evidences. If the authors of such obviously artifact-related historical studies ignore the evidence from the earth, it is hardly surprising, say, that economic and military historians do the same.

Not only must we try to improve the quality of our publishable manuscripts, but we must then make sure that the publishers do them justice. Some of you may have recently seen the journal of a state archaeological society which published a report on a colonial plantation site dug and submitted by a university faculty member, wherein seven out of twenty-four pictures were printed upside-down, and eight had no captions. As it happened, the report was so bad that it was a case of the pot calling the kettle black — and that was how the pictures were printed. But had it been a first rate report, this kind of publishing would have robbed it of its usefullness. Yet our society's own journal cannot be expected to carry the load alone, any more than we can expect that the new and excellent *Nautical Archaeology* can handle all wreck material that needs to be published. Indeed, I see a need for a journal confined to submarine and related work on post-medieval sites. It has been suggested by cynical colleagues that many people now working on underwater sites are incapable of writing reports — if so they have no business to be doing the work. No report, no license, and equally importantly, no report, no release of any artifacts for sale.

ARCHAEOLOGICAL EDUCATION

Of course, it is easy enough to stand up here and glibly say what should and should not be done, grandly tossing out occasional bouquets to the good guys with one hand while flailing away at the villains with the other. This may be the way to get through a key-note address that lacks pictures to keep you awake, but it is no way to solve our problems.

There *is* a crisis in historical archaeology, but it will not be frightened away by bombastic rhetoric, nor by pouring concrete in the gears of bulldozers, or poison in the ears of sleeping vandals. Education is our best spokesman, and we must use it to plead our case wherever anyone will listen. The fate of the Moss-Bennett Bill for Salvage Archaeology in the last Congress may not be too encouraging, but in truth the time has never been riper for legislative support at every governmental level. If we fail to take advantage of the leverage provided by the upcoming Bicentennial, we deserve to be ordered to turn in our trowels. I remain convinced that education is the best hope of gaining popular support for the study and protection of historical sites, enabling those who want to help to do so, teaching those who are going to dig anyway that there is more statisfaction in finding out than in finding, and above all making the tax-paying public and their tax-dispensing representatives believe that the dangers to our cultural environment are just as real, just as dangerous in the long run, as the destruction of the forests, the farmlands, or the rivers.

It is inevitable, but a shame nonetheless, that the tremendously varied and exciting program that Alan Woolworth and the Minnesota Historical Society have put together, is to benefit so few of us. As is the case with every national society, the people who attend the annual meetings are generally those whose professional institutions pay the freight, thus shutting out many junior professionals and, in our case, the amateurs who cannot obtain the time or afford the funds to attend. I can but hope that the day is not too far off when the use of video-tape casette players will be as common as typewriters and radios, and that the content of entire meetings can be made available for subsequent replay wherever there is someone ready to listen and learn.

The distinguished archaeologist Jaquetta Hawkes once wrote that archaeology gives a people "a sense of having roots", and this is indisputably true. But unfortunately, most people take them too much for granted. The modern Roman throws his garbage into the Forum and apathetically watches the Colosseum crack, and we let the Visigoths of commerce despoil the environs of St. Augustine, Williamsburg, Gettysburg, scything the green from virtually every piece of historically fertile American soil upon which they can encroach. This too is our problem, part of our crisis, and against it education is our only weapon.

A nation that propagates a generation which rejects the achievements and scorns the monuments of its forefathers, is a nation growing a tree without roots. And trees without roots, no matter how rich their foliage, do not bend before the winds of change. They fall — and die. I suggest to you, however, that although our tree may be leaning a bit, the fact that this society, after only six short years of existence, can come up with a program this good, and that here today, we have the privelege of sharing our problems and prospects with so many friends from other countries, is evidence enough that the roots can expect some pretty potent fertilizer in the years ahead.

ROY S. DICKENS, JR.
WILLIAM R. BOWEN

Problems and Promises in Urban Historical Archaeology: The MARTA Project

ABSTRACT

The America urban setting presents a variety of problems in the execution of archaeological surveys and assessments, while it also provides a promising and unique set of resources. Using the MARTA (Metropolitan Atlanta Rapid Transit Authority) Project as an example, some of these problems and promises are discussed. Survey, testing, and mitigation procedures are described and evaluated. Also, consideration is given to the potential uses of the urban archaeological resource, with examples of hypothesis testing, pattern delineation, identification of formation processes, and public education.

The number of archaeological projects in the American urban setting has increased dramatically in the past few years. One stimulus for this increase has been the enforcement of federal mandates for cultural resource assessment, which apply equally to projects in cities and rural areas. Another, and perhaps more important, factor has been an epistomological expansion within archaeology itself. This expansion was initiated by several American archaeologists (e.g., Ascher 1962; Fontana 1965, 1968; Deetz 1970) who recognized the research value of recent—and even modern—material remains. Their suggestions have recently been applied directly to the study of American urban culture by Salwen (1973), Schuyler (1974), Rathje (1974, 1977), Leone (1977), and others. Nonetheless, in the United States, "archaeology of the city" is still in its infancy (Salwen 1973:151).

In this paper some of the problems and promises of American urban archaeology are evaluated. Examples are drawn from a large survey-and-excavation project in Atlanta, Georgia, being conducted in conjunction with the construction of a city-wide rapid transit system. Survey and mitigation procedures are examined in relation to the unique characteristics of both the urban environment and the urban archaeological resource.

Also discussed is the potential conceptual and theoretical importance of urban archaeological research, using examples of hypothesis testing, pattern delineation, and identification of formation processes. In a larger sense this section of the paper also considers the value of urban remains in studying the evolution of material culture. Finally, there is a brief discussion of the importance of urban projects in educating the public about the goals of modern archaeology.

Problems In Urban Archaeology

Large-scale fieldwork in the urban environment is difficult for a number of reasons. There is, of course, the concrete-brick-asphalt veneer, effectively masking all that lies below. Prior disturbances are numerous and complex, often leaving little evidence of original surfaces. In addition, the areas under investigation may still be in use or surrounded by a number of on-going activities. Singly, or in combination, these factors make environmental impact archaeology especially difficult. For example, it is almost impossible to follow "normal" procedures in identifying sites, evaluating their significance, and developing a mitigation plan. Even when there is adequate lead time for field survey and testing, documentary search, and informant interviews, only a moderate percentage of the resources usually can be identified and evaluated prior to construction disturbance.

The visibility of archaeology in the urban setting exacerbates problems of vandalism and " bottle hunting." In active construction areas, there are also increased possibilities for accidental disturbance of sites while they are awaiting evaluation or excavation. Visibility also results in frequent interruption, and even occasional harassment, by the curious. Some of the difficulties encountered by archaeologists on urban construction sites have been well documented by Wilson (1975:39–43) for the Patterson, New Jersey Salvage Project. It should be said at this point, however, that visibility also produces many benefits, some of which will be discussed later.

Since urban archaeologists are in many cases researching cultural remains of only moderate age, problems also arise from the public's often mistaken image of our discipline (which may be at least partly the result of archaeology's lack of visibility in the past). The popular image includes the idea that archaeological remains must be greatly removed in time or space from our own culture to be of importance. And, there is also the esoteric view, which holds that although archaeology may be an interesting endeavor, it cannot be of any real value to people in the modern world. Consequently, urban archaeologists may have to spend valuable time justifying to agency officials and construction engineers, and even to some members of review agencies or the academic community, the importance of archaeological remains in a modern context. This problem can result in conflicts and delays when they are least needed.

The MARTA Project

As early as 1962, the City of Atlanta initiated plans to construct a large-scale rapid transportation system. Finally, in 1965, under the auspices of the federal Urban Mass Transportation Administration (UMTA), the Metropolitan Atlanta Rapid Transit Authority (MARTA) was established. The MARTA system was to be composed of four main lines and several subsidiary lines, forming a 52 mile rail network. The main lines would roughly quadrisect the metropolitan area, as they radiated north, east, south, and west from the heart of the central business district (Figures 1 and 2).

Although an environmental impact statement was prepared for MARTA in 1972–1973, the study did not include an adequate evaluation of cultural resources. In 1974, in an effort to correct this oversight and to comply with requests from the State Historic Preservation Office, MARTA contracted with historians and archaeologists for additional cultural resource assessments. Initially, Georgia State University agreed to conduct archaeological surveys on small portions of the East and West lines where clearing and construction were already underway. Later, in 1975, a contract was signed for work on larger segments of the East and West lines. Subsequent contracts, in 1976, 1977, and 1979, covered the remainder of "Phase A" construction corridors on all four lines (Figure 2). In most of the work thus far, the archaeology has been accomplished along with or only slightly ahead of construction. During the most difficult period (1975–1976), two major excavations had to be undertaken on sites where demolition and construction already were in progress.

The "salvage" element of the project has diminished during the past three years which has allowed for the development of systematic procedures and clearer research goals. Now, for example, there is usually enough lead time for documentary searches prior to fieldwork. Gradually, too, the laboratory work has caught up with the fieldwork. Currently, a computerized inventory is being developed for the more than 100,000 items that have been cataloged.

Research Design

Ideally, a large urban archaeological project should be undertaken only within the framework of a well-developed research design. Such a design would include a sampling strategy through which data could be systematically extracted from those behavioral contexts defined by the investigator. For example, if one chose to investigate socioeconomic change, he might divide the city into be-

FIGURE 1. The MARTA construction corridors are from 30–50 meters wide. This view is of the West Line as it approaches the central business district.

havioral components (e.g., industrial, commercial, residential) which could be traced chronologically. If after defining the areal boundaries of these components at prescribed time intervals through maps and other documents, stratified random sampling might then be employed in the archaeological surveys. Such a strategy would insure that each behavioral-chronological stratum would be included in the data base from which the city's socioeconomic development would be interpreted.

In the MARTA Project, boundaries of the transit corridors have determined the limits of investigation. Within these boundaries the archaeologists were asked to identify and evaluate the significance of *all* archaeological resources and to propose a plan to mitigate

adverse impact on certain of these resources. Since many areas were already under construction by the time the archaeological surveys were begun, the above steps had to be greatly accelerated. In fact, for many sites, identification, evaluation, and mitigation all had to be accomplished within a period of a few days.

In spite of these constraints, it has been possible to formulate broad research goals and to gather data in such a manner as to be applicable to those goals. The layout of the transit corridors provides for some degree of systematics in data collection. As noted earlier, the four corridors nearly quadrisect the city from east to west and north to south, which eliminates much of the bias that might develop from a less proportional arrangement.

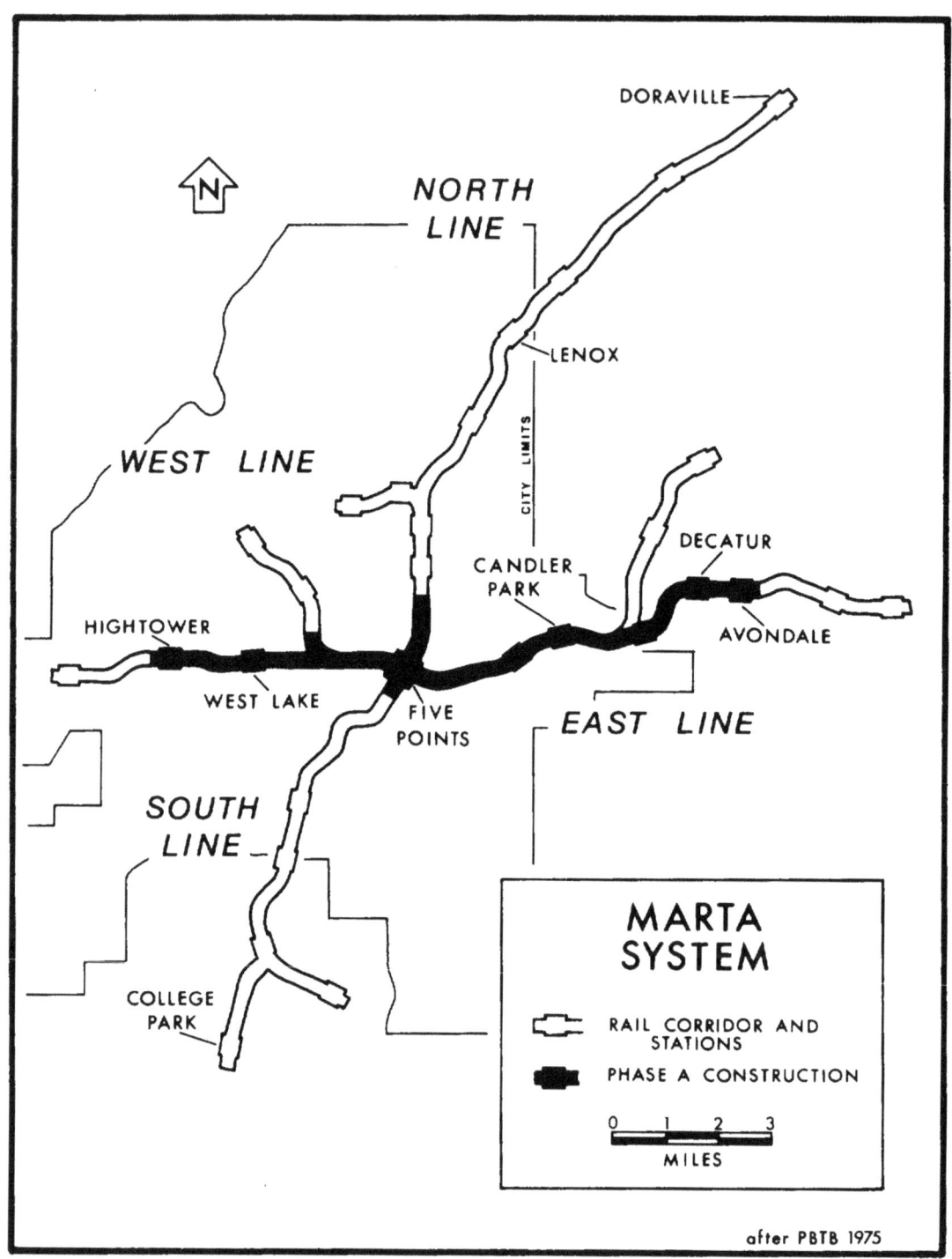

FIGURE 2. Map of the MARTA system, showing the North, East, South, and West lines.

Secondly, since Atlanta has grown in more or less concentric expansions from its point of origin (rather than along a river or major roadway), the layout of the corridors has provided transects of most chronological and behavioral strata.

In formulating research questions, there has been a tendency to rely on a structural-processual model. Atlanta is known to have undergone a transformation from a basically folk-agrarian community in the mid 1800s, to an industrial-manufcturing center of regional importance in the late 1800s, to a commercial-communications megalopolis by the mid 1900s. Sites are evaluated, and consequently receive investigative attention, on the basis of their potential for elucidating the mechanisms—technological, economic, sociological, and ideological—that underlie this transformation. In this approach, an important site or feature is one that has behavioral and chronological "integrity." For example, the recent discovery of several backfilled wells in the downtown part of Atlanta proved very important. The fill of these wells, which dated to around 1890, contained artifacts exclusively of domestic origin; after 1900, this part of the city became predominately commercial. Before this discovery it had not been possible to isolate, with certainty, the remains of central-city domestic activity. Now, these remains can be compared with those from suburban residential dumps of the same period, and questions can be asked about similar behaviors in differing urban contexts. And, finally, the information from these comparisons can be applied to the larger problem of reconstructing Atlanta's evolutionary processes.

Survey Units and Site Designation

In order to facilitate construction, MARTA divided its construction corridors into segments termed Construction Contact Units (CCUs). These units range in size from about 50,000 to 100,000m^2. A CCU is further divided into parcels, each of which consists of about 1,000 to 2,000m^2 and which represents an historically-documented unit of property ownership (Figure 3). Prior to the archaeological work, MARTA had accurately mapped the CCUs and parcels, and these maps have been adopted by the archaeological survey team. Not only has use of the CCU-Parcel maps provided controls for data collection, but it has facilitated communication with MARTA officials and construction personnel.

The urban fieldworker is confronted with an almost continuous distribution of cultural remains which must be differentiated, sampled, and evaluated, Thus, an important consideration is how to divide the "larger site" (the city) into smaller meaningful units. In the MARTA Project, "site" status has been assigned to single features (a well), groups of related features (a system of Civil War earthworks), or concentrations of artifacts (a dump). A site might consist of only a small portion of one parcel (a well or foundation) or cover portions of several parcels (a large dump or military earthwork). Where features are missing or there are no distinct concentrations of artifacts, collections are made and information recorded by parcel and CCU.

Survey, Testing, and Mitigation Procedures

When time permits, documentary and informant data are gathered prior to the field surveys. Unfortunately, there has not been sufficient time for this type of research during much of the MARTA Project. Still, the potential of historical data is reflected in the fact that, to date, 25% of the sites have been located through documentary evidence (Table 1). Although no sites have been discovered as yet exclusively from the reports of informants, such reports have been helpful in better defining and evaluating a number of sites.

All parts of the MARTA corridors are subjected to systematic surface inspection, except those already graded to subsoil. Areas obscured by existing buildings or pavement are inspected after structural demolition but prior to earth removal. Surface inspection is conducted by two or more individuals walking side-by-side at two-meter intervals (Figure 4).

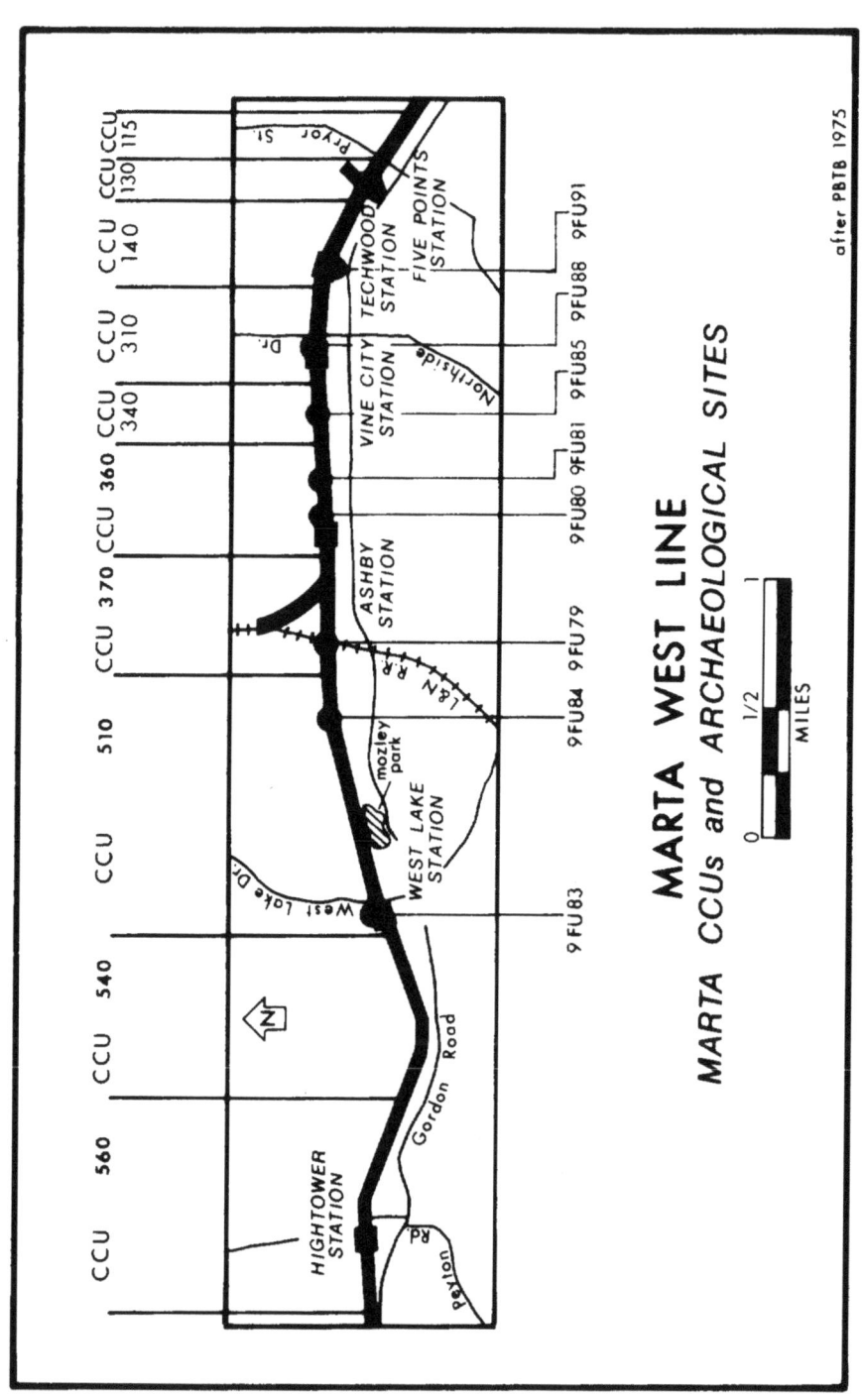

FIGURE 3. Map of MARTA West Line, showing CCUs and archaeological sites.

TABLE 1
FREQUENCIES AND PERCENTAGES OF SITES BY METHOD OF DISCOVERY, LISTED FOR
CONTRACT PERIOD AND TOTAL PROJECT.

Method of Site Discovery

Contract Period	Historical Documents		Informants		Surface Inspection		Testing		Metal Detection		Monitoring		Totals	
	Freq.	%	Freq.	%	Freq.	%	Freq.	%	Freq.	%	Freq.	%		
1975–1977	5	(31)	0	(0)	4	(25)	2	(13)	1	(6)	4	(25)	16	(100)
1977–1979	2	(17)	0	(0)	1	(8)	0	(0)	0	(0)	9	(75)	12	(100)
1979–1980	1	(25)	0	(0)	1	(25)	0	(0)	0	(0)	2	(50)	4	(100)
Totals	8	(25)	0	(0)	6	(19)	2	(6)	1	(3)	15	(47)	32	(100)

During these inspections, all artifacts, regardless of age, are collected within sample parcels. These artifacts provide a ready source of information on the periods and gross categories of land use of a parcel, information which can be used to determine if further work is needed. Of the sites recorded to date, 19% have been discovered during the surface surveys (Table 1). The productivity of surface inspection has decreased as the surveys have moved into the more obstructed downtown areas, as indicated by the differences between the number of sites found by this technique in 1975–77 and 1977–80 (Table 1).

Subsurface testing is conducted in all areas where historical research or survey observations suggest the possibility of buried surfaces or features. The tests are excavated at uniform intervals, the size of which varies according to evaluations of disturbance, prior land use, and observations in adjacent parcels. All tests are plotted on the CCU-Parcel maps. Initially, tests were excavated with post-hole diggers, but this tool has been abandoned in favor of a bucket auger with which the same task can be accomplished more quickly (Figure 5). Deeper tests are excavated by shovel or occasionally by mechanical equipment provided by the nearby construction teams (Figure 6). Thus far, 6% of the sites have been discovered through subsurface testing.

Because urban culture has made such extensive use of metals, another important tool for obtaining subsurface information in the urban setting is the metal detector. Several types of detectors have been successfully employed on the MARTA Project (Figure 7). Selected areas are set aside for systematic metal detection based on surface observations, historical research, and the extent of previous disturbance. Although only 3% of the

FIGURE 4. Surface inspections of MARTA rights-of-way occur before and after demolition of existing structures.

FIGURE 5. Shallow subsurface testing is accomplished with a bucket auger.

FIGURE 6. Deep subsurface testing is sometimes required. This backhoe test was excavated to determine the depth and composition of a turn-of-the-century municipal dump.

sites have been discovered with these instruments (Table 1), they have been useful in obtaining better information on a number of sites.

A final and very important stage of the MARTA fieldwork is on-site construction monitoring (Figures 8 and 9). This technique allows the field worker to discover sites that go undetected during pre-construction survey and testing and provides an opportunity to evaluate the effectiveness of the earlier work. Areas must be checked regularly as demolition and construction progress, which requires close communication between archaeologist and construction personnel. Thus far in the MARTA Project, 47% of the sites have been discovered through monitoring (Table 1). This technique has also provided additional information on many previously recorded sites. The value of monitoring has increased as construction has moved into the more heavily obstructed downtown areas. This is obvious in the increased number of sites located by this method in 1977–1980, as opposed to 1975–1977 (Table 1).

When sites are not discovered until construction is underway, it becomes necessary to conduct emergency excavations. On the MARTA Project this has been termed "extraordinary mitigation." Sometimes, arrangements have been made which allow construction personnel to work around an endangered site until excavations can be completed, or to shift work to another location until the significance of a find can be evaluated. Usually, with

FIGURE 7. Metal detectors are used for locating buried artifacts and features. The instrument in use here is a modified Metrotech 220.

FIGURE 9. Not all urban artifacts lie beneath the ground. This remnant of a sign for a wagon and buggy shop was discovered when a 1920s addition was removed from a 19th century building.

FIGURE 8. After construction begins, all earth removal is monitored by the field team. Here, the wall of a construction trench is examined for buried features.

good communication between archaeologist and engineer, this mitigation can be conducted properly without causing delays in construction. When delays are required, a clause in the construction contracts provides that MARTA will reimburse the affected firm for any losses directly related to the archaeological work.

Promises in Urban Archaeology

Reid, Rathje, and Schiffer (1974:125–26) have suggested that "archaeologists can apply their method and theory to the study of material culture in *modern* industrial societies for the purpose of deriving explanatory statements of *modern* human behavior." The validity of this approach has been amply demonstrated in the Tucson Garbage Project (Rathje 1974, 1977; Rathje and McCarthy 1977). However, since modern industrial societies have evolved through complex processes, the totality of that development must be considered archaeologically. Here is where the study of 19th century and early 20th century urban sites can be important. They should provide an "explanatory bridge" between interpretations of early historic material culture, where the behavior is extinct, and modern material culture, where the behavior is our own.

There exists, therefore, two complimentary values to archaeology of urban sites. This work can help to elucidate the process of urban cultural evolution, thereby making archaeology relevant to studies of present behaviors and to planning for future behaviors. It can also contribute to the development of better method and theory for all of archaeology, since those behaviors being studied are part of a still-active continuum for which the material-behavioral collaries often can be identified through documents and informants.

To follow are several examples of the directions the MARTA research is taking, along with a short discussion of the value of this kind of archaeology to public education.

Hypothesis Testing

The urban archaeological resource presents opportunities to formulate and test hypotheses about human behavior in a variety of behavioral contexts and to combine several independent sets of data in broadly-based research strategies. In addition to the archaeological collections, there is a wealth of preserved documents (newspapers, magazines, city directories, deed and title records, census reports, church records, and insurance maps, to name a few) and a fair number of surviving participants. In the MARTA Project, behavioral hypotheses sometimes have been developed from the archaeological data and were then tested with information obtained from documents or informants. At other times the documents or informants have generated hypotheses for which testable evidence was sought in the archaeological record. By employing these different resources in combination, it is possible to identify pitfalls that might plague archaeologists who have the material record as their primary or only resource.

The combined use of documents, informants, and artifacts is well illustrated in the analysis of a small garbage deposit from a suburban, "working class" neighborhood of about 1910 (Figure 10). In the middle layers of the deposit was an unusually rich accumulation of table refuse, whereas the strata above and below contained a broader range of domestic materials together with small amounts of building materials and commercial refuse. This situation suggested that the middle layers might represent a very intensive period of domestic activity. Beginning with the artifacts, the relative frequency of turkey bones in the middle layers prompted questions to elderly neighborhood residents about their use of this food resource. These informants replied that, around 1910, turkey was usually present on their tables only at Thanksgiving or Christmas. This information then led to the formulation of hypotheses about holiday-season behavior that might be checked in other areas of the archaeological and documentary record. An examination of the numbers of sherds in the various functional categories of table ceramics suggested that large serving pieces were uncommonly numerous in the middle layers. These archaeological frequencies, when compared with "ideal" frequencies of serving, eating, and drinking vessels in tableware sets listed (and illustrated) in mail-order catalogs of the period, were determined to be statistically significant, another reflection of holiday eating behavior. This prompted a return to the archaeological remains, where additional propositions were

FIGURE 10. A small, neighborhood dump of ca. 1910 was discovered during monitoring on the MARTA East Line. The remains shown here have been found to consist of holiday-season refuse.

developed with regard to expected patterning of bottles, hardware, toys, plant remains, and other faunal remains. The results of these analyses, almost without exception, provided support for the holiday interpretation.

Pattern Delineation

Pattern delineation is another important goal in modern archaeological research. South (1977:31) has stressed the importance of pattern recognition in the elucidation of behavioral processes:

"Once pattern is recognized, the archaeologist can then ask why the pattern exists, why it is often so predictive it can be expressed as laws. In so doing, he can begin to build a theory for explaining the demonstrated patterns."

Patterns are formed by the spatial distributions of artifacts and artifact classes within a site, as well as in the relative frequencies between sites. In the MARTA Project where a complete site, or even a large portion of a site, usually cannot be excavated, patterns have been defined from surface collections, individual features, or test excavations.

Some of the urban behavioral patterns recognized, or suggested, include a variety of *domestic* patterns (based on collections representing individual households, neighborhoods, municipalities, and ethnic enclaves); *commercial* patterns (tavern, hotel, meat market); *industrial* patterns (railroad, mill, foundry); and various *specialized* patterns (club, hospital, military). These are all more specific than South's (1977) "Frontier,"

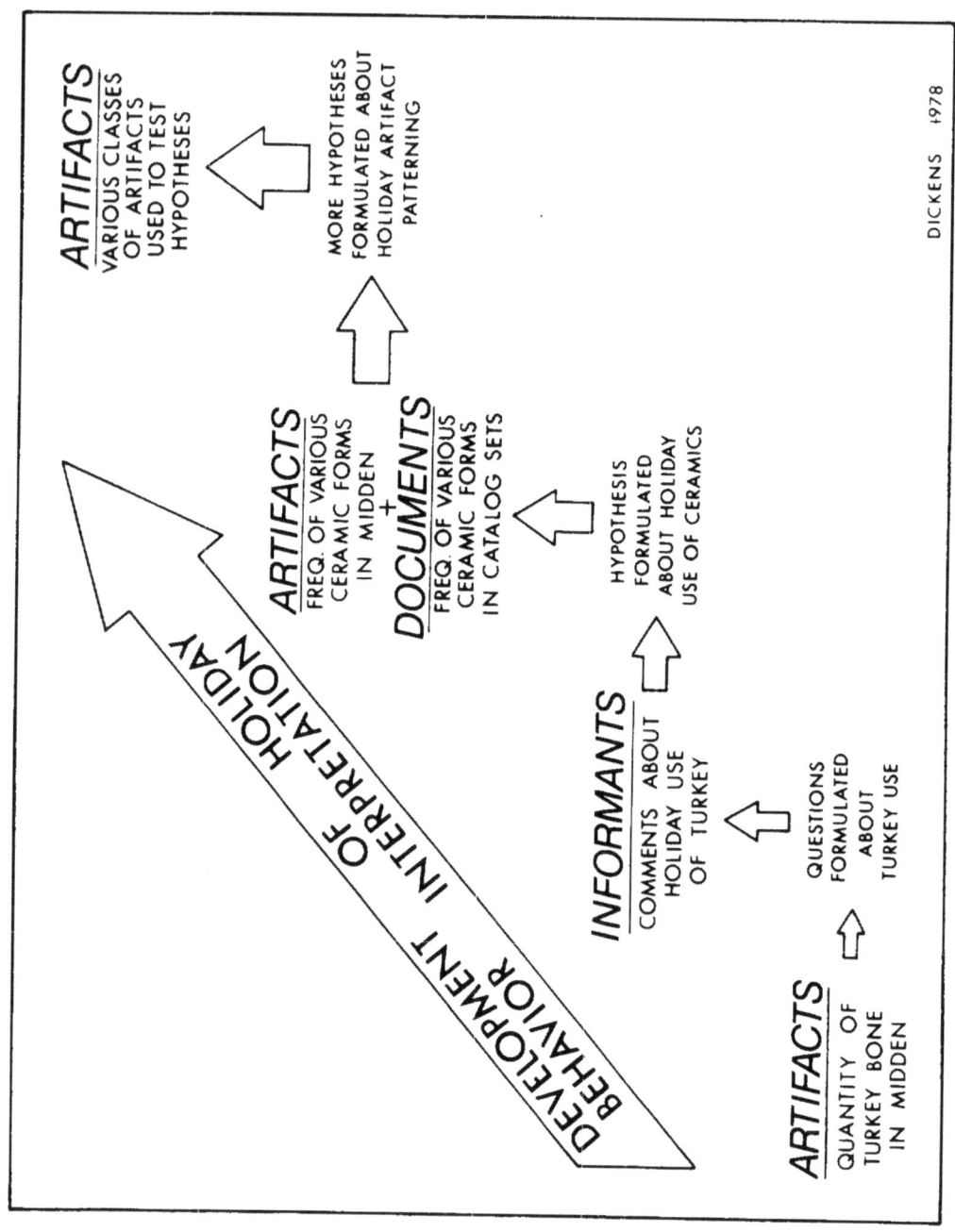

FIGURE 11. Schematic depiction of the research process through which holiday-season behavior was interpreted.

"Carolina," and "Brunswick" patterns for the Colonial Period. The complexities of urban-industrial culture, however, will require that specific intrasite patterns (as well as more general intersite patterns) be defined.

This is one area in which urban historical archaeology can provide data applicable to larger research problems. For example, when the specifics of various commercial patterns have been defined, these should be of immeasurable value to those individuals who are attempting to define various kinds of commercial districts in ancient urban sites such as those in Mexico, South America, and the Near East. This is not to say that there will be one-to-one correlations but that there should be certain underlying patterning common to specific types of commercial activity wherever and whenever they have occurred.

FIGURE 12. MARTA's excavations on the West Line intersected a turn-of-the-century municipal dump. At the location shown here, the deposit was about 15 meters deep.

Formation Processes

Formation processes, recently discussed by Schiffer (1977:13–40), are especially important in interpreting urban sites. Artifacts seldom lie in their original contexts, as one might find on early historic or prehistoric sites. Rather, individual items or even large groups of materials often have been subjected to post-mortem manipulations. Sometimes, discarded items were even retrieved for further use (possibly with a different function) before final abandonment.

Urban dumps, (Figure 12) especially, exhibit a variety of discard behaviors, through which items were "transformed from the systemic context to the archaeological context" (Schiffer 1977:19). At some of the late 19th century MARTA sites, differences in the conditions of beer-ale bottles provide an interesting example of these different discard behaviors. In dumps resulting from domestic activities, some of the bottles were whole while other were in fragments. At a tavern dump of the same period, however, all of the beer and ale bottles were broken. Initially, two explanations for the tavern situation were

suggested: either there was a regulation requiring that these bottles be broken following use, or recycling was practiced. An examination of the historical documents, along with a count of bottle corks at the tavern dump (significantly more corks than bottles), now indicates that the latter interpretation was correct. This example illustrates the differences in disposal behavior that might affect a single class of artifacts. In interpreting many archaeological remains it becomes as important to determine the behavior that brought items into the archaeological context as the behavior that accompanied them in the systemic context.

As noted earlier, redeposited cultural remains are common in the urban setting. These usually are contained in transported or bulldozed fills. Redeposited remains should not be considered unimportant simply because they are not in their original context. In the MARTA Project it has been possible in some instances to identify the original sources of fill by an examination of city and county records. It also is worthy of mention that the field team routinely records the locations of fills transported during MARTA construction. These are designated "relocated sites," and they are recorded in the same manner as other sites.

Public Education

Public archaeology often has been equated with contract (or public-funded) archaeology. Many of us working in this area would like to see the definition expanded to include public participation and education (McGimsey 1972:5–19). Some of the public's misconceptions about the goals and values of archaeological research dissolve when these activities become more visible. In the urban setting considerable visibility is insured.

Experiences in the MARTA Project attest to the fact that people are anxious to learn about the project and about archaeology in general (Figures 13 and 14). They seem to share the archaeologist's frustration with the shallow treatment that his work often receives from the media and in popular writings. Since the beginning of the project in 1974, there have been numerous visitors to the sites and to the labs and frequent interaction with agency officials and construction personnel. In the beginning there was little public understanding of the work, especially with the emphasis on

FIGURE 13. The MARTA Project often attracts public attention. Here, lunch-time visitors are given a tour of excavations on the East Line at Decatur.

recent sites and artifacts. However, through a continuing program of public lectures, responsible press coverage, and unsensational TV news reports, a genuine interest has developed in most sectors. This kind of exposure cannot hurt archaeology, and it may even create a level of public awareness that has been long desired and needed.

Conclusions

In spite of the difficulties encountered when conducting archaeological work in the urban environment, it is likely that a demand for such work will increase in coming years. The renovation of "inner cities," and the development of urban parks, shopping malls, and transit systems, will in all likelihood have federal backing and consequently will require cultural resource assessments. Some of the difficulties encountered in urban archaeology can be overcome. The MARTA Project has demonstrated that the use of historical documents and informants, multiple survey and testing procedures, on-site monitoring, and good relations between archaeologist and contractor can facilitate data recovery. It has also shown that, even in a basically salvage operation, important research goals can be formulated.

Although early historic and prehistoric sites may be rare in the urban setting, there are abundant remains of urban culture itself. These remains hold great promise for increasing our understanding of the development of American city life, as well as providing a material culture "laboratory" in which to test assumptions held by archaeologists who study temporarily remote cultures. The exposure archaeology receives in the urban setting cannot help but correct some of the misconceptions that surround the discipline, and it may serve to bring this work more completely into the "public" realm.

FIGURE 14. This sign, erected at the site of archaeological excavations on the East Line, exemplifies the public education emphasis of the MARTA Project. Visitors are urged to "talk to the team members."

ACKNOWLEDGEMENTS

The authors are grateful to Robert L. Blakely and Robert A. Rubinstein for reading and commenting on this paper. An earlier version was presented at the 43rd Annual Meeting of the Society for American Archaeology, Tucson, Arizona, May 4, 1978.

REFERENCES

ASCHER, ROBERT
  1962 Ethnography for Archaeology: a Case from the Seri Indians. *Ethnology* 1: 360–69.

DEETZ, JAMES
  1970 Archaeology as a Social Science. In current directions in anthropology, *Bulletin of the American Anthropological Association* 3(3) Pt. 2: 115–25.

FONTANA, BERNARD L.
  1965 On the Meaning of Historic Sites Archaeology. *American Antiquity* 31(1): 61–65.
  1968 Bottle, Buckets, and Horseshoes: the Unrespectable in American Archaeology. *Keystone Folklore Quarterly* 13(3): 171–84.

LEONE, MARK P.
  1977 The New Mormon Temple in Washington, D.C. In Historical Archaeology and the Importance of Material Things, edited by Leland Ferguson, pp. 43–61. *Special publications of the Society for Historical Archaeology*, Vol. 2.

McGIMSEY, CHARLES R., III
  1977 *Public Archaeology*. Seminar Press, New York.

RATHJE, WILLIAM L.
  1974 The Garbage Project: a New Way of Looking at the Problems of Archaeology. *Archaeology* 27(4): 236–41.

1977 In Praise of Archaeology: *Le project du garbage*. In Historical Archaeology and the Importance of Material Things. edited by Leland Ferguson, pp. 36–42. *Special publications of the Society for Historical Archaeology*, Vol. 2

RATHJE. WILLIAM L. AND MICHAEL MCCARTHY
1977 Regularity and Variability in Contemporary Garbage. In *Research Strategies in Historical Archaeology*. edited by Stanley South, pp. 261–86. Academic Press, New York.

REID. J. JEFFERSON. WILLIAM L. RATHJE AND MICAHEL B. SCHIFFER
1974 Expanding Archaeology. *American Antiquity* 39(1): pp. 125–26.

SALWEN. BERT
1973 Archaeology in Megalopolis. In *Research and Theory in Current Archaeology*, edited by C. L. Redman, pp. 151–63.

SCHIFFER. MICHAEL B.
1977 Toward a unified science of the cultural past. In *Research strategies in historical archaeology*, edited by Stanley South, pp. 13–40. Academic Press, New York.

SCHUYLER. ROBERT L.
1974 Sandy Ground: Archaeological sampling in a Black community in metropolitan New York. *Papers of the Conference on Historic Sites Archaeology* 7(No. 2): 12–52.

SOUTH. STANLEY
1977 *Method and theory in historical archaeology*. Academic Press, New York.

WILSON. BUDD
1975 The nature and scope of archaeological observation. In 1974 symposium on industrial archaeology, Patterson, New Jersey, edited by E. S. Rutch, pp. 39–43. *Northeast Historical Archaeology* 4(1 and 2).

ROY S. DICKENS. JR.
WILLIAM R. BOWEN
LABORATORY OF ARCHAEOLOGY
GEORGIA STATE UNIVERSITY
ATLANTA. GEORGIA 30303

PARKER B. POTTER, JR.

Critical Archaeology: In the Ground and on the Street

ABSTRACT

This paper is composed of two very different parts, linked by a single concept, the idea of recursivity. The first part of the paper deals with the construction of artifact analyses within the framework of critical archaeology. The second part discusses the public performance of critical archaeological interpretations. The link between these two seemingly disparate enterprises is an understanding that material culture has the capacity to teach its users ways of thinking and behaving. This active quality of material culture is what is called recursivity.

Introduction

This article is about the recursive quality of material culture and, in particular, the key role played by this concept in the creation of "Archaeology in Annapolis," a long-term, city-wide experiment in the application of Frankfurt School critical theory (Held 1980; Geuss 1981) to historical archaeology, a research project which has been directed since 1981 by Mark Leone. The data and interpretations presented in this paper were developed during the 4½ years the author worked for "Archaeology in Annapolis" as an assistant to Leone collecting data for a doctoral thesis (Potter 1989) and overseeing the program of public archaeological interpretation discussed later in this article.

In this article, the recursive quality of material culture is taken to be those aspects of material culture expressed in the following passages:

> Architecture, as with other types of material culture patterning, is both a product of organized action and a constraint on future action. Once a structure has been raised people must move through, toward or away from it, and experience changing morphologies and relationships. In a spatial order the social order may be visibly reinforced (Tilley 1984:137).

> The circulation of things—to the extent that they acquire the specific social properties and value of money—does not

only express production relations among men, but it creates them (Rubin 1972:10–11).

> Material culture does not just exist. It is made by someone. It is produced to do something. Therefore it does not passively *reflect* society—rather, it creates society through the actions of individuals (Hodder 1986:6).

Stated another way, the recursive quality of material culture is the capacity of objects to teach their users ways of thinking and behaving. This kind of teaching is not a matter of explicit messages located on or attached to the "surfaces" of things. Instead, such teaching takes place, often unnoticed, through the *use* of various items for whatever practical purposes they are designed to fulfill. When this teaching-through-use occurs, the result can be the partial or total enactment or recreation of a particular model for how society ought to operate. One goal of material culture studies based on the idea of recursivity is the illumination of differences between the messages on the surface of things and the models of society enacted by people's use of them or, more colloquially, the differences between what an item of material culture promises its users and what it delivers, especially when what is delivered has no apparent connection to an object's function. One part of such analyses is a side-by-side comparison of the interests of the *makers* (and marketers) of any given object and the interests of the *users* of that same item. Broadly speaking, such a research strategy is similar to the technique called "immanent critique" by the critical theorists of the Frankfurt School. In an immanent critique a social formation is judged on how well it achieves the goals it sets for itself and how well it adheres to its own self-imposed principles for operation (Held 1980:183–189).

Having defined the concept of recursivity as it is used here, it remains to introduce "Archaeology in Annapolis" and the place of recursivity in this experiment in critical archaeology. The particular critical archaeology that Leone has developed for Annapolis is a three-part strategy for conducting archaeological research that is self-consciously relevant to modern American life (Potter 1989:70–71). The first step is ethnography intended to explore the ideological aspects of life in the community in which an archaeological investigation takes place. In this discussion, the term ideology refers to those givens or taken-for-granteds of daily life that are cultural constructs but which are often treated as natural or inevitable and which, therefore, can serve to naturalize or mask social relations of dominance and inequality. The second step is archaeological research and artifact analysis dedicated to uncovering the roots of the ideologies identified by ethnography, and the goal is to give those ideologies histories, showing that since they have beginnings they are *not* natural or inevitable but cultural. The third step is a program of public interpretation that puts on display the pierced ideology, to demonstrate that certain aspects of contemporary life, normally taken for granted, can be questioned and challenged rather than simply accepted as immutable. The goal of a critical archaeology, like the goal of any critical theory, is enlightenment that enables individuals to understand better their interests, enlightenment that may serve as the basis for emancipatory social action. ''Archaeology in Annapolis'' aims to show people how history is created and does so in an attempt to help people become less susceptible to having history used against them.

In the critical archaeology developed by Leone and others for Annapolis there is a particular relationship between the idea of recursivity and archaeological attempts to penetrate ideology and put it on display. Specifically, the recursive quality of material culture, as defined here, is what makes material culture a potentially powerful instrument for communicating and teaching ideology. Further, this kind of teaching is a process that takes place in the present just as it did in the past. Consequently, the balance of this article is divided into two parts, dealing with the second and third steps in the research program for critical archaeology outlined above. First is a discussion of an archaeological analysis of material culture, arguing that through the process of being used by people, ceramic tableware taught ideology in 18th-century Annapolis. This teaching-through-use is recursivity ''in the ground.'' The two-part ancillary issue of ''agency'' is then discussed. The section that follows moves ''on the street'' to discuss the subtle

messages communicated, often unawares, by archaeologists using material culture to teach site visitors about the roots of modern ideology. And in both of these cases, what is taught by material culture is an ideology, the enactment of which may or may not be in the best interests of the people to whom it is taught.

In the Ground

As noted above, this section focuses on 18th-century ceramics to demonstrate the idea of recursivity and the ideological quality of material culture. But before working through that example, it is necessary to explain in some detail one thing that is *not* included under the rubric of recursivity.

The contrast here is between recursivity and emulation. Emulation models of society are based on the idea that wealthy or high-status individuals are the first to acquire new (and expensive) items of material culture and that such high-status goods are coveted by members of lower classes to whom those goods eventually trickle down. Allied with emulation models is the idea that the rich practice conspicuous consumption as a way of demonstrating their wealth. According to this widely-held perspective, the main thing material culture teaches people is the desire to own it. This process certainly played a significant part in what McKendrick et al. (1982) call *The Birth of a Consumer Society* in 18th-century England, but the desire to own is not the only lesson material culture has the capacity to teach. Beyond emulation and conspicuous consumption is the part played by material culture in sustaining and advancing the ideology of capitalism. Whether or not specific items of material culture taught ideology to specific users cannot be proven empirically, but one purpose of the following example is to suggest that such a process is plausible.

If material culture can teach and reinforce ideology, then the question for a critical archaeology becomes how to organize material culture studies that can help pierce or unmask past (or present) ideologies. The starting point for such studies is an idea that has been around since the New Archaeology, namely the idea that there are as many ways to describe an artifact or classify a collection of artifacts as there are individuals who attempt the task. Put more strongly, names and classifications for artifacts are not intrinsic and they are not neutral; they are imposed by the observer to enable him or her to answer specific questions (Kaplin 1964:51; Binford 1965:206; Clarke 1968:13; Dunnell 1971:117; Hill and Evans 1972:251; Fontana 1973:3; Potter 1982:6). For a critical archaeology application of this insight means finding ways of using variability in the material record to measure the penetration and power of capitalist ideology. To do this comprehensively can, but does not necessarily, involve paying attention to variables left unexamined by analysts who have other interpretive goals, and it is often the case that the variables useful for an analysis of ideology are not the variables that would be chosen by an analyst using an emulation model.

Consider, for example, a creamware plate—or a piece of one. Even a small fragment of a creamware plate has dozens of variables, some of which historical archaeologists have learned to pay attention to and measure, others of which generally have been ignored as insignificant. The key question here is: Significant or insignificant *for what*? An increasing number of historical archaeologists are asking this question, but for far too long it has gone unasked. There is so much good scholarship on the manufacture of 18th-century Anglo-American material culture, and thus so much to learn, that learning the ceramics, for example, has become a matter of mastering Noël Hume as a rite of passage. It is fine to learn Noël Hume, but it is also important to learn what learning Noël Hume is good for. To do so requires determining the point of view from which Noël Hume (1970) wrote *Artifacts of Colonial America*. Noël Hume takes the point of manufacture as his focus for understanding 18th-century Anglo-American material culture. Therefore, for answering some questions, for example questions about the distribution of the products of particular factories, Noël Hume's scheme of classification for ceramic artifacts is the best one available. But, if one's questions focus on some other point in the life span of ceramic items,

like retail sale at the local level, then perhaps another scheme of classification is more appropriate. Rubertone (1976, 1979:94) cites Cronin (1962), Deetz (1965), Hill (1970), Longacre (1970), and Plog (1977) in a discussion of this same issue in relation to studies of prehistoric and pre-industrial ceramics.

The crucial insight is this: Names and classifications for artifacts are not neutral and they are not intrinsic; they are imposed by the observer to enable him or her to answer specific questions. There can be no ''right'' or ''wrong'' way of describing an artifact outside of a particular question that the artifact is being used to answer. That is, the ability to differentiate between creamware and pearlware should not be a criterion for judging the competence of historical archaeologists—although it is often used as such—but instead is a particular skill valuable *only* if being able to tell the difference contributes to some analytical end. As has been noted, this insight has been around since the New Archaeology and it has, in fact, been put into play by an increasing number of historical archaeologists.

Historical archaeologists have invented ways to use ceramic artifacts to learn about several different aspects of life in the past, and each of these analyses requires attention to a different set of variables selected from the many that could be measured. Ceramic tableware has been used for dating (South 1977), the analysis of diet (Otto 1975, 1977), and the determination of socioeconomic status (Miller 1980). South, following Noël Hume, uses ware type primarily and surface decoration secondarily, Otto vessel form, and Miller surface decoration. But as sound as these various techniques are, and most historical archaeologists have used one or more of them, all of these ways of learning about the past through ceramics treat ceramic artifacts as simply a *reflection* of past societies. That is, these modes of analysis make no use of the recursive quality of material culture, and one result is that they do not use the material record to explore the roots of modern ideology. These ways of dealing with the artifactual record are not adequate for a critical archaeology.

How then does one do a ceramic analysis based

on the idea of recursivity? The first step is to ask what kinds of information a set of creamware plates contains and what kinds of behavior such a set of plates has the capacity to teach. Among other things, a set of creamware contains quite a bit of information about the process of its manufacture and may well have communicated such information to its 18th-century users. But what, specifically? First, there is aesthetics, but nobody would argue that archaeology is the best way to learn about 18th-century aesthetics or that art is all that one can learn from 18th-century ceramics. Then there is mind, but Deetz (1977) never really argues that plates taught people how to "think Georgian." Some would say that the history of technology was—and is—what 18th-century ceramics teach best. But the history of technology, as a perspective, often seems to take any technological change that appears to have led to contemporary life as an advancement and an unqualified good—while leaving people out of the picture. That is, the history of technology sometimes produces interpretations that act as ideology by supporting the current social and economic order without examining it.

Rather than interpreting ceramics as an instrument for teaching aesthetics, mind-sets, or technology, it could be argued that mass-produced items of material culture taught the people who used them about the organization of the labor that went into their manufacture. It may be productive to see the historical archaeological record as the history of labor. Provocative work along these lines has been initiated by Orser (1988) and Paynter (1988). Returning to the creamware plate already introduced as an example, the mark that that plate bears most clearly is the mark of the regulated, standardized, segmented—and alienated—labor that went into its manufacture. The most radical position on this issue, articulated by Leone (1988) and others, is that as 18th-century middle-class and working-class Americans ate from relatively inexpensive sets of creamware plates, they learned what E. P. Thompson (1967) calls work-discipline. Work-discipline is a series of practices including payment by the hour, that served to alienate workers from the products and

the value of their labor in the name of efficiency. By using creamware plates people were subconsciously learning and internalizing ideologically charged concepts like individualism that helped them to be good workers. In this way mass-produced mold-made plates helped to reproduce among their users the social relations of production responsible for their manufacture.

This interpretation is especially intriguing when it is contrasted with the premise of the emulation model view of 18th-century ceramics. According to McKendrick (1982) Josiah Wedgwood made sets of creamware, also called queensware, for Queen Charlotte of England and Catherine the Great of Russia, among other members of the European nobility. His idea was that royal and noble use of his wares would encourage middle-class folks to buy similar wares in an attempt to be like their social superiors. Wedgwood's message to middle-class consumers was, in essence, 'Use queensware and be like the Queen of England,' while the likely result was that buying, owning, and using creamware served to make middle-class people *unlike* the Queen of England by teaching them to accept the organization of their labor by capitalists in factories and other industrial workplaces. In this way, creamware delivered to its users something exactly the opposite of what Wedgwood promised it would, which was similarity to the segment of 18th-century European society immune to the organization of the industrial workplace. (This failure to deliver on an advertised promise is precisely the kind of phenomenon targeted by immanent critique.) The emulation model is a particularly inappropriate interpretive tool in this case because it is identical with and perpetuates the ideology of capitalism. To use Handsman's (1977, cited in Meltzer 1981) terminology, the idea that using the same kind of plates as rich people makes middle-class people more like the wealthy is the vulgar ideology of creamware plates, the surface message used by Wedgwood to sell plates and make his fortune. The sub-surface message carried by those plates, the characteristics of creamware that taught people ways of thinking that strengthened their ties to positions of social inferiority is what Handsman would call their non-vulgar ideology. It is to this level of ideology that the greatest attention needs to be paid in critical analyses of material culture.

The idea that creamware plates taught their users to be manageable members of society, that tableware trained people to work for capitalists, is a surmise rather than an historical fact but it has a basis in material culture. That basis is the striking physical regularity of creamware plates. This regularity was produced by the use of molds and by regulation in the workplace based on separating the parts of plate-making into discrete tasks performed by specialists. Along with advances in ceramic technology and marketing, the organization of labor according to the principles of mass production and task specialization was one of Wedgwood's major contributions to the ceramic industry in particular and the Industrial Revolution in general. And as noted above, creamware plates clearly bear the marks of the segmented, standardized, and regulated labor that went into them. Those marks are the symmetry, standardization, and regularity of creamware plates.

Just as there is ample documentary evidence of the regulated labor that went into creamware plates, so too is there considerable documentation of the ways in which creamware plates were likely used by at least some of the people who purchased them. That evidence is contained in the proliferation of etiquette books and other guides for behavior written and circulated during the 18th century (Shackel 1987). The etiquette books' view of the individual as separate from but equivalent to other individuals, as well as the rules for the polite behavior of individuals in society contained in these books were reinforced by ceramic tableware which provided each individual with a plate separate from and similar to the plates of all the other diners around a table. In addition, one of etiquette's secondary functions, providing a way of stratifying society by separating those who knew the social rules from those who did not, was facilitated by the production of increasingly specialized tableware forms, dessert plates, dinner plates, breakfast plates, soup plates, and so on, not to mention the various exotic serving pieces. An understanding of material culture as recursive says that by eating

from creamware plates in the ways suggested by the various etiquette books, people in the 18th century also learned to accept the principles by which their labor would be organized in a capitalist workplace by men like Wedgwood.

So far this argument has attempted to link the physical characteristics of creamware plates with the kind of labor that went into them and the kind of behavior that made use of them. Yet to be discussed is a way to use this insight for archaeological analysis.

Interestingly, Deetz's (1977) work is of assistance here, even though Deetz himself nowhere undertakes the study of ideology. Deetz's work is useful to the extent that the qualities he ascribes to the Georgian world view—balance, order, symmetry, segmentation, and standardization—are also characteristics that virtually define the industrial workplace in capitalist production. Leone (1988) has for several years used this similarity to go beyond Deetz's statements of what the Georgian world view *is* to ask what the Georgian world view *is good for*. Leone's response is, of course, that the Georgian world view was a good (i.e., profitable) way for capitalists to organize industrial labor. A worker taught at home to see standardization and segmentation as the way in which the world naturally works may have been more likely to see such organization in the workplace as appropriate. Furthermore, that same worker may have been more likely to accept the loss of control over the products of his or her labor that came along with such an organizational scheme.

Therefore, Deetz's conception of the Georgian world view may be seen as a guide to the archaeological identification of 18th-century material culture that reinforced an ideology that led workers to accept being alienated from the products of their labor. One problem with this approach is that Deetz's use of structuralism and binary oppositions greatly reduces artifact analysis to the detection of the presence or absence of Georgian traits in material culture. One is left saying that coarse-bodied, slip-decorated earthenware plates signal an unsegmented, unstandardized, pre-capitalist world view while creamware plates always signal the opposite, a world view parallel with the ideology of early industrial capitalism. Conversely, working from this point of view, one cannot possibly discover that some person or group of people in the past used creamware plates in a distinctly non-Georgian way. The central difficulty is that Deetz's work provides no sophisticated way to measure the "Georgian-ness" of any assemblage in relation to other assemblages.

This problem has been understood for some time. Handsman (1981:12–17) provides one solution in his analysis of differentiation and specialization. Another solution has been developed and extensively tested by Paul Shackel (Shackel 1987; Leone et al. 1987; Little and Shackel 1989). This second solution is a formula for quantifying segmentation by determining the amount of variety in the sizes of plates in any given ceramic assemblage.

The basis of Shackel's formula is the assumption that a person who left an assemblage of nothing but 10-in. plates ate—and thought—differently than someone who left an assemblage representing equal numbers of 6-, 7-, 8-, 9-, 10-, and 12-in. plates. An assemblage of the first kind would be difficult to use according to the prevailing rules of etiquette, particularly those that distinguished various meals from each other (e.g., breakfast vs. dinner) and which divided individual meals into separate courses. But an assemblage of the second kind represents the existence in the past of a table fully stocked with creamware plates and serving pieces. Such an assemblage also implies that someone at the table was knowledgeable enough to enforce the proper etiquette for using this array of tableware. This etiquette segmented the food that composed the meal by putting different courses on different kinds of dishes while at the same time segmenting the group of diners around the table by separating them from each other through their use of individual place settings rather than communal vessels. But by saying that both of the previously described archaeological assemblages contain few redware plates and lots of creamware plates makes them both more similar than different. Further, such a statement would mask the kind of variation described here.

Shackel's formula for ceramic variability provides the opportunity to break free from the assumption behind a great deal of archaeological analysis, the idea that most objects have their *full* meanings attached to them when they are made. The point of using the idea of recursivity is that objects considered to be artifacts today had meanings attached to them when they were made *and* when they were used (and yet again by archaeologists today). In addition, the ability to measure how different people selected differently (or similarly) from the same range of available objects provides an analytical basis for discovering *rejection* of the Georgian world view by people using material culture usually termed "Georgian." That is, a white Annapolitan in 1787 who used *all* 10-in. creamware plates would have been using tableware differently than many of his or her neighbors and would very likely have known it.

The noteworthy thing here is that the principal variable in Shackel's formula, plate size, is something that historical archaeologists have always known to be a measurable attribute but have rarely used to any particular analytical end. Many historical archaeologists have measured rim sherds to determine the sizes and the names of the plates from which they came, but most such efforts have been merely classificatory; little *additional* meaning is ever drawn from the fact that occupants of a given site used twice as many dinner plates as breakfast plates and no dessert plates at all. Most plate measurement has done little more than characterize the archaeological record in terms that would have been meaningful to Staffordshire potters without any explanation of how the potter's perspective is meaningful in terms of a specific archaeological analysis.

Returning to the issue of recursivity, Shackel's formula is a way of quantifying the potential of a ceramic assemblage in the past to teach segmentation, an important part of an ideology that supported the emergence of early industrial capitalism. This formula provides the analytical link between material culture and ideology essential for a critical archaeology.

Agency

Having argued that ceramic tableware was one channel through which ideology was taught, one ancillary issue needs to be addressed. That issue is agency, and there are two parts.

The first part concerns agency in the past. Specifically, one way of attacking a critical analytical strategy based on the idea of recursivity is to demonstrate that the particular agent responsible for the production of a given item of material culture did not intend the effects attributed to its use. In the case of the ceramic analysis presented above, such a countering argument would require only evidence that Josiah Wedgwood was not consciously trying to use the products of his factories to dominate members of the working class. In response, to the extent that Wedgwood's plates had a "life" of their own once they left the factories, what Wedgwood intended is not a sufficient explanation of what Wedgwood plates may have done as objects used by people in society. Consider Alfred Nobel; he did not intend or attempt to kill thousands of people but his intentions do not change the fact that dynamite has done just that. So, the analysis proposed here cannot be refuted by a demonstration that Wedgwood was a considerate employer and a friend to workers.

The second part of this issue concerns agency in the present. Critical archaeology, as developed in Annapolis, is concerned not only with identifying items and classes of material culture that may have taught and reinforced ideology in the past but also with examining versions of history, in the present, that continue the process of reinforcing ideology. The goal of such examination is to unmask these ideological versions of the past in a public way. This unmasking is sometimes misunderstood to be a claim that the author of an ideologically useful version of the past specifically intended the effect ascribed to his or her book, article, or film. Again, this article does not claim that a historian writing a guidebook for Annapolis in 1965 intentionally misrepresented what he or she knew to be the truth about Annapolis history in order to advance a particular political agenda. Critical analyses of artifacts and interpretations of the past need not be accusatory. Michael Wallace, an incisive radical critic of Colonial Williamsburg, says:

I will try to demonstrate that, from the mid 19th century onwward, most history museums were constructed by members of dominant classes and embodied interpretations that supported their sponsors' privileged positions. I do not contend that those who established museums were Machiavellian plotters; the museum builders simply embedded in their efforts versions of history that were commonplaces of their class's culture (Wallace 1986:137).

The position taken by Wallace is much like the position taken in this article; a critical analysis does not need to demonstrate the villainy of a writer of history, only the potential of his or her work to act as ideology. Conversely, identifying the motivations of a history writer as praiseworthy does not refute an analysis that shows the ideological usefulness of his or her writings.

This discussion of agency is a good bridge to the next section which deals with the idea of recursivity in the context of "Archaeology in Public," the program of archaeological interpretation invented to carry out the third step in a program of critical archaeology for Annapolis.

On the Street

The previous sections deal with the value of the idea of recursivity for critical analyses of archaeological materials and ideology in the ground. That same concept has a part to play in the design and implementation of an effective program of public education based on a critical approach to both archaeological material culture and historical interpretation.

The appropriateness of using the recursive quality of material culture as a basis for building a program of archaeological interpretation can be understood by reference to two articles in Gould and Schiffer's (1981) *Modern Material Culture: The Archaeology of Us*, specifically the contributions of Leone (1981) and Meltzer (1981). All of the other articles in the book are about material culture used by people in living their normal daily lives while both Leone and Meltzer discuss history museums. One could easily ask how these two papers fit into the book. The "Archaeology in Annapolis" ceramic analysis explores the ways that 200-year-old material culture communicated to people 200 years ago, and the most insightful modern material culture studies explain the ways that contemporary material culture communicates to people today. Leone and Meltzer both consider the ways in which old (or historic) material culture communicates to people today. The only thing that distinguishes the work of Leone and Meltzer from the rest of the articles in *The Archaeology of Us* is that the manufacture of the material culture Leone and Meltzer study is temporally separate from the people who learn from it; the processes by which material culture teaches people hold as much for Leone and Meltzer as they do for the rest of Gould and Schiffer's "archaeologists of us." Recursivity can be used to guide studies like Leone's and Meltzer's, to illuminate the subtextual messages encoded in presentations of the past, or it can be used to guide the creation and implementation of presentations of the past. This second path is the one followed here.

This section uses a narrower definition of recursivity than that used above. Previously two aspects of recursivity were identified: (1) that material culture teaches through its use; and (2) that some of the messages it communicates are hidden, below the surface, or subtextual. This section lays aside the first part of that definition and uses only the second.

The idea of subtextual communication is helpful in dealing with a problem encountered during the implementation of the "Archaeology in Annapolis" public program. As has been noted, this interpretive program attempts to use material culture to show members of contemporary society parts of either a past or a present ideology that may serve to thwart their interests. The idea is to pierce such an ideology in the hope that enlightenment may lead people to understand better their own interests and may even lead to emancipatory social action. In historical disciplines, a critical interpretation often entails teaching the idea that versions of the past are created by—and serve—contemporary interests. A successful educational program is one that helps enfranchise people with some control over their consumption of information about the past. A visitor who has gotten the point of such a presentation is one who has learned to ask two questions of any version of the past: What is its point of view? and, What does it try to get people to do? In comparison to traditional historical interpretation based on "true facts" and unexamined premises, the kind of historical interpretation presented here is somewhat radical. However, the problem for which recursivity is a part of the solution is the fact that a significant number of visitors fail to find the interpretations presented in Annapolis to be radical.

Since the first season of "Archaeology in Public" in Annapolis critically informed archaeological site tours have been evaluated through the use of a 1-page questionnaire that assesses both the performance quality of the tours and also their success from a critical perspective. Of interest here are the responses to a pair of short-answer questions. The questions are: "What did you learn about archaeology that you did not know before you visited the site?" and, "What connection do you see between this site and everyday life today?"

The first of these two questions was asked twice, in 1985 at the Shiplap House site and in 1986 at the Main Street site. The desired response was for people to say that they learned that archaeology was relevant to today because it could uncover the roots of contemporary ideology. Between 5 and 10 percent of the visitors who filled out evaluation forms responded this way, while well over half indicated that they had learned some fact or another about archaeological procedures and techniques. As long as what people have learned is accurate (i.e., "archaeology is painstaking") such messages are encouraging, but they do not constitute success from the standpoint of critical theory. In addition to these two categories of responses, there is one curious set of responses indicating that some people went away from the tours with a message exactly the opposite of the one that was intended. These responses are the ones in which people said that they learned that archaeology connected the past to the present by showing the continuity of evolution from the 18th century to today. Nothing could be further from the intention of a critically informed interpretation than the idea that cultural change is evolutionary. Evolution suggests that change operates beyond the agency of the individuals affected by it and, as ideology, serves to disfranchise individuals rather than enfranchise them with the means to control their lives. It is the purpose of any historical critical theory to oppose such formulations because they teach individuals to be passive victims of history rather than agents for change.

The same kind of miseducation discussed above has been identified in responses to the second question, which asked visitors what connections they saw between the archaeological site they had visited and everyday life today. This question was asked, during one season only after the tours at the Main Street site in 1986. The question had no particular "right" answer but it was hoped that visitors would say that the site contained archaeological evidence for the beginnings of some taken-for-granted element of contemporary daily life. The actual result was that a plurality of visitors who filled out evaluation forms (37.2%) gave responses like "history repeats itself." These responses, like those of people who view historical change as evolutionary, show people leaving "Archaeology in Annapolis" site tours thinking that historical change was, and contemporary social change is, beyond the ability of individuals to affect. Some visitors who respond this way could be using history to trap themselves in their present lives, and if this kind of entrapment did take place, the ideological basis for this way of thinking was so strong that these people made "Archaeology in Annapolis" site tours a part of the "trap." Talk of entrapment may overstate what is indicated by those responses; use of the concept of entrapment has concerned nearly everyone who reviewed this article. But given a choice, it seems more productive to overinterpret visitor evaluation data than to give up the goal of having a serious impact on an audience. "Archaeology in Public" costs far too much for its authors to be satisfied with providing nothing more than entertainment or "local color."

In addition, visitors used the question about archaeology and everyday life to express two very different ideas about the resemblance between the 18th century and today. Some visitors learned from the tour that the 18th century is very similar to today while a like number of visitors learned from the *same* tour that the 18th century and today are very different from each other. Both responses offer a critical theorist reason to worry. Visitors who saw the 18th century as similar may see any changes between then and now as gradual, evolutionary, and natural, that is, beyond their control. When this kind of change is naturalized it becomes difficult to locate the agents of change and even more difficult to identify the interests served by such change. Those visitors who cited the differences between then and now may see any changes as beneficial progress, leading society from some sort of "dark age" to a wonderful today. For these people, the agents of change are not hidden but glorified, yet the result is the same; the status quo is seen to be the way the world is supposed to be and is beyond question and challenge.

The basic problem represented by these various instances of miseducation is the absorptive power of capitalist ideology, the ability of a powerful ideology to co-opt, transform, and use for its own purposes even a radical critique of itself. In each of the cases of miseducation described above, the interpretations that visitors left the site with are interpretations that serve the interests of the status quo and the dominant ideology "Archaeology in Annapolis" was attempting to call into question.

This absorption and transformation of a radical critique happens in two ways. The first, mostly beyond the scope of this paper, has to do with the widespread adoption of biological evolution as a metaphor for explaining *any* instance of long-term change. This model tends to naturalize change and make it appear beyond question and human intervention in both the past and the present. One way to combat this problem is to deal explicitly with the concept of evolution and make it clear that evolution is *not*, in this context, an appropriate metaphor for long-term social and cultural change.

A second way that miseducation occurs is a result of the program's strategy for using material culture to teach. In virtually all site tours, including those that elicited the responses noted above, there have been discussions of classes of material culture like architecture and ceramics that have pointed out changes over time from less to more complexity, from less to more standardization, in short, from less to more modernity. This tactic is risky, it has been learned, because so many visitors come to the project's sites already believing that such change is inevitable and all for the best. Given this predisposition, it can be assumed that in any presentation that arranges artifacts in order from less to more complex those artifacts will teach that the status quo is good and legitimate because it is a clear improvement over the past, even if such a message is contrary to the one intended at the surface level of that interpretation. It is worth noting here that a critical interpretation does not automatically reject the status quo, but does insist on opening up for investigation all aspects of the current order, including the ideas about the past that underpin it. The understanding that artifacts can communicate on several levels is an acknowledgment of the recursive quality of material culture, at least under a narrower definition of recursivity.

There is a way to build an interpretation of archaeological material culture out of this understanding of recursivity. When asked what they would like to see in future site tours, a majority of visitors have said that they would like to see more artifacts than they saw on their initial tour. Thus the audience has presented a mandate to use artifacts to teach them about the past. Further, the fact that people have such a strong desire to see these tangible results of archaeological work is a fairly strong indication that they have some conceptual category into which to place them, some a priori argument for which these artifacts are evidence. To use artifacts effectively, to advance a critical agenda, it is necessary to learn from visitors just what those a priori arguments are. Archaeological educators may have an interpretive agenda, but many visitors come to archaeological sites already in possession of a relatively well-developed lesson plan.

Stated another way, most archaeologists know that artifacts do not speak for themselves, therefore archaeological educators must take the time to learn the frameworks that site visitors are likely to use to interpret the artifacts that are shown to them, especially when so many visitors seem to use artifacts to support a dominant ideology that disfran-chises them. Already noted are the ways in which visitors use artifacts arranged from simple to complex as evidence for the superiority of modern technology and the social forms that facilitate it. Similarly, when told of the increasing use of individual plates, utensils, and drinking vessels during the 18th century, 90 percent of all visitors who comment on this phenomenon take the change to signal an increasing concern with hygiene. This popular interpretation makes creamware plates an unqualified good, leading to modern concepts of health, even though no evidence exists to suggest that the people who made, sold, and used creamware in the 18th century did any of those things with hygiene in mind.

These are just two examples of the many interpretive frameworks that visitors use to attach meanings to artifacts. The value of the idea of recursivity is that it acknowledges the ability of material culture to communicate on several levels simultaneously. Once this quality of material culture is established, it becomes legitimate and in fact imperative for those who would teach with material culture to study carefully the ideas about material culture already held by the people they intend to teach. Archaeological educators have to discover how people think with things, and what they think, and then construct interpretations that acknowledge those modes of thought, exposing them as ideological when that is the case. Rather than presenting critical interpretations of material culture in a vacuum, it may be necessary to work comparatively, explaining how a particular interpretation works by explaining what it is not. In these ways the idea of recursivity may be vital to the creation of critical interpretations, discussions of archaeological material culture that help people liberate themselves from contemporary ideologies that thwart their interests and limit their freedoms.

Summary

This paper has attempted two goals. The first section uses the idea of recursivity to build a more sophisticated way of investigating and understanding the various ways that material culture has acted on people and society in the past. The second section is an acknowledgment that in the present, just as in the past, material culture has a capacity to guide behavior and shape society. A creamware plate in a 20th-century museum is as active recursively today as it was on an 18th-century table 200 years ago. Thus an understanding of recursivity is vital both for interpreting 18th-century material culture and also for presenting interpretations of 18th-century material culture to people today. Just like the people whom archaeologists study, people today—including archaeologists—are subject to subtextual messages already embedded in the material culture of contemporary American society, or to ideological messages embedded by archaeological interpretation in that material culture. Given that life in contemporary America is lived in the midst of an enveloping and ideologically charged material world, this article will close with two questions that are only partially answered here. First, how is it possible to construct a critique of capitalism while completely surrounded by capitalism and its artifacts? Second, how is it possible to create an alternative perspective when the very principles of the discipline's basic research technique, archaeological excavation, are order, segmentation, and standardization—principles identical to those that structure the phenomenon that archaeologists of capitalism are trying to study, and whose roots these scholars are attempting to find in the ground and interpret to the public on the street? Obviously there is more work to do.

ACKNOWLEDGMENTS

I would like to thank Mark P. Leone for inviting me to join "Archaeology in Annapolis" and Paul A. Shackel and Barbara J. Little for inviting me to participate in this volume and the symposium that led to it. Nancy Jo Chabot has listened to and improved all of the ideas that appear in this article. I would also like to thank Historic Annapolis Foundation (HAF—previously Historic Annapolis, Incorporated), a nonprofit educational and preservation organization founded in 1952 to preserve the present National Historic Landmark District of Annapolis and its history. HAF has provided funding for and has shared its research findings with "Archaeology in Annapolis," but the opinions expressed in this paper do not necessarily reflect the views of HAF.

REFERENCES

BINFORD, LEWIS R.
1965   Archaeological Systematics and the Study of Culture Process. *American Antiquity* 31(2):203–210.

CLARKE, DAVID L.
1968   *Analytical Archaeology*. Methuen, London.

CRONIN, CONSTANCE
1962   An Analysis of Pottery Design Elements Indicating Relationships between Decorated Types. In Chapters in the Prehistory of Eastern Arizona, I, edited by Paul S. Martin, John B. Rinaldo, William A. Longacre, Constance Cronin, Leslie G. Freeman, Jr., and James Schoenwetter. *Fieldiana Anthropology Series* No. 53:105–114. Field Museum of Natural History, Chicago.

DEETZ, JAMES F.
1965   The Dynamics of Stylistic Change in Arikara Ceramics. *Illinois Studies in Anthropology* No. 4. University of Illinois Press, Urbana.
1977   *In Small Things Forgotten*. Anchor Press/Doubleday, New York.

DUNNELL, ROBERT C.
1971   Comment on "The Importance of Both Analytic and Taxonomic Classification in the Type-Variety System" by Sabloff and Smith. *American Antiquity* 36(1):115–118.

FONTANA, BERNARD L.
1973   The Cultural Dimension of Pottery: Ceramics as Social Documents. In *Ceramics in America*, edited by Ian M. G. Quimby, pp. 1–13. University Press of Virginia, Charlottesville.

GEUSS, RAYMOND
1981   *The Idea of a Critical Theory*. Cambridge University Press, Cambridge.

GOULD, RICHARD A., AND MICHAEL B. SCHIFFER (EDITORS)
1981   *Modern Material Culture: The Archaeology of Us*. Academic Press, New York.

HANDSMAN, RUSSELL G.
1977   *The Bushkill Complex as an Anomaly: Unmasking the Ideology of American Archaeology*. Ph.D. dissertation, Department of Anthropology, American University, Washington, D.C. University Microfilms, Ann Arbor.
1981   Early Capitalism and the Center Village of Canaan, Connecticut: A Study of Transformations and Separations. *Artifacts* 9(3):1–22. Washington, Connecticut.

HELD, DAVID
1980 *Introduction to Critical Theory: Horkheimer to Habermas.* University of California Press, Berkeley.

HILL, JAMES N.
1970 Broken K Pueblo: Prehistoric Social Organization in the American Southwest. *Anthropological Papers* No 18. University of Arizona Press, Tucson.

HILL, JAMES N., AND ROBERT K. EVANS
1972 A Model for Classification and Typology. In *Models in Archaeology*, edited by David L. Clarke, pp. 231–274. Methuen, London.

HODDER, IAN
1986 *Reading the Past.* Cambridge University Press, Cambridge.

KAPLIN, A.
1964 *The Conduct of Inquiry: Methodology for Behavioral Science.* Chandler, San Francisco.

LEONE, MARK P.
1981 Archaeology's Relationship to the Present and the Past. In *Modern Material Culture: The Archaeology of Us*, edited by Richard A. Gould and Michael B. Schiffer, pp. 5–13. Academic Press, New York.
1988 The Georgian Order as the Order of Merchant Capitalism in Annapolis, Maryland. In *The Recovery of Meaning: Historical Archaeology in the Eastern United States*, edited by Mark P. Leone and Parker B. Potter, Jr., pp. 235–262. Smithsonian Institution Press, Washington, D.C.

LEONE, MARK P., PARKER B. POTTER, JR., AND PAUL A. SHACKEL
1987 Toward a Critical Archaeology. *Current Anthropology* 28(3):283–302.

LITTLE, BARBARA J., AND PAUL A. SHACKEL
1989 Scales of Historical Anthropology: Archaeology of Colonial Anglo-America. *Antiquity* 63(240):495–509.

LONGACRE, WILLIAM
1970 Archaeology as Anthropology: A Case Study. *Anthropological Papers* No. 17. University of Arizona Press, Tucson.

MCKENDRICK, NEIL
1982 Josiah Wedgwood and the Commercialization of the Potteries. In *The Birth of a Consumer Society: The Commercialization of Eighteenth-Century England*, edited by Neil McKendrick, John Brewer, and J. H. Plumb, pp. 100–145. Indiana University Press, Bloomington.

MCKENDRICK, NEIL, JOHN BREWER, AND J. H. PLUMB
1982 *The Birth of a Consumer Society: The Commercialization of Eighteenth-Century England.* Indiana University Press, Bloomington.

MELTZER, DAVID J.
1981 Ideology and Material Culture. In *Modern Material Culture: The Archaeology of Us*, edited by Richard A. Gould and Michael B. Schiffer, pp. 113–125. Academic Press, New York.

MILLER, GEORGE
1980 Classification and Economic Scaling of 19th-Century Ceramics. *Historical Archaeology* 14:1–40.

NOËL HUME, IVOR
1970 *A Guide to Artifacts of Colonial America.* Alfred A. Knopf, New York.

ORSER, CHARLES E., JR.
1988 Toward a Theory of Power for Historical Archaeology: Plantations and Space. In *The Recovery of Meaning: Historical Archaeology in the Eastern United States*, edited by Mark P. Leone and Parker B. Potter, Jr., pp. 313–344. Smithsonian Institution Press, Washington.

OTTO, JOHN S.
1975 *Status Differences and the Archaeological Record—A Comparison of Planter, Overseer, and Slave Sites from Cannon's Point Plantation (1794–1861), St. Simon's Island, Georgia.* Ph.D. dissertation, Department of Anthropology, University of Florida, Gainesville. University Microfilms, Ann Arbor.
1977 Artifacts and Status Differences—A Comparison of Ceramics from Planter, Overseer, and Slave Sites on an Ante-Bellum Plantation. In *Research Strategies in Historical Archaeology*, edited by Stanley South, pp. 91–118. Academic Press, New York.

PAYNTER, ROBERT
1988 Steps to an Archaeology of Capitalism: Material Change and Class Analysis. In *The Recovery of Meaning: Historical Archaeology in the Eastern United States*, edited by Mark P. Leone and Parker B. Potter, Jr., pp. 407–434. Smithsonian Institution Press, Washington, D.C.

PLOG, STEPHEN
1977 *A Multivariate Approach to the Explanation of Ceramic Design Variation.* Ph.D. dissertation, Department of Anthropology, University of Michigan, Ann Arbor. University Microfilms, Ann Arbor.

POTTER, PARKER B., JR.
1982 The Translation of Archaeological Evidence into Economic Understandings: A Study of Context, Naming, and Nineteenth-Century Ceramics in Rockbridge County, Virginia. Unpublished M.A. thesis, Department of Anthropology, Brown University, Providence, Rhode Island.
1989 *Archaeology in Public in Annapolis: An Experiment in the Application of Critical Theory to Historical Archaeology.* Ph.D. dissertation, Department of Anthropology, Brown University, Providence, Rhode Island. University Microfilms, Ann Arbor.

RUBERTONE, PATRICIA E.
1976   Interaction in Archaeology: Inferences from Ceramic Attribute Analysis. Paper presented at the Annual Meeting of the Society for American Archaeology, St. Louis, Missouri.
1979   Social Organization in an Islamic Town: A Behavioral Explanation of Ceramic Variability. Unpublished Ph.D. dissertation, Department of Anthropology, State University of New York at Binghamton, Binghamton.

RUBIN, L.
1972   *Essays on Marx's Theory of Value*. Black and Red, Detroit.

SHACKEL, PAUL A.
1987   *A Historical Archaeology of Personal Discipline*. Ph.D. dissertation, Department of Anthropology, State University of New York at Buffalo, Buffalo. University Microfilms, Ann Arbor.

SOUTH, STANLEY
1977   *Method and Theory in Historical Archeology*. Academic Press, New York.

THOMPSON, E. P.
1967   Time, Work-Discipline, and the Industrial Revolution. *Past and Present* 38:56–97.

TILLEY, CHRISTOPHER
1984   Ideology and the Legitimation of Power in the Middle Neolithic of Southern Sweden. In *Ideology, Power, and Prehistory*, edited by Daniel Miller and Christopher Tilley, pp. 111–146. Cambridge University Press, Cambridge.

WALLACE, MICHAEL
1986   Visiting the Past: History Museums in the United States. In *Presenting the Past: Essays on History and the Public*, edited by Susan Porter Benson, Stephen Brier, and Roy Rosenzweig, pp. 137–161. Temple University Press, Philadelphia.

PARKER B. POTTER, JR.
NEW HAMPSHIRE DIVISION OF HISTORICAL RESOURCES
P.O. BOX 2043
CONCORD, NEW HAMPSHIRE 03302

Part II:
Methodologies and Approaches

1997 "Leveling the Playing Field" in the Contested Territory of the South African Past: A "Public" versus a "People's" Form of Historical Archaeology Outreach. In *In The Realm of Politics: Prospects for Public Participation in African American and Plantation Archaeology*, Carol McDavid and David Babson, editors. Thematic issue, *Historical Archaeology* 31(3):52-65

PATRICE L. JEPPSON

"Leveling the Playing Field" in the Contested Territory of the South African Past: A "Public" Versus a "People's" Form of Historical Archaeology Outreach

ABSTRACT

In South Africa, the legacy of colonialism and apartheid includes a history of partisan concepts of ethnic and social identity. The long charged, sociopolitical context has also affected research questions, as well as public interpretations, about the past. Today, there are calls for a new past for the new South Africa. Historical archaeology can provide both a methodology and raw materials which South Africans can use to form their own interpretations of their past helping, in turn, to engender pride through a historical consciousness emancipated from colonial and apartheid ideology. This article presents an overview of this complex and changing research context and its implications for a historical archaeology study of South African frontier identity. Research and "public" archaeology efforts concerning material and mythical perspectives of ethnicity are discussed. Employed in a cross-context comparison with African-American research, this study highlights the need for decolonized historical archaeology outreach.

Introduction

Formal calls to incorporate the voice and the needs of "the other" in historical interpretations have become commonplace within North American archaeology and within the field of anthropology in general (e.g., Tilley 1989; Pinsky and Wylie 1989). In historical archaeology, this concern falls within the spheres of critical archaeology (e.g., Leone et al. 1987; Handsman and Leone 1989; Potter 1994) and archaeology in the public interest. South African archaeological practice has similar public responsibility concerns. However, within this regional tradition, a distinction is clearly drawn between a public archaeology which popularizes knowledge about the past and a people's archaeology based on democratizing knowledge. As Ritchie (1990:31) explains it, "a popularizing archaeology brings to light aspects of the past excluded in dominant or elitist history" while a people's archaeology "defines instead the different processes through which knowledge about the past is produced."

This difference in outreach orientation became important during the People's Education for People's Power campaign initiated in the 1980s in the fight to end Nationalist Party government rule and establish a democratic South African society (Kruss 1988; Odendaal 1991). By promoting "the values of democracy, non-racialism, collective work, and active participation" (Callinicos 1991:262), this campaign sought to create an alternative to state-directed history interpretations. In line with this need, the principle objective of a people's archaeology became "to empower communities so that they may develop the ability to produce knowledge and establish for themselves a popular memory" (Ritchie 1990:32).

The contrast between these two forms of archaeological responsibility has bearing on material culture studies of ethnicity and on historical archaeology's potential for challenging ethnic stereotypes, be it in South Africa or elsewhere. A "public" archaeology type of outreach involves cracking open the door of the past a little wider in order to incorporate "other voices" for a richer, fuller, story of the past. This endeavor also involves sharing history constructions more broadly with an audience beyond that found in the academic arena. The focus of this activity rests on exposing to the public the archaeologist's role as a caretaker of the common heritage, and this understanding, in turn, assists in archaeology's need to secure both heritage resources as well as the practice of archaeology itself. Alternatively, a people's archaeology type of outreach advocates a change in the power relations involved in the control of history interpretation and history resources. This outreach form takes the position that the art and activity of constructing the past must itself be shared. In this focus, the archaeologist's role as the authoritative voice in the practice of history interpretation is surrendered.

A look at historical archaeology research and outreach in the realm of South African politics helps to distinguish the contributions produced by these two options and highlights why historical archaeology's responsibility to the public should be based not just on archaeology's needs but on archaeology's need to meet the needs of the public.

Background

To consider this topic more fully, its context within the study of the 19th-century South African frontier and anthropology in apartheid South Africa is addressed below.

The 19th-Century South African Frontier: History, Ethnicity, Historiography, and Historicity

Few would be surprised to learn that understandings about the past in South Africa are found wanting. The existing history interpretations, whether scholarly or public, are generally Eurocentric in their orientation, their intellectual tradition, and the source data on which they are based. For a discussion on South African historiography see, among others, Smith (1988); Saunders (1988). History written about black South Africans, and black contributions to traditional Occidental history, has always been limited. Prior to colonial contact, indigenous Southern Africans chronicled their histories orally leaving no written documents for Western-style history construction. Later, during the colonial and apartheid eras, blacks were restricted both in their access to Western forms of education and in what they could be taught in Western educational institutions (Kallaway 1984).

An absent or static perception of the indigenous population in historical interpretations, and a Eurocentric concern for important people, places, and events, is not an unusual occurrence in histories produced in a post-colonial setting. But, in South Africa, the historical memory has been additionally compromised by the development of, and the opposition to, Afrikaner Nationalism and, in particular, the political historical myths constructed to support the policy of apartheid.

The place and potency of Afrikaner Nationalism in South African society and its history is easily demonstrated by the Voortrekker Monument, a prominent example of Afrikaner material culture located on a hillside outside the city of Pretoria (Figure 1). This artifact of Afrikanerdom dates to the urbanizing and industrial changes occurring in the country during the first half of this century. In particular, British capitalist imperialism and increasing competition from black migrant workers led to a minority political separatist action involving mainly rural white inhabitants (Le Cordeur 1981). This faction of society created a social group consciousness through such activities as a language movement, the creation of a new national anthem, new stamp and coin decoration, and a new flag (Moodie 1975; Adam and Gilomee 1979; Thompson 1985; Gilomee 1989). This ethnic affirmation response became crystallized in the historical myth of the Great Trek and the memorial to it, the Voortrekker Monument (Du Toit 1984).

In brief, the Great Trek story involves a Genesis-like history of frontier migration. It details the movement of Dutch colonial farmers who trekked northwards during the 1830s from the Colony of the Cape of Good Hope into the interior of Africa. The myth rests on a belief that these migrants, redefined as *Afrikaner Voortrekkers*, were a chosen people summoned by God to spread civilization and Christianity into the heart of the continent. This saga and its commemorating structure have long served as a rallying point for the descendant Afrikaner people or *volk*.

The monument's architectural features, its interior furnishings and external landscaping, and its function as a historic landmark and gathering place are reflective of, and act to fulfill, an understanding of this Afrikaner unity. The concentric-ring pattern on the interior main floor is suggestive of ripples in a pond into which a stone has been cast, and signifies to the visitor the spirit of Afrikaner sacrifice spreading throughout the country (*Sentrale Volksmonumente-Komitee En Die Sentrale Voortrekker Eeufeeskomitee[SVE]* 1938). A marble frieze adorning the nearby interior walls depicts the frontier migration story helping to indoctrinate the thousands of people who have viewed it over the past half century (*SVE* 1938). An oil lamp, reputedly used on the Great Trek, burns as an eternal flame (Bond 1949). Near to this lies a cenotaph commemorating the life of the unknown, martyred, Afrikaner soldier. This crypt is illuminated one day each year, noon on 16 December, by a ray of sunlight guided through an astronomically positioned roof aperture (Heymans 1986:7). This yearly event marks a date in Afrikaner political historical myth on which the Voortrekkers made a covenant with God.

On the outside, the fortress-like monument with its gun slit window openings and encircling wagon-train decorated wall, is reminiscent of a defensive ring encampment, or *laager* (*SVE* 1938; Heymans 1986). Beyond this wall, the hillside is richly landscaped with indigenous African plants. The various trek routes which the immigrants followed into the African interior are recreated in miniature in this "wild garden" using a landscape map model. Along these paths are markers symbolizing the obstacles and events which the Voortrekkers encountered during their journey. This configuration allows visitors to the monument to relive the Trek experience for themselves.

This Afrikaner ideology of "a sacred mission and calling for providence" was wedded, with the sanctioning of the official state church (Dutch Reformed), to the idea of a human racial taxonomy (Moodie 1975:265). In this worldview, members of the human species are perceived as separated into stable, bounded entities, each with distinctive cultural and physical characteristics. This understanding, in turn, held that the Afrikaner "people" should be separate from all others in order to maintain their position in a hierarchy of ethnic and cultural difference (Moodie 1975:265; Schutte 1989). Thus, while crucial to establishing the identity of the Afrikaner, the Genesis ideology also formed a

FIGURE 1. The Voortrekker Monument, 1990, view looking north. (Photograph by the author.)

larger social context that provided the logic for a system of ethnic segregation.

This understanding of South African society and its history became sacrosanct and ultimately formed the substructure for a "civil religion" (Moodie 1975:296) that served for over half a century as the ideological basis for apartheid, the Afrikaner Nationalist policy of "Separate Development." Under this logic, racial and/or ethnic culture groups or populations were perceived as unassimilable and incompatible each with its own character, its own potential, and its own destiny-Zulu, Afrikaner, English, Sotho, Xhosa, Venda, and so on (Thompson 1985). Legislation enforced and, in turn, justified these ethnic-based separations. These separations were furthermore supported and maintained through retroactively constructed, discrete ethnic histories (Dubow in Hall 1990:65).

For the past 50 years, until the recent political transformations, these segregated pasts were propagated through Nationalist bureaucratic rule making their way into everyday experience through school books (Auerbach 1966; Adam and Gilomee 1979; Cornevin 1980; du Preez 1983; Thompson 1985; Ashley 1989), national monuments and museums (Wright and Mazel 1987; Peires 1989; Davison 1991), and popular heroic tales (Moodie 1975; Thompson 1985;

Naidoo 1989). These political histories have helped to sever the black African from a past that provides a stabilizing and positive sense of identity: the black African heritage has itself been colonized:

> If a ruling minority can enslave the minds of the people, control their ideas and their whole way of thinking, they have found an even more efficient weapon for subjugating them than the use of force, the military and the police. For then the people themselves assist in their own enslavement. If the rulers can make the people believe that they are inferior, wipe out their past history or present it in such a way that they feel, not pride but shame, then they create the conditions that make it easy to dominate the people (Majeke 1952:Introduction).

This apartheid history point of reference remains active, residual, and latent in much of the South African public consciousness helping keep apartheid history interpretations institutionally and mentally ingrained even while political transformations have occurred. As such, the apartheid created past unconsciously, consciously, and covertly continues to shape both the South African present and its future (Kallaway 1991; Mare 1993).

Anthropology in Apartheid South Africa

One result of the apartheid and colonial heritage is that there has been a tainting of major anthropological analytical concepts including, among others, ethnicity, community, culture, and tradition, in South African based anthropological and archaeological research (Gluckman 1975; Sharp 1980a; Whisson 1981; Hall 1990, 1993). Under the social and political context of apartheid, studies that employed these constructs were perceived as representing a colonialist stance and/or collusion with the "White Regime" (Hall 1983, 1984). This represented a valid concern in this context because talking about ethnicity could create or reinforce the ethnic divisions of apartheid and colonialism (Boonzaier and Sharp 1988; Kuper 1988:50; Horowitz 1991:28–29). This "opposition" was also a response to specific disciplinary developments unique to South Africa.

Within South Africa's charged sociopolitical setting, the local anthropology tradition underwent a split into two contrasting camps, that of a British-style social anthropology in English-speaking universities, and a discipline called *Volkekunde* found at Afrikaans speaking universities, several homeland universities, and in government agencies such as the Bureau for Racial Affairs and the South African Defense force (Sharp 1980a, 1980b; Booyens and van Rensburg 1980; Pauw 1980; Sharp 1981; Kuper 1983, 1986, 1988; Gordon and Spiegel 1993). For the past 30-some years, South African anthropological research has "normally been formulated in terms of one or other of these anthropology traditions, and, as often as not, the efforts have been judged in political terms as much as by academic criteria" (Kuper 1986:4).

Liberal-thinking South Africans have commonly believed that *Volkekunde* and its practitioners were, by and large, committed to the Nationalist movement and that the discipline was the deliberate development of the intellectual underpinnings of apartheid (Moodie 1975:245; Kuper 1983:104, 1988:35). This belief was based on the particular use and understanding of ethnicity in Volkekunde known as "ethnos theory." This theoretical understanding divides humankind into *volke* (*na*tions, people) each with its own particular culture (Booyens and van Rensburg 1980; Sharp 1980a, 1981:19; Kuper 1983:33; Voorster et al. 1986). *Volkekunde*, according to a University of South Africa course study guide, involves the study of: "a) peoples as cultural groups, b) culture as the product of peoples, c) psychological features of peoples of all times as the cause or result of culture, and d) physical features of peoples of all times as the cause or result of culture" (Voorster et al. 1986:97–98). This central concern with ethnos also underlaid the *volk* mythology of Afrikanerdom, and, in its practice, *Volkekunde* essentially extended the core conception of the Afrikaner *volk* to other ethnos (Moodie 1975;

Sharp 1981:28; Butler 1989; Gilomee 1989). As a result, *Volkekunde* can be conceived of as anthropology constructed in terms of an intellectual paradigm conducive to Afrikaner consciousness (Kuper 1988:35).

The tendency towards a divergence into these two camps became marked in the 1940s with the arrival of Afrikaner Christian Nationalist rule (Sharp 1981). With this Nationalist Party victory over British imperial interests, Afrikaner intellectuals appropriated institutions to enforce the *volk* ideal (Moodie 1975; Adam and Gilomee 1979; Smith 1988:4; Pityana 1995). University of Pretoria anthropology professor W. M. Eiselen, for example, was a major architect of "separate development," serving as an administrator of apartheid policy under the new Afrikaner government (Moodie 1975:73). Other *volkekunde* anthropologists served the government on the Committee for Bantu Affairs, in the Department of Cooperation and Development, and in the Defense Force which had an ethnological section. *Volkekunde* departments, meanwhile, offered "service courses" that prepared students for civil service sector jobs in which they functioned to enforce and justify the policy of apartheid and the homelands system (Sharp 1981:5).

During this period, many South African social anthropologists strongly sought to distance themselves from the ethnos theory approach of their *volkekunde* colleagues. Several of these individuals were also politically active in opposing apartheid and several became targets and victims of the government, suffering actions ranging from harassment to even murder—including the assassinations of Ruth First and University of The Witwatersrand anthropologist, David Webster. The South African social anthropologists formally renounced apartheid by professionally stating a political position supporting a democratic society (Association for South African Anthropology in Southern Africa [AASA] 1988; Fry 1992:230).

By the time I began my own research (Jeppson [1998]), this branch of South African anthropology had come to define analytical concepts such as ethnicity, culture, and tradition as aspects of political nationalism which held no anthropological relevancy. Ethnicity was considered a "dirty word," and culture was a concept regarded as by necessity racist, a point I discovered during one of my early talks. I found that negative critiques haunted American anthropology, particularly the work of Melville Herskovits—also the father of American African Studies—whom *Volkekunde* studies heavily adopted from, and Alfred Kroeber, because of his (later retracted) paper on the "Superorganic" (Sharp 1980a, 1981:36). This anticultural anthropology sentiment condemned the holistic, four-field approach and assessed American cultural anthropology as not just inferior but immoral. As a result of this guilt by association, visiting American cultural anthropologists were sometimes avoided by local social anthropologists and, every so often, I even heard the name of Herskovits "demonized" and invoked as an epithet.

This avoidance of "culture," as a term and concept, in this regional tradition also stemmed, in part, from social anthropology's theoretical positioning—"the reluctance of the Radcliffe-Brown school to allow an independent explanatory role to cultural factors" (Kuper 1983:48; Gluckman 1975)—and a Marxist paradigm favored for the last two decades in the radical branches of South African history, sociology, anthropology, and archaeology. Moreover, the anticulture stance was reinforced and supported by black consciousness politics, by the mass democratic processes striving for national unity, and by a black nationalist position within South African anthropology that promoted the judging of research efforts on the basis of the "contribution to a national identity" (Kuper 1986:2). Adding to the equation was South Africa's isolation from metropolitan anthropology and its ideas due to its extreme geographical position, located on the southern tip of the continent, and to global politics—specifically, the decades of national economic decline and therefore loss of university funding, and the years of academic boycotts, all of which limited the information flow normally available through academic journals and scholarly exchanges (Gordon and Spiegel 1993).

A Historical Archaeology Study of 19th-Century Frontier Identity: Reassessing Ethnicity in the Search for a New South African Past

A research strategy for historical archaeology involves several components, among which are method and theory, and research and outreach in South Africa. These are addressed more fully below.

Method and Theory

So how does a historical archaeology study conducted in the American anthropological tradition effectively incorporate, and become incorporated into, such a research context? Ethnicity as a cultural term does have a complex history, a variety of meanings, and a number of uses and abuses both inside and outside South Africa. The approach I take in my investigation of the South African frontier is to illustrate the value of ethnicity and identity concepts in the study of South African society and its history (Jeppson 1993, 1995a, 1996a, [1998]). Specifically, I use excavated objects and documentary evidence from four frontier sites—a mission, a fort, a hinterland domestic site, and a colonial town site—to investigate the nature and role of material culture in frontier social dynamics: using a cross-cultural approach, I investigate how Industrial Age, mass-produced British goods are involved in the construction, reproduction, and transformation of shared cultural beliefs and values during a time of contact, conflict, and culture change (Jeppson 1987, 1988b, 1988c, 1988e, 1988f, 1990a, 1990c, 1991a, 1991b, [1998]). The recovered evidence suggests that material culture functions in 19th-century frontier society as symbols in social interaction, reflecting and actively communicating information about the making and marking of social group identities. I argue, both in the research and in related public outreach activities, that a concern with the

definition and self-definition of frontier social groupings, and the relationship of these definitions to history, is integral for an understanding of the South African past, present, and future.

Unlike apartheid's hegemonic ideology and the responding impetus to ignore ethnicity and culture, much academic and public emphasis in American society and history is concerned with questions of self-identity and collective self-consciousness, and the circumstances under which self-perceptions yield to the will of a democratic majority (Appleby et al. 1994). In the ideological understanding of the United States, studies of social group identity—ethnicity, nationalism—play an increasing part. Furthermore, while ethnicity in South Africa has long remained associated with "tribe," American anthropology long ago jettisoned this understanding, aligning with metropolitan anthropology's interest in multicultural, multiethnic, and interactive contexts. Within this research context, my investigation of South African frontier ethnicity embraces epistemological features fundamental to these paradigms and postures, that is, that ethnicity is nonisolated, contemporary, and universally applicable; that it is subjectivist, or both objectivist and subjectivist; that it exists as a unit only in relation to others; and that it has shifting boundaries and varying degrees of "systemic" quality (Cohen 1978:384–385).

Such issues of classification in cognition—social group identity, ethnicity, and nationalism—are also a central focus of an "anthropology of knowledge"; the anthropological concern for culture "as a process of acquiring and displaying knowledge"—of rules, values, and beliefs—including how it is that people learn about and create social consciousness (Crick 1982:287). Such knowledge includes how social identities come into existence, what resources may be employed in the process, what roles material culture may play in their social reproduction, and why the social identifications might be mobilized (Shennan 1989:16). An understanding of how such cultural histories and ethnic origins are experienced, remembered, and created is a relevant enterprise both in South Africa and in the modern world in general, plagued as it by racial schisms, ethnicity factionalism, and rival nationalisms.

The study of ethnicity similarly plays an important role in the development of North America historical archaeology as an academic enterprise (e.g., Deetz 1977; Schuyler 1980). Unlike the social science conducted in the apartheid context, historical archaeology studies of ethnicity are undertaken within a social and political setting that favors a multicultural heritage approach as a way to reach a more accurate understanding of the American past and present. For a discussion of this context see, among others, Takaki (1987) and Appleby et al. (1994). An interest in ethnicity is a logical outgrowth of American historical archaeology's goal of "writing the history of the inarticulate" (Ascher 1974:10). The descendants of enslaved Africans, Chinese laborers, and other American immigrants, as well as First Nations people, have strong ethnic heritage interests which form a common point for contemporary popular and political organization and definition (Glazer and Moynihan 1963).

The theoretical underpinnings of current historical archaeology ethnicity research, described elsewhere by McGuire (1982) and McKee (1984), is foreign to that found in *Volkekunde* and that long feared by the South African social anthropologists. American historical archaeologists routinely propose an adaptive nature for tradition and identity. In this approach, ethnicity is seen as something that people themselves create, as something that grows and changes. The emphasis in this understanding is placed on process, or on the consciousness that forms the starting point for the construction and maintenance of social group boundaries (Barth 1970). These boundaries are often imposed or reinforced using symbols, including material culture, putting them within the purview of historical archaeology.

Research, Outreach, and Response in the South African Context

While I propose that issues of classification and cognition should not be ignored in the study of the South African past, it has not always been the case that these interests are welcome. South Africa's turbulent social and political context presents perplexing issues for a material culture investigation of cultural identity at every stage of the research process: at the point of determining categories for data analysis, in the methodological practice of archaeological comparison, indefining the theoretical concepts of anthropology knowledge, and in the public outreach related to the research. I touch on two such examples here.

Preliminary documentary research conducted on the Wesleyan Mission Station of Farmerfield (established 1839) indicates that a complex social landscape comprised of discrete ethnic villages once existed at this site (*Graham's Town Journal*, 2 April 1840:4; Wesleyan Missionary Society, 1840, 1847, 1853:13–14; Merriman in Varley and Matthew 1957[17 August 1850]:125; Shaw 1860[July 1850]). A church building, the Catechist's home, and the common pasture lands were reputed to be surrounded by three hamlets or villages located contiguous to each other: one hamlet inhabited by individuals formerly enslaved by European colonists, another occupied by farmer-herders indigenous to the area (amaXhosa), and a third inhabited by farmer-herders from the north (Sotho). This structured residential setting constitutes one of the earliest episodes of a segregated South African landscape although the reported social divisions could have been imposed or reflected acknowledged emic differences—linguistic, racialistic, ethnic—or could have even been nonexistent.

These historically perceived, discrete, village locations make for an ideal archaeological opportunity for investigating questions of social distinctions marked by material culture variations. However, when these historically defined social groupings were juxtaposed with one another for artifact analysis and interpretation, the response among many local liberal and radical academics, those with whom I eagerly desired to share this research, was overwhelmingly negative. Among other things, I was told categorically that culture groups did not exist in the past, or the present, but were only figments of the South African

Christian National frame of reference. When I presented artifact pattern evidence and oral history testimony that could be indicative of possible "social groupings," it was suggested to me that perhaps I "could substitute the word ethnicity with a Latin or German term that sounded scientific," or perhaps I could "find a French term that had flair" (audience remarks, Southern African Association of Anthropologists conference 1988). I found that inquiries about the culture, tradition, and/or ethnicity of the inhabitants at Farmerfield constituted research that was "inherently racist" (audience remarks, Archaeology Department guest lectures, University of the Witwatersrand 1987, 1992).

As my research became crowded by the South African social and political context, it became obvious to me that the difficulties harbored valuable clues into how the past served as a resource in current South African society. Once I recognized the dominant ideologies of the research context, and their components, I found I could deal with the research context anthropologically and not as simply a situation that had to be correct or corrected for. The focus of my artifact study and the related outreach efforts shifted to include the practice of culture as a historical experience: the problematic relationship between history, ethnicity, historiography, and historicity became part of the story of investigating identity definitions and the relations of these definitions to history. In brief, I propose in this research and outreach that frontier material culture differences reflect self-generated as well as externally imposed social designations formed in response to, and partly in opposition to, the new or changing environment and encountered "others." As such, the recovered symbolic markers, and the social divisions of difference and sameness they mirror and mark, are products of intra- and inter-group relations, representing cultural resource grounded in a shared historical experience.

In this process-oriented interpretation, social identity constructs are assessed as fluid entities based on shifting, concurrent, common interests. As social categories, such classifications do not define all of a person, nor even all of a collec-

tive. Moreover, I do not perceive such material reflections of identity to be simply a matter of maintained cultural background or tradition represented by "survival" markers. They are, in fact, distinguished from social categorizations based on mere spatial variation in material remains. I do not ascribe site specific assemblages to static ethnic or cultural stereotypes as "archaeological cultures." Rather, any discovered social group identifications refer instead to self-conscious identifications that are anchored internally in experience and externally in the contingent situation, or setting, involving the mobilizing identity. Thus, while the South African frontier identities may, in their making, be in part derived from a sense of a deeper cultural past, the relationship between these colonial-era residents and their heritage of cultural beliefs and practices is not an uninterrupted one.

I suggest with this research that the borders and nature of frontier social groupings change according to the needs and social circumstances developing in culture contact and conflict. In their use as a symbol of identity definition and boundary maintenance, the material culture expressions of identity represent a form of knowledge. This knowledge is not just about social meaning alone but is also knowledge about how it is that these symbols themselves are formed and maintained (Crick 1982). Such knowledge is significant because, as Comaroff (1982:50) explains elsewhere, "in a world of marking relations, of denoting identities, it isn't the contents of those identities alone that is important but the processes of marking them, establishing with them a sociological chain of being." It is the interpreting of these boundaries and identities, providing the how and why for these material record patterns, that returns those "forgotten" to South African history in a two-directional process of culture change.

In the end, the social identities translated from the frontier material record are presented as nonstatic cultural entities that only can be understood in historical perspective. This situationally defined and historically contextualized concept of identity formation helps to expose as fallacy the notions of primordial, bounded ethnicities that have shaped the South African segregated historical consciousness. I argue that once there is an understanding of the situationalness of identity formation, the imposed, self-defined, and adopted social definitions found in apartheid South Africa can be evaluated. Employed with this aim, the frontier past constructed with historical archaeology evidence is used to challenge the present. It becomes a resource that is more effective for the general public: Historical archaeology research on frontier society holds a promise of empowerment for those whose contributions to the past and to the present have been denied, or for those who have assimilated into their self-identity the static, negative, handicapping representations created by others.

In the archaeological outreach related to this dissertation study (Jeppson 1988a, 1988c, 1989a, 1989b, 1989c, 1989e, 1990a, 1990b, 1990d, 1990e, 1991c, 1992, 1995a 1995b) I have attempted to illuminate the interconnectedness of the colonizer and colonized in frontier experience and the contingency of social othering. I combined these points with an emphasis on critical thinking skills to form a recurring theme in both public and people's types of archaeology outreach—including site tours, field and lab work with students and public volunteers, school-based presentations, public and in-house museum lectures, research-related museum exhibits, and museum education program aids.

Among my various archaeology outreach efforts is a traveling museum exhibit case that I constructed during research at the British military site of Fort Double Drift (established 1836). This exhibit case, discussed elsewhere (Jeppson 1988a, 1988d, 1989b, 1989c, 1989d, 1989e, 1995a, 1995b), was designed as a remote educational aid for the Mobile Museum Education Service at the Albany Museum in Grahamstown. This liberal-leaning institution embraced historical archaeology in the late 1980s, serving as host to numerous projects (cf. Hardwick 1989; Scott and Deetz 1990; Winer and Deetz 1990; Deetz 1993; Jeppson [1998]). The museum kindly supported the construction of this educational aid lending me materials, equipment, and the assistance of their Displays Department staff.

This exhibit, comprised of a display case and work booklet, is designed to compare and contrast history information sources—documents and excavated artifacts—and to include, within one scenario, all those present on the frontier landscape—San, Khoi, Xhosa, British settler, and British military. It is hoped that the comparison of history information sources will encourage an awareness of how interpretations about the past come about in a "method as message" approach. This approach, detailed elsewhere by Leone (1983:46), uses the concept of "how do we know what we know" to illustrate the "process of knowing." As Leone (1983:46) states, "method displays provide the public with the ability to assess and the possibility of challenging conventional conclusions about the past."

For a South African public armed with such critical thinking skills (Tunmer 1988; van Zyl 1988), apartheid history constructions, and even presently held beliefs, can come to be recognized as part of a historical process and thus be removed from a state of inviolate fact. In this manner, history no longer remains something that is static but rather becomes part of the ongoing process of making the past. Importantly, in this approach to the study of the South African frontier there is no "absolving of activities of the past" and no "correcting past history constructs" (Leone 1983:46). Likewise there is "no encouragement of a state of historical amnesia" (Leone 1983:46). In this outreach activity, the critical thinking skills used in the study of the past become important as educational messages themselves, and these skills, in turn, can be taken beyond the exhibit exercise, out into general life experience. In contrast to apartheid and colonial history constructs, this history interpretation is useful for citizens of the new South Africa. The relations between past and present and between history and modern society are exposed raising the possibility for an understanding of the conditions of modern life (Potter 1991, 1992, 1994).

It is also my hope that the broader based picture of the frontier, made possible with archaeologically recovered evidence, can help, in one small measure, to free South Africans to move beyond the ideological impasse of Nationalist and colonial interpretations and preconceptions by uniting the history of Europeans with the history of the indigenous. The interpretation of the frontier portrayed in this educational exhibit is not of an elite, a majority, or a dominant history, nor a history of only those forgotten. It is a presentation of a past that both of these partake of and help create. Such "integrating" of the past can help create potential scaffolding for a new historical social reality (cf. McDavid, this volume). The historical archaeology data and interpretations, and the methods and methodology for their recovery, are resources available for a new socialization of people into knowledge (Peponis and Hedin 1982).

This educational exhibit received positive evaluations from, among others, the curator of the Africana Museum (Nagelgast 1990), a university historian in a Teaching Credential program, museum educators at the South African National Gallery and the South African Museum (audience comments, South African Museum Associations Education Conference IX 1989), and staff at both local, then segregated, black and white elementary and high schools who were desperate to circumvent or amend government produced history texts. Despite these positive reviews, in the final analysis this educational exhibit could not be accessioned into the museum's Education Department. Not only did it not fit with the state-mandated school syllabus which formed the basis for the mobile museum service, but it also conflicted with the ideological structure of South African museums.

This ideological structure during the final years of apartheid was mandated by the Nationalist government's "Own Affairs/General Affairs" policy (Smith 1987; Owen and Holleman 1989; Webb 1989). "Own Affairs," as defined in the 1983 constitution, concerned "matters which specially or differentially affect a population group in relation to the maintenance of its identity and the upholding and furtherance of its way of life, culture, traditions, and customs"—any concerns beyond the unit of the "population group" were part of "General Affairs." Under the choke hold of this ideology and bureaucracy, museum schol-

arship, social space, and funding were divided into discrete domains: the disciplines of cultural history and *kulture geskeidens* were concerned with the history of the English colonists, their descendants and the Afrikaners; anthropology departments—also referred to as ethnology or, as a distancing measure from *volkekunde*, ethnography—performed study on black lifeways; and archaeology departments concerned themselves with pre-contact indigenous history such as that of the deep Iron Age and the Stone Age (Davison 1991).

The multicultural, multidisciplinary museum educational exhibit "confused" these commonly held, official notions of segregated South African history, and so, in essence, the exhibit could not find a home—it is, however, used by the Archaeology Department staff. As a "critical thinking"-based display, it also presented an alternative methodology to the one-sided and distorted Nationalist history narrative. In this sense, it challenged the authority of the state which was, in part, divinely sanctioned through ideological schooling and which required loyalty and obedience from its students (Ashley 1989:23). South African museums, long a tool of apartheid with their ideological history interpretations, still remained at this time, regardless of individual sentiments within the institutions, a victim of apartheid ideology and bureaucracy and the exhibit outreach effort became, in turn, a victim of this.

Conclusion

Today, a rejection of the existing historical interpretations by the majority of the South African populace, an abandonment of Afrikaner Nationalist politicized history practice, and a spate of history revisions related to the changing discourse of African and South African politics marks the state of anthropology research in South Africa and South African history construction. At the same time, the continuing ethnic strife in South Africa's Kwazulu/Natal Province has helped it become readily apparent that ethnicity cannot be washed or wished away as a factor in explaining prevailing South African social relations (Mare 1993). Now, as enforced separations between South Africans disappear, ethnicity is reemerging as a valid topic in a surge of post-Resistance activity (Fry 1992; Gordon and Spiegel 1993). This move complements the many calls made for useful histories for a changing South Africa and holds promise for anthropological historical archaeology research.

The "masses," speaking through social organizations, trade unions, political platforms, and now political leaders in departments of ministry, have specifically "demanded" an end to histories characterized by domination and by a lack of common national unity and purpose. Such requirements strike at the heart of the segregated and static ethnic histories that have formed the core of much public history and apartheid ideology, and that have long supported dehumanizing domination. The expressed desire is for a history that supports liberation and transformation from colonial and apartheid oppression and that restores a sense of historical consciousness (Ashley 1989; Kallaway 1991).

Because the past in South Africa has been a site of oppression—one reinforced through a pervasive, repressive, historical ideology—any social rather than only structural change towards a new society must include a handing over of the reins of power. This surrender must specifically include the power of the historical frame of reference, particularly that of "social group identity" which is linked to culture pride and self worth. This will free the population from the fear of difference instituted under the apartheid construction of knowledge.

Historical archaeology can contribute towards the creation of a historical past of common national unity and restored pride in heritage relevant to today's post-apartheid South Africa. The raw data recovered in such research, and the resulting broader based history interpretations, can add testimony needed for a reevaluation of self- and national identity for a new South African society. In contributing to such alternative history interpretations, historical archaeology studies of ethnicity can also make transparent the ideological realities of colonialism and apartheid oppression, helping to maintain a vigilance against their continuation in post-apartheid life.

Beyond this regional contribution, when considered at a global-level scale of comparison, historical archaeology in the realm of South African politics can also serve as a case study example against which to examine public outreach issues in African-American archaeology. The analysis of another culture is an effective way to open up areas of one's own culture in which notions of the past and cultural integrity are created and remain largely unexamined (Thornton 1988). This comparison of two, "colonial brother," nation-states helps highlight contradictions that exist in global-wide historical archaeology research contexts and, therefore, in its practices and goals. The comparison reveals, for example, how a concern for poly-vocality in North America "could" describe an American-centric need and focus. This follows an understanding that "the knowledge we formulate about 'the other' is refracted through the knowledge we have built to define ourselves" (Crick 1982:293).

Viewed within the larger, modern world context, the segregation ideology of apartheid South Africa remains unique among the ideological unity credos that evolved in other heavily European populated, post-colonial, nation states, such as Brazil, Australia, and Mexico, or even in the European "mother countries" which were formed or transformed as a result of colonial expansion and conquest. It stands, for example, as an antithesis to the American ideology of *e pluribus unum*— "one out of many"—where diversity is perceived as a source of identity and unity: a syncretic, evolving, commonality in civil culture (Fuchs 1991; Appleby et al. 1994). Whereas the concept of "multiculturalism" serves as a basis and reaffirmation of an American national identity, the Afrikaner "united as one" ideology alternatively represents one *ethnos*—Afrikaner culture—against, and above, all others (Moodie 1975).

The "multicultural" understanding of American collective identity represents a recent national meta-narrative. Based on the last quarter-century of social history scholarship, this understanding challenges the older order of Anglo-American leadership supported by objectivist science paradigms that were themselves reworked from earlier notions of manifest destiny and social progress (Appleby et al. 1994). Like those believed in before it, this defining sense of national identity gives cohesion to an aggregation of people missing a common, shared folk culture. This use of multiculturalism as an understanding for American national identity (context) is reflected in the calls for poly-vocality in history interpretations and in the responses to this need found in historical archaeology research and archaeology outreach. This national identity also endorses the inclusiveness of an open society while falling short of creating one in practice. As a result, extreme adherents of multiculturalism advocate a fragmented "identity politics," not dissimilar in structure and emphasis to apartheid politics.

The importation into South Africa of the North American concept of multiculturalism has several implications for national consciousness of which the historical archaeologist would want to be aware. In this setting, the term has been put to various context-specific uses. During the recent political transitions, multiculturalism has served a Nationalist Party political strategy in "a plan for a continued plural society with group rights" (Kallaway 1991). Used in this sense, multicultural history, or poly-vocality, would mean the continuation of special privileges and rights for particular culture groups in the new South Africa. This term-sans-concept adoption follows two earlier consequences of "relative usage" or "the penetration of [South African] intellectual culture by otherwise commonly used international, scientific ideas" (Kuper 1988:50). Decades ago, apartheid rulers tried to gain legitimacy for their policy by replacing the term "race" with the metropolitan term "culture" and replaced the apartheid term "pluralism" with "segregation." These apartheid-type uses were incompatible with an American or nationalist black majority emphasis on national heritage. More recently, in the election of a transitional government of national unity with Nelson Mandela as president, multiculturalism in South Africa was celebrated as "one nation, many cultures." This understanding encourages an appreciation of culture difference. "Unity in Diversity" forms the basis for building a "rainbow nation" identity for the new South Africa (African National Congress Information Services, 22 April 1996).

Similarly, in a cross-context comparison, the anti-American cultural anthropology sentiment once found among South African social anthropologists appears paradoxical when juxtaposed with the rhetoric of the prominent conservative wing of U.S. society, which rails against affirmative action, multiculturalism, and a broader based set of history standards (Appleby et al. 1994). Meanwhile, the most extreme right-wing factions frequently attack the "liberal scholarship" of American anthropology as the root cause for (what they perceive to be) America's social ills. For example, a member of the National Alliance—a patriot movement-aligned neo-Nazi group that shares sentiments with the Freemen, Christian Identity, some militias, and the Ku Klux Klan—said the following on a recent radio broadcast: "Herskovits . . . and other students of the cultural anthropology school headed by the communist Boas [including] Ashley Montagu, Raymond Pearl, Herbert Seligman, Otto Klineberg, Gene Weltfish, Amram Scheinfeld, Ruth Benedict, L. C. Dunn, Isador Chein, and Margaret Mead . . . propagandized the public and subverted the government with that foundation and wellspring of liberalism . . . the fraudulent doctrine of universal human equality" (McKinney 1995a, 1995b).

Transcripts of this and similar discussions are widely available on the AM dial, FM dial, and shortwave radio (e.g., the National Alliance radio broadcast, *American Dissident Voices Weekly*), in publications (e.g., the National Alliance's publication, *National Vanguard*), and on Internet Radio (National Alliance's *FreeSpeech* at http://www.natvan.com). In this rhetoric, the position is that "liberalism" is based on an anthropology-linked sociopolitical agenda responsible for "fifty years of liberal and alien subversion of our government and institutions, the moral decay, the decline of the public school system, the out-of-control immigration, the explosion of non-white crime, [and] the other consequences of diversity" (McKinney 1995b). Anthropologists have furthermore "brainwashed" the public about "the study of race": the "modern religion of equalitarianism" is presented as the Boas school's attempt to "distort and falsify science" conducted on race (McKinney 1995a). In these media forums, books such as *The Bell Curve* (Hernstein and Murray 1994) are cited extensively as "scientific" sources that valiantly attempt to expose this anthropological "brainwashing."

A comparison of historical archaeology in the realms of South African and African-American politics exposes context-specific assumptions that could potentially affect practices and goals. Edward Said (1989:210–211), among others, has cautioned about the imperialistic aspects of decolonialism in the field of anthropology, stating that "even as we strive to decolonize anthropology, with much theoretical work on textuality and discourse, American imperialism remains a factor affecting theoretical discussion. To practice anthropology in the U.S. is not just to be investigating 'otherness' and 'difference' in a large country; it is to be discussing them in an enormously influential and powerful State whose global role is that of a superpower."

This same caution is relevant for the role of poly-vocality, depending on its use and definition, in historical archaeology. A comparison of research contexts helps to make known how historical archaeology is part of itself, how any statement about culture is a statement about historical archaeology and how any practice of archaeology outreach is therefore a cultural decision involving power relations.

Once the goals and practices that exist in differing research contexts are identified, they can be reflected upon and can be fed back into historical archaeology, ultimately enriching the field of study as a whole. The resulting decolonized research will add to ongoing discussions within general, or metropolitan, anthropology and archaeology about how people define and shape their world and the approaches useful for identifying and understanding such worldviews.

ACKNOWLEDGMENTS

I thank the Albany Museum, the Department of Archaeology and the Oppenheimer Centre For African Studies at the University of Cape Town, the Institute For Social And Economic Research at Rhodes University, and the National Monuments Council of South Africa for facilitating various phases of this research. Anna Papp and Stephen Welz kindly donated materials, and Gerard Marx graciously provided artistic advice for the display case. Headmistress Qaba, Mr. Mfino, Ms. Qama, the students at Farmerfield School, Headmistress Lehr, Keith James, Virginia Burrage, George Brauer, and especially Mr. Cecil Nonqane helped with outreach activities. I owe my gratitude to Antonia Malan, Gabrielle Ritchie, Edwin O. Hanish, Simon Hall, Patrick McAllister, and Robert Thornton for helping me to refine my understanding of South African disciplinary traditions. I thank Robert Schuyler and James Deetz for their advice, support, and direction with this research. Carol McDavid made several helpful suggestions concerning this paper.

REFERENCES

ADAM, HERIBERT, AND HERMANN GILOMEE
1979 In *The Rise and Crisis of Afrikaner Power.* David Philip, Cape Town, South Africa.

AFRICAN NATIONAL CONGRESS INFORMATION SERVICES
1996 Freedom Day Celebrations: "Unity in Diversity." South African Communications Services, 22 April 1996. Johannesburg, South Africa. <http://WWW.sacs.org.za/cgi-bin/vdkw_cgi>.

AMERICAN DISSIDENT VOICES WEEKLY
1991– Radio program hosted by William Pierce and the
1996 National Alliance. Shortwave 15420 and 7355 kHz; Satellite G7 Channel 14; 7.56 MHz audio; AM radio dial Q 100 (Florida); AM 760, 890 (Alabama); AM 1230, 1180 (Texas); 1190, 490 (Arkansas); AM 1090 (Midwest and Gulf South U.S.); AM 1540 (Upper Midwest and Northern Mountain U.S.); AM 990 (Northeast); Q FM 94.3 (Texas), ADV Internet Radio on-line <http://www.natall.com/radio.html>. Hillsboro, VA.

APPLEBY, JOYCE, LYNN HUNT, AND MARGARET JACOB
1994 *Telling the Truth about History.* W. W. Norton, NY.

ASCHER, ROBERT
1974 Tin Can Archaeology. *Historical Archaeology* 8:1–16.

ASHLEY, MICHAEL
  1989 *Ideologies and Schooling in South Africa.* Pioneer Press, Mowbray, South Africa.

ASSOCIATION FOR ANTHROPOLOGY IN SOUTHERN AFRICA (AASA)
  1988 Ethical Guidelines for South African Anthropologists (as approved by the Association for Anthropology in Southern Africa at Its 1987 conference). Presented to the Membership at the Annual Meeting of the Association for Anthropology in Southern Africa Conference, Grahamstown, South Africa.

AUERBACH, FRANZ
  1966 *The Power and Prejudice in South African Education: An Enquiry into History Textbooks and Syllabuses in the Transvaal High Schools of South Africa.* Balema, Cape Town, South Africa.

BARTH, FREDERICK
  1970 *Ethnic Groups and Boundaries.* Little, Brown, NY.

BOND, J. J.
  1949 The Saga of the Great Trek. *The Star,* 16 December:Insert. Johannesburg, South Africa.

BOONZAIER, EMILE, AND JOHN SHARP
  1988 *South African Keywords: The Uses and Abuses of Political Concepts.* David Philip, Cape Town, South Africa.

BOOYENS, J. H., AND N. S. JANSEN VAN RENSBURG
  1980 Reply from Potchefstroom, Anthropology in South Africa. *Royal Anthropology Institute Newsletter* 37:3–4.

BUTLER, JEFFREY
  1989 Afrikaner Women and the Creation of Ethnicity in a Small South African Town, 1902–1950. In *The Creation of Tribalism in Southern Africa,* edited by Leroy Vail, pp. 55–81. James Currey, London.

CALLINICOS, LULI
  1991 Popular History in the Eighties. In *History from South Africa,* edited by Joshua Brown, Patrick Manning, Karin Shapiro, Jon Wiener, Belinda Bozzoli, and Peter Delius, pp. 257–268. Temple University, Philadelphia, PA.

COHEN, RONALD
  1978 Ethnicity: Problem and Focus in Anthropology. *Annual Review of Anthropology* 7:379–403.

COMAROFF, JOHN
  1982 Dialectical Systems, History and Anthropology: Units of Study and Questions of Theory. *Journal of Southern African Studies* 8:143–172.

CORNEVIN, MARIANNE
  1980 *Apartheid Power and History Falsification.* UNESCO, Paris.

CRICK, MALCOLM
  1982 Anthropology of Knowledge. *Annual Review of Anthropology* 11:287–313.

DAVISON, PATRICIA
  1991 Material Culture, Context and Meaning: A Critical Investigation of Museum Practice with Particular Reference to the South African Museum. Unpublished Ph.D. thesis, Department of Archaeology, University of Cape Town, Cape Town, South Africa.

DEETZ, JAMES
  1977 *In Small Things Forgotten, The Archeology of Early American Life.* Anchor Press/Doubleday, NY.
  1993 *Flowerdew Hundred: The Archaeology of a Virginia Plantation, 1619–1864.* University of Virginia, Charlottesville.

DU PREEZ, J. M.
  1983 *Africana Afrikaner Meestersimbole in Suid-Afrikaanse Skoolhandboeke.* Librarius, Alberton, South Africa.

DU TOIT, ANDRE
  1984 Captive to the Nationalist Paradigm: Prof. F. A. van Jaarsveld and the Historical Evidence for the Afrikaner's Ideas on His Calling and Mission. *South African Historical Journal* 16:49–78.

FREESPEECH
  1995 Monthly Newsletter for Supporters of American Dissident Voices. <http://www.natall.com/FREESP/FSDIR.HTML>. National Alliance, Hillsboro, WV.

FRY, PETER
  1992 Anthropology in Southern Africa. *Current Anthropology* 33(2)230–231.

FUCHS, LAWRENCE H.
  1991 *The American Kaleidoscope: Race, Ethnicity and the Civic Culture.* Wesleyan University, Middletown, CT.

GILOMEE, HERMANN
  1989 The Beginnings of Afrikaner Ethnic Consciousness. In *The Creation of Tribalism in Southern Africa,* edited by Leroy Vail, pp. 21–54. James Currey, London.

GLAZER, ROBERT, AND DANIEL P. MOYNIHAN
  1963 *Beyond the Melting Pot.* MIT Press, Cambridge, MA.

GLUCKMAN, MAX
  1975 Anthropology and Apartheid: The Work of South African Anthropologists. In *Studies in South African*

Anthropology, edited by Miles Fortes and S. Patterson, pp. 21–39. Academic Press, London.

GORDON, ROBERT, AND ANDREW D. SPIEGEL
  1993 Southern Africa Revisited. *Annual Review of Anthropology* 22:83–105.

GRAHAM'S TOWN JOURNAL [Grahamstown, South Africa]
  1840 Wesleyan Missions in South Africa: Extracts from the Report for 1839–1840. *Graham's Town Journal,* 2 April 1840:4

HALL, MARTIN
  1983 Tribes, Traditions and Numbers: The American Model in Southern African Iron Age Ceramic Studies. In *South African Archaeological Bulletin* 38:51–57.
  1984 The Burden of Tribalism: The Social Context of Southern African Iron Age Studies. *American Antiquity* 49:445–467.
  1990 "Hidden History": Iron Age Archaeology in Southern Africa. In *A History of African Archaeology,* edited by Peter Robertshaw, pp. 59–77. Currey, London.
  1993 The Archaeology of Colonial Settlement in Southern Africa. *Annual Review of Anthropology* 22:177–200.

HANDSMAN, RUSSELL G., AND MARK LEONE
  1989 Living History and Critical Archaeology in the Reconstruction of the Past. In *Critical Traditions in Contemporary Archaeology,* edited by Rebecca Pinsky and Alison Wylie, pp. 117–135. Cambridge University Press, Cambridge, UK.

HARDWICK, J. J.
  1989 A Comparative Study of Staffordshire Ceramics of the Nineteenth Century in America and South Africa. Unpublished B.A. honors thesis, Department of Anthropology, University of California, Berkeley.

HERNSTEIN, RICHARD J., AND CHARLES MURRAY
  1994 *The Bell Curve: Intelligence and Class Structure in American Life.* Free Press, NY.

HEYMANS, RIANA
  1986 *The Voortrekker Monument.* Board of Control of the Voortrekker Monument, Pretoria, South Africa.

HOROWITZ, DONALD L.
  1991 *A Democratic South Africa? Constitutional Engineering in a Divided Society.* University of California, Berkeley.

JEPPSON, PATRICE L.
  1987 Research Report. *Martevaan II, Cape Historical Archaeology Association Newsletter.* Antonia Malan, Newsletter Editor. University of Cape Town, Cape Town, South Africa.
  1988a Getting the Research Out. *Martevaan IV, Cape Historical Archaeology Association Newsletter.* Antonia Malan, Newsletter Editor. University of Cape Town, Cape Town, South Africa.
  1988b Historical Archaeology at Farmerfield Mission Station: Method and Theory. Paper presented at the Annual Meeting of the Southern African Association of Anthropologists, Grahamstown, South Africa.
  1988c Historical Archaeology in the Eastern Cape: Introduction to the Research Design. Paper presented at the Southern African Archaeology Association Biennial Conference, Johannesburg, South Africa.
  1988d Historical Archaeology in the Eastern Cape. Paper presented at the South African Museum Association, Eastern Cape Regional Conference, East London, South Africa.
  1988e Research Report. *Martevaan III, Cape Historical Archaeology Association Newsletter.* Antonia Malan, Newsletter Editor. University of Cape Town, Cape Town, South Africa.
  1988f South African Historical Archaeology Report. *The Society for Historical Archaeology Newsletter* 21(3):45.
  1989a Ceramics as History or Ceramics as Objects? Paper presented at the South African Museum Association Eastern Cape Regional Conference, Cradock, South Africa.
  1989b Historical Archaeology and Alternative Cultural History Interpretations. Paper presented at the South African Museum Association Educational Conference IX, Cape Town, South Africa.
  1989c Historical Archaeology and Method, Alternative Cultural History Interpretations in South African Museums. Paper presented at the Joint South African Museum Association/Cape Historical Association Symposium, Cape Town, South Africa.
  1989d Historical Archaeology, History and Archaeology of a Frontier Fort: Methods Used in the Study of the Past. Booklet prepared for Albany Museum, Mobile Museum Education Box, on file, Archaeology Department, Albany Museum, Grahamstown, South Africa.
  1989e History in a Case. *The Elephant's Child* 3:4. Newsletter of the Albany Museum, Grahamstown, South Africa.
  1990a 19th-Century Ceramics as Clues to Social Identity in the Eastern Cape Colony of South Africa. Paper presented at the Annual Meeting of The Society for Historical Archaeology Conference on Historical and Underwater Archaeology, Tucson, AZ.
  1990b Bridging the Gap—Shamans, Bains and Pembe: Archaeology as an Integrating Force in Cultural History Museums. Paper presented at the Southern African Archaeology Association Conference, Kimberly, South Africa.
  1990c Ceramics as Clues to 19th-Century Social Organization in the Eastern Cape. Paper presented at the Southern African Association of Archaeologists Biennial Conference, Kimberly, South Africa.

1990d Historical Archaeology in South African Museums. Invited plenary session paper presented at the South African Museum Association History Sectional Meeting, Pretoria, South Africa.

1990e The Way We See It: Images of Eastern Cape History—The History Behind, Within, and Outside a New Culture History Display. Report submitted to the Albany Museum, Grahamstown, South Africa.

1991a Colonial Systems and Indigenous Response: Material Expressions Discovered at Farmerfield Mission Station. Paper presented at the Institute for Social and Economic Research Seminar Series, Rhodes University, Grahamstown, South Africa.

1991b Colonial Systems and Indigenous Responses: Black Material Culture at a 19th-Century, British, Methodist Mission in South Africa. Paper presented at the Annual Meeting of The Society for Historical Archaeology Conference on Historical and Underwater Archaeology, Richmond, VA.

1991c Shaman, Bain's and Pembe: The Material Culture Approach in South African Museums. Paper presented at the South African Museum Association Annual Conference, Cape Town, South Africa.

1992 Archaeology Is a Strange Concept: Problems Encountered Teaching Archaeology at the University of Venda. Paper presented at the Archaeology and Education Workshop, conducted by Edwin Hanisch and Patrice L. Jeppson, at the Southern African Association of Archaeologists Conference, Cape Town, South Africa.

1993 Material Culture Expressions of Ethnicity and Identity on the Nineteenth-Century Eastern Cape Frontier. Paper presented at the Sociology and Anthropology Colloquium Series, California State University, Bakersfield.

1995a Archaeology in the Public Interest: Applied Historical Archaeology in a South African Museum Educational Exhibit. Paper presented at the Chacmool Conference, University of Calgary, Canada.

1995b Historical Archaeology and Alternative History Interpretations in a South African Museum Education Exhibit. Paper presented at the Annual Meeting of The Society for Historical Archaeology Conference on Historical and Underwater Archaeology, Washington, DC.

1996a "Leveling the Playing Field" in the Contested Territory of the South African Past: Prospects for Public Archaeology. Paper presented at the Annual Meeting of The Society for Historical Archaeology Conference on Historical and Underwater Archaeology, Cincinnati, OH.

[1998] Mythical and Material Perspectives of Ethnicity on the 19th-Century South African Frontier. Unpublished Ph.D. dissertation, Program in Historical Archaeology, University of Pennsylvania, Philadelphia, forthcoming.

KALLAWAY, PETER
1984 Apartheid and Education. Raven Press, Johannesburg, South Africa.
1991 Education and Nation Building in South Africa in the 1990s: Reforming History Education for the Post Apartheid Era. Paper presented at the Comparative and International Education Society Conference, Pittsburgh, PA.

KRUSS, GLENDA
1981 People's Education: An Examination of the Concept. Cape Town, South Africa.

KUPER, ADAM
1983 Anthropology and Anthropologists. Routledge and Kegan Paul, London.
1986 The Anthropologist's Vocation in South Africa. African Studies 45(1).
1988 Anthropology and Apartheid. In South Africa in Question, edited by John Lonsdale, pp. 33–52. University of Cambridge African Studies Centre, Cambridge University Press, Cambridge, UK.

LE CORDEUR, BASIL
1981 The Politics of Eastern Cape Separatism: 1820–1854. Cape Town, South Africa.

LEONE, MARK P.
1983 Method as Message. Museum News 62:34–41.
1992 "Epilogue": The Productive Nature of Material Culture and Archaeology. In Meanings and Uses of Material Culture, edited by Barbara Little and Paul Shackel. Historical Archaeology 26(3):130–133. California, PA.

LEONE, MARK P., PARKER B. POTTER, AND PAUL SHACKEL
1987 Towards a Critical Archaeology. Current Anthropology 28(3):283–302.

MAJEKE, NOSIPHO [NORA TAYLOR]
1952 The Role of the Missionaries in Conquest. Cumberwood, South Africa.

MARE, GERHARD
1993 Ethnicity and Politics in South Africa. Zed Books, London.

McGUIRE, RANDALL
1982 The Study of Ethnicity in Historical Archaeology. Journal of Anthropological Archaeology 1(2):159–178.

McKEE, LARRY W.
1984 Delineating Ethnicity from the Garbage of Early Virginians: The Faunal Remains from the Kingsmill Plantation Slave Quarter. Paper presented at the

Annual Meeting of The Society for Historical Archaeology Conference on Historical and Underwater Archaeology, Williamsburg, VA.

McKINNEY, IAN
1995a The Long March. *American Dissident Radio*, National Alliance Radio broadcast, 1 July 1995. Hillsboro, WV.
1995b The Long March. *FreeSpeech* 1(8). Monthly Newsletter for Supporters of American Dissident Voices. William Pierce, Newsletter Editor. National Alliance, on-line <http:www.natall.com/FREESP/FSDIR.HTML>. Hillsboro, WV.

MOODIE, T. DUNBAR
1975 *The Rise of Afrikanerdom: Power, Apartheid, and the Afrikaner Civil Religion.* University of California Press, Berkeley.

NAGELGAST, E. B.
1990 Letter from Africana Museum Curator requesting information concerning "the philosophy behind, and the construction and function of, the traveling exhibit by Jeppson." Submitted 11 November 1990 to Brian Wilmot, Director, Albany Museum, Grahamstown, South Africa.

NAIDOO, JAY
1989 *Tracking Down Historical Myths.* A. D. Donker, Johannesburg, South Africa.

NATIONAL VANGUARD
1993– Publication of the National Alliance, on-line <http://
1996 www/natall.com/NATVAN/NATDIR.HTML>. Hillsboro, WV.

ODENDAAL, ANDRE
1991 Developments in Popular History in the Western Cape in the 1980s. In *History from South Africa: Alternative Visions and Practices*, edited by Joshua Brown, Patrick Manning, Karin Shapiro, Jon Wiener, Belinda Bozzoli and Peter Delius. Temple University Press, Philadelphia, PA.

OWEN, D., AND W. HOLLEMAN
1989 Grey History: A Pox on General and Own Affairs. Paper presented at the South African Museum Association Annual Conference, Bloemfontein, South Africa.

PAUW, B. A.
1980 Recent South African Anthropology. In *Annual Review of Anthropology* 9:315–338.

PEIRES, JEFF
1989 Ethnicity and Pseudo-Ethnicity in the Ciskei. In *The Creation of Tribalism in Southern Africa*, edited by Leroy Vail, pp. 395–413. James Currey, London.

PEPONIS, J., AND J. HEDIN
1982 The Layout of Theories in the Natural History Museum. *Nine H* 3:21–25. London.

PINSKY, VALERIE, AND ALISON WYLIE
1989 *Critical Traditions in Contemporary Archaeology.* Cambridge University Press, Cambridge, UK.

PITYANA, SIPHO MILA
1995 HSRC'S Revolution from Above. *Weekly Mail and Guardian* 6–12 January:8. Johannesburg, South Africa.

POTTER, PARKER B., JR.
1991 What Is the Use of Plantation Archaeology? *Historical Archaeology* 25(3):94–107.
1992 Critical Archaeology: In the Ground and on the Street. *Historical Archaeology* 26(3): 117–129.
1994 *Public Archaeology in Annapolis: A Critical Approach to History in Maryland's Ancient City.* Smithsonian Institution Press, Washington, DC.

RITCHIE, GABRIELLE
1990 Dig the Herders/Display the Hottentots: The Production and Presentation of Knowledge about the Past. Unpublished M.A. thesis, African Studies Department, University of Cape Town, South Africa.

SAID, EDWARD W.
1989 Representing the Colonized: Anthropology's Interlocutors. *Critical Inquiry* 15:205–225.

SAUNDERS, CHRISTOPHER
1988 *The Making of the South African Past: Major Historians on Race and Class.* Cape Town, South Africa.

SCHUTTE, GERHARD
1989 Afrikaner Historiography and the Decline of Apartheid: Ethnic Self-reconstruction in Times of Crisis. In History and Ethnicity, edited by Elizabeth Tonkin, Maryon McDonald, and Malcolm Chapman. *Association of Social Anthropology Monographs* 27:216–231. Routledge, London.

SCHUYLER, ROBERT
1980 *Archaeological Perspectives on Ethnicity in America.* Baywood, Farmingdale, NY.

Patrice L. Jeppson

SCOTT, PATRICIA E., AND JAMES DEETZ
1990 The Transformation of British Culture in the Eastern Cape, 1820–1860. *Social Dynamics* 16(1):55–75. Cape Town, South Africa.

SENTRALE VOLKSMONUMENTE-KOMITEE EN DIE SENTRALE VOORTREKKER EEUFEESKOMITEE (SVE)
1938 *Sentrale Voortrekker-Eufees, 1838–1938.* Pretoria, South Africa.

SHARP, JOHN
1980a Can We Study Ethnicity? A Critique of Fields of Study in South African Anthropology. *Social Dynamics* 6(1):1–16. Cape Town, South Africa.
1980b Two Separate Developments, Anthropology in South Africa. *Royal Anthropology Institute Newsletter* 36:4–6.
1981 The Roots and Development of Volkekunde in South Africa. *Journal of South African Studies* 8(1):16–36.

SHAW, WILLIAM
1860 *The Story of My Mission in South Eastern Africa.* Hamilton Adams, London

SHENNAN, STEPHEN
1989 *Archaeological Approaches to Cultural Identity.* Unwin Hyman, London.

SMITH, ANDREW
1987 Museums in a Changing and Divided Society. Paper presented at Africa Seminar, Centre for African Studies, University of Cape Town, South Africa.

SMITH, KEN
1988 *The Changing Past: Trends in South African Historical Writing.* Ohio University Press, Athens.

TAKAKI, RONALD
1987 *From Different Shores: Perspectives on Race and Ethnicity in America.* Oxford University Press, NY.

THOMPSON, LEONARD
1985 *The Political Mythology of Apartheid.* Yale University Press, New Haven, CT.

THORNTON, ROBERT
1988 Culture. In *South African Keywords*, edited by Elaine Boonzaier and John Sharp, pp. 17–28. Philip, Cape Town, South Africa.

TILLEY, CHRISTOPHER
1989 Archaeology as Socio-Political Action in the Present. In *Critical Traditions in Contemporary Archaeology*, edited by Margaret Conkey and Christine Hastorf, pp. 3–84. Cambridge University Press, Cambridge, UK.

TUNMER, ROY
1988 Museum Education as Skills Education. *South African Museum Association Bulletin* 18(4):12–16.

VAN ZYL, SILVIA
1988 Guest Editorial: Museum Education within the Overall Framework of South African Education. *South African Museum Association Bulletin* 18(4):1.

VARLEY, C. H., AND H. M. MATTHEW
1957 *The Cape Journals of Archdeacon N. J. Merriman 1848–1855.* Van Riebeeck Society, Cape Town, South Africa.

VOORSTER, R., R. HAMBROCK-UKEN, AND F. C. DE BEER
1986 *Anthropology Study Guide SKA-301-6.* University of South Africa, Cape Town.

WEBB, DENVER
1989 The Cheshire Cat's Advice and the Problems of History in Museums. Paper presented at the South African Museum Association Annual Conference, Bloemfontein, South Africa.

WESLEYAN MISSIONARY SOCIETY (WMS)
1840 Missions in South Africa. *Wesleyan Missionary Notices, &c.* (September) 1(21):22–23. James Nichols, Hoxton-Square, London.
1847 Wesleyan Mission at Farmerfield, South Africa. *Wesleyan Missionary Notices, &c.* (December) 5(110):206–208. James Nichols, Hoxton-Square, London.
1853 *Report on the Auxillary Wesleyan Mission Society for the Albany and Kaffraria District for the Year Ending May 1853.* Godlonton, White, Grahamstown.

WHISSON, MICHAEL
1981 Anthropological Research in Contemporary South Africa. In *Apartheid and Social Research,* edited by John Rex. UNESCO Press/Unipub, Lanham, MD.

WINER, MARGOT, AND JAMES DEETZ
1990 The Transformation of British Culture in the Eastern Cape, 1820–1860. *Social Dynamics* 16(1):55–75. Cape Town, South Africa.

WRIGHT, JOHN, AND AARON MAZEL
1987 Bastions of Ideology: The Depiction of Precolonial History in the Museums of Natal and KwaZulu. In *South African Museum Association Bulletin* 17:301–310.

PATRICE L. JEPPSON
THE PROGRAM IN HISTORICAL ARCHAEOLOGY
UNIVERSITY OF PENNSYLVANIA
PHILADELPHIA, PA 19104

James G. Gibb

Imaginary, But by No Means Unimaginable: Storytelling, Science, and Historical Archaeology

ABSTRACT

"Imaginary, But by No Means Unimaginable," a phrase coined by L. Daniel Mouer and Ywone Edwards-Ingram at the 1998 Conference on Historical and Underwater Archaeology, epitomizes a new approach to archaeological analysis and public interpretation. The suddenness with which examples of storytelling appeared in conferences and publications has left little opportunity for comment, particularly to address the theoretical and methodological issues that underlie this hybrid of science, humanities research, and artistic expression. This commentary suggests that storytelling is more than a means of engaging public audiences: it is a form of archaeological analysis.

Introduction

Storytelling has burst into historical archaeology with as much exuberance and promise as any theoretical precept that has visited the field in the last thirty years. Unlike the purveyors of paradigms, the storytellers bring a wide range of perspectives to their craft, and they emphasize performance, not concept, product, not abstraction and they speak in the vernacular rather than in the abstruse language of philosophy. In this discovery of a too long hidden eloquence, however, the storytellers have given short shrift to two questions: why and how should archaeologists tell stories? This commentary explores the issues of theory and method in storytelling, largely through examination of a remarkable series of publications with the unremarkable title of *Los Vaqueros Project Final Report* Numbers 1 through 6. This series offers a new approach for conveying the results of archaeological research to non-specialist audiences. It also may offer—although this was not the intention of the authors—a new approach to archaeological analysis.

Archaeologists as Storytellers

The meteoric rise of storytelling as public interpretation began when Mary Praetzellis organized the "Archaeologist as Storyteller" session for the Society for Historical Archaeology's 1997 Conference on Historical and Underwater Archaeology. Comprised of nine performances sandwiched between a short introduction by Adrian Praetzellis and brief closing remarks by James Deetz, the session played to a well-filled room and since has been published as a special issue of *Historical Archaeology* (Praetzellis 1998).

Deetz (Gibb 1997a) described the session as unlike anything presented at the 29 previous meetings of the Society, "a healthy dose of humanism in an arena where we often substitute histograms and binary plots for the pulse of human life." Different, certainly. Performers moved about the stage and ballroom, two or more voices often heard rather than one, the texts interpretive rather than analytical. Each performer offered a new way to look at and interpret the past. Adrian Praetzellis brought a complexity of Asian-Euroamerican social relations to 19th-century Sacramento and an earthiness to Yankee merchant Josiah Gallop, rarely expressed in a conference paper or journal article. One could almost taste freshly baked bread toward the end of Julia Costello and Judy Tordoff's presentation on traditional Italian bread baking in and around Calaveras County, California. Many in the audience probably forgot at some point during the performance that William Harris's letter to Governor William Jeffreys was wholly fictional, a piece borne of Dan Mouer's imagination and many years of archaeological and historical research in Tidewater Virginia.

As the papers went to press Mary Praetzellis organized "Archaeologists as Storytellers II," presented at the annual meeting in Atlanta. The room, a large one, was packed. Eight presentations by 12 performers, 7 of whom had been involved in the previous year's session, gave voice to: the United State's first avocational archaeologist and third president; Lowell, Massachusetts, boarding house keeper Amanda Fox; Catryn, an enslaved South African girl in Cape Town; circuit preacher John Early in New Canton, Virginia; madams, prostitutes, and 'Johns' in fin-de-siècle Los Angeles; Californian cowboy Fermin Valenzuela and a fictitious university student; and a Caribbean planter and a slave, alternating with an American male and a Jamaican female archaeologist.

All of the papers from both sessions introduced novel ways of exploring and presenting the past. Always imaginative, sometimes surreal, these presentations are more than historical fiction, and more than "just the facts." Their influence, growing within the profession, now extends to a larger public. Despite wide dissemination, and perhaps because of the emphasis on product, historical archaeologists—me and some of the storytellers, inclusive—have misunderstood the archaeologist-as-storyteller. The cause: lack of a clearly defined theoretical underpinning that justifies storytelling and provides a basis for method.

Why Stories?

A story is a narrative, a tale, an account of events (e.g., Herodotus's fifth century BC Histories), personalities (e.g., Plutarch's Lives from 1st and 2nd centuries A.D.), or attitudes (e.g., Samuel Richardson's [1741-1742] Pamela; Or Virtue Rewarded). The word suggests fiction, but—as any journalist will aver—a story need not be fictional. A fictional account, however, can accurately represent the time and place of cultures and events past (e.g., Defoe's [1722] A Journal of the Plague Year), even if the details derive from the author's imagination rather than from direct observations or critical evaluation of documents. Technical writers, by contrast, narrate process, not product. They tell the reader how they analyzed a problem and came upon a solution, rather than rendering interpretation into narrative. After all, is not the former the job of the scientist? Is not the narrator or interpreter a popularizer, a Carl Sagan, Michael Graves, Jacob Bronowski, Ivor Noël Hume, or whatever antonomasia pleases the reader? Most archaeological data and interpretations in printed media appear as reports: detailed documents describing background material, methods, and techniques of data recovery and analysis, and interpretations. In practice, if not in theory, storytelling and technical reporting

occupy independent domains: the one literary, the other scientific.

As long as archaeologists accept these dichotomies—scientist and popularizer, report and story—the answer to the question, why stories, remains inescapable. Stories are a means by which interpreters can bring the results of scientific research to non-specialist audiences, but stories have no place in research. Stories, so conceived, educate the public and earn its support, or such was my assumption in reviewing the first of the Archaeologists as Storytellers series.

> Each of these performances was well written, beautifully so in several instances, and well presented. The stories were not so much fictitious as interpretive, carried out in an entertaining, engaging manner. These are exactly the kinds of performances that will build constituencies and help satisfy our ethical obligations to the communities that we serve (Gibb 1997a).

No mention at all of how these stories might directly serve professional audiences. Indeed, my one criticism of the 1997 session was that the performers had no plans for taking their show "on the road." They were playing to the wrong audience. The realization that stories might have analytical value came to me in an unexpected way.

In July of 1998, the London Town Foundation, operators of an historic house museum, asked me to write a play about ghosts for Halloween, drawing material from The Lost Towns of Anne Arundel Project's archaeological and archival research at the site of colonial London, Maryland. I agreed, partly intrigued by the possibilities of the genre and partly as a means of promoting archaeological research. The project staff and volunteers, however, had not yet collected enough information—archaeological and archival—to tell coherent, interesting stories about colonial London's residents. Taking a cue from Mary Praetzellis's storytellers, I developed three vignettes that integrated data through literary material, drawing on English-language novels, plays, and diaries of the period. Samuel Richardson's novels Pamela (1741-1742) and Clarissa (1747-1749), the diaries of William Byrd and James Boswell, and a number of other English language plays and novels helped flesh out personalities, motivations, and social mores and customs. They contributed to context in the absence of more site-specific contextual data.

I could not be sure that my protagonists would have used the words that I put into their mouths, acted in the ways I made them act, or even that they would have found themselves in the situations in which I placed them. The vignettes suggested, however, patterns and relationships that The Lost Towns Project staff might look for or deduce from the growing archaeological and archival databases. For example, when innkeeper Elinor Rumney gently chides her husband Edward for talking to, rather than ferrying, travelers, that raises the issue as to the appearance of the ferry and its landing. Was the landing a distinct space in which travelers could wait, meet, and interact with one another and the ferryman, observing or suspending the rules of deference? To what extent did Elinor and Edward cooperate in the operation of the tavern and ferry? Identification and study of submerged ferries and landings could contribute to a clearer understanding of Colonial Period travel and the relationship between ferries and taverns. Archival study of the wealth and position of ferrymen and their clients, and of the individuals competing for ferry licenses, could contribute to a broader understanding of colonial social relations and how those relations were expressed in travel when strangers encountered one another. The Lost Towns Project staff did not consider these questions prior to my having written the play. They will now.

Creating encounters among ghosts, and between ghosts and museum interpreters, in a way, became a form of analysis, subject to further study and hypothesis testing. Just the act of imagining the language and forms of address used by the ghosts suggested subtleties in the relations among London's residents and visitors that might have gone unaddressed by conventional research. Creating a sustainable story with believable plot and dialogue requires precision and logic no less demanding than would be required in formulating and testing hypotheses.

Attending the Archaeologists as Storytellers performances, reading the published versions of the first performances, and attempting my own interpretive historical fiction led me to two observations: (1) interpretive historical fiction holds great promise for engaging and educating specialist- and non-specialist audiences; and (2) it can provide a powerful analytical tool, an explicitly subjective, but rigorous, means of exploring archaeological and archival data.

What I did not learn from my brief experience as a playwright, was method. How do we create interpretive historical fiction that is true in scope if not in detail? The Los Vaqueros Report Series, prepared by the Anthropological Studies Center at Sonoma State University in California, provides a methodology, although not in an entirely explicit manner.

Research Design and Narrative

Archaeological stories, at least those presented in the Atlanta session and in Praetzellis (1998), derive from recently concluded or ongoing research. Several authors have revisited Cook's (1998) "Katherine Nanny, Alias Naylor": A Life in Puritan Boston with conventional scholarly papers in Cheek (1998). Yamin's (1998) "Five Points" story grew out of a substantial data recovery project report in New York City, and Beaudry's (1998a, 1998b) two Massachusetts tales were drawn from extensively documented research at the Spencer-Peirce-Little Farm in Newbury and the Boott Mill boarding houses in Lowell. To what extent these storytellers relied on a particular method, only they can answer, but their scientific research designs and rigorous analyses must have shaped the concepts and plots underlying their stories. Put another way, the stories reflect the investigators' research interests and findings. The Los Vaqueros publications more clearly illustrate the relationship between research and interpretive historical fiction.

Praetzellis et al. (1997) Tales of the Vasco includes a brief discourse on methods. They describe their five tales, in the introduction to the booklet, as fact-based works of fiction:

> Our stories are neither The Objective Truth nor . . . are they constructed out of thin air. The scenarios—an interview, meetings, and a correspondence—are pure invention, but all the historic characters actually lived on the Vasco [an area 30 mi. east of San Francisco]. We have constructed the details of their lives from a variety of sources. We will never know, however, their motivations, emotions, attitudes, or thoughts; nor whether they would approve of how we have pictured them (Praetzellis et al. 1997).

On the following page Praetzellis et al. (1997) provided a portion of one of their tales, complete with footnotes (Gibb 1997b) to illustrate how their stories derive from original research. The

Tales, however, lack footnotes, in-text citations, and the other paraphernalia of academic writing, and rightly so—the original research already had been thoroughly documented in technical reports. This snippet provides the first explicit explanation of the method underlying the product.

The Los Vaqueros Project began in 1980, a series of contracted research projects designed to identify and evaluate historic and prehistoric archaeological sites prior to reservoir construction in an arid canyon in northern California. Praetzellis et al. (1997) provided a working history that offers a chronology of human occupation of the Vasco and identifies historical contexts with which research questions might be constructed and findings interpreted. Fredrickson et al. (1997) documented linguistic, ethnographic, and some archaeological fieldwork pertaining to the aboriginal occupation of the area, as well as historic contexts for evaluating the historical significance of Native American sites. Ziesing (1996, 1997a) described archaeological investigations at four historic sites, dating largely from the second half of the 19th and the first third of the 20th centuries. Each of these technical reports posed research questions appropriate to their scope, and methods appropriate to the questions. They reviewed the history of the area, discussing such issues as: the colonial Spanish presence; the shift from livestock raising to grain agriculture during the 1870s; land speculation and litigation in the 1880s and 1890s; tenancy in the latter part of the 19th and early 20th centuries; and immigration and ethnic diversity throughout the prehistoric and historic periods.

From the historical review, Praetzellis and Praetzellis (Ziesing 1996:27-32), identified three principal research contexts for the historic sites: ranching adaptations and the environment, social relations, and modernization. For each context, they posed a primary question and as many as six secondary questions, and they identified specific data requirements and potentially contributing archaeological data sets. Subsequent chapters documented methods and findings, and offered recommendations for future research. So far, pretty standard stuff. Reports 5 and 6, however, set this series—and the entire project—apart from anything that I have seen in compliance or grant-funded archaeology.

Report No. 6, Ziesing's (1997b) "From Rancho to Reservoir: History and Archaeology of the Los Vaqueros Watershed, California," synthesizes archaeological, archival, and oral history data in a format suitable for a wide range of audiences. The contributors constructed their essays in terms of the historic contexts, questions, and results documented in the less intellectually accessible technical reports. [For the issue of intellectual accessibility see Davis (1997:85).] The Anthropological Studies Center at Sonoma State University printed 150 copies for distribution to local and state libraries, historical societies, informants, colleagues, and high schools (Mary Praetzellis 1998, pers. comm.). The volume is well designed, illustrated, and bound, and an excellent, accessible contribution to local and state history.

Report No. 5 is Tales of the Vasco (Praetzellis et al. 1997), mentioned above. The series number assigned to this publication suggests that it was written before Report No. 6, the synthesis, although the numbering may be an artifact of the review and publication process. One step removed from synthesis and two steps from the original research, Tales of the Vasco breathes life, as the cliché goes, back into the now deceased denizens of this rural community. Readable, and sometimes moving, the tales convey more about life on the Vasco, and of conducting archaeological research there, than straightforward, "just the facts" kind of reporting ever could. The authors anticipated the greater interest that this report would generate, printing 400 for local and statewide distribution (Mary Praetzellis 1998, pers. comm.).

Although innovative in building substantive synthesis from data, and public interpretation from synthesis, nothing in the Los Vaqueros Project report series suggests the analytical value of stories. Adrian Praetzellis, in his introduction to the *Historical Archaeology* volume, "Archaeologists as Storytellers," attributes this interest in storytelling to a need to indulge, to say what a site is really about without having to qualify every point; to convey impressions without undermining science. Stories, however, need not be an end product, the last, not-entirely-demonstrable word on a site and its occupants. Louis Peres' tale, told to a fictional interviewer, can redirect research and technical analyses.

When Peres, a Jewish French émigré and the subject of one of the Tales of the Vasco, states that his first wife, Maria Antonia, was a Catholic Mexican, that is a fact. Anyone researching the Peres family, or the adobe ranch house in which they lived in the 1880s, probably would have uncovered that bit of information. When Peres sends his daughter Lucy out of the parlor, and confides to the interviewer that he does not mention his ex-wife around his new wife, the devoutly Jewish Palmyra Levy, that is imagination. It also is the first step in looking at some very important social issues.

When Louis Peres arrived in San Francisco in 1860, he stayed at the Hotel de L'Europe, run by French expatriate Daniel Orlette; a logical decision since Peres did not "speak English so good." Yet when he married a couple of years later, he chose not a French woman but a Mexican, and a Catholic at that. This is a matter of public record, as is the divorce. Was their common religious heritage a factor in the marriage of Louis and Palmyra and, if so, why was it not an issue in the marriage of Louis and Maria? An ineffable affair of the heart? Or were ethnicity and religion of less concern than they would become a few years later (1870s) in a more settled society? The answer, as far as this commentary goes, is unimportant. The question, on the other hand, is very important, arrived at through a tale that uncovered a possible inconsistency, a bit of plot that perhaps does not work quite right or that needs some explanation. In the fictional interview, Louis states that Palmyra is religious, implying that he his not. Praetzellis et al. are telling their readers that at least in this case, the wife—not the husband—is concerned about a shared religious heritage. We do not know what piqued Louis' interest in Palmyra, but his Jewish identity, expressed or not, might have been important to Palmyra.

The reader can comb Tales of the Vasco for similar leaps of imagination, bits of plot—based on considerable knowledge of the history and archaeology of the region developed to bring archaeological, archival, and oral history data into a coherent story and to "explain" the inconsistencies. Hardly the products of idle or lazy minds, these Tales grew out of meticulous research and careful writing, and a commitment to creating understanding as well as knowledge. The Tales were created, not in lieu of rigorous analysis, but in addition to those analyses. The remaining challenge is to revisit the original data and analyses with the perspective gained through storytelling.

Summary and Conclusions

While some might quibble over departures from the absolutely demonstrable, none would dispute the power of a story well told. Stories can captivate and communicate, educate and inspire. But they can be written as much for the writer as for the listener. Rooted in original research, products of theory and method, stories explore new vistas and highlight subtleties of social relations overlooked in more conventional analyses. Storytelling is a form of experimentation and analysis in which the storyteller-analyst examines certain conditions, while holding others constant, determining how the actors might have behaved. Insights derived from such tales may have testable implications.

Would it be hyperbole to say that there have been more stories told around screens and excavation units than scholarly papers printed in journals? Probably not. I doubt there is a practicing field archaeologist who has not speculated about a particular artifact or deposit while excavating, screening, or recording. Sometimes serious, often facetious, these attempts at storytelling in the field lack the rigorous logic and supporting data that go into a fact-based story; but they are a good start. Tales of the Vasco serves as an excellent model for archaeologists writing interpretive historical fiction. We owe its production, in part, to the Contra Costa Water District, the sponsoring agency, for their imaginative approach to compliance with the nation's environmental laws. To my knowledge, the Los Vaqueros series is unique: may it not remain so for long.

ACKNOWLEDGEMENTS

Al Luckenbach, Jason D. Moser, and Liz West commented on an earlier version of this paper, offering clarity where there was muddle. Mary Praetzellis and Adrian Praetzellis conscientiously replied to several questions about their work: I appreciate their patience and good humor. The views expressed in this commentary, except where specifically attributed to another, are mine.

REFERENCES

BEAUDRY, MARY C.
  1998a Farm Journal: First Person, Four Voices. *Historical Archaeology* 32(1):20-33.
  1998b A Lost Memoir of a Lowell Boardinghouse Keeper. Paper presented at the The Society for Historical Archaeology Conference on Historical and Underwater Archaeology, Atlanta, GA.

COOK, LAUREN J.
1998   "Katherine Nanny, Alias Naylor": A Life in Puritan Boston. *Historical Archaeology* 32(1):15-19.

CHEEK, CHARLES D. (EDITOR)
1998   Perspectives on the Archaeology of Colonial Boston: The Archaeology of the Central Artery/Tunnel Project, Boston, Massachusetts. *Historical Archaeology* 32(2).

DAVIS, KAREN L
1997   Problems and Process: The Archaeologist and Public Interpretation. In *Presenting Archaeology to the Public: Digging for Truths*, John H. Jameson, editor, pp. 84-98. Altamira Press, Thousand Oaks, CA.

FREDRICKSON, DAVID A., SUZANNE B. STEWART, AND GRACE H. ZIESING
1997   Native American History Studies for the Los Vaqueros Project: A Synthesis. Anthropological Studies Center, Sonoma State University Foundation, *Los Vaqueros Project Final Report* 2. Rohnert Park, CA.

GIBB, JAMES G.
1997a   Archaeologists as Storytellers. *The Society for Historical Archaeology Newsletter* 30(1):7.
1997b   Tales of the Vasco: Archaeologists as Storytellers. *The Society for Historical Archaeology Newsletter* 30(4):6-7.

PRAETZELLIS, ADRIAN, GRACE H. ZIESING, AND MARY PRAETZELLIS
1997   Tales of the Vasco. Anthropological Studies Center, Sonoma State University Foundation, *Los Vaqueros Project Final Report* 5. Rohnert Park, CA.

PRAETZELLIS, MARY (EDITOR)
1998   Archaeologists as Storytellers. *Historical Archaeology* 32(1).

YAMIN, REBECCA
1998   Lurid Tales and Homely Stories of New York's Notorious Five Points. *Historical Archaeology* 32(1):14-85.

ZIESING, GRACE H. (EDITOR)
1996   Investigations of Three Historic Archaeological Sites, CA-CCO-447/H, CA-CCO-445/H, and CA-CCO-427/H, for the Los Vaqueros Project, Alameda and Contra Costa Counties, California. Anthropological Studies Center, Sonoma State University Foundation, *Los Vaqueros Project Final Report* 3. Rohnert Park, CA.
1997a   Archaeological Investigations at the Vasco Adobe Site, CA-CCO-470/H, for the Los Vaqueros Project, Alameda and Contra Costa Counties, California. Anthropological Studies Center, Sonoma State University Foundation, *Los Vaqueros Project Final Report* 4. Rohnert Park, CA.
1997b   From Rancho to Reservoir: History and Archaeology of the Los Vaqueros Watershed, California. Anthropological Studies Center, Sonoma State University Foundation, *Los Vaqueros Project Final Report* 6. Rohnert Park, CA.

JAMES G. GIBB
THE LOST TOWNS OF ANNE ARUNDEL PROJECT
PACE/PO BOX 6675
ANNAPOLIS, MD 21401

Ann Stahl, Rob Mann, and Diana DiPaolo Loren

Writing for Many: Interdisciplinary Communication, Constructionism, and the Practices of Writing

ABSTRACT

Though each of us works in different geographical areas (Ghana, the Lower Mississippi Valley, and the Great Lakes), our research is unified by our use of multiple sources to explore the history of colonial encounters and commitment to demonstrate the value of archaeological sources in exploring the materiality of those encounters. Yet, each of us has struggled with writing about these encounters, particularly as we publish in a variety of venues serving multiple audiences of historians, anthropologists, archaeologists, and lay people. We examine the "split literatures" that develop from our efforts to write for a variety of audiences and assess how tensions between scientific discourse and narrative shape these literatures. The interdisciplinary collaboration that is celebrated as part of a rapprochement among history, anthropology, and archaeology requires new approaches to writing, which we explore here.

Introduction: Writing and Interdisciplinary Communication

The last two decades have witnessed a growing rapprochement between history and anthropology that has led some to declare that we are at the "end of Ethnohistory" (Meyer and Klein 1998). So, too, has there been a convergence of interest among archaeologists and their anthropological and historical colleagues. Though differences remain between anthropologically oriented history and historically oriented anthropology (Stahl 2001), this rapprochement has resulted in a blurring of disciplinary boundaries that has implications for audience. The audience for our "academic" writing may today include historians, anthropologists, and archaeologists, as well as members of the societies about which we write. At the same time, anthropology, history, and archaeology have been affected by constructionism—the view that our interpretations of the

past are shaped by contemporary concerns. Both developments have implications for how and for whom we write. Despite the fact that writing consumes a good deal of our professional energy, archaeologists have not reflected to the same extent as practitioners in other fields on writing practices (Geertz 1973; H. White 1973; Canary and Kozicki 1978; Clifford and Marcus 1986). Here, we explore how our practices of writing are shaped by our disciplinary berths (as archaeologists, historians, or anthropologists) and, often less explicitly, by our perceived audience. Just as fundamental, however, are issues of epistemology: what we think we can know and how we think we know it. In broad brush strokes, we explore what we call the "split literatures" among disciplines (scientific/technical, historical, and popular genres) and examine how changing epistemological stances have reshaped their contours. We argue that a growing concern with representation, subjectivity, and constructionism has simultaneously blurred the boundaries among these split literatures *and* further fractured them. Though we work in different areas (Ghana, the Great Lakes, and the Mississippi Valley), we focus on common problems using diverse sources (archaeological, archival, and oral historical). Each of us has struggled to communicate our results to diverse audiences of archaeologists, historians, anthropologists, and other folks. Here we reflect on this process but begin by drawing attention to the fractures that inhibit interdisciplinary communication.

The split literatures that characterize archaeology, anthropology, and history are shaped by distinct disciplinary preoccupations that contribute to the sense that we are not "speaking the same language" (Whittenburg 1983:52). Some locate the problem in an archaeological propensity for jargon (e.g., Whittenburg's [1983:52] advice that we rely less on "'buzz words' and more on a good prose style"). But we argue that split literatures flow from foundational ideas about what we think we are doing as archaeologists, historians, or anthropologists, ideas that are more variegated than a simplistic scientific/humanist dichotomy (e.g., Wilson 1998:8–65). Yet, as

Edward O. Wilson (2002:11) argues, forms of writing reinforce perceived cleavages between "scientific" and "non-scientific" communication. A key distinction among these three genres (scientific/technical, historical, and popular) is the relationship between evidence and narrative, though they are also shaped by disciplinary berths, the goals of publication (e.g., compliance reports compared to synthetic analyses), as well as publication venues. Archaeological publications often adopt a scientific or technical discourse in which evidence (descriptive accounts of artifacts and their patternings) is dis-embedded from a discussion of its significance. Narrative follows evidence, apparently flowing from it. In historical discourse, evidence is more often embedded *within* narrative (cf. Stoler 1989). Source citations in footnotes authorize the narrative, pointing the reader to the evidence that supports narrative claims. These genres share a concern to "present the evidence," a concern shaped by the notion that our accounts should be replicable—that a knowledgeable person working from the same sources could arrive at substantially similar conclusions. Yet, when scholars (whether archaeologists, historians, or anthropologists) write for a broad audience, they feel less compelled to "show the evidence." Here authority rests on professional credentials, and it is assumed that the audience is more interested in narrative (or that they lack the expertise or interest to assess the evidence; cf. Potter 1994; Shackel, et al. 1998:4). So a third genre is characterized by popular accounts that privilege a narrative within which evidence is opaque.

These are the lines of cleavage that make historians and anthropologists impatient with descriptions of pottery, archaeologists impatient with trying to locate the appropriate footnote, and lay audiences unclear about the basis of knowledge claims (also Meyer and Klein 1998: 199). We suspect that our rather cartoonish sketch of these genres will ring familiar (see Stone 1997:23 for a four-fold classification). Despite these differences in the relationship between evidence and narrative, these genres are unified by a sense that the past is knowable. They work from the foundational premise that we can access a lived past through diverse sources—a view that Michel-Rolph Trouillot (1995:14) terms the "storage model of memory-history." This contributes to a view of historical

writing as indexical, as a mapping of historical reality "as it was." Of course, this foundational premise has been undermined by the antipositivist "linguistic turn" and the growing sense that we construct the past in the present. Critiques of positivist epistemology range from the view that texts reference rather than index past realities, to an extreme constructionist view that sees texts as constructed in the present with an arbitrary relationship to the past (for variants of historicism and associated debates, see Reill 1975; Hodder 1986; Shanks and Tilley 1987; D'Amico 1989; Vernon 1994; Joyce 1995; Eley 1996; Hamilton 1996; Spitzer 1996; Windschuttle 1996; Gallagher and Greenblatt 2000). While we do not wish to rehearse the debates that flow from postmodern and poststructural stances on history, we do want to locate ourselves in the debate and explore their effects on these split literatures.

We proceed from a view that the past is knowable, though our knowing is shaped by an interested present. We reject the view that "anything goes," that one story about the past is as good as any other, believing that evidential constraints matter (e.g., Wylie 1992, 1996). Our concern is that standard writing strategies bracket out the "nested frames" (Gallagher and Greenblatt 2000: 25) that shape knowledge of the past, thereby obscuring the interested character of our referential knowledge. The *embedded model* of writing that we explore below works to bring those nested frames into view, to present them as part and parcel of our knowledge of the past. This requires reflexivity about our position vis-á-vis our research agendas, our position in relation to the past we seek to know, and the implications of the knowledge we produce for shaping the present, particularly in relation to descendant populations.

Our approach to the colonial contexts we study has been shaped by Trouillot's (1995) *Silencing the Past: Power and the Production of History*. Trouillot (1995:22) addresses the problem of constructionism in historical inquiry, observing that historians (and we would add archaeologists and anthropologists) rarely examine the production of narratives or the processes by which "evidence" is created (cf. Stoler 1989; Comaroff and Comaroff 1992, 1997). For Trouillot (1995:27), the "mentions" that shape any historical narrative imply "a particular bundle of silences." Silences enter at multiple moments in the production of history: "the moment of fact creation (the making of *sources*); the moment of fact assembly (the making of *archives*); the moment of fact retrieval (the making of *narratives*); and the moment of retrospective significance (the making of *history* in the final instance)" (Trouillot 1995: 26; emphasis in original). These moments are shaped by power, yet Trouillot resists the extreme constructionist stance that we are simply free to make it up, insisting that "the materiality of the sociohistorical process (historicity 1) sets the stage for future historical narratives (historicity 2)" (Trouillot 1995:29).

Elsewhere we have argued (Loren 1999; Mann 1999b; Stahl 1999b, 2001, 2004) that the tension between Trouillot's historicity 1 and 2 is productive because of its simultaneous attention to history making in the present (constructionism) *and* to understanding a lived past (also Hall 1992, 1994, 1999; Potter 1994; Shackel et al. 1998). This tension between history making in the present and knowing the lived past cannot be separated into distinct moments. Rather, as Trouillot illustrates through his analysis of the Haitian Revolution, these processes are embedded in one another. In other words, he resists what we might label "soft" constructionism—the notion that we can reflexively assess and then strip away contemporary influences (including power) to arrive at a more accurate understanding of history. This *subtractive model* implies separate moments in knowing. But, along with Trouillot (1995), we resist "hard" constructionism—one that treats as irrelevant or relinquishes the possibility of knowing a lived past (e.g., Tonkin 1992), what we term an *irreducible model*. Neither do we see the question of how our understanding of the past is shaped by the present as an optional research category (Stahl 2001, 2004)—an issue that only those interested in the "politics of history" should address. As we argue below, this has implications for how we write.

We thus proceed from a different epistemological stance than that which underwrote earlier split literatures. We, too, claim a knowable past but understand that knowing is profoundly shaped by and creative of power in the present, what we termed an embedded model. Trouillot's framework has important implications for how we conceptualize the relationship between archaeology, history, and anthropology (Stahl 2001). The material residues of archaeology—conceived as

an alternate archive (cf. Comaroff and Comaroff 1992:34) shaped by its own "bundles of silences" (Trouillot 1995:26)—can be used to explore documentary silences and vice versa (Hall 1992, 1994, 1999; Lightfoot 1995; Lightfoot et al. 1998; Loren 1999; Mann 1999b; Stahl 1999a, 1999b, 2004). The approach requires retooled methodologies (Stahl 2001:19–40). But it also requires new ways of writing that are attentive to those methods. Because "evidence" is no longer a self-evident category, we need to explore how the *making* of sources, archives, narratives, and history shapes the pattern of silences and mentions that comprise an historical account (cf. Trouillot 1995). This should preclude separating evidence from the context of its production and from narrative as archaeologists are wont to do in scientific/technical discourse. Equally it raises questions about the practice of banishing evidence to footnotes in historical narrative (Meyer and Klein 1998:190, 203). In short, narratives should incorporate an assessment of evidence as a means of making more transparent how it is we know what we know (Gould 1981 for an example of an engaging narrative that simultaneously assesses evidence). From this perspective, popular accounts that present narrative but leave evidence opaque are unsatisfactory.

An embedded model requires new ways of writing that place the tension between evidence and narrative center stage, forms of writing that move beyond standard source criticism (Wood 1990) to explore the processes and contexts that shape evidence and significance (e.g., Trouillot's moments of historical production discussed above). But old habits die hard. It is striking that although many archaeologists recognize the importance of present context on our understanding of the past, discussion of those influences is typically considered in separate forums, contributing to a new form of split literatures. A number of recent volumes focus on the "politics of the past" (Gathercole and Lowenthal 1990; Kohl and Fawcett 1995; Schmidt and Patterson 1995; Diaz-Andreu and Champion 1996; McDavid and Babson 1997; Meskell 1998), but these discussions are often bracketed out of the daily business of archaeology, a bracketing that shapes a sense that this is an ancillary rather than foundational interest. Further, the "politics of the past" literature has not systematically addressed implications for archaeological writing (e.g., McDavid's [1998:96] observation about the continued use of a standard narrative style in Schmidt and Patterson 1995).

We can see parallels in the split literatures produced by structural-functionalist anthropologists. Critiques of structural functionalism focused on the inattention to the colonial context in which structural-functionalist anthropologists worked and their indifference to change wrought by colonialism (e.g., Asad 1973). But as Sally Falk Moore (1994:29–73) amply demonstrated, anthropologists like Bronislaw Malinowski, Meyer Fortes, Monica and Godfrey Wilson, and Lucy Mair were well aware of and wrote about culture contact and social change, though they treated the topic separately from their structural-functional descriptions of tribal societies. Thus the literature produced by Africanists fell into two genres:

> One was the closed description of the way of life of particular African peoples, a kind of timeless abstraction of "the way it probably was" before the colonial period, as if native life could be conceived as a self-contained system uncontaminated by outside contacts. The second mode of description was entirely different and was concerned with the historical moment at which the fieldwork was done. This genre provided data on everything from labor migration to the impact of colonial institutions (Moore 1994:39).

This split in the literature thus flowed from a sense that culture contact was ancillary to the central project of the structural-functionalists.

There are parallels with how archaeologists have dealt with the problem of writing about the past, compared to writing about the making of the past in the present, which some see as an ancillary project. With few exceptions (e.g., Potter 1991, 1994; Schrire 1995), archaeologists have treated these forms of writing as separate genres. In this sense, constructionism has contributed to further fracturing of already split literatures. This fracturing reinforces the sense that such inquiry is optional—that we can choose to be interested (or not) in the "politics of the past." An exception is provided by the sustained case that has been made by archaeologists associated with the Annapolis study over the past decade for incorporating the context of historical production into historical analysis (e.g., Potter 1991, 1994, 1997; Mullins 1998). As a result, calls for reflexivity in historical archaeology have been somewhat narrowly linked to the agenda of

critical theory and the critique of ideology (e.g., Potter 1994:26–44; 1997; South 1997). This has perhaps translated into the view that reflexivity is associated with a particular approach to an "emancipatory archaeology." However, the roots of critical reflexivity are diverse (e.g., di Leonardo 1991; Greenblatt and Gunn 1992; Herzfeld 2001:21–54), and reflexive forms of presentation need not narrowly be linked to an archaeology informed by critical theory.

An embedded model of writing works against the separation of the "politics of knowledge" from the end product. Of course, we must acknowledge positionality and politics in shaping whether or not we choose to incorporate a concern with knowledge production into our writing, for negative consequences can flow from this kind of writing, with consequences for careers and even personal safety. But building again on Trouillot (1995), we need to examine why this is considered an optional category of research, and why when we write about these issues we do it in separate spaces. Unlike the soft or weak constructionism described above, we do not see the goal of examining the processes through which history is made in the present as enabling us to peel those influences away to reveal a truer history; rather, they are part and parcel of the histories we write, and, therefore, that examination needs to be part and parcel of those histories.

History conceived in this way requires new forms of writing. We do not claim to have successfully developed such practices, but we hope that by exploring some of the difficulties we have confronted and the blind alleys we have taken, we can contribute to a dialogue about forms of writing in interdisciplinary spaces. Something that has struck us is how our impulse to write in familiar ways made it difficult for us to communicate an understanding of history and historical process that flowed from an altered epistemology. Here, by offering anecdotes about our writing experiences, we focus on the challenges of modifying writing practices to incorporate reflexivity as well as the unanticipated responses generated by these efforts.

Making History in Banda: Ann Stahl

For more than a decade, I and other members of the Banda Research Project have worked to explore how daily life in the rural Banda area of west-central Ghana was reshaped by changing geopolitical economic changes over the last seven centuries (Stahl 1991, 1994, 1999a, 2001; Stahl and Cruz 1998). I initially conceived of the project as one to document changes using diverse lines of evidence (archaeological, oral historical, and documentary). I began in 1986 by collecting family histories with the goal of learning something of the ethnic and political history of the Banda area. Banda was at the time enmeshed in a chieftaincy dispute, one that began in 1977, was partially resolved in 1997, but has lingering effects to this day. This dispute clearly shaped the contours of oral histories and community perception of our project. The archaeological phase of the project (small scale in 1989 and 1990, then expanded in 1994, 1995, and 2000) was similarly a site of periodic tension. I thus came to the recognition that history is constructed and has saliency in the present through more than a decade of involvement with Banda people. This recognition came practically, sometimes uncomfortably, rather than theoretically. For many years, I drew examples from these experiences to convey to students in a variety of courses how we come to know the past and how that knowledge is shaped by tensions in the present. Yet, I treated these as separate spheres of knowledge and, in retrospect, spoke and wrote about them as if the contemporary context of knowledge production, though important, was antecedent and separable. Once acknowledged, one could proceed to speak and write about the past and our knowledge of it in conventional ways. I was then, and am today, uncomfortable with the excesses of a constructionism that radically doubts the knowability of the past. Trouillot's (1995) volume provided me with the tools to think about these spheres as embedded and relational, rather than separable into distinct realms or moments and shaped my "re-visioning" of a recent book that explores the role of archaeology in historical anthropology through the lens of the Banda case study (Stahl 2001). Whereas an earlier version of the manuscript dealt with the chieftaincy dispute and contemporary ethnic struggles in a chapter on contemporary Banda, the revised version considers the saliency of the dispute for the construction of evidence and its effects on the "bundle" of silences and mentions (following Trouillot 1995) that framed

my interpretation of Banda history. These issues thread through the volume. At the same time, I explore the saliency of the past for contemporary Banda peoples, attempting to tease out the power of history in the present. Standard models of writing fail here—one cannot treat evidence and narrative separately, nor can one relegate evidence to footnotes. How we construct the evidence demands as much attention as what we learn from it.

In retrospect, my effort to bring into view the "nested frames" that shaped my research and the saliency of history in Banda was facilitated by anecdotes. Catherine Gallagher and Stephen Greenblatt (2000:49–74) argue for the saliency of anecdotes in historical analysis. Anecdotes encourage a form of "counterhistory," in that they "perforate the context of narrative explanation" (Gallagher and Greenblatt 2000: 49). In the context of historical literary analysis that is the subject of Gallagher and Greenblatt's volume, they suggest that anecdotes let one "sense that there is something—the 'real'—outside of the historical narrative"; in this sense, anecdotes are "irritatingly antithetical to historical discourse" (Gallagher and Greenblatt 2000:50). In retrospect, the anecdotes that I deployed in *Making History in Banda* do not so much enable a "touch of real" (in the sense of Gallagher and Greenblatt 2000:20–48); rather, by contextualizing knowledge, they forestall closure on the issues under consideration. They underscore for readers that the "truths" about Banda history that I present, though grounded in evidence, are partial, positioned, and subject to reinterpretation (Jameson 1997:15). In other words, they underscore the referential rather than indexical quality of that knowledge, a reference that is shaped by context and interest. This way of writing, while not easy, resulted in a richer account, more open to scrutiny—allowing a variety of readers to discern the basis of my knowledge claims. Yet, I continued to fall back on familiar writing practices: a relatively standard archaeological report (Stahl 1999a) lies behind and is frequently cited in the book as the place where interested readers ("real archaeologists") can go to find detailed archaeological evidence (plans, profiles, contextual information), information largely dis-embedded from the contexts in which we produced it. Still, technical reports can be richly contextualized and attentive to the nested frames that shape them (e.g., McIntosh 1995), and as a discipline, we should encourage this.

Audience, Power, and Local Narratives: Rob Mann

North American archaeologists increasingly find themselves writing for an interested lay audience because of the changing contours of cultural resource management (CRM) and public archaeology. In the U.S., CRM and other technical reports are structured according to state and federal guidelines such as those found in *The Secretary of the Interior's Standards and Guidelines for Archaeology and Historic Preservation*. Still, the resulting "gray literature" epitomizes the split literatures. Technical/descriptive findings are set off from narrative accounts of "conclusions" or "significance." The "historical background" sections that open these reports add a third split to the mix. American historians and ethnohistorians typically have not examined "the role of narrative (or other forms) as a generic class of writing within archaeology" (Pluciennik 1999: 653). Such reflexivity is more common among scholars working in academia than those working in CRM or public archaeology (e.g., Last 1995; but Gibb 1997 for an exception). History in these compliance and technical reports is structured by chronology and tends to view the past as a performed narrative that simply awaits discovery (Fogelson 1989).

Lay audiences readily accept this narrative structure because it presents history in a familiar style. The historical narratives presented in primary and secondary school conditions how we conceptualize historical writing. Patricia Galloway (1991:455) calls this the "cultural hegemony of the narrative text." "History was (and is) constructed according to a set of notions of what *constituted* a history—what it should contain, look like, teach, and cause" (Galloway 1991:461, emphasis original). These histories are presented as "factual," "truthful" and unproblematic narratives of an equally unproblematic and positively knowable past (Krech 1991:349). Certain historical narratives have become part of an Anglo-American historical consciousness and structure our ways of thinking about the past, even if the particular narrative has ceased to be widely read. These narratives are progressive and present his-

tory as a "moral success story" (Wolf 1982:5). They are part of a larger dominant ideology that endows the West with an intrinsic moral virtue such that its ultimate triumph is seen as inevitable (Wolf 1982:5; Abu-Lughod 1989:12–18). As such they serve nationalistic interests that induce a citizenry to "imagine" a lineal, progressive, and natural link between past "forefathers" and contemporary nation-states (Anderson 1983; Trigger 1985:5–6). Such histories help to legitimate and reproduce the status quo; silences are naturalized and certain groups simply drop out of history as they inevitably give way to the march of "civilization."

Fredrick Jackson Turner's (1894) seminal work, "The Significance of the Frontier in American History" is a case in point. While Turner's thesis has come under attack within some segments of academia (Limerick 1987:17–32), it seems still to hold great saliency for a broad segment of the Anglo-American population (Cronon et al. 1992: 4–5; on the persistence of the Turnerian narrative tradition in American historiography, see Klein 1997). Its role in reproducing U.S. capitalist ideology, (e.g., claims to the individualistic and democratic nature of the "frontier"; Cronon et al. 1992:14–15) has been likened to a "grand national anthem" (Warren 1999:369). Land systematically appropriated by "bullets, blades, and blood" is transformed into "free land," there for the taking by industrious and democratic Euramericans (Cronon et al. 1992:15).

At the same time, dominant narratives create spaces for the production of local histories. As Patricia Nelson Limerick (1987:21) notes, Turner's thesis makes invisible many historical actors, including, for example, French Canadian traders. Local histories can and often do seize upon the ambiguities of the dominant narratives in order to create local identities. But no less than the dominant narratives, local histories establish and aid in reproducing and legitimating local power relations (Peel 1995). However, they rarely step outside of or challenge the ideological constraints established by larger narratives, and this has implications for how local histories deal with these contradictions. The story of Zachariah Cicott provides an illustration of local narrative production and demonstrates how it is produced within the interstices of a larger historical framework.

In the early years of the 19th century, Cicott, a *Canadien* trader from Detroit, married a Potawatomi woman named Pe-say-quot and established a trading post on the central Wabash River in present-day Warren County, Indiana. Cicott, his Native American wives (he married a Brotherton Indian named Elizabeth upon Pe-say-quot's death) and their métis children lived at the post until his death in 1850. The Cicott trading post was occupied when Anglo-American expansion was increasingly and rapidly encroaching upon the fur trade society of the Wabash Valley. By the time of his death, Cicott had witnessed the complete disintegration of a way of life that had thrived in the Wabash Valley for more than a century.

During the early-19th century, Anglo-Americans viewed *Canadiens* like Cicott (and their Native American trading partners) as impediments to settlement and the development of agrarian capitalism. They considered the Canadiens to be "as lazy as the Savages" (Lajeunesse 1960: 84–85). With the gaze of the "European improving eye," and its focus on "capitalist futures," Anglo-Americans saw not a multiethnic society thriving in the Wabash Valley but, rather, a vast unimproved "wilderness" (Pratt 1992:61; Vibert 1997:84–118). By the end of his life, when Canadiens were no longer a threat to Anglo-American hegemony, Cicott's Anglo neighbors had developed a more ambivalent attitude towards the few Canadiens who remained. Later in the 19th century, many early settlers recorded this ambivalence in their reminiscences (e.g., Hanes 1880; Yount 1901, 1908; Magee 1983). These "pioneer narratives" simultaneously acknowledged the historical existence of Canadien traders, Native Americans, and the métis and denied the historical significance of the disappearance of the fur trade society they had created (Sleeper-Smith 2001:141–163). Once removed from "the context of their fur trade world," individuals such as Cicott became the romanticized "frontier exotics," so prevalent in pioneer narratives (Sleeper-Smith 2001:149). It is at such moments of retrospective significance (Trouillot 1995:26) that we see the beginnings of local historical narratives of the central Wabash Valley.

Since the late-19th century, Cicott has occupied a prominent role in the local history of the central Wabash Valley. Sparse documentary records and oral traditions, sometimes embellished, con-

tribute to competing and often contradictory versions of Cicott's life. These histories lend a folkloric aspect to Cicott's story, portraying him as both a local hero who fought with American forces during the War of 1812 and as a rogue fur trader of mixed and dubious ancestry (e.g., Goodspeed 1883; Clifton 1913; Whicker 1916, 1925, 1927). In these histories, Cicott is often celebrated as a local entrepreneur who founded the town of Independence and became the wealthiest man in the county. In 1930 these traditions were "brought to life" at a historical pageant. The proceeds of the pageant were used to erect a memorial at Cicott's grave. A bronze tablet placed on the stone commemorates the heroic aspects of the Cicott legend, dubbing him a "faithful" friend to the "white people," while at the same time maintaining a distinction between Canadiens such as Cicott and the Anglo-Americans who ultimately settled the Wabash Valley.

Thus the Canadiens, silenced in dominant histories (e.g., Barnhart and Riker 1971:127–129; Cayton 1996; Carmony 1998), can be celebrated in local narratives without ever really confronting the ideological constraints established by the dominant narratives. So while Cicott still looms large in local history and folklore as a "founding father" of the central Wabash Valley, local inhabitants do not question why no Canadiens, not to mention Native Americans, remain there today. At a higher level of historical consciousness, notions of the "inevitability" of Anglo hegemony mask this seemingly apparent contradiction. When making history in the "final instance" (Trouillot 1995:26), local narratives commemorate at one and the same time both the entrepreneurial aspects of the Cicott story that link him to contemporary concerns with progress and the heroic/tragic aspects that make the disappearance of "his kind" seem natural and unproblematic (for similar accounts of this process, R. White 1991:518–519; Sleeper-Smith 2001:141–163). Local power relations are thus legitimated and local identity is infused with a sense of uniqueness, both of which are reproduced by maintaining control over the production of local narratives.

In 1997, I unintentionally challenged the legitimacy of this local narrative and discovered first hand the power inherent in the story (Trouillot 1995). In 1990 the Warren County Park Board (WCPB) purchased the site of

Cicott's trading post. The goal of the WCPB was to establish an historical and recreational park centered on the interpretation of Cicott's post. Data concerning the physical location and extent of the Cicott occupation of the site were needed in order for the WCPB to proceed with site development and interpretation. Since 1990 I have been involved with the archaeology at the Cicott Trading Post site. Three seasons of fieldwork have focused on locating the main structure on the site and delimiting the spatial extent of the trading post (Mann 1999a:1–4). In 1997 I directed excavations at the site under the auspices of IMA Consulting, Inc., and in April 1999 submitted a final report (Mann 1999a) to the WCPB.

The report was structured in the historical background/technical descriptions/conclusions format described above. The historical background section was presented as a chronological narrative. It was, I thought, a rather straightforward account that used established frameworks for dividing up the history of the Wabash Valley (e.g., "the French period," "the British period," etc.). This traditional framework, however, partially masked my new approach to history that was operating at a barely conscious level.

Interspersed into this narrative was not only a critique of the dominant narratives but also overt references to the fact that my critique stemmed not from a mere reinterpretation of dominant histories but from a recognition that those histories were produced in the present from silences and mentions that were themselves produced in the past (Trouillot 1995). I wove into the narrative of dates, events, and happenings an account of how past power inequities shape the histories we produce in the present. I wanted to explore the contradictory nature of narratives that either silenced or mythologized Canadiens by drawing attention to processes of social and economic marginalization of Canadiens in the past (Mann 1999a:16). Canadiens did not simply disappear from the scene after the fall of New France in 1763. Nor were they the "swarthy" romantic figures of local fur trade narratives. But laying bare the process of narrative production within that very same framework had quite unintended consequences.

For some readers, my approach set up "moments of disjuncture" (Paul Reckner 1999, pers. comm.). These readers encountered ideas that challenged the notion that the past exists independently from the present in a framework that typically naturalizes that foundational premise. A park board member reacted strongly to these ideas and vehemently denounced the historical background section of my report in a letter to the WCPB. It was clear to this reader that my report was not simply a revisionist history, which sought to undermine old "facts" with new ones. That sort of process has long been part of the production of the Cicott saga (Whicker 1916, 1925, 1927; Henry 1982). Instead the author of this letter was dismayed that I had arbitrarily selected and discarded only certain "facts" in order to promote a subversive "political agenda." A charge of "postmodernism" (with vague references to the "thought and methods of Michel Foucault") meant for the author that I had abandoned the "real" past and reduced history to "a back alley cat fight over garbage."

With frequent reference to the "real" past and "historical reality," the author noted that Cicott the entrepreneur is "writ large" in the annals of the Wabash Valley. The ultimate disappearance of Cicott and fur trade society was, according to the author, inevitable as the American system of freehold land tenure was simply a more rational way to settle and exploit productive lands that the Native Americans and Canadiens had left as empty wilderness. I was shocked and dismayed when I received a copy of the letter. My first response was to write a letter to counter to these "accusations." Upon further reflection, though, I have come to see the letter not so much as a personal attack on my interpretation of history but, rather, as an illustration of the power inherent in historical narratives. I had not really challenged any of the "facts" regarding the life and times of Cicott, but I had challenged the notion that those facts existed independently of power relations, both in the past and in the present. By doing so, I had potentially undermined the power of the Cicott narrative to reproduce and legitimate local power relations and local identities that embraced Cicott the myth without ever confronting the tragedy of Cicott the man. By doing so in the guise of a traditional narrative, my report was viewed as especially pernicious and my motives were quickly ascertained to be "political" and subversive.

Constructing Local and Legal Histories
in the Lower Mississippi Valley: Diana
DiPaolo Loren

The colonial past we interpret in popular narratives and scientific literature is often tied to the legal concerns of Native Americans and indigenous peoples. All too often, it is assumed that our popular audience is comprised of the public at large and perhaps Native Americans; while the audience of site reports and academic articles includes other archaeologists and not Native Americans. Although archaeologists call attention to the growing discourse between Native Americans and archaeologists, this exchange usually occurs within a specific venue in anthropology and is often not a primary concern in the construction of scientific literature (for example, discussion between Lepper 2000 and Stapp and Longnecker 2000; also Smith 1994; Handsman and Richmond 1995; Biolsi and Zimmerman 1997).

My research on processes of creolization in 18th-century Louisiana forced me to recognize the concerns of present-day indigenous groups, especially those striving to obtain the status of a federally recognized Native American tribe (Loren 1999). My work draws on diverse sources (images, archaeology, and historic texts) to investigate and highlight the emergence of creole or mixed-blood identities in multiethnic French and Spanish colonial communities (Loren 1999, 2001). Colonial mixed-bloods have been largely silenced in popular histories of the region as well as in archaeological research of the colonial Southeast. This silence is both historical—the result of the tenuous and ambiguous positioning of mixed-bloods in colonial society—and has more recent roots in the perhaps purposeful silencing of these groups in the present. Here, as Trouillot (1995) notes, silences have entered the story at multiple moments. In the course of my research, I have tended to focus more on the creation of silences in the past, yet I continue to reflect on those silences created in the present and their political implications.

I initially envisioned that my project would add to anthropological literature on colonial contexts as well to the general knowledge of the emergence of creole identity (Loren 1999). Indigenous groups in Louisiana who are striving to obtain status as a federally recognized Native American group argue for ethnic and cultural continuity from precolonial to present times. Creolization theories counter this, noting that during the colonial period close contact between Africans, Native Americans, European, and mixed-bloods in "plural" households, communities, and colonies resulted in the emergence of new creole identities (Lightfoot 1995; Upton 1996; Lightfoot et al. 1998; Loren 1999). Nonetheless, I felt that my research would ultimately have little effect on the claims by Louisiana groups because, at the time, I was in New York and I would publish my work in scholarly journals. Requests for academic references and copies of conference papers from these groups, however, were tied to legal issues, forcing me to re-envision my role in the process of producing histories. Obtaining federal recognition requires that Native Americans use diverse sources—oral traditions, scientific evidence, and popular narratives—to legitimate indigenous identity for the federal government.

While we seek to reconcile these split literatures within anthropological discourse, we rarely consider the contradictions that emerge for people outside academia. Native Americans use all available literature (both evidence and narratives) to construct histories with regard to legal definitions surrounding federal recognition, sovereignty rights, and repatriation (Echo-Hawk 2000). Yet in constructing these literatures, archaeologists have different concerns tied to perceived audience and publication venue. In the case of popular narratives, we assume that we are disentangling a past that is poorly understood by the general public. When Native Americans are considered part of this ill-defined audience, interpretations are often structured in ways that will not incite tensions between archaeologists and indigenous groups, which are often already heightened because of recent repatriation debates. Our concern in scientific literature centers on proposing viable interpretations of the past buttressed by archaeological evidence and authoritative citations. We feel free to expose "real" evidence in this literature, and we fall back on the position that history making in the present occurs separately from the knowledge of a lived past.

Native Americans are then caught between the split literatures because we rarely write for them as a specific audience. Few articles on collaboration between archaeologists and Native

Americans appear in academic journals; they are more often published in American Anthropological Association or Society for American Archaeology newsletters (cf. Landsman and Ciborski 1992; Handsman and Richmond 1995). Additionally, the concern of constructing indigenous identity according to current federal definitions rarely affects archaeological interpretations as Native Americans are often not the perceived audience of these works. Yet indigenous groups obtain federal and state recognition, strengthen and supplement claims of sovereignty, exercise repatriation rights, and establish legal claims by adhering to federal definitions that require them to use oral traditions, historical narratives, archaeological literature (including "grey literature"), and academic volumes for which a different audience is assumed and, at times, different evidence presented (cf. Echo-Hawk 2000: 269). Any contradictions among these literatures may potentially influence constructions of indigenous identity and the ability to establish legal claims. As a result, Native Americans continue to be seen as removed from the process of history making. Yet, at the same time, one must acknowledge that many Native Americans and indigenous peoples have dismissed Western history-making to assert instead the primacy of their own oral historical traditions. Further, many Native Americans and indigenous peoples have created their own histories, using a combination of oral histories and archaeological evidence. As Laurajane Smith (1994:305) notes, "groups and individuals actively use material culture to construct ways of knowing the past and present which differ from archaeological and/or bureaucratic versions of the past." As archaeologists, do we have an obligation to incorporate these possibly discordant views into our research agendas? Or does the exclusion of these viewpoints point to further fracturing of "scientific" and "indigenous" evidence and the presumed power of archaeologists in making histories?

The disparity among split literatures speaks to issues of academic authority and the legitimization of history and certain ethnic heritages (Trigger 1984; Landsman and Ciborski 1992; Coombe 1993, 1998; Smith 1994; Jones and Graves-Brown 1996; Conklin 1997; Nason 1997; Wickman 1999). Native Americans are presently forced to structure histories and identities in terms of federal definitions that were, and

continue to be, largely constructed by anthropologists. Self-definitions of identity by indigenous groups are currently in response to, and often in conflict with, state- and federal-defined identities, which often reify indigenous groups as monolithic, bounded entities (Jones and Graves-Brown 1996:2). Although the legal, essentialist portrayal of indigenous groups has come under increasing attack in scholarly literature, there remains the tendency to portray groups as "authentic" using official definitions of identity (Landsman and Ciborski 1992:428; also Coombe 1993; Jones and Graves-Brown 1996; Churchill 1998). These federal definitions emerge from our scientific literature. In her discussion of the relationships among archaeology, ethnicity, and nationalism, Siân Jones (1997:25) notes that anthropological definitions of "indigenous identity" have commonly referred to a group's ethnicity or race that could be discerned through the identification of certain "traits." These definitions of *identity* are repeated through time and, at certain crucial moments, structure legal definitions of *indigenous*. While the laundry list of what constitutes indigenous was often based on dated and historic representations of culture and/or constructed during periods of discord between indigenous people and the government, the continuity of these traits continues to be a legal criterion for legitimizing indigenous identity (Landsman and Ciborski 1992:432; Welsh 1997: 13; Churchill 1998; also Vecsey and Starna 1988; Coombe 1993, 1998; Conklin 1997; Sider 1997). Although this issue is a central topic in the current discourse among anthropologists, museums, and indigenous groups, a compromise has not been realized (Tsosie 1997; Welsh 1997). Roger Echo-Hawk (2000:269) argues that this initiative could stem from the discipline of anthropology, especially in encouraging the production of literature for Indian tribes, museums, and federal agencies useful in implementing Native American Grave Protection and Repatriation Act. Yet indigenous groups, aware of the limitations of these legal definitions, have sought ways to work with them to exercise legal rights. For example, Beth Conklin (1997) shows how Amazonian Indians have used exotic body images that were once seen as the traits that comprised "primitive" stereotypes (such as body paint) in public, political, and legal forums to redefine indigenous identity and pursue goals of self-determination.

Although archaeologists now recognize the very political nature of archaeology in acknowledging, validating, and/or refuting often-competing definitions of identity, despite nationalist and local agendas (Trigger 1984; Landsman and Ciborski 1992; Smith 1994; Schmidt and Patterson 1995; Bernbeck and Pollock 1996; Tsosie 1997; Welsh 1997; Churchill 1998; Echo-Hawk 2000), the authority to construct indigenous history and identity continues to be assumed by archaeologists in scientific narratives. Smith (1994: 302) notes that this struggle over authority also extends to cultural sites: the contentions of different interest groups interpreting and using sites as political, social, and ideological symbols. The separation between history making in the present and the lived past has resulted in the further marginalization of certain indigenous groups from historical and legal processes. When we write for different audiences, and in particular for "scientific" audiences, we rarely include the histories of indigenous groups in our interpretations of the past, even if we assume that these audiences may include Native Americans (cf. Spector 1993; Handsman and Richmond 1995; Wickman 1999). Rather, indigenous histories appear in different contexts and are often subject to anthropological criticism.

While indigenous perspectives are a key aspect in anthropological discourse, when placed against other sources (including written histories), oral traditions are often silenced in scientific literature because of their presumed "invented" nature, especially regarding the deep past (Landsman and Ciborski 1992:434, 440; Echo-Hawk 2000:268). Yet this does not mean that indigenous histories are then included in popular narratives. As Gail Landsman and Sara Ciborski (1992) outline in their discussion of the relationship between anthropologists and the Iroquois, if native histories counter popular accounts (even if the latter serve to reify damaging stereotypes), they are often viewed as "problematic" and "inaccurate."

The construction of colonial history at the present intersection is shaped by the tensions between how Native Americans and archaeologists use the same historical events to construct history. Contemporary legal issues, such as repatriation, have forced some archaeologists to reassess their roles in the historical process and the consequences of the split literatures, but these

disjunctures among literatures signal a residual unwillingness to acknowledge processes of history making and their epistemological limits (cf. Comaroff and Comaroff 1992; Hall 1992, 1994; Smith 1994; Trouillot 1995, 1998; Zimmerman 1997; Mann 1999b; Stahl 1999b, 2001). A first step towards reconciliation is the recognition that scientific and popular literatures often tell different stories and include different silences, which may have some impact on the rights, histories, and claims of groups whose past we are constructing (Landsman and Ciborski 1992). Some have gone further to suggest that we incorporate questions of concern into our research agendas (Biolsi and Zimmerman 1997). The materiality of the past is a common ground from which both archaeologists and Native Americans can work; however, the particulars of how and why that past is constructed remain subject to future debate (for example, debate between Echo-Hawk 2000 and Mason 2000; also Trouillot 1995, 1998; Biolsi and Zimmerman 1997; Nason 1997; Wickman 1999).

I continue to write and speak about colonial Louisiana in different venues, both popular and academic, but my research is now guided by the realization that the audience of both literatures is often one and the same. Because of the implications of this research towards the legal claims of indigenous groups in Louisiana, I have chosen not to make connections from 18th-century to present-day identities. Yet, the 18th century looms large in contemporary constructions of identity, and my work on creolization could still be used to strengthen or refute claims of indigenous identity. To this end, I have not reached a compromise, yet the recognition of the legalities of making history can hopefully lead towards some resolution of these split literatures in the future.

Conclusion

Our goal in this paper has been to encourage a dialogue about writing, less as a form of poetics than as a way of rendering our accounts less opaque, producing writing that encompasses a concern with the *making* of the account into the account itself. Our accounts of the past are things "*made, composed, fashioned*" (Gallagher and Greenblatt 2000:28, emphasis original) and in this sense, "fictions" (Geertz 1973:15–16; cf.

Clifford and Marcus 1986) or, in terms more amenable to archaeologists, "artifacts" (Potter 1997:43). This does not mean that they have no reference to a lived past; what it does mean is that the process of producing the past should be brought into view (also Potter 1997:37); if histories are fashioned, they are composed in relation to our preoccupations, our archives, the position of descendant populations, and so on (e.g. Trouillot's [1995:26] four moments of historical production). Bringing these processes of historical production into view seems particularly important in a period when storytelling and narrative are gaining new prominence as instructional modes (Spector 1993; Praetzellis 1998; Gibb 2000; Gleick and Wilson 2001; Wilson 2002). Ironically, dyed-in-the-wool positivists (Wilson 2002) and poststructuralists (Hodder 1986) agree on the "power of story." For Wilson (2002:10) narrative can make "science human and enjoyable without betraying its nature." The narrative form that he advocates treats "the scientists as protagonists in a story that contains, at least in muted form, the mythic elements of challenge and triumph" (Wilson 2002:10; for examples in paleoanthropology, Leakey and Lewin 1976; Johanson 1981; for accounts that expose the nasty politics of paleoanthropology, Kalb 2001). Storytelling is engaging and entertaining; however, we share Lewis's (2000) disquiet with the emphasis on a singular product while obscuring both its production and alternative possibilities (for example, Orser's 2001:8–10 critique of De Cunzo's 1998 archaeological "story"). Yet, a deconstructionist response is not the only alternative to positivism's self-confident narratives (e.g., Gallagher and Greenblatt 2000:14). Historicism, or the recognition that context frames knowledge, need not be synonymous with the view that all the world's a text (Trouillot 1995). As Stephen J. Gould (1981) adequately demonstrated in his *Mismeasure of Man*, it is possible to explore knowledge production and its consequences in the form of an engaging story.

As we approach the question of writing and interdisciplinary communication in the context of blurred disciplinary boundaries, we need to consider several layered issues: goals, epistemology, and communication. Different academic goals and preoccupations shaped the split literatures discussed above. Yet these literatures were underwritten by a shared epistemology. In this model, interdisciplinary collaboration might be facilitated by simple adjustments in how we communicate with one another. This view is captured by the sentiment that if archaeologists wrote more like historians, mimicking a historical narrative style, it might grease the skids of interdisciplinary collaboration; however, our argument proceeds from a different sense of goals and epistemological foundations. In this context, the goals of interdisciplinary cooperation flow from a concern to overcome the limiting science/humanist dichotomy that has shaped our disciplines. This re-envisioning proceeds from a shared epistemology, one that sees history as a mosaic of silences and mentions shaped by power but grounded in the materiality of the past. By interrogating multiple lines of evidence, we are in a better position to assess and interpret those silences. From this perspective, the challenge of interdisciplinary communication confronts historians, anthropologists, and archaeologists—no one can pursue the business of writing as usual. The challenge is to develop writing strategies that lay open to scrutiny the processes through which we come to know the past and the power that inheres in that knowing, while still making claims about a lived past (also Meyer and Klein 1998; for parallel concerns in museums and site tours, Stone and Molyneaux 1994; Bograd and Singleton 1997; Potter 1997; Potter and Chabot 1997). The written accounts that emerge are potentially rich, though fraught with some of the problems of miscommunication and tension that we have briefly described.

There is a continuing need for multiple types of archaeological and historical writing. Compliance and the ethical requirements of full reporting require technical reports that "present the evidence" so that others may draw on data generated by our research. Yet, we argue that there is scope for embracing an embedded model of writing in technical reports just as in accounts directed at a broader audience (Jameson 1997:13 on the need to broaden the scope and accessibility of compliance reports; also Gibb 2000:3–5). Gallagher and Greenblatt's (2000:25) "nested frames" shape our work from the posing of questions, the conceptualization of research design, the negotiations of interested parties in accessing sites, thorough analysis and more. So far as is possible, we need to bring these nested frames into view, for they are part and parcel of the "data" that we present.

But we also draw attention to another challenge of interdisciplinary communication, one that relates to those outside the narrow ranks of disciplinary specialists and, more specifically, to the interested but often silenced people whose pasts are our focus and for whom the pasts we reconstruct matter most. These are members of our audience who may be caught between the split literatures, as Loren argues in the case of Native Americans. Held to essentialist standards of identity by federal and state bureaucrats or motivated to embrace essentialist conceptions of identity to further claims to resources, subaltern groups have drawn on these diverse literatures to root claims in the present to an authorized past. Academics who have embraced constructionism have come under sharp criticism by those who see constructionism as linked to a politics of "de-authentification" (e.g., Briggs 1996; Friedman 1996; Rogers 1996). We need to acknowledge the extent to which subaltern groups mobilize around essentialized identities as claims to authenticity in a move that Gayatri Spivak (1987:205) terms "strategic essentialism": the "strategic use of a positive essentialism in a scrupulously visible political interest." For academics, this raises the question of "when we should endorse the ennobling lie" (Appiah 1992:175).

This conundrum is shaped by another dichotomy that we have inherited from the "invented tradition" literature that followed from Eric Hobsbawm and Terence Ranger's (1983) influential volume. The authors' choice of the term "invention" was deliberate (Ranger 1993: 79), though that choice had unintended consequences. By distinguishing a marked form of tradition ("invented") from an unmarked one, the term allowed a tacit impression that there is a qualitative difference between the two—that although the colonial period witnessed considerable "invention of tradition," other times and traditions were not so marked. The resulting dichotomy shaped the soft constructionism that we described above and contributed to the notion that by stripping away invented traditions, one could reveal authentic ones, allowing, as Ranger later observed (1993:63–64), essentialism to slip in the back door.

Of course there is a growing literature that works against such a crude dichotomy, one that views tradition not as something enshrined but, rather, something that is worked at because of its relevance—something produced, reproduced, and modified in particular contexts with particular effects through practice (e.g., Ranger 1993; Dirks 1994; Cohn 1996; Stoler and Cooper 1997). This literature works against the distinction between marked and unmarked traditions, between authentic and inauthentic, by identifying the relational practices through which such distinctions are created. Though this literature is directed to an academic audience, it suggests an alternative to strategic essentialism. Though strategic use of essentialisms (Spivak 1987) may continue to be important, we need to be attentive to the ways in which they reproduce existing orders (see di Leonardo 1991, 1998; Hekman 1995). An alternative, as Kwame Appiah (1992:175) observed, is to show that essentialisms like race and national history are not simply falsehoods, "but they are useless falsehoods at best or—at worst—dangerous ones: that another set of stories will build us identities through which we can make more productive alliances." To accomplish this we need to reevaluate our writing strategies, acknowledging the need to be "writing up" and "reaching out." Essentialist notions shape historical discourse at a variety of levels—from the textbooks our children read to the dialogues about federal recognition standards among bureaucrats and politicians in the corridors of power. Here is where there is work to be done in contesting these notions. But this cannot be accomplished by adopting a soft constructionism that succumbs to the same dichotomies that have long structured historical sensibilities nor by adopting a thoroughgoing constructionism that treats the lived past as unknowable. Rather, it will require thorough case studies written in accessible language that rely less on disciplinary authority and more on laying open the logic of reconstruction, case studies that interrogate the making of evidence (sources, archives, and narratives) at the same time as they explore how past practices have shaped current possibilities. This requires that we view subaltern groups in relation to those who wielded the power to shape their lives as well as representations of them, at the same time as the powerful simultaneously made themselves (Stoler and Cooper 1997; for an earlier example, Mintz 1985). Studying the lives of those on "both sides" of the power divide is important to the equation, for it reveals how actors in a variety of positions are mutually implicated in the historical processes that shape present sensibilities and possibilities.

ACKNOWLEDGMENTS

This paper began life as a contribution to a session entitled "Interdisciplinarity: Collaboration or Competition" at The Society for Historical Archaeology Conference on Historical and Underwater Archaeology in Québec City in January 2000. We thank Mary Ellin D'Agostino for the invitation to participate in that session, an invitation that prompted conversations among the authors that might not otherwise have occurred. The final version of this paper benefited from feedback from participants in that session as well as critical readings by Reinhard Bernbeck, Barbara Little, Susan Pollock, Paul Reckner, Michel-Rolph Trouillot, and two anonymous reviewers.

REFERENCES

ABU-LUGHOD, JANET L.
1989 *Before European Hegemony: The World System AD 1250–1350.* Oxford University Press, New York.

ANDERSON, BENEDICT
1983 *Imagined Communities: Reflections on the Origin and Spread of Nationalism.* Verso, London.

APPIAH, KWAME ANTHONY
1992 *In My Father's House: Africa in the Philosophy of Culture.* Oxford University Press, New York.

ASAD, TALAL (EDITOR)
1973 *Anthropology and the Colonial Encounter.* Humanities Press, Atlantic Highlands, NJ.

BARNHART, JOHN D., AND DOROTHY L. RIKER
1971 *Indiana to 1816: The Colonial Period.* Indiana Historical Bureau and Indiana Historical Society, Indianapolis.

BERNBECK, REINHARD, AND SUSAN POLLOCK
1996 Ayodhya, Archaeology, and Identity. *Current Anthropology,* 37 (supplement): 138–142.

BIOLSI, THOMAS, AND LARRY J. ZIMMERMAN (EDITORS)
1997 *Indians and Anthropologists: Vine DeLoria Jr. and the Critique of Anthropology.* University of Arizona Press, Tucson.

BOGRAD, MARK D., AND THERESA A. SINGLETON
1997 The Interpretation of Slavery: Mount Vernon, Monticello, and Colonial Williamsburg. In *Presenting Archaeology to the Public: Digging for Truths,* John H. Jameson, Jr., editor, pp. 193–204. Altamira Press, Walnut Creek, CA.

BRIGGS, CHARLES L.
1996 The Politics of Discursive Authority in Research on the "Invention of Tradition." *Cultural Anthropology,* 11:435–469.

CANARY, ROBERT H., AND HENRY KOZICKI (EDITORS)
1978 *The Writing of History: Literary Form and Historical Understanding.* University of Wisconsin Press, Madison.

CARMONY, DONALD F.
1998 *Indiana 1816–1850: The Pioneer Era.* Indiana Historical Bureau and Indiana Historical Society, Indianapolis.

CAYTON, ANDREW R. L.
1996 *Frontier Indiana.* Indiana University Press, Bloomington.

CHURCHILL, WARD
1998 The Tragedy and the Travesty: The Subversion of Indigenous Sovereignty in North America. *American Indian Culture and Research Journal,* 22(2):16–69.

CLIFFORD, JAMES, AND GEORGE E. MARCUS (EDITORS)
1986 *Writing Culture: The Poetics and Politics of Ethnography.* University of California Press, Berkeley.

CLIFTON, THOMAS A.
1913 *Past and Present of Fountain and Warren Counties.* B. F. Bowen and Company, Indianapolis, IN.

COHN, BERNARD S.
1996 *Colonialism and Its Forms of Knowledge: The British in India.* Princeton University Press, Princeton, NJ.

COMAROFF, JOHN L., AND JEAN COMAROFF
1992 *Ethnography and the Historical Imagination.* Westview Press, Boulder, CO.
1997 *Of Revelation and Revolution,* Vol. 2: *The Dialectics of Modernity on a South African Frontier.* University of Chicago Press, Chicago, IL.

CONKLIN, BETH A.
1997 Body Paint, Feathers, and VCRs: Aesthetics and Authenticity in Amazonian Activism. *American Ethnologist,* 24(4):711–737.

COOMBE, ROSEMARY J.
1993 The Properties of Culture and the Politics of Possessing Identity: Native Claims in the Cultural Appropriation Controversy. *Canadian Journal of Law and Jurisprudence,* 6(2):249–285.

1998 *The Cultural Life of Intellectual Properties: Authorship, Appropriation, and the Law.* Duke University Press, Durham, NC.

CRONON, WILLIAM, GEORGE MILES, AND JAY GITLIN
1992 Becoming West: Toward a New Meaning for Western History. In *Under an Open Sky: Rethinking America's Western Past*, William Cronon, George Miles, and Jay Gitlin, editors, pp. 3–27. W. W. Norton, New York.

D'AMICO, ROBERT
1989 *Historicism and Knowledge.* Routledge, London.

DE CUNZO, LU ANN
1998 A Future after Freedom. *Historical Archaeology,* 32(1): 42–54.

DIAZ-ANDREU, MARGARITA, AND TIMOTHY CHAMPION (EDITORS)
1996 *Nationalism and Archaeology in Europe.* Westview Press, Boulder, CO.

DI LEONARDO, MICAELA
1991 Introduction: Gender, Culture, and Political Economy. Feminist Anthropology in Historical Perspective. In *Gender at the Crossroads of Knowledge: Feminist Anthropology in the Postmodern Era*, Micaela di Leonardo, editor, pp. 1–48. University of California Press, Berkeley.
1998 *Exotics at Home: Anthropologies, Others, American Modernity.* University of Chicago Press, Chicago.

DIRKS, NICHOLAS B.
1994 Ritual and Resistance: Subversion As a Social Fact. In *Culture/Power/History*, Nicholas. B. Dirks, Geoffrey Eley, and Sherry B. Ortner, editors, pp. 483–503. Princeton University Press, Princeton, NJ.

ECHO-HAWK, ROGER C.
2000 Ancient History in the New World: Integrating Oral Traditions and the Archaeological Record in Deep Time. *American Antiquity,* 65(2): 267–290.

ELEY, GEOFF
1996 Is All the World a Text? From Social History to the History of Society Two Decades Later. In *The Historic Turn in the Human Sciences*, Terrence J. McDonald, editor, pp. 193–243. University of Michigan Press, Ann Arbor.

FOGELSON, RAYMOND D.
1989 The Ethnohistory of Events and Nonevents. *Ethnohistory,* 36(2):133–147.

FRIEDMAN, JONATHAN
1996 The Politics of De-Authentification: Escaping from Identity, a Response to "Beyond Authenticity" by Mark Rogers. *Identities,* 3(1):127–136.

GALLAGHER, CATHERINE, AND STEPHEN GREENBLATT
2000 *Practicing New Historicism.* University of Chicago Press, Chicago.

GALLOWAY, PATRICIA K.
1991 The Archaeology of Ethnohistorical Narrative. In *Columbian Consequences*, Vol. 3: *The Spanish Borderlands in Pan-American Perspective*, David H. Thomas, editor, pp. 453–469. Smithsonian Institution Press, Washington, DC.

GATHERCOLE, PETER, AND DAVID LOWENTHAL (EDITORS)
1990 *The Politics of the Past.* Unwin Hyman, London.

GEERTZ, CLIFFORD
1973 *The Interpretation of Cultures.* Basic Books, New York.

GIBB, JAMES G.
1997 Necessary but Insufficient: Plantation Archaeology Reports and Community Action. *Historical Archaeology,* 31(3):51–64.
2000 Imaginary, but by No Means Unimaginable: Storytelling, Science, and Historical Archaeology. *Historical Archaeology,* 34(2): 1–6.

GLEICK, J., AND EDWARD O. WILSON (EDITORS)
2001 *The Best American Science and Nature Writing.* Houghton Mifflin, New York.

GOODSPEED, WESTON A.
1883 *Counties of Warren, Benton, Jasper and Newton, Indiana.* F. A. Battey and Company, Chicago.

GOULD, STEPHEN J.
1981 *The Mismeasure of Man.* W. W. Norton, New York.

GREENBLATT, STEPHEN, AND GILES GUNN
1992 Introduction. In *Redrawing the Boundaries: The Transformation of English and American Literary Studies*, Stephen Greenblatt and Giles Gunn, editors, pp. 1–11. Modern Language Association of America, NY.

HALL, MARTIN
1992 Small Things and the Mobile, Conflictual Fusion of Power, Fear, and Desire. In *The Art and Mystery of Historical Archaeology: Essays in Honor of James Deetz*, Anne E. Yentsch and Mary C. Beaudry, editors, pp. 373–400. CRC Press, Boca Raton, FL.
1994 Lifting the Veil of Popular History: Archaeology and Politics in Urban Cape Town. In *Social Construction of the Past: Representation As Power*, George Clement Bond and Angela Gilliam, editors, pp. 167–184. Routledge, London.
1999 Subaltern Voices? Finding the Spaces between Things and Words. In *Historical Archaeology: Back from the Edge*, Pedro Paulo A. Funari, Martin Hall, and Siân Jones, editors, pp. 193–203. Routledge, London.

HAMILTON, PAUL
1996 *Historicism.* Routledge, London.

HANDSMAN, RUSSELL G., AND TRUDIE LAMB RICHMOND
1995 Countering Colonialism: The Mahican and Schaghticoke Peoples and Us. In *Making Alternative Histories: The Practice of Archaeology and History in Non-Western Settings*, Peter R. Schmidt and Thomas C. Patterson, editors, pp. 87–118. School of American Research Press, Sante Fe, NM.

HANES, JACOB, SR.
1880 Early Recollections of Independence, Warren County, Indiana. *Warren Republican*, 2 September 1880.

HEKMAN, SUSAN
1995 Subjects and Agents: The Question for Feminism. In *Provoking Agents: Gender and Agency in Theory and Practice*, Judith Kegan Gardiner, editor, pp. 194–207. University of Illinois Press, Urbana.

HENRY, JOHN
1982 Zachariah Cicott. In *The Independence Sesquicentennial*, pp. 27–33. Warren County Historical Society, Williamsport, IN.

HERZFELD, MICHAEL
2001 *Anthropology: Theoretical Practice in Culture and Society*. Blackwell Publishers, Oxford.

HOBSBAWM, ERIC, AND TERENCE RANGER (EDITORS)
1983 *The Invention of Tradition*. Cambridge University Press, Cambridge.

HODDER, IAN
1986 *Reading the Past: Current Approaches to Interpretation in Archaeology*. Cambridge University Press, Cambridge.

JAMESON, JOHN H., JR.
1997 Introduction. What This Book Is about. In *Presenting Archaeology to the Public: Digging for Truths*, John H. Jameson, Jr., editor, pp. 11–20. Altamira Press, Walnut Creek, CA.

JOHANSON, DONALD C.
1981 *Lucy, the Beginnings of Humankind*. Simon and Schuster, New York, NY.

JONES, SIÂN
1997 *The Archaeology of Ethnicity: Constructing Identities in the Past and Present*. Routledge Press, New York.

JONES, SIÂN, AND PAUL GRAVES-BROWN
1996 Introduction: Archaeology and Cultural Identity in Europe. In *Cultural Identity and Archaeology: The Construction of European Communities*, Paul Graves-Brown, Siân Jones and Clive Gamble, editors, pp. 3–24. Routledge Press, London.

JOYCE, PATRICK
1995 The End of Social History? *Social History* 20: 73–91.

KALB, JON E.
2001 *Adventures in the Bone Trade: The Race to Discover Human Ancestors in Ethiopia's Afar Depression*. Copernicus Books, New York,.

KOHL, PHILIP L., AND CLARE FAWCETT (EDITORS)
1995 *Nationalism, Politics, and the Practice of Archaeology*. Cambridge University Press, Cambridge.

KLEIN, KERWIN LEE
1997 *Frontiers of Historical Imagination: Narrating the European Conquest of Native America, 1890–1990*. University of California Press, Berkeley.

KRECH, SHEPARD, III
1991 The State of Ethnohistory. *Annual Review of Anthropology*, 20:345–375.

LANDSMAN, GAIL, AND SARA CIBORSKI
1992 Representation and Politics: Contesting Histories of the Iroquois. *Cultural Anthropology*, 7:425–447.

LAJEUNESSE, ERNEST J.
1960 *The Windsor Border Region*. University of Toronto Press, Toronto.

LAST, JONATHAN
1995 The Nature of History. In *Interpreting Archaeology: Finding Meaning in the Past*, Ian Hodder, Michael Shanks, Alexandra Alexandri, Victor Buchli, John Carman, Jonathan Last, and Gavin Lucas, editors, pp. 141–157. Routledge Press, London.

LEAKEY, RICHARD, AND ROGER LEWIN
1976 *People of the Lake*. Anchor Press, Garden City, NY.

LEPPER, BRADLEY T.
2000 Working Together—or Serving Two Masters? *Society for American Archaeology Bulletin*, 18(4):22–25.

LEWIS, KENNETH E.
2000 Imagination and Archaeological Interpretations: A Methodological Tale. *Historical Archaeology*, 34(2): 7–9.

LIGHTFOOT, KENT G.
1995 Culture Contact Studies: Redefining the Relationship between Prehistoric and Historic Archaeology. *American Antiquity*, 60(2):199–217.

LIGHTFOOT, KENT G., ANTOINETTE MARTINEZ, AND ANN M. SCHIFF
1998 Daily Practice and Material Culture in Pluralistic Social Settings: An Archaeological Study of Culture Change and Persistence from Fort Ross, CA. *American Antiquity*, 63(2):199–222.

LIMERICK, PATRICIA NELSON
1987 *The Legacy of Conquest: The Unbroken Past of the American West*. W. W. Norton, New York.

LOREN, DIANA DIPAOLO
  1999 Creating Social Distinction: Articulating Colonial Policies and Practices along the Eighteenth-Century Louisiana/Texas Frontier. Doctoral dissertation, Department of Anthropology, State University of New York at Binghamton.
  2001 Manipulating Bodies and Emerging Traditions at the Los Adaes Presidio. In *The Archaeology of Traditions: Agency and History Before and After Columbus*, Timothy R. Pauketat, editor, pp. 58–76. University of Florida Press, Gainesville.

MAGEE, BENJAMIN FRANKLIN
  1983 *Recollections of Benjamin Franklin Magee, 1834–1915.* Dickinson Printing, Mooresville, IN.

MANN, ROB
  1999a The 1997 Archaeological Excavations at the Cicott Trading Post Site (12WA59). Report of Investigations Number 520 from IMA Consulting, Inc., Minneapolis, MN, to the Warren County Park Board, Williamsport, IN.
  1999b The Silenced Miami: Archaeological and Ethnohistorical Evidence for Miami-British Relations, 1795–1812. *Ethnohistory*, 46:399–427.

MASON, RONALD J.
  2000 Archaeology and Native American Oral Traditions. *American Antiquity*, 65(2):239–266.

MCDAVID, CAROL
  1998 Review of *Making Alternative Histories: The Practice of Archaeology in Non-Western Settings*, Peter R. Schmidt and Thomas C. Patterson, editors. *Historical Archaeology*, 32(4):95–97.

MCDAVID, CAROL, AND DAVID W. BABSON (EDITORS)
  1997 In the Realm of Politics: Prospects for Public Participation in African-American and Plantation Archaeology. *Historical Archaeology*, 31(3).

MCINTOSH, SUSAN (EDITOR)
  1995 Excavations at Jenné-Jeno, Hambarketolo, and Kaniana (Inland Niger Delta, Mali), the 1981 Season. *Publications in Anthropology*, Vol. 20. University of California Press, Berkeley.

MESKELL, LYNN (EDITOR)
  1998 *Archaeology under Fire: Nationalism, Politics, and Heritage in the Eastern Mediterranean and Middle East.* Routledge Press, London.

MEYER, MELISSA L., AND KERWIN LEE KLEIN
  1998 Native American Studies and the End of Ethnohistory. In *Studying Native America Problems and Prospects*, Russell Thornton, editor, pp. 182–216. University of Wisconsin Press, Madison.

MINTZ, SIDNEY W.
  1985 *Sweetness and Power: The Place of Sugar in Modern History*. Viking, NY.

MOORE, SALLY FALK
  1994 *Anthropology and Africa: Changing Perspectives on a Changing Scene.* University of Virginia Press, Charlottesville.

MULLINS, PAUL R.
  1998 Expanding Archaeological Discourse: Ideology, Metaphor, and Critical Theory in Historical Archaeology. In *Annapolis Pasts: Historical Archaeology in Annapolis, Maryland*, Paul A. Shackel, Paul R. Mullins, and Mark S. Warner, editors, pp. 7–34. University of Tennessee Press, Knoxville.

NASON, JAMES D.
  1997 Beyond Repatriation: Cultural Policy and Practice for the Twenty-First Century. In *Borrowed Power: Essays on Cultural Appropriation*, Bruce Ziff and Pratima V. Rao, editors, pp. 195–224. Rutgers University Press, New Brunswick, NJ.

ORSER, CHARLES E., JR
  2001 Race and the Archaeology of Identity in the Modern World. In *Race and the Archaeology of Identity*, Charles E. Orser Jr., editor, pp. 1–13. University of Utah Press, Salt Lake City.

PEEL, J. D. Y.
  1995 For Who Hath Despised the Day of Small Things? Missionary Narratives and Historical Anthropology. *Comparative Studies in Society and History*, 37(3): 581–607.

PLUCIENNIK, MARK
  1999 Archaeological Narratives and Other Ways of Telling. *Current Anthropology*, 40(5):653–678.

POTTER, PARKER B., JR.
  1991 What Is the Use of Plantation Archaeology? *Historical Archaeology*, 25(3):94–107.
  1994 *Public Archaeology in Annapolis: A Critical Approach to History in Maryland's Ancient City.* Smithsonian Institution Press, Washington, DC.
  1997 The Archaeological Site As an Interpretive Environment. In *Presenting Archaeology to the Public: Digging for Truths*, John H. Jameson, Jr., editor, pp. 35–44. Altamira Press, Walnut Creek, CA.

POTTER, PARKER B., JR., AND NANCY JO CHABOT
  1997 Locating Truths on Archaeological Sites. In *Presenting Archaeology to the Public: Digging for Truths*, John H. Jameson, Jr., editor, pp. 45–53. Altamira Press, Walnut Creek, CA.

PRAETZELLIS, ADRIAN
  1998 Introduction: Why Every Archaeologist Should Tell Stories Once in a While. *Historical Archaeology*, 32(1): 1–3.

PRATT, MARY LOUISE
  1992 *Imperial Eyes: Travel Writing and Transculturation.* Routledge Press, London.

RANGER, TERRENCE
1993 The Invention of Tradition Revisited: The Case of Colonial Africa. In *Legitimacy and the State in Twentieth-Century Africa: Essays in Honour of A. H. M. Kirk-Greene*, Terence Ranger and Olufemi Vaughan, editors, pp. 62–111. MacMillan, London.

REILL, PETER HANNS
1975 *The German Enlightenment and the Rise of Historicism.* University of California Press, Berkeley.

ROGERS, MARK
1996 Beyond Authenticity: Conservation, Tourism, and the Politics of Representation in the Ecuadorian Amazon. *Identities*, 3:73–125.

SCHMIDT, PETER R., AND THOMAS C. PATTERSON (EDITORS)
1995 *Making Alternative Histories: The Practice of Archaeology and History in Non-Western Settings.* School of American Research Press, Sante Fe, NM.

SCHRIRE, CARMEL
1995 *Digging through Darkness: Chronicles of an Archaeologist.* University of Virginia Press, Charlottesville, VA.

SHACKEL, PAUL A., PAUL R. MULLINS, AND MARK S. WARNER (EDITORS)
1998 *Annapolis Pasts: Historical Archaeology in Annapolis, Maryland.* University of Tennessee Press, Knoxville.

SHANKS, MICHAEL, AND CHRISTOPHER TILLEY
1987 *Re-Constructing Archaeology.* Cambridge University Press, Cambridge.

SIDER, GERALD
1997 Against Experience: The Struggles for History, Tradition, and Hope among a Native American People. In *Between History and Histories: The Making of Silences and Commemorations*, Gerald Sider and Gavin Smith, editors, pp. 62–79. University of Toronto Press, Toronto, ONT.

SLEEPER-SMITH, SUSAN
2001 *Indian Women and French Men: Rethinking Cultural Encounter in the Western Great Lakes.* University of Massachusetts Press, Amherst.

SMITH, LAURAJANE
1994 Heritage Management As Postprocessual Archaeology? *Antiquity*, 68(259):300–309.

SOUTH, STANLEY
1997 Generalized Versus Literal Interpretation. In *Presenting Archaeology to the Public: Digging for Truths*, John H. Jameson, Jr., editor, pp. 54–62. Altamira Press, Walnut Creek, CA.

SPECTOR, JANET D.
1993 *What This Awl Means: Feminist Archaeology at a Wahpeton Dakota Village.* Minnesota Historical Society Press, St Paul.

SPITZER, ALAN B.
1996 *Historical Truth and Lies about the Past: Reflections on Dewey, Dreyfus, de Man, and Reagan.* University of North Carolina Press, Chapel Hill.

SPIVAK, GAYATRI CHAKRAVORTY
1987 *In Other Worlds: Essays in Cultural Politics.* Methuen, New York.

STAHL, ANN B.
1991 Ethnic Style and Ethnic Boundaries: A Diachronic Case Study from West Central Ghana. *Ethnohistory*, 38(3):250–275.
1994 Change and Continuity in the Banda Area, Ghana: The Direct Historical Approach. *Journal of Field Archaeology*, 21(2):181–203.
1999a The Archaeology of Global Encounters Viewed from Banda, Ghana. *African Archaeological Review*, 16(1): 5–81.
1999b What is the Use of Archaeology in Historical Anthropology? In *The Entangled Past: Integrating History and Archaeology. Proceedings of the 30th Annual Chacmool Conference*, Matthew Boyd, editor, pp. 4–11. Department of Archaeology, University of Calgary, Alberta.
2001 *Making History in Banda. Anthropological Visions of Africa's Past.* Cambridge University Press, Cambridge.
[2004] Making History in Banda: Reflections on the Construction of Africa's Past. *Historical Archaeology*, in press.

STAHL, ANN B., AND MARIA DAS DORES CRUZ
1998 Men and Women in a Market Economy: Gender and Craft Production in West Central Ghana c. 1775–1995. In *Gender in African Prehistory*, Susan Kent, editor, pp. 205–226. Altamira Press, Walnut Creek, CA.

STAPP, DARBY C., AND JULIA G. LONGNECKER
2000 Dr. Lepper Is Wrong. *Society for American Archaeology Bulletin*, 18(4):22–24.

STOLER, ANN LAURA
1989 Rethinking Colonial Categories: European Communities and the Boundaries of Rule. *Comparative Studies in Society and History*, 31(1):134–161.

STOLER, ANN LAURA, AND FREDERICK COOPER
1997 Between Metropole and Colony: Rethinking a Research Agenda. In *Tensions of Empire: Colonial Cultures in a Bourgeois World*, Frederick Cooper and Ann Laura Stoler, editors, pp. 1–56. University of California Press, Berkeley.

STONE, PETER G.
1997 Presenting the Past: A Framework for Discussion. In *Presenting Archaeology to the Public: Digging for Truths*, John H. Jameson, Jr., editor, pp. 23–34. Altamira Press, Walnut Creek, CA.

STONE, PETER G., AND BRIAN L. MOLYNEAUX (EDITORS)
1994 *The Presented Past: Heritage, Museums, and Education.* Routledge, London.

TONKIN, ELIZABETH
  1992 *Narrating Our Pasts: The Social Construction of Oral History.* Cambridge University Press, Cambridge.

TRIGGER, BRUCE
  1984 Alternative Archaeologies: Nationalist, Colonialist, and Imperialist. *Man,* 19:355–370.
  1985 *Natives and Newcomers: Canada's "Heroic Age" Reconsidered.* McGill-Queen's University Press, Kingston, ONT.

TROUILLOT, MICHEL-ROLPH
  1995 *Silencing the Past: Power and the Production of History.* Beacon Press, Boston, MA
  1998 Silencing the Past: Layers of Meaning in the Haitian Revolution. In *Between History and Histories: The Making of Silences and Commemorations,* Gerald Sider and Gavin Smith, editors, pp. 31–61. University of Toronto Press, Toronto, ONT.

TSOSIE, REBECCA
  1997 Indigenous Peoples' Claims to Cultural Property: A Legal Perspective. *Museum Anthropology,* 21(3): 5–11.

TURNER, FREDRICK JACKSON
  1894 The Significance of the Frontier in American History. In *Proceedings of the State Historical Society of Wisconsin at Its Forty-First Annual Meeting, Held December 14, 1893,* pp. 79–112. Madison.

UPTON, DELL
  1996 Ethnicity, Authenticity, and Invented Traditions. *Historical Archaeology,* 30(2):1–7.

VECSEY, CHRISTOPHER, AND WILLIAM STARNA
  1988 *Iroquois Land Claims.* Syracuse University Press, Syracuse, NY.

VERNON, JAMES
  1994 Who's Afraid of the "Linguistic Turn"? The Politics of Social History and Its Discontents. *Social History,* 19(1):81–97.

VIBERT, ELIZABETH
  1997 *Trader's Tales: Narratives of Cultural Encounters in the Columbia Plateau, 1807–1846.* University of Oklahoma Press, Norman.

WARREN, LOUIS S.
  1999 Vanishing Point: Images of Indians and Ideas of American History. *Ethnohistory,* 46(2):361–372.

WELSH, PETER H.
  1997 The Power of Possession: The Case against Property. *Museum Anthropology,* 21(3):12–18.

WHICKER, J. WESLEY
  1916 Zachariah Cicot. In *Historical Sketches of the Wabash Valley.* J. Wesley Whicker, Attica, IN.
  1925 Zachariah Cicot. *Indiana Magazine of History,* 21(1): 100–08.

  1927 Pierre Moran or Chief Parish of the Potawatomi Indians. *Indiana Magazine of History,* 23(2):229–236.

WHITE, HAYDEN
  1973 *Metahistory: The Historical Imagination in Nineteenth-Century Europe.* Johns Hopkins University Press, Baltimore, MD.

WHITE, RICHARD
  1991 *The Middle Ground: Indians, Empires, and Republics in the Great Lakes Region, 1650–1815.* Cambridge University Press, Cambridge.

WHITTENBURG, JAMES P.
  1983 But What Does It Mean? A Historian's View of Historical Archaeology. In *Forgotten Places and Things: Archaeological Perspectives on American History,* Albert E. Ward, editor, pp. 49–54. Center for Anthropological Studies, Albuquerque, NM.

WICKMAN, PATRICIA RILES
  1999 *The Tree That Bends: Discourse, Power, and the Maskókî People.* University of Alabama Press, Tuscaloosa.

WILSON, EDWARD O.
  1998 *Consilience: The Unity of Knowledge.* Alfred A. Knopf, New York.
  2002 The Power of Story. *American Educator,* 26(1): 8–11.

WINDSCHUTTLE, KEITH
  1996 *The Killing of History: How Literary Critics and Social Theorists Are Murdering Our Past.* Free Press, New York.

WOLF, ERIC R.
  1982 *Europe and the People without History.* University of California Press, Berkeley.

WOOD, W. RAYMOND
  1990 Ethnohistory and Historical Method. In *Archaeological Method and Theory,* Vol. 2, Michael B. Schiffer, editor, pp. 81–109. University of Arizona Press, Tucson.

WYLIE, ALISON
  1992 The Interplay of Evidential Constraints and Political Interests: Recent Archaeological Research on Gender. *American Antiquity,* 57(1):15–35.
  1996 The Constitution of Archaeological Evidence: Gender Politics and Science. In *The Disunity of Science: Boundaries, Contexts, and Power,* Peter Galison and David J. Stump, editors, pp. 311–343. Stanford University Press, Stanford, CA.

YOUNT, N. H.
  1901 Zachariah Cicot, an Eccentric French Trader. In *Pearls along the Wabash: The Reminiscences of Newlin Hoover Yount,* Doris Holtman Cottingham, editor, pp. 3–4. Warren Graphic Printing Company, Williamsport, IN.
  1908 Reminiscences of Early Days in Warren County. *Warren Review,* 10 September 1908.

Ann Stahl, Rob Mann, and Diana DiPaolo Loren

ZIMMERMAN, LARRY J.
  1997 Anthropology and Responses to the Reburial Issue. In
        *Indians and Anthropologists: Vine DeLoria Jr. and the
        Critique of Anthropology*, Thomas Biolsi and Larry J.
        Zimmerman, editors, pp. 92–112. University of Arizona
        Press, Tucson

ANN STAHL
DEPARTMENT OF ANTHROPOLOGY
BINGHAMTON UNIVERSITY
BINGHAMTON, NY 13902-6000

ROB MANN
REGIONAL ARCHAEOLOGY PROGRAM
MUSEUM OF NATURAL SCIENCE
LOUISIANA STATE UNIVERSITY
BATON ROUGE, LA 70803-3216

DIANA DIPAOLO LOREN
PEABODY MUSEUM OF ANTHROPOLOGY AND
ETHNOLOGY
HARVARD UNIVERSITY
11 DIVINITY AVENUE
CAMBRIDGE, MA 02138-2019

Christopher N. Matthews

Public Dialectics: Marxist Reflection in Archaeology

ABSTRACT

The public dimensions of archaeological practice are explored through a new method called Marxist reflexivity. This use for Marxism draws a parallel with recent reflexive archaeologies that highlight the impact of archaeologists and archaeological processes on the creation of archaeological records. Though similar in this sense of critique, reflexive and Marxist archaeologies do not often overlap, as each is essentially driven by a distinct agenda and logic. Through a critical review of four public programs undertaken in historical archaeology, this distinction is disassembled.

Introduction

Marxist critical archaeology strives to align itself with traditions of modern criticism to rework archaeology from a scientific analysis of the human past to a practice dedicated to using the past to change the present (Leone et al. 1987; Shanks and Tilley 1987; McGuire 1992). By definition, such work is a form of public archaeology in that living cultures and concerns are intimately involved in the way archaeological investigations are designed. However, there are a variety of ways that such archaeologies can be envisioned. An examination of these approaches should shed light on their differential effectiveness and provide a way for archaeologists to better articulate their own and others' interests in the production of archaeological work. Such a review may be found below, but the purpose of this work is guided by a particular concern.

The approach developed draws on critical theory to better define archaeology in the public sphere. While public archaeology is often regarded as a key space for articulating critical theory (Potter 1994), rarely is this approach formulated so that archaeology itself is the subject of critical analysis. Too often, critical archaeologists engage with significant public issues such as nationalism (Kohl and Fawcett 1995; Meskell 1998), racism (Blakey 1987; Franklin 1997, 2001), and class conflict (McGuire and Walker 1999) and then turn to archaeology for solutions without situating its essence amidst the very social issues that are being engaged. In other words, archaeology is regarded as a separable component of the social fabrics with which archaeologists engage. Such instances objectify archaeology and its potential. They also reverse the basis of Marxist praxis, which insists on a greater sense of fluidity in how archaeology in theory relates with its everyday practical action (McGuire and Wurst 2002). Ultimately, such an approach undermines the capacity for Marxist archaeologies to sustain an active focus on social change. To develop an alternative dialectical approach to public archaeology, this article reviews why archaeology, as practice and symbol, must be the central subject of critical thinking by Marxist archaeologists. The specific effort is toward re-situating archaeology in public from a place created by and for archaeologists to the place defined in the social construction of archaeology that results from engaging archaeology with those already working for change in the modern world.

This discussion involves a consideration of reflexive hermeneutics in archaeology to understand how to recognize the existence of archaeology in the living world. It then elaborates how the dominant reflexive approach in archaeology can be made useful for developing a specifically Marxist reflexive praxis. Finally, a review of a set of public historical archaeologies at Five Points in New York, Ludlow in Colorado, Annapolis in Maryland, and Tremé in Louisiana identifies the different themes and interests that underlie the articulation of archaeology with the public. These examinations establish a four-stage approach for defining and interpreting the archaeological significance of the public interests that set archaeologists to work. The goal is to accumulate a new set of foundations for recognizing and centering archaeology's public significance so that the Marxist critique may emerge in archaeological practice rather than in just its theoretical positions.

Reflexive Hermeneutics and the Social Construction of "Archaeology"

To rethink public archaeology, it is useful to adopt the hermeneutic approach outlined by Ian Hodder (1999) in *The Archaeological Process*. While not a Marxist approach, Hodder's method, when expanded and critiqued, provides a firm foothold for dialectically situating archaeology in public in a productive and creative fashion. Hodder seeks to develop a nondichotomous method for archaeological interpretation. This means breaking down the processsualist Cartesian subject (archaeologist)-object (archaeological record) opposition so that these poles exist in a circular, essentially iterative, relationship. Hodder critiques the Cartesian dichotomy that lies at the root of processsualist archaeology for masking the contexts of archaeological finds and research agendas and thus the slippages and fluidities that are produced by the influence of such contexts on interpretation. He argues that oppositional thinking hides the important detail, that what archaeologists believe to be true now will act as a basis for any future truth claims. Hodder emphasizes that interpretation, not fact, resides at the foundation of knowledge.

In the processsualist Cartesian approach, archaeologists are instead presented with a stable archaeological record that is discovered in nature by stable archaeological techniques that reveal its contents and, with the application of normal disciplinary method and theory, produce its meaning. Here the foundation of knowledge is fact, not belief. As Hodder suggests, the Cartesian approach makes the archaeological record appear to act, when effectively examined, as is its own agent since the actions of archaeologists should be made increasingly invisible behind the facts they discover. Hodder's alternative focuses on the impossibility of removing the agency of archaeologists from archaeological work, especially their foundational interpretations that "act" as facts but are more realistically propositions of truth. The circular basis of the hermeneutic approach can accommodate this much-less-secure basis of knowledge because it questions and re-questions

assumptions based on the new knowledge gained by making them. This back-and-forth tacking, Hodder asserts, makes the interpretive basis to archaeological knowledge more secure and equally more open to productive criticism and/ or multiple interpretations.

Marxists should applaud this approach for its goals but improve on it by bringing to bear the critical eye Marxism has for understanding the real conditions that social action produces and is produced by. This means in addition to applying Hodder's ideas in practice, it is vital to critically evaluate the social positions that archaeologists assume or, more specifically, are allowed to assume when they produce interpretations of the past. Here, this means archaeology's social relations of production, including but not limited to the class positions and relations that archaeologists hold and aspire to within the larger societies of which they are a part. A Marxist reflexivity thus asks: what political economies come to bear on how archaeologists access sites, develop research questions, and even reflexively explore their own presence in archaeological work? The focus is on these sorts of "public" positions. A return to Hodder's study explains.

One means for materializing the hermeneutic circle in archaeological practice is to work against the grain of individualized archaeological analysis. While all archaeologists to a degree rely on the interpretation of archaeological remains by individual archaeologists, Hodder argues that collectivities can be developed in practice that serve as more knowledgeable agents in the interpretive process. His example from his own research project at the Neolithic tell site of Çatal Hüyük in Turkey is to establish spaces in the archaeological project for collaboration between field and lab specialists so that field interpretations of, for instance, burned bone or deposit dates can be developed in conjunction with laboratory artifact specialists. Artifact processing occurs rapidly at Çatal Hüyük, and lab specialists tour the site daily to work with field specialists so that the gulf between excavation and analysis is minimized, producing more secure bases for interpretation. Additionally, interpretations are made cooperatively using the differential sorts of expertise that define the archaeological project, overarched by the commitment by all to reflect on and keep open the assumptions these various specialists make. To assist in the latter, Hodder innovatively employs a cultural anthropologist who questions and analyzes the various project specialists to reveal and mediate underlying concerns about their own work *and* their collective work with others.

This self-reflexivity has been a hallmark of Hodder's postprocessual archaeology since the 1980s. It shows that at Çatal Hüyük he has carefully studied how archaeological knowledge is produced in excavation and analysis, and he worked hard to bring this awareness to a prominent position in the development of a new interpretive method. Yet, for such an approach to work for Marxists, archaeologists need to consider some very important additional issues: What *social* processes allow archaeologists who use such a method to exist, meaning what social positions and relations do interpretive archaeologists occupy and employ in the grander scheme of the site/project as part of the modern world? If the project is truly reflexive, has it made space for these social processes in the interpretation of the archaeological remains? In other words, does the interpretive circle make room for those social relations that allow archaeologists to claim the legitimacy of what they do to the nonarchaeological world that has made space for them? This is a vital step if researchers are to truly advance archaeology's reflexivity towards the nondichotomous status Hodder seeks. The goal of a Marxist reflexivity is to not only break down the opposition of the archaeologist and the archaeological record but also to redefine the very processes by which archaeological remains and their interpreters are related in the public sphere. One way to see the difference here is to recognize that in Hodder's collectivities the archaeological record remains an *object* of discovery and interpretation, though now by more diverse sets of specialists working cooperatively, that exists essentially outside the contemporary world. The more radical approach proposed here suggests that the record itself be established as a subject within the interpretive process. This does not mean revitalizing the agency granted it in the processualist approach but establishing a method that makes the record mediate the processes by which archaeologists and nonarchaeologists relate. The goal is to use this approach to develop a method for collective

action linking archaeologists and their publics that uses shared interests in the archaeological past as the site of common ground.

There are two implications of this approach that must be dialectically articulated for archaeology to work against its dichotomies. First, archaeologists must establish the contingency of their social position as experts within a certain prescribed system. Archaeological professionals are sustained not only by their training and the funding that supports its application but also equally by the existence in dominant society of the space they occupy to be archaeologists. This space must be examined for how it was formed, and for what archaeologists and others do now to sustain it, especially regarding public interpretations of the past. Then archaeologists must critically evaluate and incorporate these public interests into the foundations of the assumptions made in and about interpretive projects. The key here is to focus on the idea of the public significance of archaeology, and this is the focus of the reviews presented below. Second, archaeologists must recognize that the material remains of the past are the essential objects that define their living presence. Before any remain is interpreted, archaeologists should recognize that they interpret themselves into existence by referencing the material they alone control in defining it as archaeological. Following Hodder's hermeneutics, archaeologists must not only tack back and forth between objects and their meanings but also between objects and the identity claims of being an archaeologist that allow certain persons the right to be interpreters of the past in the living world. Here archaeological remains must be examined for how they legitimize the claims made on them by archaeologists and others regarding their meanings in the living world. Thus, a Marxist reflexivity expands on Hodder's hermeneutics by emphasizing the real existence of archaeological remains as part of the living social world and the use of such remains to negotiate spaces for social action, including especially the actions that legitimize and empower archaeologists.

Numerous archaeologists have worked to understand these social aspects of archaeology by looking at its history and its role in living heritage debates (Trigger 1989; Patterson 1995; Meskell 1998). Recently some have worked to better articulate the social bases of archaeology with the way archaeological research is done. The most prominent literature for this is on the responses by archaeologists and Native Americans regarding the reburial and study of ancient human remains by those who have sought to define ways for the archaeology of Native America to proceed despite its inherent colonialist origins (Zimmerman 1989, 1997; Biolsi and Zimmerman 1997; Swindler et al. 1997; Thomas 2000; Watkins 2000; Fine-Dare 2002). A very productive related approach, with firm roots in the Marxist tradition in archaeology, is research in American historical archaeology that has sought to directly identify itself with the public concerns of living and descendent communities who are currently working for social change. Three of the best public programs in historical archaeology that may be set in this vein are reviewed—the Five Points project in New York, the Colorado Coal Field War project, and the Archaeology in Annapolis project—as well as a program in New Orleans designed by the author to show different approaches to working with the public significance of archaeology. The point is to elucidate the different ways that the public resides within archaeology and to critically evaluate how archaeologists have responded to this discovery.

Myth Busting—Five Points

One of the great claims of American historical archaeology is its ability to challenge popular historical assumptions about the everyday lives of hidden and silenced peoples such as slaves, women, and members of the working class. Many archaeological studies have in fact taken their role to be myth busters in the sense that the archaeological record is used to contradict stereotypes of poverty, backwardness, acquiescence, and inferiority that surround historically marginalized peoples and that sustain their continuing subordination (Mayne and Murray 2001; Yamin 2001a, 2001b; Horning 2002; Reckner 2002). Archaeology is regarded as a public resource that describes the "way it really was" for these people, that they were better people and fared better than the popular mytho-historical accounts suggest. These studies are considered public archaeology here because they work in dialogue with popular narratives about local and regional pasts. The archae-

ology of the 19th-century working-class Five Points neighborhood in New York City, which adopted the "important goal" of constructing "a corrective to biased representations of the neighborhood while avoiding a romanticized image of poverty" (Reckner 2002:107), is an example of research where this myth-busting role was made central.

Paul Reckner (2002) discusses how the 19th-century "urban sketches" genre of reporting and writing produced powerful narratives of urban life in New York and elsewhere that continue to resonate in public today. The basic theme is the depiction of the inner-city slum as a wasteland of poverty and vice that was home to the dangerous classes. Reckner shows that the vast array of literature and analysis from the period produced a "moral causality narrative" in which the problems of the slums were seen as the result of the social and moral failings of those living there. Though his principle discussion relates the struggle of the Five Points archaeology project to overcome the influence of this narrative in the representation of their work in the local press, he cites that even project archaeologists fell prey to it by explaining that the large amount of pottery recovered at the site may be the result of theft, a common assumption about the poor when viewed through the lens of the moral causality narrative. Reckner's article clearly relates the struggle to work not only with the remains of the past but also equally with the space those remains inhabit in public today. In this case, this space was already occupied by a powerful master narrative that overdetermined much of what the public and even the archaeologists would gather from the archaeology. It became the goal of the project to provide another perspective to explain the past at Five Points and to create an alternative interpretation that could supplant the dominant mythic tropes they discovered in public. This is the first step in a Marxist reflexivity. Exploring the alternatives produced at Five Points, though, shows some of the limitations that archaeologists can face.

Among the most powerful results of the Five Points project are Rebecca Yamin's (1998, 2001a) alternative narratives produced in a semifictional storytelling style. Yamin draws from specific archaeological features associated with documented Five Points households to tell richly illustrated vignettes about individual Five Pointers. These stories are told from an insider's perspective by being written in the first person and through detailed site-specific descriptions of the everyday spaces, activities, thoughts, and desires of working-class Five Pointers. By amplifying the archaeological remains, which by themselves, according to Yamin (2001a:162,164,167), have "no story line, [and] no plot," but with "acts of imagination," the narratives are intended to provide a "process of understanding . . . the *humanity* of the people who lived at Five Points [emphasis added]."

As Reckner shows, the master tropes of the urban slum produced in the 19th century were overwhelmingly negative accounts, and Yamin and her colleagues show how their effect underwrites a public belief that past working-class lives were on the whole disrespectable. To offset this, Yamin (2001a:159) argues that Five Pointers challenged the limitations of their circumstances, which (in agreement with the 19th-century urban sketches) she identifies as "overcrowded" and "insanitary," by practicing respectable behaviors. These included purchasing ceramic figurines, gothic-style white granite tableware, and plenty of meat. Such finds, Yamin argues, shows these people enjoyed luxuries beyond the bare necessities and that they found ways, such as in the enjoyment of the clean lines of the gothic patterns, to counter the circumstances in which they lived. These are all excellent observations, but whether they challenge public beliefs about working-class lives gleaned from the popular urban sketches is doubtful. This is not just because archaeology is a marginal discourse but, rather, because it is an effect of the Five Points archaeologists' use of "respectability" as their main theme.

Regarding the diverse groups at the site, Yamin (2001a:166) writes, "they shared the stigma of living at Five Points and a penchant for respectability in spite of it." The characteristics that define respectability are never established, nor is it said whose respect these people were getting and/or desiring. Rather, whether these actions meet standards of respect has to be judged, or to follow the archaeologists, they are respectable, inasmuch as they defy the master narrative descriptions of working-class poverty and vice. In placing so much emphasis on an under-defined respectability produced

in reference to the moral causality narratives, the archaeologists inadvertently reproduce and legitimize the basis of knowledge they sought to challenge and overcome. Without further clarification, researchers can only employ the characteristics of respectability defined by the highly critical and presumably biased 19th-century middle-class authors to evaluate these past working-class lives. Although Yamin (2001a:166) argues that "seen from the inside, through the [archaeologist's] narratives, respectability appears not as an imitation of middle-class behaviours but as an important value in working-class life," it is only those middle-class aspects of respectability which the Five Pointers violated that are open for discussion. In other words, it is only possible to make the dubious and contradictory conclusion that middle-class respectability was a value in working-class lives.

Such a contradiction is sustained by the project's analysis that places heavy significance on shopping and consumption. Five-Pointer households are shown to be littered with consumer goods like ceramic plates and figurines that reflect the freedoms and pleasures that the urban marketplace offered. Rather than critically considering how the urban poor were co-opted into the market as part of the development of modern capitalist social relations of production and consumption, readers are given an imaginary insider's perspective in which the market is solely a source of wonder, freedom, and a means for acquiring respect (Wurst and McGuire 1999). For this to be the case, the working-class immigrants they write about would have to overlook the social relations that drove them from their homelands and into the overcrowded, insanitary, and notorious American slums. In other words, they would have to adopt the American middle-class ideology of upward mobility that would allow them to believe that their present circumstances were temporary and would be overcome.

What is required is a more substantial engagement with the idea of respectability as it pertains to understanding class *relations* and the way working people lived—not in an insular class-defined world but in a liminal space that balanced the capacities and limitations they had to improve the overwhelmingly harsh conditions in which they lived. More broadly, when mitigating the influence of powerful narratives, archaeologists must not simply counter with seemingly positive alternatives. A position that is cognizant of the today's role of archaeologists as storytellers must be developed. Work must be done to analyze through research how that position of archaeology is as much a product of contemporary cultural concerns, social interests, and class positions as it is a result of the archaeological record. In other words, when approaching and countering powerful myths, archaeologists need to consider that such stories serve as the basis for the powerful ideologies (and the struggles that brought them about) that legitimize equally the archaeological investigations undertaken and the myths that archaeologist seek to depose. The case here is that the narrative developed on working-class respectability appeared to be independent and alternative but was more realistically only a new component of the existing one and another middle-class attempt to articulate the problem of the working class. This limitation on producing archaeological alternatives can be handled more directly. Turning to consider other projects shows how this has been done.

Advocacy—Ludlow

Facing the challenge of knowing and acting in the terms and interests of subordinate people, some archaeologists have proactively engaged with social movements to define their public position. This effort involves analyzing the living world to understand the public organizations and perspectives that constitute it and working to "fuse" (Ludlow Collective 2001:95) archaeology with the movements that archaeologists seek to promote. This work is not positioned within the realm of the public discourse on the past as defined by master narratives but within the social structures that serve to locate people (and their perspectives on the past) in the living world. An example of this sort of approach is the Archaeology of the Colorado Coal Field War of 1913–14 being undertaken by the Ludlow Collective (Duke and Saitta 1998; Ludlow Collective 2001; McGuire and Reckner 2002; Walker and Saitta 2002; Wood 2002a, 2002b). The distinction of this project is its self-defined basis in activism and advocacy. As Philip Duke and Dean Saitta (1998:4) write, "we are tired of . . . pretensions to a value-free

and politically neutral archaeology . . . We are interested in the radical class transformation of society, and we seek in all of our scholarly work to provide some tools for accomplishing this." Such a clear-cut political stance is the first step to fusing archaeology with alternative public interests, and this project clearly defines what interests they support.

The most basic public connection forged by the Ludlow Collective is between their research at the site of the Ludlow massacre and the neighboring company town of Berwind and the interests in the memorialization of the massacre by workers today, especially the United Mine Workers (UMW). The story of the Ludlow massacre is shocking. Working under oppressive and dangerous conditions, miners organized and struck in 1913 demanding "the right to unionize, higher pay, and that existing Colorado mining laws be enforced" (Ludlow Collective 2001: 96). Because of the strike, the Colorado Fuel and Iron Company (CFI) forced the miners out of company housing, and most moved to UMW tent camps nearby, the largest of which was at Ludlow. The strike persisted through the winter of 1913–14, climaxing in April 1914 with the killing at the Ludlow camp of 20 people including 2 women and 11 children by company guards armed with machine guns and under the command of the Colorado National Guard. The massacre captured the nation's attention as progressives demonized John D. Rockefeller, Jr., chair of CFI, for violating the rights of miners and their families (Ludlow Collective 2001:96–98).

Such a catastrophe caused not only national concern but also altered national consciousness regarding workers' rights. Questions were asked by all about what effect the killing of essentially innocent strikers and their families meant for American democracy. Although for union workers the meaning was clear: as union workers visiting the site told Saitta, the story of the Ludlow Massacre is just part of the story of the American working class being suppressed (Duke and Saitta 1998:3). This reaction has led the archaeologists to emphasize the often overlooked importance of class in archaeological research. Duke and Saitta (1998) argue that class is the most vital relation for understanding social action, but it is also the one major social marker (others being, e.g., race, ethnicity, gender, and sexuality) that has received only scant attention by archaeologists. They conclude that class is not only a marker of subjectivity for archaeological subjects but is also a key component for defining archaeologists themselves:

> Archaeology has typically served middle-class interests. It is part of the intellectual apparatus (things such as schools, books, magazines, organizations, and arts) that produces the symbolic capital (things such as esoteric knowledge, shared experience, certification, and social skills) that individuals need to be part of the middle class. This apparatus, including archaeology, developed as part of the historical struggles that created the capitalist middle class . . . Because it is set in the middle class, archaeology attracts a middle-class following, and often does not appeal to working-class audiences (Ludlow Collective 2001:95; also McGuire and Walker 1999).

The argument is that an uncritical archaeology reproduces middle-class norms and expectations, even regarding events like the massacre at Ludlow, and thus significantly distorts the story, stealing its usefulness to develop a productive working-class consciousness today. The Ludlow Collective seeks to challenge this class-based limitation by explicitly working to produce and represent a working-class perspective, and to do this it draws on both theory and collaboration.

Theoretically, the Ludlow Collective employs a Marxist praxis for archaeology "that entails knowing the world, critiquing the world, and changing the world" (Ludlow Collective 2001: 95; also McGuire and Wurst 2002). This perspective leads archaeologists to explore how class consciousness was formed in the traditionally masculine spaces of the mines and saloons and, equally and perhaps more substantially, in the feminine spaces of the workers' homes, both at the company town and the Ludlow tent colony itself (Wood 2002a). As they describe it, this perspective explores "how mundane experience shaped the strike," a process that "*humanizes* the strikers because it talks about them in terms of relations and activities that our modern audiences also experience [emphasis added]" (Ludlow Collective 2001:95,103).

The Ludlow project works in collaboration with the UMW and other working-class audiences. Most specifically, this collaboration taught project members that typical archaeological questions about human origins or the rise of civilizations garner little interest among the working class. Instead, they found that a focus on everyday life "including who produces what, how production is accomplished, who benefits from the distribution of the social product, and how these arrangements are ideologically justified" carries much more weight (Duke and Saitta 1998:5). Through such collaboration, the project has learned to place a great deal of emphasis on writing in plain language and developing programs for the public, the media, and Colorado public schools that teach and advocate the story of everyday working lives, especially so an understanding of the harshness of past working-class lives may be disseminated (Ludlow Collective 2001:103–104).

The driving force of this approach—being based in an explicit theoretical agenda and working in collaboration with acknowledged public interests—also describes the next essential step in developing a Marxist reflexivity. The Ludlow Collective has not only identified a publicly formed political space (working-class consciousness) with which it hopes to connect its work, but it has sought to turn that discovered perspective on archaeology itself by challenging that archaeology's public basis is already class-defined. A suggestive example of this is the fact that many of the visitors to Ludlow's public excavations had been drawn to the site by a highway sign pointing to the Ludlow Massacre Memorial (there is a monument at the site erected by the UMW), which was thought to be identifying the site of an Indian war, not a class war! This story, however, does not apply to the visitations made by hundreds of living miners and other union members who attend the annual memorial service held at the site by the UMW. This disjunction between union and nonunion publics was a factor in the project's decision to focus on the everyday lives of the strikers. This approach allows the strikers' lives to resonate with the contemporary public who can imagine these past people by making comparisons with their own familiar practices and thus gain some sense of their consciousness. It is this approach that allows the archaeology at Ludlow to "become a powerful form of memory and action" (Ludlow Collective 2001:100).

At this point, however, some limitations can be seen in the project's approach. As the collective argues, archaeology is seen as a form of social action that can, but not often does, allow a working-class perspective to be used in the interpretation of the archaeological record. Yet, to do this, the project "humanizes" the strikers at Ludlow, a process that they argue bridges the gulf between past working-class lives and present working-class interests. The expected result here is that a farther reaching comprehension of the very compelling story of the Ludlow massacre, its causes, and its effects will, in essence, automatically result in increased class consciousness. The concern here is that the tie between raising class consciousness and the humanization of the strikers fails to disassemble the class bias of archaeology that the project identifies and seeks to overcome. The impulse of the project does not disseminate from the working class but, rather, from its memorialization—i.e., its production as a subject of memory—a discourse that requires a great deal more critique for such an activist project to succeed.

When the Ludlow Collective states that archaeology can be a form of memory and action, it is suggesting that archaeology is not already and always such. Drawing from its own critique of the class bias of archaeology, it is important to recognize that archaeology always serves its audiences by being an active source for memory building, but that action is typically by and for the middle class and about memories typically created in the abstract as stories of "the other." It is not sufficient to simply assert that the project is *not* doing this for an alternative to be materialized. Nor is it sufficient to seek out what interests among the working class differ from the middle class that may allow a research project to take on a working-class perspective. Rather, a project must engage more deeply with the roots of the class-formation process. In this case, what real conditions caused conflicting capitalist social classes to form and be reproduced, despite such intense violence and public outrage in the past? An archaeology project must then consider how class differences serve to establish the spaces for memory that make class interests produce historic and living perspectives: How may memorial reflection be situated within this class formation process? In other words, a project must respect, comprehend, and represent the social difference that class formation creates and the *partial* perspective on both past and living

experience it produces. The turn to the common humanity of the strikers undermines this effort since the social processes of difference created by class formation are masked.

It would be helpful then to abandon the abstraction of humanity and to embrace the more concrete, though partial, perspective of the working class. This would allow the memorials produced by the archaeology to be made by the working class and not just about them. By resorting to the anthropological abstraction of shared humanity as a way to relate class experience, the Ludlow Collective produces a public space that can work as much against working-class interests as for them because the Ludlow strikers remain in this analysis an "other" defined as an object of study. Their partial class-defined subjectivities are reduced to abstractions based on what any human would do given those conditions. Drawing on the postcolonial historical criticism of Dipesh Chakrabarty (2000), the most significant trouble with this approach is that it mirrors the abstraction that lies at the foundation of capital: the commodification of labor (Sayer 1987). "To organize life under the sign of capital is to act *as if* labor could indeed be abstracted from all the social tissues in which it is always embedded and which make any particular labor—even the labor of abstracting—concrete [emphasis in original]" (Chakrabarty 2000:54). In a capitalist society, this "labor of abstracting" is the defining practice of the middle class for whom "the abstraction . . . becomes true in practice" (Chakrabarty 2000:54, citing Marx 1973:104–105). Yet, unlike the middle class, the working class does not require abstraction to know that their forebears were abused and exploited (Duke and Saitta 1998:3).

A more effective public approach for the collective would be to situate the strikers in less of an abstract time and space called "Ludlow 1913–14" and to tell the story by collapsing the time difference that archaeology commonly presupposes. By focusing on the inherent archaeological act of memorialization (by making "then" into "now"), the project can better make the archaeological record (which exists now) into a living social agent and a subject in its own right that is not just useful to working-class struggles but is a participant in them. This way the objectification of the strikers as an anthropological object is dissolved, the othering habit of time difference in archaeology is denied, and the memory of the massacre is not a memory of visiting the site but of actively producing its meaning in living social action. To do this, the idea of the public and public interest in archaeology must be articulated from the very start of the project in the present.

Engagement—African American Annapolis

This sort of presentist approach was defined by the Archaeology in Annapolis project when it decided to explore the archaeology of African American Annapolis. The project had long been employing critical theory to explain the Annapolis past (Leone et al. 1987, 1995; Little 1994; Potter 1994; Leone 1995; Shackel et al. 1998; Mullins 1999; Warner 2001; Matthews 2002a) when it turned to the archaeology of African Americans. Like the Colorado Coal Field War project, Archaeology in Annapolis is driven by an explicit political agenda that is critical of the status quo in both Annapolis and archaeology. The goal was to use both public excavations and traditional archaeological research to challenge modern capitalist social relations, especially those that formed in Annapolis in the 18th century. These included slavery and the production of the modern American ideology based on natural law and self-evident truths (Leone 1984, 1995). A major focus was on the way these lessons from the past were used to educate modern tourists about the historical significance of Annapolis (Potter 1994). In addition to basic historical information on the role of Annapolis in the American Revolutionary era (its Golden Age), the stories tourists heard provided them with models, such as visits by George Washington, for how to properly behave as tourists and appreciate the inherent value of the historic landscape and the stories it contained. With these models, tourists to Annapolis were expected to observe the past, treat it with dignity, and leave it as they found it. As a resource for all Americans, the tourists' role in Annapolis was to accept the stories they were told as true and move on apparently better off with their American identity confirmed.

The critical archaeology tours in Annapolis sought to challenge this tourist-knowledge relationship by encouraging visitors to question what they were being told (Leone 1983; Potter 1994). So that visitors would be given insight into the way archaeologists arrived at interpretations of the past, site tours explained the methods used in archaeology to produce the archaeological record and how archaeologists developed research questions to examine the remains. Specifically, it was hoped that the archaeological record could be used to unmask modern ideologies by prompting site visitors to question the validity of the stories they were being told and to critically reflect on their role in the way these histories were made. Tourists were asked to consider the ideas of work and the vacation and their relationship to personal discipline. Tourists were also shown that the archaeological record identified the historical contingencies that produced these self-evident norms. For example, archaeology showed that the taken-for-granted aspects of modern lives such as going to work, being paid by the hour, living apart from work, and going on vacation were norms developed only in the last two centuries as part of the way industrial capitalism came to dominate the social order by normalizing time-discipline. It was hoped that this critical approach would lead to a more fully formed historical consciousness among site visitors that they could use to pierce the ideologies that were used to rationalize their subordination to the status quo.

This lofty goal failed to materialize. Site visitors were not convinced of the connections archaeologists were making between the past and the present or of the relationship between interpretations of archaeological remains and the stories of their own lives. In order to interpret what they heard, visitors employed and reproduced the ideological separations (Barnett and Silverman 1979; Matthews et al. 2001) that lay at the foundations of modern capital. Specifically, tourists embraced their position as doubly removed from the Annapolis past. First, they believed that these stories were unconnected to their lives, except as consumable entertainment. Second, their role was by definition one of passive consumption; if this was somebody's history, it was certainly not theirs. Facing these ontological roadblocks, the Archaeology in Annapolis project redesigned its public approach.

Turning to consider African American archaeology in Annapolis, the project was aware of the limitations it faced in producing a critical archaeology. They also realized that the African American past was even more politically volatile than the middle-class and elite archaeologies they had undertaken thus far. African American archaeology presented both a new opportunity and a challenge for an archaeology program dedicated to critiquing the status quo. Reflecting on their experience with modern tourists, Archaeology in Annapolis sought in the new work to confront the limitations imposed on their agenda by the modern ideologies that interact with presenting archaeology in public. The project sought a means to undermine the basic separations that allow tourists to keep the past at arm's length. They also had to find a way to move from providing a route into the past for the public to finding the routes that already exist in the way the modern public lives now in relation to the past. They then followed these guideposts in making archaeological decisions. This work decentered the role of archaeology so that what archaeologists do and the spaces they occupy became more publicly produced. This is exactly what the Ludlow project did in reference to living working-class interests and concerns, but the Annapolis project took a different path.

This path was to engage directly with the African American descendent population in Annapolis to talk with them, not on the site but before excavations began, about what archaeology is and how it could be of service to their interests. Then the project took a vital next step: they asked what the community would like to know from archaeology. They heard the following:

1. Do we have an archaeology?
2. Is there anything left from Africa?
3. Tell us about freedom, not about slavery (Leone et al. 1995).

Answering these questions became the agenda for the project, and the research that has resulted has produced novel archaeological interpretations of the African American past (Leone and Fry 1999; Mullins 1999; Warner 2001). This direct engagement allowed the project to

share the authorization of its work with the community whose contemporary interests in the past were being explored. This differs from the Ludlow project because the engagement was not with abstract working-class interests but with specific contemporary concerns that were articulated by the public as archaeological research questions. The difference is that the Annapolis project rejected the viability of the separation between past and present in the way they approached the archaeological record. Following their approach, it can be said that it is not the lessons that were learned about the past to challenge the dominant histories and ideologies of today that matter, but, more directly, what matters is how past lives may be brought to bear on living now and, more specifically, how the living world uses such past-present connections in the way they live today. Thus, the African American public interests that drove the Annapolis research became the means for the project to explicitly state what from the present they brought with them as they explored the past. This was Leone's question more than two decades ago regarding interpretation at public history museums. Here, though, the point was to learn and employ how challenges to the status quo made by African Americans in their everyday lives today were in part derived from the way they related to and used the past. This relevant critique of contemporary society was allowed to guide archaeologists as they worked. This project followed the guidelines discussed by Chakrabarty and other postcolonial scholars whose interest is to challenge aspects of Western dominance by de-stabilizing and redefining its categorization of knowledge (Said 1979; Spivak 1987; Bhabha 1994). In this case, archaeology was transformed from a discourse about the past that can have relevance in the present to a discourse specifically located in the present that uses public relations with the past to change the way people are perceived and actually situated in modern social and power relations.

The limitations of the approach in Annapolis appear in the way that archaeology was presented and how the African American perspective was represented. To learn about African American public interests, the Annapolis Project established a space for dialogue between archaeology and African Americans in Annapolis. This space produced three guiding research questions but was not itself considered a factor in the way these questions emerged. Archaeology was presented as neutral resource, as something that could be put to use by anyone with an interest in the past. The impact of the power that archaeologists have by virtue of the social construction of archaeology to create this space for African Americans to learn about and use archaeology is not discussed. This oversight sets up a confrontation between the inherent biases of an unexamined social archaeology and the perspectives of those whose interests are normally excluded. It runs the risk in this case of forcing African American interests to fit with more powerful archaeological interests in order to be acted on.

To handle this problem, the project might have paused between learning about what exactly African Americans sought to know and the initiation of research to examine these concerns. In this moment, the archaeologists could have defined the hermeneutic relationship between archaeology and this public to see more clearly how each was implicated in the other. On the one hand, what specifically did the project gain from taking the approach it did to learning about African American interests in the archaeological past? How was the social consequence of this approach for archaeology and its constituents defined? On the other hand, what benefit did African Americans take from working with archaeologists? How did the creation of this new relationship affect and/or produce their agenda?

This line of questioning leads archaeology to not only engage with and act on articulated public interests but also to *interpret* those interests in light of the spaces that brought them to archaeology's attention. This critique is not to suggest that archaeologists need to tease out buried conspiracies; rather, they are encouraged to make the social relations that are increasingly defining the character of public archaeology more critically framed so that the actual authorization of archaeological interpretation may be more substantially brought into view. Put another way, archaeologists should not seek to be set to work by interested publics but to realize that the hope to connect with these people is a sign that researchers are already at work. This is how the representation of African Americans in this project is problematic. No one can

deny that a unique historical path produced the modern African American community in Annapolis. However, the goal of developing an archaeology to understand and serve that community requires more thought. Just as with the projects regarding class relations discussed above, there needs to be a careful examination of the social relations that are embedded in the claim to being African American. The social space that produced the three research questions thus needs critical review so that the histories and assumptions that produced it (i.e., the difference between African Americans and archaeologists) may be challenged as well as employed. In this way a sense is established that the work of African American archaeology is about the historical development of a social perspective rather than a study of an objectified type of people.

In order to put archaeology in the service of groups in such a manner, archaeologists need to do more than learn how the critical perspectives of such groups may be appropriated. They need to be sure that the spaces these groups have created for talking back, which result from the strategic and incidental partiality of their perspective, are an integral part of the way archaeology forms itself through these groups. Archaeological publics must be able to talk back at archaeology as much as archaeologists would like to talk back at the social limitations and inequalities that are defined by studying others. To do this, archaeology should bring to the surface the foundational assumptions it employs to realize and represent the multiple partial perspectives that drive its investigations of the past and, as suggested below, do this through a critical reflection on the production of archaeology in public.

Hybridity—Archaeology in Tremé

One last example can be made of the work done by the Greater New Orleans Archaeology Program (GNOAP) housed in the College of Urban and Public Affairs at the University of New Orleans. The GNOAP studies the archaeology of New Orleans for the specific purpose of public outreach and education. In 1999, as director of the GNOAP, the author organized a program called Archaeology in Tremé based on excavations at the St. Augustine site in the predominantly and historically African American neighborhood of Tremé. In 1998, residents in Tremé began the work to have their neighborhood recognized as an historic district by the city of New Orleans. It was hoped that a public archaeology program could assist this effort and be able to capitalize on the historical consciousness that the nomination would promote. Following the lead of the Annapolis and Ludlow projects researchers sought to identify in present social action the specific histories that mattered in contemporary Tremé and that could direct archaeological research in the neighborhood.

To develop the program, conversations were held with several interested parties about the Tremé neighborhood to learn exactly what people were interested in identifying as the basis for Tremé's historical significance. This research showed that Tremé differed from Annapolis where the dominant historic tropes are either clearly pronounced (Annapolis' role in the American Revolution) or are invisible as they relate to those who are left out of the dominant story (African Americans who did not know they had an archaeology). In Tremé the story was neither visible nor invisible, it was instead a web of different stories and interests regarding the meaning of making an historic Tremé. In order to capture this complexity in the archaeology program, the questions explored were organized around a central theme that articulated the concerns people had about relating their interests in the present and the past. Specifically, the focus was on the social action involved in producing an awareness of archaeology.

To do this required retracing how the GNOAP entered the neighborhood. This had initially involved working with a local preservationist who had been a regular GNOAP volunteer since its inception and who had been championing the importance of archaeology in the preservation of New Orleans' heritage since before the GNOAP was created. When it was explained why the GNOAP should work in Tremé, she made the arrangements with Father LeDoux of St. Augustine Church, which properly owned the site, to show him the significance of its archaeological potential. The site is located on a grassy lot adjacent to the church building now used as a parking area for the congregation and a playground for the neighborhood. Historically, this

was the first part of Tremé to be built when the Company of the Indies located a brick and tile works on the site in the 1710s. The works was run as a plantation with a manor house for the foreman and the work done by resident enslaved Africans. After the company abandoned Louisiana in 1731, the works passed to Charles Morand, the foreman who (along with the subsequent family that obtained the site in the 1750s) continued its operation with enslaved labor until the 1790s. The works was then shut down and the property subdivided by Claude Tremé, the new owner who remained in residence at the manor house until the 1810s. The house then passed through several owners including the College d'Orleans who used it as part of its school and, later, the Sisters of Mount Carmel who used it as their convent house and a school for free girls of color. Ultimately, the house was damaged by a hurricane in the 1920s and demolished in 1926 after the Carmelites moved to a new location. Since then, the site of the manor house has been an open lot (Matthews 1999).

This history fascinated Father LeDoux who knew some of it, but he did not know anything about the early colonial brickworks component, which was the aspect that the preservationist was most excited about. For preservationists, the site was significant because examples of early French architecture are actually quite rare in Louisiana due to two 18th-century fires in New Orleans and the slow development of the colony prior to the 19th century. Furthermore, much of the early habitation area of the city has been repeatedly built over, destroying most of the early archaeological deposits. The St. Augustine site was thus a vital resource for recovering a lost history of the region. Clearly, this was something to consider when developing the research, but it was only one among many interests that were revealed.

To understand these other interests, it was necessary to stay rooted in the present to explore exactly how other people expressed interest in the site. For example, it was intriguing that Father LeDoux did not know the colonial story of the site that the preservationist emphasized. In fact, this was the case for most residents of Tremé. Everyone knew the St. Augustine churchyard, many knew about and were proud of the site's heritage as a school for free girls of color, and a few knew that the site was associated with Claude Tremé. No one knew that the site was a slave-based plantation before all of that. Yet, it was clear that most Tremé residents were not interested in that part of story either since they did not see it as part of their heritage. This pattern of knowledge and interest was also a worthwhile issue to explore through archaeological research. It represents a disjuncture that mirrors the one between the tourists and union workers at Ludlow but reverses the roles. At Ludlow the working-class interest in the site was well formed as it was memorialized in a monument and through annual commemorations. In Tremé, those with the most complete knowledge were outsiders who saw it as a resource for amplifying the established narratives of Louisiana's French heritage and was not the local community, whose heritage was being considered for historical designation and who seemed to have little interest in contributing to the city's colonial period.

From these discoveries the research for the project became based on the question "what made the site archaeological?" Framing the work through this question made the project a reflection on the relative social knowledge of the site and its significance today to those who directed the GNOAP to it. For preservationists, archaeology is an established form of historical research that legitimizes their function in society. Through archaeology they would provide a history for Tremé that would fold the Tremé story into a grander Louisiana historical narrative. The archaeological character of the site to Tremé residents, however, was not about tying their neighborhood to dominant statewide narratives. While those in Tremé had lived without the plantation's history, they were not living without history per se. Their desire for historic recognition was driven by their identification of Tremé as an historic African American place, and in fact the point of this designation for many was explicitly to challenge the standard historical narratives in New Orleans that had as yet insufficiently represented the African American past. The archaeological project would bring attention to and similarly help legitimize this effort. While it is too much to say these are conflicting histories, it is clear that they emerge from different contemporary perspectives on the past. The goal, therefore, was to make the project a means for exploring not just the past but also for articulating in the present public culture how interests in and knowledge about the past in Tremé define the way differing and partial perspectives inform those living in New Orleans today. To accomplish this, these differing interests in archaeology were made a guide for how the actual archaeology was to be done. Specifically, this approach would allow researchers to find out how some interests in the site are muted or silenced in the present by the way these differing perspectives have formed through time. This question was asking of the archaeological record (as both a data source and a symbolic representation of reality) if, how, and why historical knowledge is collectively shared.

Additionally, employing this approach, the project was better able to assess the meanings for doing archaeology in light of the most significant difference between the communities being worked with—race. While the interests that drove the work were not exclusively defined by race, it was clear that race mattered since those who knew the history of the site (preservationists) were predominantly white and those who lived without this knowledge (residents) were predominantly African American. Thus, in determining the implications of the primary question, the research explored through archaeology how race framed the partial social knowledges that would make an awareness of archaeology and its potential significance to those who seek to know and use the past unevenly shared. As such, for the excavation of the St. Augustine site a dialectical archaeology was developed of race formation and cultural production, both in the remains uncovered (Matthews 2001, 2002b) and in the way the social meanings of archaeological discoveries were defined in public today.

Articulating the particular ways that archaeology enters the world of a project adds another dimension to Marxist reflexivity. It elicits from public engagements not only research questions and sources of insight into the ways that the past and present relate but also a way of incorporating the specific and varied uses for archaeology that in part define the social relations that must be understood in order to represent the contemporary world, which guides exploration of the past. This approach expands on the destabilizing basis of the African American archaeology project in Annapolis. While the adoption of African American interests in the formation of archaeological research questions brought the critique of modern American society embedded in African American identities to bear on archaeological research, the Tremé project stepped through and beyond such a critique to analyze the relational partiality from which such perspectives on the past emerge. The preservationists and the Tremé community shared a great deal in terms of what they hoped to gain from archaeology, but they failed to recognize this mutual interest because of contemporary race relations. Therefore, a way to articulate how archaeology revealed these interests and conditions and a way for the research to be about the dialogues that drive interest in archaeology today was found.

It is vital to see that the archaeology here was situated in the interstices of this living cultural production process as something related to the partiality of each group's perspective and, more importantly, to how each group, in relating to archaeology and archaeologists, established their difference from the other. Archaeological research questions can reflect this interstitial location, for even though archaeology and archaeologists have their own partialities, archaeologists also are the only ones responsible for representing in public the archaeological interests that drive them to work. In this manner, their voices may emerge from the social dynamics, such as race and class relations, that are fueling the present social action that grabbed their attention or, better put, that drove an interest in the constructions of reality that archaeology produces. It is not the spaces claimed by living social actors from which work should emerge; these are for the most part inaccessible, given already established positions in modern society. Rather, their work should emerge from the processes of social debate and cultural production that condition and create these living identities.

This approach to the discovery of public meanings may be seen as an application of Homi Bhabha's (1994) postcolonial emphasis on hybridity. The GNOAP discovered and recorded a range of public interests regarding archaeology in Tremé and then interpreted these interests as evidence of the contemporary cul-

ture that the archaeology project was to interpret and represent. It was not just one or the other perspective that made this project work; the work brought out how they were each formed in relation to each other and how archaeology itself was implicated in the production of this social knowledge. Bhabha's argument is that such other-referencing used in order to know ourselves is the way partial perspectives are formed because the other is not known on its own terms but solely in the terms of the self. The related point is that every self is then in part formed through its other and exists as a hybrid. While modern culture largely suppresses the recognition of this hybrid condition, it nevertheless resides within all. To discover the way social formations produce the spaces occupied should be reflected upon. For archaeology this means keying in on how archaeological knowledge relates to the manner in which diverse constituencies define themselves and working to learn the archaeological questions that can be developed, given the nature of the social relations that condition access to and presence in these public cultural worlds. Archaeology may be hybridized with other interests (as in the advocacy of the Ludlow project or in the engagements that produced the research questions in Annapolis), but in this effort the already hybrid situations should be recognized that determine any sense of self assumed or encountered.

Conclusion: Decolonizing Archaeology

Four archaeology projects in a sequence have been reviewed to show the different sorts of public archaeology that inform a Marxist reflexivity. While these projects have been criticized, critique was not the point. Each of these projects is regarded as among the best in archaeology when considering the position of archaeologists in relation to the public cultural worlds in which they operate. Furthermore, each has based its work, especially its theorizing, on challenging the professionally conceived relations between the public and archaeology that need to be rethought if archaeology could make a difference in the living world.

The research has identified that a Marxist reflexivity may be developed through a process of critical reflection on the role of doing public archaeology in the modern world. The foundation is the idea of *myth busting* or of a confrontation with dominant tropic narratives that marginalize minority perspectives. Public archaeology can be a corrective that can balance the effects of these narratives and work to replace them with alternatives. The Five Points project illustrates this approach but was challenged to rethink the use of "respectability" as a source for an alternative narrative. It was suggested that the archaeologists question more carefully the basis they used to situate their alternatives. The key is awareness of the class position of archaeology and thus making a focus of the research to be a critique of archaeology as a myth-maker as well as any public uses of its conclusions.

A deeper degree of public engagement was identified as *advocacy* in which archaeologists specifically align their work with active social movements. The Ludlow Collective has done this by advocating capitalist working-class and union interests. This position led them to focus on the everyday lives of the Ludlow strikers to better understand how class consciousness was formed. This focus also served as a bridge between the past and present and between archaeology and the public so that working-class struggles and consciousness could be disseminated and the status quo of modern social relations challenged. It was argued, however, that this approach complicated the project's goals by reproducing the othering techniques embedded in the creation of archaeological subjects, making the Ludlow strikers unapproachable, except through the middle-class process of abstraction. It was suggested that the project more explicitly challenge the temporal implications of archaeology and conceive of a more presentist consideration that draws on contemporary working-class interests rather than the memorialization of those interests through an archaeological dig.

To break the hold on archaeology by middle-class interests, an even deeper level of public *engagement* is required. The approach to African American archaeology by the Archaeology in Annapolis project exemplifies this level by basing its approach on a living public interest and by allowing members of the African American community who subscribe to that interest to produce archaeological research questions. These specific community concerns contrasted

with the more-generalized class interests defined at Ludlow and bring to bear on the archaeological record the established criticisms of modern social relations that included specific means for knowing (or not knowing) and using the past. This method challenges archaeology to be more open to public authority for the purpose of making room in archaeological work for explicit criticisms of archaeology's capacity to serve alternative public interests. The Annapolis project was urged to be more aware of the power involved in the creation of the dialogic spaces that allow the identification of archaeological publics and their interests. Specifically, archaeology itself must remain open to the critique it seeks to understand and employ by focusing on marginalized people and groups.

A last step was defined as *hybridity* and explained in the work of the GNOAP in the New Orleans neighborhood of Tremé. The GNOAP expanded on the Annapolis approach by critically analyzing multiple present interests in the archaeological past. This work was based in the discovery of archaeological questions stemming from the interstices of modern social relations as they pertained to race and archaeological knowledge. From there, the uneven sharing of historical and archaeological knowledge within the living community was questioned. These varied interests in archaeology then became the force that guided the archaeological work. This deeper engagement worked at the level of social and cultural production so that the perspectives in the living world were not only engaged and critiqued through archaeology but also more fully exposed for their hybridity, especially in the way each used their interests in archaeology to define themselves as different from the other. These hybrid categorizations of public archaeological knowledge were framed as central, yet accepted as partial, and then defined as the proper means for archaeology to enter to the social world.

These approaches exemplify the sort of Marxist reflexivity described in the first section. Each project challenges the Cartesian subject-object opposition that underlies most archaeology by working with the public to establish an archaeological perspective. The analysis, however, suggests that the route towards a more-radical public practice for archaeology is the one that sustains the critical dialogue of the hermeneutic relationship between archaeology and its publics, especially for seeing exactly how archaeology already works within the cultures and communities that sustain it. There is much to learn from postcolonial criticism to make sense of the differences between the projects. Thus, one overarching goal of Marxist reflexivity is to decolonize archaeology (cf. Harrison 1991; Apffel-Marglin and Marglin 1996). All of the projects discussed seek to do this, but the more successful are those that take aim at not only the interpretation of the past, even given diverse and competing public interests, but also at the signifying practices embedded within archaeology that make it a legitimate discourse that people may use to define their positions in the world today. To decolonize archaeology is to challenge the means it employs to produce its subjects as knowable and to critique the colonialist and essentialist politics that these representations often involve. Thus, aspects that make archaeology appear stable in public, such as the regular passage of time, the distant location of the past, or the viability of working-class and African American identities, require the attention of archaeologists as much as the social issues they seek to connect with and allow archaeology to serve.

Decolonizing archaeology, furthermore, requires that archaeologists strive to know the meanings and purposes of archaeological research and practice in the partial terms of the publics. Archaeologists must be able to articulate why others find archaeological work interesting and useful to understanding and challenging their current conditions. With this awareness a rationale for the work can be established that draws on the interpretations made of the cultural worlds and social matters engaged with by initiating archaeological research. In this way, the social constructions produced by working in public remain active in the manner that hermeneutics encourages, so that as researchers work and produce new understandings, they can continue to tack between their knowledge of the world and the way that knowledge guides them towards archaeological interpretation.

Finally, decolonizing archaeology means that archaeologists should work to elicit the critical alternatives that already exist to knowing the past and that these will be found among those already positioned to talk back to the modern world. The Ludlow project found this in unions; the Annapolis project found this in the African American community; and the GNOAP found it in the critiques of race that produced partial knowledge of a local past. These alternatives are not simply signs of difference but are routes for seeing how the past works in the way the world is constructed by those struggling for change today. Archaeologists committed to social change must learn and embrace these alternative perspectives on the past and then use them to direct how archaeology is done. The most significant impact that can be made is thus to redefine the location and responsibility of archaeology in public from the past to the present, or from the other to the self, so that an archaeological voice is produced through a critical engagement with the cultural worlds that allow archaeologists to have a public voice at all.

ACKNOWLEDGMENTS

Earlier versions of this paper were presented at the Fifth World Archaeological Conference in Washington, DC, in June 2003 and at the RATS conference in Binghamton, NY, in October 2003. I wish to thank Randy McGuire for his invitation to prepare this paper for both conferences and for his comments on earlier drafts. The paper has also benefited from the readings of two anonymous reviewers, Kurt Jordan, Paul Mullins, Zoë Burkholder, Jenna Coplin, and the support of Mark Leone and Ian Hodder. While I hope these readers see their suggestions incorporated here, any mistakes or shortcomings remain my own responsibility.

REFERENCES

APFFEL-MARGLIN, FRÉDÉRIQUE, AND STEPHEN A. MARGLIN (EDITORS)
    1996 *De-Colonizing Knowledge: From Development to Dialogue.* Oxford University Press, New York, NY.

BARNETT, STEVEN, AND M. G. SILVERMAN
    1979 *Ideology and Everyday Life.* University of Michigan Press, Ann Arbor.

BHABHA, HOMI K.
    1994 *The Location of Culture.* Routledge, London, England.

BIOLSI, THOMAS, AND LARRY J. ZIMMERMAN (EDITORS)
    1997 *Indians and Anthropologists: Vine Deloria Jr., and the Critique of Anthropology.* University of Arizona Press, Tucson.

BLAKEY, MICHAEL L.
1987 Skull Doctors: Intrinsic and Political Bias in the History of American Physical Anthropology. *Critique of Anthropology*, 7(2):7–35.

CHAKRABARTY, DIPESH
2000 *Provincializing Europe: Postcolonial Thought and Historical Difference*. Princeton University Press, Princeton, NJ.

DUKE, PHILIP, AND DEAN SAITTA
1998 An Emancipatory Archaeology for the Working Class. <http://www.shef.ac.uk/assem/4/> University of Sheffield, Sheffield, England. 31 October 2004. Originally published in *Assemblage: The Sheffield Graduate Journal of Archaeology*, 4 (Oct).

FINE-DARE, KATHLEEN S.
2002 *Grave Injustice: The American Indian Repatriation Movement and NAGPRA*. University of Nebraska Press, Lincoln.

FRANKLIN, MARIA
1997 Why Are There So Few Black American Archaeologists? *Antiquity*, 71:799–801.
2001 A Black Feminist Inspired Archaeology? *Journal of Social Archaeology*, 1(1):118–125.

HARRISON, FAYE V. (EDITOR)
1991 *Decolonizing Anthropology: Moving Further toward an Anthropology for Liberation*. Association of Black Anthropologists, American Anthropological Association, Washington, DC.

HODDER, IAN
1999 *The Archaeological Process: An Introduction*. Blackwell, Oxford, England.

HORNING, AUDREY
2002 Myth, Migration, and Material Culture: Archaeology and the Ulster Influence on Appalachia. *Historical Archaeology*, 36(4):129–149.

KOHL, PHILIP, AND CLARE FAWCETT (EDITORS)
1995 *Nationalism, Politics, and the Practice of Archaeology*. Cambridge University Press, Cambridge, England.

LEONE, MARK P.
1983 Method as Message: Interpreting the Past with the Public. *Museum News*, 62:35–41.
1984 Interpreting Ideology in Historical Archaeology: Using the Rules of Perspective in the William Paca Garden in Annapolis, Maryland. In *Ideology, Power, and Prehistory*. Daniel Miller and Christopher Tilley, editors, pp. 25–35. Cambridge University Press, Cambridge, England.
1995 A Historical Archaeology of Capitalism. *American Anthropologist*, 97(2):251–268.

LEONE, MARK P., AND GLADYS-MARIE FRY
1999 Conjuring in the Big House Kitchen, An Interpretation of African American Belief Systems Based on the Uses of Archaeology and Folklore Sources. *Journal of American Folklore*, 112 (445): 372–403.

LEONE, MARK P., PAUL R. MULLINS, MARION C. CREVELING, LAURENCE HURST, BARBARA JACKSON-NASH, LYNN D. JONES, HANNAH J. KAISER, GEORGE C. LOGAN, AND MARK S. WARNER
1995 Can an African-American Historical Archaeology Be an Alternative Voice? In *Interpreting Archaeology: Finding Meaning in the Past*, Ian Hodder, Alexander Alexandri, Victor Buchli, John Carman, Jonathan Last, and Gavin Lucas, editors, pp. 110–124. Routledge, New York, NY.

LEONE, MARK P., PARKER B. POTTER, JR., AND PAUL SHACKEL
1987 Toward a Critical Archaeology. *Current Anthropology*, 28(3):283–302.

LITTLE, BARBARA J.
1994 "She Was . . . an Example to Her Sex": Possibilities for a Feminist Historical Archaeology. In *Historical Archaeology of the Chesapeake*, Paul A. Shackel and Barbara J. Little, editors, pp. 189–204. Smithsonian Institution Press, Washington, DC.

LUDLOW COLLECTIVE
2001 Archaeology of the Colorado Coal Field War, 1913–1914. In *Archaeologies of the Contemporary Past*, Victor Buchli and Gavin Lucas, editors, pp. 94–107. Routledge, London, England.

MARX, KARL
1973 *Grundrisse: Foundations of the Critique of Political Economy*, Martin Nicholas, translator. Penguin Books, Harmondsworth, UK.

MATTHEWS, CHRISTOPHER N.
1999 Management Summary of Excavations at the St. Augustine Site (16OR148), New Orleans, Louisiana. Report to the Louisiana Division of Archaeology, Baton Rouge, from the Greater New Orleans Archaeology Program, University of New Orleans, LA.
2001 Race and Political Economy: Comparative Archaeologies of Annapolis and New Orleans in the Eighteenth Century. In *Race and the Archaeology of Identity*, Charles E. Orser, editor, pp. 71–87. University of Utah Press, Salt Lake City.
2002a *An Archaeology of History and Tradition: Moments of Danger in the Annapolis Landscape*. Kluwer/Plenum, New York, NY.
2002b Black, White, Light, and Bright: A Narrative of Creole Color. *The Stanford Journal of Archaeology* <http://archaeology.stanford.edu/journal/newdraft/matthews/index.html>, Stanford Archaeology Center. 31 October 2004.

MATTHEWS, CHRISTOPHER N., MARK P. LEONE, AND KURT A. JORDAN
2001 The Political Economy of Archaeological Cultures: Marxism in American Historical Archaeology. *Journal of Social Archaeology*, 2(1):109–134.

MAYNE, ALAN, AND TIM MURRAY, (EDITORS)
2001 *The Archaeology of Urban Landscapes: Explorations in Slumland*. Cambridge University Press, Cambridge, England.

McGuire, Randall H.
1992 *A Marxist Archaeology*. Academic Press, San Diego, CA.

McGuire, Randall H., and Paul Reckner
2002 The Unromantic West: Labor, Capital, and Struggle. *Historical Archaeology*, 36(3):44–58.

McGuire, Randall H., and Mark Walker
1999 Class Confrontations in Archaeology. *Historical Archaeology*, 33(1):159–183.

McGuire, Randall H., and LouAnn Wurst
2002 Struggling with the Past. *International Journal of Historical Archaeology*, 6(2):85–94.

Meskell, Lynn (editor)
1998 *Archaeology Under Fire*. Routledge, London, England.

Mullins, Paul R.
1999 *Race and Affluence: An Archaeology of African America and Consumer Culture*. Kluwer/Plenum, New York, NY.

Patterson, Thomas C.
1995 *Towards a Social History of Archaeology*. Harcourt Brace, Forth Worth, TX.

Potter, Parker B., Jr.
1994 *Public Archaeology in Annapolis*. Smithsonian Institution Press, Washington, DC.

Reckner, Paul
2002 Remembering Gotham: Urban Legends, Public History, and Representations of Poverty, Crime, and Race in New York City. *International Journal of Historical Archaeology*, 6(2):95–112.

Said, Edward
1979 *Orientalism*. Vintage, New York, NY.

Sayer, Derek
1987 *The Violence of Abstraction: Analytical Foundations of Historical Materialism*. Basil Blackwell, London, England.

Shackel, Paul A., Paul R. Mullins, and Mark S, Warner (editors)
1998 *Annapolis Pasts: Historical Archaeology in Annapolis, Maryland*. University of Tennessee Press, Knoxville.

Shanks, Michael, and Christopher Tilley
1987 *Reconstructing Archaeology: Theory and Practice*. Routledge, New York, NY.

Spivak, Gyatri
1987 *In Other Worlds: Essays in Cultural Politics*. Routledge, London, England.

Swindler, Nina, Kurt E. Dongoske, Roger Anyon, and Alan S. Downer (editors)
1997 *Native Americans and Archaeologists: Stepping Stones to Common Ground*. AltaMira Press, Walnut Creek, CA.

Thomas, David H.
2000 *Skull Wars: Kennewick Man, Archaeology, and the Battle for Native American Identity*. Basic Books, New York, NY.

Trigger, Bruce G.
1989 *A History of Archaeological Thought*. Cambridge University Press, Cambridge, England.

Walker, Mark, and Dean Saitta
2002 Teaching the Craft of Archaeology: Theory, Practice, and the Field School. *International Journal of Historical Archaeology*, 6(3):199–207.

Warner, Mark S.
2001 Ham Hocks on Your Cornflakes. *Archaeology*, 54(6): 48–52.

Watkins, Joe
2000 *Indigenous Archaeology: Native American Values and Scientific Practice*. AltaMira Press, Walnut Creek, CA.

Wood, Margaret
2002a Women's Work and Class Conflict in a Working-Class Coal-Mining Community. In *The Dynamics of Power*, Maria O'Donovan, editor, pp. 66–87. Center for Archaeological Investigation, Southern Illinois University, Carbondale.
2002b Moving towards Transformative Democratic Action through Archaeology. *International Journal of Historical Archaeology*, 6(3):187–198.

Wurst, LouAnn, and Randall H. McGuire
1999 Immaculate Consumption: A Critique of the "Shop 'Till You Drop" School of Human Behavior. *International Journal of Historical Archaeology*, 3(3):191–199.

Yamin, Rebecca
1998 Lurid Tales and Homely Stories of New York's Notorious Five Points. *Historical Archaeology*, 32: 1:74–85.
2001a Alternative Narratives: Respectability at New York's Five Points. In *The Archaeology of Urban Landscapes: Explorations in Slumland*, Ian Mayne and Tim Murray, editors, pp. 154–170. Cambridge University Press, Cambridge, England.

Yamin, Rebecca (editor)
2001b Becoming New York: The Five Points Neighborhood. *Historical Archaeology*, 35(3):1–135.

ZIMMERMAN, LARRY J.

1989 Made Radical by My Own: An Archaeologist Learns to Accept Reburial. In *Conflict in the Archaeology of Living Traditions*, Robert Layton, editor, pp. 60–67. Routledge, London, England.

1997 Remythologizing the Relationship between Indians and Archaeologists. In *Native Americans and Archaeologists: Stepping Stones to Common Ground*, Nina Swindler, Kurt E. Dongoske, Roger Anyon, and Alan S, Downer, editors, pp. 44–56. AltaMira Press, Walnut Creek, CA.

CHRISTOPHER N. MATTHEWS
DEPARTMENT OF ANTHROPOLOGY
HOFSTRA UNIVERSITY
HEMPSTEAD, NY 11549

Timothy Baumann
Andrew Hurley
Lori Allen

Economic Stability and Social Identity: Historic Preservation in Old North St. Louis

ABSTRACT

Since the 1950s, the Old North St. Louis neighborhood in St. Louis, Missouri, has suffered population loss and disinvestment due to failed urban renewal initiatives, the construction of a new interstate highway that bisected the community, and suburbanization. Under the auspices of a U.S. Housing and Urban Development Community Outreach Partnership Center grant, the Public Policy Research Center at the University of Missouri-St. Louis partnered with the Old North St. Louis community to assist it in attaining economic growth, social stability, and a cultural identity through archaeological research and interpretation. Building off existing historic preservation initiatives, this partnership employed "true acts of inclusion" in developing with the community the major goals and the "questions that count." Archaeological work in conjunction with oral histories and archival research was used to strengthen the sense of community through development of K–12 educational programming, a local neighborhood museum, a video documentary, a published history, a website, and an historic bike trail. These products provided the tools to attract new residents, investors, and visitors to the neighborhood and served as cultural glue, connecting people to place. The project advances the concept of public archaeology by demonstrating how research and interpretation can be aligned with specific urban revitalization goals.

Introduction

Archaeology has contributed significantly to many facets of historic preservation in the United States, including economic development (tourism and revitalization of the urban landscape), education and outreach, and the creation of a sense of community and social identity. Much of this work falls under the term "public archaeology," which has been defined recently as "archaeological research that includes any kind of engagement with the public" (McKee 2002: 456). In Edward Staski's (1987:ix) introduction to *Living in Cities*, he argues that one of the "ever-growing" responsibilities of archaeologists working in the urban environment is in "*public relations*," and that "in the next several years urban archaeologists should have developed a comprehensive and effective set of procedures for meeting public needs and desires." At this time, there are no "set procedures" for engaging the public, but, instead, various models and examples have been developed over the past 25 years (Cressey 1983, 1987, 1991, 2002, 2005; Cressey and Henry 1990; Potter 1994; Jameson 1997, 2004; McDavid and Babson 1997; McKee and Thomas 1998; Shackel et al. 1998; Smardz and Smith 2000; Little 2002; Marshall 2002; Derry and Malloy 2003).

It is from these precedents that the Old North St. Louis community developed a public-oriented urban archaeology initiative. Here, in a distressed innercity neighborhood, scholars and students have collaborated with local citizens to integrate archaeological research into an urban revitalization strategy that revolves around the preservation of an historic landscape. The historical preservation approach adopted in Old North St. Louis demonstrates some of the creative ways in which archaeological and historical research can be employed to both stimulate economic investment and reconnect people to the places in which they live.

Historic Preservation Movement: Missouri and St. Louis

The archaeological project in Old North St. Louis flows directly from local concerns and is embedded in a broader historic preservation agenda that has achieved considerable success in the city of St. Louis as well as the state of Missouri. St. Louis is typical of cities that have witnessed tremendous sprawl and have attempted to reverse it by preserving and showcasing historic urban landscapes. Between 1950 and 1990, land use in the metropolitan area increased by 455% while the population grew by only 33% (East-West Gateway Coordinating Council 1994: 90). Moreover, all of this population growth occurred in suburban areas. Within the city, population decreased by 146%, from 856,796 in 1950 to 348,189 in 2000 (City of St. Louis

2004). This population loss, due to urban renewal clearance and disinvestment, was greatest in those neighborhoods surrounding the downtown core. Yet, St. Louis is also a place where history has been used to revitalize neighborhoods. Although the restoration of 19th-century homes and the publicizing of history have brought new life to several distressed innercity communities by luring tourists and affluent homeowners, historic preservation initiatives have fluctuated in importance and occurrence. In the late 1970s and early 1980s, federal tax-credit programs assisted in revitalizing dozens of buildings, including Union Station—the central train station for St. Louis, which was rehabilitated into a major retail and restaurant center in 1985. After the passage of the Federal Tax Reform Act in 1986 and a decline in the city's population, historic preservation programs in St. Louis dwindled. Instead, developers preferred to demolish older buildings for parking lots.

Starting on 2 January 1998, Missouri's historic preservation movement was jump-started again with the development of the Missouri Historic Preservation Tax Credit program (Missouri Alliance for Historic Preservation 1997; Missouri Department of Economic Development 1999). This program is available for commercial and residential use, providing a credit towards Missouri state taxes on 25% of the cost of renovation. In order to be eligible for this program, a structure must be listed on the National Register of Historic Places as an individual or as a contributing building within a National Register district or a local historic district certified by the U.S. Department of the Interior.

Since its inception in 1998, the tax credit program has generated nearly $295 million in historic rehabilitation with about $74 million in state tax credits. The national multiplier effects from this program have created 11,789 person-years of work, $391 million in income, $578 million in gross domestic product, and $122 million in taxes (Listokin et al. 2001). The majority of these tax-credit projects have been in the City of St. Louis with approximately $183 million in project costs and $46 million in tax credits equaling 62% of the total program activity. Most of these rehabilitation costs have occurred in the central downtown business district of St. Louis, but neighborhoods like Old North St. Louis have also benefited from this program.

Historic Preservation in Old North St. Louis

The application of historic preservation in Old North St. Louis dates back to 1980 when several families formed a homeowner's organization called the Old North St. Louis Restoration Group (ONSTLRG) to stem the tide of urban decay. Located just two miles north of downtown, the neighborhood had been victimized by postwar urban renewal programs and rampant disinvestment (Figure 1). During the 1950s, highway construction for Interstate 70 destroyed more than 10 blocks, including several churches that served as community anchors. As families left, homes were obtained by absentee landlords, many of whom refused to maintain their properties. During the late 1970s and early 1980s, an outbreak of arson further diminished the housing supply. Population declined rapidly as the outflow of older residents exceeded the influx of low-income families who might occupy the remaining rental units. By 2000, only 1,500 people lived in an area that had supported 10 times that number 60 years earlier. Boarded-up buildings and vacant lots came to dominate a landscape that was once filled with densely packed row houses, thriving churches, and bustling shops.

During its first 10 years of existence, members of the ONSTLRG devoted their energies to "helping each other in the rehabilitation of homes, creating and maintaining community gardens, and participating in a variety of neighborhood organizations and activities" (ONSTLRG 2004). The families who formed the restoration group were convinced that their efforts would be futile if the community lacked respect for the physical environment. Furthermore, they concluded that an appreciation for the area's rich history was essential to the process of cultivating that respect. This conviction was strengthened by the success of historic preservation campaigns in the Soulard Market and Lafayette Square districts just south of downtown where urban pioneers moved back from the suburbs and restored dozens of Victorian-era homes during the 1970s and 1980s. Hoping to achieve similar results, the restoration group campaigned successfully in 1984 to get the neighborhood placed on the National Register of Historic Places and began sponsoring tours of historic homes in the area. Around this same time, the organization embarked on a program to

FIGURE 1. Aerial view of Old North St. Louis with the original and current boundaries. (Drawing by Timothy Baumann, 2006.)

purchase, rehabilitate, and sell some of these historic homes. In addition, the group created the Wright Thing Street Festival, an annual street fair with food, performances, art exhibitions, and educational booths designed to reinforce community bonds and support networks.

The restoration group's efforts have produced mixed results thus far. Although several younger families have purchased and rehabilitated homes in the last decade, the pace of change has been limited largely due to the racial stigma of St.

Louis's "North Side," which is considered a predominantly African American community characterized by crime and poverty. Among the brighter improvements has been the commitment of a developer to build more than 100 new homes on empty lots in the North Market Street section of the neighborhood. These new homes will mimic the architectural styles of the surrounding 19th-century structures, thereby preserving the historical character of the neighborhood. The extant homes in this redevelopment corridor will also be rehabilitated for modern residential and commercial use. The new housing will accommodate both low- and middle-income families with the purpose of attracting new residents and retaining the current community base.

Old North St. Louis Neighborhood Partnership

In September 2001, the University of Missouri-St. Louis (UMSL) Public Policy Research Center received a Housing and Urban Development (HUD) Community Outreach Partnership Center (COPC) grant. The center works to develop partnerships with St. Louis area community and neighborhood organizations in order to create "livable communities" and is part of an UMSL Urban Neighborhood/University Partnership initiative, created in September 1998 to link university resources with urban neighborhood needs and priorities, to develop mutually respectful research and action partnerships, and to strengthen the capacity of both the university and the community to build flourishing alliances.

The HUD COPC grant was designed to link the physical, economic, intellectual, and creative resources of the university to the Old North St. Louis neighborhood. Throughout this project, students, faculty, and Public Policy Research Center staff worked with residents of the Old North St. Louis neighborhood to engage the community in a productive manner. This collaborative process has benefited the neighborhood and has changed the way that students are taught, using a service-learning approach. The project aimed to preserve the character, quality, and culture of the Old North St. Louis neighborhood as well as to strengthen community programs and further enable residents to be self-sufficient. Archaeological research represented only one component of a multifaceted approach to urban revitalization, and its utility can only be understood in the context of the total package.

Given the ONSTLRG's commitment to historic preservation, it is not surprising that most of the tasks outlined support the goal of protecting and rehabilitating historic homes. For example, a home maintenance and financial literacy program taught local renters how to develop a financial strategy that will lead to local home ownership. Another series of courses offered in the neighborhood and taught by faculty from UMSL covered the economics of restoring older homes. The environmental health and safety component of the grant offered expertise about some of the dangers involved with remodeling older homes, such as lead poisoning. A community organizing and leadership training initiative helped the community identify and publicize its assets through maps, databases, and a website. Public archaeology fell under a fourth broad category, neighborhood stabilization and historic preservation, the object of which was to conduct and publicize historical research in order to promote tourism and nurture a greater appreciation for the built environment among current residents. In addition to archaeological excavations, this section of the grant called for the development of a website, a local history trail, an oral history project, a video documentary, K–12 educational programs, a community museum, and a published history (Rectenwald and Hurley 2004). The various components specified in the HUD COPC grant were designed to support each other in the effort to bring attention and investment to the neighborhood's historic landscape.

Public archaeology was viewed as tool for community building. More specifically, project participants hoped that an inclusive public archaeology project would help repair rifts that had developed between lower-income renters and more-affluent homeowners over the previous decades. Tension between these two groups stemmed from the Model Cities initiatives of the late 1960s and 1970s. The Model Cities program, part of President Lyndon Johnson's "war on poverty," was an attempt to reduce unemployment, provide better housing, and improve education in distressed inner cities. In Old North St. Louis, the major thrust of the program involved tearing down older homes and building new low-income townhouses that clashed with the area's architectural heritage (Kaitz and Hyman 1970; Howard 1972; Gilbert 1973; Washnis 1974; Brown and Frieden 1978; Wood 1990). Many original members of ONSTLRG objected to the Model Cities approach, while the social service agencies involved with Model Cities saw the restoration group's efforts as, at best, tangential to the interests of the area's growing low-income population. Today, a consensus has emerged around the conviction that the neighborhood's political clout hinges on the full mobilization of the local population. A major goal of the project was to employ history and archaeology in a manner that resonates with and unifies all segments of the community.

Archaeology in Old North St. Louis

The archaeology component of the HUD COPC grant assisted with ONSTLRG's neighborhood stabilization and historic preservation programs by helping create a link between the past and a sense of place in the present. This project drew upon previous public archaeological models such as those pioneered in Alexandria, Virginia (Cressey 1983, 1987, 1991, 2002, 2005), and Annapolis, Maryland (Potter 1994; Shackel et al. 1998), but the ultimate guidance for the Old North St. Louis archaeology program came from the collective desire of the living community to revitalize its specific neighborhood. In this effort, the university partners met regularly with a citizen advisory committee that reflected the community's current ethnic mix. Admission to this committee was open to everyone in the neighborhood, but those with an interest in local history and who had previously been active in ONSTLRG were strongly encouraged to participate. Over three years this committee met once a month to discuss not only the goals of the archaeology project and how to integrate them with the larger public history program but also the even larger HUD COPC grant initiatives (environmental health and safety, home maintenance and financial literacy, community organizing and leadership, and expanding university/community partnerships). Archaeology was not the centerpiece of this overall project but was a primary mechanism used to help improve the social and economic conditions in this community.

Overall, this archaeology program was a collaborative research project, combining the concerns and interests of the descendant and academic communities. Archaeology was used in conjunction with archival research and oral interviews to recover a lost history and generate artifacts and information that could be interpreted and exhibited in the neighborhood.

The descendant community participated in this program by conducting volunteer research, developing research themes, selecting archaeological sites, and interpreting this information for the living community today.

The first step of the public archaeology project was to establish the community advisory committee, which then assisted in creating a research design outlining an historical context of the neighborhood, developing major historical themes and research questions, and conducting a neighborhood survey to determine its archaeological integrity. This information was used to make recommendations on archaeological sites to test and to help nurture companion education and economic development programs.

Site selection was based on the following criteria, which were jointly decided between the academic and local community: (1) accessibility and legal permission, (2) archaeological integrity (bulldozed or relatively undisturbed), (3) close proximity to the local elementary and secondary schools to enable student interaction, (4) threat of future development, and (5) addressing the "questions that count" to the public (Derry 1997). Among the potential research topics and sites discussed in community meetings were public institutions, socioeconomic status, settlement patterns, transportation systems, and gender relations. Consistent with the objective of using history as a community-building tool, local residents gave priority to the neighborhood's tradition of ethnic diversity and its capacity to incorporate newcomers.

Old North St. Louis has long served as a "gateway" or "port-of-entry" neighborhood, a place where people of diverse backgrounds came from afar to gain a foothold in the city before moving on to other parts of the metropolis (Figure 2). The neighborhood as it exists today dates back to 1816 when three landowners, William Chambers, William Christy, and Thomas Wright, incorporated the Village of North St. Louis. Their civic venture was rooted in the hope that a favorable location on the Mississippi River would attract commerce and investment. The town grew slowly in its early years as most new settlers to the area gravitated to the adjacent City of St. Louis. Rapid growth awaited the town's annexation to the City of St. Louis in 1841 and the ensuing influx of immigrant settlers from Europe. For the remainder of

FIGURE 2. Bird's-eye view of Old North St. Louis (Compton and Dry 1876.)

the 19th century, German and Irish immigrants were the dominant groups in the neighborhood. Unlike some areas of St. Louis that were known for their ethnic concentrations, North St. Louis became home to a multitude of nationalities, professions, and religious groups, including free African American families (Rectenwald and Hurley 2004).

By the beginning of the 20th century, North St. Louis was a bustling working-class neighborhood with its social life organized around ethnic associations and churches. The population continued to diversify as new immigrant groups from Poland, Italy, and Russia replaced many of the original residents. While many children and grandchildren of the earlier German and Irish inhabitants remained, others climbed the social ladder by purchasing homes in more prestigious neighborhoods to the north and west. This pattern of geographic mobility and displacement was repeated during World War II when European Americans and African Americans from the rural south migrated to the area in large numbers in search of defense industry jobs (Rectenwald and Hurley 2004).

Drawing on this diverse history, the community (voiced through the citizen advisory committee) wanted to know how ethnicity shaped the day-to-day life of prior inhabitants. Did German families live differently from Irish, Italian, or African American families? Did foreigners retain Old World customs in the New World? Did ethnic attachments wane with the passing of generations? On the other hand, local residents also wanted to explore the social relationships that developed among these ethnic groups. In particular, the current community was eager to learn more about the social relationship between the German Americans and African Americans before and after the Civil War. In the decade prior to the Civil War in St. Louis, German immigrants were viewed as strong antislavery proponents. This political perspective was quite evident in the German language press of the time (Rowan 1983, 1992; Boernstein 1997), but did these antislavery viewpoints reflect anything about the social relationships that developed between ordinary Germans in Old North St. Louis and those of African descent? Did the largely German presence in the neighborhood influence the opportunities available to recently freed slaves in the aftermath of the Civil War?

Starting in 2002, UMSL archaeological field schools and additional historical research, which included participation by middle school and college students as well as the community at large, were conducted to address some of these questions. Three sites were selected: German American households at 1204–1208 Hebert Street (23SL1229), a mixed ethnic block at 1102–1112 Chambers Street (23SL1230), and a postbellum African American school and community along the 1200 block of Hadley Street (23SL1231), formerly North Twelfth Street.

Hebert Street Site

The Hebert Street site consisted of three two-story, brick row houses with a razed alley house and outbuildings. In the 19th century, primarily first- and second-generation ethnic German families occupied these homes. By 1910 other cultural groups had begun to move in, including those from Hungary, Austria, and France. Most of these residents were renters. In the U.S.

census records the male occupations at this site varied between blue- and white-collar jobs (blacksmith, cabinet maker, chemical worker, drayman, machinist, painter, porter, printer, riverboat pilot, salesman, and teamster). Female occupations were typically listed as keeping house or as a servant, but Emily Mund was employed in 1900 as a saleswoman of ceramics; Sophia Ponath was listed in 1910 as working in a hattery; and Lillian Lemke was working at a dress and dye company in 1920.

A view of the Sanborn Fire Insurance map of 1909 reveals a stable and several sheds along the alleyway (Figure 3). Archaeological work focused on the rear yard area of this site to document general yard refuse and these outbuildings. Excavations in 2002 uncovered portions of the razed alley house, a stable, a shed, and a fence. An analysis of the artifacts recorded ceramics, food remains, toys, bottles, and architectural material. Perry Jaynes (2003) conducted a detailed analysis of the ceramic assemblage (Table 1), focusing on socioeconomic indicators and secondarily on ethnicity. A total of 216 sherds with a mean ceramic

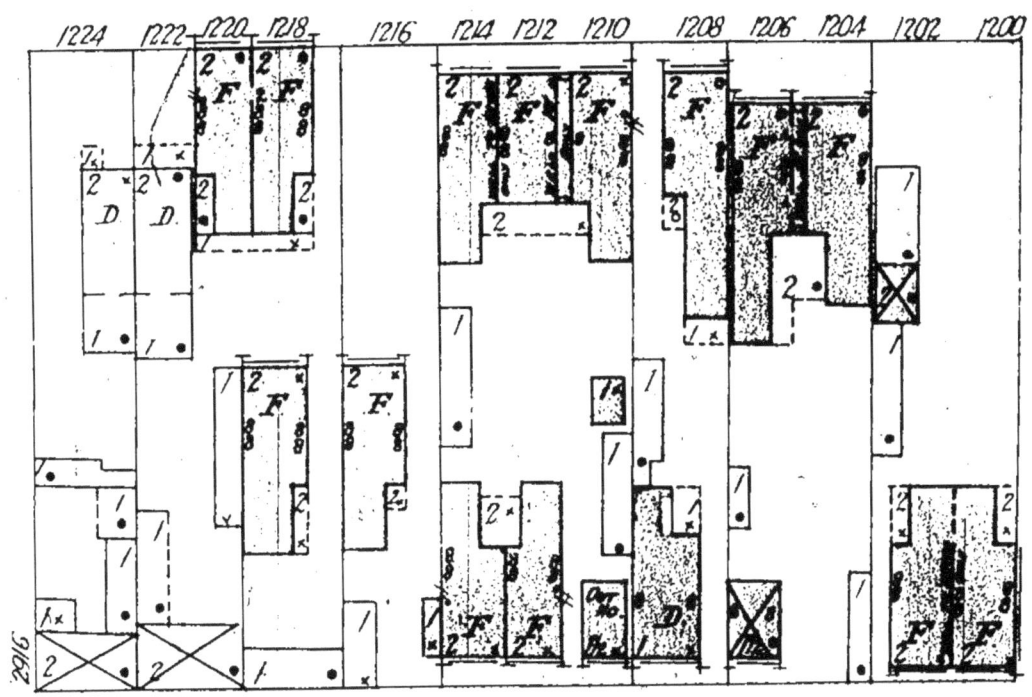

FIGURE 3. 1909 Sanborn Fire Insurance map highlighting the 1200 block of Hebert Street in Old North St. Louis.

TABLE 1
OLD NORTH ST. LOUIS CERAMIC ASSEMBLAGES

Ware Type	Hebert Street Site (%)	Chambers Street Site (%)
Earthenware	4 (2%)	1 (1%)
Ironstone	9 (4%)	13 (12%)
Porcelain	59 (27%)	19 (18%)
Redware	42 (19%)	18 (17%)
Stoneware	18 (8%)	30 (28%)
Whiteware	79 (37%)	21 (20%)
Yellowware	5 (2%)	4 (4%)
Total	216 (100%)	106 (100%)

date of 1882 were collected from this site. Using George Miller's (1980, 1991) ceramic economic index, Jaynes hypothesized that the Hebert Street site would have a middle-class index value, similar to that found at the Franklin Glass Works site (Miller 1980). The results calculated instead a lower-class index of 1.34, which was equivalent to Miller's (1980) Tenant Farmers and Frontier Log Cabin class indices. This was unexpected because of Old North St. Louis's urban location but may be explained by the occupants' renter status as well as the lack of Miller index values for porcelain, stoneware, and redware, which were not used in factoring the Hebert Street site economic index. Of these ceramic types, porcelain represented 27% of the total assemblage with 69% as tableware. With porcelain normally as one of the most expensive wares, the economic status of these households may have been higher. In contrast, redware and stoneware, the least expensive of ware types, represented 19% and 8% of the assemblage, which could counterbalance the value of porcelain.

The redware and stoneware recovered included mostly hollowware forms (drain pipe, crocks, flowerpots) but also included a flat redware vessel with lead glazing. Ethnically, redware vessels like this one have also been linked to a German cultural tradition. In particular, Pennsylvania Germans had a long tradition of producing lead-glazed redware for use as tablewares from the 1600s to the 1800s (Lasansky 1979; Zug 1986; Ketchum 1991). In a rural context, redware has also been found in higher percentages on German farms that produced butter and other milk by-products (Groover 2003:256–267). Is the greater use of redware a German ethnic tradition or one associated with an occupation or class? Charles Zug (1986) argued that even though Pennsylvania Germans were known for their production and use of redware, other cultural groups equally produced and used redware. Is this a German tradition that continued in Old North St. Louis? If so, then what does this mean with regard to German foodways as well as German immigrant resistance to other ethnic lifeways? Unfortunately, answers to these questions were not obtained from this project and will require further archaeological testing and historical research on additional German and other ethnic households in St. Louis and elsewhere. In an attempt to collect additional data from other ethnic contexts, work on two additional sites in the Old North St. Louis neighborhood was undertaken. Excavations were conducted in the 1100 block of Chambers Street, an ethnically diverse area, and in the 1700 block of Hadley Street, an African American neighborhood.

Chambers Street and Hadley Street Sites

The Chambers Street site once contained a row of brick homes with outbuildings, dating back to 1859, that was occupied by a mixed community of German, Irish, and Polish families. The 19th-century German households consisted of brothers George and Karl [Charles] Bernays. The Bernays were part of the German Forty-Eighters who immigrated to North St. Louis before the Civil War. The Forty-Eighters were typically well-educated professionals (doctors, lawyers, musicians, and writers) who fled the collapse of the German Revolution in 1848. George was a physician, and Karl worked primarily as a newspaper writer and editor for the *Anzeiger des Westens*, the *Republican*, and the *Anzeiger* newspapers in St. Louis (Hyde and Conard 1899:142). Ideologically, the Forty-Eighters believed in artisan republicanism, free thought, democracy, and anticlericalism. They were not Marxist and therefore not concerned with systematic class exploitation as a result of capitalist wage labor. Because of this ideological base, most German Americans saw the Confederacy as a direct threat to the democratic ideal on which the United States had been founded. Even more importantly, they saw slavery as a grave economic threat to artisan republicanism. As independent artisans and craftsmen, they could not compete economically in a system that allowed the competition access to the free labor of slaves. German Americans supported civil rights for blacks because slavery presented a direct political and economic threat to the their lifestyle as small business owners and skilled tradesmen (Shore et al. 1992).

Karl Bernays, along with his friend and boss Heinrich [Henry] Boernstein, personally pleaded the case for arming the newly formed German militia in St. Louis to President Lincoln. The formation of this militia was in direct response to the pro-Confederate state government of Missouri, the slave-holding Little Dixie area of rural Missouri, and the nativist whites in St. Louis as well as the Irish, who made up the second largest immigrant population group in the city (Boernstein 1997). Bernays and Boernstein argued successfully to Lincoln that if the militia was not armed, the geographically important Missouri and St. Louis rivers, along with St. Louis's Federal arsenal, would surely fall to the Confederacy, a tactical and strategic disaster. Boernstein, although decidedly middle-aged, took an active role in the corps. He wrote of the troops under his command being verbally abused as well as having rocks pelted at them and even being fired upon while transporting Federal prisoners through the city until they reached the safety of the German-inhabited districts. American-born whites and the Irish were particularly virulent. German American civilians were also forced to arm themselves because the Irish American police chief expressed some disinterest in enforcing the laws to protect the Union sympathizers (Boernstein 1997).

Along with the German American radicals, a significant number of white Republicans in St. Louis politically supported black civil rights in the postwar era. One result of this position was increased educational opportunities for African Americans and the creation of Dessalines School in 1866 in North St. Louis (Figure 4). Originally known as Colored School no. 2, it was the second school for educating African American children in St. Louis. Prior to this time, an 1847 state law prohibited free and or enslaved African Americans from attending schools in the city. For the first few years of its existence, the school operated out of a church basement. In 1871, the city purchased the former home of a local lumber merchant and converted it into a schoolhouse. In its first year of operation, more than 300 students attended classes at this schoolhouse. A small African American community developed around the Dessalines school. In the subsequent decades, more than two dozen African American families made their homes in the blocks surrounding the school, which was a source of great pride. In the 1900 U.S. census, all of the African Americans listed in this neighborhood were renting property, and most were working in blue-collar occupations as domestic servants, a fireman, day laborers, laundresses, porters, or teamsters. There were some exceptions, including John Stone, a teacher; William Perny, a physician; and Dalla Hill, a nurse at the city jail. In a foreshadowing of the urban renewal upheavals of post-World War II, the African American residential enclave was wiped out by the construction of an interurban rail line in 1930, connecting St. Louis with towns across the Mississippi River in Illinois. The school

FIGURE 4. Dessalines School in Old North St. Louis, ca. 1876 (Photo courtesy of the St. Louis Public Schools Records Center/Archives.)

remained active until 1974 but was demolished shortly after its closure.

The presence of this school and black community, largely unknown to current inhabitants, has sparked a great deal of curiosity today, particularly among African American residents. People wanted to know why the school was located in their neighborhood, how the attitudes and political views of German and Irish immigrants may have influenced the decision, and to what extent the African American residents were integrated into the wider community.

In 2003, archaeological work was conducted at 1112 Chambers Street to explore an Irish household adjacent to Karl Bernays's home and at 1750 Hadley Street to determine if any intact remains from the African American community survived the construction of the 1930 rail line. The Irish home site at 1112 Chambers was owned and occupied by first- and second-generation Irish families who rented out extra rooms to both small families and unmarried male boarders. The boarders worked in neighboring businesses and industries as railroad and factory workers, machinists, clerks, and bookbinders. The 1112 Chambers Street address was selected for four reasons. First, it was the least disturbed of the lots between 1102 and 1112 Chambers. Second, previous studies of German households had been done at the Hebert Street site. Third, the Irish community of North St. Louis was the second most populous ethnic group in 19th-century North St. Louis. Last, the Irish were often at odds with the German and African American communities over politics and employment.

Excavations at the 1112 Chambers Street address uncovered an ash pit, a waterline trench, and a shallow pit feature. Abundant artifacts included ceramics, bottle fragments, doll parts, buttons, and both faunal and floral remains. Despite the neighborhood's reputation as a place where people could walk to their jobs, a work tag from the East St. Louis Stone Company was also recovered at this site, suggesting that by the 20th century some people traveled outside the neighborhood to their place of employment. The East St. Louis Stone Company was across the Mississippi River in the State of Illinois and operated there as early as the 1920s. By this time, an extensive metropolitan streetcar network facilitated the movement of people throughout the region and across the river, thereby widening employment opportunities. The history of the neighborhood was and continues to be tied to the history of other places. Rather than developing in isolation, the community was shaped by broader economic, social, and demographic forces.

Catherine Barnes (2004) completed a ceramic analysis of the 1112 Chambers Street assemblage, recording 109 sherds (Table 1). Using Miller's (1980, 1991) ceramic economic index, an overall value was calculated at 1.4, which was only slightly higher than the ceramic value of 1.34 at the Hebert Street site. Ceramic comparisons with the Hebert Street site suggested that whiteware, redware, and porcelain were less frequent, while ironstone and stoneware were more common. How these data relate to differences in ethnic affiliation is unclear at this time. Additional data are needed from other urban sites in St. Louis as the sample size was too small to document any definitive patterns. Part of this additional data may have been recovered in summer 2005 by the Archaeological Research Center of St. Louis that conducted a mitigation of two city blocks on the southern edge of the Old North St. Louis neighborhood (Harl 2005). These excavations were part of the Cochran Gardens housing project, a HUD development, and they uncovered thousands of artifacts primarily from the cisterns and privies of an ethnically diverse neighborhood that included Germans, Irish, Poles, Russians, and African Americans. Analysis of this material is ongoing and will be completed in 2007.

Archaeological work at 1750 Hadley Street was chosen because it was the least disturbed homestead in this postbellum African American neighborhood. Unfortunately, archaeological research at the Dessalines School was not possible because a new cinder block industrial building was constructed at that site in 2001. The 1750 Hadley Street residence sat immediately across the street from the school at the corner of Hadley and Brooklyn streets. After the 1930 rail line construction, a coal yard and loading dock were placed at this address. Investigators used surface collection techniques and a systematic posthole testing survey across the site. The posthole tests documented a layer of cinder/coal just below the ground surface that was up to 1 ft. thick. Few artifacts were found below this lens, and no cultural features were encountered that were associated with the period of African American occupation. These results suggest that this site was severely damaged by the rail line construction and did not warrant additional testing. Despite a failure to uncover any intact remains at this site, future research will continue to explore the neighborhood for additional information that could aid understanding of the social relationships among its diverse people.

Connecting the Past to the Present

One of the primary goals of the Old North St. Louis project was to connect the past to the present community, creating a sense of place. In this process, history and archaeology were used to raise historical consciousness in the neighborhood. This historical ownership was accomplished through various methods of conversational and reflective approaches to the past (Potter 1994; McKee and Thomas 1998). These methods were first applied through an oral history project conducted by UMSL faculty and students in 2002. Differing in age, gender, and ethnic background, approximately 30 people who had some firsthand knowledge of the neighborhood were interviewed. Some of these informants grew up in Old North St. Louis and then moved away, while others spent their entire lives there. Some never lived in the neighborhood at all but worked, worshiped, or shopped there.

Interviewees were presented with artifacts recovered from the archaeological digs and were asked to identify the functions of these objects and to reflect on any life stories related to these materials. The objective was to have the individuals attach personal meaning to these artifacts and claim historical ownership. For example, numerous marbles were unearthed at the German American homes at 1204–1208 Hebert Street. They were presented to the interviewees who shared memories about playing with marbles. A rich assemblage of marble stories was created, with informants describing the specific games they played, the types of marbles they used, and, perhaps most importantly, with whom they played. The recollections revealed that marbles were a means of transcending the ethnic divisions that otherwise organized social life; children played marbles with other youngsters who lived nearby, regardless of their ethnic backgrounds. Moreover, the conversations about marbles yielded some unanticipated information about the ways in which gender organized childhood recreation. Several informants noted that only boys played with marbles.

In addition to the marbles, ceramic and bottle fragments were also offered for inspection. Interviewees were asked whether the artifacts were recognizable and how they were used. When presented a coffee pot fragment that was uncovered in the backyard of a German American household, one startled woman of Italian descent pointed to her glass showcase to indicate that she still owned an intact version. She explained that the pot was part of a coffee and tea set acquired by redeeming coupons from the Jewel Tea Company in the 1950s. Although this woman maintained many Italian customs in her home, especially with regard to foodways, the coffee and tea set was an example of engagement with a consumer culture that crossed ethnic lines. In this particular case, the interview also proved instrumental in identifying the ceramic fragment. The utility of the direct inspection technique went beyond the precise identification of artifacts. In most cases, informants were familiar with the objects and were able to describe their use or origin in a way that enhanced understanding of daily life. Through direct inspection, the interviewees assumed interpretive authority over the artifacts. Moreover, by repeating the process with several interview subjects, the project accommodated multiple perspectives on past events.

Another example of direct inspection occurred in an interview with Ollie Garger, whose Austrian-born parents had founded the Garger Bottling Company in Old North St. Louis in 1919. He was presented with various soda bottle fragments recovered from the excavations. His response proved illuminating with respect to the changing relationship between the local and national consumer economy. The Gargers originally manufactured and bottled soda in their home and sold their product door to door by wheelbarrow. Although the family maintained the business into the 1980s, consumer allegiance to national brands such as Pepsi Cola and Coca Cola eroded the vitality of local producers like the Gargers in the post-World War II era. Reflecting the growing participation in mass consumer culture, many artifacts of more recent vintage were manufactured far from Old North St. Louis. Archaeological evidence also revealed a longstanding engagement with global consumption networks, dating back to the 19th century. For example, one ceramic fragment recovered at the Hebert Street site was identified as part of an ironstone bowl manufactured by Charles Meakin in Hanley, England, between 1883 and 1889. For Christian and Maria Rolf, who inhabited the house at that time, the imported bowl, likely part of a matching set, represented a link to a flowering culture of mass consumption. Although it is unknown where the Rolfs purchased their bowl, wares produced by the Meakin family were routinely sold through Sears, Roebuck and Company catalogs around this time (Israel 1993:678).

With regard to themes of ethnicity and wider connections, archaeological evidence complicated historical assumptions held by many people in the community. The notion of a completely self-sufficient community, governed by stark ethnic segmentation, was challenged by the archaeological record. The community's ability to incorporate new interpretations was greatly enhanced by the openness of the research process and the trust it engendered. Inviting residents to participate in the excavations nurtured a respect for production of knowledge. Involving residents in interpretive processes not only invested them with authority but also cultivated among them an obligation to get the story right. Indeed, striving for a truth based on hard evidence, no matter how elusive, proved integral to developing consensus on a broad range of issues.

Information collected from oral histories was combined with archaeological data and historical documents to create a website, a heritage bicycle tour, a community museum, K–12 educational programs, a video documentary, and a published history (Rectenwald and Hurley 2004). Assisted by USML faculty and students, residents of Old North St. Louis developed the heritage bicycle tour. The trail was a spur of the Riverfront Bike Trail, which connects to the National Park Service's Jefferson National Expansion Memorial (the Arch) and includes 30 historic sites throughout the neighborhood, ranging from prehistoric mounds to a present-day butterfly garden. The citizen advisory committee worked diligently, designing the route as well as selecting photos and writing text for a brochure and historic markers. This information was also published in the popular history book *From Village to Neighborhood: A History of Old North St. Louis* (Rectenwald and Hurley 2004:101–120). The process of creating this heritage trail was one of the most time-consuming and emotional aspects of this project. Lengthy discussions were had over which historic sites to select and how to describe their importance through narratives. In the end, the advisory committee had a greater understanding of and respect for the neighborhood's diverse heritage as well as the multivocal perspectives of its citizens.

The advisory committee also designed a small community museum from the archaeological, oral history, and archival research. The museum was enhanced by donations of material objects from current residents. The proposed exhibit, parts of which have been put into operation, includes an introductory panel introducing viewers to archaeological methodology and explaining the utility of interpreting the past through material culture. Thematic displays highlight the destruction and renewal of the physical landscape, the struggle to define a sense of place, African American heritage, the process of earning a living, and childhood experiences.

Soliciting donations of material artifacts from local residents provided yet another mechanism for community involvement and served to integrate current residents into the flow of history. Just as the actions of previous generations shaped the present, their actions will determine the future. Framed in this manner, the archaeological displays link past, present, and future in a very personal way. Donated items included old menus from a local soda fountain, piano sheet music, a sewing machine, a dresser,

and an assortment of kitchenware. The incorporation of donated items is particularly valuable because many people in Old North St. Louis cannot trace their own history back very far in the neighborhood and have no direct connection to many of the excavated artifacts. This approach to collecting reinforces the idea that the history of a place is the history of many places. By attaching stories about the owners to the artifacts, both donated and excavated, present-day inhabitants can compare their lives with the lives of those who preceded them and develop a sense of connection to place through a sequence of past lives and material culture.

In conjunction with the museum exhibit, a K–12 archaeology activity book and resource kit was created for local schools (Schmidt 2005a, 2005b). The activity books include lesson plans that were designed to encourage learning by using local history/archaeology examples from local neighborhoods. Previous studies have shown that students will become more engaged in education if they can personally connect to the subjects studied (Ruffin 2002; Simmons et al. 2003). Resource kits provide supplementary books, videos, basic analytical tools (ruler, magnifying glasses), and unprovenienced historic artifacts (chamber pot, soda bottle, clay pipe). UMSL faculty and students conducted teacher workshops in spring 2004, introducing educators to these new resources and their possible classroom uses.

A major goal of the Old North St. Louis project was also to publicize the neighborhood's history more broadly in the metropolitan area. The history book, heritage trail, museum, and documentary were employed as marketing tools to lure St. Louisans to a part of the city they might not otherwise visit. ONSTLRG hopes that the idea of cultivating community through history will inspire some visitors to purchase and rehabilitate some of the many endangered historic homes or buy one of the new homes and thus contribute to the organization's goal of neighborhood stabilization.

Conclusion

Critiques of contemporary urbanism in the U.S. frequently emphasize the destructive impact of the sprawling metropolitan form. The phenomenon of suburban sprawl has been attacked on a number of grounds: (1) despoiling natural habitats on the fringes of cities, (2) creating costly inefficiencies in the provision of public services, and (3) draining vital resources from the urban core. In the eyes of many critics, privileging the periphery at the expense of the core has impoverished the metropolitan landscape to the extent that cities can no longer nurture vibrant and sustainable communities. In rapidly growing suburbs and "edge cities" (Garreau 1991), shopping malls, fast food outlets, and superhighways have produced what James Kunstler (1993:10) calls the "geography of nowhere." Devoid of unique identifying features, suburban subdivisions and commercial strips have denied people the opportunity to establish intellectual and emotional attachments to places where they live and work. As a result, no common ground exists upon which the bonds of community can develop and flourish.

Meanwhile, diversion of investment from core to periphery has vanquished inner city landscapes. The flip side of outward dispersal has been abandonment of the center. Not only has this phenomenon exacerbated social inequalities, but it has also destroyed the very places most capable of generating strong communities. In his recent book, *A Place to Remember: Using History to Build Community*, Robert Archibald (1999) notes that older inner city neighborhoods have something very precious that fringe developments lack—a rich history. When long-established shops, churches, and schools submit to bulldozers or fall into disrepair, not only buildings but also the shared memories they embody are lost. "What is happening in cities and towns all over this land," he writes, "is a forgetting, a truncation of narratives that attached people to each other and to their places and gave them a sense of lives lived before their own and lives that will be lived later" (Archibald 1999:149). Archibald takes the argument one step further when he insists that strong communities are founded on mutually accepted values and that by establishing standards of appropriate social behavior, history can reinforce shared ideals. From this perspective, one can see how the process of preserving the past becomes an act of reinvigorating community. Deciding what history to recover and evaluating actions taken by previous generations serve as a mechanism for defining a community.

While writers like Kunstler (1993) and Archibald (1999) make a compelling argument for historic preservation as an act of community building, economic arguments have been even more effective in encouraging cities to protect and restore historic landscapes (Advisory Council on Historic Preservation 1979; National Trust for Historic Preservation 1982; Lichfield 1983; Leithe et al. 1991; Rypkema 1994). In the wake of failed urban renewal programs of the 1950s and 1960s, urban planners and policymakers sought alternative strategies for bringing new investment and middle-class taxpayers back to the city (Kettler and Paseltiner 1983; St. Louis Urban Investment Task Force 1985; Peterson and Robinson 1988). Many cities discovered that rehabilitated historic districts had the capacity to augment tourist revenue (Heudorfer 1975; Hayes 1987; Hammer, Siler, George & Associates 1990; Kaylen 1999). At the same time, dozens of inner city neighborhoods across the country began to encourage rehabilitation of historic houses as a means of boosting property values and attracting affluent homeowners. By the late 1970s, historic preservation had become a well-established urban revitalization tool (Murtagh 1997; Hamer 1998; Tyler 2000).

From a financial standpoint, even successful, economically driven historic preservation campaigns have not always contributed to community cohesion. Indeed, they have served as much to divide and disrupt communities as to unify them. Problems inevitably arise when the reconstructed physical environments envisioned by preservationists clash with the needs and values of contemporary residents. Rising property values in "gentrified" districts have often led to displacement of poorer residents, making historic preservation a divisive issue in many cities. The impulse to freeze a landscape in time can alienate residents whose lives bear little resemblance to those who lived and thrived in the era selected for veneration. In some instances, local residents have thwarted heritage tourism proposals out of fear that an influx of visitors would threaten community tranquility (Hamer 1998:95–99,105–06,122; Miller and Tucker 1998:125–137). Using history to simultaneously build community and revitalize local economies remains a major challenge for those involved in the preservation movement.

Old North St. Louis residents attempt to meet this challenge by tying physical rehabilitation of older homes to community-based public history and archaeology initiatives. Building on recent innovations in the field of public archaeology, faculty and students at the UMSL have helped local citizens research, interpret, and exhibit their past in a manner that was consistent with the community's social and economic objectives for revitalization. The underlying philosophy of the project was that effective historic preservation requires broad citizen engagement. Drawing upon earlier models, historic preservation in Old North St. Louis has attempted to stimulate economic investment and reconnect people to the places where they live.

In the effort to make history relevant to people who currently inhabit the neighborhood, this project emphasized the recent past as much as the era in which most of the restored homes were built. Drawing attention to changes in the neighborhood over the past half-century served two purposes. First, it allowed current residents to see that they are part of the neighborhood's history. Second, it made the remote past more meaningful by making it part of a continuous linear narrative leading to the present. Archaeology facilitated this approach as many of the objects recovered were of recent vintage. The stories behind 20th-century artifacts were compared and combined with the stories behind 19th-century artifacts to create comprehensive historical narratives on particular themes such as children's recreational activities or domestic food preparation. Linking the remote past to both the recent past and the present was encouraged further by displaying recovered artifacts in a community museum alongside items that people use in their homes today.

In the end, archaeology alone cannot save the Old North St. Louis neighborhood or the world for that matter, but it can help to improve the economic and social health of a community as a part of a multidisciplinary project. This approach asks archaeologists to step away from the laboratory microscope and become social activists. In doing this, archaeology *in* and *of* the city must address the urban population's interests and concerns, but working with the public is no easy task (Salwen 1973; Staski 1982). To be honest, it is much easier to conduct research without addressing public needs, but the results in such projects are only heard in conference papers or found in the grey literature of state

or federal agencies. When the public is offered "true acts of inclusion," they can be empowered by their collective heritage, which in turn may result in tourism and urban renewal as well as change views about social relationships in the past and present (Edwards-Ingram 1997). Results of the Old North St. Louis project are far from complete and partially unknown, but lessons learned from this St. Louis example can help with future projects in other cities. From the ground up, neighborhoods like Old North St. Louis can be rejuvenated with a renewed sense of economic stability and restored neighborhood identity.

References

ADVISORY COUNCIL ON HISTORIC PRESERVATION
  1979 *Contributions of Historic Preservation to Urban Revitalization.* Advisory Council on Historic Preservation, Washington, DC.

ARCHIBALD, ROBERT R.
  1999 *A Place to Remember: Using History to Build Community.* Rowman & Littlefield, Walnut Creek, CA.

BARNES, CATHERINE M.
  2004 Broken Dishes: A Ceramic History of Old North St. Louis. Senior thesis, Department of Anthropology, University of Missouri, St. Louis.

BOERNSTEIN, HEINRICH [HENRY]
  1997 *Memoirs of a Nobody: The Missouri Years of an Austrian Radical 1849–1866,* Steven Rowan, translator and editor. Missouri Historical Society Press, St. Louis.

BROWN, LAWRENCE D., AND BERNARD J. FRIEDEN
  1978 *Guidelines and Goals in the Model Cities Program.* Brookings Institution, Washington, DC.

CITY OF ST. LOUIS
  2004 Census 2000 Results. City of St. Louis, Missouri < http://stlouis.missouri.org/census/>.

COMPTON, RICH J., AND CAMILLE N. DRY
  1876 *Pictorial St. Louis.* Compton & Company, St. Louis, MO.

CRESSEY, PAMELA J.
  1983 *Approaches to Preserving a City's Past.* National Park Service and City of Alexandria, VA.
  1987 Community Archaeology in Alexandria, Virginia. *Conserve Neighborhoods,* 69:1–6. [National Trust for Historic Preservation, Washington, DC.]
  1991 Landmarks: 30 Years of Archaeology in Alexandria. Abstract, No. 3, Alexandria Archaeology, Office of Historic Alexandria, City of Alexandria, VA.

2002 *Walk and Bike the Alexandria Heritage Trail: Guide to Exploring a Virginia Town's Hidden Past.* Capital Books, Dulles, VA.
2005 Community Archaeology in Alexandria, Virginia. In *Unlocking the Past: Celebrating Historical Archaeology in North America*, Lu Ann De Cunzo and John H. Jameson, Jr., editors, pp. 97–102. University of Florida Press, Gainesville.

CRESSEY, PAMELA J., AND SUSAN L. HENRY
1990 *Archaeological Significance in Cities: Developing Contexts and Criteria for Decision Making.* Alexandria Archaeology Publications, 21, City of Alexandria, VA.

DERRY, LINDA
1997 Pre-Emancipation Archaeology: Does It Play in Selma, Alabama? *Historical Archaeology* 31(3):18–26.

DERRY, LINDA, AND MAUREEN MALLOY
2003 *Archaeologists and Local Communities: Partners in Exploring the Past.* Society for American Archaeology, Washington, DC.

EAST-WEST GATEWAY COORDINATING COUNCIL
1994 *Transportation Redefined: A Plan for the Region's Future.* East-West Gateway Coordinating Council, St. Louis, MO.

EDWARDS-INGRAM, YWONE
1997 Toward "True Acts of Inclusion": The "Here" and the "Out There" Concepts in Public Archaeology. *Historical Archaeology* 31(3):27–35.

GARREAU, JOEL
1991 *Edge City.* Doubleday, New York, NY.

GILBERT, NEIL
1973 *The Model Cities Program: A Comparative Analysis of Participating Cities, Process, Product, Performance, and Prediction.* U.S. Office of Community Development, Washington, DC.

GROOVER, MARK D.
2003 *An Archaeological Study of Rural Capitalism and Material Life: The Gibbs Farmstead in Southern Appalachia, 1790–1920.* Kluwer Academic / Plenum Publishers, New York, NY.

HAMER, DAVID
1998 *History in Urban Places: The Historic Districts of the United States.* Ohio State University Press, Columbus.

HAMMER, SILER, GEORGE & ASSOCIATES
1990 Economic Impact of Historic District Designation, Lower Downtown, Denver, Colorado. Report to the Office of Planning and Community Development, Denver, CO, from Hammer, Siler, George & Associates, Silver Spring, MD.

HARL, JOSEPH
2005 Cochran Gardens Hope VI, Tract I Housing Project. *MAPA Newsletter* 3(1):11.

HAYES, TRACY
1987 *Tourism and Historic Preservation in the South.* National Trust for Historic Preservation, Southern Regional Office, Charleston, SC.

HEUDORFER, BONNIE SMYTH
1975 A Quantitative Analysis of the Economic Impact of Historic District Designation. Master's thesis, Pratt Institute, Brooklyn, NY.

HOWARD, DICK
1972 A Comparison of the Model Cities Programs of St. Louis and Kansas City, Missouri. Doctoral dissertation, Department of Political Science, University of Missouri, Columbia.

HYDE, WILLIAM, AND HOWARD L. CONARD (EDITORS)
1899 *Encyclopedia of the History of St. Louis: A Compendium of History and Biography for Ready Reference.* Southern History Company, St. Louis, MO.

ISRAEL, FRED L. (EDITOR)
1993 *1897 Sears Roebuck & Co. Catalogue.* Chelsea House, Philadelphia, PA.

JAMESON, JOHN H., JR. (EDITOR)
1997 *Presenting Archaeology to the Public: Digging for Truths.* AltaMira Press, Walnut Creek, CA.
2004 *The Reconstructed Past: Reconstructions in the Public Interpretation of Archaeology and History.* AltaMira Press, Walnut Creek, CA.

JAYNES, PERRY
2003 In Our Own Backyard: An Analysis of the Old North St. Louis Ceramic Assemblage. Senior thesis, Department of Anthropology, University of Missouri, St. Louis.

KAITZ, EDWARD M., AND HERBERT H. HYMAN
1970 *Urban Planning for Social Welfare: A Model Cities Approach.* Praeger, New York, NY.

KAYLEN, MICHAEL
1999 *Economic Impact of Missouri's Tourism and Travel Industry: Annual Report.* Tourism Research and Development Center, University of Missouri, Columbia.

KETCHUM, WILLIAM C., JR.
1991 *American Redware.* Henry Holt & Company, New York, NY.

KETTLER, ELLEN, AND DEBORAH PASELTINER
1983 *Zoning and Historic Preservation: A Survey of Current Zoning Techniques in U. S. Cites to Encourage Historic Preservation.* Landmarks Preservation Council of Illinois, Chicago.

KUNSTLER, JAMES HOWARD
1993   *The Geography of Nowhere: The Rise and Decline of America's Man-Made Landscape.* Simon and Schuster, New York, NY.

LASANSKY, JEANNETTE
1979   *Central Pennsylvania Redware Potter, 1780–1904.* Union County Oral Traditions Projects, Lewisburg, PA.

LEITHE, JONI L., THOMAS MULLER, JOHN E. PETERSON, AND SUSAN ROBINSON
1991   *The Economic Benefits of Preserving Community Character: A Methodology.* Government Finance Research Center of the Government Finance Officers Association, Chicago, IL.

LICHFIELD, NATHANIEL
1983   *Economics in Urban Conservation.* Cambridge University Press, Cambridge, MA.

LISTOKIN, DAVID, MIKE L. LAHR, KEVIN ST. MARTIN, NOMEL FRANCISCO, AND MICHELE B. McGLYN
2001   *Economic Impacts on Historic Preservation in Missouri.* Center for Urban Policy Research, Rutgers University, New Brunswick, NJ.

LITTLE, BARBARA J. (EDITOR)
2002   *Public Benefits of Archaeology.* University Press of Florida, Gainesville.

MARSHALL, YVONNE (EDITOR)
2002   Community Archaeology [theme issue]. *World Archaeology* 34(2).

McDAVID, CAROL, AND DAVID W. BABSON (EDITORS)
1997   In the Realm of Politics: Prospects for Public Participation in African-American and Plantation Archaeology [theme issue]. *Historical Archaeology* 31(3).

McKEE, LARRY
2002   Public Archaeology. In *Encyclopedia of Historical Archaeology,* Charles E. Orser, Jr., editor, pp. 456–458, Routledge Press, London, England, UK.

McKEE, LARRY, AND BRIAN THOMAS
1998   Starting a Conversation: The Public Style of Archaeology at the Hermitage. *Southeastern Archaeology* 17(2):133–139.

MILLER, GEORGE L.
1980   Classification and Scaling of Nineteenth-Century Ceramics. In *Historical Archaeology* 14:1–40.
1991   A Revised Set of CC Index Values for Classification and Economic Scaling of English Ceramics from 1787 to 1800. In *Historical Archaeology* 25(1):1–25.

MILLER, ZANE, AND BRUCE TUCKER
1998   *Changing Plans for America's Inner Cities.* Ohio State University Press, Columbus.

MISSOURI ALLIANCE FOR HISTORIC PRESERVATION
1997   *Proposed State of Missouri Historic Rehabilitation Investment Tax Credit: Analysis of Costs and Benefits.* Missouri Alliance for Historic Preservation, Columbia.

MISSOURI DEPARTMENT OF ECONOMIC DEVELOPMENT
1999   *Missouri Historic Preservation Tax Credit Program.* Missouri Department of Economic Development, Jefferson City.

MURTAGH, WILLIAM J.
1997   *Keeping Time: The History and Theory of Preservation in America.* John Wiley & Sons, New York, NY.

NATIONAL TRUST FOR HISTORIC PRESERVATION
1982   *Economic Benefits of Preserving Old Buildings.* Preservation Press, Washington, DC.

OLD NORTH ST. LOUIS RESTORATION GROUP (ONSTLRG)
2004   Old North St. Louis: An Urban Village on the Edge of Downtown. Old North St. Louis Restoration Group, St. Louis, Missouri < http://www.onsl.org/>.

PETERSON, JOHN E., AND SUSAN G. ROBINSON
1988   *The Effectiveness and Fiscal Impact of Tax Incentives for Historic Preservation: A Reconnaissance for the City of Atlanta.* Government Finance Research Center of the Government Finance Officers Association, Chicago, IL.

POTTER, PARKER B., JR.
1994   *Public Archaeology in Annapolis: A Critical Approach to History in Maryland's Ancient City.* Smithsonian Institution Press, Washington, DC.

RECTENWALD, MIRANDA RABUS, AND ANDREW HURLEY
2004   *From Village to Neighborhood: A History of Old North St. Louis.* Missouri Historical Society Press, St. Louis.

ROWAN, STEVEN
1992   From Forty-Eighter Radicalism to Working-Class Press: Franz Schmidt and the Freie Blätter of St. Louis, 1851–1853. In *The German-American Radical Press: The Shaping of a Left Political Culture, 1850–1940,* Elliot Shore, Ken Fones-Wolf, and James P. Danky, editors, pp. 31–48. University of Illinois Press, Urbana.

ROWAN, STEVEN (TRANSLATOR)
1983   *Germans for a Free Missouri: Translations from the St. Louis Radical Press, 1857–1862.* University of Missouri Press, Columbia.

RUFFIN, MONYA
2002   The Acquisition of Inquiry Skills and Computer Skills by Eighth Grade Urban Middle School Students in a Technology-Supported Environment. Doctoral dissertation, School of Education, University Missouri, St. Louis.

Timothy Baumann, Andrew Hurley, and Lori Allen

RYPKEMA, DONOVAN D.
   1994 *The Economics of Historic Preservation: A Community Leader's Guide.* National Trust for Historic Preservation, Washington, DC.

ST. LOUIS URBAN INVESTMENT TASK FORCE
   1985 *The Impact of the Investment Tax Credit on Neighborhood, Commercial, and Downtown Development and Historic Preservation in St. Louis.* St. Louis Urban Investment Task Force, St. Louis, MO.

SALWEN, BERT
   1973 Archeology in Megalopolis. In *Research and Theory in Current Archaeology*, Charles L. Redman, editor, pp. 151–163. John Wiley and Sons, New York, NY.

SCHMIDT, SARAH M.
   2005a *Archaeology Adventures in Old North St. Louis: A Supplementary Activity Book for the Old North St. Louis Community Museum Traveling Archaeology Education Kit.* Public Policy Research Center, University of Missouri, St. Louis.
   2005b *Archaeology Adventures in Old North St. Louis: Teacher Handbook.* Public Policy Research Center, University of Missouri, St. Louis.

SHACKEL, PAUL A., PAUL R. MULLINS, AND MARK S. WARNER
   1998 *Annapolis Pasts: Historical Archaeology in Annapolis, Maryland.* University of Tennessee Press, Knoxville.

SHORE, ELLIOTT, KEN FONES-WOLF, AND JAMES P. DANKY (EDITORS)
   1992 *The German-American Radical Press: The Shaping of a Left Political Culture, 1850–1940.* University of Illinois Press, Urbana.

SIMMONS, PATRICIA, MONYA RUFFIN, JOSEPH POLMAN, CRISSIE KIRKENDALL, AND TIMOTHY BAUMANN
   2003 If Stones Could Talk. *The Science Teacher* 70(5): 52–54.

SMARDZ, KAROLYN, AND SHELLEY J. SMITH
   2000 *The Archaeology Education Handbook: Sharing the Past with Kids.* AltaMira Press, Walnut Creek, CA.

STASKI, EDWARD
   1982 Advances in Urban Archaeology. *Advances in Archaeological Method and Theory.* Vol. 5, Michael Schiffer, editor, pp. 97–150. Academic Press, New York, NY.
   1987 *Living in Cites: An Introduction.* In *Living in Cities: Current Research in Urban Archaeology*, Edward Staski, editor, pp. ix–xi. Special Publication Series, No. 5, The Society for Historical Archaeology, California, PA.

TYLER, NORMAN
   2000 *Historic Preservation: An Introduction to Its History, Principles, and Practice.* W. W. Norton, New York, NY.

WASHNIS, GEORGE J.
   1974 *Community Development Strategies: Case Studies of Major Model Cities.* Praeger, New York, NY.

WOOD, ROBERT
   1990 Model Cities: What Went Wrong, the Program or Its Critics? In *Neighborhood Policy and Programs: Past and Present*, Naomi Carmon, editor, pp. 61–73. St. Martin's Press, New York, NY.

ZUG, CHARLES G.
   1986 *Turners and Burners: The Fold Potters of North Carolina.* University of North Carolina Press, Chapel Hill.

TIMOTHY BAUMANN
DEPARTMENT OF ANTHROPOLOGY
MISSOURI VALLEY COLLEGE
500 E. COLLEGE ST.
MARSHALL, MO 65340

ANDREW HURLEY
DEPARTMENT OF HISTORY
UNIVERSITY OF MISSOURI-ST. LOUIS
ST. LOUIS, MO 63121

LORI ALLEN
PUBLIC POLICY RESEARCH CENTER
UNIVERSITY OF MISSOURI-ST. LOUIS
ST. LOUIS, MO 63121

Helaine Silverman

Epilogue: Perspectives on Community Archaeology

ABSTRACT

Historical archaeology has promoted dramatic changes in its fields of endeavor over the past quarter century. Theoretical sophistication, international scope, particular attention to the subaltern, and manifold engagement with living stakeholder communities now characterize the profession. This epilogue considers the history of this intellectual progression, interweaving it with consideration of the specific contributions in this themed volume.

Background

Civic engagement, public outreach, and community collaboration appear to have exploded onto the archaeological scene following passage of the Native American Graves Protection and Repatriation Act (NAGPRA) by the U.S. Congress in 1990, although there were outstanding earlier individual efforts, such as the Ozette archaeological project discussed by Marshall (2002:212–214), and certainly prior joint institutional efforts by the Society for American Archaeology (SAA), Society for Historical Archaeology, and American Anthropological Association in the 1980s. In particular, the valiant efforts of the Public Relations Committee and Public Education Committee of the Society for American Archaeology in a series of reports in the late 1980s to the early 1990s can be highlighted.

Evidence of the shift to a socially responsible and ethically engaged archaeological practice became fully evident in the field with the initiation of a regularly appearing "Working Together" column in the *Bulletin* of the Society of American Archaeology (Aldenderfer 1993; Echo-Hawk 1993), renamed *The SAA Archaeological Record* (*TSAA-AR*) in 2000. Today it is commonplace and expected that archaeologists will interact meaningfully with the descendants of the Native American societies they study. Moreover, not only is "Working Together" still a vibrant part of *TSAA-AR*, its coverage has expanded to consider archaeologists' engagement of indigenous communities and local stakeholders outside the United States as well (Stanish and Kusimba 1996; Nicholas 1997; Smith 1997; Stothert 1998; Christen 2008; Grier and Shaver 2008). Articles published in another *TSAA-AR* section, called "Exchanges," address similar issues in the U.S., Latin America, and elsewhere (McClung de Tapia 2002; Weissel 2003; Meyers 2004:23).

Various historical archaeologists were actively engaged in a public outreach approach as far back as the 1970s. Speaking selectively, mention can be made of some 40 years of archaeology at Weeksville, an impoverished African American neighborhood of Brooklyn, New York, where archaeology has contributed to "trigger diverse memories, recollections, and re-interpretations of a nineteenth century historic space as a way for people to understand, connect to, and address contemporary conditions and concerns, and to reclaim their space" (Scott 2009). Other examples can be found in Deetz's classic *In Small Things Forgotten* (1977) and his work at Parting Ways. Of course, there are the successful collaborations of contract and historical archaeologists with various African American church groups, notably the work of John Milner Associates in Philadelphia, such as the Vine Street Cemetery rescue project. Since the 1980s Pamela J. Cressey, city archaeologist for Alexandria, Virginia, has worked with volunteers and professionals to create a vibrant and constantly expanding community-archaeology project. Similarly, in Baltimore, Elizabeth Comer, director of the Baltimore Center for Urban Archaeology, has generated a range of projects promoting public archaeology as a tool for community preservation and empowerment. Today, many historical archaeologists regularly attend and present papers at the annual meeting of the Society for Applied Anthropology based on the nature of their research and professional practice (see below). This perspective is readily seen in Shackel and Chambers's (2004) recent volume, *Places in Mind: Public Archaeology as Applied Anthropology*.

In the late decades of the 20th century American archaeology overall was being affected by the discussions and debates leading up to the formulation of a set of "Principles of Ethics" in the Society for American Archaeology (Lynott and Wylie 1995, 2000). In this regard it is also important to note that ICAHM (UNESCO's International Committee on Archaeological Heritage Management), under the new copresidency of Douglas C. Comer and Willem Willems, is about to undertake a major program of discussion and consultation concerning the dissemination of international standards to which various national archaeological bodies will contribute. Within the SAA, the Public Education Committee (PEC)—founded "to reach larger audiences through projects that promote understanding of and respect for other cultures and encourage preservation of heritage resources"—also was refocusing archaeology (PEC 2004). Although not restricted to U.S. archaeologists and the U.S. past, the PEC is largely composed of archaeologists working in the United States, where its efforts have been creative, consistent, visible, and highly successful thanks to an effective network of state and local archaeology-education coordinators who actively communicate with each other and with their constituencies. In the 1990s and through 2002 the PEC published *Archaeology and Public Education*, a newsletter providing an array of information for practitioners.

Into this exciting mix can be placed the founding, in 1997, of *The International Journal of Historical Archaeology* (*IJHA*) to provide a forum for the similar changes in subject matter and professional practice occurring specifically in that field. While *IJHA* was not founded exclusively to address public outreach, from its beginning, the *IJHA* has promoted scholar-community engagement of the kind discussed in this volume. Moreover, the journal has adopted a global purview (a notable change in the scale of analysis of historical archaeology), enthusiastically publishing work being done outside the United States by American and local archaeologists. To date this includes research in Mexico, Brazil, Bolivia, Argentina, South Africa, Nigeria, Ireland, Britain, Scandinavia, Sicily, China, various states of Southeast Asia, the Philippines, many Pacific Islands, Australia, New Zealand, regions of the former Ottoman Empire, Cyprus, and Greece.

Change toward an applied perspective entered university programs at the same time. In 1993 Anne Pyburn, Karen Vitelli, and Richard Wilk organized the Center for Archaeology in the Public Interest (CAPI), a not-for-profit organization supported by Indiana University, that became a vanguard of the new social archaeology movement. Subsequently, a graduate track called "Archaeology in Social Context" was instituted in Indiana University's Department of Anthropology. For a while, in the mid-1990s, CAPI published *Public Archaeology Review*, a meritorious agenda-promoting minijournal with big ideas. Since then, CAPI scholars and associates have published four important edited volumes: *Archaeological Ethics* (Vitelli 1996), *Archaeological Ethics, Second Edition* (Vitelli and Colwell-Chanthaphonh 2006), *Ethical Issues in Archaeology* (Zimmerman et al. 2003), and *Ethics in Action* (Colwell-Chanthaphonh et al. 2008).

Other archaeologists have created analogous centers at their own universities. One of these, the Center for Heritage Resource Studies (<http://www.heritage.umd.edu>), founded in 2000 at the University of Maryland by Paul Shackel, Erve Chambers, Mark Leone, and Michael Paolisso, has been particularly successful institutionally, with coordinated teaching, research, and funding programs and targeted international collaboration (especially with the Ename Center in Belgium). The Collaborative for Cultural Heritage and Museum Practices at the University of Illinois, created in 2005 by D. Fairchild Ruggles and Helaine Silverman, specifically added museums to its purview and has achieved a notable record of annual conferences (<http://champ.anthro.illinois.edu>) and the start of a publication series resulting from these (Silverman and Ruggles 2007; Ruggles and Silverman 2009; Ruggles [2011]; Silverman 2010). More recently, in 2007, the College of Design at the University of Minnesota partnered with UNESCO's World Heritage Centre to create a Center for World Heritage Studies (<http://worldheritage.cdes.umn.edu>).

In addition to university centers, it is very important to note the creation of new journals such as *The African Archaeology Diaspora Newsletter* (online), *Public Archaeology* (beginning in 2000), and from the World Archaeology Congress, *Archaeologies* (beginning in 2005). Each of these emphasizes social archaeology (to use this term as an umbrella for "engaged," "public," "community," "outreach," etc.).

This opening up of historical archaeology is also occurring in the field of historic preservation, whose concern traditionally has been the building but not the peopled environment in which it exists—what Kaufman (2004) calls "the diversity deficit." Kaufman advocates consideration of how historic preservation can present racially, ethnically, and culturally diverse historical experiences and how it should serve diverse constituencies.

American historical archaeology is part of the trajectory summarized above. Previously, the field had largely focused on elites and supporting dominant narratives and was rather unconcerned with issues of race, class, gender, minorities, personhood, power, and inequality. American historical archaeology began evolving dramatically in the 1980s into a holistic discipline informed by critical theory, however (Leone et al. 1987). Interest shifted from plantation owners to African American subalterns (Leone et al. 1987; Leone and Potter 1988; Ferguson 1992; Handler and Gable 1997; Shackel 2000, 2001; Cuddy 2005; Fennell 2007). This focus now dominates the field and has expanded to attend to all of America's minority or materially less-visible peoples and communities (McGuire 1982; Yamin 2001; Costello 2004; Maniery 2004; Wall et al. 2004). Turner and Young (2007) have used the expression "concealed communities" and "people at the margin" to describe historical archaeology's new focus on the lives of the ordinary people comprising the vast majority of the world's population. They are the focus of this volume's articles. Furthermore, and related to this perspective, historical archaeology's time frame has expanded to encompass pasts as recent as yesterday (Zimmerman, this volume).

Terms and Concepts

The articles herein are a major contribution to the growing corpus of projects concerned with civic engagement, public outreach, community collaboration, and community building. Each of these activities is a meaningful term, although often the words are used interchangeably and in combination. The definitions in this section are certainly open to revision.

McManamon (2005:23) defines *civic engagement* as the use of archaeological materials, including sites, "as tools for a civic dialogue about the issues that face the American people today." Archaeology provides substance for this public dialogue, observes McManamon (2005:23). Gallivan et al., in this volume, also emphasize

dialogue—about the past and its contemporary consequences—specifically between researchers and their various "publics." The overriding sense of civic engagement is that it prepares all people to participate better as citizens in society through collective action, to take active roles in advancing the public good, making the world a better, more hopeful, healthier, more equitable place.

McManamon's *public engagement* is the "wringing [of] interesting public interpretation opportunities from the individual projects" (in his case, the daily cultural resource management projects undertaken by the National Park Service) (McManamon 2005:22). This author prefers the term *public outreach*, for it suggests not just the interpretive efforts necessary to engage the public, but also pragmatic actions such as inviting local community members to a roundtable so that their interests and concerns are addressed, and goodwill and desire for knowledge is generated. Public outreach became an especially recognized endeavor of value in the mid-1990s when it was codified in Principle 4 of the 1996 "Principles of Ethics of the Society for American Archaeology," stating that archaeologists should "communicate archaeological interpretations of the past. Many publics exist for archaeology ... [including] cultural groups who find in the archaeological record important aspects of their cultural heritage" (Lynott and Wylie 2000). Jameson (1994:17) argues that public outreach is an "ethical imperative," stating that unless archaeologists "communicate effectively with the general public, all else is wasted effort." Archaeologists must "make the past accessible and ... empower people to participate in a critical evaluation of the pasts that are represented to them" (Jameson 1994:17). Through "opening" archaeological research to public view and critique, multiple voices are added to archaeological interpretation, and that democratizes archaeology (Jameson 1994:17). Tully (2007:155) calls this dialogic public outreach "community archaeology," emphasizing that it "seeks to diversify the voices involved in the interpretation of the past" (Marshall 2002). One of the most rewarding aspects of the dialogue is that communities may raise questions about the past that archaeologists might not even have contemplated, thereby leading them "to see archaeological remains in a new light and think in new ways about how the past informs the present" (Marshall 2002:218).

The embrace of multivocality leads to true *community* collaboration—the recognition by archaeologists that stakeholders (whether descendant communities or geographically proximal neighbors) should be consulted and ought to have a voice in a project (in which they may or may not wish to actively participate), and should derive some benefit from it (or at least not be negatively impacted), whether this be material or ideological (Little 2002). An understanding and recognition of the values held by a community toward the past (in whatever tangible and intangible forms that might take) is vital (De la Torre et al. 2005; Mathers et al. 2005; Spennemann 2006) if there is to be effective collaboration. Marshall (2002:211) argues that archaeologists must relinquish at least partial control of their projects to the local community. Community collaboration, then, has two partners: the archaeologists and the community.

In the best of cases, community collaboration is not generated top down by the scholars but rather is the product of nonhierarchical discussion. Collaboration may take a number of forms. It could be archaeologists hiring people from the community to work on the project in various ways or offering school children the opportunity to learn new skills, such as photography, mapping, and computerized data entry, thereby opening their vistas beyond manual labor. Collaboration could be the community offering a building as a lab for the project or getting enthused about providing ethnographic information, perhaps oral history. Certainly community collaboration could be the construction of a site museum by both parties (Silverman 2006). It most especially would be the community participating in the archaeologist's research design, and the archeologist meeting the needs of the community in this manner (Gallivan et al., this volume).

Community building may be a highly desirable outcome of public outreach, civic engagement, and community collaboration. It is an aspect of "community archaeology" as discussed by Tully (2007:158), for it is engages "the general process of social cohesion, for example where the inhabitants of modern towns and villages can be brought together through a sense of ownership of their local heritage." Community building carries with it a sense of identity based on heritage, memory, and constructive uses of the past. Sense of place also may be involved. A

community, perhaps imagined—using Anderson (1983) loosely—begins to construct itself socially through recognition of a shared past, a heritage that it may seek to preserve. This heritage may be culturally lineal, as in the case of descendant communities, or it may be fictive, yet useful. Given that heritage is so often contested and, therefore, perversely, a basis for conflict (Ayodhya, India, springs to mind), and given that many disparate social, political, and economic forces—local, regional, and national—inevitably constitute the operational context, the active stimulation of community building and participation in community building by archaeologists on the basis of the revelation of heritage by their archaeological work must be undertaken with caution. For indeed, once put into the public domain—as well it should be—heritage takes on a life of its own in the hands of its stakeholders (the play on words is deliberate).

Thus, the interface of the archaeological site and the local community/community of stakeholders is a "contact zone," to borrow the phrase from Peers and Brown (2003); their usage is different from that made famous by Pratt (1992)—"a place that source community members enter for the purposes of consultation and collaboration." The author would bring their concept more into line with Pratt's original usage. She defines the contact zone as "social spaces where disparate cultures meet, clash, and grapple with each other, often in highly asymmetrical relations of domination and subordination" (Pratt 1992:4). That is the true challenge faced by archaeologists intent on good deeds: can they adequately relinquish their positions of authority so as to engage the community as equals—for the culture referred to by Pratt also implicates different interpretive schemata of the world, different epistemologies, histories, memories, and subjectivities.

Pyburn and Wilk (2000) offer excellent advice in this regard (Pyburn 2006). They observe that archaeologists' most noble intentions to aid local people (typically underprivileged, whether in the U.S. or a foreign country) and acknowledge their rights, nevertheless, may result in "foisting our value system rather thoughtlessly onto others in the guise of good deeds," and thereby cause unintended problems for the people the archaeologists are trying to help (Pyburn and Wilk 2000:79). Pyburn and Wilk do not advocate aloofness, only that archaeologists be aware of the many ethical issues that exist in a community's or region's social, political, and economic milieu. For instance, in the most ostensibly benign way, archaeologists might inadvertently exacerbate internal divisions within the community by whom they hire for their projects.

Pyburn and Wilk recommend that archaeologists work with trained applied anthropologists in trying to meet their ethical responsibilities. Either with professional assistance or on their own, archaeologists need to obtain (or generate for themselves) significant ethnographic knowledge (social, cultural, economic, political, ideological) about the area in which and people with whom they are going to work, before archaeological investigation and certainly before becoming involved in any kind of beneficent endeavor. Goldstein (2000) has observed that assistance to communities can take many forms, some of which potentially may create difficulties for the recipients. I can envision a situation in which an archaeologist unwittingly puts two towns in tourist, economic, and heritage competition with each other by assisting in the building of a community museum in one place but not the other.

But lest my colleagues be scared off from undertaking public sphere actions, they should recognize that archaeologists, like everybody else in that domain, already are

> political actors and it's better to be conscious about the social ramifications of archaeological practice and risk some "danger," than not to think about the contemporary context to all. Archaeology *always* impacts communities in one way or another, so it's best for archaeologists to focus the force of that effect (Paul Shackel 2008, pers. comm.).

Shackel (2004:10–12, this volume) is well aware of the abovementioned issues when he identifies "heritage development" as a positive basis for working with the communities affected by archaeological research. He specifically advocates this activity as "applied archaeology," drawing the term from the well-established field of applied anthropology. As explained by the Society for Applied Anthropology (SfAA), practitioners of applied anthropology seek "the integration of anthropological perspectives and methods in solving human problems throughout the world [so as] to advocate for fair and just public policy based upon sound research" (SfAA 1999). Applied anthropologists are concerned with

problems of biological variability, cultural diversity, ethnicity, gender, poverty, class, and imbalances in resources, rights, and power, among other topics. In order to address these issues the SfAA advocates that anthropologists build partnerships at the community, national, and international levels and acknowledge the perspectives of all people involved (SfAA 1999). Applied anthropologists are typically strong policy advocates and deeply involved in development projects among the disenfranchised, the poor, and minorities, wherever these populations are. But their field of action, and that of applied archaeologists, need not be restricted solely to disadvantaged groups, inasmuch as all peoples have a heritage, for example Handler (1988) in Quebec, Herzfeld (1991) in a Cretan town, Lowenthal (1985) among the English, and Orser (2004) with the diasporic Irish.

Although not intrinsically unproblematic, heritage is an important grounding essence for living in the present. Indeed, that is why bellicose actors will often seek to physically eradicate or performatively suppress the tangible/intangible heritage of others, and why elites (understood as those in/with power) may actively (or even casually) rescript or unwrite pervasive popular understandings of the past, including the space of everyday life. Shorn of its moorings, a heritage-denied or heritage-impeded population may eventually or perhaps more rapidly succumb to new ideologies and practices—at least such would be the hope of the perpetrators. But empowered (sensu stricto) with their heritage, a community may resist, survive, and succeed under duress, and prosper even more when not so challenged. For even in the most benign circumstances, quite simply, heritage "feels good." As Rosenzweig and Thelen (1998) demonstrated with personal survey data, Americans feel a connection to the past—their past and more general pasts. The past constitutes an important part of their everyday lives, framing their understanding of the present and being the foundation for anticipating the future. It is in this sense that the author has used the word "moorings."

Clearly, the concern with *sustainability* running throughout this volume is one of the most important contributions the authors make to applied/community archaeology, and in this concept the reader sees the linkage to heritage development noted above. Development work is never undertaken with the intent that it achieve a one-time impact in the lives of those affected. Rather, the whole rationale of intervention is that the development be sustained, particularly once the agents of its instigation are gone from the scene and with them, possibly, financial resources. This issue of sustainability has plagued many of the well-intentioned site-museum projects undertaken by archaeologists intent on helping the communities in which they work (Silverman 2006). Too often, once the archaeologist is gone, the community falls to internal bickering over museum management and distribution of its scarce resources, and the infrastructure becomes difficult to sustain, and with it the jobs that had been provided and possibly the site that was being protected. Shackel (this volume) correctly sees the key to sustainability in community building. If this cohesion can be achieved, development and other projects will likely be sustained, for they will exist in a stable, socially reproducing environment.

The Articles

Applied archaeologists are anthropologists whose database resides in the past but who recognize that their subsurface involvement with ancient societies occurs in contemporary contexts that must be understood and engaged. This realization is, as said earlier, recent in archaeology, particularly among American archaeologists in underdeveloped countries where conditions of colonialism or imperialism or the local elite power structure did not encourage a deep engagement with the peoples among whom the investigators worked. Castañeda (1996:97–122) scathingly conveys the self-containment of the Carnegie Institution projects in Yucatan in the 1920s and 1930s; their maps effaced the contemporary Maya from the settlements in which they lived so as to represent only the ancient sites. Castillo Butters and Holmquist Pachas (2006:table 10.1) even tabulate the lack of development work *not* conducted by foreign projects on the Peruvian north coast, which has seen a century of intensive excavation. Nor are Americans alone in their previous state of unenlightenment. Hollywood's *The Mummy* (1932), starring Boris Karloff, depicts quite well the fraught relationships between British archaeologists and the Egyptians of various classes among whom they circulated. The change (albeit not universal or even

pervasive) in archaeological practice that began in the 1980s was codified in 1996 in some of the "Principles of Archaeological Ethics of the Society for American Archaeology." "Principle No. 2: Accountability" states, among other points, that

> responsible archaeological research ... requires an acknowledgment of public accountability, and a commitment to make every reasonable effort, in good faith, to consult actively with affected group(s), with the goal of establishing a working relationship that can be beneficial to all parties involved (Lynott 2000:29).

The contributors to *Places in Mind* (Shackel and Chambers 2004) and to the present volume are archaeologists who share the goals of the field of applied anthropology (discussed above) and are competent to effect the desired results within the guidelines of the SfAA and the ethical principles of the SAA.

But effecting results, as desired by a community, may actually run counter to archaeological ethics. This is the conundrum discussed by Gallivan, Moretti-Langholtz, and Woodard in their nuanced consideration of how native communities in Virginia tried to gain federal recognition by deploying strategic essentialism (identities that move through time unchanged), which runs counter to anthropology's constructivist notions of social identity. Archaeological excavation and its associated historical research were able to demonstrate that Werowocomoco had been the capital of the Powhantan chiefdom at the time Jamestown was founded. But after more than 400 years of mistreatment by Anglo society (including "violence, dispossession, and shifting power dynamics") it is impossible for the Powhatan descendants to demonstrate their historical and political continuity from contact times to the present, as required by U.S. law for legal tribal recognition ("a group with a continuous history linked by blood ties to an ancestral community that resides in a narrowly-defined region"). The archaeologists have been able to demonstrate, however, that the legal requirement is itself flawed, based on scholarly reconstruction of the centuries of cultural and social evolution of the Powhatan peoples and distortion of Anglo colonial documentary sources representing native life in 1607. The archaeological project has collaborated closely with Tidewater native societies to create greater historical awareness, to further native empowerment, and to build community around the archaeological and historical counterfacts revealed by the Werowocomoco research, thereby balancing and hopefully redressing the bias inherent in mainstream America's Jamestown mythical narrative. The site of Werowocomoco itself has become "a locus of reconnected and reordered social relations among six of the seven Powhatan-descended tribes." The pluralistic character and relations among the contemporary descendants demonstrably parallels their pluralistic political networks prior to the Jamestown intrusion. The archaeologists are in a position to legitimately question existing federal recognition criteria. They have found a productive fulcrum-point balance between scientific honesty and ethical activism towards the Tidewater native peoples.

Nash, Colwell-Chanthaphonh, and Holen are also concerned with native peoples of the U.S., but from the perspective of a progressive museum philosophy seeking to bring stakeholders into manifold aspects of the professional world of research. These curators have created the "Indigenous Inclusiveness Initiative" and the "Collections Synthesis Project" at the Denver Museum of Nature and Science. Among their goals are to resituate Native Americans from objects of nature to societies that engaged nature through cultural practices; use the museum collections to generate respect, reciprocity, justice, and dialogue between native and nonnative stakeholders; promote beneficence ("anthropology should do some good") and stewardship (rather than ownership); make accessible the objects "held for the public good" so that they truly serve the public; and, of course, include Native American perspectives and voices at the museum so that "indigenous cultural treasures can be appreciated from every perspective—aesthetic, historical, scholarly, and cultural." In my opinion, the most laudable innovation at the museum is the creation of a Visiting Indigenous Fellowship Program, for this is where and when native peoples drive the agenda. The museum benefits because of what it learns from native peoples' concerns; native fellows benefit by being able to take advantage of museum resources for the purposes that they regard as important to themselves and their communities. The fellows are able to take back to their communities ideas and knowledge that build and strengthen community and a sense of Indian identity as they, the native people, wish it to be. The museum also is promoting exposure of Native American youth to science careers, including a science scholarship program. But opening the museum, inviting in native people, and directing them to careers in science and archaeology is still a top-down endeavor. Nowhere is the conflict of cultural schemata clearer than in the incident the authors relate about a very expensive gala dinner that the museum used to host for the native community, the funds for which the museum sought to redirect toward an investment in education programs, a move many local Native Americans opposed in favor of continuing the four-hour blowout. These differing cultural values reflect different ways of building community, and a full museum commitment to civic engagement means letting Native Americans decide what best serves them.

McDavid tells us about Houston's inner-city neighborhoods, where a process of intensive gentrification conflicts with grassroots efforts to maintain and reclaim control of landscapes of historical significance to the African American community and their narratives. Although McDavid's work is not archaeological as is commonly understood, she does "excavate" meanings held by multiple publics through participation in historical societies, commissions, and committees. She discovers that well-meaning attempts to discuss, celebrate, and preserve African American history may actually serve to "perpetuate and reproduce race/class inequities and power imbalances." She is exceptionally sensitive to the extent to which the archaeologist's work may contribute to or hinder the empowerment of African Americans. Empowerment may be achieved when, for instance, an archaeological project recovers evidence of a formerly thriving, albeit materially poor, community, the voices of which can be enhanced through oral history production. This would greatly increase a subaltern community's control over the narratives told about it.

Here is seen a direct intersection with Chidester and Gadsby's work in Baltimore, where an historically white working class in the neighborhood of Hampden, with the assistance of archaeologists, seeks to recover and assert its history. In this case it is former mill workers who constitute the subaltern, with voices unheard because of the few descriptions of their lives and living conditions. Their history is being erased through gentrification that concentrates only on building facades, whose interior space is resignified as middle class through conversion to a sanitized, commodified, tourist simulacrum of a mill town. Instead of grime there is "The Avenue," with gift and antique shops, restaurants, boutiques, and artist studios. Names allusive to the poverty-stricken past now adorn upscale real-estate developments such as "The Clipper Mill." The remaining working-class residents in Hampden and nearby cannot afford to patronize the new mill landscape.

Chidester and Gadsby make several important generalizations: heritage is an active process, tourist marketing may perversely privilege place over people, and marketable heritage too often comes under the control of outsiders rather than its stakeholders. What can be done? Chidester and Gadsby advocate activist archaeology, i.e., community development and social action underwritten by the actual archaeological recovery of history, which demonstrates the prior existence of a healthy, hardworking, community neighborhood. Like McDavid, their goal is empowerment so that a "more just and equitable future" may be achieved.

McDavid suggests other strategies for achieving that goal. I found her argument for what I will call "subversion" or "infiltration" particularly compelling. She argues that archaeologists have academic skills that can be readily redeployed to the real world of urban politics in the form of public service. Archaeologists can volunteer at museums, in historical societies, and serve on various boards and commissions in which they can be powerful voices advocating racially diverse participation, more inclusive docent and exhibition scripts, and a fair balance between the needs of the African American community and that of more privileged others.

The case presented by Mullins and Jones is particularly interesting because it is underwritten by an entire academic department's and university's commitment to civic engagement, the latter in veritable penance for the expropriation of significant tracts of historically black neighborhoods required for the expansion of Indiana University-Purdue University at Indianapolis (IUPUI). As Mullins (2007:94) has previously explained, "dispossession of the campus' former residents is today largely invisible to the campus community." But now the university administration is keen "to address this experience and their institutional role in it; and many community

groups feel some vested interest in both university and community heritage." Over the course of several years, Mullins and his collaborators have undertaken a "constituent-driven archaeology that is based in community interests" (Mullins 2007:94). This approach, notably pursued in Ransom Place, an historically African American neighborhood that was not destroyed by the expansion of IUPUI, has permitted Mullins and Jones to practice a truly productive community-group civic engagement. Of particular interest is how active the neighborhood association is (representing all of the 150 households). Mullins and Jones ponder grassroots expressions of community identity and heritage and the political interests that these implicate from the perspective of their African American constituencies. The latter are not monolithic—not politically, and certainly not in terms of the social identities that are constructed. Mullins and Jones are well aware of the political nature of their project and see it as inevitable in working with a marginalized population in a climate of racial inequality. But, they argue, civic-engagement archaeology must necessarily have an activist aspect.

Regardless of race, McDavid, Chidester and Gadsby, and Mullins and Jones are all concerned with situations of dispossession. In the cases of Houston and Baltimore it is the result of gentrification. In the case of IUPUI it is the result of university expropriation (which amounts to much the same thing).

McDavid and Mullins and Jones work with urban African American communities so as to return their heritage of place to them, enabling them to achieve this through their own efforts of interpretation and involvement. This ceding of "power" to the community is particularly necessary in these two case studies because the scholars are white. Both teams work alongside the community in an attempt to lessen the impact of their own outside, dominant positions.

The African American situation dealt with by Delle and Levine in urban Lancaster, Pennsylvania, is different from Houston and Indianapolis, for here the focus is on "long ago." Lancaster has a development mission of its own in an area that "offers fun" for everyone, according to its tourism literature (Lancaster is located in the center of the trademarked "heart of the Pennsylvania Dutch country"). The city has smart-growth programs, cultural-heritage planning initiatives, and community-action groups. It consciously promotes its historical sites as part of urban revitalization premised on marketing itself as a new tourist destination (Britt 2007:154). With great hopes for tourism, the city undertook construction of a hotel and convention center downtown. In so doing, archaeologists were provided with an exciting opportunity to investigate materials pertaining to the homes of the 19th-century Radical Republican antislavery resident Thaddeus Stevens, and his antislavery mulatto housekeeper and friend, Lydia Hamilton Smith. They had been largely forgotten by Lancaster when Delle and Levine began their project. The excavations recovered numerous finds, among them a cistern that may well have been a physical element in the Underground Railroad. As explained by Delle and Levine, the Stevens/Smith archaeological legacy now has developed into a key component of an emerging heritage narrative in the city. The new historical knowledge recovered through archaeological excavation has generated interest in and debates about the local past in Lancaster, even painful acknowledgment that some Lancaster County residents had been slaveholders. The new history is of particular interest to the city's African American population.

Delle and Levine dedicated themselves to public outreach. Through public presentations during excavation, community-service learning in the public schools, grade-school workshops, walking tours, excavation visits, lectures, and other activities Delle and Levine reached many residents. They regard their classroom efforts with children as the centerpiece of their community-outreach program. Children, it is hoped, have been inspired to participate in community action. The entire city is aware of and officially (though not uniformly among the populace) embraces its antislavery past, constructing it as heritage through incorporation of the Stevens/Smith site into a convention center and museum complex.

Another dimension of the Delle and Levine project in Lancaster concerns "a significant shift in the heritage narrative of downtown ... which had previously focused on a narrow band of time in which retail consumerism in large department stores shaped the identity of many Lancastrians." Delle and Levine trace a fascinating history of urban development plans and their intersection with Lancastrians' strong sense of place, intangible heritage, and local identity. I am fascinated by

their discussion of Penn Square's shopping spaces as "social spaces central to identity formation, negotiation, maintenance, and reproduction in Lancaster." Although it is, perhaps, a stretch, I am reminded of Benjamin's (2002) discussion of the arcades of Paris and their role in the formation of a new urban identity, the flâneur, as well as the opportunity offered to women, the *flâneuse*. I also find relevance to my own analysis of local protests in the 1990s concerning the potential remodeling of the colonial-period Plaza de Armas in Cuzco, Peru, in which a strongly felt community identification with the plaza as a social space, customary space, and Roman Catholic space defeated a progressive mayor's attempt to recover the original Inca identity of the plaza (Silverman 2008). In Cuzco, tourism had generated service businesses around the plaza (restaurants, diverse handicraft shops, money-exchange booths, internet cafés, bars), no longer relevant or economically accessible to the city's residents, but a reality irrelevant to the locals in the maintenance of their affection for the plaza's central fountain and familiar building facades.

Tourism is also an important factor in Baumann's discussion of how Arrow Rock, Missouri, transformed itself over the course of the 20th century from a river town into a major heritage-tourism site. It achieved National Historic Landmark Site recognition in 1963 and the designation of "Distinctive Destination Site" in 2006 from the National Trust for Historic Preservation. This remarkable story suggests comparison with Santa Fe, New Mexico—and, in fact, Arrow Rock was connected to the Santa Fe Trail, which became a basis for historic preservation efforts there. In both cases, grassroots "white, rich" private citizen/residents were in control of the heritage initiative. But, in the case of Arrow Rock, the interpretive heritage script originally obviated African American (read: poor, disenfranchised) history, whereas in Santa Fe the Anglo newcomers commodified Native American and Hispanic cultures (Wilson 1997). In both places tourism is currently the driving force, but whereas Santa Fe celebrates its cultural diversity, "Arrow Rock still has not completely embraced its diverse heritage [and t]he legacy of slavery and the social segregation of the Jim Crow Era continue to affect how history is interpreted." Baumann reports on how archaeology, exhibitions, and educational programs seek to correct the existing "interpretive inequity" (and residual racism) so as to engage and empower the previously marginalized African American community that originated in slavery.

Perhaps the most interesting issue about Arrow Rock is its dramatic decline in population, from 1,000 before the Civil War to 78 now, of whom only one is African American. There is no descendant community in situ. One might think, then, that the effort to preserve and celebrate Arrow Rock's African American heritage would be unsuccessful. Since the late 1990s African Americans have returned to Arrow Rock to tell their story, however, collaborating with professional archaeologists and historians, as are many in the white descendant community. Archaeological, historical, and interpretive work is ongoing in a collaborative manner between the descendant communities, the local historical society, and the Missouri State Parks. Baumann says this has resulted in a renewed sense of community identity. The results of these years of research and engagement will be displayed in a new museum.

Arrow Rock resonates significantly with the New Philadelphia project being conducted by Paul Shackel, Christopher Fennell, Terry Martin, and Anna Agbe Davies (*Historical Archaeology* 44[1]). Although Arrow Rock still physically exists, whereas New Philadelphia, Illinois, is extinct and buried, I am struck by the community-generating results of both projects, as the archaeologists and historians have actively sought out members of the African American descendant community to create a major collaboration. New Philadelphia also has achieved National Historic Landmark status, as well as inscription in the National Register of Historic Places.

In terms of greater significance, Baumann is quite clear:

> The legacy of slavery has continued to impact how and where African American history is interpreted. This has been a problem not only in Arrow Rock, but nationally, as museums and historic sites struggle with how to interpret "uncomfortable history" ... that might offend a tourist, benefactor, or the descendant community.

It is this uncomfortable history that has also motivated Praetzellis and Praetzellis to focus on a different U.S. minority population: Asian Americans. Their Heinlenville (San Jose, California) project deals with the communities created by Japanese and Chinese immigrants who occupied overlapping urban sites and faced similar episodes of discrimination by mainstream white society. Through archaeology, the physical remains of these communities are being recovered and rediscovered, which is to say, put into the contemporary public sphere of Heinlenville's descendants. Although Chinatown and Japantown were torn down in the 1950s and built over with the City Corporation Yard, the descendant communities retain memories and associational sentiments toward that once thriving landscape. Their oral histories have been collected by the Heinlenville project with a view toward subsequent public interpretation through traveling exhibitions, a website, and elementary school curriculum enrichment. Of particular interest is the argument that Heinlenville is a Site of Conscience under the rubrics of racism and displacement followed by the International Coalition of Historic Site Museums of Conscience. This labeling will facilitate a broader context for the study and marketing of Heinlenville, beyond its direct significance for the descendant community.

Of the nine fascinating case studies in this volume, I consider Zimmerman and Welch's the most remarkable, a milestone in archaeology. They explore how the homeless nevertheless enable the feeling and tangibility of home in their nomadism and semipermanent camps, with all that implies in terms of material culture warming the heart and creating a hearth. They argue that the homeless, whom they call displaced persons and who politically are largely invisible, "still manage to retain a cultural heritage of sorts. They carry some materials with them ... while caching other elements." Can what is so ephemeral be treated or conserved in the same way as other heritage resources? Should it be?

Certainly, they argue, the police should be aware of the material culture of homelessness. Through application of archaeological method and theory Zimmerman and Welch have identified route sites, short-term sites, and campsites. They recognize a caching behavior that the outside world perceives as trash, but whose materials are, for the homeless, the "stuff" that helps them live materially and defines each one as a person socially and emotionally. Therefore, no matter how distasteful to the rest of urban society, the officially misidentified trash of the homeless should not be taken away. Zimmerman and

Welch forcefully demonstrate that the information generated by archaeological study can be useful to city officials in providing better supplies and delivery of social services to homeless people. Here is where their study becomes civic engagement. Ultimately, however, it is up to city (and state and national) officials to definitively resolve the pathology of homelessness by generating income-sufficient jobs such that the healthy homeless can acquire homes, and the mentally ill homeless can be moved off the streets into permanent shelters or institutions.

The Zimmerman and Welch essay is a reminder of the brilliant 1936 screwball comedy and biting social commentary, *My Man Godfrey*. Godfrey (played by actor William Powell) has left his Brahmin Boston home to become what the other wealthy characters in the film call one of the "forgotten men" who lives on the city garbage dump. Taking place at the height of the Great Depression, the forgotten men (whose reasons for their current condition vary) have created a viable community of mutual support. Their material culture is mostly scavenged and largely the same in terms of what is needed for basic survival. The city decides to evict them. If forced to leave the dump (itself a midden in the making), their meager material culture would become the top stratum of the stratified deposit. Godfrey solves the issue by turning the dump into a successful nightclub, employing the forgotten men and thereby correcting their situation of homelessness.

Conclusions

Colwell-Chanthaphonh has argued that "archaeologists should play an active role in the pursuit of justice" (2007:25). This pursuit transcends concerns with democracy, inclusivity, and reciprocity so as to overcome archaeology's colonial legacy. Archaeology must, he argues, now embrace applied problems that will truly benefit communities, such as ameliorating resource claims, improving agricultural technology, and furthering economic development (Colwell-Chanthaphonh 2007:29). In so saying, Colwell-Chanthaphonh resonates with all of the essays in this volume as well as numerous others (Shackel and Chambers 2004; Little and Shackel 2007) that seek to promote an agenda of real-world archaeology: civic engagement, public outreach, and community building. A significant and growing number

of archaeologists passionately believe that their work should serve the public, particularly those who are marginalized. Some archaeologists, such as the authors in this volume, are brave enough to actually put their ideology into practice. As indicated earlier, this is not without risk. Yet the authors in this volume overwhelmingly appear to have been successful in their civic engagement, public outreach, community collaboration, and participation in community building.

Today, U.S. historical archaeology is almost everywhere being conducted with sensitivity to descendant communities and local stakeholders and eager involvement of these communities in the projects (Mullins 2004; Shackel and Chambers 2004; Wall et al. 2004; LaRoche 2005; <http://www.histarch.uiuc.edu/>). Far from pandering to multivalent constituencies, the incorporation of these groups' interests in historical archaeology projects is significantly enhancing archaeologists' interpretation of data—indeed collaboration is generating more data, often through recovered memory (Shackel 2005, 2008). Moser et al. (2003:21) praise "the contribution that 'others' can make to the intellectual dimensions of archaeological practice." Speaking of the enthusiastically pursued engagement of stakeholders in New Philadelphia, which was founded by a freed slave, Christopher Fennell (2008) stated,

Our oral history project provides evidence about what people today see as important community stories. ... In addition, our recording of oral history interviews provides important stories about racialization and how the town existed as a multiracial community into the 1920s. We are designing this collaborative archaeology, history, and oral history project to be as democratic as possible.

This participatory transparency has given New Philadelphia importance far beyond its revised historical conclusions and new National Historic Landmark status, for the site is now significant to a large number of people; they are vested in it and, by extension, favorable to and even proactive toward archaeology's study of the past. This approach is consistent with the National Park Service's "shared competency" model (Little 2005) in which archaeologists are not the only truth holders and disseminators, and with the overall approach of community archaeology expounded in this volume (Marshall 2002; Moser et al. 2003; Tully 2007).

Uniting all of these academic and applied pursuits, individual scholars, and organized programs is an overwhelming commitment to social justice and the belief that archaeologists must actively seek to promote it and redress its absence through real-world engagement. Each author in this volume exemplifies that position.

Archaeologies of Engagement, Representation, and Identity is an exceptionally successful grouping of articles that sets an agenda and opens new vistas for what is not only possible in the field of historical archaeology, but what is fundamentally and ethically necessary for its continued success and growth.

References

ALDENDERFER, MARK
1993 Introducing a New Column. Working Together: Exploring Avenues for Cooperation Between Archaeology and Native American Peoples. *SAA Bulletin* 11(4):2.

ANDERSON, BENEDICT
1983 *Imagined Communities: Reflections on the Origin and Spread of Nationalism.* Verso, London, UK.

BENJAMIN, WALTER
2002 *The Arcades Project.* Belknap Press/Harvard University Press, Cambridge, MA.

BRITT, KELLY M.
2007 Archaeology—the "Missing Link" to Civic Engagement? An Introspective Look at the Tools of Reinvention and Reengagement in Lancaster, Pennsylvania. In *Archaeology as a Tool of Civic Engagement*, Barbara J. Little and Paul A. Shackel, editors, pp. 151–172. AltaMira Press, Lanham, MD.

CASTAÑEDA, QUETZIL
1996 *In the Museum of Maya Culture: Touring Chichén Itzá.* University of Minnesota Press, Minneapolis.

CASTILLO BUTTERS, LUIS JAIME, AND ULLA SARELA HOLMQUIST PACHAS
2006 Modular Site Museums and Sustainable Community Development at San José de Moro, Peru. In *Archaeological Site Museums in Latin America*, Helaine Silverman, editor, pp. 130–155. University Press of Florida, Gainesville.

CHRISTEN, KIMBERLY
2008 Working Together: Archival Challenges and Digital Solutions in Aboriginal Australia. *SAA Archaeological Record* 8(2):21–24.

COLWELL-CHANTHAPHOHN, CHIP
2007 History, Justice and Reconciliation. In *Archaeology as a Tool of Civic Engagement*, Barbara J. Little and Paul A. Shackel, editors, pp. 23–46. AltaMira Press, Lanham, MD.

COLWELL-CHANTHAPHOHN, CHIP, JULIE HOLLOWELL, AND DRU MCGILL
2008 *Ethics in Action: Case Studies in Archaeological Dilemmas.* SAA Press, Washington, DC.

COSTELLO, JULIA G.
2004 The Chinese in Gum San ("Golden Mountain"). *The SAA Archaeological Record* 4(5):14–17.

CUDDY, THOMAS W.
2005 African Americans in Archaeology in Annapolis. *The SAA Archaeological Record* 5(2):6–10.

DE LA TORRE, MARTA, MARGARET MACLEAN, RANDALL MASON, AND DAVID MYERS
2005 *Heritage Values in Site Management: Four Case Studies.* Getty Conservation Institute, Los Angeles, CA.

DEETZ, JAMES
1977 *In Small Things Forgotten.* Anchor Books, New York, NY.

ECHO-HAWK, ROGER C.
1993 Working Together: Exploring Ancient Worlds. *SAA Bulletin* 11(4):5–6.

FENNELL, CHRISTOPHER
2007 *Crossroads and Cosmologies: Diasporas and Ethnogenesis in the New World.* University Press of Florida, Gainesville.
2008 New Philadelphia Archaeology Project: Updates on Project Progress. Department of Anthropology, University of Illinois, Urbana-Champaign <http://www.anthro.uiuc.edu/faculty/cfennell/NP/updates.html>. Accessed 15 June 2008.

FERGUSON, LELAND
1992 *Uncommon Ground: The Archaeology of African America, 1650–1800.* Smithsonian Institution Press, Washington, DC.

GOLDSTEIN, LYNNE
2000 The Potential for Future Relations Between Archaeologists and Native Americans. In *Ethics in American Archaeology*, 2nd edition, Mark J. Lynott and Alison Wylie, editors, pp. 118–125. Society for American Archaeology, Washington, DC.

GRIER, COLIN, AND LISA SHAVER
2008 The Role of Archaeologists and First Nations in Sorting Out Some Very Old Problems in British Columbia, Canada. *The SAA Archaeological Record* 8(1):33–35.

HANDLER, RICHARD
1988 *Nationalism and the Politics of Culture in Quebec.* University of Wisconsin Press, Madison.

HANDLER, RICHARD, AND ERIC GABLE
1997 *The New History in an Old Museum: Creating the Past in Colonial Williamsburg.* Duke University Press, Durham, NC.

HERZFELD, MICHAEL
    1991 *A Place in History: Social and Monumental Time in a Cretan Town.* Princeton University Press, Princeton, NJ.

JAMESON, JOHN H.
    1994 The Importance of Public Outreach Programs in Archaeology. *SAA Bulletin* 12(3):16–17.

KAUFMAN, NED
    2004 Heritage Places and the Diversity Deficit in Historic Preservation. *CRM: The Journal of Heritage Stewardship* 1(2):68–85.

LAROCHE, CHERYL JANIFER
    2005 Heritage, Archaeology, and African American History. *The SAA Archaeological Record* 5(2):34–37,44.

LEONE, MARK, AND PARKER B. POTTER (EDITORS)
    1988 *The Recovery of Meaning: Historical Archaeology in the Eastern United States.* Smithsonian Institution Press, Washington, DC.

LEONE, MARK, PARKER B. POTTER, AND PAUL A. SHACKEL
    1987 Toward a Critical Archaeology. *Current Anthropology* 28(3):283–292,299–302.

LITTLE, BARBARA J.
    2005 Archaeologists and Interpreters Working Together. *The SAA Archaeological Record* 5(2):19–21.

LITTLE, BARBARA J. (EDITOR)
    2002 *Public Benefits of Archaeology.* University Press of Florida, Gainesville.

LITTLE, BARBARA J., AND PAUL A. SHACKEL (EDITORS)
    2007 *Archaeology as a Tool of Civic Engagement.* AltaMira Press, Lanham, MD.

LOWENTHAL, DAVID
    1985 *The Past is a Foreign Country.* Cambridge University Press, Cambridge, UK.

LYNOTT, MARK J.
    2000 Ethical Principles and Archaeological Practice: Development of an Ethics Policy. In *Ethics in American Archaeology*, 2nd edition, Mark J. Lynott and Alison Wylie, editors, pp. 26–34. Society for American Archaeology, Washington, DC.

LYNOTT, MARK J., AND ALISON WYLIE (EDITORS)
    1995 *Ethics in American Archaeology: Challenges for the 1990s.* Society for American Archaeology, Washington, DC.
    2000 *Ethics in American Archaeology*, 2nd edition. Society for American Archaeology, Washington, DC.

MCCLUNG DE TAPIA, EMILY
    2002 A First Look at Public Outreach in Mexican and Guatemalan Archaeology. *SAA Archaeological Record* 2(2):27–29.

MCGUIRE, RANDALL H.
    1982 The Study of Ethnicity in Historical Archaeology. *Journal of Anthropological Archaeology* 1(2):159–178.

MCMANAMON, FRANCIS P.
    2005 The Public Interpretation of America's Archaeological Heritage. *The SAA Archaeological Record* 5(2):22–23.

MANIERY, MARY L.
    2004 The Archaeology of Asian Immigrants: 35 Years in the Making. *The SAA Archaeological Record* 4(5):10–13.

MARSHALL, YVONNE
    2002 What is Community Archaeology? *World Archaeology* 34(2):211–219.

MATHERS, CLAY, TIMOTHY DARVILL, AND BARBARA J. LITTLE (EDITORS)
    2005 *Heritage of Value, Archaeology of Renown.* University Press of Florida, Gainesville.

MEYERS, ALLAN
    2004 The Challenge and Promise of Hacienda Archaeology in Yucatan. *The SAA Archaeological Record* 4(1):20–23.

MOSER, STEPHANIE, DARREN GLAZIER, JAMES E. PHILLIPS, LAMYA NASSER EL NEMR, MOHAMMED SALEH MOUSA, RASCHA NASR AIESH, SUSAN RICHARDSON, ANDREW CONNER, AND MICHAEL SEYMOUR
    2003 Transforming Archaeology Through Practice: Strategies for Collaborative Archaeology and the Community Archaeology Project at Quseir, Egypt. In *Museums and Source Communities: A Routledge Reader*, Laura Peers and Allison K. Brown, editors, pp. 208–226. Routledge, London, UK.

MULLINS, PAUL R.
    2004 The Invisible Landscape: An Archaeology of Urban Renewal and the Color Line. *The SAA Archaeological Record* 4(4):25–28.
    2007 Politics, Inequality, and Engaged Archaeology: Community Archaeology Along the Color Line. In *Archaeology as a Tool of Civic Engagement*, Barbara J. Little and Paul A. Shackel, editors, pp. 89–108. AltaMira Press, Lanham, MD.

NICHOLAS, GEORGE
    1997 Working Together: Archaeology, Education and the Sewepemc. *SAA Bulletin* 15(2) <http://www.saa.org/publications/SAAbulletin/15-2/SAA8.html> Accessed 21 September 2009.

ORSER, CHARLES E.
    2004 Archaeological Interpretation and the Irish Diasporic Community. In *Places in Mind. Public Archaeology as Applied Anthropology*, Paul A. Shackel, editor, pp. 171–191. Routledge, New York, NY.

PEERS, LAURA, AND ALISON K. BROWN (EDITORS)
    2003 *Museums and Source Communities: A Routledge Reader.* Routledge, London, UK.

PRATT, MARY LOUISE
    1992 *Imperial Eyes: Studies in Travel Writing and Transculturation.* Routledge, London, UK.

PUBLIC EDUCATION COMMITTEE (PEC)
2004 Public Education. Society for American Archaeology <http://www.saa.org/Pubedu/index.html>. Accessed 4 June 2008.

PYBURN, K. ANNE
2006 Exhibiting Archaeology: Site Museums and Cultural Resource Management in Latin America. In *Archaeological Site Museums in Latin America*, Helaine Silverman, editor, pp. 256–266. Springer, New York, NY.

PYBURN, K. ANNE, AND RICHARD WILK
2000 Responsible Archaeology is Applied Anthropology. In *Ethics in American Archaeology*, 2nd edition, Mark J. Lynott and Alison Wylie, editors, pp. 78–83. Society for American Archaeology, Washington, DC.

ROSENZWEIG, ROY, AND DAVID THELEN
1998 *The Presence of the Past: Popular Uses of History in American Life*. Columbia University Press, New York, NY.

RUGGLES, D. FAIRCHILD (EDITOR)
[2011] *Heritage Cities*. Springer, New York, NY.

RUGGLES, D. FAIRCHILD, AND HELAINE SILVERMAN (EDITORS)
2009 *Intangible Heritage Embodied*. Springer, New York, NY.

SCOTT, JENNIFER
2009 Placing Weeksville in the Past and Present: Documenting and Interpreting the Stories of Brooklyn's Forgotten 19th-Century African American Community. Paper presented at electronic symposium, Places of Meaning, Meaning in Place: Tangibility, Controversy and Conscience at Historic Sites, 42nd Conference on Historical and Underwater Archaeology, Toronto, ON.

SHACKEL, PAUL A.
2000 *Archaeology and Created Memory: Public History in a National Park*. Springer, New York, NY.
2004 Working with Communities: Heritage Development and Applied Archaeology. In *Places in Mind: Public Archaelogy as Applied Anthropology*, Paul A. Shackel and Erve J. Chambers, editors, pp. 1–16. Routledge, New York, NY.
2005 Memory, Civic Engagement, and the Public Meaning of Archaeological Heritage. *The SAA Archaeological Record* 5(2):24–27.
2008 Memory Studies in Historical Archaeology. *The SAA Archaeological Record* 8(1):10–11.

SHACKEL, PAUL A. (EDITOR)
2001 *Myth, Memory, and the Making of the American Landscape*. University Press of Florida, Gainesville.

SHACKEL, PAUL A., AND ERVE J. CHAMBERS (EDITORS)
2004 *Places in Mind: Public Archaeology as Applied Anthropology*. Routledge, New York, NY.

SILVERMAN, HELAINE
2008 Daniel Estrada and the Plaza de Armas in Cuzco, Peru. *Heritage Management* 1(2):181–217.

SILVERMAN, HELAINE (EDITOR)
2006 *Archaeological Site Museums in Latin America*. University Press of Florida, Gainesville.
2010 *Contested Cultural Heritage: Religion, Nationalism, Erasure and Exclusion in a Global World*. Springer, New York, NY.

SILVERMAN, HELAINE, AND D. FAIRCHILD RUGGLES (EDITORS)
2007 *Cultural Heritage and Human Rights*. Springer, New York, NY.

SMITH, MICHAEL E.
1997 Working Together: Archaeology in the Middle of Political Conflict in Yautepec, Mexico. *SAA Bulletin* 15(4) <http://www.saa.org/publications/SAAbulletin/15-4/SAA8.html>. Accessed 21 September 2009.

SOCIETY FOR APPLIED ANTHROPOLOGY (SFAA)
1999 Mission. Society for Applied Anthropology <http://www.sfaa.net/sfaagoal.html>. Accessed 3 May 2008.

SPENNEMANN, DIRK H. R.
2006 Gauging Community Values in Historic Preservation. *CRM: The Journal of Heritage Stewardship* 3(2):6–20.

STANISH, CHARLES, AND CHAPURUKHA M. KUSIMBA
1996 Working Together: Archaeological Research and Community Participation. *SAA Bulletin* 14(3) <http://www.saa.org/publications/SAAbulletin/14-3/SAA15.html>. Accessed 21 September 2009.

STOTHERT, KAREN E.
1998 Working Together: The New Role of the Ancient Lovers of Sumpa. *SAA Bulletin* 16(2) <http://www.saa.org/publications/SAAbulletin/16-2/SAA15.html>. Accessed 21 September 2009.

TULLY, GEMMA
2007 Community Archaeology: General Methods and Standards of Practice. *Public Archaeology* 6(3):155–187.

TURNER, SAM, AND ROB YOUNG
2007 Concealed Communities: The People at the Margins. *International Journal of Historical Archaeology* 11(4):297–303.

VITELLI, KAREN D. (EDITOR)
1996 *Archaeological Ethics*. AltaMira Press, Walnut Creek, CA.

VITELLI, KAREN D., AND CHIP COLWELL-CHANTHAPHOHN (EDITORS)
2006 *Archaeological Ethics*, 2nd edition. AltaMira Press, Walnut Creek, CA.

WALL, DIANA DIZEREGA, NAN A. ROTHSCHILD, CYNTHIA COPELAND, AND HERBERT SEIGNORET
2004 The Seneca Village Project: Working with Modern Communities in Creating the Past. In *Places in Mind: Public Archaeology as Applied Anthropology*, Paul A. Shackel and Erve J. Chambers, editors, pp. 101–117. Routledge, New York, NY.

WEISSEL, MARCELO
2003   A Needle in a Haystack: Buenos Aires Urban Archaeology. *The SAA Archaeological Record* 3(4):28–30.

WILSON, CHRIS
1997   *The Myth of Santa Fe: Creating a Modern Regional Tradition.* University of New Mexico Press, Albuquerque.

YAMIN, REBECCA (EDITOR)
2001   Becoming New York: The Five Points Neighborhood. *Historical Archaeology* 35(3):1–135.

ZIMMERMAN, LARRY J., KAREN D. VITELLI, AND JULIE HOLLOWELL-ZIMMER (EDITORS)
2003   *Ethical Issues in Archaeology.* AltaMira Press, Walnut Creek, CA.

HELAINE SILVERMAN
DEPARTMENT OF ANTHROPOLOGY
UNIVERSITY OF ILLINOIS
109 DAVENPORT HALL
URBANA, IL 61801

Part III:
African American Archaeology and the Public

PARKER B. POTTER, JR.

What Is the Use of Plantation Archaeology?

ABSTRACT

This essay is a commentary on plantation archaeology inspired by a recent article by William H. Adams and Sarah Jane Boling (1989). By asking what is the use of plantation archaeology, this author does not mean to reject this increasingly popular archaeological enterprise. Rather, the purpose is to provoke serious reflection on two issues: (1) the reasons for doing plantation archaeology and (2) the audiences for such studies. The essay has three main parts: a general discussion of the status of self-reflection in plantation archaeology; a specific critique of Adams and Boling's piece; and a set of four suggestions for improving on Adams and Boling's work, *not* by changing their analysis but by paying greater attention to the contexts in which slave-owned ceramics existed in the past and the contexts in which these same objects exist today, as archaeological finds. This commentary is based on critical theory, and on the proposition that, whether it is explicitly interpreted for the public or not, any archaeological project is a public performance. Whenever archaeologists go about their archaeological work, they perform, at the very least, their own training and biases, their sources of funding and support, *and* the history of their research subjects, a history to which they may have only the most tenuous connections.

Introduction

It would be an overstatement to say that there is a revolution afoot in American archaeology, but there is enough of an honest difference of opinion within the field for Robert Preucel to have organized a Southern Illinois University/Center for Archaeological Investigations Visiting Scholar's Conference on what he terms the "processual/postprocessual debate" (Preucel 1991). Given this way of characterizing the current debate(s), it is important to note that postprocessual archaeology is less a coherent movement than it is a collection of kindred perspectives. Among the various postprocessual archaeologies, there is critical archaeology (Wylie 1985; Leone 1986; Leone et al.

1987; Washburn 1987; Potter 1989; Pinsky and Wylie 1990) which is based on the critical theory of the Frankfurt School (Held 1980; Geuss 1981; Arato and Gebhardt 1982). This commentary uses two elements of critical archaeology to form a critique of the recent article by Adams and Boling (1989) entitled "Status and Ceramics for Planters and Slaves in Three Coastal Georgia Plantations." Specifically, it is argued: (1) that Adams and Boling's article is not adequately self-reflective and (2) that this lack of self-reflection significantly impedes the authors' ability to understand the implications of their work and to anticipate the possible uses to which their conclusions could be put.

Adams and Boling's Conclusion

This critique begins with the last two sentences of Adams and Boling's article:

> Indeed, on such plantations slaves may be better understood within the context of being peasants or serfs, regarding their economic status. Their legal status was still as chattel slave, of course, but their economic freedoms were much greater than most people realize (Adams and Boling 1989:94).

The question here is a simple one. To whom is this statement directed? Or, stated another way, who is the audience for Adams and Boling's analysis and the conclusions they draw? Or, more aggressively, who would gain and who would lose as a result of social action based on a conclusion like this? This last question is a vital one, given the Frankfurt School understanding of the inseparability of knowledge and human interests.

These questions are asked because it is not evident from their article that Adams and Boling have asked them, either of themselves or of contemporary African Americans, the audience most likely to be affected by their work. These questions matter because it would be relatively easy for someone advocating a racist position to use a statement like Adams and Boling's conclusion as a starting point from which to claim that slavery was not such a bad deal for enslaved African Americans. This claim, in turn, could be used to argue that if slave life was not so bad, then contemporary

African Americans do not have as much to complain about as they think they do. This hypothetical argument may sound far-fetched, but one lesson in David Duke's recent political success in Louisiana is that there are plenty of people out there who would be more than happy to buy into an argument like the one just outlined. Moving from today's front pages to the academic literature, one can find many examples of the political use (and/or misuse) of archaeology and history. Clark (1957:259–260) on Nazi Germany, Silverberg (1968, 1974) on the Moundbuilder myth, Trigger (1980) on Native Americans, and Hall (1984, 1988) on South Africa are just several of the growing number of archaeologists who have turned their attention to the social use of archaeological knowledge in the societies that sponsor or support archaeological research. In addition, this issue seems to be a central theme in several volumes of the recently published "One World Archaeology" series (Layton 1988, 1989; Gathercole and Lowenthal 1990; Stone and MacKenzie 1990).

The only point here is that Adams and Boling's article would have been a more socially responsible piece of scholarship if they had considered and acknowledged the potential usefulness of their conclusions, particularly to those who would try to minimize the enormity of slavery in order to deny the legitimacy of current claims of racial discrimination against African Americans and to thwart the efforts of African Americans to achieve and preserve full civil rights. At this point, the term "social responsibility" needs to be defined.

This writer's intention is *not* to equate social responsibility with one particular theoretical or political viewpoint. Rather, in this situation, social responsibility means having a full awareness of the contexts and the consequences of the work one does, the conclusions one reaches, and the modes of expression one chooses. The entire academic enterprise and archaeologists' own professional lives are based on the idea that words are powerful things, and meaning resides at several levels in the texts researchers produce. Thus, as defined here, social responsibility means nothing more than using the most sophisticated methods available to mean what is said and to say what is meant, to an acknowledged audience. In early drafts of this article, the use of the term "social responsibility" troubled some readers. During the course of revision, this writer has discovered a good clear statement on this issue. Writing in the *Winterthur Portfolio* Forum, Edward Chappell (1989:287) says, "My argument, simply put, is that museums have a responsibility for the broad social implications of what they present, as well as for the accuracy and clarity of the subject with which they are dealing." He also notes that "most of us are too involved in a headlong pursuit of the past to glance over our shoulders at the effects that we and our predecessors have had on the world around us" (Chappell 1989:248–249)."

Finally, near the end of his article, Chappell argues the point on which this commentary is based:

> Clearly it is the responsibility of museum planners to anticipate . . . misreadings as well as to ensure the accuracy of the presentation and the physical setting. We must consider how exhibitions may be misinterpreted, as well as how we intend them to be understood (Chappell 1989:263).

Chappell's comments are directed toward the museum profession, but as already argued, it is reasonable to consider any instance of archaeological activity—and the products that result—as a public performance, as an exhibition in Chappell's sense.

As Sinclair emphasizes in a discussion of archaeology in Mozambique, controlling the uses of archaeological work is by no means a sure thing: "We are faced with a situation (which seems to occur widely) where the producer of even relevant scientific knowledge does not control the ambits within which such information is to be used" (Sinclair 1990:157). While researchers may sometimes (or frequently) lose control of the knowledge produced, they are *always* free to anticipate its potential impacts, and failure to do so is, in Chappell's terms, socially irresponsible.

To return to Adams and Boling, the irony in their article is that they have provided a potential weapon for a social and political position they no doubt find repugnant. The key to this irony is their apparent lack of self-reflection. The qualifier "apparent" is used because Adams has indeed presented these conclusions to African-American audiences (Adams 1989, pers. comm.). That fact needs to be *in the article itself*, as a part of an internal mechanism designed to protect the article's powerful conclusion from blatant misuse by those with an agenda that runs counter to the intentions of the authors. What Adams and Boling fail to provide is precisely what Epperson *does* provide when he characterizes his work in plantation archaeology as "addressing the construction of race within what remains a largely racist society" (Epperson 1990:35). Archaeologists may argue with Epperson's assessment of contemporary American society (this writer does not), but at least it is there to be examined; Adams and Boling give no clue as to their view of the world into which they are sending their research and its conclusions. Furthermore, Epperson is not shy about articulating his agenda, which is to help inform "the fundamental critique of oppression and domination, both historically and in the present" (Epperson 1990:35). This critique constitutes a "social and political commitment . . . to help create a more humane social order" (Epperson 1990:35). In contrast, Adams and Boling provide neither a reflexive commentary on their intentions nor a consideration of any of the various social agendas for which their work could be a tool.

Plantation Archaeology as Unreflective

A lack of self reflection is hardly unique to Adams and Boling. To the contrary, an unreflective viewpoint is exactly the perspective adopted in much of the plantation archaeology that has been carried out over the last 15 years (Leone and Potter 1988:307–312) and in fact, much of American archaeology (Potter 1989:21–45, 1991). For example, there is virtually no acknowledgment of contemporary social context in any of the articles in Singleton's (1985) edited volume, *The Archaeology of Slavery and Plantation Life*. Two particularly telling instances of this lack of reflection are William Kelso's (1984) book on Kingsmill Plantation and the large body of work inspired by John

Otto's (1984) book on Cannon's Point Plantation, based on his dissertation (Otto 1975).

The second chapter of Kelso's book, called "Above Ground," contains three sections: "Context," "Things," and "People." What is interesting is that most of Kelso's discussion of slaves and slave life appears in the section called "Things." The section on "People" is mostly reserved for slave-owning *white* people. This understanding of slaves as things certainly characterizes the time period about which Kelso is writing, but the way Kelso uses this 18th-century understanding, unreflectively, to form his own narrative strategy serves to perpetuate those categories today. That is, Kelso acknowledges neither the source of the categories he uses nor the historical justification for calling slaves "things." Thus, the idea that slaves were things is expressed in Kelso's own, living authorial voice. As a result, the reader is left with no logical alternative other than to conclude that Kelso himself, as an active member of 20th-century society, considers African Americans to have been things. Of course this is absurd, but Kelso invites this inappropriate interpretation by failing to understand that how one says something is a part of what one says. This point is far from esoteric, and has been made in discussions of archaeological education in Venezuela (Vargas Arenas and Sanoja Obediente 1990:51–52) and the United States (Kehoe 1990:213) as well as in discussions of museum exhibits on Native American topics (Lester 1987; Blancke and Slow Turtle 1990:125). In the case of Kingsmill Plantations, this writer would argue that no matter how sympathetically or humanistically slave life is presented in a section called "Things," there is no avoiding the implication that African Americans were things, that it was appropriate to think of them as such, and that it *still is* appropriate to think of African-American people as things.

This writer's solution to this problem is not to ignore or deny the 18th-century viewpoint, but instead to clearly label it both culturally and temporally and then to separate it carefully from the contemporary perspective that informs a particular piece of work on 18th-century slavery. In this case, since his section headings say otherwise,

Kelso should have told his readers explicitly that *he* does not think that African Americans are not people, that his section headings are intended to represent *only* a particular 18th-century viewpoint and not his own. Instead of assuming this category, Kelso could have explored its origins and history, working as Epperson does to "denaturalize" the category of race by demonstrating "that it is not a universal, natural, or inevitable aspect of the human condition" (Epperson 1990: 35). The starting point for all of this is self-reflection. If Kelso had considered the implications of his section headings, it is doubtful that he would have used them the way he did. The self-reflective question he could have asked himself is: "are my feelings on the humanity of African Americans accurately represented by these section headings?" Thus, this writer is not telling Kelso what to think or say, but only asking whether or not he *meant* to say what it seems that he *did* say, subtextually.

With regard to Otto's Cannon's Point work, this writer's criticism is somewhat different but also rooted in an unreflective viewpoint. Furthermore, the argument lies more with those who have followed Otto's example than with Otto himself, but because the issue to be dealt with was introduced to historical archaeology through Otto's work, that will be the focus of this discussion. Otto's goal in analyzing the archaeological record at Cannon's Point has been to investigate and describe the living conditions on an ante-bellum plantation, as a way of augmenting discussions of "the legal or social aspects of slave treatment" (Otto 1975:2) based on written records. The three principal realms of material culture Otto uses are houses, artifacts (such as ceramic and glass tableware), and food remains. The problem is that Otto's basic question and his analytical framework, used unreflectively, constitute a dangerous trap for plantation studies.

The spring in this trap is the idea of quality of life. While Otto is very careful to limit himself to *describing* the conditions of slave life, others have taken the logical step to *judging* the quality of slave life. Otto (1975:2), Singleton (1985:7), and Reitz et al. (1985:185) have all characterized the nutritional analyses of Fogel and Engerman (1974)

as controversial if not problematic. But the real problem with *Time on the Cross* is not the accuracy of the answers it provides, which is where the debate is currently being carried out. Rather, the problems with studies like *Time on the Cross* lie with the questions they ask and in their inattention to the sources of these questions. Put simply, is it really reasonable to pose *any* research question that could be answered with a statement that slave life was not all that bad? Is it reasonable to reach a conclusion along the lines of "everyone knows that these people were slaves, *but* they had nutritious food, adequate housing, and/or stylish tableware" as if food, living space, or ceramics could ever, under any circumstances, obviate the condition of involuntary servitude? Otto's questions and answers are not of this sort, but intentionally or not, Otto has set an agenda for plantation archaeology, and his work has encouraged others, including Adams and Boling, to think in this way.

As suggested above, the ability to ask questions that logically entail these seemingly unreasonable answers is based on a failure of reflection, and this failure is composed of several parts. First, the quality of slave life is invariably judged in western scientific terms that may or may not be appropriate to the lives being judged. Without demonstrating that these measures of quality of life are meaningful in terms of an 18th-century African-American worldview, their use constitutes a continuation—albeit an intellectual one—of the domination of master over slave. Lilla Watson, an indigenous Australian (or Murri) who is also a western trained academic, pinpoints this issue when she says:

> It is still a case of white academics and writers describing us and our culture, generally using Western concepts, categories, and definitions—i.e., white terms of reference. The areas of study undertaken represent white preoccupations, perspectives, and priorities. . . . We have had enough of being defined and described by whites, of having others determine what is relevant and important in Aboriginality. We will say who and what we are. It has taken a long time for white Australia to reach the point of being ready to hear what we say, rather than what others say about us (Watson 1990:92).

In discussing various western perspectives on Australian aboriginal culture, Barlow (1990:76–

78) goes well beyond the neutral term "etic," referring instead to "colonial knowledge," which he sees as a specific body of information used as a tool for cultural oppression. Watson and Barlow both identify *two* problems with Western categories. They are inappropriate to the people whose cultures are being studied *and* they are potentially injurious to the literal and cultural descendants of those research subjects. That is, the use of such categories is both bad science and bad politics.

Returning to plantation studies in the American South, there is the additional problem of false comparability. Many archaeological analysts of plantation slavery have followed Otto and Stanley South (1977, 1978, 1979, 1988) in adopting a radically functionalist approach. Orser (1989) provides a commentary on this trend. Archaeological plantation studies are so tied to a functionalist approach that it is probably a good idea to wonder about the degree to which the current popularity of plantation studies is driven by the fact that plantations lend themselves so readily to functionalism; it may well be the case that current archaeological studies of plantation slavery have far more to say to functionalist social scientists than they have to say to African-American descendants of plantation slaves. A principal by-product of all this is a systems-based mode of analysis that compares planters, overseers, and slaves on the basis of differential deposits of various classes of artifactual material. In such analyses, things stand for the people who used them—a plate for a planter and so on, and it is this identity between people and things that gives rise to the problem of false comparability.

Because they were made out of the same materials, or were the same objects, plantation houses, meals, and dishes are analytically interchangeable today in a way that the people who used those objects were absolutely *not* socially interchangeable 200 years ago. Furthermore, on most plantations, ceramic types circulated much more freely from table to table than did the people who ate at those tables. The probability of *any* kind of plate turning up on the table of a planter, overseer, or slave was far greater than the probability of a slave eating at a planter's table or a planter eating at a slave's table. To take this problem one step further, the ability to "translate" from slave life to overseer life to planter life through the use of scales based on ceramics, architecture, or food remains is dangerous because such translation is, in fact, the basis for judging the quality of life rather than simply describing the conditions of life. Slave-owned ceramics can be compared with planter-owned ceramics by means of Miller's (1980) price indices, but such an analysis, with ceramics in the foreground, ignores the fact that ceramics were not the glue that held a plantation together, slavery was. For both of these reasons, artifacts do not stand for the people who used them, or do so in a very limited way, *unless* they are examined in the context of a theory that gives precedence to the economic and social relations of slavery and which explicitly contradicts the social mobility implied by functionalist material culture analyses. This fallacy of letting things stand for people is the same issue Marx identifies as the fetishism of commodities when he says, "There it is, a definite social relation between men, that assumes, in their eyes, the fantastic form of a relation between things" (Marx 1977:246).

The key issue here is not quality of life, but rather *who controlled* the quality of life, the very issue that is obscured in analyses like Adams and Boling's. In effect, Adams and Boling argue that the ability of both planters and slaves to buy similar tableware is a more powerful social fact than the ability of planters to buy and sell slaves. Rather than studying the workings of slavery, analyses like these *assume* slavery and jump past it into one or another material culture subsystem. However, it is likely that on most plantations, most of the realms of material culture measured to determine the quality of life were controlled by white owners and overseers, indirectly if not directly. If slaves hunted their own game or bought their own ceramics, it is probably because their owners allowed them to do these things, and owners *certainly* had the power to prohibit these activities. This applies as well to the Africanisms that plantation archaeologists have worked so hard to identify. It is also likely that these limited "social freedoms," "cultural freedoms," and "economic freedoms" were carefully monitored, calculated, balanced, and traded off *by plantation owners* against other, more powerful unfreedoms. It was within the power of *any* plantation owner to grant (or restrict) a range of "economic freedoms," but it was most definitely *not* within the power of any slave to achieve the "freedoms" available to some slaves. Thus, slavery is a more significant social fact here than the possession of pearlware or porcelain. Slavery structured ceramic acquisition in a way that ceramic possession could not structure or affect the social relations of slavery; no amount of porcelain on his or her table could transform a slave into a planter. Discussions of quality of life, which *assume* slavery and therefore ignore its workings, can serve to mask the more profound material culture issue which is how material culture, some of it representing certain limited "economic freedoms," was used both overtly and covertly to control slaves and to enforce the dominance of their masters.

Having asserted the dominance of slave owners over slaves, and the pre-eminence of slavery among the various social facts of plantation life, one crucial distinction needs to be made. Specifically, acknowledging the ultimate power of slave owners over slaves is not the same thing as ignoring the fact that slaves were often able to improve their circumstances and shape many aspects of their daily lives. This writer clearly intends the former and rejects the latter. Without question, some slaves went to great lengths to preserve their own cultural traditions *and to create new ones*, but they usually did so within the larger context of a social and economic institution over which they had relatively little control. In this matter this archaeologist follows Orser (1989:35) who says, "Although plantation slaves helped create their world within the plantations of their bondage . . . it would be oversimplistic to state that they did so in isolation of the prevailing plantation social fields, or relations of production." On this point, Epperson (1990:36) states that "archaeologists must . . . struggle to recognize and celebrate the unique African-American heritage without glossing the context of oppression within which this oppositional culture was, and continues to be,

forged." Epperson borrows a solution to this conundrum, or at least a name for the solution, from feminist scholarship. This solution is the "double strategy" of "learning to fight inequality and injustice while preserving and fostering diversity" (Epperson 1990:35). In Epperson's approach to plantation archaeology, this double strategy consists of two goals, "valorization of the African-American culture of resistance and the denaturalization of essentialist racial categories" (Epperson 1990:36). This writer's intention here is to oppose the position, held in some quarters, that it is somehow paternalistic to acknowledge the dominance of slave owners over slaves.

As already argued with respect to Kelso, this writer does not believe Otto to be an apologist for slavery or for contemporary racism and is only suggesting that by failing to be adequately self-reflective, Otto and, more importantly, those who have followed his lead have chosen a set of questions and an analytical framework that perpetuates the worldview of the masters at the expense of representing the worldview of the enslaved. And they have done so without adequately considering the interests of the people most likely to be affected by their conclusions. While a working plantation is a perfect example of a social or economic system, it is a system that worked far better for some participants than for others. One solution to this classic dilemma of functionalism would have been to identify clearly the source of these questions and frameworks in 20th-century scholarship rather than in some continuity with or sympathy for antebellum slaveowners who justified slaveowning through paternalistic demonstrations of the "good" living conditions in their quarters. Otto could have used self-reflection to identify the highly problematic nature of his research orientation by asking himself: "how would a group of African Americans in former plantation country respond to a talk based upon my inquiry into the quality of life enjoyed/endured by their slave ancestors?" Or more pointedly, "of what use is it to contemporary African Americans to know the quality of the dishes used by their enslaved ancestors?" Relatively few plantation archaeologists have asked themselves questions like these, nor—

more importantly—have they asked such questions directly of the descendants of the people they are studying.

Furthermore, the point of this article is not to provide answers to these questions; this writer does not have any. The best that can be offered is a method (critical archaeology) that contains procedures for identifying constituencies, generating socially relevant research questions, and presenting results. Whatever answers may seem to be implied flow from the use of a social theory (Marxism) that assumes economic exploitation, as identified by class analysis. The hypothetical audience of African Americans invoked from time to time throughout this discussion is constituted by a use of critical theory. While it is clearly inappropriate for this writer to speak for African-American interests, this article has been written because it is even more inappropriate for Adams and Boling not to have considered contemporary African-American interests, a failure this writer attributes to a lack of reflection. To state this point another way, it is absolutely not appropriate to assert that Adams and Boling's potential African-American audience thinks about its cultural heritage in the same way that Lilla Watson thinks about Murri history, but it should have been Adams and Boling's place to *ask* whether this is the case or not. At this point, it is important to recognize that while this writer speaks of African Americans as if they all feel the same way and share the same interests, they clearly do not. For this reason, any effort to understand African-American interests in the archaeology of African-American heritage must be local, ongoing, and directed to specific communities.

Having touched on one of the ways in which Adams and Boling's article is of a piece with previous attempts at plantation archaeology, this writer would like to return to the article itself and will begin by describing the article's major flaw, its failure of reflection. This will be followed with four suggestions for solving this problem.

A Failure of Reflection

The principal criticism of Adams and Boling's article is its failure of reflection. There is simply no evidence in this article that Adams and Boling have made any effort to understand the needs and interests of an audience made up of the descendants of their research subjects. At the same time, however, Adams has given at least three talks based on his attempt "to provide blacks with a heritage they would otherwise not have known about" (Adams 1989, pers. comm.). Specifically, Adams has

> addressed several African-American audiences and made the same conclusion to them that the slaves on Georgia plantations had the ability to exercise a greater amount of freedom than is generally recognized; these audiences liked to hear that slaves could buy and sell many items and did not have to rely on massa for it (Adams 1989, pers. comm.).

There are two problems here. First, it is important to distinguish between the appreciation Adams' audiences have shown him for his scholarly interest in their past, which is no doubt quite real, and the more important goal of providing these audiences with interpretations they can use, in their own interests. These are two very different things, and Adams has demonstrated only the first. Adams and Boling's failure to fulfill this second responsibility may be rooted in the idea of their "giving" a heritage to African Americans rather than working with African Americans to create a place for them in the process of heritage production. The simplest way to achieve this would be to involve African Americans in the development of research questions rather than just presenting them with research conclusions based on questions that may or may not be relevant to their interests.

In such an endeavor, the point of reflection is not simply to anticipate how African Americans will react to a set of research results, but rather, it is to consider as broadly as possible the issue of what a particular community of African Americans can do with such results to advance their own interests. Stated another way, the pivotal question is not, "Did the audience applaud?" but instead, "Was the audience able to do anything with what they heard, after they left the auditorium?" As already noted, this line of reasoning is based on the Frankfurt School idea that knowledge is inseparable from human interests and social action.

Given this concern, it is reasonable to ask what is the use of analyses that downplay the institution of slavery while focusing on the ways that slaves were able to work around the dominance of their masters. Again it is important to remember that neither the ownership of porcelain nor the retention of Africanisms could *ever* deliver a slave from bondage. If the value of historical knowledge is its usefulness as a basis for future action, archaeologists have two choices in doing the historical archaeology of slavery. They can either present a version of the past that teaches people to outwit their oppressors while leaving the basis for oppression intact—which is what some plantation archaeology does—or present a version of the past that focusses directly on the structures of oppression. The hope is that this second approach will help people *of all races* to recognize contemporary vestiges of past domination and therefore to challenge and change the institutions that support domination rather than accepting domination and simply circumventing it. Placing too much emphasis on the limited freedoms available to some slaves and the ability of slaves to create certain aspects of their own world could do a disservice to contemporary African Americans engaged in the attempt to identify and challenge the racial discrimination that still exists in contemporary American society. From the standpoint of critical theory, studies like Adams and Boling's do little to foster the empowerment of contemporary African Americans.

Furthermore, if knowledge like the conclusion drawn by Adams and Boling is not especially useful to contemporary African Americans or is irrelevant to them, then this knowledge has the potential to be quite useful to opponents of equal rights for African Americans. If one accepts the Frankfurt School position that knowledge is never neutral, then knowledge is either for or against. And in this writer's opinion, it is nothing short of unethical to dig up the artifacts of a people's past if the resulting representation of that past is likely to be used against them. Wilcomb Washburn (1988) has recently, and publicly, scoffed at the idea that, "if, in excavating a site, the evidence seemed to suggest that the slaves, for example, were not so badly off, that line of work should be broken off for fear of

hurting the interests of blacks." While one would argue, in such a case, for reanalysis based on the premise that *by definition* slaves could never be well off, the position that Washburn ridicules really amounts to little more than an adaptation of the most basic standard of anthropological ethics: the injunction against ethnographers doing harm to their informants.

To sum up this argument, this writer finds fault with Adams and Boling for failing to reflect on the circumstances in which their archaeological work has been conducted. Specifically, they are conducting plantation research in the midst of a social, economic, and political environment in which the reverberations of plantation slavery are still echoing. By failing to listen to these echoes, Adams and Boling have chimed in without knowing what tune they are playing. In the criticisms already made above and in the four suggestions that follow, this writer is disputing neither the analytical competence Adams and Boling bring to their task *nor* their right to draw the conclusions they draw but is only suggesting avenues they might have wished to explore had they carefully considered the implications of those conclusions.

Four Approaches to Reflection

Interestingly, one way of improving Adams and Boling's article may be found in the article that follows theirs in *Historical Archaeology* 23(1). In his cogent and persuasive discussion of ceramic use by the métis in the Northwestern Plains of Canada, David Burley (1989) goes a step beyond determining who had what by paying careful attention to the various audiences for the cultural messages conveyed by ceramic use. Through the use of historical and ethnohistorical data, he is able to make considerable progress toward understanding ceramic artifacts in terms of their native meanings rather than simply in terms of the Spode/Copeland pattern books or Miller's (1980) CC index. By searching out a native point of view through a consideration of the audience for slave quarter ceramic use, Adams and Boling could have made a more compelling case for why African

Americans today should care about the monetary values of their ancestors' ceramic holdings. Furthermore, had they been looking in an appropriate way, Adams and Boling may have been able to find ways of seeing resistance to slavery, even in the use of Euroamerican objects by slaves. In fact, Otto (1975, 1984) has already had some success with this general kind of research in plantation archaeology. One of his principal conclusions from Cannon's Point is that different classes of material culture (architecture and ceramics) served different functions in representing and enacting the complex web of relationships that enmeshed planters, overseers, and slaves; similarities in architecture linked planters and overseers while similarities in ceramic holdings linked overseers and slaves.

Ironically, a second way of improving upon Adams and Boling's article may be found in the article that comes just *before* their piece. In his discussion of plantation archaeology in the Low Country of Georgia and South Carolina, J.W. Joseph pays some attention to the broader historical context of plantation slavery. Specifically, he sees a connection between the 1808 ban on the importation of slaves and the improvement of living conditions of plantation slaves (Joseph 1989:64–65). He realizes that after 1808 slaves were required not only to produce agricultural products, they were also required to reproduce the labor force of which they were a part. It is very likely that an improved "quality of life" contributed to the efficiency of this unique reproduction of the means of production. That is, the allegedly high quality of slaves' lives served the interests of their owners. Given this, Adams and Boling could have strengthened their analysis by considering more fully the broader context in which they found evidence for the economic freedom of some slaves. To their credit, Adams and Boling do consider the differences between gang-based labor and task-based labor but there are still important questions they leave unasked. How did slaves come to attain their economic freedoms? What was in it for their masters? The point here is the same one that Joseph recognizes: economic freedom for slaves, such as it was, or good living conditions, did not exist in a vacuum on the plantation. They were connected to

other social and historical factors which need to be considered before a collection of porcelain shards can have any real meaning.

With respect to both of these criticisms, self-reflection would have shown Adams and Boling the narrow, acontextual data base with which they chose to work and the lack of weight this lack of context imposes on their conclusions. By ignoring the context of ceramic use and display as well as the social and historical context of slave life, Adams and Boling allow themselves to use a slender data base to arrive at conclusions that would be amusing if they were not potentially dangerous. In the final two suggestions, this writer goes beyond *Historical Archaeology* 23(1) and discusses two deeper issues which have been discussed in the work of Charles Orser and Theresa Singleton.

The logic that underlies Adams and Boling's conclusion is "sure they were slaves, *but*. . . ." It is precisely this readiness to separate the fact of slavery from various aspects of slave life that prevents Adams and Boling from framing an analysis that is useful to any African-American audience imaginable. As noted above, once one chooses to peel slavery off from diet or ceramic holdings or architecture, it becomes possible to ignore slavery completely and thus fail to see, or even to ask about, its role in these various aspects of life. Again, Vargas Arenas and Sanoja Obediente (1990) discuss the political power of the categories and compartments used to "hold" and discuss the past. An alternative approach, and the one taken by Orser (1987, 1988a, 1988b), is Marxian analysis that sees slavery as the key organizing factor behind *all* aspects of slave life. That is, Orser does not ghettoize slavery as just another independent variable in the lives of slaves. Thus, for Orser, the main material culture research question becomes: "how did this or that element of material culture contribute to the maintenance of a slave-based economy?" It is highly unlikely that the economic freedoms Adams and Boling identified came at no cost to the slaves who enjoyed them. Adams and Boling's analysis would have been more powerful if they had explored the question of how porcelain-buying slaves paid for the privilege of buying their own dishes. What was the trade-off? What did the slave owner get, or think that he or she got, by allowing this small measure of economic freedom? This line of inquiry is very likely one that Adams and Boling would have explored had they made a commitment to providing information that was potentially useful to an audience composed of African-American descendants of slaves instead of an audience composed of historical archaeologists whose primary agenda is refining and applying George Miller's ceramic indices.

The fourth suggestion for improving upon Adams and Boling comes from the work of Singleton and her key insight that African Americans today have relatively little interest in archaeology (Singleton 1988:364). In the same vein, Charles Fairbanks has said,

> I would like to admit to a personal lapse in the results of my work in slave and plantation archaeology. While it is certainly important to let other archaeologists and historians know what we have done, we have a larger and more imperative duty. That is to inform the people we are studying of those results. Throughout the country there is a large body of Black persons who should know what we have found out about their past. That they have not shown a great deal of interest until now is surely our fault (Fairbanks 1984:12).

Singleton's response to this problem is her argument, by example, that it is important for archaeologists to study carefully the popular environments in which their work is displayed, discussed, and used. In particular, Singleton discusses the place of plantation archaeology in the museum world and in the lives of contemporary African Americans.

Archaeologists would all do well to follow her lead by understanding that data are likely to have use-lives that extend beyond the immediate utilizations of them in site reports and scholarly articles. If an archaeologist does not take control over how her data are presented to the public at large, it is certain that control over the meaning of those data will fall to others with interests that may or may not be those of the archaeologist. This idea that knowledge is usually knowledge for a purpose gets back to the idea of social responsibility that was introduced earlier. Keeping track of the public representations of data, in the loci identified by Singleton, is simply a way of making sure that data always say what researchers mean and, in the case

of plantation archaeology, are never used to prolong the victimization of those who are already acknowledged to be history's victims. Historical archaeology should not contribute to making the descendants of victims *in* history victims *of* history and historical scholarship.

To follow up on Singleton's insight that historical scholars should attend to the public performance of the data they create, she also notes that slavery is being seen less and less as a taboo subject in museums. There are at least two parts to this phenomenon. First, history museum educators generally are starting to come to grips with a wide variety of controversial or painful aspects of the American past (Baker and Leon 1986; Patterson 1986; Crosson 1988; Sellars 1988; Brown 1989). In addition to this, and more specifically, museum educators are beginning to learn that there are ways of teaching about domination in the past without endorsing, encouraging, inviting, or inspiring more of the same, in the future. First among these techniques is the straightforward step of anticipating, openly acknowledging, and clearly rejecting any readily apparent yet inappropriate conclusion that could be drawn from a body of archaeological data. That is, archaeologists can try to predict the most egregious potential misuses of their work and then tell people what they mean, in part, by telling them what is *not* meant. This may sound simplistic or unnecessary, but perhaps Adams and Boling should have told readers explicitly not to use their analysis to conclude that slavery was not such a bad life. Dennis Pogue (1990:4) takes this very step when, after presenting archaeological evidence for a higher-than-expected degree of "material comfort," he clearly states that "the bottom line of all this is that they were still slaves, and this [finding] does not imply that their daily life was any less onerous." Without this kind of statement, it is difficult to distinguish between propositions Adams and Boling intend to test and beliefs they assume they hold in common with their readers.

Conclusion

This commentary concludes by taking the step that this writer has criticized Adams and Boling for not taking. Namely, this writer wants to be absolutely explicit about what this article is, and what it is not. First and foremost, and despite what the subtext may *seem* to say, this writer is not accusing Adams and Boling of racism, nor implying that they are apologists for slavery. Rather, it is suggested that they have framed a conclusion that could easily be used to advance a racist argument and that they have not done enough to anticipate and guard against such a misuse of their conclusion.

To restate the main point, this all flows from a failure of reflection. It is this failure of reflection that allows Adams and Boling to speak of the ability of slaves to purchase ceramics as "economic freedom" while ignoring the fact that the same set of equivalencies used to attach a monetary value to a teapot was also used to attach values to slaves. One must question the "economic freedom" of a $500 slave buying a $2.50 teapot from a shopkeeper who could not even conceive of calculating his or her own value as a purchase price in dollars and cents.

While Adams and Boling's conclusion might pass muster at a meeting of the Society for Historical Archaeology, it simply does not make a case for its usefulness to an audience made up of descendants of slaves. They would likely reject the notion that a few shards of porcelain equal economic freedom. And so too would the Daughters of the American Revolution. Archaeological collections from the homes of the Signers of the Declaration of Independence are full of shards of porcelain. The so-called "Fathers of Our Country" were free to make considerable fortunes before the Revolution, but they risked these fortunes in order to attain a greater freedom. If one accepts, at the level of popular historical discourse, that the freedom to make a great deal of money was not enough for this nation's greatest cultural heroes, one certainly should not accept an archaeological analysis that allows the ability of slaves to spend a little bit of money on a few pieces of porcelain to overshadow the fact of their bondage. Is so partial a freedom any kind of freedom at all?

Finally, if this essay was purely a rhetorical exercise, the previous sentence would have been its conclusion, but it is not. So far this writer has made a case for making plantation archaeology good politics. However, these same steps can make plantation archaeology good archaeology. As Epperson (1990:35) notes, "a social and political commitment will not only improve the quality of current archaeological research and interpretations, but also help to bridge the gap between academic disciplines and the communities archaeologists purportedly study and serve." At every point, the kind of self-reflection advocated herein will lead in two parallel directions. It will clearly lead to a plantation archaeology that is more useful to the hypothetical audience of African Americans that has been repeatedly invoked. And, importantly, this version of plantation archaeology will be better received *not just* because it is good politics. Self reflection, as discussed here, always involves a push for greater contextuality. To make Adams and Boling's ceramics really meaningful, this writer would have tried to analyze them in terms of a set of multiple contexts including: (1) aspects of ceramic use and display beyond simple possession, as indicated solely by discard; (2) the use of other classes of material culture; (3) the broad flow of the history of slavery; (4) the nature of localized attempts to preserve the institution of slavery; and (5) the enactment of serious attempts at resistance. All of this contextuality makes for good politics but also for good scholarship.

ACKNOWLEDGMENTS

I would like to thank Mark Leone for introducing me to many of the ideas that form the theoretical basis for this paper. I would also like to thank Gary Hume and Richard Boisvert of the New Hampshire Division of Historical Resources for their thoughtful readings of early drafts. Thanks are also due to Don Hardesty and the anonymous reviewers, whose work has made this a better paper. Finally, I would like to thank Nancy Jo Chabot, who is right about things more frequently than I take her good advice. For all the results of good advice not taken, I take full responsibility.

REFERENCES

ADAMS, WILLIAM H., AND SARAH JANE BOLING
   1989 Status and Ceramics for Planters and Slaves on Three Georgia Coastal Plantations. *Historical Archaeology* 23(1):69–96.

ARATO, ANDREW, AND EIKE GEBHARDT (EDITORS)
1982 *The Essential Frankfurt School Reader*. Continuum, New York.

BAKER, ANDREW, AND WARREN LEON
1986 Old Sturbridge Villiage Introduces Social Conflict into Its Interpretive Story. *History News* 41(2):6–11.

BARLOW, ALEX
1990 Still Civilizing? Aborigines in Australian Education. In *The Excluded Past,* edited by Peter Stone and Robert MacKenzie, pp. 68–87. Unwin Hyman, London.

BLANCKE, SHIRLEY, AND CJIGKITOONUPPA JOHN PETERS SLOW TURTLE
1990 The Teaching of the Past of the Native Peoples of North America in U.S. Schools. In *The Excluded Past*, edited by Peter Stone and Robert MacKenzie, pp. 109–133. Unwin Hyman, London.

BROWN, PATRICIA LEIGH
1989 Away from the Big House: Interpreting the Uncomfortable Parts of History. *History News* 44(2):8–11.

BURLEY, DAVID
1989 Function, Meaning, and Context: Ambiguities in Ceramic Use by the *Hivernant* Metis of the Northwestern Plains. *Historical Archaeology* 23(1):97–106.

CHAPPELL, EDWARD A.
1989 Social Responsibility and the American History Museum. *Winterthur Portfolio* 24(4):247–265.

CLARK, GRAHAME
1957 *Archaeology and Society. Third Edition.* Methuen, London.

CROSSON, DAVID L.
1988 Museums and Social Responsibility: A Cautionary Tale. *History News* 43(4):6–10.

EPPERSON, TERRENCE W.
1990 Race and the Disciplines of the Plantation. *Historical Archaeology* 24(4):29–36.

FAIRBANKS, CHARLES H.
1984 The Plantation Archaeology of the Southeastern Coast. *Historical Archaeology* 18(1):1–14.

FOGEL, ROBERT W., AND STANLEY L. ENGERMAN
1974 *Time on the Cross: The Economics of American Negro Slavery.* Little, Brown, Boston.

GATHERCOLE, PETER, AND DAVID LOWENTHAL (EDITORS)
1990 *The Politics of the Past.* Unwin Hyman, London.

GEUSS, RAYMOND
1981 *The Idea of a Critical Theory: Habermas and the Frankfurt School.* Cambridge University Press, Cambridge.

HALL, MARTIN
1984 The Burden of Tribalism: The Social Context of Southern African Iron Age Studies. *American Antiquity* 49(3):455–467.

1988 Archaeology under Apartheid. *Archaeology* 41(6):62–64.

HELD, DAVID
1980 *Introduction to Critical Theory: Horkheimer to Habermas.* University of California Press, Berkeley.

JOSEPH, J.W.
1989 Pattern and Process in the Plantation Archaeology of the Low Country of Georgia and South Carolina. *Historical Archaeology* 23(1):55–68.

KEHOE, ALICE B.
1990 "In Fourteen Hundred and Ninety-two, Columbus Sailed . . .": The Primacy of the National Myth in U.S. Schools. In *The Excluded Past,* edited by Peter Stone and Robert MacKenzie, pp. 201–216. Unwin Hyman, London.

KELSO, WILLIAM M.
1984 *Kingsmill Plantations, 1619–1800: Archaeology of Country Life in Colonial Virginia.* Academic Press, New York.

LAYTON, R. (EDITOR)
1988 *Who Needs the Past?* Unwin Hyman, London.
1989 *Conflict in the Archaeology of Living Traditions.* Unwin Hyman, London.

LEONE, MARK P.
1986 Symbolic, Structural, and Critical Archaeology. In *American Archaeology Past and Future: A Celebration of the Society for American Archaeology, 1935–1985,* edited by David J. Meltzer, Don D. Fowler, and Jeremy A. Sabloff, pp. 415–438. Smithsonian Institution Press, Washington, D.C.

LEONE, MARK P., AND PARKER B. POTTER, JR. (EDITORS)
1988 *The Recovery of Meaning: Historical Archaeology in the Eastern United States.* Smithsonian Institution Press, Washington, D.C.

LEONE, MARK P., PARKER B. POTTER, JR., AND PAUL A. SHACKEL
1987 Toward a Critical Archaeology. *Current Anthropology* 28(3):283–302.

LESTER, J.A.
1987 Lowering Curatorial Blinders. Paper Presented at the Annual Meeting of the American Association of Museums, San Francisco. Tape cassette, Vanguard Systems, Inc., Shawnee Mission, Kansas.

MARX, KARL
1977 The Fetishism of Commodities and the Secret Thereof. In *Symbolic Anthropology: A Reader in the Study of Symbols and Meanings,* edited by Janet L. Dolgin, David S. Kemnitzer, and David M. Schneider, pp. 245–254. Columbia University Press, New York.

MILLER, GEORGE L.
1980 Classification and Economic Scaling of 19th-Century Ceramics. *Historical Archaeology* 14:1–40.

ORSER, CHARLES E., JR.
1987 Plantation Status and Consumer Choice: A Materialist Framework for Historical Archaeology. In *Consumer Choice in Historical Archaeology*, edited by Suzanne M. Spencer-Wood, pp. 121–137. Plenum Press, New York.
1988a The Archaeological Analysis of Plantation Society: Replacing Status and Caste with Economics and Power. *American Antiquity* 53(4):735–751.
1988b Toward a Theory of Power for Historical Archaeology: Plantations and Space. In *The Recovery of Meaning: Historical Archaeology in the Eastern United States*, edited by Mark P. Leone and Parker B. Potter, Jr., pp. 313–343. Smithsonian Institution Press, Washington, D.C.
1989 On Plantations and Patterns. *Historical Archaeology* 23(2):28–40.

OTTO, JOHN SOLOMON
1975 *Status Differences and the Archaeological Record: A Comparison of Planter, Overseer, and Slave Sites from Cannon's Point Plantation (1794–1861), St. Simon's Island, Georgia.* Ph.D. dissertation, Department of Anthropology, University of Florida, Gainesville. University Microfilms, Ann Arbor.
1984 *Cannon's Point Plantation, 1794–1860: Living Conditions and Status Patterns in the Old South.* Academic Press, New York.

PATTERSON, JOHN
1986 Conner Prairie Refocuses Its Interpretive Message to Include Controversial Subjects. *History News* 41(2): 12–15.

PINSKY, VALERIE, AND ALISON WYLIE (EDITORS)
1990 *Critical Traditions in Contemporary Archaeology.* Cambridge University Press, Cambridge, England.

POGUE, DENNIS
1990 News from Across Virginia. *Virginia Preservation* [The Newsletter of the Preservation Alliance of Virginia] (June):4.

POTTER, PARKER B., JR.
1989 *Archaeology in Public in Annapolis: An Experiment in the Application of Critical Theory to Historical Archaeology.* Ph.D. dissertation, Department of Anthropology, Brown University, Providence, Rhode Island. University Microfilms, Ann Arbor.
1991 Self-Reflection in Archaeology. In *Processual and Postprocessual Archaeologies: Multiple Ways of Knowing the Past*, edited by Robert W. Preucel. Center for Archaeological Investigations, Carbondale, Illinois, in press.

PREUCEL, ROBERT W. (EDITOR)
1991 *Processual and Postprocessual Archaeologies: Multiple Ways of Knowing the Past.* Center for Archaeological Investigations, Carbondale, Illinois, in press.

REITZ, ELIZABETH J., TYSON GIBBS, AND TED A. RATHBUN
1985 Archaeological Evidence for Subsistence on Coastal Plantations. In *The Archaeology of Slavery and Plantation Life*, edited by Theresa A. Singleton, pp. 163–191. Academic Press, New York.

SELLARS, RICHARD WEST
1988 The Texas School Book Depository Building: Preserving the Dark Side of History. *History News* 43(6): 24–26.

SILVERBERG, ROBERT
1968 *Moundbuilders of Ancient America: The Archaeology of a Myth.* New York Graphic Society, Greenwich, Connecticut.
1974 *The Moundbuilders.* Ballantine, New York.

SINCLAIR, PAUL
1990 The Earth Is Our History Book. In *The Excluded Past*, edited by Peter Stone and Robert MacKenzie, pp. 152–159. Unwin Hyman, London.

SINGLETON, THERESA A.
1988 An Archaeological Framework for Slavery and Emancipation, 1740–1880. In *The Recovery of Meaning: Historical Archaeology in the Eastern United States*, edited by Mark P. Leone and Parker B. Potter, Jr., pp. 345–370. Smithsonian Intitution Press, Washington, D.C.

SINGLETON, THERESA A. (EDITOR)
1985 *The Archaeology of Slavery and Plantation Life.* Academic Press, New York.

SOUTH, STANLEY
1977 *Method and Theory in Historical Archaeology.* Academic Press, New York.
1978 Pattern Recognition in Historical Archaeology. *American Antiquity* 43:223–230.
1979 Historic Site Content, Structure, and Function. *American Antiquity* 44:213–237.
1988 Whither Pattern? *Historical Archaeology* 22(1):25–28.

STONE, PETER, AND ROBERT MACKENZIE
1990 *The Excluded Past.* Unwin Hyman, London.

TRIGGER, BRUCE G.
1980 Archaeology and the Image of the American Indian. *American Antiquity* 45(4):662–676.

VARGAS ARENAS, IRAIDA, AND MARIO SANOJA OBEDIENTE
1990 Education and the Political Manipulation of History in

Venezuela. In *The Excluded Past*, edited by Peter Stone and Robert MacKenzie, pp. 50–60. Unwin Hyman, London.

WASHBURN, WILCOMB E.
1987 A Critical View of Critical Archaeology. *Current Anthropology* 28(4):544–545.
1988 Announcing the ''Guerrilla Archaeologist.'' Ms. on file, New Hampshire Division of Historical Resources, Concord, New Hampshire.

WATSON, LILLA
1990 The Affirmation of Indigenous Values in a Colonial Education System. In *The Excluded Past*, edited by Peter Stone and Robert Mackenzie, pp. 88–97. Unwin Hyman, London.

WYLIE, ALISON
1985 Putting Shakertown Back Together: Critical Theory in Archaeology. *Journal of Anthropological Archaeology* 4:133–147.

PARKER B. POTTER, JR.
NEW HAMPSHIRE DIVISION OF HISTORICAL RESOURCES
P.O. BOX 2043
CONCORD, NEW HAMPSHIRE 03302-2043

1997   Pre-Emancipation Archaeology: Does It Play in Selma, Alabama? In *In the Realm of Politics: Prospects for Public Participation in African-American Archaeology*, special issue of *Historical Archaeology*, edited by C. McDavid and D. Babson. vol. 31:3, pp. 18-26

LINDA DERRY

Pre-Emancipation Archaeology: Does It Play in Selma, Alabama?

ABSTRACT

This paper is a first-person narrative of one archaeologist's struggle to achieve public participation in the archaeology of pre-emancipation Alabama. This account details the difficulties of working in a polarized community, famous both for its plantation past and its 20th-century racial strife. Successful participation by local African Americans was only possible after the archaeologist's academic interest in slavery took a back seat to the needs of the community. Ten years of failures and some successes are summarized. Concluding remarks outline the lessons learned.

Introduction

Travel brochures declare that "History lives in Selma, Alabama!" During the Civil War, Selma was one of the South's main military manufacturing centers. Here, the naval ordnance turned out Confederate warships, including the ironclad *Tennessee*. War relics are on display in local museums and other public buildings. A driving tour of the Old Town Historic District highlights the grand antebellum town homes of Dallas County's planter elite.

In 1965 thousands gathered in Selma and overcame violence and hardship to launch the Selma to Montgomery march for civil rights. The march ultimately led to the voting rights act of that same year. Tourists can visit the Brown Chapel AME church where Dr. Martin Luther King launched the march. They can retrace his historic steps across the Edmund Pettus Bridge. The Voting Rights Museum near the bridge displays photographs and artifacts from this historic event.

Community relations have vastly improved since the media focused on Selma and the "Bloody Sunday" of 7 March 1965. However, in many respects the community, and its history, remain segregated in two camps. While residents of African descent celebrate Selma's illustrious voting rights history, residents of European descent cling to the white pillared antebellum past. Selma's historical showplace, Sturdivant Hall, has been accurately furnished to reflect its opulent antebellum lifestyle, yet the kitchen and slave quarters house a gift shop. During the 25th anniversary of the Voting Rights March, white officials were shut out of the celebration planning process (Benn 1990:3A). Few white faces are seen at the annual bridge-crossing festival; even fewer faces of color are in the crowd at the battle of Selma reenactment. Apparently, representations of each other's history threaten both groups. And now, with the rapid growth of Alabama's black heritage tourism business and the promise of federal highway dollars to develop a historic trail and interpretive centers along the 1965 march route, the festering question of ownership of the past will predictively develop into unpleasantness (*Selma Times Journal* [STJ] 1995:1A).

This is the environment in which I live and work. I often describe myself as an interpretive archaeologist (Hodder 1991). The Alabama Historical Commission (AHC) employs me to develop and manage an archaeological park, Cahawba (1DS32; sometimes spelled Cahaba), located just 10 mi. from Selma. The mission of the AHC is "to foster an awareness of the value of historic structures, sites, and objects that reflect the heritage of all Alabamians and to facilitate the preservation and documentation of these resources for the use, enjoyment, and education of present and future generations" (AHC 1993:1). My specific tasks are many. Beyond archaeological and historical research, I am in charge of land acquisition, construction of park facilities, fund-raising, sustaining public support, and interpretation. As a state employee, public participation is important to every aspect of my work.

My European descent, the topic of pre-emancipation archaeology, and the politics of my setting were roadblocks to achieving public participation. Various academic approaches were applied to the participation problem and failed. Only when questions were asked that were meaningful to the local community was a workable solution found.

The Site

Cahawba was created in 1819 to become Alabama's first official state capital. Cahawba later became the market and social center of the wealthy cotton planters of Dallas County and their enslaved laborers. Today Cahawba is a dead town, and the remains of that antebellum society are well preserved beneath a landscape of relics and ruins. It has been a dead town since Reconstruction times. On the other hand, Cahawba does have one true descendant, Selma. After the Civil War, Selma inherited Cahawba's county seat and its inhabitants. Many structures in Selma's historic district once stood in antebellum Cahawba. These homes were dismantled, transported by river barge, and reassembled again in nearby Selma.

Uncovering the Problem

When I arrived at Cahawba 10 years ago, my initial method reflected my professional belief that historical archaeologists should be historians as well as archaeologists. Since I was dealing with a protected site, I started my work not by excavating but by building a historical context. I typed verbatim into the computer every available historical document, deed, local newspaper column, and diary. Later the computer reassembled this information by town lot so I could prioritize lot purchase, then by family names so I could recreate biographies and community networks.

Early in this process, one fact became immediately obvious: Cahawba's population had always been at least 63 percent African American. However, this majority was seldom mentioned in written histories of the town. Furthermore, a previously ignored Reconstruction era for the town emerged. Although most of the white residents of the town fled to Selma after the war, many freed persons set up residence in Cahawba. Cahawba became the "Mecca of the Radical Republican party," a haven for black politicians and schools.

An unexpected bonus of our new computer files was their attraction to genealogists. Cahawba descendants from all over the nation began to write and even visit my office for information. Their favorite items were articles from Cahawba's antebellum newspaper because the editor filled the local column with town gossip (*Dallas Gazette* 1853–1859). These records provided descendants much more than standard birth and death dates. Descendants invariably returned our kindness with an influx of family papers, pictures, artifacts, and even cash donations for the project! Our work was repaid fourfold. These items rounded out Cahawba's history in a way we never imagined, and they also provided interpretive material for exhibits. Cahawba descendants became frequent visitors, but these visitors were always of European descent. Cahawba's 63 percent majority still had no voice, and our exhibits, now full of pictures, had no faces of color.

About this time, we began some test excavations as a prelude to park development. We had media coverage, including the *National Geographic World* (1987:19–23), and many visitors. Again, however, the only African Americans were people "forced" to attend due to work assignments or advisory board appointments. The lack of visitor interest by the African-American community puzzled me. After all, the park's fundraising group, "Cahawba Concern," was conspicuously biracial, in a community with few integrated organizations. If they had no interest in the history or archaeology of the place, why were they working so hard to "Save Cahawba," as they proclaimed on their popular bumper sticker? I began to reanalyze the situation and came to the disappointing but illuminating conclusion that our black volunteers, who were almost exclusively from an adjacent rural black community, were not interested in Cahawba for its history. Rather, their interest in Cahawba centered on the potential economic benefits for the living community and the close-to-home recreational benefits for their children. While I was grateful for their support, regardless of the reason for it, I still hoped for more local recognition of the site as the important African-American historical and cultural resource that it was.

The Search for a Solution

I looked to The Society for Historical Archaeology (SHA) for help in attracting the interest of the black community. I joined the newly formed African-American archaeology forum and attended their first "cross-cultural" workshop held at the 1992 SHA annual meeting in Jamaica. Scholars from Africa, America, and the Caribbean were invited to discuss the complex relationship between African-American material culture and the traditions of a diverse African continent. With this academic model in mind, I returned home and prepared a temporary exhibit for a statewide Black Heritage Month. I paired historic photos of local African-American cemeteries with a picture of a Congo chief's burial. Both photos showed a similar placement of grave goods. The point of the display was to celebrate African traditions. Before I even placed the exhibit, the look on the faces of our African-American employees and volunteers told me this was a big mistake. As they explained, to their fundamentalist Christian community, these traits were considered pagan and certainly not something to celebrate during Black Heritage Month.

Cahawba has three cemeteries. When I first arrived, I found that preservationists had fenced, cleared, and maintained two of them over the years. They had left the third, labeled "Negro Burial Ground" on historic maps, overgrown and inaccessible (Dallas County Office of Probate 1883). With this in mind, I listened intently at another SHA workshop. The speaker stressed that African Americans did not necessarily share the concept of perpetual care for cemeteries. She suggested that my desire to clear the brush from this third graveyard was merely a reflection of my own cultural preference (Carrel Cowen-Ricks 1993, pers. comm.). After considering her

argument, and asking some of my local African-American supporters what they thought about it, I found that this idea did not play very well at home. Apparently there is a long tradition in rural Alabama that involves an annual gathering to scrape the earth clean around the graves. My support group went so far as to tease me about listening to those "big city blacks." After all, one said, "what did they know about things down here?" One man, in particular, spoke with exceptional authority since his family had been in the funeral business for three generations, and he had personally interred several bodies at Cahawba's burial ground.

I took to heart Abdul-Karim Mustapha's (1995:1–2, 4) comments in the *African-American Archaeology Newsletter,* suggesting that Mount Vernon or Monticello be regarded as a piece of African-American material culture because, after all, "we helped dig the first foundation" (Mustapha 1995:54). So, I started to consider ways to present the material culture of Cahawba as African American, since it had been built largely by African Americans. On the other hand, I also took to heart an editorial in the local newspaper that had been written by a black county commissioner. He insisted that public money *not* be spent on structures built and maintained with slave labor (Varner 1993:4). Friends, scholars, and advisory board members of African descent told me that slavery was too painful a topic to consider. For many of them, their history began only in 1965 with the voting rights movement. The history before, simply put, belonged to someone else.

After years of trying, I was demoralized, depressed, and decided it was time to give up. I was interested in pre-emancipation archaeology, SHA was interested in pre-emancipation archaeology; but the African-American community in which I lived and worked apparently was not. Of course, I could keep an "inclusive" interpretive theme for my established white visitors (McDavid, this volume). After all, adding some faces of color to their traditional view of history could only be a positive move (Farnsworth

FIGURE 1. St. Paul's School, abandoned in 1952. St. Paul's is one of three historic structures still standing on the archaeological site of Old Cahawba.

1993:115–116). However, I would have to find something else to draw in the black community.

The Solution: Asking the Questions that Count

I needed to find something about the history of Cahawba that would interest this segment of the community. *I had to find someone willing to talk to me, and I had to start listening.* First, I looked at my staff —did it include voices that might open doors in the community? I used a staff opening to hire a descendant of a black Cahawbian as the welcome center manager, and also began a long-term program to hire local youth as summer office staff and park workers. Second, I looked at members of "Cahawba Concern," the volunteer group mentioned previously. Of the African-American members, most also attended the Beloit community center, located just 3 mi. from Cahawba. Our most avid volunteers from the Beloit center were retired school teachers. They were always advocating more activities for children, especially at our

annual festival. Third, I took a long, hard look at Selma's current events. At the time, the news media was focusing on a school boycott. Black activists charged that "tracking" in the school system was effectively creating segregation within the schools. Ironically, school violence associated with the boycott caused white flight to private schools, essentially returning the community, at least temporarily, to a completely segregated school system (Smothers 1990:5D).

The St. Paul's Project

Out of this community context, we created the St. Paul's project. St. Paul's school is one of three historic structures still standing on the archaeological site of Old Cahawba. The other two are antebellum. St. Paul's was built in this century, constructed out of salvaged material from older buildings (Figure 1). It stands close by the ruins of an antebellum Methodist church. When the church burned in 1954, it was functioning as an African Methodist Episcopal (AME) church (*STJ* 1954:1–2). An old sign calls St. Paul's the "Boys Academy." In truth, the Cahawba Boy's Academy did stand here in the 1850s. However, the current structure was a segregated schoolhouse for children of more recent black tenant farmers. The school board closed the doors at St. Paul's in 1952.

I knew very little about this school and no

FIGURE 2. Students interviewing Mrs. Mattie Arthur, now deceased, about St. Paul's School.

one seemed willing to talk much about it. I learned, for example, that a woman in the Beloit community had taught there as her first job; however, she was always "too busy" to make time for an interview. As odd as it seems, the only record the county school board or the state department of education had of this school or its students was a report calling for its closure. All the historical records could tell us was that it was a public school, that it closed in 1952, and that it was just one of 80 similar segregated black schools located in the county (Alabama State Department of Education 1951).

I wanted to learn more about the school, but also realized that I needed to address the community's interest in finding more activities for young people. So, my next step was to interest a Selma middle school teacher in helping us with a project designed to do both. We took her students and paired them up with former teachers, parents, students, and a white school superintendent from the period (Figure 2). Their job was to salvage the school's oral history before it was too late. We armed them with 35 mm. cameras and measuring tools so they could record the physical evidence on site. Several experts donated their talents to the project. An architect from Tuskegee Institute showed them how to make Historic American Building Survey-quality measured drawings. An English professor from the University of Alabama spoke to them about the importance of language and oral traditions to African Americans. A folklorist from the Alabama Department of Traditional Culture shared effective methods for oral interviews.

These middle school students did a great job. Their work culminated in a photographic exhibit, a trip to Washington, DC, to learn about the National Register, and the creation of a three-dimensional representation of the school. They taped and transcribed their interviews for posterity. I learned that informants who were reluctant to talk to me were quite willing to share their memories with these children. From these informants, students learned about the insidious aspects of segregation and racism in the segre-

gated schools of the past, including the substandard physical structure of most schools, the short school year for young farm laborers, and the extremely low graduation rate. But they also learned other things about St. Paul's and other schools of the past: that people had a greater sense of community, that parents took more responsibility for their childrens' schooling, that classrooms had fewer discipline problems, and that religion and the black church played a large role in the segregated public school system (Forging Opportunities for Children United in Selma 1995).

The Pay-off

Working with these children opened many doors for me. People began to perceive that I played a role in the preservation of their community, and that I was interested in more than just the preservation of old things. I became a functioning member of the community, and was therefore worthy of trust. I also started to receive more unsolicited information. One day, in the mail from Detroit, I received a church publication outlining a preacher's remembrances of his childhood in our school (Whitt n.d.). Later I experienced a visit from a fascinating man who had interviewed hundreds of African-American students in the Cahawba area during 1952 to assess their anxiety over anticipated desegregation.

On the other hand, I had to learn to barter for access to some kinds of information. After the abandonment of St. Paul's School in the 1950s, a burial society used the structure as a meeting hall. At monthly meetings, each burial society member enjoyed singing, prayer, and fellowship, and then contributed 15 cents toward a burial fund. When a member died, the fund paid for burial expenses. A descendant let me borrow the society's records (Christian Benevolent Society [1959]) only after I promised to type a church homecoming bulletin on my office computer. As a state employee, I probably violated state policy in doing this. From a community standpoint, however, I was recognizing, respect-

FIGURE 3. Drawing of Ezekiel Arthur, reportedly drawn about the time of emancipation. This portrait was given to the project by Ezekiel's daughter-in-law, Mrs. Mattie Arthur.

that white people cannot be trusted or should be avoided since, in the past, they have been a source of misery.

Participation from the local African-American community has continued to increase after the St. Paul's project. I now have some faces of color for our exhibits. For example, one family brought me a drawing of Ezekiel Arthur, a resident of Cahawba, reportedly done about the time of emancipation (Figure 3). His descendants have lived in the area ever since, and one of his descendants, Mattie Arthur, participated in the St. Paul's project (cf. Figure 2). Later when the caretaker of a small neighborhood 'Archive of Black History' passed away, his family gave me a stack of books and papers he had set aside for me. Contained in this gift was a 1908 drawing of the Cahawba home place of the Hatcher family (Figure 4). During slavery, the Hatchers were carpenters, wheelwrights, and blacksmiths who hired out their own time. During Reconstruction, they became important political and religious leaders (Duncan 1908:12–21).

Other positive things began to happen. With the signatures of black descendants, we petitioned the county commission to force a white land owner to open an access road to the "Negro Burial Ground." A Lutheran church inner city youth mission plans to travel from St. Louis

ing, and valuing the community's sense of ownership in the material. In other words, I did not take without recompense.

By working with these middle school children, I learned a lot about St. Paul's. I can now offer an interpretation that has some value and relevance to the African-American communities in the area. Even better, I now have some standing in the community. Individuals now believe I can be trusted with family history more dear to my initial research interests, pre-emancipation history. After we finished the school project, black descendants began to share these older stories with me. Once I heard a few of these stories, I understood why families had been reluctant to share them with an unfamiliar white woman. Oral traditions about family history often contain more than genealogical information. Most also relate a moral or lesson to the younger generation. Frequently that lesson is

FIGURE 4. This drawing of the Hatcher family home was found in a 1908 church publication by George Braxton. The publication was written by a Hatcher descendant, and Mr. Braxton gave the publication to the project (Duncan 1908:15).

to help us carefully clean grave markers and open an interpretive trail into the cemetery. Best of all, at a recent Selma tourism council meeting, I was amazed to hear the Brown Chapel AME group promoting Cahawba as a black heritage site. They called it "our Cahawba." Perhaps pre-emancipation archaeology will play in Selma after all.

Postscript

Heady with success and thinking of myself as a paragon of open-mindedness, I welcomed a summons by a Selma community organization. At their meeting, I summarized the developing archaeological park at Cahawba. After the presentation, I received no questions about my talk, which discussed archaeology, economic development, educational programs, community involvement, and the recording of oral traditions. Instead the African-American members of this group immediately bombarded me with questions about plans to acquire property near the park currently owned by African Americans. They wanted me to know that if any such plans existed, they were dead set against it. Finally, one man stood and asked me about one particular house in Cahawba: "Had it not burned down shortly after a black family refused to sell their lot to the state?" His tone was clearly accusatory. I was so stunned that I was unable to explain that, in fact, the house had burned several years prior to the state's involvement in Cahawba. I could not compose my thoughts fast enough to tell him the full story about what had actually happened, that, when I had originally asked the family about buying the lot on which the house had stood, the family told me they did not want to sell it because the burned remains of their father had not been reclaimed from the ashes. Respecting their wishes, my agency simply reworked the park plans and asked our lawyer to purchase an adjacent lot instead; we did not pursue the purchase of the lot at all. However, during the meeting, all I could say was how personally hurt I was by this

accusation. I also assured them that nothing could be further from the truth.

After reflecting on this encounter, I realized that I was stunned not only by the horrible insinuation about arson, but by the realization that I had fallen victim to the "you people syndrome." I had met the needs of the local rural church-going community that surrounded my site, but these urban activists had little in common with Cahawba's neighbors. Their downtown perspective was not driven by the needs of African Americans living in or near Cahawba. Friends from the Beloit community assured me that these Selma people did not even know the Cahawba families they thought they were defending. Instead they were verbalizing a national agenda, which was, at the time, developing around a question of ownership of interpretive rights and compensation at Martin Luther King's home in Atlanta (*Jet* 1995:12–14; Greenwald 1995:37). This experience, although painful, forced me to realize that I had fallen victim to the myth of the monolithic African-American culture —but then, so had the African-American members of the Selma audience by assuming that the rural black community did not support our efforts.

Conclusion

In summary, the lessons I have learned about public participation in pre-emancipation archaeology over the last 10 years in Selma are as follows:

1. An archaeologist's main concern, in terms of public archaeology, should not be only to disseminate his or her findings to the public *after* excavation. Instead, the target audience needs to be involved in the project from the very beginning. If the community does not help define the questions, the answers probably will not interest them.

2. Do not look only to professional associations, such as SHA, for an approach. Serve your

community. Ask the questions that count to them.

3. Take a holistic approach; be part of the community. The cold, detached, scientific approach will get you nowhere. Unfortunately, acceptance is not achieved overnight. It takes a long-term commitment and a willingness to work through difficult issues *with* the community.

4. If you can use an oral history program in your project that promotes intergenerational pairings, do so. This means of "passing on" history is a respected tradition in many African-American communities and families.

5. Recognize diversity in the African-American community in which you work or live.

These conclusions are little more than just plain, old common sense. Archaeologists and other preservationists have heard much of it before (Logan 1992; [Polley] 1994). However, it is often easy to lose sight of one's principles in the face of complex situations. Perhaps the specifics of the Selma/Cahawba experience can be a reminder to other interpretive archaeologists finding themselves in similar situations.

ACKNOWLEDGMENTS

I wish to thank Carol McDavid for her insightful comments and suggestions regarding the manuscript. I would also like to thank Cahawba Concern, the Archaeological Conservancy, the Alabama Historical Commission, the Selma-Dallas County Historic Preservation Society, local chapters of the Boy Scouts of America, and the park staff for working hard to preserve, protect, and interpret the archaeological resources of Old Cahawba.

REFERENCES

ALABAMA STATE DEPARTMENT OF EDUCATION
  1951 A Survey Report of the Dallas County Schools, School Year 1950–1951. *Research and Survey Series 109.* Alabama State Board of Education, Montgomery.

ALABAMA HISTORICAL COMMISSION
  1993 Alabama Historical Commission Strategic Plan.

Manuscript on file, Alabama Historical Commission, Montgomery.

BENN, ALVIN
  1990 Selma Still Struggling to Gain Racial Unity. *Montgomery Advertiser and Alabama Journal,* 11 February:1A–3A.

CHRISTIAN BENEVOLENT SOCIETY [CAHABA, AL]
  [1959] Christian Benevolent Society Record Book. Duplicate on file, Old Cahawba Archaeological Park, Alabama Historical Commission, Orrville.

DALLAS COUNTY OFFICE OF PROBATE [AL]
  1883 Map of Cahaba, Alabama, Showing the Property of Samuel Kirkpatrick. *Map Book* 1:184. Selma, AL.

DALLAS GAZETTE
  1853– Local News. *Dallas Gazette.* Cahaba, AL.
  1859

DUNCAN, SARA J.
  1908 *Progressive Missions in the South and Alabama with Illustrations and Sketches of Missionary Workers and Ministers and Bishop's Wives.* Franklin Printing and Publishing, Atlanta, GA.

FARNSWORTH, PAUL
  1993 "What Is the Use of Plantation Archaeology?" No Use at All, If No One Else Is Listening! *Historical Archaeology* 27(1):114–116.

FORGING OPPORTUNITIES FOR CHILDREN UNITED IN SELMA [FOCUS] (COMPILER)
  1995 Transcripts of St. Paul's School Oral History Interviews. Manuscript on file, Old Cahawba Archaeological Park, Alabama Historical Commission, Orrville.

GREENWALD, JOHN
  1995 Controversy: Not Fit for a King. *Time* 145 (January 16):37.

HODDER, IAN
  1991 Interpretive Archaeology and Its Role. *American Antiquity* 56 (1):7–18.

JET
  1995 King Family Order Park Agency to Stop Tours in Dispute over Property. *JET* 87 (January 16):12–14.

LOGAN, GEORGE C.
  1992 African-American Archeology, Public Education, and Community Outreach. *CRM* 15(7):9–11.

MUSTAPHA, ABDUL-KARIM
  1995 (dis)Owning the Emperor's Robe. *African-American Archaeology Newsletter* 14(Summer):1–4. Tom

Wheaton, newsletter editor. New South Associates, Stone Mountain, GA.

NATIONAL GEOGRAPHIC WORLD [Washington, DC]
1987   Digging for the Past. *National Geographic World* 144 (August):19–23.

[POLLEY, CLAUDIA]
1994   *Communities for the Future: Preservation of African American Heritage in the United States, Summation Report From First Symposium.* Manuscript on file, National Association for African American Heritage Preservation, Indianapolis, IN.

SELMA TIMES JOURNAL [Selma, AL] (*STJ*)
1954   Old Methodist Church at Cahaba Swept by Flames. *Selma Times Journal*, 26 May:1–2.
1995 $1.5 Million Set Aside for March Route. *Selma Times Journal*, 21 December:1A.

SMOTHERS, RONALD
1990   In Pupil 'Tracks' Many See a Means of Resegregation. *New York Times*, 18 February:5D.

VARNER, PERRY
1993   Your Opinion: Restoration of St. James Unneeded. *Selma Times Journal*, 16 November:4.

WHITT, REV. ROBERT, JR.
n.d.   The Big Old Teaching Snake. ECHOES Sunday School Literature. Wheaton, IL. Undated publication on file, Old Cahawba Archaeological Park, Alabama Historical Commission, Orrville.

LINDA DERRY
OLD CAHAWBA ARCHAEOLOGICAL PARK
ALABAMA HISTORICAL COMMISSION
9518 CAHABA ROAD
ORRVILLE, AL 36737-0566

1997 "Power to the People": Sociopolitics and the Archaeology of Black Americans. In *In the Realm of Politics: Prospects for Public Participation in African American and Plantation Archaeology*. Thematic issue, *Historical Archaeology* 31(3):36-50

MARIA FRANKLIN

"Power To The People": Sociopolitics and the Archaeology of Black Americans

ABSTRACT

This article is concerned with the sociopolitics of African-American archaeology. The intent here is to prompt archaeologists to think more about how our research affects black Americans today, and therefore why it is necessary that they be encouraged to take an interest in archaeological endeavors. The success or failure of our attempts to establish ties with black communities depends on us. The main emphases of this article are, therefore, focused on raising our level of awareness to the challenges we face, and increasing understanding as to the variable histories and perspectives that the diverse and knowledgeable black American public possesses and will hopefully share with archaeologists.

Introduction

The question of "Why do historical archaeology?" is often answered with the discipline's ability to give "people without a history" a "voice" (Little 1994:6; Orser and Fagan 1995:37–38). Indeed, while historical archaeology initially focused on the "rich and famous" of America's past, the discipline's growth is most notably due to the study of historically oppressed groups: Native Americans, African Americans, immigrants, and women. The emphasis on a more inclusive American history is an important goal, and this goal is often cited by archaeologists in order to substantiate the relevance of historical archaeology to today's society. Yet we seldom question our intentions in "giving a voice" to people of the past. Is it simply so that people of the present can better understand and appreciate their cultural heritage and national identity? Are we to assume that the American public is interested in the same questions that we are, and that our research both serves public interests and positively affects our society (Potter 1994:14)? Archaeologists seldom

reflect upon these questions, even though we are aware that the practice of manipulating the past to serve social, economic, and political agendas is probably as ancient and as widespread as human interest in the past itself. The addition of archaeology to the repertoire of "means to study the past" gave imperialists, nationalists, and racists one more weapon in their arsenal for re-penning histories better suited to legitimate and support their oppressive regimes (Trigger 1989). As archaeologists, we may recognize the open-ended potential for abuse through the control and subsequent distortion of historical and archaeological interpretations (Schmidt and Patterson 1995). Such an unconscionable act, we believe, could only be carried out by those politically motivated in order to further secure their privileged position in a society. We stop short of questioning our own position as guardians of the past: our inherent biases, our personal agendas (Pyburn and Wilk 1995:73), and our role in creating pasts which serve the present. It is as if we are unaware that the social and political context within which we operate has any influence on our interpretations and representations of the past. As Christopher Tilley (1989:110) warns, "an apolitical archaeology is a dangerous academic myth. The problem is not that archaeology is a political discourse, but that its politics largely take place on a tacit or unconscious level."

The unreflective practice of archaeology has had detrimental social and political effects upon people everywhere and throughout time (e.g., Hall 1984; Handsman and Leone 1989; Layton 1989; Gathercole and Lowenthal 1990; Stone and MacKenzie 1990; Potter 1991). Those who remain unwilling to reflect upon the social and political implications of their work will only escalate further alienation of archaeologists from the public. Either people will increasingly learn to live quite contentedly without archaeology (McManamon 1991:127) or, if we are not willing to change, we may eventually be forced to change (Zimmerman 1995:67). This article, then, is an attempt to challenge an uncritical

African-American archaeology primarily through consciousness-raising.

The question I pose is, has the black archaeological past been colonized by white, middle-class specialists? I begin by briefly summarizing some of the troubling aspects of archaeological practice exposed through "critical" sociopolitical analyses which are relevant to this critique of African-American archaeology. A critical approach is necessary if African-American archaeology is to be made relevant to black Americans in particular, and American society in general. I then focus on African-American archaeology, and why it is necessary that we make more of an earnest effort to involve black Americans in research and interpretations. I discuss some of the issues that we can address as we initiate a discourse with black Americans, including the question of legitimate claims to cultural resources and dealing with a multivocal black community. The success or failure of our attempts to establish ties with black Americans will hinge upon *our* level of sensitivity, openness, and understanding of the histories and viewpoints that they bring to the exchange. For this reason, most of this discussion is meant to prompt archaeologists to reflect upon and question the current and highly problematic state of African-American archaeology. While the suggestions here are not fully developed, they can serve as a point of departure for future action in transforming our discipline.

Sociopolitics and Critical Archaeologies

> The tendency for archaeological interpretation to be influenced by society does not appear to be diminishing as archaeology becomes more theoretically sophisticated, as some archaeologists have suggested it would (Clarke 1979:154). Instead it appears to remain one of archaeology's permanent features (Trigger 1989:380).

The sociopolitical analyses of archaeology are fairly recent phenomena (Wylie 1989:95) that, while increasing in momentum and influence, cannot be labeled a unified trend (Gero 1985:342; Wylie 1985:134). As Handsman and Leone (1989:118) have observed, "the relevant literature is diverse and inconsistent in orienta-

tion." Such analyses generally involve exposing and critiquing the connections between archaeological knowledge claims and how they are "constituted" by the social and political contexts within which we practice archaeology (Wylie 1989:94). There are two ways in which this occurs, as Wylie (1983:120) further explains: "On one hand, there is a concern with the way in which contextual factors condition or control the archaeological enterprise, complemented on the other hand by a concern with the way archaeology, so conditioned, serves interests dominant in this context." The critique of sociopolitics has been carried out with varying emphases (cf. Gero 1985:342). There is, however, a unifying bond to these approaches: "They are, above all, critical" (Handsman and Leone 1989:118). Cases exist where archaeologists have been effectively critical without even referring to "sociopolitics." In these examples archaeologists have variously challenged the authority of academic knowledge claims (Klesert and Powell 1993; Zimmerman 1994), the control of cultural resources (Messenger 1995:68), and the need to actively involve descendant groups in archaeological endeavors (Spector 1993). Then there is the other end of the spectrum where lies the well-developed "philosophical" approach of the critical theorists (Wylie 1989:94). Developed by German sociologists—the Frankfurt school—in the 1920s and '30s, critical method and theory is grounded in Marxism (Leone 1984:1). Critical theorists are interested in challenging the ways in which historical interpretations are used against the dispossessed in the form of a "masking ideology;" to obscure and hence perpetuate class differences within a capitalist system where domination is assumed (Wylie 1983, 1985, 1989; Leone 1984, 1992; Handsman and Leone 1989; Tilley 1989; Potter 1994:36–39). Leone (1984:1) has observed that although critical theory is not widely used by archaeologists, "many of its insights have entered piecemeal."

By whatever means, confronting the sociopolitics of archaeology has had the effect of transforming the ways in which many of us think about, practice, and advocate our discipline (e.g., Gero et al. 1983; Gero 1985, 1989; Handsman and Leone 1989; Layton 1989; Pinsky and Wylie 1989; Tilley 1989; Wylie 1989, 1991; Gathercole and Lowenthal 1990; Stone and MacKenzie 1990; Gero and Conkey 1991; Potter 1991; Leone 1992; Spector 1993; Lynott and Wylie 1995; McDavid, this volume). This transformation owes its impetus to the initial repudiation by post-processualists of New Archaeology's unrealistic goal of a neutral, "value-free" archaeology, and an intense critique of futile attempts to achieve it (Handsman and Leone 1989:118; Tilley 1989:110–111; Trigger 1989:381; Wylie 1989:93–94). Critical archaeologists charge that interpretations and representations of the past are at all times "interest-constituted" (Handsman and Leone 1989; Wylie 1989:94). The interests served by an unreflective archaeology are of those in power who seek to tighten control of the dispossessed through history and archaeology by purchasing "an empirical substantiation of national mythology" (Leone 1973:129). An uncritical, unreflective archaeology therefore, whether we intend it or not, "sustains rather than challenges the contemporary social order" (Tilley 1989:105). In the United States, this translates to the support and legitimization of a social order permeated by racism, classism, and gender bias.

A Word on Reflection

The point of departure for critical approaches is the recognition that all forms of knowledge are interest-constituted. Next, through self-reflection, critical archaeologists attempt to demystify the relationship between sociopolitics—both within and without the discipline—and archaeological practice (Potter 1994:36). What does it mean to be "self-reflective" or "reflexive"? Reflection involves contemplation. Reflection is the means by which the archaeologist raises his or her level of awareness regarding the focus and meaning of their research: what is the subject, what are the questions, who is the intended audience, and to whom would the interpretations be most useful? An archaeology conditioned by its sociopolitical context does not readily reveal

which interest it serves. Only through reflection can we come to understand how our research could potentially serve to legitimate dominant interests at the expense of everyone else (Handsman and Leone 1989). Wylie offers this interpretation of self-reflection as a strategy employed by critical theorists:

> Critical theory is 'critical' in two senses. First, it involves critical reflection on the knowledge-producing enterprise itself. This encompasses . . . two forms of self-consciousness . . . self-consciousness about the extent to which knowledge claims are conditioned by their social context and serve interests and beliefs that comprise this context. Second, where this self-consciousness reveals the form of a dominant ideology and social order as mediated by the scientific production of knowledge, it provides a basis for reflective understanding and criticism of the social context of research; it takes the form of prospective social criticism and action (Wylie 1985:137).

Self-reflection is therefore "central" to critical theorists (Potter 1994:29), and without it, according to Potter (1994:30), "archaeologists cannot understand the relationships between their work and contemporary life." For this reason, reflection is central to all critical archaeology.

Critical, Responsible, and Accountable

Emotional confrontations between archaeologists and indigenous peoples during the last decade have prompted most of us at some time or another to reflect upon our research. Native American concerns regarding repatriation (Powell et al. 1993; Worl 1995) provoked a growing number of archaeologists to critique an archaeological enterprise "conditioned" by elitism and ethnocentrism (Klesert and Powell 1993). This line of sociopolitical analyses confronts dilemmas such as the "ownership" of cultural resources (Powell et al. 1993; Messenger 1995:68), as well as the primacy granted Anglo- or Euro-centered knowledge claims (Layton 1989; Gathercole and Lowenthal 1990; Zimmerman 1994, 1995) and archaeological knowledge claims in general. Non-archaeologists would currently find that there is little room for opposition. As academically-trained experts on the material record, our interpretations are viewed as authoritative; especially within the profession (Gero 1989). Although cultural resources are considered a "public trust" (Lynott and Wylie 1995:23), archaeologists are the self-imposed guardians of archaeological remains, and in most instances we are in the position to dictate who is allowed access to those remains. Even site reports with the requisite data tables and site information are "coded" in language often so obtuse as to be intelligible only to other archaeologists. We essentially have a monopoly on archaeological data and interpretations, which are then "packaged" and "sold" via museum exhibits or National Geographic Society articles to "passive consumers," namely, the public (Tilley 1989:107).

Sociopolitical analyses, all of which are methodologically critical, urge archaeologists to "level the playing field" (Jeppson, this volume). The general consensus among critical archaeologists is that control of archaeological resources and knowledge must be shared with descendant groups, other impacted communities, and the public at large. Critical theorists in particular contend that impacted groups must be active participants in the process of constructing histories (Handsman and Leone 1989; Potter 1994). As these insights are put into practice through public outreach and involvement, we must remain flexible, accessible, and willing to approach each situation with an open mind. To conclude, although the aforementioned issues are more often associated with the archaeology of indigenous peoples, they are increasingly entering the discourse concerning the archaeology of black Americans.

Black Americans and African-American Archaeology

Our basic need is to reclaim our history and our identity from what must be called cultural terrorism (Carmichael and Hamilton 1970:166).

The sociopolitical climate of the 1960s and early '70s rattled the walls of academia when civil rights proponents, and most notably Black Power advocates, insisted on the institution of black studies programs nationwide (Genovese 1970:242). Black voices were the strongest in setting the agenda, which in essence insisted that American black culture and history finally be recognized as unique, valuable, and hence worthy of serious scholarship. It was no coincidence that Charles Fairbanks undertook the first anthropologically based study of an African-American site during this period of great change (Fairbanks 1984a; Ferguson 1992:xxxvi). Yet seeing as how blacks were largely responsible for igniting interest in their own histories, it is a sad irony that archaeology is perhaps the only discipline involved in the study of early black lifeways which has yet to incorporate significant contributions from any segment of black society.

The current social climate warns that the time to develop a more critical approach to African-American archaeology is past due. Our public visibility has increased as a result of the dramatic rise in the number of historical archaeologists excavating African-American sites. While the few who have made earnest efforts to communicate with black communities managed to maintain mostly positive relations (Henley et al. 1983; Leone 1992; Franklin 1996), there have been instances of conflict. Friction between white archaeologists and members of the black public over the New York African burial ground (Harrington 1993; Blakey 1995; LaRoche and Blakey, this volume) and the Venable Lane excavations (Leeds 1994; Patten, this volume) are the most notable. These examples serve to underscore the point that our research and public education efforts must be viewed within the context of contemporary American race relations. If we continue to ignore the needs and interests of descendant groups, we will foster antagonism, and our research will mean little to nothing to those segments of society whose ancestors we choose to study. If we are truly intent on using archaeology to create more meaningful histories whereby Americans of all backgrounds have the opportunity to participate in the process and, in the end, come to better understand themselves and each other, we have to start by standing in judgment of our own sociopolitics. The following observations were borne out of my initial reflective steps towards a more critical African-American archaeology. Although this critique is not fully developed, there are areas which can potentially serve as points of departure for current and future research.

Towards an Inclusive Archaeology

To start, American society remains profoundly polarized by racism. Of course most, if not all of us, realize this, but how many of us actually reflect upon how our work could potentially legitimate racism? As archaeologists, we must question how racism conditions our discipline and, in so doing, how an unreflective archaeology is fed right back into a racist society without challenging it (Potter 1991). With African-American archaeology, the potential for abuse is staggering given the uncritical state of the discipline (Potter 1991:96, 1994:15), the overwhelming number of whites excavating African-American sites, and the relatively weak efforts to involve black Americans through outreach (Fairbanks 1984b:12). This is not a statement accusing white archaeologists of racism, but to get us to think about social responsibility and ensuring that our research does not serve racist interests. This is highly likely to happen where members of descendant groups are excluded from all aspects of archaeology, including the conception of research questions, excavation, data analysis, and interpretation.

Those who have the most to gain from the current dismal state of race and class relations would continue to have only whites interpret the black archaeological past. The issue of a white majority studying and writing the histories of blacks is only beginning to be debated among historical archaeologists (Potter 1991; McKee 1994; Franklin 1996), and black Americans have generally not participated in this debate at any significant level. Yet we can look to the discourse between archaeologists and indigenous peoples to try and understand why a diverse perspective is the crucial element in the reconstruction of histories that are more relevant to

the latter (Layton 1989; Stone and MacKenzie 1990; Messenger 1995; Zimmerman 1995). Many of the concerns that blacks will have regarding the treatment of black sites will be similar to those traditionally expressed by Native Americans, as the New York African burial ground controversy demonstrated (Harrington 1993; Blakey 1995; LaRoche and Blakey, this volume). The initial lack of communication between white archaeologists and black Americans fostered mistrust, as did what was perceived to be insensitive treatment of the human remains. We are learning the hard way that archaeologists are not the only people interested in the past (Fairbanks 1984b:12), and that descendant groups have a vested interest in archaeological sites (Layton 1989; Gathercole and Lowenthal 1990; Ayau 1995; Naranjo 1995; Wylie 1996:180–183). Moreover, it is we who must bear the responsibility for bringing diverse perspectives into the discipline (Pyburn and Wilk 1995:72).

Most archaeologists agree that we have a responsibility to educate the public, but some may question the degree to which we are obligated to include the public in the research process at the level called for by critical archaeologists (McKee 1994). Fundamentally, however, our failure to establish ties with black Americans—whether they be from the local community, scholars, or members of interest groups—serves to further subjugate them, for they are in turn fully implicated in any historical interpretations concerning the black past. That is, historical and archaeological research affects *all* black Americans, not simply those whom archaeologists or others deem to be culturally, historically, or ancestrally linked to a historic site or era under study. For example, when Colonial Williamsburg's reconstructed slave quarter at Carter's Grove first opened to tourists, there were watermelons being grown in the yard, and rinds were present among the cabins' foodstuffs. Black interpreters complained that this representation of past foodways served to perpetuate negative stereotypes regarding blacks, and these items were subsequently removed (Gable et al. 1992:802). This one aspect of early black lifeways at

Carter's Grove could easily have evoked in the minds of white tourists the racist "black-face" images popularized by minstrel shows that stereotyped blacks as slow, lazy, and stupid. As this brief example demonstrates, the past does serve the present. Given this, it would not only be arrogant, but unethical, to insist that interested black Americans be able to demonstrate any sort of legitimate claim to a site before we actively involve them in a project. They are collectively impacted by our research results, and in this crucial sense, they are *all* connected to the pasts we reconstruct.

Some archaeologists might be tempted to proclaim that "history belongs to everybody" to shrug off any accountability to descendant groups, or to the general public. History belongs to everyone ideally, perhaps, but in actuality it belongs to those who have access to its material remnants, to those who control its penning, and to those who possess the power to authorize and disseminate it. History *should* belong to everyone, and that is the goal archaeologists must reach for if we are intent on archaeology being relevant to non-archaeologists.

On Relevance

Potter (1994:16) asserts that "the first responsibility of the archaeologist is not to try to make his or her research relevant but rather, it is to be conscious of how that work *is* potentially relevant, what it is relevant to, and the uses to which such work could be put." So all research is relevant, and in this case, we must determine how our research can be made relevant to black Americans. The suggestions for doing so have varied.

Much of African-American archaeology centers on the institution of slavery. Potter, a critical theorist, insists that in order for plantation archaeology to be relevant to black Americans today, it must "focus on the structures of oppression" (Potter 1991:101). That is, if through plantation archaeology we all come to "recognize contemporary vestiges of past domination," we can more effectively challenge oppression in today's society (Potter 1991:101). Potter

(1991:100) further suggests that archaeologists and African Americans come together in developing research questions to ensure that the research be in the interest of the latter. Potter's method is the most direct and effective means for instituting social action through archaeology. It aims right at the system, and therefore holds the most potential for prompting people to reflect upon and challenge the system, and hopefully institute change for the better. But here I agree with McKee (1994:5) that we must be careful about confining ourselves to only certain questions. I realize that critical theory embodies a neo-Marxist critique, and therefore systems of domination and class inequalities are emphasized. A *critical archaeology*, however, need not have the same emphasis on class structure. There are other research questions which black Americans may be more interested in where the "structures of oppression" are not immediately the focus. Leone (1992:7) refers to archaeology where "local people define the questions" as archaeology through "local empowerment." I am often questioned by other blacks about the material evidence for the roots of black culture. For many, understanding where they came from is the same thing as understanding who they are, and this knowledge is the legacy that they wish to pass on to future generations (Figure 1).

In the end we must involve black Americans in archaeology. As individuals and as a people who have much to gain or lose depending on how reflective and critical we are as archaeologists, we have an obligation to ask that they be a part of any project. In so doing, we must never assume what direction their questions and concerns might take for, as Potter (1994:225) warns, "critical archaeologies are intensely local; one size does not fit all." Black Americans constitute a culturally, socially, and politically diverse and multivocal group. In working with local black communities, we must therefore be prepared for different reactions among them.

Engaging a Diverse Black Public

Ruffins (1992) observed that collections of black memorabilia assembled by black collectors during the 19th and early 20th centuries did not contain any items pertaining to slavery for a reason. Slavery was a painful and degrading memory for blacks, and its offspring Jim Crow ensured that further humiliation through racial oppression would continue. Why, then, collect the material reminders of a system so brutal? The tendency was to try and move away from this past by moving onto and up the social ladder. Although we might lament this decision by early black collectors to exclude artifacts which now would be invaluable to our understanding of American history, it is easy to sympathize with them. Slavery was a not-so-distant memory back then. But some 130 years have passed since slavery, and American society has changed. Slavery should no longer be a subject that we sweep under the rug, for that smacks of ignorance. Or does it? Scholars are discovering that there are black Americans who still feel that slavery is a shameful topic and still too sensitive to be discussed or displayed openly. Some fear that whites would only trivialize the anguish and suffering of enslaved Africans, and the brutality of slave-owning whites. Others resent how many whites continue to ignore black contributions to history by essentially "white-washing" the past by excluding blacks. Commenting on the "total plantation experience" promised by ads of Charleston, South Carolina, plantations, black tourist guide Al Miller stated: "They might tell you that blacks used to shine the brass door-knobs. Blacks built almost all the buildings in Charleston, but you don't hear that" (Wrolstad 1994). Being systematically excluded from the process of historical and archaeological research surely only exacerbates the anxiety and resentment. But not all blacks feel that the enslaved past should remain shrouded.

Black people are currently divided over what is deemed appropriate for discussion, study, and disclosure with regard to black history (Potter 1991:100; Leone 1992; McDavid, this volume). As many more black Americans move towards dealing with slavery and its prevailing social effects, confrontations between opposing black voices resound. For example, in St. Mary's County, Maryland, members of the black community debate the future of the slave quarter at Sotterley Plantation (Figure 2). George Forrest, a descendant of enslaved Africans from another St. Mary's plantation, and a trustee of the Sotterley Foundation, sums up the problem: "Some think it is a painful part of history that needs to be torn down and forgotten about. The other [approach] is to take this structure and use it as a memorial to those folks who struggled here" (Hill 1995). In another case, the Library of Congress shut down a new exhibit titled "Back of the Big House: The Cultural Landscape of the Plantation." Curated by John Michael Vlach, the exhibit was meant to show the "slaves' perspective" on the plantation (Nicholson 1995). Hours after the exhibit opened, however, a group of black employees found the exhibit offensive and demanded the exhibit's closure. David Nicholson, a black editor for the *Washington Post*, condemned the shutdown as irresponsible. Nicholson felt that slavery would remain "a psychic wound that black Americans, and only black Americans, can heal." Despite the antagonism within black society, these case studies and others demonstrate that blacks on both sides are very much emo-

FIGURE 1. "African to American," *Daily Press*, 21 August 1994:B1. (Courtesy of the *Daily Press*, Williamsburg, VA.)

Maria Franklin

FIGURE 2. "Coming to Grips With Painful Past," *Washington Post*, 2 April 1995:B3. (Courtesy of *Washington Post*,.)

tionally bound to the issue of how to deal with the legacy of slavery. These mixed emotions surfaced during the reenactment of a slave auction at Colonial Williamsburg in October 1994 (Clawson 1994; Mathews, this volume) (Figure 3). A racially mixed crowd of 2,000 supporters and protesters, including representatives from the NAACP and the Southern Christian Leadership Conference, gathered for the event (Boyd 1994; Jones 1995). Although the majority of blacks present that day supported what was deemed an educational program, the tension in the air was heavy.

Whenever black Americans have attempted to understand what it took enslaved ancestors to survive, the words "opening the wounds" and "healing," "pain," and "struggle" are invoked to describe the emotional transformation and catharsis associated with coming to terms with a slave heritage (Hill 1995; Jones 1995; Nicholson 1995). All disagreements aside, there is a

shared compassion within black society when it comes to reckoning with the experiences of their enslaved ancestors, and this is evidenced in the above examples where the debates were similarly impassioned. These emotions arise out of a shared sense of connection to the past, and with a particular sense of commitment to rising above past and present oppression.

As archaeologists, we must not take sides in these conflicts. It is important that we do not simply dismiss the voices of opposition to our work, most of which currently involves the topic of slavery, for, as I have previously argued, all black Americans are connected to the pasts we unearth. Further, most of us have not given black society much reason to feel that archaeology should be important to them. But is it our responsibility to do so? After all, archaeologists are not the only specialists involved with constructing histories, and nonprofessionals have created their own versions of the past and then

230

Perspectives from the Society for Historical Archaeology:

FIGURE 3. "CW auctions slaves." (Courtesy of the *Daily Press*, Williamsburg, VA.)

"imposed" them upon others. Unlike the latter, however, many archaeologists recognize that this profession exists for, and because of, the public. Along with the privilege and authority that we possess as professional archaeologists, we must bear the burden of social responsibility and set an example; for if not us, then who?

Roots, Remembrances, and Contributions

> Black scholars must remember their sources, and by this I mean no technically historical sources. I mean human sources. They are the products of their source—the great pained community of the Afro-Americans of this land. And they can forget the source only at great peril to their spirit, their work, and their souls (Harding 1986:279).

As academics we often think about how our scholarship can enrich the lives of others. Seldom do we consider how our own lives, including our research, could benefit from the knowledge and experiences of nonarchaeologists. Much of the time this occurs because we have fooled ourselves into thinking that we are in the business of "giving" a history to the public. Instead, our discipline is but one cog in a machine that has been churning out histories long before we came along, and it will continue to do so if we are no longer around to participate in the process. I firmly believe that archaeology can be valuable and worthwhile to everyone else, but I still recognize that people would not be without history, culture, or tradition should archaeologists and anthropologists vanish from the face of the earth. Where black Americans are concerned, we have a long-standing tradition of studying ourselves, as evidenced by the pioneering work of individuals such as Zora Neale Hurston, Carter G. Woodson, and W. E. B. Du Bois. African-American archaeology must be seen as not only an extension of the disciplines of archaeology and anthropology but also of the vast body of scholarship on black American history and culture, much of it conducted by blacks themselves.

Archaeologists are in the enviable position of potentially benefiting from the exchange of information with insightful and knowledgeable black

Americans. What we must first overcome is the presumption that because we might be experts on the archaeological record, this makes us experts on black history and culture. Most practitioners of African-American archaeology do not even have a formal background in any sort of African or African-American studies. The resources that we do have within arm's reach, we often fail to call upon: black scholars and members of the black communities in which we work.

One suggestion for bridging the gap between archaeologists and black Americans has been to recruit more black archaeologists. While this goal should certainly be pursued, the diversification of archaeology will take time. At the same time, we often overlook the possibility of networking with black scholars with similar research interests in fields which largely overlap with ours: history, literature, folklore, cultural anthropology, black studies, cultural geography, museum studies, genealogy, and so on. In all of my exchanges with other black academics, I walked away with more than I arrived with. They were in turn eager to learn more about archaeology. I have also benefited greatly from the wisdom of nonacademics who were willing to share their insights and life experiences in order to enrich my research on early black culture. Archaeologists who have discovered that a "plural archaeological environment" can benefit research (Leone 1992:7; Agbe-Davies 1995; Franklin 1996; Powell 1996) are joined by other scholars who have also found enlightenment beyond the walls of academia.

Historian George McDaniel (1982) discovered an immeasurable wealth of memories and cultural traditions within the black families of

First-hand reflections

Local man source for many historians

By Jennifer Andes
Daily Press

FIGURE 4. "First-hand reflections," *Daily Press*, 17 March 1993. (Courtesy of the *Daily Press*, Williamsburg, VA.)

Perspectives from the Society for Historical Archaeology:

Mitchellville, Maryland. When a turn-of-the-century black tenant farm house was taken down and rebuilt within the walls of the Smithsonian, McDaniel invited black families from Mitchellville to view the house. Their collective reaction? While at the Smithsonian for 10 years, the house had been displayed backwards by curators; the front of the house was supposed to be the rear, and the kitchen and living room were reversed (McDaniel 1982:26–27). McDaniel, a white historian interested in black history, found his interviews with descendants to be invaluable. With regard to his attempts to approach and talk to people he stated: "Though I have met with a few hostile receptions, the overwhelming majority of people have been co-operative because *they have been concerned about recording the history they knew* [emphasis added]" (McDaniel 1982:xv).

Individuals as well as whole communities can help to make the difference between histories viewed through a single lens, and bolder, fuller histories viewed through multiple lenses. Scholars from the Smithsonian and the College of William and Mary have interviewed Alexander Lee to help in recounting the lives of descendants of freedmen who settled in Yorktown, Virginia, after the Civil War (McDonald et al. 1992; Andes 1993) (Figure 4). When Lee was a child, the U.S. Navy used the process of "eminent domain" to seize property that had long been settled by 600 black families and as many as 200 white families (McDonald et al. 1992:43, 75). Although the government paid some compensation to landowners, unlike the whites, many blacks could not prove that the land was theirs. Some had inherited land from family members who worked the property under slavery and were then given parcels of plantation land upon emancipation without ever receiving a deed (McDonald et al. 1992:15). Their descendants therefore ended up with nothing despite the fact that they had lived on the property for years without dispute. The land is now home to the Yorktown Naval Weapons Station. Yorktown's written history and public interpretations are dominated by glorious military events such as the surrender at Yorktown during the Revolution.

The naval base serves as a constant reminder of this grand military past. In turn, Lee's memories serve to keep alive a more grim side of Yorktown's history: the disrupted lives of those who were torn from their place of birth and way of life by a system of oppression deeply rooted in American society.

Within black communities, there are living ties to the past, both historical and cultural. And while we may be the experts when it comes to the archaeological record, this does not necessarily make us experts, or the only experts, on black history and culture. Consulting with black Americans, both scholars and nonacademics, can only broaden our base of understanding of the past. This is not to say that we should privilege knowledge on the basis of skin color. Hopefully these examples simply demonstrate that black Americans possess perspectives, insights, and lifeways, the knowledge of which could benefit archaeological research.

Conclusions

The discipline of historical archaeology is not a timeless, static entity, just as the cultures that we study were and are not. The positive growth and transformation of our field depends upon the continual reexamination of our objectives. The goals of archaeologists in general have been confined to ensuring professional responsibility to other archaeologists, to protecting cultural resources, and to dictating proper field conduct. It is only recently that archaeologists have come to debate among themselves about the privileged "ownership" of archaeological knowledge and cultural resources, and the potent effects of the social and political implications of our research. The Society for American Archaeology, for example, has recently revised its ethics statements to include principles on accountability, public education and outreach, and stewardship (Lynott and Wylie 1995; Kintigh 1996:5, 17; Wylie 1996:184–187). The statement on accountability reads: "Responsible archaeological research, including all levels of professional activity, requires an acknowledgment of public accountability and a commitment to make every reasonable

Maria Franklin

effort, in good faith, to consult actively with affected group(s), with the goal of establishing a working relationship that can be beneficial to all parties involved" (Kintigh 1996:7).

The World Archaeological Congress and the American Anthropological Association both have similar edicts in their bylaws. Yet, the bylaws of The Society for Historical Archaeology have no such specific clause in Article VII, its statement of "ethical positions." This is likely due to the fact that historical archaeologists have generally studied Anglo-Americans, and cases where whites are studying other whites are not perceived as a threat by most Americans who are white. For now, the study of African Americans by historical archaeologists goes virtually unnoticed by black Americans, mainly due to a lack of concerted efforts to bring this research to their attention. It is as if we are biding our time; waiting for more heated confrontations with black Americans before we are finally forced through public opinion and governmental regulations to engage them as equals in archaeological research. But why let push come to shove? No one stands to benefit through forced relations, where the long-held feelings of mistrust and resentment between blacks and whites are then further fueled by struggles to control archaeological interpretations of multiple black pasts.

In the end, it is up to archaeologists to make the initial effort of extending an open invitation to members of the black community to participate in the construction of their histories. Our interpretations of black history can potentially serve to legitimate and perpetuate racism in American society, and are more likely to do so should black Americans be excluded from the process of researching histories. We must take every measure to identify who benefits from our particular projects, and to whom our research is relevant. With an active, critical analysis of our research, and with the input from impacted groups, we are more likely to produce archaeological results which serve to uplift and empower communities which still suffer under racial and political hegemony.

For those who are still unsure about whether archaeologists should be accountable to black Americans, and whether we should have to actively involve them in archaeological endeavors, just ask ourselves why it is that we want to study black history and culture. But be warned, for there is far too much at stake to answer that one simply finds it interesting.

ACKNOWLEDGMENTS

I would like to thank Ywone D. Edwards and Marley R. Brown III for their enthusiastic support and critical feedback during the writing of this article. Carol McDavid and David Babson, I thank you for the herculean effort in getting this volume together. I owe sincere gratitude to Elizabeth Prine, Robin Sewell, Julie Endicott, Julie King, and anonymous reviewers who took the time to provide thoughtful comments which really helped to bring this article together. I also benefited greatly from exchanges with Anna Agbe-Davies, Garrett Fesler, James Deetz, Margaret W. Conkey, Michael Blakey, Cheryl La Roche, Alison Wylie, and Whitney Battle. Your passion for archaeology and your commitment to doing the right thing are inspiring. Thank you, Ronald L. Michael and James Gibb, for helping me locate sources necessary for completing this article. Any and all mistakes and oversights are, of course, my sole responsibility.

REFERENCES

AGBE-DAVIES, ANNA
1995 African American Archaeology in the Public Eye. Paper presented at the Annual Meeting of The Society for Historical Archaeology Conference on Historical and Underwater Archaeology, Washington, DC.

ANDES, JENNIFER
1993 First-Hand Reflections: Local Man Source for Many Historians. *The Daily Press*, 17 March. Williamsburg, VA.

AYAU, EDWARD HALEALOHA
1995 Rooted in Native Soil. *Federal Archaeology* 7(3):30–33. Departmental Consulting Archeologist and Archeological Assistance Program, National Park Service, Washington, DC.

BLAKEY, MICHAEL L.
1995 The Unity of Past and Present: Understanding the New York African Burial Ground Phenomenon. Paper presented at the University of California Faculty Seminar Series, Berkeley, CA.

BOYD, BENTLEY
1994 CW Auctions Slaves: Re-enactment Provokes Emotional Debate. *The Daily Press*, 11 October:A1–2. Williamsburg, VA.

CARMICHAEL, STOKELY, AND CHARLES V. HAMILTON
1970 Black Power: Its Need and Substance. In *What Country Have I?: Political Writings by Black Americans*, edited by Herbert J. Storing, pp. 165–181. St. Martin's Press, NY.

CLARKE, DAVID L.
1979 *Analytical Archaeologist*. Academic Press, NY.

CLAWSON, MICHELLE CARR
1994 In a Different Tongue. *Colonial Williamsburg* 17(2):32–33.

FAIRBANKS, CHARLES H.
1984a The Kingsley Slave Cabins in Duval County, Florida, 1968. *Conference on Historic Sites Archaeology Papers, 1973* 7:62–93.
1984b The Plantation Archaeology of the Southeastern Coast. *Historical Archaeology* 18(1):1–14.

FERGUSON, LELAND
1992 *Uncommon Ground: Archaeology and Early African America, 1650–1800*. Smithsonian Institution Press, Washington, DC.

FRANKLIN, MARIA
1996 Owners and Stewards, and Innocent Bystanders: Archaeologists and the Past as Property. Paper presented at the Annual Meeting of The Society for Historical Archaeology Conference on Historical and Underwater Archaeology, Cincinnati, OH.

GABLE, ERIC, RICHARD HANDLER, AND ANNA LAWSON
1992 On the Uses of Relativism: Fact, Conjecture, and Black and White Histories at Colonial Williamsburg. *American Ethnologist* 19(4):791–805.

GATHERCOLE, PETER, AND DAVID LOWENTHAL (EDITORS)
1990 *The Politics of the Past*. Unwin Hyman, London.

GENOVESE, EUGENE D.
1970 The Influence of the Black Power Movement on Historical Scholarship: Reflections of a White Historian. In *In Red and Black: Marxian Explorations in Southern and Afro-American History*, edited by Eugene D. Genovese, pp. 230–255. Pantheon, NY.

GERO, JOAN M.
1985 Socio-politics and the Woman-at-Home Ideology. *American Antiquity* 50(2):342–350.
1989 Producing Prehistory, Controlling the Past: The Case of New England Beehives. In *Critical Traditions in Contemporary Archaeology*, edited by Valerie Pinsky and Alison Wylie, pp. 96–116. Cambridge University Press, Cambridge, England.

GERO, JOAN M., DAVID M. LAACY, AND MICHAEL L. BLAKEY (EDITORS)
1983 *The Socio-Politics of Archaeology*. University of Massachusetts, Amherst.

GERO, JOAN M., AND MARGARET W. CONKEY (EDITORS)
1991 *Engendering Archaeology: Women and Prehistory*. Basil Blackwell, Oxford.

HALL, MARTIN
1984 The Burden of Tribalism: The Social Context of Southern African Iron Age Studies. *American Antiquity* 49(3):455–467.

HANDSMAN, RUSSELL G., AND MARK P. LEONE
1989 Living History and Critical Archaeology in the Reconstruction of the Past. In *Critical Traditions in Contemporary Archaeology*, edited by Valerie Pinsky and Alison Wylie, pp. 117–135. Cambridge University Press, Cambridge, England.

HARDING, VINCENT
1986 Responsibilities of the Black Scholar to the Community. In *The State of Afro-American History: Past, Present, and Future*, edited by Darlene Clark Hine, pp. 277–291. Louisiana State University Press, Baton Rouge.

HARRINGTON, SPENCER P. M.
1993 Bones and Bureaucrats: New York's Great Cemetery Imbroglio. *Archaeology* 46(2):28–38.

HENLEY, LAURA A., ANN M. PALKOVICH, AND JONATHAN HAAS
1983 The Other Side of Alexandria: Archeology in an Enduring Black Community. In *Approaches to Preserving a City's Past*, pp. 41–44. Alexandria Urban Archeology Program, Alexandria, VA.

HILL, RETHA
1995 Coming to Grips with Painful Past. *Washington Post*, 2 April:B3. Washington, DC.

JONES, CHARISSE
1995 Bringing Slavery's Long Shadow to the Light. *New York Times*, 2 April:A1, A3.

KINTIGH, KEITH W.
1996 SAA Principles of Archaeological Ethics. *Society for American Archaeology Bulletin* 14(3):5, 17. Mark Aldenderfer, Newsletter Editor. Santa Barbara, CA.

KLESERT, ANTHONY L., AND SHIRLEY POWELL
1993 A Perspective on Ethics and the Reburial Controversy. *American Antiquity* 58(2):348–354.

LAYTON, ROBERT (EDITOR)
1989 Who Needs the Past?: Indigenous Values and Archaeology. Unwin Hyman, London.

LEEDS, JEFF
1994 Blacks Protest Excavation Team. *Washington Post*, 18 January:D–4.

LEONE, MARK P.
1973 Archaeology as the Science of Technology: Mormon Town Plans and Fences. In *Research and Theory in Current Archaeology*, edited by Charles Redman, pp. 125–150. Riley and Sons, NY.
1984 Critical Theory in Archaeology. Paper presented at State University of New York, Binghamton.
1992 A Multicultural African-American Historical Archaeology: How to Place Archaeology in the Community in a State Capital. Paper presented at the Annual Meeting of the American Anthropological Association, San Francisco, CA.

LITTLE, BARBARA J.
1994 People with History: An Update on Historical Archaeology in the United States. *Journal of Archaeological Method and Theory* 1(1):5–40.

LYNOTT, MARK J., AND ALISON WYLIE (EDITORS)
1995 *Ethics in American Archaeology: Challenges for the 1990s.* Society for American Archaeology, Washington, DC.

MCDANIEL, GEORGE W.
1982 *Hearth and Home: Preserving a People's Culture.* Temple University Press, Philadelphia, PA.

MCDONALD, BRADLEY M., KENNETH E. STUCK, AND KATHLEEN J. BRAGDON
1992 "Cast Down Your Bucket Where You Are": An Ethnohistorical Study of the African-American Community on the Lands of the Yorktown Naval Weapons Station, 1865–1918. Report prepared by William and Mary Center for Archaeological Research, College of William and Mary, Williamsburg, VA. Submitted to Atlantic Division, Naval Facilities Engineering Command, Yorktown.

MCKEE, LARRY
1994 Is It Futile to Try and Be Useful?: Historical Archaeology and the African-American Experience. *Northeast Historical Archaeology* 23:1–7.

MCMANAMON, FRANCIS P.
1991 The Many Publics for Archaeology. *American Antiquity* 56(1):121–130.

MESSENGER, PHYLLIS MAUCH
1995 Public Education and Outreach. In *Ethics in American Archaeology: Challenges for the 1990s*, edited by Mark J. Lynott and Alison Wylie, pp. 68–70. Society for American Archaeology, Washington, DC.

NARANJO, TESSIE
1995 Thoughts on Two Worldviews. *Federal Archaeology* 7(3):16. Departmental Consulting Archeologist and Archeological Assistance Program, National Park Service, Washington, DC.

NICHOLSON, DAVID
1995 The Costs of Cultural Blackmail: Shutting Down the Slavery Exhibit Only Denies Our Suffering and Triumph. *Washington Post*, 24 December:C2.

ORSER, CHARLES E., JR., AND BRIAN M. FAGAN
1995 *Historical Archaeology*. HarperCollins College, NY.

PINSKY, VALERIE, AND ALISON WYLIE (EDITORS)
1989 *Critical Traditions in Contemporary Archaeology.* Cambridge University Press, Cambridge, England.

POTTER, PARKER B., JR.
1991 What Is the Use of Plantation Archaeology? *Historical Archaeology* 25(3):94–107.
1994 *Public Archaeology in Annapolis: A Critical Approach to History in Maryland's Ancient City.* Smithsonian Institution Press, Washington, DC.

POWELL, LEAH CARSON
1996 Traditional Narratives and Oral History. In *Home Herafter: An Archaeological and Bioarchaeological Analysis of an Historic African-American Cemetery (41GV125)*, edited by Helen D. Dockall, Joseph F. Powell, and D. Gentry Steele, pp. 231–219. *Reports of Investigation* 5. Center for Environmental Archaeology, Texas A&M University, College Station.

POWELL, SHIRLEY, CHRISTINE E. GARZA, AND AUBREY HENDRICKS
1993 Ethics and Ownership of the Past: The Reburial and Repatriation Controversy. In *Archaeological Method and Theory*, edited by Michael B. Schiffer, pp. 1–42. University of Arizona Press, Tucson.

PYBURN, K. ANNE, AND RICHARD R. WILK
1995 Responsible Archaeology Is Applied Anthropology. In *Ethics in American Archaeology: Challenges for the 1990s*, edited by Mark J. Lynott and Alison Wylie, pp. 71–76. Society for American Archaeology, Washington, DC.

RUFFINS, FATH DAVIS
1992 Mythos, Memory, and History: African American Preservation Efforts, 1820–1990. In *Museums and Communities: The Politics of Public Culture*, edited

by Ivan Karp, Christine Mullen Kreamer, and Steven D. Lavine, pp. 506–611. Smithsonian Institution Press, Washington, DC.

SCHMIDT, PETER R., AND THOMAS C. PATTERSON (EDITORS)
1995   Making Alternative Histories: The Practice of Archaeology and History in Non-Western Settings. School of American Research Press, Santa Fe, NM.

SPECTOR, JANET D.
1993   What This Awl Means. Historical Society Press, St. Paul, MN.

STONE, PETER, AND ROBERT MACKENZIE (EDITORS)
1990   The Excluded Past: Archaeology in Education. Unwin Hyman, London.

TILLEY, CHRISTOPHER
1989   Archaeology as Socio-political Action in the Present. In Critical Traditions in Contemporary Archaeology, edited by Valerie Pinsky and Alison Wylie, pp. 104–116. Cambridge University Press, Cambridge, England.

TRIGGER, BRUCE G.
1989   A History of Archaeological Thought. Cambridge University Press, Cambridge, England.

WORL, ROSITA
1995   NAGPRA: Symbol of a New Treaty. Federal Archaeology 7(3):34–5. Departmental Consulting Archeologist and Archeological Assistance Program, National Park Service, Washington, DC.

WROLSTAD, MARK
1994   Re-examining a Past Built on Slavery. Atlanta Journal/ Atlanta Constitution, 13 March:M6. Atlanta, GA.

WYLIE, ALISON
1983   Comments on the Sociopolitics of Archaeology: The Demystification of the Profession. In The Sociopolitics of Archaeology, edited by Joan M. Gero, David M. Lacy, and Michael L. Blakey, pp. 119–130. University of Massachusetts, Amherst.
1985   Putting Shakertown Back Together: Critical Theory in Archaeology. Journal of Anthropological Archaeology 4:133–147.
1989   Introduction: Socio-political Context. In Critical Traditions in Contemporary Archaeology, edited by Valerie Pinsky and Alison Wylie, pp. 93–95. Cambridge University Press, Cambridge, England.
1991   Gender Theory and the Archaeological Record: Why Is There No Archaeology of Gender. In Engendering Archaeology: Women and Prehistory, edited by Joan M. Gero and Margaret W. Conkey, pp. 31–54. Basil Blackwell, Oxford.
1996   Ethical Dilemmas in Archaeological Practice: Looting, Repatriation, Stewardship, and the (Trans)formation of Disciplinary Identity. Perspectives on Science 4(2):154–194.

ZIMMERMAN, LARRY
1994   Sharing Control of the Past. Archaeology 47(6):65, 67–68.
1995   Regaining Our Nerve: Ethics, Values, and the Transformation of Archaeology. In Ethics in American Archaeology: Challenges for the 1990s, edited by Mark J. Lynott and Alison Wylie, pp. 64–67. Society for American Archaeology, Washington, DC.

MARIA FRANKLIN
DEPARTMENT OF ARCHAEOLOGICAL RESEARCH
THE COLONIAL WILLIAMSBURG FOUNDATION
WILLIAMSBURG, VA 23187-1776
AND DEPARTMENT OF ANTHROPOLOGY
UNIVERSITY OF CALIFORNIA, BERKELEY
BERKELEY, CA 94720

1997 Seizing Intellectual Power: the Dialogue at the New York African Burial Ground. In *In The Realm of Politics: Prospects for Public Participation in African American and Plantation Archaeology*, Carol McDavid and David Babson, editors. Thematic issue, *Historical Archaeology* 31:3:84-106

Errata

In haste of attempting to obtain a timely publication for the following article, several errors occurred.

ARNOLD, J. BARTO III
    1996   The Texas Historical Commission's Underwater Archaeological Survey of 1995 and the Preliminary Report on the *Belle*, LaSalle's Shipwreck of 1686. *Historical Archaeology* 30(4): 66–87.

Missing References

BALL, DAVID, AND BRETT PHANEUF
    1995   Preliminary description of instrumentation and survey areas for Matagorda Bay magnetometer survey of 1995. Manuscript on file, Texas Historical Commission, Austin, Texas.

GUEROUT, MAX
    1995   Le canon de Matagorda Bay et l'artillerie de bronze française. Manuscript on file, Texas Historical Commission, Austin, TX.

LESSMANN, ANNE
    1995   Preliminary ceramic analysis of samples raised from the seventeenth-century French shipwreck *LaBelle* (1686), Matagorda Bay, Texas. Manuscript on file, Texas Historical Commission, Austin, TX.

MEIDE, CHUCK
    1995   A preliminary analysis of cask remains from the shipwreck *LaBelle*: the 1995 excavation. Manuscript on file, TX. Historical Commission, Austin, TX.

Figure Caption Error

FIGURE 5. The drawing of the touchmark inset in this figure is by Sara Keyes rather than Chuck Meide.

CHERYL J. LA ROCHE
MICHAEL L. BLAKEY

Seizing Intellectual Power: The Dialogue at the New York African Burial Ground

ABSTRACT

The New York African Burial Ground Project embodies the problems, concerns, and goals of contemporary African-American and urban archaeology. The project at once has informed and has been informed by the ever-watchful African Americans and New York public. It is a public that understands that the hypothetical and theoretical constructs that guide research are not value-free and are often, in fact, politically charged. An ongoing dialogue between the concerned community, the federal steering committee, the federal government, and the archaeological community has proved difficult but ultimately productive. The project has an Office of Public Education and Interpretation which informs the public through a newsletter, educators' conferences, and laboratory tours. The public, largely students, attends laboratory tours which often provide initial exposure to archaeology and physical anthropology. Much of this public involvement, however, was driven by angry public reaction to the excavation of a site of both historical prominence and spiritual significance.

Introduction

Excavation of the New York African Burial Ground has brought scholars, academicians, researchers, cultural resource managers, politicians, religious leaders, community activists, school children, and the general public together in a complex and often contentious philosophical and ideological relationship. The dynamics of the relationship and the shape of the project have been determined to a large extent by the relentless determination of the African-American descendant community to exercise control over the handling and disposition of the physical remains and artifacts of their ancestors. This relentless determination also ensured that the spiritual aspects of the site would not be lost in the face of scientific inquiry (Laura 1992; S&S Reporting 1993). Excavation of the African Burial Ground has global and universal implications which tran-

scend urban archaeology, physical anthropology, or the concerns of any one group.

Background

When the United States General Services Administration (GSA) contracted for the construction of a 34-story office building at Broadway, Duane, Elk, and Reade streets, New York City, on a site that historical maps indicated had been an 18th-century "Negroes Burying Ground" (Figure 1), it did not anticipate the storm of controversy that lay buried and moribund beneath nearly 30 ft. of fill. The cemetery, which was renamed the African Burial Ground in 1993 (Figure 2; Landmarks 1992), dates from before 1712 until 1794 (Howard University and John Milner Associates [HUJMA] 1993), and as the nation's earliest and largest African burial ground, holds great interest for anthropologists and historians as well as for the descendant communities. Although historians had long known of the African Burial Ground, the rediscovery was a revelation that struck a deep chord among many people of African descent in New York (Harrington 1993:33).

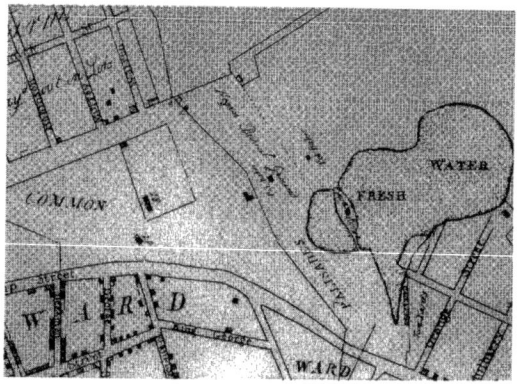

FIGURE 1. Detail of "A Plan of the City of New York from an Actual Survey," by Maerschalck, 1755. This is one of the few historic maps which specifically delineates the Burial Ground although the ravine and pertinent topography are absent. The palisades and the blockhouses for cannons are also shown. (Courtesy of the New York Historical Society, New York.)

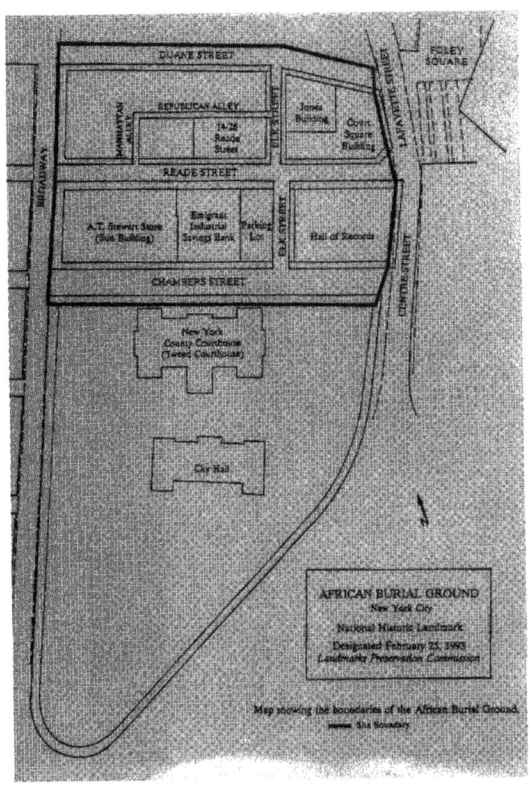

FIGURE 2. Map of lower Manhattan, outlining the original five- to six-acre boundaries of the African Burial Ground. (Reprinted with permission from National Historic Landmark Designation for the African Burial Ground, New York, February 1993.)

Excavations of the African Burial Ground began in the summer of 1991 and continued through July 1992. Early projections indicated that 50 burials would be recovered from an undisturbed area beneath Manhattan and Republican Alleys (Rutsch 1992:12). More than 400 burials were eventually disinterred from what was once the six-acre burial ground before a collaborative effort among influential and determined African Americans, and others, combined to halt excavation, take moral responsibility, and seize intellectual power.

Activism and the African Burial Ground

As chairperson of the Subcommittee on Public Buildings and Grounds, Congressman Gus

Savage brought the influence and power of the U.S. Congress to challenge the GSA. Allocation of building funds for the federal government was controlled by this subcommittee, and it was Congressman Savage's gavel that signaled the end of the excavation (Finder 1992). New York City Mayor David Dinkins combined with Congressman Savage to bring considerable political weight to bear upon the project. New York State Senator David Paterson, 29th District Member, used his influence to form the Task Force for the Oversight of the African Burial Ground (Committee on Public Works and Transportation [CPWT] 1992; Paterson 1995). This task force, many members of which later served on the federal steering committee, was originally composed of concerned citizens who monitored pertinent activities and events that surrounded the site. Peggy King Jorde, Mayor Dinkins's Liaison for the Foley Square Project, and the New York City Landmarks Commission contributed municipal power and were largely responsible for alerting and updating the public about the burial ground (CPWT 1992; Jorde et al. 1993:6).

Other African Americans were also uniquely positioned for a collaborative "power play" that changed the course and direction of the project. Journalists brought the power of the press. The late jazz violinist Noel Pointer led an organization of artists. Local New York clergy members led a committee of religious leaders. Architects, lawyers, and scores of concerned citizens, many of whom represented institutions which were dedicated to taking responsibility for the spiritual, physical, and intellectual control of the site, contributed a community activism that forced the GSA to stop the excavations, alter building plans, and change the composition and direction of the professional leadership of the project (Harrington 1993:30). In the end, power was also wrested from the government by individual elderly African Americans, who understood, through life experience, the false hope of rhetoric and the emptiness of promises (Figure 3).

A team led by Michael Blakey of Howard University brought the final necessary component, intellectual power and technical expertise (HUJMA 1993). The research team based at

Howard University began presenting its proposal to direct the site's analysis in April 1992 (Blakey 1992a, 1992b). By that time, it was apparent that no contract had been let for analysis and that the research design developed by Historic Conservation and Interpretation, Inc. (HCI), the original cultural resource management firm hired to excavate the site, (revised in March of 1992) had been rejected by review agencies. The original research design of approximately 12 pages (Rutsch 1992) had devoted two pages to the site's African or African-American bioarchaeology, and it gave virtually no substantive discussion of New York's black history. The limited approach of the initial research design underestimated the enormous analytic value of the cemetery site.

In June 1992, negotiations were taking place between Blakey as Howard University's representative and Daniel G. Roberts of John Milner Associates (JMA). JMA was in the initial phases of replacing HCI, which was having difficulty administering a project of this magnitude (Cook 1993). By submitting a more appropriate research design Howard University and JMA simultaneously shared with the community and GSA the potential value of anthropological research which could at least be known, and, at best, might be retrieved.

By July 1992, after a constant barrage of petitions, angry rhetoric and community dissension, congressional hearings, professional meetings, lobbying, and political action, leadership and control of the entire project was eventually awarded to more sympathetic institutions with greater experience and which were better developed for research of this kind. The ancestral remains were subsequently sent to the Cobb Biological Anthropology Laboratory, Howard University, Washington, DC (Figure 4), and placed under the care and direction of Michael Blakey as scientific director.

Howard University has engaged a national and international team of Africanist and African-Americanist scholars for archaeological and historical analysis. JMA established an office in

FIGURE 3. Protestors gathered for one of the many rallies concerning the excavation of the African Burial Ground. The $3 million refers to monies allocated by Congress for memoralization. (Photo by Richard Brown.)

New York City and is assisting Howard University with laboratory processing and conservation of artifacts. JMA, Blakey, and Lesley Rankin-Hill had worked together on the First African Baptist Church Cemetery project in Philadelphia, in which they had facilitated reburial of 140 skeletons of African Americans (Angel et al. 1987; Parrington and Roberts 1990; Rankin-Hill 1990; Blakey et al. 1994). Each had experience in public archaeology and community consultation. Furthermore, within the American Anthropological Association (AAA) and the World Archaeological Congress, Blakey had been deeply involved in the development of position statements on repatriation issues of indigenous peoples. For several previous years he had been working with an AAA panel that would propose an anthropology of "public engagement" (Foreman 1994).

Research Questions

The research design (HUJMA 1993) specifies three major research questions about the people buried at the site: what are the origins of the population, what was their physical quality of life, and what can the site reveal about the biological and cultural transition from African to African-American identities? In 1995, the project's specialists added the examination of "modes of resistance" as a fourth major question. The methods employed to answer these questions are both anthropological and multidisciplinary. Molecular genetics, bone chemistry, skeletal biology, history and archaeology (American and African), ethnology, conservation, and African art history represent the range of fields within which this work, now underway, is concerned.

The African presence in colonial New York is approached from an African diasporic perspective, taking into account the African societies from which most of the population is derived and placing New York within the context of the broader American diaspora. The scientific approach is also biocultural and biohistorical. It examines the historical interactions of biology and culture such that data on each inform the other and, most importantly, such that human biology is interpreted within historically-specific sociocultural contexts.

The significance of the site, according to the research design, should be understood in relation to the "vindicationist" effort (Schomburg 1929) and the critical intellectual, educational, and political concerns of the African-American community. This comprehensive research plan therefore integrates the most contemporary scientific approaches and African-American intellectual traditions. The design was developed in systematic consultation with representatives of the descendant community and the anthropological community, following the African-American tradition of scholar activism as well as recent anthropological approaches to "public engagement." By acting on an interpretation of the AAA Statement on Ethics and Professional Responsibility and in consistence with the World Archaeological Congress's First Code of Ethics, the project's new leadership adhered to the right of the descendant community to accept, modify, or reject the research design. The design was approved by the federal steering committee, with some modification, and was subsequently accepted by the General Services Administration in 1993.

Professional Issues and Background

An adequate understanding of the scholarly and public concerns relating to the African Burial Ground must be informed by an awareness of long-standing debates about the politics of the past among African Americans. These debates intersect development in American anthropology and history. The theoretical precepts that guide the fields of physical anthropology, history, and archaeology converged at the African Burial Ground. But these are three areas of study which, historically and to varying degrees, have been used to either systematically victimize or alternately ignore (Fredrickson 1971:71–96;

FIGURE 4. Program from the welcoming ceremony at Howard University commemorating the transfer of the ancestral remains from New York City to the Cobb Laboratory, Howard Unversity.

Fraser and Butler 1986; Potter 1991:95; Deloria 1995; Fountain 1995) the population which scholars were now so eager to study.

Academic Anthropology and History

The skeletal population excavated from the African Burial Ground represents the remains of some of the first Africans brought to North America. These ancestral remains were of great interest to the New York Metropolitan Forensic Anthropology Team (MFAT), the original physical anthropologists working with HCI. MFAT was greatly concerned with the morphometric data (Cook 1993:26–27; GSA 1993) this baseline population contained for the development of "racing" methods. This emphasis on the application of methods of racial identification coupled with a paucity of previous African and African-American studies research characterized the approaches of the archaeologists and physical anthropologists who had excavated the site.

The potential for stereotypical, sterile, and denigrating interpretations of the site based on morphometric analysis became increasingly apparent to the African-American community. The primacy of this interest, coupled with a perceived disrespect on the part of the physical anthropologists and the GSA for the wishes of the descendant community, led to much of the conflict that has surrounded the African Burial Ground Project (CPWT 1992:34; Scarupa 1994).

Distortions of the African and African-American past by anthropologists and historians have been a prominent concern of African Americans for nearly 150 years. As early as 1854 Frederick Douglass pointed to the works of the first American physical anthropologists and Egyptologists as an effort to show blacks to be uncivilized and subhuman for the purpose of legitimating the institution of slavery (Douglass 1950[1854]). Aleš Hrdlička, the first curator of physical anthropology at the United States National Museum, Smithsonian, stated that physical anthropology was intended to have practical ap-

plication through racial eugenics (Hrdlička 1918), while much of physical anthropology was being used to justify racial segregation laws which institutionalized discrimination against blacks.

Members of MFAT seemed keen on demonstrating to the public their technical knowledge by showing the cranial and post-cranial traits they used to classify the race of skeletons. Members of the New York descendant community often identified these explanations of facial and pelvic traits as troubling. Why should a grandmother have been disturbed at such demonstrations to her granddaughter? Why should an architect have asked, perplexed, how it could be possible for a femur to represent her ancestry? What has caused these negative reactions to simple biological approaches to racing? We have no certain answers to these questions, as indeed those who expressed these concerns seemed unable to explain them.

The intellectual background to the issues of racial determination may shed some light, however. There are historical precedents for objections to anthropological studies of race in the African-American community, and the Smithsonian's early racial research is representative of broader trends to which objections were made (Blakey 1987, 1996). In 1916, Hrdlička (1928) had great difficulty in obtaining cooperation from African Americans, particularly women, for his study of "The Full-Blood American Negro," whom he described as "suspicious." African Americans were generally aware of the demeaning uses of such data, which were generally used to show their inferiority and social distance, while "elite" Euroamericans clamored to be included in such research, which was generally used to demonstrate their superiority and social position. Hrdlička had a preconceived notion of full-bloods as the objective unit of biological analysis, yet most African Americans were not included in that type which he sought to measure and characterize. For African Americans today, "racing" has been associated with arguments in support of black inferiority, social and biological distance, and stereotypical images that reflected little of the range of variation that they knew of themselves.

The similarities between this historical example and the forensic approaches initially proposed for the African Burial Ground can be very informative. Forensic approaches assume the existence of a real racial biological type. While a broader range of African Americans can be captured within the black, or Negroid, classification used today, the assumption persists that there are some discrete traits that represent the features of a pure type (for example, nasal "guttering," extreme prognathism, large teeth). Morphological assessment in which MFAT was immediately involved during excavation focused on such discrete, stereotypical traits or their absence. These were the features that were being described to the public.

Furthermore, the use of inadequately tested post-cranial measurements for determining race raised both scholarly and public questioning. The MFAT method involved measures of the bones of the thigh and hip. The accuracy of this method has not been demonstrated on populations other than the Americans of the Terry Collection at the Smithsonian, with which the method had been developed (DiBennardo and Taylor 1983). The tautological nature of that test was questioned at the time of the original study. Moreover, even the more reliable cranial methods of racing that are based on African-American populations have been shown to be wholly inadequate for the study of West African populations, which are morphologically different from African Americans, different from other African populations, as well as regionally diverse. To reduce the biological identity of the African Burial Ground population to these narrow typologies was to assume, if applied, to construct a stereotype of the ancestral population. This is not far from Hrdlička's limitations at the turn of this century.

Biological race—Negroids, Caucasoids, Mongoloids—was viewed by forensics experts as the most objective or scientific means of classifica-

tion. The methodologically constructed black or "Negroid," however, is dissociated from any particular culture and history. Racing thus constructs an identity that is culture-less, history-less, and biologically shallow. Here, racing was being proposed by anthropologists who had engaged, as the community and scholars soon became aware, in very little study of Africana history and culture.

The proposed alternative combined morphological, morphometric, and molecular genetic data to assess specific breeding population affiliations (Blakey 1992a, 1992b; HUJMA 1993). Historical, archaeological, and stable isotope data would be used to interpret the cultural and ecological characteristics of the places of origin. The result should produce information about affiliated populations that have culture histories such as the Ashanti, Yoruba, Dutch, Lenape, English, and other potential origins of the people buried in the African Burial Ground. The descendant community's reaction to this biocultural approach was far more favorable than to forensic classification. Many physical anthropologists, however, objected to the rejection of MFAT's racing methods (Cook 1993; GSA 1993; Epperson 1997). In our case, it was the descendant community that would ultimately choose.

Embedded in the context of the New York African Burial Ground phenomenon is a sophisticated awareness on the part of the general African-American public regarding the demeaning abuses of anthropology and history by Euroamericans. The descendant community immediately understood the parallels between the mishandling of the bones and the racial reality of their lives (Wright and Brown 1992; Davila et al. 1994). If race follows the African descendant population beyond the grave, then racism, by definition, follows as well.

Public Engagement Through History

During the excavation phase of the project, the public was kept informed through a "grassroots," community-based newsletter, *Ground Truth*, by word of mouth, and by contacting the GSA directly for information. As leadership of the project changed, public education became a major component of the African Burial Ground project.

Sherrill D. Wilson was named director of the Office of Public Education and Interpretation (OPEI), formerly known as the Liaison Office. Prior to her work on this project, Wilson had developed an effective approach to public history through her African-American historic sites tours of New York City, "Reclaim the Memories." Her business, which she had been operating for five years, reflected the fact that African-American scholars were developing compatible resources and approaches that were informed by common understandings of the relationship of anthropology and history to the needs of their community. Her focus on public history was consistent with public engagement initiatives. The African Burial Ground Project would ultimately benefit from that preparation.

By focusing on the need to fill the gaps of omission left by Eurocentric public history in New York City, Wilson was participating in the long tradition of what St. Claire Drake termed "vindicationism." Throughout the 19th and 20th centuries, African-American and African scholars could usually be characterized as "vindicationists" because the most persistent thread running through their work was the attempt to correct the demeaning distortions of the culture, biology, and history of the Africana world (Schomburg 1929; Drake 1980). See also Rankin-Hill and Blakey (1994) for histories of anthropological contributions to the vindicationist effort; Diop (1974[1967]) and Van Sertima (1986) treat recent vindicationist efforts relating to archaeology, linguistic, and classical studies that are currently broadly read among the African and African-American public.

Eurocentric distortions of Africana history have been viewed not as accidental flaws of individual researchers but as politically motivated and systemic means of social, intellectual, and cultural control. While seminal historical works have contributed to correcting this legacy, Euroamericans rarely have had an understanding of the depth and dimension of African-American intellectual life (Hine 1986):

In virtually every area where evidence from the past is needed to support the validity of a given proposition, a historian can be found who will provide the evidence that is needed. Historians have usually been prepared to provide facile and quick explanations for the subordinate place of African Americans in American life. From the time Africans were brought as indentured servants to the mainland of English America in 1619, the enormous task of rationalizing and justifying the forced labor of peoples on the basis of racial differences was begun; and even after legal slavery was ended, the notion of racial differences persisted as a basis for maintaining segregation and discrimination (Franklin 1989[1965]:132).

Carter G. Woodson, perhaps the most important single African-American historian, founded the Association for the Study of Negro Life and History in 1915 and published the *Journal of Negro History* as the first outlet for the dissemination of black history. His efforts led to the formation of Negro History Week in 1926, which was later to become Black History Month. His most prominent book, *The Mis-education of the Negro* (Woodson 1933), speaks directly to the historiographic influences of the ideology of white supremacy.

Throughout the civil rights and black nationalist movements of the 1950s, '60s, and early '70s, "Black Studies" programs were fought for by African Americans and established at many universities (Hine 1986). During the 1980s and 1990s, an Afrocentric educational movement emerged in the black community in response to the distorted global and American history African-American children are continually taught. That history frequently presents a romantic view of European and Euroamerican identity and an omitted African and African-American presence in important societal developments, of which they were an integral part.

Indeed, New York's African Burial Ground was a vivid example of the omission of the colonial Africans' presence and contribution to the building of the city and the nation. The African-American public could at once turn to the abundant and tangible physical remains of the people omitted from the city's deficient school curricula. By omission, northern slavery and racism were denied.

The African-American public interested in the African Burial Ground was usually quite aware of bodies of "vindicationist," Africana studies and Afrocentric literature which held greater intellectual relevancy, while exposing the biases of "mainstream" or Eurocentric historiography and anthropology. Many among the New York public were influenced by extensive travel to various African countries, some of which was done with Afrocentric organizations. To quote Miriam Francis, one of the most active members of the federal steering committee, "If it was an African find, we wanted to make sure that it was interpreted from an African point of view" (Harrington 1993:34).

When vindicationist motivations were explained as part of the site's significance for the African-American community, Euroamericans, including members of the New York City Landmarks Preservation Commission and the Advisory Council for Historic Preservation, expressed fears and objections, characterizing the approach as ethnocentric bias. Yet the vindicationist tradition was posed as a corrective for persistent Eurocentric bias and misrepresentation, and as a search for truth and accuracy.

Archaeology and Cultural Resource Management

Although the impetus for the project was cultural resource management, the implications have been broad and complex. New Yorkers sought and still seek authority, defined by Kertzer (1988:110) as the right to exercise influence over behavior, with African and African-American archaeologists and anthropologists directing the research. As previously stated, there were concerns that the guiding methodologies, theories, and ideologies that govern the primary research disciplines (e.g., Hodder 1986, 1992; Leone and Potter 1988; Trigger 1989; Blakey 1990:38; Yoffee and Sherratt 1993; deMaret 1994:183; Leone and Potter 1994; Orser 1996) would be misapplied in studying the skeletal and artifactual remains from this site (Harrington 1993:36; Foster 1994:4). This concern certainly extended to archaeological theory and practices, particularly since problems that potentially have contributed to the loss of data occurred as a result of rapid excavation and inadequate stabilization of remains. Although never explicitly stated, the sentiment among the descendant community was that the importance, particularly the spiritual importance that the site held, was too great to allow field excavation techniques to be the sole criterion of competence (Harrington 1993:33). The question was not whether these individuals were qualified scientists, but whether they would be qualified to direct research on an important African-American bioarchaeological site.

African Americans in and Through Archaeology

For approximately the first 75 years of the history of American archaeology, until 1946, African Americans as well as other groups without an independent income were largely excluded from the profession. During the depression it was discovered that archaeology could usefully employ large numbers of individuals to move earth. The Works Progress Administration (WPA) projects of the 1930s, and later the GI Bill, allowed a broader segment of America's social classes exposure to archaeology. Most of the first archaeologists without independent wealth were World War II veterans who benefited from the GI Bill (Barbour 1994). During the 1960s and 1970s the Ford Foundation and other funding sources established fellowships to correct the underrepresentation of African-American scholars, which led to an increase in African-American anthropologists (Drake 1980), the vast majority of whom were cultural anthropologists.

The development of Cultural Resource Management (CRM) has fostered the growth of African-American archaeology since the 1960s (Ferguson 1992; Barbour 1996), particularly in the South. Until the excavations of the African Burial Ground, African-American archaeology in the North had concentrated on finds that reflected the interests of individual archaeologists and were largely of local interest (Barbour 1996).

Some of the early work in the North included Robert Schuyler's (1972) study of oyster fisherfolk of Sandy Ground, Staten Island; Bert Salwen's (Bridges and Salwen 1980) study at

Weeksville; James Deetz's study of black households in Massachusetts including Parting Ways (Deetz 1977) and Black Lucy's Garden (Bullen and Bullen 1945; Baker 1980); and Mark Leone's (1984) public archaeology program at Annapolis. Recently, CRM firms have added significantly to recovery of African-American history, including JMA's excavations at the two First African Baptist Church cemeteries in Philadelphia (Kelley and Angel 1989; Parrington et al. 1989; Crist et al. 1995).

CRM archaeologists have, however, been accountable to governmental and other clients who frequently are not principally interested in anthropological research, a problem which has pointed to the risk of "deskilling" (Paynter 1983) and to oftentimes inadequate resources for careful analysis (Lacy and Hasenstab 1983). The extent to which CRM archaeologists uphold disciplinary standards (Schuldenrein 1995) is also not the same as the extent to which they uphold the standards of African-American studies. The predominantly Euroamerican field of CRM archaeology and the predominantly African-American field of African-American studies remain far apart. Generally, CRM archaeologists need have little academic preparation or interest in African-American research. CRM archaeologists rarely seek academic preparation in African-American studies departments and very few faculty of African-American studies departments have been contracted by archaeologists. Is the view of African-American history and culture so deficient, so simple, that one need have no specialized training to conduct research in that culture area?

Philosophical Divergence

Philosophical divergence occurs in several areas including methods of analysis and interpretation, semantics, and social interpretation. Each is addressed more fully below.

Analysis and Interpretation

In the informally segregated United States, archaeology and African-American Studies have developed as ethnically distinct disciplines, the former mainly white and the latter mainly black, with little interaction. Theresa Singleton, the Smithsonian's leading historical archaeologist, and Ronald Bailey, chair of Northeastern University's African-American Studies Department, attempted to bring the two fields together in Oxford, Mississippi, in 1989. Singleton (1994) and Singleton and Bograd (1995) recognize that the ethnic and black studies movement of the 1960s and '70s spurred initial interest in African-American archaeology, along with historic preservation legislation and bicentennial interests. They find that "the problem [of African-American archaeology] is that the field is theory poor, not data poor" (Singleton and Bograd 1995). Samford (1996:113) has also observed, "In the two decades that archaeologists have been excavating African American slave sites, they have accumulated a substantial body of data. Unfortunately data recovery has outpaced both analysis and the reformulation of research goals."

While several important studies have certainly been done, year after year, archaeologists and physical anthropologists, some with a superficial understanding of African-American history and culture, profit from the conduct of research on archaeological sites that influence how African Americans are defined. This was clearly the case, and a major source of contention, surrounding the original excavation team at the New York African Burial Ground project.

Understandably, New Yorkers feared that the cultural significance often hidden from the boundaries of social contact and daily interaction would be unrecognized and overlooked (McGuire and Paynter 1991) and that obvious interpretations would become problematic in terms of recognition. This is particularly so since far fewer African descendant sites have been excavated or identified in the North as compared to the frequency with which southern plantation sites are excavated. Comparatively little archaeological evidence exists for 17th- and 18th-century New York Africans, suggesting that much groundwork will have to be laid in the study of this population.

Seizing intellectual control has meant that the criteria for competency have been expanded to include an affinity for African-American culture, past and *present*, and comfort with and knowledge of the politics of African descendant populations, their cultures, and their histories (CPWT 1992:34–41; Harrington 1993:33; Wilson 1995:3). As was sometimes the case at the African Burial Ground excavations, there was evidence of discomfort and uneasiness with African Americans among some excavators and archaeologists (McGowan and Brighton 1995, pers. comm.), further contributing to concerns that current racial attitudes would influence interpretations of the historical population being studied.

Furthermore, questions which reflect the general sentiment "should white people study black people?" (Nobile 1993; Wayne 1994:6; Curtin 1995) and an insistence on "racing skeletons" (GSA 1993; Epperson 1997) give the impression that simplistic questions are being asked rather than complex, insightful queries that also acknowledge the entangled philosophical and theoretical dilemmas archaeology must resolve with respect to the demands of descendant communities (Robertshaw 1995).

As Jamieson (1995:39) correctly observes regarding study of the remains from the African Burial Ground: "The developments in New York City . . . have demonstrated that contract archaeologists are required to deal with such remains, and that a solid understanding of the historical and anthropological aspects of African-American mortuary practices is necessary before interpreting them." In a field where African Americans have been largely invisible and the documentary evidence unsupportive, methodologies that uncover the archaeological visibility of African Americans are sorely needed (Barbour 1996).

According to Hodder (1986:7), "It is only when we make assumptions about the subjective meanings in the minds of people long dead that we can begin to do archaeology." This view of archaeological interpretation again would have left the New York descendant community dependent upon the largely Euroamerican researchers who would consider themselves qualified for such an interpretation (Klima 1992:20). As a result, New Yorkers insisted on African-American leadership and involvement in all aspects of this project.

Yet, Larry McKee (1995:4) argues in "Commentary: Is It Futile to Try and Be Useful? Historical Archaeology and the African American Experience" that "studying African-American life from just an African-American perspective would end up one-sided and ultimately sterile." Presumably, then, the dearth of African-American archaeologists, which he also acknowledges, implies that archaeological interpretation of African-American sites to date must be one-sided and ultimately sterile since primarily Euroamericans interpret these sites. After 125 years of American archaeology as an organized discipline, there are fewer than six African Americans who hold Ph.D.s in the field (Barbour 1994), with an equal number currently in graduate programs around the country.

There was a concern among African Americans that what would be deemed the important avenues of inquiry would be hollow and irrelevant for the African-descendant community (Muhammad et al. 1993:3). Entrenched, long-held philosophical positions of power are not easily relinquished, and new perspectives are often difficult for scholars to develop or embrace without dialogue or outside influence. As the changing archaeological perspective weds archaeological findings with interdisciplinary research and oral history, perhaps scholars and others outside the discipline may begin to access and find relevance in the body of work produced by our efforts. African-American historians, in particular, can be informed by accurate archaeological research and interpretation.

Semantics

Semantics and the use of descriptive language has been a constant theme in New York. Insistence on the use of the word African in the renaming of the "Negroes Burying Ground" demonstrates the descendant community's understanding of the power and influence of language as well as the need to eschew European descriptive terminology. These African Americans chose to call the Africans what they chose to call themselves—African Mutual Relief Society, African Free School, African Methodist Episcopal Church, for example (Stuckey 1987:199–200; Wilson 1995:11). The descendant community has insisted that "slaves" not be identified by their condition of servitude but rather by the conditions imposed upon them (S&S Reporting 1993). It is particularly telling that the term slave is never specifically defined in dictionaries to refer to enslaved Africans, although this is the most pervasive use of the word in the United States. The term "enslaved African" is perhaps more accurate than servant, bondspersons, bond chattel laborers, or slave and conveys the involuntary aspect of enslavement.

Not all linguistic restructuring is so easily accomplished, however. In many instances, the English language is limiting when one attempts to accurately convey the African-American experience. The continued use of the term "master" in anthropological (e.g., Blassingame 1972; Stuckey 1987; Meillassoux 1991; Holloway 1991) and historical (e.g., McManus 1966; Johnson 1969; Franklin 1989) writings is a clear example of the romantic use of language which reflects a Eurocentric approach indicative of a reluctance to divest of euphemistic language. The term "master" is defined as "one with the ability or power or authority to control; one who is highly skilled, superior; a victor, a conqueror; to rule or direct; an individual having predominance over another; having all others subordinate to oneself" (*Illustrated Heritage* 1967; *Oxford English Dictionary* 1971; *Webster's* 1971, 1991, 1994; *Scribner-Bantam English Dictionary* 1979; *World Book Dictionary* 1984; Merriam-Webster 1994). Jesus Christ is often referred to as "*the* Master" (*Webster's* 1983). Nowhere within the various definitions is the word "master" ever defined to accurately reflect the specific, traditional colloquial usage of the word. Never is "the master" defined as enslaver, or as one who enslaves, principally African descendant populations, or one who deprives Africans of their humanity, or one who coerces the labor and social actions, most specifically of African descendant populations.

Recently, scholars have attempted to avoid the use of the term master by using the term "slave

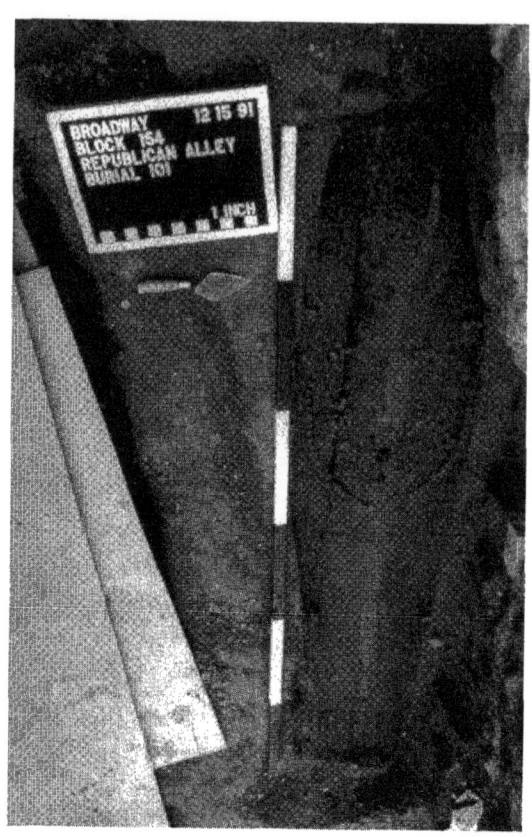

FIGURE 5. Burial 101 had tack heads arranged on a coffin in a shape that has been interpreted to be either a heart or to represent an Adinkra symbol. (Photo by Dennis Seckler; courtesy of U.S. General Services Administration.)

holder" (cf. Blassingame 1972; Meier and Rudwick 1986; Stuckey 1987; White 1991) or "planter" rather than enslaver as the descriptive which encompasses the slave-owning aspects inherent in the plantation system (e.g., Moore 1985; Singleton 1985; Ferguson 1992; Mintz and Price 1992). This term, however, lacks accuracy or visceral, emotive power and in no way conveys the hideousness of the institution of slavery or the function and actions of its principal perpetrator. Moreover, the term is misleading, since "the planter" might rarely plant. Intellectual empowerment equips African Americans with the ability to confront ideological justifications and rationalizations pertaining to use of traditional language.

Similar to language usage, analysis of material culture within archaeology is also an area that can be subjective and open to interpretation.

The interpreter's specialized knowledge and familiarity with the culture being studied should and does affect analysis in obvious ways. At the African Burial Ground, for example, a pattern of nail heads formed a symbol on a coffin which was widely recognized as a heart (Figure 5). An African-American scientist, while not at all a specialist in African symbolic systems, recognized the ornate heart shape as closely resembling one of the Asanti *Adinkra* symbols whose use was growing in popularity in African-American culture. When a Ghanaian historian of African art looked at this same symbol, he too saw *Sankofa*, one of the *Adinkra* symbols, and could explain the appropriateness of its temporal, cultural, and mortuary context: "The symbol expresses the Akan social thought that espouses the essence of tying the past with the present in order to prepare for the future" (Ofori-Ansa 1995:3).

While it is difficult to interpret or extrapolate meaning from a culturally ambiguous symbol within the archaeological context, *Adinkra* symbolism is more appropriate to the population buried in the African Burial Ground and demonstrates the divergent perspectives which shape interpretation. The introduction of relevant African systems of thought provides evidence of why African and African-American scholars felt compelled to broaden the prospective of this project. Myopic interpretation of the comparatively few diagnostic artifacts excavated from the site would contribute to a superficial understanding of New York's African colonial population.

Social Politics of the African Burial Ground

The African Burial Ground is often seen as an example of whites and blacks perceiving issues so differently as to merely exist together in physical space while operating in very different worlds of thought and action. African Americans succeeded as they did because their critical view of the issues was more accurate, relative to most Euroamericans involved with the project. While some Euroamericans directly involved with the controversy, and who were closely aligned with the African-American community,

did have a fundamental understanding of issues, and while many others empathized with the issue of desecration, most sought only to contain the inconveniences being fostered by black protest, a protest whose justifications they could scarcely have comprehended.

Equally significant for African Americans were the metaphorical and symptomatological meanings of the conflicts in which they were embroiled. Here were the historical and the current, day-to-day problems of racial discrimination being played out on a small scale. Audible racial epithets were not being slung, but that has not been the dominant or accepted mode of racist social relations in the United States for some time now. Instead, the federal government and its previous consultants were seen as pursuing a course of obstruction that reflected a dismissive attitude toward blacks whom they sought to control by denying access to substantive power. Both the consultants and the GSA underestimated the African-American community's resolve to establish authority over the disposition of the site and its analysis. When African-American community leaders and scientists repeatedly asserted those intentions, glaring attempts were made to ignore them or to placate them with shallow offerings.

Most of the Euroamerican government officials and their consultants acted without apparent recognition that blacks understood exactly what was being attempted and had effective strategies for surmounting those obstacles. Exclusion, dismissive attitudes, tokenism, and claims of unfairness and "reverse racism" when African Americans seek full access to resources are commonplace interactions with white Americans. The effectiveness of the sophisticated African-American lobby at the city, state, and national levels demonstrates a lack of realism on their opponents' part. Where in other aspects of daily life individual African-American citizens would be limited in their ability to roundly address such circumstances, here in the important moment and symbolism of their ancestor's dignity, white racism would be addressed in microcosm. The United States government's role as antagonist, along with that of the discipline that defined racial differences and African culture, could not have been more appropriate foils for African-American empowerment.

Despite the longer track record and established credentials of Howard University's program of research in African-American bioanthropology, members of the original excavation team characterized Howard's efforts as "reverse racism," a characterization that immediately eliminated the multitude of intellectual issues. Many of the whites who had represented anthropological and preservation concerns in New York City and who had supported greater participation by African-American scholars at the site began to object to Howard University's plan to remove the remains from New York City to its Washington laboratory. These New Yorkers thus attempted to stand in the way of African-American intellectual control, in the interests of their own access to a prominent historical resource.

Since New Yorkers can be extremely provincial (Muhammad et al. 1993), the choice on the part of the descendant community to remove what must have been viewed as "their" cultural resource to an environment where their interests could be understood, respected, and empowered is a dramatic indictment of the status quo. The need to place the remains at Howard University also speaks to the dearth of local options and the lack of investment in African-American bioarchaeology in New York City.

The Federal Steering Committee

In response to provisions set forth in Section 106 of the National Historic Preservation Act (36 CFR 800) requiring the consultation of interested parties, a federal steering committee composed of concerned community activists and various experts and professionals was formed to foster the dialogue between the GSA, archaeologists, and community members (Jorde et al. 1993). The New York descendant community was given an official voice in the project; future archaeological requirements were explained, and the government was seemingly accountable. The wishes of the descendant community could be directly articulated. Unlike their ancestors,

today's African Americans have been able to speak for themselves (Wall 1995).

The federal steering committee meetings were among the most virulent encounters associated with the African Burial Ground project (S&S Reporting 1992–1994; Schomburg Center 1992–1994). Many of the Euroamericans originally in control of the project were unaccustomed to or uncomfortable with emotional displays, and demonstrated a dismissive attitude when unable to contend with the emotionally charged, angry responses of a descendant community whose earlier moderaton was met only with betrayal.

More often, however, it was the need for "sensitivity" toward African Americans that whites recognized, but did not understand. While the issue of sensitivity toward the sacred was apparently shared by Euroamericans and African Americans alike, it was unclear whether the meanings of the concept were the same for both. African Americans were insisting on "respect" for the dead and the living. In a society imbued with racist stereotypes of blacks as overly emotional, irrational, and hyperpolitical, however, even liberal white concerns for "sensitivity" easily can be based upon a patronizing attitude whose assumptions are racist, further adding to an atmosphere of mistrust (Kutz 1994). African Americans sought control, not sympathy.

The charter of the federal steering committee was not renewed once the newly constructed federal office building was occupied in November 1994, leaving many with the impression that the federal government's only interest in addressing community concerns was expediency and that clearly no lasting changes had occurred. There are several specific issues which were never resolved by the steering committee. The areas of concern beyond the direction of the research included the establishment of a world-class museum, an appropriate memorial, and reinterment on the site (Jorde et al. 1993). This last issue, reinterment, could prove as onerous as the excavation of the cemetery if the GSA again misjudges the gravity and depth of importance African Americans attach to this final phase (Cohen 1992:21). There are a number of engineering constraints associated with site stabilization that render reburial on-site a major problem, requiring careful planning and strategy, professional expertise, and a timetable.

By disbanding the steering committee, expressed interests of the descendant community and issues which require time to resolve have been left unanswered. These unresolved issues are of continuing concern, although the force with which they are currently being addressed has diminished. Senator Paterson has convened a committee to address the issue of the museum (Paterson 1995), but progress has been slow. Although major concessions have been won on the part of the African descendant community, several unresolved issues such as reburial, memorialization, and the level of funding for scientific and historical research specified in the research design, in conjunction with unfulfilled commitments, leave the question of ultimate success unanswered.

Although the ancestral remains have been moved to Howard University and the federal steering committee is no longer in existence, New Yorkers have not relinquished stewardship of nor their desire to be closely involved in every aspect of the project (Muhammad et al. 1993:3). To quote Senator David Paterson, "The descendant community of African Americans has been left spellbound by the discovery, and impatient for results" (Assael 1993:18). Through ceremonies, symposia, lectures, demonstrations, and meetings, they have been relentless and diligent in their devotion, as have researchers in their commitment to public engagement. This is the scope and magnitude of activism that excavation of this archaeological resource has engendered.

Current Status

Today, New York no longer has a black mayor (Willen and Moses 1996), Gus Savage is no longer chair of the Subcommittee on Public Buildings and Grounds, and Congress is contemplating a decrease in funding and support for CRM (Craib and Johnson 1995). Since the federal steering committee no longer exists, much of the responsibility for fulfilling the descendant community's mandate now rests in the hands of the researchers and scientists in conjunction with the GSA. The struggle for control of the African Burial Ground site was a struggle to have the voice of the community heeded. Exclusion of direct community involvement as the project progresses removes ethical, moral, spiritual, and social issues and obligations from community control. The work of holding the GSA accountable to previous agreements with the community has been largely assumed by the anthropologists directing the project.

The Office of Public Education and Interpretation

The Office of Public Education and Interpretation (OPEI) opened in March 1993 for the express purpose of informing the New York and national communities about the ongoing status of the African Burial Ground project. Although the future of this office is unclear (Strickland-Abuwi 1996), it has provided information through its monthly reports to more than 40,000 interested persons from around the world (OPEI 1995–1996).

The OPEI conducts on-site and off-site historical slide presentations about the African Burial Ground project and the complementary history of Africans in colonial New York, archaeological laboratory tours, and educators' symposia for teachers, researchers, and other interested persons. The OPEI has trained more than 80 volunteers to help inform local communities of issues and current events relating to the project. The office also accepts high school and college students as semester interns in exchange for academic credit. Howard University also conducts laboratory tours in Washington, DC, and has trained a team of more than 25 volunteers in its efforts to make the research accessible to the public.

The OPEI publishes *Update*, a quarterly newsletter that has a readership of more than 10,000 persons per issue. As a direct result of the excavations, the African Burial Ground project has introduced the topics of archaeology, physical anthropology, and conservation to scores of children and adults who otherwise would not have been exposed to these disciplines.

The OPEI has supported Richard Brown, former steering committee member, in a community-engineered campaign to have the U.S. Postal Service issue an African Burial Ground commemorative stamp (Devieux 1995). As of August 1997, more than 104,000 signatures had been collected from 40 states and 16 countries (OPEI 1995–1996; Devieux 1997, pers. comm.). The goal of this commemorative stamp campaign was to collect 100,000 signatures for submission to the Citizens Stamp Advisory Committee in April 1996 (OPEI 1995–1996). This petition has been denied for the second time by the committee and will not be eligible for consideration again until late 1997. Such defeats only strengthen the resolve of the New York community and of the stamp campaign workers who understand the political and bureaucratic obstacles as well as the economic concerns of the committee associated with the stamp approval process (McAllister 1996a, 1996b).

Media Coverage

Media coverage of the African Burial Ground project has been extensive in documenting this unique colonial-era archaeological site. *The African Burial Ground: An American Discovery* (Kutz 1994) is an award-winning film produced by GSA; *Unearthing the Slave Trade* aired in 1993 on the Learning Channel; and *Slavery's Buried Past* aired in 1996 on the Public Broadcasting System. More than 500 newspaper and magazine articles have been published in media attempts to fill the historical voids relating to an African presence in colonial New York, and to tell the story of the New York African-American descendant community's struggle to preserve the site and disseminate its history (Citations 1995; Pearce 1995).

The African Burial Ground has also been included in at least two recent historical publications, *The Encyclopedia of New York City* (Jackson 1995) and *The Historical Atlas of New York City* (Homberger 1994). This new inclusion,

however, has not eliminated misinterpretation or misrepresentation. Bucolic depictions of the African Burial Ground in the *New York Times* (Dunlap 1992) and in the *Historical Atlas of New York City* (Homberger 1994:44–45) each misrepresent the visual imagery of the location by depicting a lush, flat pastoral landscape rather than the hilly, ravined location near New York's noxious industries. Situated on undesirable land and originally located outside the city limits, the cemetery was, by mid-18th century, beyond a gated, 14-ft.-high palisades; the hills and deep ravine described in Stokes (1915–1928:591), the National Historic Landmark Designation (Landmarks 1992:5), and other historical documents are not in evidence. Presenting such incorrect images negates the power of the African Burial Ground and the hardships faced by New York's early African community. This type of distortion reinforces the notion that African-American New Yorkers must be relentless in their insistence on accuracy in all aspects pertaining to the site.

The image (Figure 6) from *The Historical Atlas of New York City* (Homberger 1994) was approved by cartographic consultant Alice Hudson, head of the Map Division of the New York Public Library. When the inaccuracies were referenced during a lecture, Hudson stated that this bucolic scene was drawn by modern English artists and that the drawing does indeed look more like the English countryside than 18th-century New York City (Hudson 1995, pers. comm.).

Furthermore, most cartographers of the period also misrepresented the African Burial Ground by eliminating specific identification of the six-acre cemetery from the majority of the historical maps, further contributing to the geographical and topographical misinterpretation that has plagued the site (Edwards and Kelcey 1990,1, 3:147; Jorde et al. 1993:6). Since historical archaeology relies on documentary evidence as well as archaeological data for interpretation of sites, current visual misrepresentations and omissions of the past have implications for the discipline and reveal the continual problems of cultural bias.

Diversity and Divergence

Intellectual sophistication beyond the narrow limits of customary Eurocentrism requires the participation of people of diverse ethnicities in the practice of anthropology in general (Blakey 1989) and of archaeology and museology in particular (Blakey 1990:45). Thus, the intellectual evolution of the field; non-white participation; anti-Eurocentrism; and community engagement and empowerment are mutually reinforcing. As the situation in New York evolved, the African Burial Ground became apparent as a practical and dramatic case for the development of the theory and practice of inclusion and engagement. In the case of the African Burial Ground, engagement was also powerfully informed by the long tradition of African-American vindicationist critique (Foster 1994), as discussed previously, and by scholarly activism, the latter being a somewhat more assertive version of the engaged scholar or public intellectual. The interests of the Howard University initiative and those of the African-American public seemed to largely correspond, but these could not be realized until the public took control of the situation.

While spirituality is an issue that was at the core of the African-American struggle for control (S&S Reporting 1993), there are several other issues of concern that African-American New Yorkers brought to this site. Foremost among them is the philosophical divergence among African Americans. Although there is general unity surrounding the major issues, the African descendant community speaks with many voices (*Update* 1993–1996). The Muslim community, for example, is constant in their reminders that Muslims were also enslaved and could have been buried at the cemetery (Hatim 1995).

Various religious communities approach the site from divergent philosophical as well as divergent political perspectives. The political forces active within the African-American community also have been diverse, ranging from

FIGURE 6. Idyllic modern depiction of the African Burial Ground, which was located southwest of the Collect Pond (after Homberger 1994).

black nationalists and Afrocentric organizations to individuals with strong personal beliefs. It is particularly interesting that older African Americans, some of whom have retired from professional and scientific careers, have been among the most persistent. Additionally, divergent religious, political, and scientific perspectives and philosophies in approaching the problems relating to the African Burial Ground have, at times, been the most threatening to the cohesion and resolve of the African-American community.

Conclusion

For African-American New Yorkers, the excavation of our ancestors has been a cathartic and wrenching experience. The anxiety caused by the excavations and post-excavation project management provoked anger, outrage, and cynicism. The descendant community is still highly pained and deeply offended by the desecration of this ancestral site (Daughtry 1992; Scarupa 1994).

Outraged by the fact that this population, mistreated in life, was continuing to be mistreated beyond death (Dunlap 1992), New York's African Americans were driven by a sense of responsibility for the protection of ancestral heritage and a desire to ensure that the dead were honored and memorialized (Wright and Brown 1992; Jorde et al. 1993; Wilson 1995; Devieux 1995). This sense of responsibility and descendancy rapidly spread to the national African-American communities, and to African communities as well. A royal Ghanaian delegation visited the site and Howard University in 1995, and a briefing was held for the United Nation's Human Rights Commission in Geneva in 1996.

Realization of the global importance and of the overwhelming spiritual, historical, anthropological, and scientific importance of the site has led the African descendant community to take extraordinary measures to seize intellectual control of the project. It sought power and control, not the afterthought of inclusion. With many important issues still unresolved, perhaps the true test of that power is yet to come.

Archaeology is not an end in itself. For many African Americans, it is a conduit, an avenue leading to spiritual rebirth and renewal of our history. Our history is in the bones and in the artifacts excavated from the African Burial Ground. It is tangible, it is real, and it lives through the dead: "Black people see those remains from the Burial Ground as life and death and as part of the continuum of our experience rather than a data pool to be objectified" (Nelson 1993). According to former Mayor David Dinkins:

> Millions of Americans celebrate Ellis Island as the symbol of their communal identity in this land. Others celebrate Plymouth Rock. Until a few years ago, African-American New Yorkers had no site to call our own. There was no place which said, we were here, we contributed, we played a significant role in New York's history right from the beginning . . . . Now we—their descendants—have the symbol of our heritage embodied in lower Manhattan's African Burial Ground. The African Burial Ground is the irrefutable testimony to the contributions and suffering of our ancestors (Dinkins 1994).

Noted historian John Henrik Clarke characterizes the African Burial Ground as a holistic space that touches the lives of African people in this country and might touch the lives of African people all over the world (CPWT 1992:34). The African Burial Ground project has benefited from the participation and interest of people from around the world, from all walks of life, and from many ethnic backgrounds. The project's OPEI and the archaeological and bioanthropology laboratories have been visited by scholars from Japan, East Germany, Korea, the Caribbean, Canada, England, and Ireland, as well as from a multitude of African nations and other countries.

While all African Americans are culturally affiliated, New Yorkers have an immediate and special relationship with the African Burial Ground. No one person or group, however, can speak for the dead. This project and the historical and anthropological resource it represents, can only be enhanced when people with different agendas and ideologies enter into a deeper dialogue as they raise their voices in chorus. The African Burial Ground was designated a National Historic Landmark in February 1993.

ACKNOWLEDGMENTS

We would like to thank Dr. Sherrill D. Wilson, Director of the Office of Public Education and Interpretation for the African Burial Ground, for her contribution to and critique of this work. The contributions of Dr. Warren T. D. Barbour, Dr. Warren R. Perry, and Daniel G. Roberts are also greatly appreciated. We acknowledge the financial support of the U.S. General Services Administration. Noel Pointer and Edmund Francis, two active and dedicated members of the African-American community, have both gone on to join the Ancestors during the course of the African Burial Ground project; may they rest in peace.

REFERENCES

ANGEL, J. LAWRENCE, JENNIFER OLSEN KELLEY, MICHAEL PARRINGTON, AND STEPHANIE PINTER
1987 Life Stresses of the Free Black Community as Represented by the First African Baptist Church, 8th and Vine Streets, Philadelphia, 1824–1846. *American Journal of Physical Anthropology* 74:213–229.

ASSAEL, SHAUN
1993 Warring Archaeologists Scrape Graveyard Booty: No Indiana Jones or King Tut as PhDs ID Slavery's Moldy Bones. *New York Observer*, 7 June:1, 18.

BAKER, VERNON G.
1980 Archaeological Visibility of Afro-American Culture: An Example from Black Lucy's Garden, Andover, Massachusetts. In *Archaeological Perspectives on Ethnicity in America: Afro-American and Asian American Culture History,* edited by Robert Schuyler, pp. 29–36. Baywood, Farmingdale, NY.

BARBOUR, WARREN
1994 The Hidden Heritage of Africa's Descendants. *Federal Archeology Report* 7:1.
1996 African-American Archaeology: Its Past, Present and Future. Invited paper for Conference *Opening Doors,* February 16–17. South Carolina African American Heritage Council and South Carolina Department of Archives and History, Charleston.

BLAKEY, MICHAEL L.
1987 Skull Doctors: Intrinsic Social and Political Bias in the History of American Physical Anthropology. *Critique of Anthropology* 7(2):7–35.
1989 The Future of Anthropology. *Anthropology Newsletter* 30(7):8. David Givens, Newsletter Editor. American Anthropological Association, Washington, DC.
1990 American Nationality and Ethnicity in the Depicted Past. In *Politics of the Past,* edited by Peter Gathercole and David Lowenthal, pp. 38–48. Unwin Hyman, London.
1992a Testimony Before the City Council of New York Concerning the Role of the Howard University Laboratory for Biological Anthropology in the Negro Burying Ground Archaeological Project, 12 April.
1992b Research Design for Temporary Curation and Anthropological Analysis of the "Negro Burying Ground" (Foley Square) Archaeological Population

at Howard University, 11 June. On file with the author.
1996 Skull Doctors Revisited: Intrinsic Social and Political Bias in the History of American Physical Anthropology, with special reference to the work of Aleš Hrdlička. In *Race and Other Misadventures: Essays in Honor of Ashley Montagu in His Ninetieth Year,* edited by Larry T. Reynolds and Leonard Lieberman, pp. 64–95. General Hall, Dix Hills, NY.

BLAKEY, MICHAEL L., TERESA E. LESLIE, AND JOSEPH P. REIDY
1994 Frequency and Chronological Distribution of Dental Enamel Hypoplasia in Enslaved African Americans: A Test of the Weaning Hypothesis. *American Journal of Physical Anthropology* 95(4):371–383.

BLASSINGAME, JOHN W.
1972 *The Slave Community: Plantation Life in the Antebellum South.* Oxford University Press, New York, NY.

BRIDGES, SARA T., AND BERT SALWEN
1980 Weeksville: The Archaeology of Black Community. In *Archaeological Perspectives on Ethnicity in America,* edited by Robert L. Schuyler, pp. 38–47. Baywood, Farmingdale, NY.

BULLEN, ADELAIDE K., AND RIPLEY P. BULLEN
1945 Black Lucy's Garden. *Bulletin of the Massachusetts Archaeological Society* 6(2):17–28.

CITATIONS
1995 Citations on the New York African Burial Ground, 1991–1995. Compiled by the Office of Public Education and Interpretation of The African Burial Ground, New York, NY.

COHEN, PATRICIA
1992 Feds Won't Rebury Remains at Site. *Newsday,* 15 May:21.

COMMITTEE ON PUBLIC WORKS AND TRANSPORTATION (CPWT)
1992 Foley Square Construction Project and the Historic African Burial Ground, New York, NY. *Hearings Before the Subcommittee on Public Buildings and Grounds of the Committee on Public Works and Transportation, House of Representatives.* New York, 27 July. 102nd Congress, second session, Document 102–80. Washington, DC.

COOK, KAREN
1993 Black Bones, White Science: The Battle Over New York's African Burial Ground. *The Village Voice,* 4 May:23–27.

CRAIB, DONALD, AND RALPH JOHNSON
1995 The First Session of the 104th Congress: Examining National Priorities for Archaeology. *Society for American Archaeology Bulletin* 13(4):18.

CRIST, THOMAS A. J., REGINALD H. PITTS, ARTHUR WASHBURN, JOHN P. McCARTHY, AND DANIEL G. ROBERTS
1995 "A Distinct Church of the Lord Jesus": The History, Archeology, and Physical Anthropology of the Tenth Street First African Baptist Church Cemetery, Philadelphia, Pennsylvania. Report prepared by John Milner Associates, Inc., West Chester, PA. Submitted to Caudet/O'Brien Associates and the Pennsylvania Department of Transportation, Philadelphia.

CURTIN, PHILIP D.
1995 Ghettoizing African History. *Chronicle of Higher Education,* 3 March.

DAUGHTRY, REV. HERBERT
1992 Remarks at an Ecumenical Service for the African-American Burial Ground. *Ground Truth* 1(1), 3 April.

DAVILA, YVETTE, KEVIN FOSTER, AND D. PERRY
1994 Twelve Voices. In *Update: Newsletter of the African Burial Ground and Five Points Archaeological Projects* 1(3):4–5, 11–12. Sherrill D. Wilson, Newsletter Editor. OPEI, New York, NY.

DEETZ, JAMES
1977 *In Small Things Forgotten: The Archeology of Early American Life.* Anchor Press/Doubleday, New York, NY.

DELORIA, VINE, JR.
1995 *Red Earth, White Lies, Native Americans, and the Myth of Scientific Fact.* Scribner, New York, NY.

deMARET, PIERRE
1994 Archaeological and Other Prehistoric Evidence of Traditional African Religious Expression. In *Religion in Africa,* edited by Thomas D. Blakely, Walter E. A. van Beek, and Dennis L. Thomson, pp. 182–195. Heinemann, Portsmouth, NH.

DEVIEUX, MARIE-ALICE
1995 Stamping Grounds. *Update: Newsletter of the African Burial Ground and Five Points Archaeological Projects* 1(8):6, 13. Sherrill D. Wilson, Newsletter Editor. OPEI, New York, NY.

DiBENNARDO R., AND J. V. TAYLOR
1983 Multiple Discriminant Function Analysis of Sex and Race in the Postcranial Skeleton. *American Journal of Physical Anthropology* 61:305–314.

DINKINS, DAVID
1994 Preface. In *Reclaiming Our Past, Honoring Our Ancestors: New York's 18th-Century African Burial Ground and the Memorial Competition,* edited by Edward Kaufman. African Burial Ground Competition Coalition, NY.

DIOP, CHEIKH ANTA
1974 *The African Origin of Civilization: Myth or Reality.* Reprint of 1967 edition. Lawrence Hill, Chicago, IL.

DOUGLASS, FREDERICK
1950 The Claims of the Negro Ethnologically Considered. Reprint of 1854 edition. In *The Life and Writings of Frederick Douglass,* edited by P. S. Foner, pp. 289–309. International, NY.

DRAKE, ST. CLAIRE
1980 Anthropology and the Black Experience. *The Black Scholar* 11:2–31.

DUNLAP, DAVID W.
1992 Mistake Disturbs Graves at Black Burial Ground: Despite Promises, Workers Unearth Bones. *New York Times,* 21 February:B3, 5.

EDWARDS AND KELCEY
1990 *Draft Environmental Impact Statement.* Foley Square Proposed Federal Courthouse and Federal/Municipal Office Building. Edwards and Kelcey Engineers, Inc., New York, NY.

EPPERSON, TERRENCE W.
1997 The Politics of "Race" and Cultural Identity at the African Burial Ground Excavations, New York City. *World Archaeological Bulletin* 7:108–117.

FERGUSON, LELAND
1992 *Uncommon Ground: Archaeology and Early African America, 1650–1800.* Smithsonian Institution Press, Washington, DC.

FINDER, ALAN
1992 U.S. Permanently Halts Digging at Cemetery Site. *New York Times,* 31 July:B3.

FOREMAN, SHEPARD (EDITOR)
1994 *Diagnosing America: Anthropology and Public Engagement.* University of Michigan Press, Ann Arbor.

FOSTER, KEVIN
1994 Dry Bones Gonna' Rise: Black Thought and the African Burial Ground of New York. Unpublished M.A. thesis, Department of Anthropology, University of Texas, Austin.

FOUNTAIN, DANIEL L.
1995 Historians and Historical Archaeology: Slave Sites. *The Journal of Interdisciplinary History* 26(1).

FRANKLIN, JOHN HOPE
1989 *Race and History: Selected Essays 1938–1988.* Louisiana State University Press, Baton Rouge.

FRASER, GERTRUDE, AND REGINALD BUTLER
1986 Anatomy of a Disinterment: The Unmaking of Afro-American History. In *Presenting the Past Essays on History and the Public,* edited by Susan Porter Benson, Stephen Brier, and Roy Rosenzweig, pp. 121–132. Temple University Press, Philadelphia, PA.

FREDRICKSON, GEORGE M.
1971 *The Black Image in the White Mind: The Debate on Afro-American Character and Destiny, 1817–1914.* Wesleyan University Press, Hanover, NH.

GENERAL SERVICES ADMINISTRATION (GSA)
1993 *Comments of the Draft Research Design for Archaeological, Historical, and Bioanthropological Investigations of the African Burial Ground and Five Points Sites, New York, NY.* General Services Administration, Region 2, 26 Federal Plaza, New York, NY 10013.

HARRINGTON, SPENCER P. M.
1993 Bones and Bureaucrats: New York's Great Cemetery Imbroglio. *Archaeology* 16(2):28–38.

HATIM, IMAM MUHAMMAD
1995 Comments by Imam Muhammad Hatim, UN/NGO Representative, Admiral Family Circle Islamic Community. *Fall Educators Symposium on the New York African Burial Ground,* 4 November, New York, NY.

HINE, DARLENE CLARK (EDITOR)
1986 *The State of Afro-American History: Past, Present, and Future.* Louisiana State University Press, Baton Rouge, LA.

HODDER, IAN
1986 *Reading the Past: Current Approaches to Interpretation in Archaeology.* University of Cambridge, Cambridge, UK.
1992 *Theory and Practice in Archaeology.* Routledge, London, UK.

HOLLOWAY, JOSEPH E. (EDITOR)
1991 *Africanisms in American Culture.* Indiana University Press, Bloomington and Indianapolis.

HOMBERGER, ERIC
1994 *The Historical Atlas of New York City: A Visual Celebration of Nearly 400 Years of New York City's History.* Alice Hudson, Cartographic Consultant. Henry Holt, NY.

HOWARD UNIVERSITY AND JOHN MILNER ASSOCIATES INC. (HUJMA)
1993 *Research Design for Archeological, Historical, and Bioanthropological Investigations of the African Burial Ground (Broadway Block) New York, NY.* 14 December. Howard University, Washington, DC, and John Milner Associates, Inc., New York, NY.

HRDLIČKA, ALEŠ
1918 Physical Anthropology: Its Scope and Aims, Its History and Present Status in America. *American Journal of Physical Anthropology* 1:3–34.
1928 The Full-Blood American Negro. *American Journal of Physical Anthropology* 12:15–30.

ILLUSTRATED HERITAGE
1967 *The Illustrated Heritage Dictionary and Information Book.* Houghton Mifflin, NY.

JACKSON, KENNETH T. (EDITOR)
1995 *The Encyclopedia of New York City.* Yale University Press, New Haven, CT, and The New York Historical Society, NY.

JAMIESON, ROSS W.
1995 Material Culture and Social Death: African-American Burial Practices. *Historical Archaeology* 29:4.

JOHNSON, JAMES WELDON
1969 *Black Manhattan.* Atheneum, NY.

JORDE, PEGGY KING, MARSHA SIMMS, AND FEDERAL STEERING COMMITTEE
1993 *Final Recommendations Report to the U.S. Congress on the Memorialization of the African Burial Ground.* 6 August. On file with the Federal Steering Committee.

KELLEY, JENNIFER OLSON, AND J. LAWRENCE ANGEL
1989 The First African Baptist Church Cemetery: Bioarcheology, Demography, and Acculturation of Early Nineteenth-Century Philadelphia Blacks. Vol. 3, Osteological Analysis. Report prepared by Smithsonian Institution, Washington, DC. Submitted to Redevelopment Authority of the City of Philadelphia, PA.

KERTZER, DAVID I.
1988 *Ritual, Politics and Power.* Yale University Press, New Haven, CT.

KLIMA, DON L.
1992 Construction of Federal Courthouse and Federal Office Building at Foley Square, New York, NY (excerpted letter). *Ground Truth* 1:3.

KUTZ, DAVID (DIRECTOR)
1994 *The African Burial Ground: An American Discovery.* Film, written by Christopher Moore. On file with the Office of Public Education and Interpretation, NY. Also available from National Technical Information Services, National Audio Visual Center, 5285 Port Royal Road, Springfield, VA 22161, (703) 487-4650. Reference Number AVA 19619-VNB1.

LACY, DAVID, AND ROBERT HASENSTAB
1983 The Development of Least Effort Strategies in CRM: Competition for Scarce Resources In Massachusetts. In *The Sociopolitics of Archaeology,* edited by J.

Gero, D. Lacy, and M. Blakey, pp. 31–50. University of Massachusetts, Department of Anthropology, Amherst.

LANDMARKS
1992   National Historic Landmark Designation. Landmarks Preservation Commission, 100 Old Slip, New York, NY.

LAURA, EMILY [EMILYN L. BROWN]
1992   Honoring the Dead: A Bridge Between Two Worlds. *Ground Truth* 1(1).

LEONE, MARK P.
1984   Interpreting Ideology in Historical Archaeology: The William Paca Garden in Annapolis, Maryland. In *Ideology, Power, and Prehistory*, edited by Daniel Miller and Christopher Tilley, pp. 25–35. Cambridge University Press, Cambridge, UK.

LEONE, MARK P., AND PARKER B. POTTER, JR.
1994   Historical Archaeology of Capitalism. *Society for American Archaeology Bulletin* 12(4):14–15. Mark Aldenderfer, Editor. Washington, DC.

LEONE, MARK P., AND PARKER B. POTTER, JR. (EDITORS)
1988   *The Recovery of Meaning*. Smithsonian Institution Press, Washington, DC.

McALLISTER, BILL
1996a Post Office Jumps at Help from Bugs. *The Washington Post*, 17 May:A21.
1996b Georgia on Their Minds. *The Washington Post*, 17 May:Weekend 70.

McGUIRE, RANDALL H., AND ROBERT PAYNTER (EDITORS)
1991   *The Archaeology of Inequality*. Blackwell, Oxford, UK.

McKEE, LARRY
1995   Commentary: Is It Futile to Try and Be Useful? Historical Archaeology and the African American Experience. *Northeast Historical Archaeology* 23:1–7.

McMANUS, EDGAR J.
1966   *A History of Negro Slavery in New York*. Syracuse University Press, Syracuse, NY.

MEIER, AUGUST, AND ELLIOTT RUDWICK
1986   *Black History and Historical Profession, 1915–1980*. University of Illinois Press, Urbana, IL.

MEILLASSOUX, CLAUDE
1991   *The Anthropology of Slavery*. The University of Chicago Press, Chicago, IL.

MERRIAM-WEBSTER
1994   *The Merriam-Webster Dictionary*. Merriam-Webster, Springfield, MA.

MINTZ, SIDNEY, AND RICHARD PRICE
1992   *The Birth of African-American Culture: An Anthropological Perspective*. Beacon Press, Boston, MA.

MOORE, SUE MULLINS
1985   Social and Economic Status on the Coastal Plantation: An Archaeological Perspective. In *The Archaeology of Slave and Plantation Life*, edited by Theresa A. Singleton, pp. 141–162. Academic Press, Orlando, FL.

MUHAMMAD, AMAL, ESTER DAWSON, CLAUDIA MILNE, AND CHRIS MOORE
1993   Twelve Voices. *Update: Newsletter of the African Burial Ground and Five Points Archaeological Projects* 1(2):3. Sherrill D. Wilson, Newsletter Editor. OPEI, New York, NY.

NELSON, DOVILLE
1993   Twelve Voices. *Update: Newsletter of the African Burial Ground and Five Points Archaeological Projects* 1(2):4. Sherrill D. Wilson, Newsletter Editor. OPEI, New York, NY.

NOBILE, VINCE
1993   White Professors, Black History: Forays into the Multicultural Classroom, in Teaching Innovations Forum. *Perspectives, American Historical Association Newsletter* 31:6.

OFFICE OF PUBLIC EDUCATION AND INTERPRETATION (OPEI)
1995– Monthly Reports. Reports on file, OPEI, 6 World
1996   Trade Center, New York, NY.

OFORI-ANSA, KWAKU
1995   Identification and Validation of the Sankofa Symbol. *Update: Newsletter of the African Burial Ground and Five Points Archaeological Projects* 1(8):3. Sherrill D. Wilson, Newsletter Editor. OPEI, New York, NY.

ORSER, CHARLES E., JR.
1996   *A Historical Archaeology of the Modern World*. Plenum, NY.

OXFORD ENGLISH DICTIONARY
1971   *Oxford English Dictionary*. Compact edition. Two volumes. Oxford University Press, Oxford, UK.

PARRINGTON, MICHAEL, AND DANIEL G. ROBERTS
1990   Demographic, Cultural, and Bioanthropological Aspects of a Nineteenth-Century Free Black Population in Philadelphia, Pennsylvania. In A Life of Science: Papers in Honor of J. Lawrence Angel, edited by Jane E. Buikstra. *Scientific Papers of the Center for American Archeology* 6:138–170. Kampsville, IL.

PARRINGTON, MICHAEL, DANIEL G. ROBERTS, STEPHANIE A. PINTER, AND JANET C. WIDEMAN
1989   The First African Baptist Church Cemetery:

Bioarcheology, Demography, and Acculturation of Early Nineteenth-Century Philadelphia Blacks. Vol. 1, Historical and Archeological Documentation; Vol. 2, Artifact Catalog/Faunal Analysis. Report prepared by John Milner Associates, Inc., Philadelphia, PA. Submitted to Redevelopment Authority of the City of Philadelphia, PA.

PATERSON, DAVID A.
1995 Letter to LaRoche, regarding reinstatement of the Task Force for the Oversight of the African Burial Ground, 31 October. Letter on file with Cheryl J. LaRoche.

PAYNTER, ROBERT
1983 Field or Factory?: Concerning the Degradation of Archaeological Labor. In *The Socio-Politics of Archaeology*, edited by J. Gero, D. Lacy, and M. Blakey, pp. 31–50. University of Massachusetts, Department of Anthropology, Amherst, MA.

PEARCE, SUSAN
1995 Collective Amnesia, Knowledge Recovery: The Significance of the African Burial Ground for the Descendant Community. Paper presented at the Annual Meeting of the American Association of Anthropology, Washington, DC.

POTTER, PARKER B., JR.
1991 What Is the Use of Plantation Archaeology? *Historical Archaeology* 25(3):94–107.

RANKIN-HILL, LESLEY M.
1990 Afro-American Biohistory: Theoretical and Methodological Considerations. Unpublished Ph.D. dissertation, Department of Anthropology, University of Massachusetts, Amherst, MA.

RANKIN-HILL, LESLEY M., AND MICHAEL BLAKEY
1994 W. Montague Cobb (1904–1990); Physical Anthropologist, Anatomist, and Activist. *American Anthropologist* 96:74–96.

ROBERTSHAW, PETER
1995 *Knowledge and Power*. Department of Anthropology, California State University, San Bernardino, CA.

RUTSCH, EDWARD S., AND STAFF
1992 *A Research Design for the Broadway Block Including an In-Progress Field Work Summary Report*. Historic Conservation and Interpretation, Inc. Newton, NJ.

S&S REPORTING
1992– Minutes of the Steering Committee on the African
1994 Burial Ground of the City of New York. S&S Reporting, 132 Nassau Street, New York, NY.

1993 *A Public Forum on the Draft Proposal to the U.S. Congress for Commemorating the African Burial*

Ground. City Hall, Public Hearing Chambers, 14 June. S&S Reporting, 132 Nassau Street, New York, NY.

SAMFORD, PATRICIA
1996 The Archaeology of African-American Slavery and Material Culture. *The William and Mary Quarterly*, third series, 53(1):87–114.

SCARUPA, HARRIET JACKSON
1994 Learning from Ancestral Bones. *American Visions* 9:1.

SCHOMBURG, ARTHUR A.
1929 The Negro Digs Up His Past. In *Anthology of American Negro Literature*, edited by V. F. Calverton, pp. 299–323. Modern Library, New York City, NY.

SCHOMBURG CENTER
1992– Minutes. Sound recordings of Federal Steering
1994 Committee Meetings, NY. Schomburg Center for Research in Black Culture, New York, NY.

SCHULDENREIN, JOSEPH
1995 The Care and Feeding of Archaeologists: A Plea for Pragmatic Training in the 21st Century. *Society for American Archaeology Bulletin* 13(3):22.

SCHUYLER, ROBERT L.
1972 Sandy Ground: Archaeological Sampling in a Black Community in Metropolitan New York. *Conference on Historic Sites Archaeology Paper* 7:13–51.

SCRIBNER-BANTAM ENGLISH DICTIONARY
1979 *The Scribner-Bantam English Dictionary*. Revised edition. Bantam, NY.

SINGLETON, THERESA A.
1994 The African-American Legacy Beneath Our Feet. In *African-American Historical Places*, edited by Beth Savage, pp. 33–40. Preservation Press, Washington, DC.

SINGLETON, THERESA A. (EDITOR)
1985 *The Archaeology of Slavery and Plantation Life*. Academic Press, Orlando, FL.

SINGLETON, THERESA A., AND MARK D. BOGRAD
1995 The Archaeology of the African Diaspora in the Americas. *Guides to the Archaeological Literature of the Immigrant Experience in America* 2. The Society for Historical Archaeology, California, PA.

STOKES, I. PHELPS
1915– *Iconography of Manhattan Island, 1498–1909*, Vol. 4.
1928 Robert H. Dodd, NY.

STRICKLAND-ABUWI, LULA
1996 Raise Some Dust: Oppose Burial Ground Office Ousters. *The City Sun*, 3–9 July, 12(25):4, 7.

STUCKEY, STERLING
1987 *Slave Culture: Nationalist Theory and The Foundations of Black America.* Oxford University Press, NY.

TRIGGER, BRUCE G.
1989 *A History of Archaeological Thought.* Cambridge University Press, NY.

UPDATE
1993– *Update: Newsletter of the African Burial Ground and*
1996 *Five Points Archaeological Projects.* Sherrill D. Wilson, Newsletter Editor. OPEI, New York, NY.

VAN SERTIMA, IVAN
1986 *Great African Thinkers.* Transaction, New Brunswick, NJ.

WALL, DIANA DIZEREGA
1995 Silent Witnesses. *Seaport: New York's History Magazine* 29:3.

WAYNE, LUCY B.
1994 Letters. *African-American Archaeology: Newsletter of the African-American Archaeology Network* (summer) 11:6–7. Thomas R. Wheaton, Newsletter Editor. New South Associates, Stone Mountain, GA.

WEBSTER'S
1971 *Webster's Third New International Dictionary of the English Language, Unabridged.* G. and C. Merriam, Springfield, MA.
1983 *Webster's New Universal Unabridged Dictionary.* Second edition. Simon and Schuster, NY.
1991 *Webster's College Dictionary.* Random House, NY.
1994 *Webster's New World Dictionary of American English.* Third college edition. Prentice Hall, NY.

WHITE, SHANE
1991 *Somewhat More Independent: The End of Slavery in New York City, 1770–1810.* University of Georgia Press, Athens, GA.

WILLEN, LIZ, AND PAUL MOSES
1996 At Top, Blacks Scarce: Few Hold Key Jobs on Rudy's Staff. *Newsday,* 29 April:A2–3.

WILSON, SHERRILL D.
1995 African American Beginnings. *Update: Newsletter of the African Burial Ground and Five Points Archaeological Projects* 1(7):11–12. Sherill D. Wilson, Newsletter Editor. OPEI, New York, NY.

WOODSON, CARTER G.
1933 *The Mis-education of the Negro.* Associated Publishers, Washington, DC.

WORLD BOOK DICTIONARY
1984 *World Book Dictionary.* World Book/Scott Fetzer, Chicago, IL.

WRIGHT, HOWARD D., AND EMILYN L. BROWN (EDITORS)
1992 *Ground Truth.* Concerned Citizens for the Preservation of African-American Heritage, NY.

YOFFEE, NORMAN, AND ANDREW SHERRATT (EDITORS)
1993 *Archaeological Theory: Who Sets the Agenda?* Cambridge University Press, Cambridge, UK.

CHERYL J. LAROCHE
JOHN MILNER ASSOCIATES
6 WORLD TRADE CENTER B-26A
NEW YORK, NY 10048

MICHAEL L. BLAKEY
NEW YORK AFRICAN BURIAL GROUND PROJECT
COBB LABORATORY
DEPARTMENT OF SOCIOLOGY AND
ANTHROPOLOGY
HOWARD UNIVERSITY
WASHINGTON, DC 20059

1997 Descendants, Decisions, and Power: The Public Interpretation of the Archaeology of the Levi Jordan Plantation. In *In The Realm of Politics: Prospects for Public Participation in African American and Plantation Archaeology*, Carol McDavid and David Babson, editors. Thematic issue, *Historical Archaeology* 31(3):114-131

CAROL McDAVID

Descendants, Decisions, and Power: The Public Interpretation of the Archaeology of the Levi Jordan Plantation

ABSTRACT

Archaeological data from the Levi Jordan plantation in Brazoria County, Texas, indicate that the African Americans who lived on this plantation participated in many activities, several of African origin, that functioned to insure this community's survival in an increasingly oppressive outside world. Ethnographic data indicate that many descendants of the plantation's residents, African American and European American, still live in the Brazoria area, and that these descendants continue to negotiate issues of power and control. Any public interpretation of this archaeology will necessarily deal with diverse understandings of race and history in present-day Brazoria County. This paper will describe the political and organizational strategies being employed by a team of descendants, archaeologists, and other community members to plan and implement public interpretations that are "inclusive" of the various histories and archaeologies of the plantation's ancestors: pre- and post-emancipation African Americans as well as planters.

Introduction

This paper addresses the social character of theory and practice (Tilley 1989:114) when academics and local communities work together to plan the public interpretation of archaeology. In this case, the archaeology is that of the Levi Jordan plantation (Brown and Cooper 1990; Brown 1995). The primary question addressed here is whether or not it is feasible to create a public interpretation of this archaeology in the geographic vicinity of the (still standing) plantation house.

Three small towns—Brazoria, Sweeny, and West Columbia—are near the site, located about 60 mi. south of Houston, Texas. Many of the black and white descendants of the plantation's original black and white residents still live within 13 mi. of the site, either in one of these towns or in the rural area surrounding them. My collaborators in this project include several of these descendants as well as other community members; we are working together to decide how to interpret, publicly, the material culture of slavery, tenancy, and racism. This work is political because it reflects the ways in which contemporary people, descendants of people who owned and were owned by each other, continue to negotiate social and political power. It is also political because it incorporates ways that these people are affected, or feel that they could be affected, by the public presentation of "sensitive" archaeological and historical material.

Organization of the Research

The research for this project, which began after much of the archaeological work was complete, was designed to take place in two phases (McDavid 1994a, 1994b, 1995a, 1995b, 1995c, 1995d, 1996). The goal of the first phase, addressed here, was to determine if it would be feasible to interpret this archaeology to the public. This phase attempted to understand the ways in which local residents understood their own histories, in order to discover the constraints and opportunities, ideological and otherwise (Potter 1994:38) that might effect the public presentation of this archaeology. The second phase of the research was to involve members of the community in planning and implementing the public interpretation, with the particular goal of insuring that both black and white descendants of the original residents participated in the planning process. That phase is still underway and will be touched upon here, but only insofar as participation decisions continue to affect the feasibility question.

My goals were proactive; first, to outline a different, "inclusive" approach and, then, to apply it to the feasibility question in the study area. I conducted interviews, participated in community meetings, and took advantage of ongoing informal encounters to determine what the people in the study area thought of an "inclusive" approach and to find out how they viewed their own histories, and their places in those histories. How were their views of history constricted? Would a public interpretation of this archaeology exacerbate present-day social divisions, or assist in healing them? How did people who lived in the area surrounding the site of the interpretation deal with each other? How would the archaeology itself, rooted in a historical event that members of the community probably remember differently, affect how the archaeological story could be told?

"Public interpretation," "Public/s," and "Inclusivity"

This paper will use the terms "public interpretation," "public/s," and "inclusivity" throughout. Although they are commonly understood, they need to be clarified for this particular research. First, I refer to "public interpretation" as any museum, display, public talk, site tour, slide show, brochure, educational program, or other activity that attempts to "tell the story" of a site and the people who lived there. Second, "inclusivity" here means "mutual inclusivity"; that is, it refers to a public interpretation that encompasses the perspectives of *both* the plantation owners *and* its pre- and post-emancipation African-American residents.

Third, in using the term "public" or "publics" in Brazoria, Texas, I refer to several "publics": the descendants of Levi Jordan, the descendants of the African Americans who lived on the site, other European American and African-American members of the surrounding region, community leaders, local educators, people interested in history and archaeology, academics who study history and archaeology, and others. Occasionally people who identify with one of these groups also identify with others. Members of all of these groups form the social and political context surrounding the Jordan site, and it is hoped that to one degree or another all will participate and claim a voice in the creation of whatever interpretation takes place.

Some Brazoria "publics" were not invited to express an opinion in determining what happens at this plantation. For example, some interview data revealed a common assumption that white

supremacist groups still operate in the area. No attempts were made to solicit opinions from people known to be members of these groups, nor will such attempts be made. However, I suspect that sometimes the people would not meet with me because they just "weren't interested" may have supported some of the ideas associated with white supremacy. Their opinions may surface if plans for a public interpretation progress; they, as well as more benign "publics," are elements of the social and political milieu in which people in Brazoria live.

The implications of reactions from these kinds of groups, as well as the reactions from the plantation's descendants and other community people, go beyond a simple decision about whether or not to publicly interpret these artifacts. The question is whether they can be interpreted *in Brazoria*, and, more specifically, at the site of the original plantation. The daily reality of confronting a physical manifestation of the history of the plantation south, in the form of a museum or whatever, could be uncomfortable for the descendants of the people who lived with the realities of slavery and tenancy. Most of this paper will deal with feedback from those descendants, black and white. However, a public interpretation at this site could also generate negative, potentially harmful reactions from people who may or may not accept the premise that the history of the South is something that should be looked at "inclusively."

Another group that forms a significant "public" for this study is the community of historical archaeologists. Historical archaeologists frequently deal with the archaeologies of disenfranchised peoples whose living descendants continue to negotiate issues of social and economic power. Some of these descendants have begun to realize that their lives can be changed by the ways that other people tell their family histories, and they are, increasingly, demanding a voice in presenting the archaeologies and histories of their ancestors. Although this paper deals with a particular community, and a particular social and political context, the ethical and practical concerns that apply to it could also apply elsewhere: to other archaeologies, histories, and communities.

Moving from Past to Present

Recent historical research (Powers 1994) has shown that the power relationships of 19th-century Brazoria, Texas, continue, in large measure, today. The local communities surrounding the plantation are still dominated by white descendants of 19th-century planters, while the African-American community is largely, though not exclusively, restricted to secondary positions in community leadership and social control. Powers (1994:122) has argued that this current situation springs directly from the particular history of the region and that after the Civil War, the "white power structure acted quickly and decisively to prevent any inversion of the antebellum social order. Southern whites were committed to retaining the status quo." She describes a number of strategies with which whites maintained their domination well into the present historical period, and points out how blacks reacted to this continued domination: they created a strong, insular, cohesive social system that operates largely outside the dominant white social and political system. Powers' analysis is also supported by recent oral history research in the area immediately surrounding the plantation (Wright 1994). According to Powers (1994:304), blacks "withdrew and isolated themselves from the Anglo residents of Brazoria; to some extent the retraction was voluntary, but overall it was in response to the treatment whites dealt them."

The separate, divided nature of present-day social and political Brazoria, rooted in the oppression and domination of the past, could well have an impact on the feasibility of creating a public interpretation of this plantation site. As the data will indicate, many people in the area derive at least part of their historical and social identities from an understanding of how they fit into the history of the region. In addition, I found that there was a great deal of local familiarity with the written histories of the region in the early 20th century, which spoke of slavery mainly in terms of economic loss, such as, "The freeing of the slaves deprived the Southern people of about two thousand million dollars" (Strobel 1926:15). These sources often characterized white supremacist groups, which were comprised of ex-confederate soldiers, as heroes who "stood like a stone wall for White supremacy and preserve and gave us our present civilization, to whom we owe a debt of gratitude that can never be repaid" (Strobel 1926:1). Indeed, it did not take formal research to realize that most of modern Brazoria is racially, socially, and economically segregated; there is a great deal of continuity between past and present power relationships in the area. The question of social and political continuity between the "old" and "new" South has been the subject of considerable debate among historians; Woodward (1951) and Weiner (1978) provide introductions to both sides of the question.

This is not to say that most Brazorians today have exactly the same racial attitudes as their 19th-century ancestors and early 20th-century historians. Some whites have reacted to earlier attitudes by rejecting them altogether, stating that they consciously attempt to avoid being "like" their ancestors. Others carry a burden of guilt, which, in part, drives their actions and decisions. Similarly, many black Brazorians speak of "moving on," and frequently they, too, consciously reject the attitudes of the past. However, the world that present-day Brazorians inhabit derives from a broader historical and social context, and it is likely that their deep-rooted assumptions about power are, in part, shaped by the historical milieu in which they live.

In addition, historical relations between the two main branches of Jordan's descendants, the Martin and the McNeill families, have been strained since the 19th century (Brown 1993, 1995). These strained relationships still form part of the present-day social and historical context of the community. Some members of each branch of the family still regard each other with attitudes ranging from mild mistrust to, in some cases, outright animosity. Complicating this, the archaeological deposit in the former slave and tenant quarters of the Jordan plantation indicates that the African-American tenants left their homes suddenly, and left in such a manner that they could take very little with them (Brown 1995:98). The site was owned by the Martins at the time of this "abandonment," and historical evidence suggests that the sudden departure of the tenants from the site was provoked by the actions of some of the Martin ancestors. In addition, these same Martins were among the most active in local white supremacist movements of the late 19th century (Powers 1994; Wright 1994). Therefore, "telling the story," in archaeological terms—that is, why the tenants' possessions were abandoned in the first place, entails discussing some rather unsavory behaviors on the part of some of the Martins. Some of their living descendants object to exposing any information about the past that would "rewrite history," as some have put it.

However, the people who support archaeological research at the plantation are also from the Martin side of the family, and they are among the most vocal in demanding that the "whole truth" be publicly told and dealt with, as interview data later in this paper will indicate. Nonetheless, plans for public interpretation have already been constrained by personal and familial agendas, even though some family members approve of an "inclusive" interpretation of the site, extending even to acknowledging and dealing with actions of some of their ancestors.

Theoretical and Ideological Perspectives

The intent here is to develop this research within the broad framework of what is known as a "critical" perspective and to incorporate a mutually inclusive *both/and*, as opposed to *either/or*, point of view.

Critical Theory

The use of critical theory in the public interpretation of history and archaeology has been addressed elsewhere (Wylie 1985; Leone et al. 1987; Handsman and Leone 1989; Potter 1994) and will not be discussed at length here, except

to point out how this approach has been useful within the context of this particular project.

Critical theory is concerned with the ways in which the production of knowledge is historically situated, and with understanding how archaeological findings are relevant to particular social and political interests, whether or not the archaeologist attempts to make those findings relevant (Tilley 1989:2; Potter 1994:39–40). Traditional public interpretations of plantation life, which have tended to focus almost exclusively on the lives of planter class, have the effect of reinforcing the idea that planter class values and ideologies were natural and inevitable. Expanding the focus to include the lives of *all* the people who lived on a plantation is one way of deconstructing the dominant planter ideologies. Doing so, and doing so in explicit terms, allows the consumers of archaeological and historical knowledge to see how our understanding of the past is, in part, a function of how it is presented (Tilley 1989:114).

A central element of critical theory is a concern with the particular (Potter 1989). A critical approach, therefore, requires that the social and political constraints (Leone et al. 1987) existing in any particular community be taken into account when deciding whether or not to do a public interpretation within that community. As mentioned previously, the social and political constraints in present-day Brazoria are very much a function of those that existed the past. A "critical" approach attempts to understand the "interests and conflicts" (Leone and Potter 1994) existing within the community of Brazoria, Texas, and to incorporate them into any public interpretations that take place—even if incorporating them means that the public interpretation does not take place on the site itself.

Critical theory also calls for self-reflection by the social analyst and, I would argue, by other participants in the public interpretation process; each social actor is a "part of the societal process analyzed" (Held 1980:191). The approach here has been for each actor (academic, community member, board member, volunteer, and visitor) to recognize how his or her individual bias influences the knowledge presented about this site, and to consider how this knowledge serves their own, or other, interests (Potter 1994:39, citing Geuss 1981:78). For example, my research method included asking several project participants to become familiar with my academic biases—with critical theory and its application to this project. Without exception, all agreed that a "critical" approach, as described here, was appropriate and useful. However, all also felt that dealing explicitly with the roots of this approach, and its derivation from Marxist and neo-Marxist thinking, would be counterproductive within the conservative context of present-day Brazoria, Texas. In Brazoria, ideas about individualism, family, work, class, race, and power are constructed within modern capitalist frameworks (Handsman and Leone 1989:119), even though they may be differently perceived within black and white segments of the larger community. Although any public interpretation of this site would work toward achieving enlightenment about past and present-day issues of domination and power, it would need to do so within local frames of reference to be accepted by the community in which it takes place.

Unlike some critical archaeologies, which call for a concrete plan of social action and emancipation (Handsman and Leone 1989; Tilley 1989) the purpose of a critical approach here is simply to create a path for a public interpretation that will challenge and expand traditional ways of understanding the history of the plantation South. As such, we are "willing to accept enlightenment as an adequate result" (Potter 1994:38). This is a rather broad view of critical theory, and some may find that this project is not sufficiently "critical," in that it does not deal with issues of "class interests and exploitation" only in terms of economic domination (Blakey 1987:292). While there may be economic ramifications of all forms of oppression, "particular situations of dominance may involve sexual, political, or social exploitation without any direct economic consequence" (Spencer-Wood 1992a:3).

Critical theory also rejects views that privilege the scientific method over other ways of producing knowledge. It does not say that stringent empirical-analytical methods should be rejected (Handsman 1981; Wylie 1985:141–142; Tilley 1989:112), only that by itself positivism produces an inadequate view of the world (Potter 1994:32). The archaeological investigations at this site have used the empirical methods of the "New Archaeology," applied within the contextual, interpretive theoretical frameworks of postprocessual archaeologies (Hodder 1986; Brown 1995). Related research (Wright 1994; Taylor 1996; Hill 1997) has employed interpretive anthropology, oral history, and genealogy to illuminate the same historical period as that addressed by the archaeology. The assumption among all project participants is that science is an important way, but not the only way, to understand the past.

A "both/and" Point of View

Besides critical theory, a *both/and*, rather than *either/or*, approach (Spencer-Wood 1991, 1992a, 1992b, [1993], 1996) has also been useful in this work. Put simply, this approach will attempt to develop ways to talk about *both* black history *and* white history in the plantation South, without doing either at the expense of the other. A *both/and* approach provides a framework to explore, publicly, the interaction of dominant and non-dominant groups, and to explore the many ways that people dealt with societal restraints to form ideologies, identities, and behaviors to empower themselves. It rejects simplistic definitions of non-dominant individuals as "victims who react, negatively motivated by dominance, without any positive viewpoints or ideology of their own" (Spencer-Wood 1992b:4). Similarly, it also rejects definitions of all dominant individuals as oppressors and villains. It is hoped that this approach to public presentation will provide a way for diverse "publics" in Brazoria to be comfortable with the expression of their divided, sometimes contested, histories and that it will promote an appreciation of the contributions of *all* the people who lived on this plantation.

Method

Several data-gathering procedures were employed during this study: fact-finding trips to other interpretive sites; formal but unstructured interviews with community residents; participation in community meetings and presentations to community organizations; informal encounters with respondents; and active participation in professional associations concerned with the presentation of historical materials. The fact-finding trips took place in the summers of 1992 and 1993 and will not be addressed here, except to say that they affirmed my initial impression that most public interpretations of the history of the plantation South—despite a few well-known exceptions, some of which are included in this volume—tend to focus almost exclusively on the owners' homes, furniture, and wealth. Formal taped interviews began in October 1993 and continued into the fall of 1994. In the fall of 1994 I determined that the formal interview process had ceased to be productive; the reasons for this will be explained later in this narrative. Many informal conversations and meetings took place during the entire time and are, even now, part of an ongoing research process.

I attempted to interview representatives from various "publics" previously described: descendants of Levi Jordan, descendants of the African Americans who lived on the plantation, members of communities surrounding the plantation, persons interested in Texas history and tourism, and community leaders. Selection criteria were based on my perception of family and community influence, such as family elders, community leaders, and people actively involved in historical interpretation, and on the respondent's willingness to participate.

As mentioned previously, part of my method was to state my personal and professional agendas very clearly. Interview transcripts reveal that I sometimes did almost as much talking as my respondents—explaining what I meant by a *both/and* approach, talking about work being done at other sites, explaining what our goals were in terms of community empowerment, and so on. I usually revealed something of my own "baggage" during these interactions—there were many discussions about what it was like to grow up as southerners in a racially polarized culture, our feelings about the Civil Rights movement, how the legacies of slavery affect people in the present, and similar topics. I always made it clear that "we," meaning the core group of people initially involved in this project (the archaeological project director and two white Jordan descendants) wished to see if it would be feasible to create an inclusive, *both/and* public interpretation at this site. I made it clear that the core group would rely on community input to decide whether to support such a public interpretation. If it chose not to support it, then the public interpretation, if any, would take place elsewhere.

These transcripts revealed extremely interactive conversations, not one-sided "objective" question/answer sessions. I wanted my respondents to be able to trust me, but neither they, nor I, could ignore that I was a white, urban, university affiliated outsider—I was, and continue to be, "the other." If I had attempted to position myself as an insider, or to hide behind a mask of objectivity, I would have been seen as less trustworthy, not more. One African-American businessman commented, "Well, I don't want to interview *you*, but I think this has changed you . . . your attitude about things. And I really don't know what they were before, but I sense that since you've been doing this thing you see things differently, you know, as you really search and find out the truth about things . . . and, then, I do sense that you are sensitive, maybe more sensitive, to people since you've done this."

An African-American minister commented, after I asked for his support and told him why I felt that this project was important, that "the only way this will work is if people believe that you have a good heart . . . but I can tell you have a good heart." This kind of comment reassured me that my reflective, proactive approach had a direct and positive effect on the kind and amount of information I received during my interviews. My willingness to own my otherness—to talk about it openly and to reveal personal reasons for doing this research—led to franker, more open communication than would have been possible otherwise. It was sometimes essential in getting people to talk to me at all.

Data: Interviews, Community Meetings, and Informal Encounters

Data were gathered in several contexts: interviews, community meetings, and informal encounters. Each is discussed further below.

The Interview Process

Most of my early interviews were with Jordan's descendants; they had already been identified through attendance at family reunions and personal introductions. They were usually very eager to provide their ideas, and there was no difficulty in arranging meetings. The same held true for meetings with local community leaders—most were eager to hear about a new source of potential tourist dollars. I knew it might not be as easy to arrange interviews with African-American descendants and other community residents but had confidence that it would occur at some point. I did have some good contacts in the African-American community who had said they would be willing to introduce me to other people.

I have already mentioned that I stopped the formal interview process early in that stage of the research. To explain why, and to contextualize the summary of interview data that follows, I will now describe the legal entity that was formed to direct all public activities deriving from the plantation's archaeology. The formation of this organization was not intended to be a part of the feasibility phase of the research because it was not originally perceived to have much to do with the specific questions I was asking in my interviews—questions about how to talk about slavery and tenancy, how to teach

history, and the like. However, the existence of this organization and, more importantly, its composition, had a direct impact on my efforts to obtain candid feedback from the local African-American population.

In 1993 two Jordan descendants, including the site owners' representative, and the archaeology director, Dr. Kenneth L. Brown, set up the Levi Jordan Plantation Historical Society, a 501(c)3 tax-exempt, non-profit corporation. My role in the organization was to arrange for pro bono legal work, to serve as the organization's secretary, and to function as an unofficial organizer and "expediter." I did not serve on the board of directors because we all agreed that it should be dominated by local individuals; the only "outsider" on the board was the archaeology director. The job of the organization would include, but would not be limited to, planning the public interpretation, if it was determined to be feasible. It would also include house restoration, loaning artifacts to museums, fundraising, and similar activities. We all agreed that no substantive planning would take place—such as writing a mission statement, applying for National Register status, and so on—until the board had learned what it could from my interviews, and, more importantly, until it could expand to include people to represent the plantation's African-American ancestors. At that point we had not identified many of the African-American descendants and had no idea who might be willing and able to be involved; my research was seen as a way to get community input as well as to identify people who might be interested in participating on a formal basis.

So, I began to conduct interviews with people in the African-American community. Some interviews went very well, and the comments they generated were very useful in establishing themes that could guide us later in planning a public interpretation. During these interviews, I usually felt that I had been able to connect, to start forming a basis of mutual understanding and trust, and so on. It proved to be extremely difficult to arrange appointments, however. Only one person ever said "no" to an interview request, but many had some reason not to meet with me, citing reasons such as not having time, busy schedule, and illness. The people I interviewed were unfailingly polite and gracious, but I kept sensing a wariness, a reluctance to tell me what they really thought. One African-American respondent, who had been active in community affairs and local government, warned me that I would have trouble getting candid opinions from members of his community: "sometimes the people who would have real influence in the black community would be same ones who wouldn't want to be involved . . . you have to realize that people will tell you what they think you want to hear."

During these interviews I sensed that my own ethnicity was only part of the reason for this apparent wariness. When we started talking about racial issues, and about the shared aspects of our experiences as southerners in the late 20th century, my own openness seemed to reassure people that I was sincere and basically trustworthy. I knew there was "something else" besides my being a white, urban outsider that was affecting the success of arranging interviews in the first place.

In the summer of 1994 I finally got a glimpse of why people might have been skeptical when hearing my statements about "involving the African-American community early on." I started to hear, indirectly and never with specific examples, about other history-related community projects in which blacks had been asked to participate after most of the substantive planning had already taken place. One person mentioned a museum that had neglected to include blacks on its board, except in a token fashion, and another mentioned a parade in which blacks participated, but after most plans had already been made. Some also noted that the other local plantation museum had recently attempted to do some programming about African-American history, but that this effort had been restricted to a small display in one outbuilding on the site, and had been poorly funded by the state agency that manages the site. The blacks had been told they were "welcome" to do some kind of display, but

it was evident that there was no intent to change the more general planter-class focus of the site.

All of the African Americans who alluded to the history of tokenization in the community were very circumspect about mentioning names and specific events. Only one ever discussed the issue on tape:

> Well, [once] when we had a parade . . . the Negro was never just told "Okay, we want you all in this" . . . We live here . . . this is our home and we want to be a part of it. I told them that at meetings . . . that kind of thing, you know. But the persons who are in leadership . . . they forget about that . . . so for that reason, I think we're left out of whatever there is here to be . . . I think to a marked degree we have not been represented in the organizations as [much as] we should have been.

I started to realize that it was not surprising that my naive requests for interviews and appeals for opinion were regarded with suspicion. It became obvious that interviews were not going to be a productive way of getting input from the African-American community until members of that community were fully empowered to act on any suggestions they might make. One encounter, in particular, clarified this situation. In the fall of 1994 I attempted to make an appointment to speak with an African-American woman who is a retired educator. This individual had obviously come across university researchers before, and stated flatly that she would not meet with me until I had answered, in writing, the following questions: 1) What would I actually do with the results of our interview? Would the community be able to put it to use, or would I just get my thesis written and put the book on a shelf somewhere? 2) What would the university's role be in the process down the line? Would the archaeologist help plan the interpretation, or would he simply pack up his trowel and move on? and 3) What likelihood was there that the project would ever actually happen? Who would benefit from the project — the community or the university?

I finally realized that these kinds of questions must have been on the minds of many of the people I attempted to interview, even if they did not come right out and ask them. I did respond in writing to this individual, of course, and decided to terminate the formal interview process. I then recommended that the board of directors of the Levi Jordan Plantation Historical Society concentrate *all* its efforts on recruiting new members before any more planning, or talk of planning, took place. They readily agreed, and now, two years later, the society has a seven-person board that includes African-American descendants as well as other members of the black community.

It is important to point out that the original, three-member board did not identify and select the new members. The first new member was selected by a local African-American service organization whose membership includes several plantation descendants, including the person most active in helping us recruit. The new board member, who happens to be the same person who posed the questions above, then helped us to find additional volunteers.

So, even though the formation and composition of the Levi Jordan Plantation Historical Society turned out to have little to do with community opinions about archaeology museums and public interpretation, they had a great deal to do with community perceptions of empowerment, voice, and authority. I realized that I could interview as many white descendants, mayors, chamber presidents, and the like as I wanted to, but until African Americans were vested in the process, and empowered to make policy-level decisions, feedback from them would be extremely hard to obtain. Unless power was perceived to be held equally with the white descendants and other residents, I would probably continue to "hear what they thought I wanted to hear," to paraphrase the respondent mentioned earlier.

In spite of that difficulty, however, a number of themes emerged in interviews and other encounters which would have a direct bearing on whatever public interpretation could be created, provided that the issues of power and control discussed above are addressed. The rest of this section will highlight a few of these themes; their implications for the public interpretation of

this site, and the implications of the power question, will be addressed in the Conclusion. All names, of course, have been changed.

The Themes

Most respondents, black and white, had a strong sense of family and regional history, although it played out in different ways. One common theme was that geography seemed to play a significant role in how people defined themselves and their histories. The Jordan plantation, and the communities of Brazoria, Sweeny, and West Columbia, are located in western Brazoria County, in an area that was central to the development of early Texas history (Creighton 1975). The Brazos River divides the county into east–west sections; people living there frequently acknowledged themselves as having a "West of the Brazos" identity. There is a "West of the Brazos" phone book, for example, and a strong sense that people are keenly aware of their own history.

There also seems to be as much competition between these three small towns as there is solidarity. All have separate historical societies and separate historical museums, but there is also a museum association for the three museums that meets on a regular basis. People from West Columbia seldom neglect to mention that their town was the first capital of Texas, and people in Brazoria frequently refer, with some degree of resentment, to the time back in the 1930s that the present county seat was "stolen" in the "dead of night" and moved to Angleton (east of the Brazos). As one local resident put it after I made a presentation at a local Chamber of Commerce meeting, "this project would be a good idea — because, after all, "we" are more historical than those towns on the other side of the river."

As mentioned previously, many people I met were very informed about the early history of the county, and much of their pride had to do with the fact that the region was the locus of Stephen F. Austin's first settlement in the 1830s (Creighton 1975). The original white settlers formed what became known in this century as the "Old 300", and I heard this term many times when speaking with local residents. Once I saw a bumper sticker that declared proudly that the car's driver was "One of the old 300!," and one evening in a local bar/cafe I noticed that there were two mugs emblazoned with Austin's image nestled amongst the beers displayed for sale. The Brazoria County Historical Museum has a permanent exhibition about the original Austin settlement and lists the names of the "old 300" settlers on a prominently featured sign at the exit to the exhibition.

I also had the impression that while all respondents recognized the term "West of the Brazos" and identified themselves with being a part of that area, as opposed to "the other side of the river," the use of the term was regarded by many African Americans as more of a "white" thing, which is not surprising, since it seems to be connected to the "old 300" idea. From Mr. Alexander, a middle-aged African-American businessman: "Well, I think it is something distinctive . . . something their family has done to establish roots in this country . . . they want to say that they were part of the old 300, which I think is prestigious as a family who have developed this country . . . as well as it is for black Americans who have contributed things to this country . . . to have that same amount of prestige and distinction about what they've done . . . and so, that's why I say we have to balance the two."

My research showed that most African Americans in Brazoria were not interested in helping to plan a public interpretation that would perpetuate the stereotypic view that slaves and tenants were passive in their response to oppression and victimization. Some were skeptical when asked whether or not their community would accept a public interpretation that would focus on black history—some asked, "why do you want to stir all that slavery stuff up again?" Some expressed the idea that "just telling the truth" could be "dangerous," and several commented on the need to have interpretations that were, in their words, "non-polarizing." Again from Mr. Alexander: "You have to incorporate

the two [points of view] and then go from there . . . because otherwise it would be like all one of this and all one of that . . . you know, and it would polarize people . . . so I think that the only way you are going to really get the essence of the thing is . . . to let them work together . . . and maybe the authority would come from both . . . they can both say things about it, and they'll be more open to say it, and then I think there would be less criticism saying, well, it's all this black or all white."

When I began to talk about using a "both/and" approach, and to describe the kinds of inclusive programming underway at other sites, the response to the Jordan project warmed considerably. While most blacks I met frequently commented on the need to avoid emphasizing what they called "the punishments," they also talked about the importance of positive role models, and there was usually great enthusiasm as we explored ideas about incorporating this archaeology into history curricula in local schools. As one local African-American minister put it, when talking about how we might involve young people, "you have to show connections between what's in the ground and what people have accomplished since then." Earlier, Mr. Alexander commented that "I think it [the both/and approach] would be the only way it would survive . . . and what we need to focus on is how we're going to make it better . . . that's what I think of how it should work, and I think that's the way it would survive in the long run."

Later, Mr. Alexander and I also discussed how a public interpretation should address the "ugly" parts of history, and he said, "Well, if you did present that, it'd have to be real gentle . . . you know, something where a small kid, say six or seven, would understand it. I don't think it has to be . . . you wouldn't want to overblow that kind of thing, because some people are still sensitive about it . . . I think it would just have to be something gentle." This kind of conversation frequently led to discussions about the importance of black history and Black History Month. Whites sometimes commented that "well, it's OK, but maybe we should also have White History Month." Blacks, on the other hand, sometimes said "maybe it would be better if black history was studied all year, not just in February." The common thread in both kinds of responses, however, was that a public interpretation at this site could provide a way for students to learn about everyone's history all year long.

While whites did not generally criticize traditional interpretations, they did respond favorably to learning about the inclusive approaches being explored at other sites. Some whites expressed an enthusiasm for "telling the whole truth," although they also sometimes asked, "Is this [project] only going to be about black history"? This question may be especially pertinent to the Jordan descendants, because, as mentioned previously, the archaeological deposit itself suggests that the tenants were forcibly evicted by one of their ancestors, and because many ancestors were active in various white supremacist groups of the postbellum period. While most white descendants were quite willing to acknowledge the roles their ancestors played in the racial turbulence of the past, they also wanted to make sure that the other, "better" stories are told, such as the stories—recounted by both blacks and whites—about the friendships that sometimes developed between black and white plantation residents, and stories about the courage and fortitude of the women in the planter's family.

Most people I met thought that history, and learning about one's ancestors, was important and valuable. Mrs. Moore, a middle-aged African-American businesswoman and church worker commented that "I want my children to know all what happened during slavery . . . . I want them to get out there and know that we did this, we didn't do this, what was done . . . it's good education, and my daughter has grown strong in knowing these things." And Mr. Alexander, in his comments addressing the same issue, alluded to the importance of understanding the complex relationships that frequently existed between the enslaved and their enslavers: "Just the way these people lived . . . most of the things they had, you know, they had to do it in a creative way . . . you know, there were certain things they could do, certain things they couldn't do .

. . you know, and they survived. But . . . there were the relationships between the two [groups of people] . . . . I think there's a lot of things that we don't really see about what really went on . . . other than just master and slave . . . it wasn't just all, you   know, Afro-American or European American."

Kay, an older college student and white McNeill descendant, was also asked how she felt about publicly interpreting the archaeological materials from the quarters area. She said that "learning about it could be very healing for both sides because I do believe there's a kind of collective guilt that I feel or just sort of a guilt for, you know, things wouldn't be where they were today if they hadn't been the way they were back then."

On the whole, community leaders, such as mayors, chamber of commerce members, and museum directors, liked the idea of a plantation interpretation that would involve all members of the community—one that would increase local appreciation of the African Americans who made the planters' fortunes possible. As one local (white) leader put it, "If planning this kind of project will help us to have better ongoing contact with the leaders of the black community, then that's reason enough to do it." However, I also heard, in non-taped interviews with African Americans, that some of the people who stated their support of an "inclusive" interpretation had exhibited very different attitudes when a local group attempted to build a public swimming pool. Some whites fought the swimming pool project, and the strong perception among blacks was that the whites did not want a pool because that would mean that black children would swim with white children. On the basis of non-taped conversations with some of these individuals, my guess is that this perception was correct.

However, while many whites' support of an "inclusive" interpretation was apparently sincere, there was also awareness of the difficulties that would be involved in creating such an interpretation. Margaret, an elderly white descendant, when asked "what do you think about having the project planned by descendants of both black and white residents of the plantation?," responded that "I think that's the only approach that you can take to get cooperation from everybody, and I think they're [the black descendants] are going to have to be convinced from the first that they're not token . . . and that's not going to be an easy time."

Discussion and Conclusions: Is a Public Interpretation of This Site Feasible?

On one level of decision-making, interview data and other community input revealed that it would be feasible to create a successful public interpretation of this site if, and only if, it is truly multivocal—inclusive of black, white, Martin, McNeill, diverse "public," and archaeologist viewpoints. There was a great deal of support for an "inclusive" approach to interpreting the archaeology and history of this site, and people I met and interviewed are now more aware of what a "different" kind of plantation interpretation might be like.

However, in the long run, feasibility will have more to do with how issues of power and control are resolved than it will with whether people like the idea of an "inclusive" interpretation. A major result of this work was the realization that, before the answer to the feasibility question can ever be an unqualified "yes," the following questions will need to be addressed: 1) How can the planning group (the Levi Jordan Plantation Historical Society) continue to find ways to share power in authentic, credible ways? And, no less important, 2) How can it find ways to convince its various "publics" that power and control are genuinely shared?

While my own awareness of the importance of the power issue was one result of this work, an even more important result was the increased awareness and articulation of it within the local planning group, the board of directors of the Levi Jordan Plantation Historical Society. This is not to say that local members of this group were not aware of how power was vested in their community; obviously they were, and more profoundly than I would ever be. However, knowing something on an intuitive, common-sense level is one thing. Expressing this knowledge in explicit terms, and incorporating it into the infrastructure of an organization, is very different. The collaborative nature of this project gave definition and vocabulary to the power/control issue; project participants now share a common understanding of its importance to the success, or lack of success, of this project. As one African-American descendant put it to me recently, "It's going to be a long journey . . . but at least we've started."

At some point it will be necessary for exhibit designers, including archaeologists, to understand how local people view themselves and their histories, how they think issues like slavery should be addressed, how young people should be taught history, and so on. These themes, which were explored in my interviews—for an in-depth analysis of interview data, see McDavid (1996)—will be useful in creating a public interpretation, but they will only be useful if the power issues can be negotiated successfully. Only in a setting of shared power can sensitive, "ugly" parts of history be dealt with openly and productively—*it is a question of what comes first*. In this case, the public perception and acceptance of shared power must come first, before any public interpretation can be implemented.

For example, some of the artifacts themselves will lead to difficult choices about how to present them publicly. One such artifact is a shackle, still embedded in the brick wall in which it was found. Handling the emotional reaction that this artifact initially provokes will be a difficult challenge for the people implementing a public interpretation. How can one be "multivocal" about a shackle? At first glance the shackle would seem to be a clear-cut, unambiguous testament to white oppression, offering little opportunity for public interpretation other than to acknowledge its painful origins and then move on. However, its presence, and its location *in the quarters area*, could also provide pathways to discuss other, related issues—How did people resist oppression? How were stereotypical attitudes toward blacks responses to strategies of black resistance to white domination?

If this part of the quarters was used at some point to confine people (Kenneth L. Brown 1996, pers. comm.), this artifact could provide an opportunity to discuss how blacks might have dealt with the presence of a "jail" in the midst of their living area, and could also offer opportunities to discuss the difficult, ambiguous roles of slaves and tenants who also functioned as overseers, drivers (Genovese 1976:365–388), and, in this case, possibly jailers. It is perhaps true that these related issues are just as difficult to deal with as the presence of the shackle, but using the shackle as a point of departure could offer possibilities to discuss how the lives of the people on this plantation "overlapped, combined, and changed in different cultural contexts and over time" (Spencer-Wood [1993]). The shackle could also be used to examine the ways in which oppression and domination take many different forms, and how people take individual actions to deal with that oppression and domination (Spencer-Wood 1994).

As previously mentioned, most present-day Brazorians, including descendants of the original slaveholders, do not agree with their ancestors' attitudes towards slavery. Most, though not all, as discussed below, are willing to discuss and acknowledge their ancestors' roles in the slave and tenant system. The common view is that the old attitudes were, simply, wrong, and there is no suggestion here that the viewpoints of oppressors and oppressed should be presented as equally valid. However, presenting "good" and "bad" parts of history in an open-ended, inclusive way, rather than a closed, "this is the way it was" fashion, could help people to see for themselves how much people and attitudes have changed. More importantly, it could also allow them the space to see for themselves, without preaching or polemics, how present-day attitudes are rooted in those of the past, and begin the process of acknowledging their own participation in the perpetuation of racist, classist, and sexist social attitudes (see Blakey's discussion of white denial of racism, this volume).

One historical artifact that has already been painful for local descendants to deal with relates to the manner in which African Americans appear to have left the plantation. The objects they left behind are a positive, compelling testament to the ways that African Americans coped with slavery and tenancy, but their very existence could well bring up questions of ownership. While the legal documents setting up the Levi Jordan Plantation Historical Society provide that all artifacts will be controlled by the planning group, not by the site's white owners, in the future, descendants of the people who left the artifacts behind could easily wish to contest the legal fact that they still do not own them.

It will also be necessary to deal with the demands of white descendants who have expressed angry reactions to archaeological interpretations that attempt to explain why the deposit exists. For example, one local newspaper, while generally supportive of local historical projects, occasionally tends to emphasize the negative, sensational aspects of the plantation's history—that is, the abandonment episode. A recent story, headlined "Excavation Slowly Uncovers History's Scars," began with the sentence, "The ghosts of former slaves are whispering of an injustice done more than 100 years ago on a plantation near Brazoria" (VanDerSlice 1996). Not surprisingly, several white plantation descendants reacted very angrily to this article; one commented that "just because you found some stuff in the ground doesn't give you the right to destroy [my] family." Most of them did not dispute the relative accuracy of the article—they are quite aware of the roles that their ancestors had in the turbulence of the past. However, they blamed the archaeology director, not the newspaper reporter, for the content and tone of the article, and have begun a campaign to stop plans to publicly interpret the site. The board of directors of the planning group (Figure 1), which, as already mentioned, is composed of both European American and African-American descendants, was also very unhappy about the inflammatory tone of the article, and recognized its potential to further polarize an already segregated community.

The only way that these kinds of situations will have any hope of being resolved is for the planning group to have credibility within the local communities of *both* African-American *and* European American descendants—for it to be publicly recognized as an organization in which power and control are genuinely shared. Whether this can happen is very much an open question. Its activities have only recently begun to develop this type of positive public recognition, and the damage caused by the recent newspaper article may not be able to be contained. In addition, given the dichotomized manner in which power is still distributed within the community, the public recognition of shared power will probably be only the first, most difficult,

step in dealing with these kinds of interpretation issues.

Despite these threats to the process of community empowerment and inclusive history-writing, I will close this paper by emphasizing the positive, productive aspects of the community story, and describe the present structure and work of the board of directors of the Levi Jordan Plantation Historical Society. It is in the work of this board that the ideas about critical theory and a *both/and* approach have been incorporated into the infrastructure of this project—*theory and practice have merged.*

Facts photo: Robert J. Reed

Historical Society looks to future

Directors of the Levi Jordan Plantation Historical Society stand in front of the plantation homestead in Sweeny. Pictured, from left, are Ginny Raska, Hazel J. Austin, Carol McDavid, Dorothy Cotton, Morris Richardson and Julia Mack. The Levi Jordan house was built about 1849 and is one of the few original plantation houses still standing in the county. The group plans a history day for the fall and is formulating plans for a membership drive which will begin Aug. 1. For more information on the plantation or the historical society, call Raska at 798-1628 or Austin at 964-3823.

FIGURE 1. Photograph of some members of the Levi Jordan plantation board of directors, taken in front of the plantation house (after *The Brazosport Facts*, 22 July 1995; reprinted with permission of *The Brazosport Facts*).

Last year the new seven-member board, described earlier, began to work together (Figure 1). Their first job was to write a formal mission statement. This statement was designed to be somewhat global in nature—to allow flexibility while giving an overall direction for the organization. This statement, in particular, embodies the *both/and* approach that I had proposed, and that the board adopted. It is as follows:

MISSION STATEMENT
The primary mission of The Levi Jordan Plantation Historical Society is to preserve and interpret the archaeologies and histories of all the people who lived and worked on this plantation after its inception in the mid-19th century.
The secondary mission of the Society is to preserve and interpret the history of Brazoria County and the surrounding region, to complement the primary purpose and to offer a more thorough understanding of contributions of the people of this plantation and of this region to the history of Texas and the United States.
The tertiary mission of the Society is to utilize the public interpretation of historical and archaeological research to promote understanding and appreciation of the diverse histories of the people who built this plantation, this region, and this country.

After writing the mission statement, and expanding it into a long range plan with many specific ideas about educational programming, restoring the plantation house, and the like, the group realized that these documents did not state, in explicit terms, the ideas that formed the basis of planning—the ideas embodied in the critical, "*both/and*" approach described earlier. Therefore, the long range plan now includes a section that outlines these ideas; they comprise in effect, an ideological statement in which each member of the group believes. Here is how the idea statement appears in the printed brochures (Figure 2) that are distributed at public meetings and similar occasions:

OUR MISSION STATEMENT STATES OUR "BIG GOALS," BUT WHAT OTHER IDEAS HAVE GUIDED OUR PROPOSED PLANS TO ACCOMPLISH THAT MISSION?
That there are many different, but complementary, ways of learning about the past—archaeology, history, genealogy, oral history, literature, and others—and that each offers a different kind of "lens" through which we can

The Levi Jordan Plantation Historical Society

Long Range Plan

Preliminary Draft
for Community Review

BOARD OF DIRECTORS
Hazel J. Austin
Kenneth L. Brown, PhD.
Dorothy D. Cotton
Bruce Gotcher
Julia Mack
Ginny McNeill Raska
Morris Richardson

MAILING ADDRESS

P.O. Box 4011
Brazoria, TX 77422
(409) 798-1628

FIGURE 2. Cover of mission statement and long range plan document, including line drawing of a carved shell "cameo" found in the slave and tenant quarters of the site.

"see" the past.
That what we call "history" was not inevitable: that along the way individuals and groups made choices, and all of those choices affected what we are today.
That it is important to respect the idea that some objects from the past may have different kinds of spiritual and emotional importance to different people.
That historical truth may be defined in a variety of ways—what one person or family perceives as important about "what really happened" may be different from what another person or family perceives, and it is possible that these different perceptions may be, in some ways, equally true.
That people in the past were, in some ways, different from people now–that their decisions, conversations, and social relationships were different from ours today.
That people in the past were, in some ways, the same as people are now–that they too had work lives, family lives, spiritual lives, creative lives, and intellectual lives, and they made choices about those lives.

That the decisions we make now about how we present history will influence what we know about the past, and that all of our local communities should have a voice in making those decisions.

The people involved in this project hope that the diverse composition of the planning group, along with the mission statement, long range plan, and statement of ideas, will provide a way for people with different perspectives to see the Jordan project as something they can support and appreciate. We hope that public meetings held to present these documents, along with associated slide presentations and conversations, will offer testimony to local "publics" about how power is shared within the planning group, and will counter the negative public response to more divisive elements of the plantation's history. If this occurs, planning the public interpretation of this archaeology could begin to provide the public with "the intellectual means to assess, criticise, define, and redefine" the past (Tilley 1989:114). It could also provide a way to begin positive, meaningful communication between the various community groups who have a stake in the past, present, and future of this plantation and, in the most hopeful sense, could provide one context in which the real renegotiation of community power can finally begin to take place.

ACKNOWLEDGMENTS

Thanks to Kenneth L. Brown, for his ongoing support of my research, past and present. Thanks also to Norris Lang, Amilcar Shabazz, John McIntyre, and the board of directors of the Levi Jordan plantation (Hazel Austin, Ken Brown, Dorothy Cotton, Bruce Gotcher, Julia Mack, Ginny Raska, and Morris Richardson), for ongoing support during this research. Thanks to Parker Potter and Suzanne Spencer-Wood, whose work inspired the approaches applied here—with special appreciation to Spencer-Wood for insights on this paper; in particular, for comments about the both/and feminist perspective and its application to the conflict resolution and inclusivity issues discussed here. Thanks to Herman Kluge, Betty McDavid, Gene McDavid, Patti Jeppson, Mary Lynne Hill, Cheryl Wright, Cheryl LaRoche, Linda Derry , Ywone Edwards, and Amy Young for personal and scholarly support. All omissions and errors are, of course, my responsibility. Most of all, thanks go to the people who lived and worked on the Levi Jordan plantation from 1848 to 1892. I hope that this work helps make it possible for their stories to be told.

REFERENCES

BLAKEY, MICHAEL E.
1987 Comments in Response to Leone, Potter, and Shackel, "Toward a Critical Archaeology." *Current Anthropology* 28(3):292.

BROWN, KENNETH L.
1993 A Brief History of the Levi Jordan Plantation. Paper presented at the Antebellum Texas, Brazos Style, Conference. Center for the Arts and Sciences, Lake Jackson, TX.
1995 Material Culture and Community Structure: The Slave and Tenant Community at Levi Jordan's Plantation, 1848–1892. In *Working Toward Freedom: Slave Society and Domestic Economy in the American South*, edited by Larry E. Hudson, Jr., pp. 95–118. University of Rochester Press, Rochester, NY.

BROWN, KENNETH L., AND DOREEN C. COOPER
1990 Structural Continuity in an African-American Slave and Tenant Community. *Historical Archaeology* 24(4):7–19.

CREIGHTON, JAMES A.
1975 *A Narrative History of Brazoria County, Texas.* Brazoria County Historical Commission, Waco, TX.

GEUSS, RAYMOND
1981 *The Idea of Critical Theory: Habermas and the Frankfurt School.* Cambridge University Press, Cambridge, UK.

GENOVESE, EUGENE D.
1976 *Roll, Jordan, Roll: The World the Slaves Made.* Vintage, NY.

HANDSMAN, RUSSELL G.
1981 Early Capitalism and the Center Village of Canaan, Connecticut: A Study of Transformations and Separations. *Artifacts* 9:1–21.

HANDSMAN, RUSSELL G., AND MARK LEONE
1989 Living History and Critical Archaeology and the Reconstruction of the Past. In *Critical Traditions in Contemporary Archaeology*, edited by Valerie Pinsky and Alison Wylie, pp. 117–135. Cambridge University Press, Cambridge, UK.

HELD, DAVID
1980 *Introduction to Critical Theory: Horkheimer to Habermas.* University of California Press, Berkeley.

HILL, MARY LYNNE
1997 *The Discipline of Social Corsets: Negotiation of the Gender Typification of the Southern Lady by Female Descendants of Levi and Sarah Stone Jordan.* M.A. thesis, Department of Anthropology, University of Houston, Houston, TX. University Microfilms International, Ann Arbor, MI.

HODDER, IAN
1986 *Reading the Past: Current Approaches to Interpretation in Archaeology.* Cambridge University Press, Cambridge, UK.

LEONE, MARK P., AND PARKER B. POTTER, JR.
1994 Historical Archaeology of Capitalism. *Bulletin of the Society for American Archaeology* 12(4):14–15.

LEONE, MARK P., PARKER B. POTTER, JR., AND PAUL A. SHACKEL
1987 Toward a Critical Archaeology. *Current Anthropology* 28(3):283–302.

McDAVID, CAROL
1994a From Archaeological Context to Public Contexts: The Public Interpretation of the Archaeology of the Levi Jordan Plantation. Paper presented at the Annual Meeting of the Society for Historical Archaeology Conference on Historical and Underwater Archaeology, Vancouver, BC.
1994b From Archaeological Context to Public Contexts: The Public Interpretation of the Archaeology of the Levi Jordan Plantation. Paper presented at the Southeastern Archaeological Conference, Lexington, KY.
1995a Descendants and Decisions: Planning the Public Interpretation of the Archaeology of the Levi Jordan Plantation. Paper presented at the Southeast Region Annual Meeting of the Association of Living History Farms and Museums, Tallahassee, FL.
1995b Descendants, Collaboration, and Consensus: The Public Interpretation of the Archaeology of the Levi Jordan Plantation. Paper presented at the 28th Annual Chacmool Conference: Archaeology into the New Millennium: Public or Perish. Calgary, AB.
1995c Many Pasts and Many Presents: Collaboration in Planning the Public Interpretation of the Archaeology of the Levi Jordan Plantation. Paper presented at the Southeast Preservation Conference, Birmingham, AL.
1995d The Importance of Archaeology in the Preservation of African American Heritage: The Levi Jordan Plantation Project. Paper presented at the African Americans and Heritage Preservation Conference: Practical Strategies for Livable Communities. Texas Historical Commission, Houston.
1996 *The Levi Jordan Plantation: From Archaeological Interpretation to Public Interpretation.* M. A. thesis, Department of Anthropology, University of Houston, Houston, TX. University Microfilms International, Ann Arbor, MI.

POTTER, PARKER B., JR.
1989 *Archaeology in Public in Annapolis: An Experiment in the Application of Critical Theory to Historical Archaeology.* Ph.D. dissertation, Department of Anthropology, Brown University, Providence, RI. University Microfilms International, Ann Arbor, MI.
1994 *Public Archaeology in Annapolis: A Critical Approach to History in Maryland's Ancient City.* Smithsonian Institution Press, Washington, DC.

POWERS, BETSY J.
1994 *From Cotton Fields to Oil Fields: Economic Development in a New South Community.* Ph.D. dissertation, Department of Anthropology, University of Houston, Houston, TX. University Microfilms International, Ann Arbor, MI.

SPENCER-WOOD, SUZANNE M.
1991 Toward a Feminist Historical Archaeology of the Construction of Gender. In *The Archaeology of Gender: Proceedings of the Twenty-Second Annual Conference of the Archaeological Association of the University of Calgary*:234–244. Dale Walde and Noreen D. Willows, editors. Calgary, AB.
1992a Introduction to Critiques in Historical Archaeology. Paper presented at the Annual Meeting of The Society for Historical Archaeology Conference on Historical and Underwater Archaeology, Kingston, Jamaica.
1992b Class and Ethnicity in Domestic Reform. Paper presented at the Annual Meeting of The Society for Historical Archaeology Conference on Historical and Underwater Archaeology, Kingston, Jamaica.
[1993] Toward the Further Development of Feminist Historical Archaeology. *World Archaeological Bulletin* 7, forthcoming.
1994 Diversity and Nineteenth-Century Domestic Reform: Relationships Among Classes and Ethnic Groups. In *Those of Little Note: Gender, Race, and Class in Historical Archaeology*, edited by Elizabeth M. Scott, pp. 175–208. University of Arizona Press, Tucson.
1996 Feminist Historical Archaeology and the Transformation of American Culture by Domestic Reform Movements, 1840–1925. *Proceedings of the 1991 Winterthur Conference*:397–445. Lu Ann De Cunzo, and Bernard L. Herman, editors. Winterthur Museum, Wilmington, DE.

STROBEL, A.
1926 The Old Plantations and Their Owners. In *A History of Brazoria County, Texas*, edited by T. L. Smith, pp. 15–62. Union National Bank, Houston, TX.

TAYLOR, BARBARA
1996 Genealogical Research in the Brazoria Community. Unpublished notes and interview data. On file, Anthropology Department, University of Houston, Houston, TX.

Carol McDavid

TILLEY, CHRISTOPHER
    1989   Archaeology as Socio-political Action in the Present.
            In *Critical Traditions in Contemporary Archaeology*,
            edited by Valerie Pinsky and Alison Wylie, pp. 104–
            116. Cambridge University Press, Cambridge, UK.

VANDERSLICE, PHILLIP
    1996   Plantation's Past Life: Excavation Slowly Uncovers
            History's Scars. *The Brazosport Facts*, 6 June:1A,
            5A. Brazosport, TX.

WEINER, JONATHAN M.
    1978   *Social Origins of the New South: Alabama, 1860–
            1885.* Louisiana State University Press, Baton Rouge.

WOODWARD, C. VANN
    1951   *The Origins of the New South.* Louisiana State
            University Press, Baton Rouge.

WRIGHT, CHERYL
    1994   *I Heard It Through the Grapevine: Oral Tradition in
            a Rural African American Community in Brazoria,
            Texas.* M. A. thesis, Department of Anthropology,
            University of Houston, Houston, TX. University
            Microfilms International, Ann Arbor, MI.

WYLIE, ALISON
    1985   Putting Shakertown Back Together. *Journal of
            Anthropological Archaeology* 4:133–147.

CAROL MCDAVID
CLARE HALL
UNIVERSITY OF CAMBRIDGE
CAMBRIDGE CB3 9AL, UNITED KINGDOM

COMMENTARY

THERESA A. SINGLETON

Facing the Challenges of a Public African-American Archaeology

Introduction

As archaeologists debate their social responsibilities to descendant African-American communities, it may be insightful to examine this issue within the larger context of public history. The role museums and the other cultural institutions play in the representation of cultural "others" has become a subject of considerable critique over the past decade. This justifiable criticism is forcing museums to rethink their purpose and has inspired a few to implement changes in their research, exhibitions, and collecting programs.

Despite these efforts, however, the public history of African-American life at historically white institutions is still in its infancy. Many institutions are in a quandary as to how to best represent African-American history, while the pioneering efforts of other institutions have come under attack. In this essay, I address some issues raised in the preceding articles by examining them within the larger discourse of museum representation. My aim is to illuminate ways that could lead to an enriched public archaeology of African-American life. I focus here on the public history of African-American life at historically white, "mainstream" museums and historic sites rather than those of African-American museums, historical societies, or preservation organizations. The contributions of these black institutions to the development of African-American public history have been detailed elsewhere (Stewart and Ruffins 1986; Horton and Crew 1989; Ruffins 1992). While I refer to some of the literature on this subject, my discussion is drawn from my own observations as a participant in exhibition projects, workshops, and review panels; through formal and informal museum visits; and ongoing dialogues with museum professionals and their constituencies over the past 15 years.

How Is African-American Public History Changing?

Why has African-American public history been so slow to develop at mainstream institutions?

Given the history of race relations in this country, some readers may consider the answer to the first question obvious. From a museum perspective, however, the answer is more complicated than simply attributing this development to racism. To be sure, racist ideologies were responsible for the failure of the museums to systematically collect objects and interpret African-American life prior to the Civil Rights Movement (Ruffins 1992:521–523), but racism alone does not explain the more recent reluctance of museums to interpret African-American life.

Museums have relied and, for the most part, continue to rely upon collections for exhibitions. Because active collecting of African-American material culture is a post-1960s development, collections of African-American objects are scarce and frequently uneven in scope. This is particularly true for objects dating to the 18th and 19th centuries. Thus the void of African-American objects presents a challenge to developing exhibitions consisting of traditional artifact displays. The scarcity of pre-20th-century objects combined with many museums' desire to exhibit only "authentic" objects—those with well-documented provenances—relegates the representation of African-American life to a few black-specific items. Repositories of collections emphasizing the decorative arts—furniture, silverware, textiles, so forth—are notorious for following this practice. Many house and plantation museums fall within this category, and they take pride in owning a black-made quilt or a piece of furniture. Too often, however, exhibiting these one or two items is the extent to which African-American life is interpreted.

In the absence of large collections of African-American objects predating 1900, museums are finding alternative ways of developing exhibits on African-American topics. White history exhibitions in general are increasingly reliant on multimedia presentations, those representing African-American life tend to emphasize visual and documentary materials, audio programs, or staged performances rather than objects. Photographic images of African-American form the focus for many exhibitions. While photographic sources dealing with the pre-emancipation era are limited, those of later periods remain an underutilized resource. Images captured by black photographers are particularly important because they usually depict aspects of African-American life that are virtually absent in the Public Works photographs of the 1920s and 1930s.

Findings from archaeological and other material culture studies of African-American life are being used to recreate living areas at historic sites. The Slave Quarter exhibit at Colonial Williamsburg Carter's Grove is one of the best known, and other similar recreations are now emerging. Excavated sites offer another possibility for interpretation. Monticello initiated a tour in 1995 of the exposed foundations from the structures that once housed the enslaved community at Mulberry Row, the industrial complex at Monticello. Archaeological materials are also finding their way into traditional artifact displays, particularly as archaeologists become more interested in producing popular formats of their research (e.g., Alexandria Archaeology 1992; Deagan and MacMahon 1995; Leone et al. 1995).

By canvassing numerous repositories for 18th- and 19th-century African-American materials, traditional exhibitions organized around objects are also possible. The traveling exhibition *Before Freedom Came: African American Life in the Antebellum South* (Campbell and Rice 1991), brought together over 250 objects, including archaeologically-recovered materials, from more than 90 public and private collections. Many of these objects had never been previously exhibited, and had thus generated interest in locating others possibly hidden away in collections.

Other exhibitions utilize extant collections containing items similar to ones African Americans owned. This strategy was successfully implemented in *Field to Factory: Afro-American Migration 1915–1940* (Crew 1987). Recreating a room setting, for example, was based upon extensive photographic and historical research. The actual objects used had no established connection with African Americans or the migration; however, they were historically correct and provided an accurate image of working-class African-American life (Crew and Sims 1990:171).

In the exhibition *Mining the Museum* (Corrin 1994), curator Fred Wilson takes an innovative approach to the reexamination of a museum collection for insights into the African-American experience. Framed as a critique of museum collecting and exhibiting practices, Wilson evaluates how and where African Americans are represented in the collection of the Maryland Historical Society in Baltimore. The institution's collection is characteristic of decorative arts museums. The exhibition exposes evidence of African-American identity in unexpected materials and restores that history by raising questions about the meaning of objects. Although public reactions to the exhibition have been mixed, even an eight-year-old child liked the exhibit because "Wilson asks more questions than he answers" (Corrin 1994:18).

Whereas the lack of collections no longer presents an insurmountable obstacle to developing museum programs on African-American life, limitations in funding and staff expertise in African-American history and culture pose continuing problems. Of the 8,200 museums in this country approximately 80 percent are classified as small organizations with annual incomes of less than $100,000 (American Association of Museums 1994:32). These small institutions frequently employ only one or two professionals who must be able to carry out a multitude of responsibilities. Oftentimes these individuals are not knowledgeable in African-American history, and do their best to organize an occasional program on African-American life, usually during Black History Month.

Even when funding and staff constraints are not major concerns, some museums are reluctant to develop programs in African-American life because previous efforts failed to attract black visitors. While the success or failure of any program varies with local circumstances, low black visitation is often an indicator of the absence of black participation in the project or neglecting to advertise in the black media and other venues within the black community. To encourage the visitation of diverse audiences, museums are involving these prospective audiences in the planning stages of exhibits. In some projects, community groups are organized to review exhibition ideas and plans. In others, museum staff have gone out into the community to solicit opinions on upcoming projects. Many museums use questionnaires about exhibitions to solict feedback on how the exhibits can be improved.

In a survey of museums across the country, James Horton and Spencer Crew found that museums with the most successful public programs in African-American history had a long-term commitment to developing African-American public programs; on-staff specialists in African-American studies or a black museum professional; and well-established ties with the local black communities for their input and support. These institutions also reported the highest levels of black visitation to their museums of all of those participating in the survey. For institutions with limited staff and resources, Horton and Crew (1989:227–229) recommended that special fundraising for African-American programming may be necessary.

What Does This Mean for Archaeology?

The previous discussion has significant implications for developing a public archaeology of African-American life. The lack of objects, of course, is not a problem for archaeological interpretation of African-American life. But how archaeologists interpret artifacts and sites remains a problem. For example, just as museums of decorative arts are narrowly focused on the few surviving objects made by African Americans, archaeologists are sometimes too narrowly focused on the few objects suggestive of African origins. Linda Derry's experience at Cahawba

illustrates this point. Black community members at Cahawba were not interested in their African heritage, but in stories that were relevant to their most recent history. This is not to say that archaeologists should abandon understanding the African heritage in the formation of African America, but an overemphasis of this issue may inhibit other lines of inquiry that are of interest to the communities we serve.

Similarly, the preoccupation in archaeology with classifying sites into cultural "types" oversimplifies our understanding of social interactions. Drake Patten argues that applying the label "African American" to the site once occupied by Catherine Foster obscures her identity as a mulatto both in the past and in the present. The revelation that Foster's present-day descendants identify themselves as white reaffirmed Patten's initial skepticism about labeling the site African American. Not only did the meaning of the site change for the black community, it also changed for the archaeologists who now lament adopting the t-shirt slogan—"ask me about African-American archaeology in Charlottesville." Patten's discussion raises several questions regarding the definition and purpose of African-American archaeology: How are African-American sites defined? If the Foster descendants considered themselves black or biracial—the current, popular term used to refer to persons of black-and-white heritage, would that fact have validated the site as African American? Is African-American archaeology simply the study of black-occupied sites? Can it also be a frame of reference within which sites are interpreted?

Like many archaeologists, Patten considers African-American archaeology to be the study of material culture recovered from black-occupied sites rather than as a lens through which material culture is interpreted. Horton and Crew (1989:228) remind us that "what is important about black history is the perspective and commentary it offers on the American experience." Archaeology should aim to capture this perspective. To accomplish this goal, African-American archaeology should be seen primarily as a way of framing questions pertinent to the African experience in the Americas. It is not necessary to restrict such questions to sites with an identifiable or discrete black provenience, but to any site that can illuminate aspects of African-American history and culture. This could very well include sites occupied by Euroamericans, for example, slaveholders, abolitionists, or laborers, as well as sites occupied by persons of mixed cultural or "racial heritage."

The Foster site may arguably not be an African-American site because it is unknown whether or not Catherine Foster acknowledged her African ancestry. Nonetheless, the site is important to African-American history and archaeology as it provides an opportunity to address questions concerning cultural identity and the construction of race. Patten takes issue with the fact the black community appropriated a mulatto as an African American; African Americans have historically claimed mulattoes because white America historically has not. At the same time, many mulattoes accepted the identity they shared with the blacks, and were often activists for the combined community. African-American archaeology at the Foster site should focus on how Catherine Foster perceived of her identity. Census records only provide indications of her physical appearance, not her cultural identity. It may be possible to infer Catherine and her family's cultural identity from records of the institutions—churches, mutual aid societies, schools, so forth—with which she and her family associated. These institutions played a key role in producing and in reproducing African-American culture.

Developing a public archaeology of African-American life must also consider the findings of Horton and Crew's museum survey. Of the issues raised in the survey, the one that deserves greater attention in archaeology is the need to employ black professionals and African Americanists in public archaeology programs. Black criticism of all-white archaeological teams conducting investigations of African-American sites should not be dismissed as "reverse racism." As La Roche and Blakey observe from their study of the African Burial Ground, such criticism stems from concerns that white archaeologists have a superficial knowledge of African-American history and culture, and are likely to interpret the archaeological record in such a way as to reinforce stereotypes of black life. These legitimate concerns have not received serious attention in archaeological practice. This should not be taken to mean that whites will deliberately misinterpret the archaeological record, but that white perspectives and those of blacks will not necessarily be the same.

An excellent illustration of the differences between black and white interpretations of archaeology is evident in the steel "hot comb" recovered from the Gott Court site in Annapolis, Maryland. Gott's Court was a series of connected houses built around 1906 and occupied by African-American tenants into the early 1950s. After an all-white archaeological team failed to identify the function of the artifact, an African-American woman explained to archaeologists that the steel comb was heated to straighten hair. With knowledge of the artifact's function, the archaeologists suggested that straightening hair was an effort to assimilate. The African Americans they consulted rejected that notion and proposed that the comb was used to give the appearance of assimilation (Leone et al. 1995:113–114).

Differences in the "hot comb" interpretation also point to the need for specialists in African-American studies to be engaged in archaeological research projects. Scholars have studied the African-American beauty tradition of which "hair straightening" is a part (e.g., Robinson 1984), and they could critically analyze the meaning of this practice. The "hot comb" may have initially arisen from an ideology of assimilation or one intended to give the appearance of assimilation, but it was later popularized and adopted by millions of black women worldwide. Even today, the "hot comb" and its chemical equivalents are widely used. At what point did the meaning of this artifact change? What does it mean today? Specialists in African-American studies are needed to raise and address the kinds of questions required in robust interpretations of the archaeological record.

There is an obvious need to incorporate black perspectives in African-American archaeology.

The question is how? The authors of all the essays included in this volume are to be commended for taking their research to the community, but community participation is not enough. Patten is correct in saying that communities look to scholars as the authorities. More importantly, communities are not the ultimate decision makers on how archaeology will be interpreted for either the academy or the public. The inclusion of specialists in African-American life increases the likelihood that black perspectives will be given a voice and receive critical treatment. It goes without saying that every project in African-American archaeology should aim to include specialists of African-American studies as part of the research team.

Celebratory or Social History of African-American Life?

A recurrent theme found in several of essays here and elsewhere (e.g., Leone et al. 1995) concerns the focus for public interpretations of African-American life. Several black communities informed the archaeologists that they were not interested in slavery, but in topics that "celebrated" their heritage. A celebratory history is derived from an ideology of success, and usually emphasizes well-known persons or events, individual achievements, and contributions to a society (Stewart and Ruffins 1986:307). The public history of "mainstream" America emerged from a focus on "celebrated" historical figures and events, and the thrust of most African-American public history, until the past 20 years, has also been celebratory (Stewart and Ruffins 1986; Ruffins 1992).

With the advent of the "new social history" of the 1970s, museums began to redirect their focus from celebrated people and events to the everyday lives of ordinary women, children, ethnic minorities, immigrants, slaves, mill workers, gays, and lesbians. Some museums have successfully made this transition, but many others have not. A recent critique suggests that social history is hard to find at American historic sites; what visitors confront are new themes of celebratory history:

Our monuments are still intended to be "inspiring"; to revere heroic ancestors more than understand their complexity; to forget the invisible labor of those who built much of the environment; to anchor us in a comfortable past, even if that past requires a carefully scaled replica to hide its flaws. Our desire is to have heroes who, though imperfect, are tragic because of the circumstances that crushed them, not because of personal shortcomings or the usual tonic of hubis. This is as true in our appraisal of George Washington as it is of Crazy Horse, Frederick Douglass, Junipero Serra, or Elizabeth Cady Stanton (Burham 1995:206).

Simply put, our goal in public archaeology should be to present social histories. Celebratory histories may offer the initial "hook" to get local communities interested in archaeology and public history, but in the long run, this kind of history is a disservice. Consider, for example, the exhibition on the slave trade, *Transatlantic Slavery: Against Human Dignity* (Tibble 1994), at the Merseyside Maritime Museum in Liverpool, England. Audience surveys taken before and after the exhibition opened revealed that many visitors were unaware of England's role in the slave trade. In fact, many thought slavery was an institution largely confined to the southern United States, according to Alison Taubman (1994, pers. comm.), project manager of the Transatlantic Slavery gallery, Mersyside Maritime Museum in Liverpool. As scholars, we know Great Britain had a major stake in the transatlantic slave trade, made huge profits from it, and imported many more slaves to the sugar islands than to all of North America. We cannot assume, however, that the general public has this knowledge. Without a public history based on social history, historical subjects remain invisible and eventually get lost in public memory.

Slavery is too important a topic in the African-American experience to push aside. Increasingly, museums are interpreting slavery. Monticello has taken a lead in organizing a network of museum professionals to discuss how to best interpret it. Although public interpretation of this subject is increasing, these presentations are still problematical. At many plantation museums, visitors are introduced to social history in tours of the slave quarters, but celebratory history persists in the tour of the "big house."

Similarly, a study of interpretation at Colonial Williamsburg revealed that the history of whites is presented as factual, making it appear more truthful than black history, which is presented as conjectural (Gable et al. 1992). The public interpretation of slavery or of all African-American life will not be effective unless efforts are taken to reconcile these competing histories. The schism between the two histories may also explain why some black communities have no desire to see slavery represented in public history.

Implementation of a public history based upon social history will require changing what people perceive as important about the past. Heroic deeds, success stories, and contributions to society only tell part of the story. Uncomfortable topics such as miscegenation or "passing," or the ugly issues of the brutalities of the slave trade or land evictions, are aspects of the past that need to be interpreted. Reenactments of slave auctions or recreations of slave ship interiors may not be the best techniques to convey these ideas, but avoiding these topics increases the chances that they will be misremembered or forgotten. Social history can often be incorporated into existing museum interpretation, as Philip Burnham illustrates using an example from a house tour: "A simple cupboard can lead us to talk about the craftspeople who built it; the kind of community they live in; where the raw materials were found; how the object was transported for sale; who moved the piece from the dock; what kind of god their children believed in; and how the owner accumulated the wealth that permitted him (or her) to buy it in the first place" (Burnham 1995:215).

What Can Archaeology Do?

Obviously, archaeology cannot resolve the tension between celebratory and social history, nor can it provide answers to the questions which developing an African-American public history poses. Archaeology, however, does resonate well with many African Americans, something I have discovered over the years when introducing African-American archaeology to black audiences. For African Americans, archaeology offers a tangible association with real places and the people who once lived at those places; it partially restores the artifactual legacy of African-American life that museum curators, field researchers, and black intellectuals dismissed as unimportant and did not collect; it unveils stories missing from official records and other documents written by people who did not understand African-American culture; and it empowers communities to have a voice in the interpretation and preservation of their heritage.

The essays in this volume attest to the difficulties of developing a public archaeology of African-American life for which there are no easy solutions: black and white perspectives will differ; advocates for celebratory history and those for social history will collide; archaeologists will disagree on how to involve communities, what constitutes African-American archaeology, and whether or not archaeology can be apolitical.

African-American archaeology is clearly moving into a new realm where its public is helping to set the agenda. While some archaeologists appear to be uncomfortable about this development (e.g., McKee 1994), it is nonetheless making us more socially responsible and credible about what we say and do. In time, the public's influence may help us recognize that African-American archaeology is more than the study of black-occupied sites, but a way of framing issues pertinent to understanding the African diaspora.

REFERENCES

ALEXANDRIA ARCHAEOLOGY
  1993 To Witness the Past: African American Archaeology in Alexandria, Virginia. *Catalogue of Exhibition.* Alexandria Archaeology Museum, City of Alexandria, VA.

AMERICAN ASSOCIATION OF MUSEUMS
  1994 *Museums Count.* American Association of Museums, Washington, DC.

BURNHAM, PHILIP
  1995 *How the Other Half Lived: A People's Guide to American Historic Sites.* Faber and Faber, Boston, MA, and London.

CAMPBELL, EDWARD D. C., JR., AND KYM S. RICE (EDITORS)

1991   *Before Freedom Came: African American Life in the Antebellum South.* University Press of Virginia, Charlottesville.

CORRIN, LISA G. (EDITOR)

1994   *Mining the Museum: An Installation by Fred Wilson.* The Contemporary, Baltimore, MD, in cooperation with the New Press, NY.

CREW, SPENCER

1987   *Field to Factory: Afro-American Migration 1915–1940.* National Museum of American History, Smithsonian Institution, Washington, DC.

CREW, SPENCER, AND JAMES E. SIMS

1990   Locating Authenticity: Fragments of a Dialogue. In *Exhibiting Cultures*, edited by Ivan Karp and Steven D. Lavine, pp. 159–175. Smithsonian Institution Press, Washington, DC.

DEAGAN, KATHLEEN, AND DARCIE MACMAHON

1995   *Fort Mose: Colonial America's Black Fortress of Freedom.* University of Florida Press, Gainesville.

GABLE, ERIC, RICHARD HANDLER, AND ANNA LAWSON

1992   On the Uses of Relativism: Fact, Conjecture and Black and White Histories at Colonial Williamsburg. *American Ethnologist* 19:791–805.

HORTON, JAMES O., AND SPENCER R. CREW

1989   Afro-Americans and Museums: Toward a Policy of Inclusion. In *History Museums in the United States: A Critical Assessment*, edited by Warren Leon and Roy Rosenzweig, pp. 215–236. University of Illinois Press, Urbana.

LEONE, MARK P., PAUL R. MULLINS, MARIAN C. CREVELING, LAURENCE HURST, BARBARA JACKSON-NASH, LYNN D. JONES, HANNAH JOPLING KAISER, GEORGE C. LOGAN, AND MARK S. WARNER

1995   Can African-American Historical Archaeology Be an Alternative Voice? In *Interpreting Archaeology:*

Finding Meaning in the Past, edited by Ian Hodder, Michael Shanks, Alexandra Alexandri, Victor Buchil, John Carman, Jonathan Last, and Gavin Lucas. Routledge, London.

MCKEE, LARRY

1994   Commentary: Is It Futile to Try and Be Useful? Historical Archaeology and the African-American Experience. *Northeast Historical Archaeology* 23:1–7.

ROBINSON, GWEDOLYN

1984   *Class, Race, and Gender: A Transcultural Theoretical and Sociohistorical Analysis of Cosmetic Institutions and Practices to 1920.* Ph.D. dissertation, Department of History, University of Illinois, Chicago. University Microfilms International, Ann Arbor, MI.

RUFFINS, FATH DAVIS

1992   Myths, Memory, and History: African American Preservation Efforts, 1820–1990. In *Museums and Communities: The Politics of Public Culture*, edited by Ivan Karp, Christine Mullen Kreamer, and Steven D. Lavine, pp. 506–611. Smithsonian Institution Press, Washington, DC.

STEWART, JEFFERY, AND FATH D. RUFFINS

1986   A Faithful Witness: Afro-American Public History in Historical Perspective, 1828–1984. In *Presenting the Past: Essays on History and the Public*, edited by Susan Porter Benson, Stephen Brier, and Roy Rosenzweig, pp. 307–336. Temple University Press, Philadelphia, PA.

TIBBLES, ANTHONY (EDITOR)

1994   *Transatlantic Slavery: Against Human Dignity.* National Museums and Galleries on Merseyside. HMSO, London.

THERESA A. SINGLETON
DEPARTMENT OF ANTHROPOLOGY
SYRACUSE UNIVERSITY
SYRACUSE, NY 13244

ANNA S. AGBE-DAVIES

An Engaged Archaeology for Our Mutual Benefit: The Case of New Philadelphia

Of all of the factors to shape archaeological practice—curiosity about the peoples and events of the past, a desire for a more scientific approach, or the willingness to embrace ambiguity, just to name a few—it may be that the most revolutionary of all will be the discipline's halting realization that archaeologists do not practice in a vacuum. In reviewing the research output for the first three seasons of historical research, excavation, and analysis of the site at New Philadelphia, one is struck by how profoundly this project has been shaped in a positive manner by the principals' attention to the contexts within which they work, and the way in which their work reverberates in the world. Archaeologists have become accustomed to asserting that their work improves the world: ancient wisdom is revived to solve modern problems; lost or neglected stories are brought to light by the "democratic" discipline; and the roots of current social conditions are revealed, the better to transform the present. These beliefs sustain many archaeologists in their work, and examples of such benefits can be found within this volume. But here is also an extended case study, with detailed examples, that demonstrates not only how archaeology can save the world, but how engagement with the world can save archaeology. The authors contributing to this volume provide a multifaceted description of one particular research project, and in doing so demonstrate how community engagement shapes and benefits archaeological practice.

The ways in which this phenomenon is manifested can be grouped, for the purposes of this essay, under several mutually inclusive headings. One might consider how community engagement touches upon themes at the forefront of current archaeological research, or how that engagement intersects with enduring themes that have shaped the field for many years. One could examine the juxtaposition of various stakeholder perceptions of, and uses for the past and its residues. Finally, one can contemplate how this transformed archaeology fits with the categories customarily used to partition archaeological work—period, region, cultural group, and social institution. These various stances are used to frame the remarks which follow.

At whatever scale it is considered—archaeology, historical archaeology, African diaspora archaeology—the New Philadelphia project reflects the themes and concerns that shape contemporary archaeological practice. This aspect is of particular interest to me, as I joined this long-term project as a co-director starting in 2008. Researchers are animated by a variety of questions. How can technology be harnessed to wrest interpretations from the landscape? What new ways of thinking about material culture will allow greater insight into the lives of those who made, used, and discarded those things? How to best communicate project findings? Researchers also reconsider the topics and institutions investigated and the research questions that drive the work, in part because of increased attention to, and appreciation for the complexity of relationships with stakeholders.

The traditional means of publication and dissemination of archaeological knowledge through monographs, conference presentations, and journal articles has been joined by a number of other forums and venues that extend the reach of scholarship, and bring it to the attention of broader and more diverse audiences. The New Philadelphia team maintains two websites, available at <http://www.heritage.umd.edu> and <http://www.anthro.uiuc.edu/faculty/cfennell/NP/>. Both sites present material for a lay readership, as well as the standard technical reports, and in doing so join a number of other recent projects notable for the accessibility of raw data and incremental developments, as well as working interpretations (McDavid 2004; African Burial Ground 2007; Digital Archaeological Archive of Comparative Slavery 2007). The New Philadelphia project made these electronic resources broadly accessible long before the publication of the present volume. This is not an accident, as observed by Paul Shackel in his introduction to this volume. An engaged archaeology is an accountable archaeology. Ready access to data and transparent interpretive procedures build trust and credibility among stakeholders, no less than they do within the profession. Likewise, in responding to the challenges of non-archaeologists, researchers are compelled to consider their own ideologies and the partial perspectives that are part of archaeology's culture.

The fact that archaeology is being undertaken at sites like New Philadelphia, where one learns about emancipation and interracial relations, as opposed to slavery and its attendant social distinctions, is itself a response to the interests of the public, particularly a black public, which is sometimes, but not always as fascinated by "the peculiar institution" as are social scientists (Derry 1997; Watters 2001; Leone et al. 2005). Indeed, other institutions are coming to the fore in African diaspora archaeology, including schools (Sprinkle 1994; Agbe-Davies 2002; Helton, this volume). In the process of developing a research program on the archaeology of the African diaspora in Chicago, I have been struck by the number of requests by community members to investigate sites other than residences. This runs counter to long-term trends in African diaspora archaeology, in which homes and graves have been the predominant focus—the latter being a mixed bag as far as many stakeholders are concerned. Rather, people seek an archaeological perspective on important community institutions: clubs, businesses, theaters, churches, or "institutional" residences. An example of the last is the Phyllis Wheatley Home for Girls, where for the last two years archaeologists and students from DePaul University have had the privilege of working with community educators and preservation activists to remind the city of the struggles and triumphs of the women who founded, and those who resided in the Home (Bobbie Johnson 2006, pers. comm., 2007, pers. comm.; Joann Tate 2006, pers. comm., 2007, pers. comm.; Agbe-Davies [2008]). Think of the expanded picture of American lives that is obtained when not just houses, but the array of spaces in which people spent their days is considered!

With this infusion of new subjects and increased openness to research questions that inspire a general audience, comes a more complex relationship among the various stakeholders in an archaeological project or site. An interesting discussion of the very term "stakeholder" occurred at the annual conference of the Society for Historical Archaeology in 2007, which included an open-forum discussion of research designs and methods in African diaspora archaeology (Fennell 2007). As I recall, the conversation began with an assertion from the floor that to use the term "stakeholder" was to engage in gratuitous and politically correct wordsmithing, and that the customary term "audience" was perfectly adequate. I do not remember how the question was resolved, but it did get me thinking. What role do archaeologists envision for those who witness their efforts? What makes the New Philadelphia project—and any number of its contemporaries—notable is the fact that the term "stakeholder" is no mere lip service or jargon, but reflects an actual appreciation for the stake—the risk, the investment, the claim—that such individuals and groups do indeed hold in the research and its outcomes. Audiences look and listen. Stakeholders engage and often challenge, a dynamic that may encourage archaeologists to see themselves as stakeholders as well (LaRoche and Blakey 1997; Epperson 2004). Throughout the contributions to this volume one observes the traces of the ways in which various stakeholders—including descendants of New Philadelphia residents, McWorter family members, current inhabitants of the region, scholars in other fields, and collectors and providers of oral history testimony—have done more than just absorb the information that emanates from the archaeological team working at New Philadelphia. Instead, they have asked difficult questions and pushed for clarity in analysis and interpretation, doubtless to the benefit of the final result.

As archaeologists become more explicit about the impact they hope their scholarship will have on "the real world" (see, for example, the contributions to "community archaeology" in *World Archaeology*, vol. 34, no. 2), they have also sought mechanisms to inculcate these values in the next generation of researchers. As Michael Nassaney (2004:89) notes, archaeologists were advocates for experiential learning long before it became a pedagogical buzzword, and their work is often conceived as serving some larger purpose. Projects like New Philadelphia bring the processes of service learning explicitly into archaeological instruction (such as the contributions to Nassaney and Levine 2007). The students who participate in the Research Experience for Undergraduates program at New Philadelphia certainly learn state-of-the-art archaeological methods, but true to the model of service learning, their education comes through the process of serving a function useful to some constituency, namely those who wish to perpetuate and enlarge upon the legacy of Frank McWorter and his neighboring townsfolk (Martin et al. 2004; Christopher Fennell, Terrance Martin, and Paul Shackel 2005, pers. comm., 2007, pers. comm.).

Despite the many ways in which the endeavors described in this volume point towards the future of archaeological practice, one can also see traces of themes that have endured for years and continue to shape the field. For example, there is a continued pursuit of ways in which material culture might be used to distinguish among the former occupants of the town site, whether along racial/ethnic lines, or in terms of regional origin, occupation, or gender. Also apparent is the tension that often exists between various local and traditional understandings of a site and its contents, and the archaeologists' interpretations of that evidence, not to mention conflicting descendant perceptions of the site and its meanings.

As Shackel (this volume) notes in his contribution on ceramics, African diaspora archaeology has often been preoccupied with the persistence of traditions. Yet the artifacts of New Philadelphia, like so many other sites, frustrate attempts to find clear differences between, for example, assemblages associated with African American and European American occupants. Although the problems associated with a focus on patterns, or Africanisms, or markers is acknowledged (Howson 1990; Edwards 1994; Singleton 2006), in analyses archaeologists often revert to familiar tropes that arguably have shaped anthropology and archaeology since their inception—that by their works you shall know them (Morgan 1877). To use the examples at hand, this volume includes not only the comparison of ceramic assemblages from white and black households, but also a discussion of distinctive features of

black cemeteries (King), and distinctive faunal assemblages that may signal the racial/ethnic, or perhaps regional roots of the features' creators (T. Martin and C. Martin).

The questions may be traditional, but I see interesting ways forward, in this volume and elsewhere, that avoid an essentialist "pots = people" equation. These ways are grounded in concepts of ethnicity reaching back to Barth (1969), and even Weber (1978). This concept of ethnicity can be expanded for analytical purposes to encompass categories of "race," with a resulting focus on "racial/ethnic" contours (Agbe-Davies 1999). Following such frameworks, archaeologists can begin to consider the work that ethnic categories do, and how material culture might be implicated in that work. Such a perspective requires, first, a new flexibility about the variables relied on to construct analyses of difference versus sameness among material items (Brown and Cooper 1990; Barile 2004). Second, archaeologists must stop trying to use material culture to do what texts can do better (Schuyler 1988). For example, a census can label the members of a household "white," "black," or "mulatto." Archaeologists should use *their* toolkit to consider how material culture might have been deployed to maintain these stated boundaries, or in competition among people so labeled, or as traces of the prizes won or lost (Mullins 1999). As Theresa Singleton (2006:265) observes, essentialist interpretations do speak to the questions and interests of some stakeholders. Nevertheless, it is the responsibility of archaeologists to ensure that their analyses and interpretations acknowledge the simultaneous mutability and rigidity of social categories (Armstrong 2008; Mullins 2008).

Another enduring theme, one that appears with an updated twist in these collected contributions, is the tension between local/popular/traditional/community narratives of New Philadelphia's past, and those that emerge from research by historical archaeologists. The contributors discuss how they have negotiated the terrain between memories of racial harmony and recollections of structural racism, bigotry, and indeed, race-based terrorism. These efforts go a long way toward "complicating our national narrative" (Paul Shackel 2007, pers. comm.). As a result of the New Philadelphia project, a great deal has been learned about slavery and race-based servitude in a "free" state. To be sure, all of these complications are entering the public sphere through a concerted program of undergraduate instruction, but perhaps more significantly, also through the engagement of local community members and descendants with the research process, rather than their receipt of the research team's interpretations as faits accomplis.

In fact, the involvement of "local community members" and "descendants" also brings to the fore interesting and productive tensions. Against claims of integration and amity can be set descriptions of segregation (in the cemetery and in the school, King, Christman, and Helton in this volume). Should the reader be surprised by the diversity of recollections? Ask any ten people if affirmative action is still necessary, or what constitutes a "hate crime," and one will see the possibilities for wildly ranging interpretations of *current* social conditions, let alone those translated through generations and through memory. The analyses described here take that tension and use it to forge stronger, more nuanced, and perhaps ultimately truer interpretations of the oral, written, and material records.

Discussion of the disjuncture between local residents, New Philadelphia descendants, and McWorter descendants does beg the questions: Who are the African American residents of this region today? Do they have any links with New Philadelphia? Whether they do or do not, what do they think of the project, and what does it mean to them? Also worthy of notice is the enthusiasm of most oral-history interviewees and non-archaeologist stakeholders for the excavation and associated research (Christman, this volume). Perhaps it is only to be expected, given that the project's impetus lay in the recruitment of academic specialists by the local community (Shackel's Introduction, this volume), but it speaks to the diligence and goodwill of all parties that the relationship continues to be fruitful.

I wish to conclude with a brief discussion of how the contributions to this volume, and the ongoing project that they represent, fit with and advance several genres of archaeological investigation. A number of keywords might be used to categorize the articles assembled here: "19th century," "African diaspora," "frontier," "interracial," "Midwest," and "townsite" come to mind. It is my hope that the assembled data and resulting interpretations from New Philadelphia

will push the boundaries of archaeological thinking of all of these fields.

The apparent lack of segregated districts within the town could help advance the appreciation of how boundaries were maintained, transgressed, and challenged in the United States from the antebellum through Jim Crow eras. Studies of the New Philadelphia site provide a wonderful contrast with studies of residential and social segregation available from other communities of the same period. Furthermore, the emerging story of the town is a useful comparison to other "all black" towns and communities of the rural Midwest (McCorvie 2005; Demel and Kusimba 2007; Wood 2007).

I would also like to see New Philadelphia as a model for deconstructing notions of homogeneity and defeatist attitudes about the possibility of using mass-produced material culture to say anything useful about culturally patterned behavior. Such notions seem to pervade archaeological studies of the 19th and 20th centuries, and of the Midwest in particular (Wilson 1990; Barile 2004). Of course, such lofty goals cannot be accomplished using the same variables, criteria, and analytical strategies that have led to the conclusion that somehow *mass production + marketing + consumerism = homogeneity*. This is where the hard work of devising novel analytical techniques comes in. Evidence of this creativity is present throughout the assembled articles. Let the readers judge the contributors' efforts and how they might transform the readers' own practices.

References

AFRICAN BURIAL GROUND

2007   The African Burial Ground: Return to the Past to Build the Future. National Parks Service, New York, NY <http://www.africanburialground.gov/ABG_FinalReports.htm>.

AGBE-DAVIES, ANNA S.

1999   The Legacy of "Race" in African-American Archaeology: A Silk Purse from the Wolf's Ears? Paper presented at World Archaeology Congress 4, Cape Town, South Africa <http://www.wac.uct.ac.za/wac4/symposia/papers/S074gbd1.pdf>.

2002   Archaeology of the Old Elliot School. *Bermuda Journal of Archaeology and Maritime History* 13:129–154.

2008   Public Archaeology and the Continuing Legacy of Uplift and Female Empowerment at the Phyllis Wheatley Home for Girls, Chicago. Paper presented at the 14th Annual Berkshire Conference on the History of Women, Minneapolis, MN.

[2008] Community Archaeology in Bronzeville: The Phyllis Wheatley Home for Girls. *Ohio Valley Historical Archaeology* 23:23–29.

ARMSTRONG, DOUGLAS V.
2008 Excavating African American Heritage: Towards a More Nuanced Understanding of the African Diaspora. *Historical Archaeology* 42(2):123–127.

BARILE, KERRI S.
2004 Race, the National Register, and Cultural Resource Management: Creating an Historic Context for Postbellum Sites. *Historical Archaeology* 38(1):90–100.

BARTH, FREDRIK
1969 Introduction. In *Ethnic Groups and Boundaries: The Social Organization of Cultural Differences*, Frederik Barth, editor, pp. 9–38. George Allen and Unwin, London, UK.

BROWN, KENNETH L., AND DOREEN C. COOPER
1990 Structural Continuity in an African-American Slave and Tenant Community. *Historical Archaeology* 24(4):7–19.

DEMEL, SCOTT J., AND CHAPURUKHA M. KUSIMBA
2007 Reconstructing Heritage in Central Illinois. The Field Museum, Chicago, IL <http://www.fieldmuseum.org/expeditions/chap_expedition/about.html>.

DERRY, LINDA
1997 Pre-Emancipation Archaeology: Does It Play in Selma, Alabama? *Historical Archaeology* 31(3):18–26.

DIGITAL ARCHAEOLOGICAL ARCHIVE OF COMPARATIVE SLAVERY
2007 Digital Archaeological Archive of Comparative Slavery (DAACS). Thomas Jefferson Foundation, Charlottesville, VA <http://www.daacs.org>.

EDWARDS, YWONE D.
1994 Beyond "Africanisms": Recent Approaches to African-American Archaeology. Paper presented at the Annual Meeting of the National Association of African-American Studies, Petersburg, VA.

EPPERSON, TERRENCE W.
2004 Critical Race Theory and the Archaeology of the African Diaspora. *Historical Archaeology* 38(1):101–108.

FENNELL, CHRISTOPHER C. (ORGANIZER)
2007 Research Designs for Atlantic Africa and African Diaspora Archaeologies. Forum held at the Annual Meeting of the Society for Historical Archaeology Conference on Historical and Underwater Archaeology, Williamsburg, VA.

HOWSON, JEAN E.
1990 Social Relations and Material Culture: A Critique of the Archaeology of Plantation Slavery. *Historical Archaeology* 24(4):78–91.

LA ROCHE, CHERYL J., AND MICHAEL L. BLAKEY
1997 Seizing Intellectual Power: The Dialogue at the New York African Burial Ground. *Historical Archaeology* 31(3):84–106.

LEONE, MARK P., CHERYL JANIFER LA ROCHE, AND JENNIFER J. BARBIARZ
2005 The Archaeology of Black Americans in Recent Times. Annual Review of Anthropology 34:575–598.

MARTIN, TERRANCE J., PAUL A. SHACKEL, AND CHRISTOPHER FENNELL
2004 New Philadelphia: The XYZs of the First Excavations. *Living Museum* 66(4):8–13.

McCORVIE, MARY
2005 Archeological Griots: An Environmental History Program at Miller Grove, a Free Ante-Bellum African American Community in Southern Illinois. *African Diaspora Archaeology Newsletter*, December African Diaspora Archaeology Network, University of Illinois, Urbana-Champaign <http://www.diaspora.uiuc.edu/news1205/news1205.html#1>.

McDAVID, CAROL
2004 From "Traditional" Archaeology to Public Archaeology to Community Action. In *Places in Mind: Public Archaeology as Applied Anthropology*, Paul A. Shackel and Erve Chambers, editors, pp. 35–56. Routledge, New York, NY.

MORGAN, LEWIS HENRY
1877 *Ancient Society or Researches in the Lines of Human Progress from Savagery through Barbarism to Civilization.* Charles H. Kerr & Co., Chicago, IL.

MULLINS, PAUL R.
1999 A Bold and Gorgeous Front: The Contradictions of African America and Consumer Culture. In *Historical Archaeologies of Capitalism*, Mark P. Leone and Parker B. Potter, Jr., editors, pp. 169–193. Kluwer Academic/Plenum Publishers, New York, NY.
2008 Excavating America's Metaphor: Race, Diaspora, and Vindicationist Archaeologies. *Historical Archaeology* 42(2):104–122.

NASSANEY, MICHAEL, AND MARY ANN LEVINE (ORGANIZERS)
2007 Archaeological Practice and Community Service Learning. Symposium held at the Annual Meeting of the Society for Historical Archaeology Conference on Historical and Underwater Archaeology, Williamsburg, VA.

NASSANEY, MICHAEL S.
2004 Implementing Community Service Learning through Archaeological Practice. *Michigan Journal of Community Service Learning* 10(3):89–99.

SCHUYLER, ROBERT L.
1988 Archaeological Remains, Documents, and Anthropology: A Call for a New Culture History. *Historical Archaeology* 22(1):36–42.

SINGLETON, THERESA A.
    2006   African Diaspora Archaeology in Dialogue. In *Afro-Atlantic Dialogues: Anthropology in the Diaspora.* Kevin A. Yelvington, editor, pp. 249–287. School of American Research Press, Santa Fe, NM.

SPRINKLE, JOHN
    1994   Manassas Industrial School. *African-American Archaeology Newsletter* 10(Spring).

WATTERS, DAVID R.
    2001   Historical Archaeology in the British Caribbean. In *Island Lives: Historical Archaeologies of the Caribbean.* Paul Farnsworth, editor, pp. 82–99. University of Alabama Press, Tuscaloosa.

WEBER, MAX
    1978   Ethnic Groups. In *Economy and Society*, Vol. 1, pp. 385–398. University of California Press, Berkeley, CA.

WILSON, JOHN S.
    1990   We've Got Thousands Of These! What Makes an Historic Farmstead Significant? *Historical Archaeology* 24(2):23–33.

WOOD, MARGARET
    2007   Wake Nicodemus: African American Settlement on the Plains of Kansas. National Park Service, Washington, DC <http://www.nps.gov/archeology/sites/npSites/nicodemus.htm>.

ANNA S. AGBE-DAVIES
DEPARTMENT OF ANTHROPOLOGY
DEPAUL UNIVERSITY
2343 N. RACINE AVE.
CHICAGO, IL 60614

2011 Archaeologies of Race and Urban Poverty: The Politics of Slumming, Engagement, and the Color Line. In *Archaeologies of Engagement, Representation, and Identity*, Paul A. Shackel and David A. Gadsby, editors. Thematic issue, *Historical Archaeology* 45(1):33-50

Paul R. Mullins
Lewis C. Jones

Archaeologies of Race and Urban Poverty: The Politics of Slumming, Engagement, and the Color Line

ABSTRACT

For more than a century, social reformers and scholars have examined urban impoverishment and inequalities along the color line and linked "slum life" to African America. An engaged archaeology provides a powerful mechanism to assess how urban-renewal and tenement-reform discourses were used to reproduce color and class inequalities. Such an archaeology should illuminate how comparable ideological distortions are wielded in the contemporary world to reproduce longstanding inequalities. A 20th-century neighborhood in Indianapolis, Indiana, is examined to probe how various contemporary constituencies borrow from, negotiate, and refute long-established urban impoverishment and racial discourses and stake claims to diverse present-day forms of community heritage.

Introduction: Reimagining the Slum

Soon after the turn of the 20th century, a massive wooden tower rose in the Indianapolis, Indiana, backyard at 458–460 Agnes Street. The tightly packed near-Westside neighborhood had been quickly built up after about 1870, when waves of European and Southern immigrants settled throughout the area and built homes along the city's western edge. As in many late-19th- and early-20th-century neighborhoods, residents and landlords soon built extra stories, expanded into yard spaces, and even converted stables and alley outbuildings into makeshift homes. Constructed in the 1870s as a single-story double, the home on Agnes Street had been expanded upward into a four-unit residence just after 1900, and the household expansion demanded additional outhouse space. While surrounding residents dug, cleaned, and redug a patchwork of outhouses throughout their ever-shrinking yards, the residents at 458–460 Agnes Street erected a comparatively colossal two-story outhouse (Figure 1). The brick-lined privy, 8 ft. to a side, could be accessed from the ground level or a second-floor walkway that extended into the yard, where the large outhouse loomed over the neighboring outbuildings and even some of the nearby homes. The outhouse remained in the yard until just after 1955, when it was finally dismantled not long before most of the block itself was razed.

In 1970 an administrator at Indiana University-Purdue University, Indianapolis (IUPUI) described the outhouse as an "architectural and engineering marvel," but by then the outhouse had been dismantled for 15 years and its brick foundation sat beneath a university parking lot. In the subsequent years the outhouse has fascinated faculty, students, and community members, but most of that fascination has revolved around the mechanics of the tower, fostering a string of jokes about which campus constituency deserved the upper-story seat (Gray 2003:43). The superficial humor in the outhouse discourse reflects understandable wonder about the structure as an engineering feat as well as curiosity about such a seemingly alien sanitary mechanism. Yet the outhouse jokes also betray many of the ways in which historical experiences are evaded or even misrepresented for particular contemporary purposes. For example, the outhouse is sometimes inelegantly offered as a symbol evoking neighborhood poverty and celebrating city and university progress. A 2004 volume comparing historical and contemporary Indianapolis photographs of the same spaces used this approach, borrowing stale slum-clearance terms that when placed beneath a 1941 image of the outhouse refer to the outhouse's neighborhood as "poverty stricken" and "blighted." The grainy black-and-white picture of the Agnes Street outhouse contrasted radically with a picturesque contemporary campus image on the facing page that proclaimed: "Out with the outhouses, in with IUPUI, one of the nation's largest urban campuses. The site of the former outhouse is now the $32 million IUPUI library" (Price 2004:89).

The outhouse (which was not actually under the library) was excavated in 2003, and the dynamic and often-contested interpretations of the archaeological assemblage, the neighborhood's history, and the outhouse itself reveal the complex heritage claims made in most cities.

Paul R. Mullins and Lewis C. Jones

FIGURE 1. In September 1941 realtor Howard W. Fieber took this picture of the two-story outhouse at 458–460 Agnes Street. (Photo courtesy of IUPUI University Library Special Collections and Archives, 1941.)

Slum caricatures that long legitimized urban displacement through references to race, space, and affluence are today relatively untenable, yet the Agnes Street outhouse is still routinely invoked as a symbol that risks distorting the community's heritage, placing poverty at the heart of community heritage, and rationalizing the neighborhood residents' mass displacement. Selective incorporation of slum history has furthered a vast range of contemporary material and social interests in many similar communities, turning many former slum landscapes into gentrified neighborhoods and urban university campuses while linking "slum" identities to community heritage and the color line.

Archaeology offers one mechanism to dissect such discourses, but slum narratives should not be reduced simply to misrepresentations that are contradicted by the historical and material realities revealed through archaeology. Alan Mayne (2007:321) champions a complex notion of slum stereotypes that acknowledges the concrete effects of the bourgeois imagination of space

and social identity. Mayne acknowledges that slum discourses certainly were self-interested rationalizations that were not necessarily especially reliable representations of material context. Nevertheless, urban narratives have always been profoundly shaped by these frameworks for defining, framing, and discussing poverty, space, and race on urban landscapes. Archaeology provides a mechanism to examine reflectively the concrete material conditions of urban marginalization, but especially interesting insights still come from examining the ways in which contemporary stakeholders, ranging from former residents to the university, define and claim the near-Westside's community heritage, often reacting against slum stereotypes even as they borrow from or accept forms of impoverishment in such narratives.

These stakeholders have conflicting visions of community, much like a century of urban reformers, slum ideologues, and residents before them. The contradictions within neighborhood historical discourses and archaeological material

296

culture reveal how history has been wielded along various lines of inequality, so it makes little sense to attempt to resolve dissentious notions of community and heritage and replace them with a monolithic archaeological narrative or an imposed notion of community. In this discourse on community heritage, the Agnes Street outhouse figures as a multivalent symbol. For instance, defining the outhouse as a material vestige of "slum life" hazards reproducing stale stereotypes and posing an ambiguous notion of urban improvement; that is, the outhouse is used to demonstrate the reader's contemporary distance from poverty while it ignores the roots of present-day social privilege. Other constituents may be uncomfortable with linking the outhouse to poverty's social stigmatization at all, but the outhouse demonstrates a profound color-based inequality in the very recent past, and evading the realities of impoverishment sidesteps these inequalities in favor of a transparent American Dream story. Still other university constituencies are simply dismayed that an academic institution with significant scholarly accomplishments and ambition has its heritage repeatedly tied back to an outhouse instead of many other more appealing histories.

Since 2000, archaeological excavations have been conducted in Indianapolis's near-Westside to illuminate the displacement of neighborhood residents and examine how archaeological insight might temper the stereotypes that rationalized urban renewal and continue to reduce community heritage to class and racial caricatures. After World War II the Indiana University Medical Center expanded into the neighborhood containing the outhouse, armed with the slum stereotypes used to rationalize wholesale displacement in much of postwar urban America (Mullins 2003). After IUPUI was officially established in 1969, the new campus quickly took aim at the surrounding neighborhoods to accommodate suburban-commuter parking and the growth of the university, which soon enveloped several hundred acres of former neighborhoods. Archaeological fieldwork and oral historical research has been conducted in partnership with neighborhood elders, university constituencies, and other city residents who stake various claims to the community's heritage, and much of the discussion, of the outhouse in particular and near-Westside heritage in general, revolves around slum stereotypes and poverty. During excavations of

the Agnes Street site in 2003, elders who lived in the near-Westside were interviewed about life in these neighborhoods that local historical discourses simply reduce to slums. Former residents acknowledge the material realities of impoverishment, but they paint poverty in ways that reveal it to be an important but not deterministic backdrop to their lives, much as racism is often portrayed. Elders sometimes use poverty as a rhetorical foil to underscore the magnitude of their ambitions and accomplishments and stress that the black community's distinctive contemporary character reflects shared African American negotiations of material scarcity and color-line segregation. This position is less a refutation of poverty than it is a rejection of ideologically loaded slum caricatures that present urban poverty as a reflection of essential African American attributes or a structural framework that determined the lives of African Americans. The contentious history of the neighborhood's landscape, the discourses over urban space, and the apparently prosaic materiality of the outhouse promise an interesting, if complex, picture of the intersection of race and heritage.

"Slumming" and the Aesthetics of Urban Poverty

Privileged thinkers have routinely "slummed" it in urban neighborhoods, using forays into marginalized communities to champion particular moralistic visions of community (Mayne 1993; Dowling 2001; Ross 2001; Feerst 2005). When a typical *New York Times* (1859:2) scribe ventured into the city's "abodes of the poor" in 1859, the anonymous author was quick to suggest that "[t]here is no pleasure in visiting the haunts of wretched men and women," but the writer nevertheless concluded that "it is wholesome to know how humanity suffers in our midst, how it even contents itself amidst its sufferings." Such "slumming" sometimes devolved into a condescending spectacle in which privileged outsiders reveled in the aesthetics of marginality and their link to the color line. For example, English traveler William Archer (1899) concluded that New York's

slums have a Southern air about them, a variety of contour and colour—in some aspects one might almost say a gaiety. ... For one thing, the ubiquitous balconies and fire escapes serve of themselves to break the monotony of line, and lend, as it were, a peculiar texture to the scene; to say nothing of the opportunities they afford for the display of multifarious shreds and patches of colour. Then the houses themselves are often brightly, not to say loudly, painted; so that in the clear, sparkling atmosphere characteristic of New York, the most squalid slum puts on a many-coloured Southern aspect.

Ray Stannard Baker (1904:61) noted that in Southern cities: "The temperament of the Negro is irrepressibly cheerful, he overflows from his small home ... and his squalour is not unpicturesque." In 1896, slum tourist H. C. Bunner (1896:90) even noted that "I have missed art galleries and palaces and theatres and cathedrals (cathedrals particularly) in various and sundry cities, but I don't think I ever missed a slum." A 1911 history of Indianapolis's "old-time slums" inventoried a host of the city's earliest ethnic neighborhoods, and one neighborhood's typical resident was described as "a compound of brilliant colors with red, blue and yellow stripes on his trousers, a red undershirt crossed with bright hued suspenders, and a gaudy neckerchief, with cowhide boots upon his feet and a broad-brimmed brown hat surrounding all" (Cottman 1911:170). In these examples, poverty was an aesthetic attraction that could be toured, imagined in slum tourists' accounts, or viewed through photographs like the 1941 image of the Agnes Street outhouse (Figure 2).

Reformers routinely bemoaned slum and tenement dwellers' inability or unwillingness to conform to universal material and moral standards, and they often took explicit aim at outhouses and sanitation conditions. A 1900 study of Chicago tenement dwellers lamented the "almost universal unsanitary condition of privies and water closets" and decried the "utter apathy of the tenants," concluding that the residents were "ignorant as to even normal sanitary conditions" (Embree 1900:358). The study noted that "the lowest grade of tenement dwellers know nothing of decent living, and there are instances where sanitary contrivances have been removed because the use was totally misunderstood" (Embree 1900:362). Some observers believed that slum dwellers simply could not reproduce such standards and broader genteel moralities because of racially determined attributes. Louis Albert Banks (1892:172), for example, concluded in 1892 that

[g]reat numbers of the incompetent, vicious, idle, deformed, or starved-brain class have been poured into

this country by immigration during the last fifty years, and have filled our slums and tenement houses, our hospitals, asylums, alms-houses, and jails to overflowing. They cannot escape the results of their physical organization, which, in its turn, is an inherited result of ancestral degeneration.

Focusing solely on the parasitic dimension of slumming ignores the concrete sociopolitical interests that drove urban discourse and had a genuine impact on material life for over a century. As in many other communities, initial slum-analysis projects in Indianapolis were focused on providing adequate housing for inner-city residents, a commitment to reforming tenement life that followed the lead of progressive advocates like Jacob Riis (1890). Unlike New York and many other big cities, though, very few of Indianapolis's marginalized neighborhoods were like high-density tenements in New York and Chicago. A 1917 study concluded that "Indianapolis is fortunate, in that it has not developed a serious tenement or lodging house problem. Its citizens live in one or two-family houses. Few houses ... are occupied by several families, but the houses are not crowded and means of ventilation are provided" (Bureau of Municipal Research 1917:341). A 1935 study indicated that 95% of the housing in the city's "blighted" areas was single-family dwellings, as compared to 36% in Chicago (where 32% was still multifamily dwellings) (Achinstein 1935:45). Certainly many of the dilemmas of metropolises were commonplace in Indianapolis, but the problem for many observers was not really poverty, which often was painted as an inevitable structural reality. In 1937, for instance, housing reformer Edith Elmer Wood (1937:15) argued that families "live in the slums because they are poor. ... Better health may increase earning power, and better environment stimulate ambition, but no one should expect the disappearance of slums to abolish poverty." Such housing reformers simply hoped to improve living conditions and restrict the spread of poverty into other areas, and they devoted little attention to structural class and color inequalities.

In 1924 social-work student Nelda Weathers ventured into Indianapolis's near-Westside and conducted a typical study that focused on the material details of life in the neighborhood, assessing housing quality and cost, street condition, utilities, and sanitation (Figure 3). This methodology densely painted the details of

"FOR THE RECORD"
PARAGUAYAN STUDEN DOCUMENTS NEED FOR CLEAN-UP CAMPAIGN.
HE THEN HELPED TO DEVELOP MATERIALS GET AREA CLEANED UP. - 1960

FIGURE 2. In 1960, this unidentified Paraguayan student joined a long tradition of visual representation of slums, trading still images for film. (Photo courtesy of IUPUI University Library Special Collections and Archives, 1960.)

FIGURE 3. Many Indianapolis residents continued to use outhouses like this row found in a series of near-Westside backyards sometime after 1940. (Photo courtesy of IUPUI University Library Special Collections and Archives.)

slum life and linked residents' material conditions to their morality in hopes of appealing to the observers' sense of justice, but like many commentators Weathers equated slum life with black housing (Meyer 1973). Outhouses often were seized upon as symbols of slum life and employed to explain the social and moral shortcomings of residents, and Weathers followed suit. In her survey of 137 houses Weathers found only 6 had "inside toilets" and 16 others used outhouses linked to the city sewers; the remainder used enclosed privy-vault outhouses. Thirty of the houses Weathers examined had "joint" outhouses used by between two and six households (which would describe the multiseat outhouse on Agnes Street), and she questioned "the injurious influence upon morals of the joint toilet." In 1908 Albion Fellows Bacon

(1908:377–378) drew similar links between "privacy and decency" when she noted that in South Bend, Indiana, "[o]ne yard closet is often used by from fifteen to twenty people." W. E. B. Du Bois's (1899:292–293) ambitious Philadelphia study surveyed the living conditions of 2,441 households and reached similar conclusions about the social and moral impact of shared outhouses, finding that 507 households had an "outhouse in common with the other denizens of the tenement or alley." A 1912 study in the south side of Chicago surveyed 682 African American homes and assumed that "[s]ince most of the houses are one- and two-family houses, it might be expected that a large proportion would have private toilet facilities" (Comstock 1912:248). Instead, about one-third of the houses surveyed in the study did not have indoor "closets" (toilet facilities) "and use yard, basement, and hall closets" that are not "conducive to the good health or morals of the tenants" (Comstock 1912:248).

A wave of codes governing sanitation swept through many American cities in the second half of the 19th century (Stottman 1996, 2000). New York City led the way in developing sanitary legislation, especially after a thorough 1865 study of city tenements cataloged a host of horrific conditions (Citizens Association of New York 1865; Stone 1979:288). One 1914 commentator argued that subsequent sanitation laws were "forced by the lamentable unsanitary conditions of the earlier types of tenement houses" (De Forest 1914:8), but uneven enforcement left much of New York and many other communities relatively unchanged well into the 20th century. Chicago, for instance, enacted a tenement housing code that required all buildings constructed after 1902 to include a water closet in each apartment with more than two rooms, but earlier structures were not required to meet the same standards (Comstock 1912:248). In 1912 the city's chief sanitary inspector estimated that Chicago still had 8,250 privy vaults in use (Ball 1912:23). A year later a reformer in one five-block swath of the city's Italian neighborhoods reported that 237 "yard closets" were found that were "dark, dirty, and most frequently out of repair" (Norton 1913:525). These Chicago outhouses were attached to buildings that predated 1902, so they were not "illegal but are as dangerous to the health and to the morals of the tenants, especially of the children, as if they were forbidden by law" (Norton 1913:525).

The Agnes Street outhouse was constructed in about 1910, and by contemporary sanitary standards the 8 × 8 ft. brick-lined privy vault with no city sewer connection lagged well behind the model sanitation systems championed in or legally required by most cities. Indianapolis built a modest sewer system in 1870, but the city had little interest in compelling residents to connect privies to the system (Holloway 1870:130–131; Bicknell 1893:46; Scarpino 1994:202). Jay Stottman (1996:42) paints a similar picture in Louisville, Kentucky, where a 1917 law requiring toilets to be connected to the sewers did not eliminate many outhouses until the eve of World War II. Despite high rates of communicable disease and clearly outlined sanitation practices in contemporary cities, Indianapolis was slow to expand the sewer system and enforce

an 1873 privy-vault code, instead licensing contractors to remove "night soil" privy waste. A 1908 study of 207 African American homes in Indianapolis "showed a sickening lack of sanitation: dark sleeping rooms without windows, alley houses without yards or sewer connection, sinks overflowing, yard closets crowded against the houses so that doors and windows have to be kept closed to shut out the stench" (Bacon 1908:378–379). In 1914 a report by the Indiana State Board of Health (1914:244) indicated that "[i]n all the cities on the White River [including Indianapolis] the hauling of night soil is done by private concerns and paid for by the householder." The report indicated that the "most unsanitary practice in the disposition of night soil was found in Indianapolis," where privy deposits were dumped into the river south of the city. An Indianapolis Water Company official estimated that the city had more than 10,000 privy vaults in use in 1914 (Indiana State Board of Health 1914:233). The authors of an extensive 1917 study of Indianapolis were surprised to find that "[t]he health department has not the power to compel householders to make sewer connections even if sewers exist, or to prescribe a sanitary privy" (Bureau of Municipal Research 1917:326). The study found that Indianapolis had the nation's highest typhoid rate among the 29 cities with more than 200,000 residents, and it argued that "[t]he main causes of this condition are undoubtedly the pollution of the streams by sewage and the large number of yard privies" (Bureau of Municipal Research 1917:326). Its authors concluded that

> Indianapolis has been exceedingly shortsighted not to realize that it cannot be a healthy city without pure water and sanitary sewers. ... It would also be a wise provision for the city itself to make the privy connections and assess the cost thereof upon reasonable annual installments. It is cheaper for the city itself to make rigid regulations as to sewer connections than to run the perennial risk of a high typhoid fever case and death rate (Bureau of Municipal Research 1917:342).

These conditions were common throughout most of Indianapolis, but they lingered in the near-Westside until the 1940s, reflecting the city's disinterest in sanitation in predominately African American neighborhoods. Basketball player Oscar Robertson (2003), for instance, lamented that in the 1940s his family's Colton

Street home two blocks north of the Agnes Street outhouse still had "no indoor plumbing, and the city came around just once a year to empty out all the waste, so the air was perpetually full of bad smells and festering diseases." In 1947 a *Saturday Evening Post* article on Indianapolis painted an even more unpleasant picture, concluding that [a]lthough some of the Negroes live in moderately pleasant circumstances ... the majority live in squalid surroundings. In certain sections ... families live in tumble-down shacks, with outdoor privies and, sometimes, with one outside tap the only source of water for fifteen or so families. Pigs, chickens and goats wander in garbage-littered yards" (Ellen and Murphy 1947:116). In 1952 an observer agreed that Indianapolis was composed of "streets and streets of hovels. ... Many of these hovels have no toilets and no running water" (Stark 1952:9).

One of the most interesting material commentaries on sanitation came from an apparently prosaic knickknack excavated on the Agnes Street site in a house neighboring the two-story privy. The excavations of the Agnes Street two-story outhouse were conducted during an excavation of 10 neighboring homes that included several wells, outhouses, and cisterns with a relatively typical range of 20th-century household discards that included several pieces of bric-a-brac. Bric-a-brac's numerous motifs from the 19th century onward most commonly included subjects from nature and historical and pseudohistorical motifs, but they also included many idiosyncratic subjects like a tiny chamber-pot curio found at 444 Agnes Street. The Agnes Street chamber pot is emblazoned "The Smallest," and at less than an inch in diameter it is indeed quite tiny (Figure 4). When indoor toilets began to replace privies in many 19th-century communities, the manufactured chamber-pot curios began, making light of the most universal of needs while also establishing some symbolic distance from outhouses and staking a household's claim to modernity (Mullins 2004:85–86). The example from 444 Agnes Street was made in interwar Japan. The two modest houses that sat alongside each other at 444 and 442 Agnes Street shared a single lot, and by the time the curio was discarded, after World War II, they appear to have had indoor toilets with a city sewer connection. Nevertheless, the house apparently still had a privy in the 1930s. The two-story privy lorded over the

neighbors' yard at 458–460 Agnes into the 1950s, and a foray into some of the surrounding neighborhood would have found many vault privies in use when the chamber pot was manufactured.

The diminutive curio made light of consequential sanitation issues by rendering the once-universal chamber pot an aesthetic object disassociated from the most unpleasant dimensions of sanitation. Most elders with memories of privies likewise tend to use humor to remember outhouses and the trappings of earlier sanitation methods. For instance, in 1937 Richard Crenshaw's family moved into the newly built Lockefield Gardens, an exclusively black public-housing project two blocks north of the Agnes Street outhouse. Crenshaw (2005:4) remembered that "[f]or their time Lockefield was a magnificent place to live. A wonderful place to live. They had hot and cold running water in the house and toilets in the house." In Crenshaw's celebration of the "magnificence" of indoor plumbing he laughed, "I can remember outhouses when I was a kid, you didn't want to walk by them." Kenneth Adams (2005:5) also lived in Lockefield and shared Crenshaw's sentiments about the quality of the Lockefield homes. Adams noted that in many other Indianapolis neighborhoods residents "had to go out and use an outhouse, but we had running water, hot and cold running water. We had indoor toilets. ... We were living good."

The tiny chamber pot in an Agnes Street living room brought the topic of sanitation into discussion through levity, but it still underscored the household's distance from the unpleasant realities of outhouses that were fresh in the experiences of household members and visitors alike. Elders often seize on such significant material shifts as key transformations in their lives. Crenshaw (2005), for example, pointed to the Lockefield homes' steam-heating system as a vast improvement over the wood- and coal-heated homes covering most of the near-Westside: "It's hard to imagine somebody getting excited about steamed heat today, but in the day it was a wonderful invention. ... It was very sufficient in heating the apartments, but another thing is you didn't have to go out and chop wood or bring coal in and carry ashes out and clean out a fireplace or furnace."

Elders rarely characterize these changes as movements from poverty to affluence or from slum life to a settled "middle-class" life, but they clearly recognize that they and many of

FIGURE 4. This modest chamber-pot curio used humor to illuminate significant sanitation concerns. (Photo by Kathryn Christine Glidden, 2008.)

their neighbors faced unpleasant and challenging conditions that were significantly diminished by everyday material conveniences like toilets and running water. In this sense, these former residents are not championing an archaeology that simply romanticizes the past and ignores the concrete realities of poverty. In her study of archaeological constructions of poverty, Sarah Chicone (2006:51) argues that some archaeological studies of slum life focus on the ideological distortions of popular portrayals of slum life to illuminate the consequential agency of slum dwellers. Chicone suggests that such a focus on how impoverished peoples' lives contrasted to the ideological pronouncements of social reformers risks evading the real social and material effects of impoverishment. Near-Westside elders, though, do not argue that poverty was utterly "imagined" by middle-class reformers, and, in fact, former residents typically concede its existence, understand its effect on their communities, and recognize its prominence in their heritage.

Reconstructing Privy and Slum Heritage

Many 20th-century observers seemed to believe that there was a concrete distinction that granted some neighborhoods the status of slum, but the specific material, aesthetic, and social dimensions defining slum life were ambiguous and directly linked to state interests and prevailing prejudices. Alan Mayne (2007:322) concurs that the "slum" was a subject fashioned to serve various public policies while it reproduced broader popular sentiments about social and individual identity. In the 1930s, for instance, Indianapolis's slum discourses tended to focus on economic analyses of poverty, a maneuver that quantifiably grounded slum life in black materiality to legitimize wholesale neighborhood removals. When Asher Achinstein (1935:46) wrestled with the definition of a slum area in 1935, he canvassed nine major cities and concluded that more than half of Indianapolis's African Americans lived in what he classified as "blighted" neighborhoods (the next highest percentage was in Baltimore, where 38% of African Americans lived in such neighborhoods). Achinstein (1935:39) decided that the most reliable measure of blight was median rentals, arguing that "where the lowest rents are paid, there the poorest housing exists." In contrast, in 1911 George Cottman (1911:170) suggested that Indianapolis's slums had already been eradicated, concluding that the slum landscape had been erased by "the moral sanitation which may fairly be said to have taken place in our community. It is said that Indianapolis is to-day, for a city of its size, exceptionally free from slum conditions. Whatever vice flourishes here makes at least a show of hiding its head and not flourishing in the more respectable quarters." This was a more indefensible position by the 1930s, when the Indianapolis Real Estate Board objected to the federal government's plans to construct the exclusively African American

Lockefield Gardens, the first public housing in Indianapolis (*Indianapolis Recorder* 1933a, 1933b). The *Indianapolis Recorder* (1933c:1) reported that the real estate board and "certain owners of properties located in the area chosen for the slum clearance ... sought to convince officials at Washington that no Negroes of Indianapolis were living in slum areas and that 'they would not appreciate better surroundings if they could get them.'" The real estate board did not evade the presence of genuine poverty, conceding that "certain sections of the city should be rebuilt, but it should be left in the hands of a private business" (*Indianapolis Recorder* 1933d:1). The realtors argued that the new homes' rental prices would be "prohibitive to those now living in this district and would force these residents to blight other areas" (Barrows 2007:146).

For elders, the question is less about whether the neighborhood constituted a "slum" than it is about residents' ambition and dignity. Very few elders accord poverty an especially prominent position in their memories of the near-Westside, but almost all acknowledge its presence, even if they are quick to refute slum stereotypes. For instance, Thomas Ridley (2002:5) grew up in the neighborhood in the 1920s, and he acknowledged that his family's modest rented home "had an outdoor toilet." Such conditions associated with slum life were often linked to renting, which was associated with community "instability" and often viewed as an insubstantial claim to citizenship. Ridley (2002:5) stressed that

> very few people owned homes, they rented. ... But that didn't mean you didn't take care of your house. You did, because you had pride. ... I don't know any side of town that didn't have a pocket, some pockets of slum area of poverty stricken homes. ... They were not modern homes most of them, but they were nice homes and kept nice by the people that lived in them.

The homes Ridley remembered were almost all vernacular houses built from the late 19th century onward, and many of the stylish 20th-century streetscapes in the African American near-Westside were by most measures model genteel communities. Booker T. Washington (1909:173) painted such African American domesticity as accommodationists' refuge from public racism, arguing that "[w]e sometimes complain about the Jim Crow cars, but, although we may not have the most agreeable part of the car in which to ride, all of us, as I have said, can have a beauti-ful home in which to live, in which to rear our children." Washington's confidence that genteel homes would provide an essential foothold to African American citizenship was misplaced in many communities, though, because black archi-tectural respectability often inspired apprehension among white observers (Mooney 2002:64).

A 1946 study of a near-Westside neighbor-hood targeted for slum clearance linked com-munity identity to genteel housing, arguing that "[a]lmost all of the families were living in houses which needed major repairs and few of them had adequate plumbing facilities" (Black-burn 1946:95). The study's author, Cleo W. Blackburn (1946:52), argued that his "analysis of community life shows little understanding or concern on the part of the people with regard to such factors as community health or sanitation." Blackburn (1946:96) concluded that the challenge was "how to co-ordinate housing building and community development in such a way as to assure a new type of life in the community as well as a better appearance in housing."

Following models he had learned at the Tuskegee Institute in the 1930s, Blackburn was a proponent of slum clearance and advocated "sweat equity" redevelopment of slum tracts, with a community of model African American homeowners building new homes in place of former slums (Pierce 2005:67–69). Blackburn believed that African Americans in the near-Westside would learn new social discipline as they transformed the community's material living conditions. The project eventually built over 330 homes between 1950 and 1964, but Blackburn's rebuilding project was intentionally peopled by solidly middle-income homebuilders, favoring families with stable work histories, spotless records, and good credit (Pierce 2005:70). Most displaced African Americans who once lived in the area were compelled to migrate to equally marginal housing elsewhere.

The material conditions along Agnes Street in the 1950s had declined significantly from Thomas Ridley's childhood, and as he acknowledged, they had been difficult for some near-Westside house-holds for most of the 20th century. By the 1950s, Agnes Street had declined as a result of wartime migration into the city, a half century of landlord disinterest in maintaining the homes, and the city's persistent failure to extend basic utilities to

residents. Eventually this decline was seized upon as the key reason to uproot thousands of house-holds throughout the near-Westside. After World War II the Indiana University Medical Center expanded into the surrounding neighborhood, armed with slum stereotypes used to rationalize wholesale displacement in much of postwar urban America. In some communities slum clearance was a rapid and utter razing of whole swaths of city, but in Indianapolis it was a protracted process of mostly modest land acquisitions. In 1956 one large tract of 19 ac. was acquired by the city's redevelopment commission, an area in which the building commissioner said the "houses are structural, fire and health hazards and many have no plumbing" (*Indianapolis Star* 1956:1). The city rationalized the displacement by stress-ing that of the 116 families living in the area, 29 had no running water, 33 had no indoor plumb-ing, 63 lacked baths or showers, and 36 were using outhouses. While the city professed that "the clearance was ordered solely on the basis of blight there and not for the convenience of the school," Indiana University repaid the city's costs on the project and took possession of the land. After IUPUI was officially established in 1969, the small campus quickly took aim at surround-ing neighborhoods to accommodate suburban-commuter parking and the growth of the univer-sity, which soon enveloped several hundred acres of former neighborhoods. The home at 458–460 Agnes Street and its monumental outhouse even-tually fell to the wrecking ball during this 1960s transformation of the campus landscape. The privy's *terminus post quem* comes from a bottle, manufactured in 1954, found in the lowest exca-vated level, reflecting that even in the neighbor-hood's last moments sewer connections still had not been extended to every Agnes Street home. A 1958 map shows the outhouse removed, so it was razed and filled sometime between 1954 and 1958, with the house and its neighbors follow-ing soon afterward (Rosenberg 2008). Eventually Agnes Street was renamed University Boulevard, further distancing the campus community from the heritage of the former residents.

Consuming Poverty

The concrete consumption tactics reflected in the Agnes Street assemblage provide a more illuminating picture of the residents' lives than simply framing the analysis in terms of how the artifacts either support or refute the residents' poverty and position on a slum landscape. For instance, the privy included 1,042 bones, and more than 75% of those are pork. The predominance of pork indicates a strong preference for it over other meats, and it does not surprise African American elders who concur with the vast volume of archaeological scholarship that reveals a similar African American devotion to pork. Somewhat surprisingly, many former residents assume that such households were consuming inferior cuts like feet elements, linking pork, however circuitously, to poverty. The Agnes Street assemblage, though, is dominated by the most costly pork loin and rib chops, while it also includes less-desirable vertebral scraps, rib tips, and feet. While elders tend to deemphasize poverty in their memories of their youth, some still assume that economic scarcity will be reflected in archaeological material culture.

Community descendants stake a complicated position on the assemblage that rejects some dimensions of economic determinism even as it accepts the powerful influence of material marginalization. On the one hand, elders almost always acknowledge material want in many of these neighborhoods. On the other hand, though, they resist framing the analysis in terms of a deterministic notion of poverty that ignores households' tactical consumption patterns and clever resource management. On Agnes Street, for example, the predominance of pork likely reflects such circumspect consumption tactics by residents Max Folley and Oscar Roddy. By the mid-1950s the Agnes Street apartments were home to Oscar Roddy, who worked at Kingan's meat-packing plant, and Max Folley, who lived at 458½ Agnes Street from 1948 until the 1960s and also worked at Kingan's. From 1862 to 1966, Kingan's was one of the largest pork plants on the face of the planet, in which, by the company's own count, more than 10,000 hogs met their ends each day. Neighborhood residents and employees often took discarded meat from Kingan's, which is suggested by many of the smaller cut bones, although distinguishing slaughterhouse discards from market purchases is infeasible. Nevertheless, pork loins certainly were not routinely discarded into Kingan's glue vats. Folley and Roddy were probably bringing at least some of this food home from Kingan's

and apparently mixed some desirable cuts in alongside the feet and bone scraps normally pilfered from the glue vats.

Such tactics produce a picture of material consumption that resists being reduced simply to deterministic frameworks or agency disconnected from impoverishment and the color line, and similar tactics are reflected in other dimensions of the assemblage. For example, during World War II, many ideologues renewed the call for home food preservation, and the Agnes Street glass assemblage provides an opportunity to see how such entreaties played out in at least one set of households. Since the 19th century champions of home food preservation had often celebrated the thrift and material discipline provided by home food preservation, but such consumption dictates were often dropped in the face of inexpensive and convenient mass-produced canned goods. Many African American domestics, for instance, did home food preservation for white employers and were not eager to do the same unpleasant labor in their own homes when canned foods were widely available and quite cheap (Mullins 1999:178–180). In 1887 Maria Parloa's (1887:87) popular household manual was already willing to decree that "taken for all and all, canned foods, especially fruits and vegetables, are a great blessing." In 1918 over 7.5 million cases of corn alone were canned in the United States, and by 1940 16.6 billion pounds of vegetables were sold in cans (Judd and Marshall 1918:64; Halper 2003:1,371). During World War II, though, canned food was rationed to preserve tin resources, reviving lagging interest in home food preservation (Halper 2003:1,371–1,372). In Indianapolis, Cleo Blackburn's Flanner House social service agency built a massive cannery in 1944 to serve its predominately African American constituency in the near-Westside (Figure 5). Preserving a vast range of vegetables in glass mason-style jars, Flanner House reported that "20,000 cans of food were processed" in 1944, almost all of which were canned vegetables grown in one of Flanner House's 250 family garden plots (Allen 1945). A 1955 pamphlet proudly noted that "[i]n its community gardens, open to Negroes and whites alike, hundreds of families grow their own vegetables, and can them in the Flanner House cannery" (High 1955). Despite such rhetoric, most households before and after the war opted for inexpensive

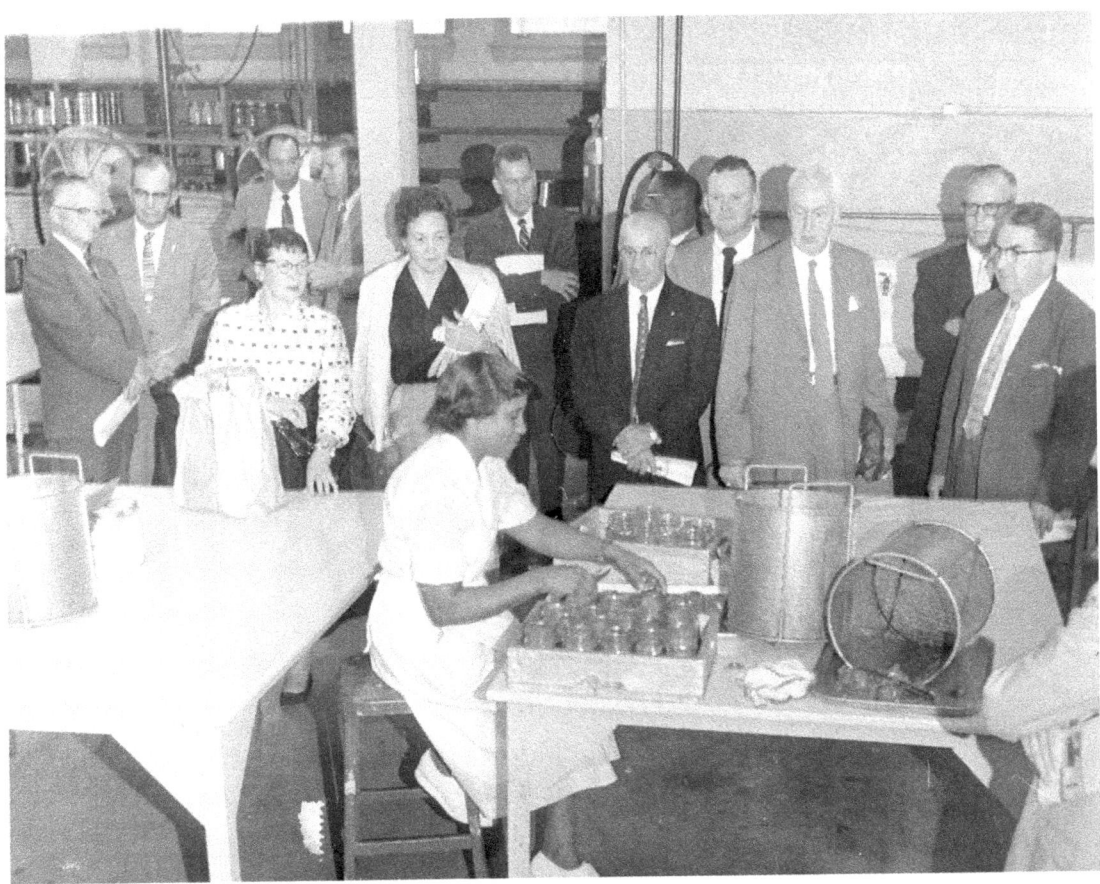

FIGURE 5. Sometime after World War II, this woman posed at the Flanner House cannery for an unidentified touring group. While such visits might not strictly be considered "slumming," this demonstration of Flanner House's thrift and uplift programs certainly was in a tradition of slum tourism across class and color lines. (Photo courtesy of IUPUI University Library Special Collections and Archives.)

mass-produced canned foods, and the Agnes Street assemblage had a significant volume of corroded metal that likely came from such vessels. Nevertheless, the glass assemblage indicates that the households at 458–460 Agnes Street also were consuming home-preserved food. Of 240 bottles in the Agnes Street outhouse, 31 (12.9%) were preserving jars, which were the second most common vessel type. The mean production date of the 31 preserving jars was 1943.09, which is slightly earlier than the assemblage's mean production date of 1944.21; consequently, there may have been modest reuse of some preserving jars, but extensive reuse would be reflected in an earlier production date. The Agnes Street residents may have seen such food production and consumption as "thriftiness," they may have adopted canning

as an economically prudent tactic, or their home food production could have been some combination of those sentiments. Thriftiness was routinely bandied about in moralizing consumption literature from the 19th century onward, but along the color line it often implied that black consumers would largely remove themselves from white consumer space as full participants. In 1913 the white sociologist Robert Park (1913:152) suggested that many African American tenant farmers mired in poverty might improve their circumstances with more disciplined planning and consumption: "The average tenant farmer will spend as much money during the cropping season as the grocer or the banker who is advancing him will permit. ... A thrifty farmer, however, can reduce the amount of his purchases at the store to almost nothing." Booker T. Washington was the best-known African American champion of thrift as part of a "racial uplift" discourse promoted most extensively in the wake of Emancipation but continually revived in the 20th century as well (Gaines 1996; Daugherty 2004). Thrift and racial uplift were rather ambiguous notions, but they were often linked closely to the material details of everyday life. Washington (1900:174), for example, noted that "[w]hile the great bulk of the race is still without money and property, yet the signs of thrift are evident on every hand. Especially is this notable in the large number of neat little homes which are owned by these people on the outer edges of the towns and cities in the South." Tuskegee's outreach programs to rural women included training in a wide range of household skills, including home food preservation as well as dressmaking, poultry raising, and "moral" amusements (Washington 1904:123).

Indianapolis's own Flanner House was a persistent advocate of "self-help" programs fashioned after similar uplift models at Tuskegee Institute, where Executive Director Cleo Blackburn had served as a research assistant. Flanner House touted its cannery as a mechanism to foster material discipline, encouraging prospective canners to "enjoy the glorious feeling of thrift and efficiency by having a grocery of your own canned goods in your own home. ... [Y]ou will save money, time, and energy, and you will enjoy a deep pride in your saving when you can at the Flanner House cannery" (Flanner House [1950]). The Agnes Street residents may have agreed that home food preservation materialized self-sufficiency, but this does not mean that such household production was not also a reflection of impoverishment. Elders often stress the relationship between material penury and individual aspiration; this maneuver constructs a heritage that recognizes community impoverishment but stresses how personal and family initiative and discipline allowed some households to advance materially and socially. Some neighborhood ideologues saw such material ambition and discipline as an essential element in the reconstruction of former slum communities. In 1952, for instance, a Flanner House advocate argued that construction of "sweat equity" homes built by neighborhood residents was "not the end of their aspirations, but only a step towards the

formation of a community where each family will be in a position to live best and serve most" (Kimbrough [1952]:5). This position applauded ambition and disciplined labor and stressed relationships with neighbors, vesting community in the shared willingness to work toward common aspirations.

Conclusion

The spot on which the Agnes Street outhouse once sat is today home to a new Campus Center, a gleaming monument of steel and glass that lords it over the parking lots and buildings that now populate the IUPUI campus. The outhouse provides a stark contrast to the new Campus Center that makes the latter structure and the university itself appear to be a justifiable improvement on the neighborhood that it displaced. Most sober observers will agree that eliminating many of the most unpleasant dimensions of impoverished neighborhoods had a positive impact on subsequent generations, and most elders have no nostalgia for impoverishment. Yet for elders, the community that once populated these neighborhoods was not defined simply by material conditions or the narrowly defined and ideologically distorted slum discourses that sought to displace the community. The dilemma is that certain material forms defined as slum life are recurrently resurrected to legitimize the social and political displacements related to urban renewal and to avoid the sticky questions of how such displacement has a powerful contemporary legacy. In the face of a radically reshaped campus landscape that bears no material traces of historic architecture and is no longer populated by a descendant community, stereotypes and historical ignorance have tended to replace reflective and critical pictures of the many residents that populated the neighborhood for more than 150 years. Contemporary perceptions of the near-Westside hazard lapsing into the same class, cultural, and racist distortions that have characterized slumming for well over a century.

Archaeology may lend some concrete material presence to these former neighborhoods and productively establish the heritage of the landscape before it became a campus and ocean of parking lots. This materiality would unite a fine-grained archaeological picture of the things and spaces that made up the near-Westside landscape while recognizing how they were concretely shaped by, understood through, and inseparable from social discourses such as those on slum life, race, and poverty. Establishing that historical presence is only the first move in creating an engaged picture of the community, one that still needs to examine how a vast range of residents' lives were significantly influenced but not determined by racism, economic marginality, and material circumstance. The challenge is to temper the archaeological narrative in ways that recognize marginalization and acknowledge the power of racism without letting those structural influences drive the analysis or eliminate the collectively meaningful agency of the near-Westside's residents. The ultimate goal of such scholarship is not necessarily to forge a clearly defined community based on archaeological analysis, because monolithic notions of community usually have been wielded by urban-renewal advocates, racists, and even universities in order to make particular social subjects conform to particular dominant interests. Instead, seemingly prosaic archaeological materials like those from the Agnes Street outhouse should reveal communities actively negotiating numerous forms of difference. The outhouse can mean many different things, and in fact it is perhaps most valuable as an element of neighborhood heritage when it reveals dissentious views of history and the contemporary world. Piercing the distorted and simplistic pictures of the outhouse as a symbol of poverty projected onto racism is a critical first step, but it should ultimately make this and similar contexts mechanisms that interrogate contemporary social interests.

Acknowledgements

Thanks to Kenneth Adams, Daisy Borel, Richard Crenshaw, and Thomas Ridley for the time they have taken to discuss Indianapolis history with us. Although she passed away before we completed this article, Shirley Ross also shared many of her thoughts and was always keen to contribute. Various ideas in this article were planted by Bob Barrows, Melissa Bingmann, A'Lelia Bundles, Chris Glidden, Sue Hyatt, Liz Kryder-Reid, Craig Lee, Lynn Meskell, Wilma Moore, Seth Rosenberg, Jay Stottman, and Larry Zimmerman. Todd Daniels-Howell, Greg Mobley, and Stephen Townes in the IUPUI University Archives have given lots of research help and ideas on the neighborhood. Paul Shackel and David Gadsby provided comments and direction on a first draft. Chris Glidden conducted the faunal analysis with the support of an IUPUI School of Liberal Arts Langsam-Oswald Summer Fellowship. Three anonymous reviewers provided thoughtful suggestions for revising the article. Of course, none of those folks bear any responsibility for the shortcomings of the article.

References

ACHINSTEIN, ASHER
1935 Some Economic Characteristics of Blighted Areas. *Journal of Land and Public Utility Economics* 11(1):38–47.

ADAMS, KENNETH
2005 Interview by Craig Lee, 12 April. Manuscript, Bethel AME Oral History Project, Department of Anthropology, IUPUI, Indianapolis, IN.

ALLEN, ROWLAND
1945 Letter to Will Alexander, 12 April. Rowland Allen Papers 1830–1972, Indiana Historical Society, Indianapolis.

ARCHER, WILLIAM
1899 *America To-Day, Observations and Reflections.* Charles Scribner's Sons, New York, NY. Project Gutenberg <http://www.gutenberg.org/files/7997/7997-h/7997-h.htm>. Accessed 5 February 2008.

BACON, ALBION FELLOWS
1908 The Housing Problem in Indiana. *Charities and the Commons* 21(5 December):376–383.

BAKER, RAY STANNARD
1904 *Following the Color Line: An Account of Negro Citizenship in the American Democracy.* S. S. McClure Company, New York, NY.

BALL, CHARLES B.
1912 Privy Vaults. Safe Disposal of Bodily Wastes a Necessity. *Proceedings of the Academy of Political Science in the City of New York* 2(3):21–28.

BANKS, LOUIS ALBERT
1892 *White Slaves, or The Oppressions of the Worthy Poor.* Lee and Shepard, Boston, MA.

BARROWS, ROBERT G.
2007 The Local Origins of a New Deal Housing Project: The Case of Lockefield Gardens in Indianapolis. *Indiana Magazine of History* 103(2):125–151.

BICKNELL, ERNEST P.
1893 *Indianapolis Illustrated.* Consolidated Publishing, Indianapolis, IN.

BLACKBURN, CLEO W.
1946   A Study of 454 Negro Households in the Redevelopment Area, Indianapolis, Indiana, October, 1946. Flanner House, Indianapolis, IN.

BUNNER, H. C.
1896   Jersey Street and Jersey Lane, Urban and Suburban Sketches. Charles Scribner's Sons, New York, NY.

BUREAU OF MUNICIPAL RESEARCH
1917   Report on a Survey of the City Government of Indianapolis, Indiana. William B. Burford, Indianapolis, IN.

CHICONE, SARAH JANE
2006   Feeding, Clothing and Sheltering Southern Colorado's Working Class: Towards an Archaeological Analysis of Poverty. Doctoral dissertation, Department of Anthropology, Binghamton University, State University of New York. University Microfilms International, Ann Arbor, MI.

CITIZENS' ASSOCIATION OF NEW YORK
1865   Report of the Council of Hygiene and Public Health of the Citizens' Association of New York Upon the Sanitary Condition of the City. A. Appleton and Company, New York, NY.

COMSTOCK, ALZADA P.
1912   Chicago Housing Conditions, VI: The Problem of the Negro. American Journal of Sociology 18(2):241–257.

COTTMAN, GEORGE S.
1911   Old-Time Slums of Indianapolis. Indiana Magazine of History 7(2):170–173.

CRENSHAW, RICHARD
2005   Interview by Craig Lee, 5 October. Manuscript, Bethel AME Oral History Project, Department of Anthropology, IUPUI, Indianapolis, IN.

DAUGHERTY, ELLEN KATHLEEN
2004   Lifting the Veil of Ignorance: The Visual Culture of African American Racial Uplift. Doctoral dissertation, Department of Art History, University of Virginia. University Microfilms International, Ann Arbor, MI.

DE FOREST, ROBERT W.
1914   A Brief History of the Housing Movement in America. Annals of the American Academy of Political and Social Science 51(1):8–16.

DOWLING, ROBERT M.
2001   Slumming: Morality and Space in New York City from "City Mysteries" to the Harlem Renaissance. Doctoral dissertation, Department of English, City University of New York. University Microfilms International, Ann Arbor, MI.

DU BOIS, W. E. BURGHARDT
1899   The Philadelphia Negro: A Social Study. University of Pennsylvania Series in Political Economy and Public Law, No. 14. Philadelphia.

ELLEN, MARY, AND MARK MURPHY
1947   Indianapolis. Saturday Evening Post 221(6):16–17, 115–117.

EMBREE, FRANCES BUCKLEY
1900   The Housing of the Poor in Chicago. Journal of Political Economy 8(3):354–377.

FEERST, ALEX JONATHAN
2005   Bowery Beautiful: Progressive Slumming and Ghetto Aesthetics, 1880–1930. Doctoral dissertation, Department of English, Duke University. University Microfilms International, Ann Arbor, MI.

FLANNER HOUSE
[1950] Save at Flanner House Cannery. Flanner House, Indianapolis, IN.

GAINES, KEVIN KELLY
1996   Uplifting the Race: Black Leadership, Politics and Culture in the Twentieth Century. University of North Carolina Press, Chapel Hill.

GRAY, RALPH D.
2003   IUPUI—The Making of an Urban University. Indiana University Press, Bloomington.

HALPER, EMANUEL B.
2003   Shopping Center and Store Leases. Law Journal Press, New York, NY.

HIGH, STANLEY
1955   Cleo Blackburn's "Grand Design." Digital Collections of IUPUI University Library, Indianapolis, IN <http://indiamond6.ulib.iupui.edu/cdm4/document.php?CISOROOT=/Flanner&CISOPTR=1990&REC=3>. Accessed 1 April 2008.

HOLLOWAY, WILLIAM R.
1870   Indianapolis: A Historical and Statistical Sketch of the Railroad City. Indianapolis Journal, Indianapolis, IN.

INDIANA STATE BOARD OF HEALTH
1914   Thirty-Second Annual Report of the State Board of Health for the Fiscal and Board Year Ending September 30, 1913. William B. Burford, Indianapolis, IN.

INDIANAPOLIS RECORDER
1933a   City to Clean-up Negro Slums. Indianapolis Recorder 16 September:1.
1933b   Wipe Out the Slums. Indianapolis Recorder 9 December:4.
1933c   Local Group Scores Objectors to Federal $5,000,000 Slum Clearance Project. Indianapolis Recorder 16 December:1.
1933d   Many Organizations and Individuals Announce Support of Slum Clearance Plan. Indianapolis Recorder 23 December:1.

INDIANAPOLIS STAR
1956   Medical Center to Build on Slum Cleared Acres. Indianapolis Star 4 October:1,9.

JUDD, CHARLES H., AND LEON C. MARSHALL
1918 Lessons in National and Community Life, Series C, For the Intermediate Grades of the Elementary School. Department of the Interior, Washington, DC.

KIMBROUGH, JOYCE
[1952] An Adventure in "Self Help" Building. Manuscript, Indiana Historical Society, Indianapolis.

MAYNE, ALAN
1993 The Imagined Slum: Newspaper Representation in Three Cities 1870–1914. Leicester University Press, New York, NY.
2007 Tall Tales but True? New York's "Five Points" Slum. Journal of Urban History 33(2):320–331.

MEYER, DAVID R.
1973 Blacks in Slum Housing: A Distorted Theme. Journal of Black Studies 4(2):139–152.

MOONEY, BARBARA BURLISON
2002 The Comfortable Tasty Framed Cottage: An African American Architectural Iconography. Journal of the Society of Architectural Historians 61(1):48–67.

MULLINS, PAUL R.
1999 Race and Affluence: An Archaeology of African America and Consumer Culture. Kluwer/Plenum, New York, NY.
2003 Engagement and the Color Line: Race, Renewal, and Public Archaeology in the Urban Midwest. Urban Anthropology 32(2):205–230.
2004 Consuming Aspirations: Bric-a-Brac and the Politics of Victorian Materialism in West Oakland. In Putting the "There" There: Historical Archaeologies of West Oakland, Mary Praetzellis and Adrian Praetzellis, editors, pp. 85–115. Anthropological Studies Center, Sonoma State University, Rohnert Park, CA.

NEW YORK TIMES
1859 The Abodes of the Poor. New York Times July 1:2.

NORTON, GRACE PELOUBET
1913 Chicago Housing Conditions, VII: Two Italian Districts. American Journal of Sociology 18(4):509–542.

PARK, ROBERT E.
1913 Negro Home Life and Standards of Living. Annals of the American Academy of Political and Social Science 49(1):147–163.

PARLOA, MARIA
1887 Miss Parloa's Kitchen Companion, 19th edition. Clover Publishing Company, Boston, MA.

PIERCE, RICHARD B.
2005 Polite Protest: The Political Economy of Race in Indianapolis, 1920–1970. Indiana University Press, Bloomington.

PRICE, NELSON
2004 Indianapolis Then and Now. Thunder Bay Press, San Diego, CA.

RIDLEY, THOMAS
2002 Interview by Paul Mullins, 5 November. IUPUI Archaeology and Oral History Project, Department of Anthropology, IUPUI, Indianapolis, IN.

RIIS, JACOB A.
1890 How the Other Half Lives: Studies Among the Tenements of New York. Charles Scribner's Sons, New York, NY.

ROBERTSON, OSCAR
2003 The Big O: My Life, My Times, My Game. Rodale Press, Emmaus, PA.

ROSENBERG, SETH ANDREW
2008 Corner Stores and Bottles: African-American Consumption in Indianapolis. Master's thesis, Department of Anthropology, Ball State University, Muncie, IN.

ROSS, ELLEN
2001 Slum Journeys: Ladies and London Poverty, 1860–1940. In The Archaeology of Urban Landscapes: Explorations in Slumland, Alan Mayne and Tim Murray, editors, pp. 11–21. Cambridge University Press, New York, NY.

SCARPINO, PHILIP V.
1994 Urban Environment. In The Encyclopedia of Indianapolis, David J. Bodenhamer and Robert G. Barrows, editors, pp. 199–208. Indiana University Press, Bloomington.

STARK, IRWIN
1952 Jewish Work-Camp in Indianapolis: The Younger Generation Rolls Up its Sleeves. Commentary 13(1):7–13.

STONE, MAY N.
1979 The Plumbing Paradox: American Attitudes toward Late Nineteenth-Century Domestic Sanitary Arrangements. Winterthur Portfolio 14(3):283–309.

STOTTMAN, M. JAY
1996 Out of Sight, Out of Mind: An Archaeological Analysis of the Perception of Sanitation. Master's Thesis, Department of Anthropology, University of Kentucky, Lexington.
2000 Out of Sight, Out of Mind: Privy Architecture and the Perception of Sanitation. Historical Archaeology 34(1):39–61.

WASHINGTON, BOOKER T.
1900 The Future of the American Negro. Small, Maynard and Company, Boston, MA.
1904 Working with the Hands: Being a Sequel to Up from Slavery: Covering the Author's Experiences in Industrial Training at Tuskegee. Doubleday, Page and Company, New York, NY.
1909 Some Results of the Armstrong Idea. Southern Workman 38(3):170–181.

Paul R. Mullins and Lewis C. Jones

Wood, Edith Elmer
1937 The Costs of Bad Housing. *Annals of the American Academy of Political and Social Science* 190(1):145–150.

Paul R. Mullins
Department of Anthropology
Indiana University-Purdue University,
    Indianapolis
Cavanaugh Hall 413B
Indianapolis, IN 46202

Lewis C. Jones
Department of Anthropology
Indiana University
701 E. Kirkwood Avenue
Bloomington, IN 47405

Part IV:
Archaeology, Heritage, and Justice

Tracy Ireland

"The Absence of Ghosts": Landscape and Identity in the Archaeology of Australia's Settler Culture

ABSTRACT

This article is a case study investigating archaeology as a practice embedded in a complex web of culturally constructed codes of meaning or discourses. A distinctive form of discourse concerning the landscape and its role in determining national identity characterizes Australian culture. This discourse has been central to the construction of the idea of the nation and its past: in particular, concepts of the land as hostile and empty, of the bush as the essence of Australia, and of the landscape as feminine. The paper considers the ways in which this landscape discourse has operated within historical archaeological research and heritage management and discusses the implications of these discursive relationships for past and future research.

Introduction

> It was the fearful loneliness of the place that most affected her—the absence of ghosts. Till they arrived, no other lives had been lived here. It made the air that much thinner, harder to breathe. She had not understood, till she came to a place where it was lacking, the extent to which her sense of the world had to do with the presence of those who had been here before, leaving signs of their passing and spaces still warm with breath—a threshold worn with the coming and going of feet, hedges between fields that went back a thousand years, and the names even further; most of all, the names on the headstones, which were their names, under which lay the bones that had made their bones and given them breath (Malouf 1994:110).

This discussion of landscape, identity, and Australian historical archaeology considers certain discursive themes within the Australian cultural tradition, which have particular relevance to the way in which archaeologists have studied the historic past in Australia. Representations of landscape in the Australian imagination have constructed a powerful discourse through which the landscape and human behavior within it has, subsequently, been understood. Landscape discourse has, therefore, been central to the narrative construction of the Australian settler nation

and its past. In particular, the landscape is seen as a determinant of not only the course of colonial history but also of the distinctive characteristics of national identity. In her comparison of bicentennial commemorations in Australia (1988) and the United States (1976), Lyn Spillman has pointed out how central the landscape was to expressions of national identity in the Australian celebrations. This contrasted markedly with the United States where the land had formed only "a minor part of the symbolic repertoire." She also noted that the Australian land was more important in national iconography in 1988 than it had been in the centennial celebrations of the previous century (Spillman 1997:125).

It is important to clarify that in studies of Australian cultural traditions, the term "landscape" is used often and broadly. It may cover a grab bag of concepts from the biophysical environment, to a natural backdrop in films and literature, or the more specific genre of landscape painting. Generally, the term is used to describe representations of nature. Nature in this context is the opposite to culture, and in the Australian settler context, nature is the enemy of culture and the opponent of civilization (Gibson 1993:212). Tom Griffiths suggests that "the competing realities of geography and history, land and culture, have stood for a fundamental, persistent tension between origins and environment in Australian life" (Griffiths 1997:11). This concept of an environment somehow opposed to the fostering of cultural development is central to colonial narratives of settler history in Australia.

However, concepts of landscape and environment are also elided into metaphors of settler self-representation and the identity of the nation. Australian nationalism of the 20th century is characterized by an escalation of the value and meaning attributed to the special characteristics of the Australian environment: the visual qualities of the landscape and the unique native flora and fauna. Settler identification with landscape is, however, ambiguous and full of contradictions. To the largely urbanized settler population, nature (the Outback or the bush) is the source of the genuine Australian experience, yet it is seen, simultaneously, as the indigenous wilderness from which they are alienated (Morton and Smith 1999:175).

For the purposes of definition however, it is important to note here that *archaeological* understandings of landscape as a cultural palimpsest or, more simply, as a human constructed or influenced environment cannot be overlaid upon concepts of landscape in Australian culture generally. For instance, the idea of *pristine wilderness* (that is, nature unaltered by humans) is so prominent in Australian culture that conservationists and land managers still struggle with the idea that most of the continent is a cultural landscape, shaped by a long history of human occupation. In historical archaeology, understandings of cultural landscape compete with the colonialist construction of the expanding of a frontier that is not simply geographical but also a major ontological disjunction between the beginning of history and the end of prehistory (Rose 1999: 9). The colonial inheritance of the institutional and academic division of history, prehistory, and historical archaeology has left little conceptual territory within which to explore hybrid cultures and landscapes (Colley and Bickford 1996; Murray 1996c).

Hence, there is a complex entanglement of culturally constructed ways of knowing the Australian landscape, landscape-based expressions of national identity, and the historical and archaeological research that is both constructed through these cultural traditions, while also seeking to explain them. This analysis is less concerned with critiquing the basis in reality of these constructions concerning landscape and identity than with understanding the way in which they operate within culture as discourses or self-perpetuating codes of meaning (Foucault 1972; Schaffer 1988).

An important context for this analysis is recent critiques of identity discourse and archaeology, including literature on archaeology, ethnicity, and nationalism (Bond and Gilliam 1995; Kohl and Fawcett 1995; Atkinson et al. 1996; Diaz-Andreu and Champion 1996; Graves-Brown et al. 1996; Jones 1997). These critiques spring from widespread intellectual interest in the social context of knowledge production and, in particular, the use of knowledge about the past in maintaining or subverting power in society. American historical archaeologists have pursued this issue more vigorously in the arena of investigating capitalism, both in the past as well as the way in which it

forms the context for question formulation in the present (Leone and Potter 1999).

Following postcolonial theorists, this paper approaches nationalism as a significant form of cultural identity that may be expressed through and constituted by all kinds of cultural practice (Anderson 1983; Bhabha 1990; Brennan 1990; Parker et al. 1992; Ashcroft et al. 1995). The Australian nation was created through the events of British colonial expansion and through the eventual transferal of colonial control from the founding metropolitan country to the colony itself, where it has been maintained through the unity and complicity of the settler group (McClintock 1994:258). Nationalism and colonialism cannot be considered as two separate or opposing ideologies in Australia; they remain fundamentally intertwined. Australia experienced no war of independence and still maintains the Queen of England as the head of state. The 1992 High Court of Australia's Mabo decision concerning lands rights for indigenous people has been claimed by some to be the most significant disruption of ongoing colonialism in this nation's history (Attwood 1996a:109).

Rather than looking at archaeology as a discipline that may be impacted upon, to greater or lesser degrees, by external influences such as nationalism, this paper seeks to understand traditions of understanding that are embedded within Australian historical archaeology and the subtle, multilayered relationships between archaeology and other cultural discourses. Such analysis necessarily relates to debates concerning disciplinary objectivity, relativism, and academic responsibilities (Kohl and Fawcett 1995; Lampeter Archaeology Workshop 1997). Discourse analysis, as employed here, accepts that all ideas, theories, and explanations are created within and through a complex historic, socio/cultural, and linguistic situation. Further, this analysis is admittedly political in that it addresses current social and ethical concerns about how nationalist/colonialist pasts are used to promote restrictive and oppressive identities in the present.

The quotation at the beginning of this paper comes from David Malouf's novel *Remembering Babylon*, a recent re-examination of what is, perhaps, the most dominant theme in Australian settler art and literature—the question of the land and its role in shaping national identity. Malouf takes the trope of Australia's hostile environment and explores the real effects of this culturally constructed perception in the day-to-day lives of settlers. In this way, he disrupts the familiar colonialist narratives, which center on success or failure in the battle against the environment. In the passage quoted above, Malouf describes how a settler from Scotland feels about her surroundings on a remote Australian farm. He catalogues what is absent from the place: the features of the European landscape that formed her cultural identity and to which her culture gives symbolic meaning. Malouf's settlers *do* see the land as empty and threatening, and this is based on the European perception that property involves improvement and exploitation of resources rather than simply living with the land as the Aborigines are seen to do (Fletcher 1997:177). The novel, in fact, employs a conceit whereby Aborigines become literally invisible to the settlers, as invisible as the ecological balance of the land that they struggle to make more like home. This invisibility was also found in the historical narratives of colonial settlement before the appearance of challenging revisionist histories such as those by Henry Reynolds (1981, 1987). Despite the impact of Aboriginal histories, some sections of the community reject these interpretations of the national past as "black armband" history, a view reinforced by the Australian Prime Minister in a famous 1996 speech (Howard 1996, Birch 1997).

In the phrase "the absence of ghosts," Malouf describes the cultural foundations of the concept of *terra nullius* in the minds of settlers. This concept is central to the understanding of colonialist representations of and responses to Australian land and, therefore, a crucial component of what is called landscape discourse in this paper. *Terra nullius* was the legal description of the concept that the continent of Australia was vacant and wilderness before the possession of the land by the British, based on the belief that Aborigines and Torres Strait Islanders, as hunter-gatherers, did not improve the land and, thus, had no proprietorial rights to it. This legal doctrine was finally overthrown by the High Court's Mabo land rights decision in 1992, which provided the first legal basis for the recognition of prior ownership of Australian land by indigenous people. Malouf's settlers' perception of the Australian landscape as hostile and without a human dimension results in a con-

stant and unhappy emphasis on survival and on the hardships associated with changing or battling the land to conform to their understanding of civilization and progress. It also results in the formation of a group identity based primarily upon fear of their opponents: nature or the environment and Aborigines as nature's strange envoys in human form (Fletcher 1997:176).

The paradigm of *terra nullius* is crucial to the foundational histories and popular understandings of Australia as a nation of settlers rather than conquerors. Although no longer upheld by law, the concept remains deeply embedded within Australian culture, from beliefs about pioneers and settler identity through to understandings of traditional Aboriginal culture, the land, nature, and so-called wilderness (Langton 1995). Recent studies have attempted to understand the significance of *terra nullius* and its subsequent overturning in the Mabo decision to Australian settler culture and national identity through a consideration of how the term has operated within various fields of discourse such as colonial history, science, politics, literature, and Aboriginal archaeology (Attwood 1996b; Murray 1996a; Griffiths and Robin 1997; Gelder and Jacobs 1998). The main aim of this analysis of historical archaeology is to draw out the way in which landscape discourse has operated within and through research and writing. However, the research that is critiqued in this paper should not be considered to be without value because it has perpetuated colonialist constructions of the past. Analysis of the cultural and social context of research, which is not just an interesting subfield of the history of archaeology, enables constructive new readings of research and allows past research to be built upon rather than being simply dismissed as outdated.

Landscape and Identity in the Australian Cultural Tradition

This section briefly reviews key elements of Australian settler history and intellectual traditions that have contributed to understanding the landscape in particular ways. Settling Australia was an imaginary as well as a physical process. The culture of the settlers provided the forms and descriptions through which the landscape was given a meaning and shape that was comprehensible to them. Australian settlers were predominately from Britain and Ireland, more than 160,000 arriving as convicts until transportation finally ceased in 1868. Free immigrants were also predominantly English, Scottish, and Irish, although some Europeans were encouraged, especially Germans, thought to be culturally and racially closest to the British. Chinese immigration, largely associated with the gold rushes of the 1850s and 60s, caused immense social debate in the late-19th century. Consequently, one of the first acts of the newly federated nation in 1901 was to pass legislation that was to become the basis for Australia's notorious White Australia Policy, which persisted until 1966 (Curthoys 1999b: 279). However, despite this predominance of settlers of Anglo-Celtic heritage, it should be remembered that the settler group was still ethnically, religiously, and politically diverse (Melleuish 1998:10). Postwar migration radically changed the ethnic composition of Australian society. Since the late 1940s, there has been a steady widening of the potential countries-of-origin of immigrants, and this has engendered a diverse society, which struggles in a search for appropriate expressions of cultural identity and national unity (Pettman 1992). In the absence of a common cultural legacy, the experience of place has been described as central to identity constructions in settler societies (Ashcroft et al. 1995:152). In Australia, the ideology of colonialism has constructed the land as the prime object of desire, and it is the consequences of this desire that provides the clearest basis for a community identity that is different from the idea of the mother country.

The Land As Empty

A philosophical rationale for the colonization or invasion of Australia in 1788 was in part provided by the Scottish Enlightenment philosophers, such as Adam Smith and Adam Ferguson, who expounded an influential theory of the evolution of human society (Attwood 1996b:ix). This four-phase explanation saw hunter-gatherers as the first stage in a natural evolution that concluded with commerce and empire. Hunter-gatherers, they proposed, had no conception of property and so their lands were deemed desert or waste—*terra nullius*. Interest in cultural evolution was one of the scientific rationales for the

journeys of exploration into the Pacific. "The Moral Philosopher ... who loves to trace the advances of his species ... draws from voyages and travels the facts from which he is to deduce his conclusions respecting the social, intellectual, and moral progress of Man" (Jacques Julien de Labillardiere, 1800, quoted in Dixon 1986:6). These journeys were, therefore, conceived of as travel into the ancient past that could be used to complete knowledge of "the history of man."

Within this framework, Aborigines were thought of as living in a different time from the Europeans: a time before history. Brian Attwood (1996b) has analyzed the implications of the epistemological framework of the European discourse of history for both the act of colonization and the subsequent construction of Australian colonial history. European historical discourse, following enlightenment and evolutionary thinking, aligns time with progress in an inevitable linear progression. This discursive alignment formed part of the mental framework that enabled the British to see the Australian landscape as wilderness and available for possession. Attwood (1996b:viii) therefore claims that "History was not only the discourse of the colonizers; it was also a colonizing one." Colonization and its attendant Christianity, civilization, and progress enabled history, therefore, to begin on a continent where time in European terms had previously been meaningless.

In 1828, Sir Thomas Mitchell was appointed as Surveyor General of New South Wales. A man of great energy, Mitchell saw his mission as translating the tracts of wilderness into intellectually defined objects through a process of survey and naming. At that time, settlement was confined to areas close to Sydney, but the whole of the east coast had been claimed for Britain. Mitchell undertook extensive journeys of exploration in eastern Australia in order to lay the necessary framework for this imperial possession. His exploration diaries detail how each expedition was led by Aboriginal guides who negotiated with the various tribes encountered along the way. Although Mitchell records daily encounters with different groups of Aboriginal people, he was, nevertheless, able to write that he saw "a country which is yet in the same state as it was when formed by its maker ... . A land so inviting, and still without inhabitants" (Lines 1991:71). Mitchell named the lush valleys of

Victoria "Australia Felix" and wrote, "Of this Eden it seemed that I was the only Adam and it was indeed a sort of paradise to me" (Schaffer 1988:60).

The Land As Hostile:
Explorers and Pioneers

Mitchell and the early explorers wrote of Australia in rapturous terms; however, as settlement and exploration progressed, as explorers perished, and farmers experienced drought, the land came to be seen as harsh and threatening. As early as 1849, when Charles Sturt published an account of his failed journey to locate an inland sea in the center of the continent, visions of rapture were replaced with a perception of the continent as inhospitable to civilization (Gibson 1996:92). But the dangerous and threatening character of the land was to be construed as the test of Empire and the test from which Australian manhood would emerge ennobled:

> To successfully plant a young Colony ... seems to require special qualities, physical, moral and intellectual, which are possessed in their highest form by the Anglo-Saxon people. It is a small matter to supplant the Aboriginal inhabitants of a barbarous country and to secure possession of their land ... . It is battling with Nature, conquering the soil, holding on against capricious seasons, fighting with the elements and compelling the earth to yield ... . (William Harcus's 1876 emigration guide, quoted in Schaffer 1988:84).

Sir Keith Hancock's 1930 history *Australia* is seen as a crucial text in establishing and giving academic authority to a nationalist history connecting the land with national character. Hancock's history was centrally concerned with land settlement and the pastoral industry as the instrument of colonial possession. The battle for possession is the battle to establish European agricultural systems in the Australian environment. The enemy in this battle is, therefore, nature, not international trade, economic depression, or the inequities of the colonial administration (Schaffer 1988:87). Failure on the land, through drought, bushfire, and flood, came to be seen as the mythical forge for national character. Pioneers were the free immigrants from Britain and Ireland (as opposed to the non-free convicts) who fought to establish new lives free of Old World class prejudices and poverty. The settler's "failure" in material terms is compensated by the spiritual benefits of pioneering strength, stoicism, and love of the land, love of the nation.

Anne Curthoys interprets Australia's pioneer legend as an essentially "victimological narrative," which, she argues, resonates meanings derived from Judeo-Christian history and from biblical stories such as the Exodus (Curthoys 1999a:4). The inheritance of these pioneer and land myths, Curthoys claims, underlies the inability of many Australians to deal with a history that paints them as colonial aggressors, rather than as the victims or survivors of a history of struggle.

The Bushman and the Bush
As the "Essence" of Australia

The 1890s have been constructed through later historiography as the decade in which a true national culture was crystallized. By this time, 70% of the settler population was Australian-born, and the six colonies were instigating the process of federation, which led to the creation of the continent nation in 1901 (Byrne 1996). Australian writers, artists, journalists, and politicians began to consciously articulate descriptions of a unique national character at this time, using imagery that, although reinvented, remains current and influential at the start of the 21st century. The results of the settler experience became essentialized in the myth of the "bushman." The bushman was a model of masculinity created by the effects of the Australian landscape, resulting in a typical national character that was defined in Russell Ward's *The Australian Legend* as the antiauthoritarian larrikin, practical and independent, but loyal to his mates (Ward 1958:1–2). The Great War of 1914–1918 saw this same national type heroized as the Digger or the Anzac (White 1981; Lake 1992:313).

Henry Lawson's stories and poems are perhaps the best-known exemplars of the bushman genre. One form of the bush hero beloved by Lawson is the Swagman, an out-of-work man who wandered the roads of rural Australia carrying nothing but his swag, or bedroll. Lawson writes: "The Australian swag was born of Australia and no other land—of the Great Lone Land of magnificent distances and bright heat: the land of Self-reliance and Never give in and Help your mate" (Hodge and Mishra 1990:153). This sentence is a distillation of Lawson's ideology of the bush, clearly articulating how facets of the environment—distance, isolation, and harsh climate—shaped a unique Australian character that was built on egalitarian, masculine mateship.

The main aspect to note about the myth of the bushman is that its most famous exponents were a group of urban writers and the magazine the *Bulletin*, which was a mouthpiece for the urban liberal bourgeois *against* the interests of powerful rural pastoralists. In contrast to the pioneer myths of settlement discussed above, which are more centrally concerned with the process of imperial possession, the bush myths link more strongly with these nationalist, democratic ideologies. The bush or the land is used as an allegory for the masculine freedom that was the political agenda of the writers. However, this allegorical function of the bush within the political context of the 1890s is a largely forgotten aspect of this construction as it was reproduced throughout the 20th century as a key aspect of national identity. This is designed, despite significant critical scholarship that has shown the bush myth and the "The Australian Legend" to be an ideological construct, to reproduce the authority of masculinist, political interest groups (Davison 1978; White 1981; Lake 1986).

The bush myth has also been constituted through and perpetuated by landscape art. In particular, the images of the Heidelburg School of the 1880s and 1890s remain icons in Australian culture today. These landscape images, often employing a heroic figure dwarfed by open surroundings, so dominated Australian art that they led prominent art historian Bernard Smith to state in 1976, "This preoccupation with landscape has been largely responsible for the creation and maintenance of a false consciousness of what it is to be Australian" (Hodge & Mishra 1990:143). The idea that national character is a result of our, or our ancestors', experience of the bush and its hardships still pervades Australian culture today, exemplified in recent films such as *Crocodile Dundee*, *The Man from Snowy River*, and even *Priscilla, Queen of the Desert*. Libby Robin has recently pointed out how the meaning of the bush in national culture has changed since the 1970s. The value of a rural life on the frontier, as conceived of by the *Bulletin* writers, has transmuted into the concept of the spiritually restorative wilderness, required as an escape for suburban Australians from "economy and history" (Robin 1998:123). Of particular interest in Robin's work in this context is her argument

that current meanings of bush and wilderness, associated with the environmental conservation movement, have been developed through the power and meaning of the earlier bush myths, revitalizing in some ways their ongoing centrality in national culture. Further, the texts and representations that created the bush myth, and that were so self-consciously created to express the emergence of a new national culture, are also pervaded by a description of gender relations that continued to resonate in Australian culture in the 20th century (Rowley 1993:186).

The Land As Feminine

If the bushman has represented the nation, then the nation's "other" has been seen as the land or the body of Australia itself. Analysts of cultural nationalism have outlined how the nation develops conceptions of itself in opposition to a perceived other, an object that may be simultaneously both desired and despised. In Australian nationalist traditions, the other can take many forms: it may be Britain, it may be Aborigines or Asians, but frequently the other is the landscape itself. The linguistic signification of Australia as mother and the land as the body of a woman was studied in detail in a groundbreaking analysis published by Kay Schaffer in 1988. In essence, it is the colonialist framework of desire, to possess, master, and tame, which casts the object of this desire, the land, in a feminine role. Historical rhetoric of the 19th and early-20th centuries constantly eroticizes the love/hate relationship between the settlers and the land. The explorers "lift her veils of mystery" and penetrate the vast recesses of the interior. In contrast to the benevolent European construction of Mother Earth, Australia is often personified as a "witch mother," experimenting on her helpless victims.

The consequence of this discourse, which casts the nation as masculine and its other as feminine, is that women as subjects have been almost totally absent from constructions of national identity. In the 1970s, Anne Summers and Miriam Dixson initiated an ongoing analysis into what they considered was an ethos of subtle contempt for women that pervaded the Australian cultural tradition (Summers 1975; Dixson 1976). As has been seen, the bushman is a loner, just a man and the wide-open spaces; freedom is paramount as is loyalty to his mates. The ties of wife and family were construed as the antithesis to this freedom (Lake 1986:118; Lake 1992:312). Significantly, the bush myth casts the battle with the land as establishing the territory of the nation. This creates an inherent tension between the ties of family and nation-building work on the land. As Sue Rowley points out, when women are present in bush literature, their labor is not marked on the land but on their own bodies, which Henry Lawson habitually described as "gaunt" and "haggard": "these women are positioned not as the heroes of the battle, but as its casualties" (Rowley 1993:188).

This construction has since been the subject of much historical explanation. It has led to an overwhelming focus on bush work, mineral prospecting, droving, and pastoralism for instance, as the work that made the nation. Revisionist histories have successfully "discovered" women in the past, included them in popular historical accounts, and even established their contribution to nation building (Margarey et al. 1993; Grimshaw et al. 1994). However, the ongoing power of this discourse, which establishes a relationship between men and the national territory based on patriarchal gender relations, continues to resonate in Australian national life (Reekie 1992:17).

Landscape and Identity As Discourses within Archaeological Interpretation

Landscape discourse is not only a set of ideas about the landscape but also about settler men and women who are constructed in various roles in opposition to it, about history that is seen as a result of it, and about Aborigines who are viewed as part of it. The idea of landscape is so central to the national cultural tradition that research, which takes the settler landscape as its subject, must develop a critical capacity regarding its historical and literary construction. This critique should also be turned back upon the discipline of historical archaeology itself, not only to inform approaches to the historic landscape or the past in general but also in order to understand the cultural context of established research questions and fields of interest.

Historical Archaeology and Heritage

The following review of historical archaeological research suggests that landscape discourse operates

within the discipline in a number of ways. First, there is a fundamental and entrenched relationship between the practice of historical archaeology and identity discourse, through the philosophy and institutions of the heritage movement. Historical archaeology, as a practice that studies the physical remains of Australia's history, cannot be considered in isolation from the processes that resulted in the attribution of value to the material remains of the national past. Its emergence as a field of interest in the 1960s and 1970s can be historically located within a national revival of interest in Australian history, literature, art, and material culture (Bennett 1993:236). This, in turn, was linked to local and international conservation and environmental movements and the bolstering of national and regional identities in the face of perceived cultural globalization. The environmental movement, which emerges in Australia in the 1960s, has been described as "a fusion of romanticism, nationalism, and science, but ... also an attempt to reject colonialism" (Morton and Smith 1999:172). Although today environmental conservation and settler heritage movements have many tensions and divergent aims, their roots in essentially nationalistic concerns seem to be clear. The idea that landscape and settler identity are linked has been accepted as a fact within environmental and heritage conservation movements—as a taken-for-granted, spiritual association rather than a historically constructed idea. It is also significant that in Australian conservation legislation, heritage is often termed environmental heritage (as in the New South Wales Heritage Act, 1977) and is constituted in legislation as a part of the environment. This implies that heritage, like biodiversity, exists independently of human thought and is not ideologically constructed. Hence cultural resource management has concentrated on developing empirical methodologies to "discover" heritage and organize it into taxonomies of relative value rather than to approach it as culturally constructed or examining the role it plays in community life.

The ethnographic and archaeological interest in Aboriginal cultural heritage has a very different history, which is beyond the scope of this paper. It is important to note however, that this interest developed out of 18th- and 19th-century interest in the natural history of Australia, within Enlightenment concepts of evolution and amateur traditions of collecting and antiquarianism. Historical archaeology, although now linked to Australian prehistory institutionally and methodologically, draws its concepts of value and significance from a process that historicized the settler nation and constructed ideas of national heritage and identity. This is not to say that, as a practice, historical archaeology has not absorbed ways of constructing meaning and attributing value from other fields of discourse; it is obvious that it has. However, the idea that the material remains of the recent past are worth studying at all is one that has been established within the community predominantly through the discourse of national heritage and identity rather than through discourses concerned with the universal value of knowledge, such as history, science, and archaeology in general.

Griffiths (1996:195) and Graeme Davison (1991:3) argue that what was new about the heritage movement of the 1960s and 1970s was not its nationalistic focus, as heritage and nationalism can be seen as strongly linked in the 19th century, but the redefinition of heritage as a material rather than a spiritual concept. The idea of a material heritage, and its accompanying concepts of collecting, curation, and conservation, gave archaeological methodologies an obvious role in the newly defined heritage movement. Griffiths has shown that an archaeological sense of the past, a belief that scientific methodologies may be used to recover material remnants and decode their meaning, is integral to the nature of the modern preservation movement (Griffiths 1996:196). This linking of materiality with heritage ensured that archaeology as a practice became more deeply involved in the discourse of heritage and, of course, in heritage management work than was the case with the related disciplines of history and anthropology (Byrne 1996:101). Archaeologists, such as Jim Allen, Judy Birmingham, Anne Bickford, Isabel McBryde, Rhys Jones, and John Mulvaney, who were specifically concerned with the potential of the new field of historical archaeology also played a significant role in the formative history of the Australian Heritage Commission, the national body responsible for heritage administration since 1974. Their involvement ensured that historical archaeology defined a strong niche as a discipline responsible for an important component of the nation's heritage (Bonyhady and Griffiths 1996:9).

Historical archaeology in Australia still possesses a limited base in universities and receives relatively little funding from sources that traditionally fund research in Old World archaeology or prehistory (Egloff 1994). Consequently, most historical archaeological work is funded through private clients complying with cultural resource management requirements embodied in legislation, which varies from state to state (Colley 1996; Connah 1998:3). Thus, historical archaeological research must justify itself in terms of its ability to address themes enshrined as important within heritage management frameworks. This in itself need not and, of course, in many cases has not prohibited creative responses to archaeological research issues. However, as some of the examples discussed below will demonstrate, it has tended to link historical archaeological research to a framework of national history, which has traditionally supported dominant identity constructions and which reflects colonialist myths about the nature of the land and men's relationship to it (Ireland 1996:92).

Town and Country

As we have seen, art and literature that valorized men's lives in the bush in the 19th century, for the purpose of allegory supporting a political standpoint, has been taken as evidence of historical experience, as a reflection of reality rather than as a construction for a political purpose. In addition to this, the colonialist history of the "progressive mastery" of the land—peopling it, making it useful through industry and agriculture—has dominated accounts of Australia's national development. This construction of the past can be shown to have constrained and influenced archaeology in a number of ways, but also, significantly, there is some suggestion that the archaeological evidence itself has provided some resistance to it.

"Of the Hut I Builded," Graham Connah's 1988 overview of Australian historical archaeology, is an example of how a variety of archaeological research and interpretation may be structured within a framework that tacitly reproduces colonialist and nationalist constructions of the past (Connah 1988, later published under the title *The Archaeology of Australia's History*). The purpose of the following discussion of this text is to analyze its discursive context, not to criticize it for omissions identified with the hindsight of a decade of revisionist history and in the light of a significantly different intellectual climate.

It should be noted that the book was published with assistance from the Australian Bicentennial Authority, a body that funded a host of history and heritage-related projects to mark 200 years of colonization in 1988.

The book mirrors the tendency for historical archaeological research, especially that linked to heritage management projects and funding sources, to follow the popularly understood themes of nationalist history: the centrality of rural expansion in the process of founding the nation, the importance of industrialization, and the hostility of the environment to these processes. The rhetorical style of the text reinforces this thematic structure: for instance, the settlement of Sydney is where the "birth of a new nation can be observed from the archaeological evidence," while convicts are celebrated for their "vital role in the settlement of this nation" (Connah 1988:35,62). The implication of considering the archaeology of early Sydney as a foundation for the nation closes our eyes to the other histories being played out at that time. For instance, the first annexation of Australia clung to the eastern coast, integrating Sydney in a colonial adventure that in the minds of many included the adjacent Pacific islands for as far as Tahiti (Crowley 1974:48). The Australian nation, based on the continental landmass, was not a foregone conclusion in 1788.

The book instantly invokes the mythology of the bush by taking the Henry Lawson poem, *Reedy River*, as its leitmotif. The poem revisits many of Lawson's prominent themes concerning man's insignificance in the Australian landscape, its intractability, and dual status as desired object and hated foe. Three of the book's eight chapters dealing with archaeological evidence are devoted to industry and rural production. Although whaling is discussed briefly in one chapter, maritime industry and trade economies, which account for critical, early transferals of capital into the colony, do not feature as a theme of this land-centered narrative. Evidence from maritime archaeology, covering only the wrecks of Dutch East Indiamen, is confined to a chapter dealing with "pre-colonial contact" and is seen as an interesting prolegomenon to the business of colonization from 1788. However, as Wayne Johnson's paper in this volume shows, the continent of Australia was certainly implicated in European colonial politics from well before this

date. Schuyler has also usefully shown that interaction prior to actual settlement also changes cultural landscapes, and recognition of this interaction allows richer archaeological interpretations than may be achieved within the confines of nationalist history (Schuyler 1991). The evidence of Dutch East India Company shipwrecks is construed by Connah as precolonial because it predates the settlement of Australia by the British. This highlights the understanding of colonization as settlement and nation building rather than as a complex phenomenon including colonial trade, military, and cultural activities.

Although research in urban archaeology and contact archaeology (archaeology of contact between settler and indigenous people) is referred to in the final chapter of the book, much of this research existed in unpublished reports at the time that the text was written. Connah's book also reflects a preference for the analysis of structural and technological remains rather than artifact and material culture analysis, which remains a poorly published issue in Australian historical archaeology (Lawrence 1998b). The incompatibility of the overall themes of land settlement and industry in Connah's text with the social issues addressed by urban archaeology and material culture studies, may be another reason why attempts were not made to address what was then a burgeoning interest in the urban archaeology of the 19th century (Karskens and Thorp 1992; Lydon 1993).

The romance of the bush, then, continues to seduce those seeking the essential qualities of the Australian historical experience. Stephanie Moser has suggested that Australian prehistory sought its disciplinary identity through the rigors of fieldwork in the remote outback, archaeologists themselves reliving Lawson's promise of masculine fulfillment in the arms of the bush (Moser 1995). Historical archaeologists, rather than reliving this tradition, have given much attention to explaining it.

No Place for a Woman

It is in the area of urban archaeology that the realities of the material evidence have drawn archaeologists into directions that challenged the dominant discourses of national development. Historical archaeology's concentration on rural work and industry continued to reconstruct the idea of Australia as "Manzone Country" (Summers 1975). Its focus on pioneer technology and the success or failure of technological processes perpetuated an almost tacit understanding that this was the work that had made the nation, and it was man's work. An analysis of the contents of the *Australian Journal of Historical Archaeology* (now *Australasian Historical Archaeology*) shows how research implicitly reinforced this construction. Since it was first published in 1983, this journal has published 65 case studies on Australian rural or industrial sites or groups of sites, and only eight case studies on urban archaeology (the balance of articles, on other subjects such as conservation and theory, numbers 60).

The alternative thread in historical archaeological research has come from within the heritage management industry rather than from the academy. The creation of legislation protecting historical archaeological relics, particularly in NSW in 1977, has seen a gradual growth in compliance, which has resulted in numerous, large-scale excavations of urban sites and neighborhoods and also in Melbourne (Mayne and Lawrence 1998; Murray and Mayne this volume). Much of this work exists in unpublished reports (but compare Proudfoot et al. 1991; Lydon 1993; Karskens 1999). This paper contends that the explosion in urban archaeology, which began in Sydney in the late 1980s, occurred because of the creation of a solid legislative footing. It also occurred because of the commitment of the cultural resource managers responsible for implementing this legislation and educating the public on the heritage value of historical archaeological material (Temple 1988). However, the debates about the value of these urban excavations suggest that archaeological researchers themselves were struggling for the conceptual and methodological frameworks required to make sense of this kind of archaeology (Birmingham 1990; Karskens and Thorp 1992; Egloff 1994; Mackay 1996; see in particular Thorp quoted in Mackay 1996): "The relics provisions of the NSW Heritage Act allows archaeologists to be lazy. If a relic exists ... it can be the subject of an archaeological excavation. That does not ensure that the site, or object, is significant or worthy of excavation." What this means is that the heritage management infrastructure, through its insistence on the potential value of all archaeological material, forced archaeologists to move in new directions.

Because of the exigencies of the consulting archaeological industry, the lack of full-time researchers, and the fact that these sites produced such huge numbers of artifacts, work from urban sites was slow to be published. Artifact analysis was an overwhelming and expensive proposition, and it took some years for a grounding in analytical skills and an orientation in material culture theory to be established in the professional community (Birmingham 1990; Lawrence 1998b). There are many practical issues that made it difficult for academic and postgraduate researchers to participate in urban archaeological research. The value of inner city land means that it will rarely, if ever, be available for the sort of long-term, planned research that can be scheduled into the university calendar. Rural sites, removed from the pressures of development, suit the academic far better in terms of arranging successive seasons of fieldwork separated by periods of writing and analysis.

However, the material evidence of urban life *has* encouraged consulting archaeologists into productive partnerships with academic archaeologists and social historians in order to interpret and interrogate the material culture (Karskens and Thorp 1992; Mayne and Lawrence 1998; Karskens 1999). The new focus on the domestic sphere has led to a reconsideration of the roles of women as consumers, mothers, homemakers, publicans, and boardinghouse keepers. Growing interest in feminist theory had a major impact in defining the key fields of interest for urban archaeologists (Lydon 1995a; Karskens 1997). Jane Lydon has explained historical archaeology's tardiness in adopting feminist themes in terms of its dominant theoretical approaches, which favored economic and technological explanatory frameworks (Lydon 1995b). The evidence presented here also suggests that nationalist discourse shaped this aspect of practice, reflecting its particular concerns with settling the land, the hostile environment, the bushman as hero, and the absence of women as subjects within this discourse.

The way in which urban archaeology raised issues such as women's lives, ethnicity, and the relationship between identity and material culture, has now provided evidence that reveals the "flatness" of dominant nationalist discourses, the homogenizing effect that narratives of unity and progress have on the heterogeneity of lives and social relationships in the past (Karskens 1999, Lydon 1999). At the same time, Susan Lawrence has chosen to meet the myths head on and has used material culture and archaeological evidence to examine the nature of men's lives in the bush (Lawrence 1998a, 1998b, 1999). Lawrence takes the construction of the lone bushman and shows that the reality is likely to have been far more complicated. She sheds light on the social and sexual tensions of 1890s society by demonstrating the conflicting constructions of masculinity apparent in the context of archaeological and historical evidence. Lawrence's work on various bush sites has also approached industry in its social context, addressing issues raised by revisionist social and feminist historians, as well as aspects of material culture theory, to reveal that "Whalers, miners, and pastoral workers were physically remote from the main stream of society, but they were none the less integrated with it. A habitus that incorporated domestic ideology, and domesticated masculine identity, informed the lives of men, and sometimes women, in the bush" (Lawrence 1998a:5).

Success and Failure

Colonization is underpinned by an understanding of settlement as transformative: wasteland into productive land, nature into culture. As discussed earlier, the construction of the landscape as hostile has its roots in the imagery of the late-19th century and was promulgated through later history writing that emphasized the "battle" against nature as the only battle involved in the process of building the settler nation. Griffiths has shown how successive Australian governments ignored advice on the nature of arid inland environments and continued to promote the spread of settlement on the basis of "national and racial anxiety" (Griffiths and Robin 1997: 11). Nationalistic rhetoric, therefore, construes the Australian environment as hostile, rather than construing the policies of government as wrong headed or as being able to ignore human suffering in order to achieve political ends.

Within historical archaeological interpretation, the idea of the "battle" to settle the land and make it productive has generated a marked tendency to consider sites and landscapes in terms of success or failure. Studies carried out in the 1970s and 1980s aimed to establish a field of

interest for the emerging practice of historical archaeology, and their focus was solidly on the abandoned relics of agricultural and industrial technology (Birmingham et al. 1979, 1983). Further, abandoned rural and industrial sites were under threat from decay, expanding urban settlement, and modern industry, so the recording of such places became established not only as a core interest of the practice but also as a conservation imperative. Abandoned rural and industrial sites now form an important research genre, or field of interest, in Australian historical archaeology, as the number of case studies published in the *Journal of Australian Historical Archaeology* shows. The fact that sites were interpreted within a predominantly economic framework, such as that proposed by Judy Birmingham and Dennis Jeans (1983), also predisposed interpretation towards the success/failure question.

Thus, we see that archaeologists have effectively established a circular and self-perpetuating relationship between the myth of the hostile environment and the battle to establish the nation and the research that seeks to examine it. Abandoned and notionally unsuccessful enterprises are sought out in order to explain their failure. Obviously, research on "successful" sites still in operation is more problematic, and although examples can be found, they are less dominant. Individually these case studies of "failure" often provide insightful analyses. The fact that success/failure becomes a self-evident structuring device in interpretation, however, with the greater weight of evidence falling on the side of failure, means that archaeological research continues to reproduce the idea that the environment in Australia is hostile and the intent of colonization is benign.

The success/failure model has also been employed more broadly: in *Of the Hut I Builded*, Connah devotes a chapter to the archaeology of failed settlements, sites that have held obvious fascination for historical archaeologists, not least as early remains undisturbed by later development. One of the examples reviewed in this chapter is the military outpost of Victoria, Port Essington (in Arnhem Land, northern Australia), which was the subject of a detailed study by Allen in the 1960s and 70s. Allen's interpretation of this site was as a "successful strategic maneuver rather than a failed attempt at colonization" (Allen 1973:44). While Connah refers to Allen's interpretation, he further concludes, "strategic and political considerations were not a sufficient basis on their own for colonial success" (Connah 1988:49). This suggests a moral difference between the motives for establishing a settlement that are purely "strategic" and "political" and motives that are described as a *genuine* interest in colonization" (Connah 1988:49, emphasis added). As pointed out earlier, in this terminology, "colonization" is synonymous with "nation building," while strategic and political aims appear to be associated more with protecting the selfish interests of remote imperial authorities. Here the success/failure concept invokes not only the idea of battling the hostile environment but also the understanding of colonization as progress towards an outcome of meaning and value, in this case the birth of the nation. This equation is founded in Enlightenment historical discourse and Judeo-Christian narrative structures through which colonization imagines its successful transformation of wilderness into useful, productive land (Rose 1999:8).

Shared Landscapes

The most significant changes in Australian archaeology over recent decades have occurred due to the deconstruction of colonial precepts in Aboriginal prehistory and in the ethics involved in archaeologists working with Aboriginal communities. As part of international interest in the implications of colonialism, there has been a recent spate of papers on how to "decolonize" Australian archaeology (Murray 1992, 1996a, 1996b, 1996c; Pardoe 1992; Byrne 1996; Head 1996, 1998). Historical archaeologists showed an early interest in the issue of contact and in Aboriginal historic sites (Allen 1973 and Birmingham 1992 on the site of Wybalenna investigated between 1969–71). It is only recently, however, that Aboriginal culture since 1788 has begun to be seriously investigated (Murray 1993, 1996c; Colley and Bickford 1996). Sarah Colley and Anne Bickford (1996) have clearly outlined some of the institutional and theoretical barriers that have hindered the development of contact archaeology. These include the fact that settler and Aboriginal heritage are often protected under different legislation. In compliance archaeology, one set of consultants look at Aboriginal cultural heritage, while others are employed to examine settler heritage. Therefore, in day-to-day work,

there have been few arenas in which the cultural landscape of colonialism, the historic period, could be studied in a holistic way. These disciplinary and legislative boundaries are colonial artifacts in themselves, a result of seeing Aborigines as a part of the environment and as a people with no history. Denis Byrne has pointed to the potential power of the historical archaeology of Aboriginal people in countering nationalist constructions of the past and acting for reconciliation (Byrne 1996:102). However, traditional archaeological approaches to studying both prehistoric sites and landscapes and settler landscapes as evidence of agricultural and technological processes have not provided any framework within which to approach what must, in many cases, have been shared Aboriginal and European landscapes. In most contact studies, the point has been to assess the impact of settler culture upon Aboriginal behavior and technology. Traditional archaeological methodologies are not well suited to accommodate attempts to understand complex cultural exchanges and, for instance, impact upon settlers by Aboriginal culture. It is notable that in the history of settler culture, settlers are impacted upon by the environment but rarely by Aboriginal culture. The assumption that colonial activities overwrite and obliterate indigenous cultural landscapes is simplistic—an artifact of a worldview that sees progress and modernity as wiping out all evidence of the past, of the impact of colonialism as fatal and total rather than potentially creative of hybrid forms.

Hybridization of social landscapes requires us to imagine new ways to analyze historical and archaeological data. Nationalist discourse operates to simplify power relations between the colonizers and the colonized in the past. By contrast, Lydon's study of Chinese people living in Sydney, showed how these relationships were "contested and contingent," with the "possibility for shared systems of meaning" (Lydon 1999:174). Lydon contextualizes material culture within an "ethnographic collage" to reveal the way in which Chinese people at the turn of the century could both mimic dominant white cultural practices, while also altering them to accommodate the needs of their traditional cultural forms.

Landscape discourse in the Australian cultural tradition ensured that the Australian landscape was imagined as a purely natural creation: a wilderness without cultural meaning. Ross Gibson's (1993) analysis of recent landscape cinema shows that Australian culture remains fascinated by the idea of the intractability of the Australian landscape; the fact that two hundred years of colonization has made little impact upon "the timeless land." As with Malouf's Scottish settlers, the culture of "others" remains invisible when viewed through the ideology of colonialism, which constructs the land as a commodity, a source of fear and desire. This paper made an argument that the realities of urban archaeology, within the heritage management framework, helped to disrupt a circularity of research within historical archaeology, where research was constructed through landscape discourse while also seeking to explain it. This is not to say that the evidence of the bush should be avoided in future in favor of urban subjects, which are more representative of settler experience. This would imply that urban studies do not have to deal with historical mythologies of their own, when much of this work concerns highly mythologized "slum" sites, characterized as the opposite of the healthy rural lifestyle idolized by Lawson and his fellow writers and artists. While it may be time to go back to the bush and re-examine the communities who lived there, it is also appropriate to reconsider cities and towns as shared spaces of multiple meanings, as advocated by Byrne in this volume and as has been demonstrated by Lydon's study of urban Chinese (Lydon 1999). Contact studies, in both rural and urban Australia, may access a rich array of material, textual, oral, and historical evidence to produce the "ethnographic collage" that is required to retheorize contact (Head and Fullagher 1997; Rose 1999). On the other hand, this may also help to re-examine and to begin to understand the human consequences of colonialism for the settlers who saw only "an absence of ghosts."

Conclusion

This paper demonstrated the discursive relationship between cultural representations of the land and the environment in Australia and the practice of historical archaeology. The ideology of colonialism constructs the land as the object of desire in Australia. In return, archaeological research has contributed to historicizing and perpetuating this colonial act of possession. The result of this conceptual circularity is that far from revealing any disciplinary objectivity, discursive relationships between archaeology, history, and national identity contrive to actually "create a reality that they appear to describe" (Schaffer 1988:171). However, there is also some evidence that individual practitioners can break out of this conceptual circularity and that archaeological evidence may provide some resistance to erroneous and complicit interpretations.

Deconstruction of colonialist and nationalist discourses has as its central motivation a concern with the ethical implications, in our day-to-day lives, of allowing our own work to promulgate systems of belief and action that oppress and exclude. Lesly Head has recently identified some of the tensions that are felt within Australian archaeology arising from political imperatives and revisionist movements across a range of disciplines. She warns about "... the danger lies in seeing such tensions as differences that need to be resolved, rather than as the problematic from which much of our creativity is springing" (Head 1998:3).

How can this warning to refuse the seduction of comfortable, resolved narratives of the past be heeded? How is it possible to open ourselves to dialogue and risk, when historical archaeology as a practice is so closely defined by the nation, and while the concept of nation itself implies some element of resolved wholeness? In this paper, the response has been to give close attention to the foundational stories of the nation and to the foundations of the way that historical archaeologists think about the Australian past. In doing this, the smooth surface of the road leading back into the past of the settler nation becomes rough and dangerous. Eventually, there is no road at all but a network of crossing paths, leading in all directions, towards untold stories.

ACKNOWLEDGMENTS

A first version of this paper was presented at the University of Glasgow, Department of Archaeology's Seminar Series in December 1998. Thank you to Professor Bernard Knapp for the invitation and to staff and students for discussion and comments. Thank you also to colleagues Wayne Johnson and Matthew Kelly who contributed to some ideas developed here, and to the editors and three anonymous referees who made many useful and challenging suggestions.

REFERENCES

ALLEN, JIM
1973 The Archaeology of Nineteenth-Century British Imperialism: An Australian Case Study. *World Archaeology,* 5(1):44–59.

ANDERSON, BENEDICT
1983 *Imagined Communities: Reflections on the Origin and Spread of Nationalism.* Verso, New York, NY.

ASHCROFT, BILL, GARETH GRIFFITHS, AND HELEN TIFFIN (EDITORS)
1995 *The Post-Colonial Studies Reader.* Routledge, London, England.

ATKINSON, JOHN, IAIN BANKS, AND JERRY O'SULLIVAN (EDITORS)
1996 *Nationalism and Archaeology.* Scottish Archaeological Forum. Cruithne Press, Glasgow, Scotland.

ATTWOOD, BAIN
1996a Mabo, Australia, and the End of History. In *In the Age of Mabo,* Bain Attwood, editor, pp. 100–116. Allen and Unwin, Sydney, NSW, Australia.
1996b Introduction, The Past as Future: Aborigines, Australia and the (Dis)course of History. In *In the Age of Mabo,* Bain Attwood, editor, pp. vii–xxxviii. Allen and Unwin, Sydney, NSW, Australia.

BENNETT, TONY
1993 History on the Rocks. *In Australian Cultural Studies: A Reader.* John Frow and Meaghan Morris, editors, pp. 222–241. Allen and Unwin, Sydney, NSW, Australia.

BHABHA, HOMI K. (EDITOR)
1990 *Nation and Narration.* Routledge, London, England.

BIRCH, TONY
1997 "Black Armbands and White Veils": John Howard's Moral Amnesia. *Melbourne Historical Journal,* 25: 8–16.

BIRMINGHAM, JUDY
1990 A Decade of Digging: Deconstructing Urban Archaeology. *Australian Journal of Historical Archaeology,* 8:13–22.
1992 *Wybalenna: The Archaeology of Cultural Accommodation in Nineteenth-Century Tasmania.* Australian Society for Historical Archaeology, Sydney, NSW.

BIRMINGHAM, JUDY, IAN JACK, AND DENNIS JEANS
1979 *Australian Pioneer Technology: Sites and Relics. Towards an Industrial Archaeology of Australia.* Heinemann, Melbourne, VIC, Australia.
1983 *Industrial Archaeology in Australia: Rural Industry.* Heinemann, Melbourne, VIC, Australia.

BIRMINGHAM, JUDY, AND DENNIS JEANS
1983 The Swiss Family Robinson and the Archaeology of Colonisation. *Australian Journal of Historical Archaeology,* 1:3–14.

BOND, GEORGE CLEMONT, AND ANGELA GILLIAM (EDITORS)
1995 *Social Construction of the Past: Representation as Power.* Routledge, London, England.

BONYHADY, TIM, AND TOM GRIFFITHS
1996 The Making of a Public Intellectual. In *Prehistory to Politics: John Mulvaney, The Humanities and the Public Intellectual,* Tim Bonyhady and Tom Griffiths, editors, pp. 1–19. Melbourne University Press, VIC, Australia.

BRENNAN, TIMOTHY
1990 The National Longing for Form. In *Nation and Narration,* Homi K. Bhabha, editor, pp. 44–70. Routledge, London, England.

BYRNE, DENIS
1996 Deep Nation: Australia's Acquistion of an Indigenous Past. *Aboriginal History,* 20:82–107.

COLLEY, SARAH
1996 Australian Archaeology: Colonialism and Postcolonial Theory. Presented to the Department of Archaeology and Anthropology Seminar Series, Australian National University, Canberra, ACT.

COLLEY, SARAH, AND ANNE BICKFORD
1996 "Real" Aborigines and "Real" Archaeology: Aboriginal Places and Australian Historical Archaeology. *World Archaeological Bulletin,* 7:5–21.

CONNAH, GRAHAM
1988 *"Of the Hut I Builded": The Archaeology of Australia's History.* Cambridge University Press, Cambridge, England.
1998 Pattern and Purpose in Historical Archaeology. *Australasian Historical Archaeology,* 16:3–7.

CROWLEY, FRANK (EDITOR)
1974 *New History of Australia.* Heinemann, Melbourne, VIC, Australia.

CURTHOYS, ANN
1999a Expulsion, Exodus, and Exile in White Australian Historical Mythology. *Journal of Australian Studies,* 61:1–18.
1999b An Uneasy Conversation: Multicultural and Indigenous Discourse. In *The Future of Australian Multiculturalism,* Ghassan Hage and Rowanne Couch, editors, pp. 277–293. Research School for Humanities and Social Sciences, University of Sydney, NSW, Australia.

DAVISON, GRAEME
1978 Sydney and the Bush: An Urban Context for the Australian Legend. *Historical Studies,* 18(71): 191–209.
1991 The Meanings of "Heritage." In *A Heritage Handbook,* Graeme Davison and Chris McConville, editors, pp. 1–13. Allen and Unwin, Sydney, NSW, Australia.

DIAZ-ANDREU, MARGARITA, AND TIMOTHY CHAMPION (EDITORS)
1996 *Nationalism and Archaeology in Europe.* UCL Press, London, England.

DIXON, ROBERT
1986 *The Course of Empire: Neo-Classical Culture in New South Wales 1788–1860.* Oxford University Press, Melbourne, VIC, Australia.

DIXSON, MIRIAM
1976 *The Real Matilda.* Penguin, Ringwood, VIC, Australia.

EGLOFF, BRIAN J.
1994 From the Swiss Family Robinson to Sir Russell Drysdale: Towards Changing the Tone of Historical Archaeology in Australia. *Australian Archaeology,* 39:1–9.

FLETCHER, M. D.
1997 Political Identity in Contemporary Australian Literature: David Malouf and Peter Carey. In *The Politics of Identity in Australia,* Geoffrey Stokes, editor, pp. 175–184. Cambridge University Press, Cambridge, England.

FOUCAULT, MICHEL
1972 *The Archaeology of Knowledge.* Pantheon, New York, NY.

GELDER, KEN, AND JANE M. JACOBS
1998 *Uncanny Australia: Sacredness and Identity in a Postcolonial Nation.* Melbourne University Press, VIC, Australia.

GIBSON, ROSS
1993 Camera Natura: Landscape in Australian Feature Films. In *Australian Cultural Studies: A Reader,* John Frow and Meaghan Morris, editors, pp. 209–221. Allen and Unwin, Sydney, NSW, Australia.
1996 Ocean Settlement. In *Exchanges: Cross-Cultural Encounters in Australia and the Pacific,* Ross Gibson, editor, pp. 89–112. Historic Houses Trust of NSW, Sydney, Australia.

GRAVES BROWN, P., SIAN JONES, AND CLIVE GAMBLE (EDITORS)
1996 *Cultural Identity and Archaeology: The Construction of European Communities.* Routledge, London, England.

GRIFFITHS, TOM
1996 *Hunters and Collectors: The Antiquarian Imagination in Australia.* Cambridge University Press, Cambridge, England.
1997 Ecology and Empire: Towards an Australian History of the World. In *Ecology and Empire,* Tom Griffith and Libby Robin, editors, pp. 1–18. Melbourne University Press, VIC, Australia.

GRIFFITHS, TOM, AND LIBBY ROBIN (EDITORS)
1997 *Ecology and Empire.* Melbourne University Press, VIC, Australia.

GRIMSHAW, PATRICIA, MARILYN LAKE, ANN MCGRATH, AND MARIAN QUARTLY
1994 *Creating a Nation 1788– 1990.* McPhee Gribble, Melbourne, VIC, Australia.

HANCOCK, KEITH
1930 *Australia.* Ernest Benn, London, England.

HEAD, LESLEY
1996 Headlines and Songlines. *Meanjin,* 55(4):736–743.
1998 Risky Representations: The Seduction of Wholeness and the Public Face of Australian Archaeology. *Australian Archaeology,* 46:1–4.

HEAD, LESLEY, AND RICHARD FULLAGAR
1997 Hunter-Gatherer Archaeology and Pastoral Contact: Perspectives from Northwest Northern Territory, Australia. *World Archaeology,* 28(3):418–428.

HODGE, BOB, AND VIJAY MISHRA
1990 *Dark Side of the Dream: Australian Literature and the Postcolonial Mind.* Allen and Unwin, Sydney, NSW, Australia.

HOWARD, JOHN
1996 Confront Our Past, Yes, But Let's Not Be Consumed by It. *The Australian,* 19 November:13.

IRELAND, TRACY
1996 Excavating National Identity. In *Sites: Nailing the Debate: Archaeology and Interpretation in Museums,* pp. 85–106. Historic Houses Trust of NSW, Sydney, Australia.

JONES, SIAN (EDITOR)
1997 *The Archaeology of Ethnicity.* Routledge, London, England.

KARSKENS, GRACE
1996–1997 Crossing Over: Archaeology and History at the Cumberland/Gloucester Street Site, The Rocks 1994–1996. *Public History Review,* 5/6:30–48.
1999 *Inside the Rocks: The Archaeology of a Neighbourhood.* Hale and Iremonger, Sydney, NSW, Australia.

KARSKENS, GRACE, AND WENDY THORP
1992 History and Archaeology in Sydney: Towards Integration and Interpretation. *Journal of the Royal Australian Historical Society,* 78(3/4):52–75.

KOHL, PHILLIP, AND CLARE FAWCETT (EDITORS)
1995 *Nationalism, Politics, and the Practice of Archaeology.* Cambridge University Press, Cambridge, England.

LAKE, MARILYN
1986 The Politics of Respectability: Identifying the Masculinist Context. *Historical Studies,* 22(86):116–131.
1992 Mission Impossible: How Men Gave Birth to the Australian Nation—Nationalism, Gender, and Other Seminal Acts. *Gender and History,* 4(3):305–322.

LAMPETER ARCHAEOLOGY WORKSHOP
1997 Relativism, Objectivity, and the Politics of the Past. *Archaeological Dialogues,* 2:164–184.

LANGTON, MARCIA
1995 The European Construction of Wilderness. *Wilderness News,* Summer 1995/96:16–17.

LAWRENCE, SUSAN

1998a Becoming Australian: Material Life in the Bush. Paper presented at the Annual Meeting of the Australian Historical Association, Sydney, NSW.

1998b The Role of Material Culture in *Australasian Archaeology*. Australasian Historical Archaeology, 16:8–15.

1999 Approaches to Gender in the Archaeology of Mining. In *Redefining Archaeology: Feminist Perspectives*, Mary Casey, Denise Donlan, Jeanette Hope, and Sharon Wellfare, editors, pp. 126–133. ANH Publications, Research School of Pacific and Asian Studies, Australian National University, Canberra, ACT.

LEONE, MARK, AND PARKER B. POTTER, JR. (EDITORS)

1999 *Historical Archaeologies of Capitalism*. Contributions to Global Historical Archaeology series, Charles E. Orser, Jr., editor. Kluwer Academic/Plenum Publishers, New York, NY.

LINES, WILLIAM J.

1991 *Taming the Great South Land: A History of the Conquest of Nature in Australia*. Allen and Unwin, Sydney, NSW, Australia.

LYDON, JANE

1993 Archaeology in The Rocks, Sydney 1979–1993: From Old Sydney Gaol to Mrs. Lewis' Boarding House. *Australasian Historical Archaeology*, 11:33–44.

1995a Boarding Houses in The Rocks: Mrs. Ann Lewis' Privy, 1865. *Public History Review*, 4:73–88.

1995b Gender in Australian Historical Archaeology. In *Gendered Archaeology: The Second Australian Women in Archaeology Conferenc*e, Jane Balme and Wendy Beck, editors, pp. 72–79. ANH Publications, Research School of Pacific and Asian Studies, Australian National University, Canberra, ACT.

1999 *Many Inventions: The Chinese in The Rocks, Sydney, 1890–1930*. Monash Publications in History, Clayton, Victoria, ACT, Australia.

MACKAY, RICHARD

1996 Political, Pictorial, Physical, and Philosophical Plans— Realising Archaeological Research Potential in Urban Sydney. In *Sites: Nailing the Debate: Archaeology and Interpretation in Museums*, pp. 123–138. Historic Houses Trust of NSW, Sydney, Australia.

MALOUF, DAVID

1994 *Remembering Babylon*. Vintage, London, England.

MARGAREY, SUSAN, SUE ROWLEY, AND SUE SHERIDAN (EDITORS)

1993 *Debutante Nation: Feminism Contests the 1890s*. Allen and Unwin, Sydney, NSW, Australia.

MAYNE, ALAN, AND SUSAN LAWRENCE

1998 An Ethnography of Place: Imagining "Little Lon." *Journal of Australian Studies*, 57:93–107.

McCLINTOCK, ANNE

1994 The Angel of Progress: Pitfalls of the Term "Postcolonialism." In *Colonial Discourse/Postcolonial Theory*, Francis Barker, Peter Hulme, and Margaret Iversen, editors, pp. 253–267. Manchester University Press, England.

MELLEUISH, GREGORY

1998 *The Packaging of Australia: Politics and Culture Wars*. University of New South Wales Press, Sydney, Australia.

MORTON, JOHN, AND NICHOLAS SMITH

1999 Planting Indigenous Species: A Subversion of Australian Eco-Nationalism. In *Quicksands: Foundational Histories in Australia and Aotearoa, New Zealand*, Klaus Neumann, Nicholas Thomas, and Hilary Ericksen, editors, pp. 153–175. University of New South Wales Press, Sydney, Australia.

MOSER, STEPHANIE

1995 Archaeology and Its Disciplinary Culture: The Professionalisation of Australian Prehistoric Archaeology. Doctoral dissertation, Department of Prehistoric and Historical Archaeology, Classics and Ancient History, University of Sydney, NSW, Australia.

MURRAY, TIM

1992 Aboriginal (Pre)History and Australian Archaeology: The Discourse of Australian Prehistoric Archaeology. In *Power, Knowledge, and Aborigines*, Bain Attwood and John Arnold, editors, pp. 1–19. A special edition of the *Journal of Australian Studies*. Latrobe University Press in association with the National Centre for Australian Studies, Bundoora, VIC.

1993 The Childhood of William Lanne: Contact Archaeology and Aboriginality in Tasmania. *Antiquity*, 67:504–519.

1996a Creating a Post-Mabo Archaeology of Australia. In *In the Age of Mabo: History, Aborigines, and Australia*, Bain Attwood, editor, pp. 73–86. Allen and Unwin, Sydney, NSW, Australia.

1996b Aborigines, Archaeology, and Australian Heritage. *Meanjin*, 55(4):725–735.

1996c Contact Archaeology: Shared Histories? Shared Identities? In *Sites: Nailing the Debate: Archaeology and Interpretation in Museums*, pp. 199–216. Historic Houses Trust of NSW, Sydney, Australia.

PARDOE, COLIN

1992 Arches of Radii, Corridors of Power: Reflections on Current Archaeological Practice. In *Power, Knowledge, and Aborigines*, Bain Attwood and John Arnold, editors, pp. 132–141. A special edition of the *Journal of Australian Studies*. Latrobe University Press in association with the National Centre for Australian Studies, Melbourne, VIC.

PARKER, ANDREW, MARY RUSSO, DORIS SOMMER, AND PATRICIA YAEGER (EDITORS)

1992 *Nationalisms and Sexualities*. Routledge, New York, NY.

PETTMAN, JAN

1992 *Living in the Margins: Racism, Sexism, and Feminism in Australia*. Allen and Unwin, Sydney, NSW, Australia.

PROUDFOOT, HELEN, ANNE BICKFORD, BRIAN EGLOFF, AND ROBYN STOCKS
  1991 *Australia's First Government House*. The Department of Planning, New South Wales, and Allen and Unwin, Sydney, Australia.

REEKIE, GAIL
  1992 Contesting Australia. In *Images of Australia*, Gillian Whitlock and David Carter, editors, pp. 145–55. University of Queensland Press, St. Lucia, QLD, Australia.

REYNOLDS, HENRY
  1981 *The Other Side of the Frontier.* Penguin, Melbourne, VIC, Australia.
  1987 *Frontier.* Allen and Unwin, Sydney, NSW, Australia.

ROBIN, LIBBY
  1998 Urbanising the Bush: Environmental Disputes and Australian National Identity. In *Australian Identities*, David Day, editor, pp. 116–127. Australian Scholarly Publishing, Melbourne, VIC, Australia.

ROSE, DEBORAH BIRD
  1999 Hard Times: An Australian Study. In *Quicksands: Foundational Histories in Australia and Aotearoa, New Zealand,* Klaush Neumann, Nicholas Thomas, and Hilary Ericksen, editors, pp. 2–19. University of New South Wales Press, Sydney, Australia.

ROWLEY, SUE
  1993 Things a Bush Woman Cannot Do. In *Debutante Nation: Feminism Contests the 1890s*, Susan Margarey, Sue Rowley, and Sue Sheridan, editors, pp. 185–198. Allen and Unwin, Sydney, NSW, Australia.

SCHAFFER, KAY
  1988 *Women and the Bush, Forces of Desire in the Australian Cultural Tradition.* Cambridge University Press, Cambridge, England.

SCHUYLER, ROBERT L.
  1991 Historical Archaeology in the American West: The View from Philadelphia. *Historical Archaeology,* 25(3):7–17.

SPILLMAN, LYN
  1997 *Nation and Commemoration: Creating National Identities in Australia and the United States.* Cambridge University Press, New York, NY.

SUMMERS, ANNE
  1975 *Damned Whores and God's Police: The Colonisation of Women in Australia.* Penguin, Melbourne, VIC, Australia.

TEMPLE, HELEN
  1988 Historical Archaeology and Its Role in the Community. Master's (honours) thesis, Inter-Departmental Committee for Historical Archaeology, University of Sydney, NSW, Australia.

WARD, RUSSELL
  1958 *The Australian Legend.* Oxford University Press, Melbourne, VIC, Australia.

WHITE, RICHARD
  1981 *Inventing Australia.* Allen and Unwin, Sydney, NSW, Australia.

TRACY IRELAND
DEPARTMENT OF PREHISTORIC AND HISTORICAL ARCHAEOLOGY
SCHOOL OF ARCHAEOLOGY
MAIN QUAD A14, UNIVERSITY OF SYDNEY
SIDNEY, NSW 2006 AUSTRALIA

Denis Byrne

The Ethos of Return: Erasure and Reinstatement of Aboriginal Visibility in the Australian Historical Landscape

ABSTRACT

Aboriginal efforts to secure the repatriation and reburial of their ancestors' remains represent an undoing of the colonial project of collection. It is but one element of an ethos of "return" that challenges white-settler society's turning of a blind eye to the continued presence of Aboriginal people in the post-1788 landscape. Archaeologists in Australia, along with heritage professionals generally, have for the most part not deployed their skills and knowledge in the interests of revealing the historical coexistence and entanglement of settler and Aboriginal cultures. Rather, archaeologists have practiced a form of segregation that finds no room for Aboriginal people and their story in the historical landscape as archaeology constructs it. The case is put for archaeologists themselves to embrace an ethos of return that reverses this erasure.

Archaeology in Reverse

Over the last two decades or so, indigenous minorities in Australia, the U.S., and elsewhere have used what power and persuasion they have to facilitate a return to their custody of human and cultural remains. The original process of collection has been reversed. Bones and artifacts now flow from collections in the former imperial centers back to the former colonies; they also flow from collections in the cities of the former colonies back to local indigenous communities. These communities may choose to house them in keeping places or local cultural centers or to ferry them back to their ultimate destination: the multitude of points in the landscape from which they were originally collected.

It is, thus, the spatial dimension of collection, the movement of objects through space, which is foregrounded here. Some archaeologists, however, see this as secondary in importance to the act of science. They would see the fact that the remains ended up in centralized vaults, laboratories, and display cases as incidental to the quest for knowledge about what happened in the past. Indeed, many archaeologists have felt that if those pressing for repatriation would focus more on the knowledge and revelations that archaeology has been able to produce from these remains—knowledge that has the potential to enhance respect for indigenous culture and history—the repatriators would be less concerned about the precise spatial disposition of the remains (for an overview of the reburial issue, see Hubert 1989).

There are two things one might say about this. The first point is that if archaeologists now see little significance in the spatial location of collected material, then this certainly was not the case in the past. The archaeological and ethnological work of collection had a context in the great enterprise of "collecting the world" that was critical to the West's ability to know, exploit, and dominate the non-West during the Age of Imperialism. This is particularly so when we consider that the early work of archaeology functioned to legitimize, through the doctrine of cultural evolutionism, that very arrangement of global political space that had put white archaeologists and ethnologists into far-flung parts of the world, like Australia, and maintained them there. In colonial Australia, archaeology was practiced in the context of a world system busy with center-periphery movement, a world system that was a giant catchment system for objects, information, and wealth. Regardless of whether the material flowed into private or public collections, there was nothing random about the direction in which it moved: it moved resolutely to where power lay.

The second point is that indigenous minorities are acute observers of where power lies. And in the current case, they see that the presence of their cultural remains in museums and other repositories is not merely improper or offensive in their own terms, but it also strategically undermines their moral claim to land. Historically, the concept of ethnic or racial identity coalesced in the European mind around the idea of "the nation." Under the terms of this notion, there cannot be identity without land. In places like New South Wales (NSW), Australia, where indigenous people have been very largely dispossessed of land, this mindset has forced them to emphasize the physical traces of

Denis Byrne

their former tenure as landholders—to emphasize, in our terms, the archaeological evidence
of their former presence. This may account
for the way indigenous peoples regard collections, which to us represent convergences, as
dispersals. From their point of view, the act
of collection evaporates the evidence of their
entitlement to land, since this evidence loses
efficacy the moment it ceases to be in situ. In
appropriating the discourse of heritage, Aborigines in places like NSW have reworked it into
a discourse of land.

This Aboriginal discourse of land competes
with and responds to that dimension of the
colonial project that seeks not merely to inhabit
the new landscape but to confer a depth on this
habitation by narrativizing and naturalizing it.
In settler societies, the settlers become "new
natives" (Byrne 1998a:96). Needless to say,
it is helpful to this project if the indigenous
natives are either absent from the landscape
or remain out of sight. It will be argued later
that this invisibility was achieved in Australia in
two ways: physically, by marginalizing Aboriginal people on reserves and in institutions and,
discursively, by constructing a heritage landscape
in which traces of the post-1788 experience of
Aboriginal people were rendered invisible. It is
here that historical archaeology takes on a particular relevance, a particular urgency, because
in the context described here, there can be no
neutrality. By attending to postcontact artifacts
and sites, historical archaeology gives visibility
to the Aboriginal presence; by ignoring them,
it is complicit in the discursive erasure of that
presence. To date, with some notable exceptions,
Australian historical archaeologists have chosen
the latter course.

This essay addresses what will be termed
"the ethos of return." Its intention is to radically expand our understanding of an ethos
that we catch sight of in the restricted contexts
of reburial and repatriation but that informs a
whole panorama of indigenous practices and
priorities. It is proposed that there is great,
though at present almost unrealized, scope for
archaeologists to engage positively with this
ethos. The essay pays particular attention to
the situation in NSW, but it may have relevance
to the relationship between archaeologists and
indigenous minorities in other places.

Aboriginal Cemeteries
in New South Wales

The notion of an ethos of return has presented itself to the author partly as a result of a
research project, begun in 1997, which aims at
understanding the history and conservation needs
of Aboriginal postcontact-period cemeteries in
NSW and the attachment that Aboriginal people
have to these places. The project is based at
the NSW National Parks and Wildlife Service,
the state government agency mandated to protect
and conserve Aboriginal heritage sites in NSW.
It may help here to briefly sketch in the history
of these cemeteries.

From the founding of the colony of NSW in
1788, white settlement radiated out from Sydney
until, by about 1880, even the most distant and
inhospitable areas had some degree of white
presence. At first Aboriginal people continued
to be buried in traditional locations and in traditional modes, most commonly in mounded graves
with associated carved trees. But as the mosaic
of settler farms crept across the landscape, these
locations became inaccessible, and people began
to bury their dead in or near the homestead
graveyards of settler families, in church and
municipal graveyards in the white towns and
villages (Figures 1 and 2) or in unofficial burial
grounds on land not yet taken up by settlers.

Beginning in the 1880s, the most dramatic
result of the new government policy of segregation was the concentration of Aboriginal people
on small reserves, the 22 largest of which were
designated "stations" and presided over by white
managers appointed by the government's Aborigines' Protection Board (Goodall 1996). Most
Aboriginal Stations and many of the smaller
reserve communities had their own cemeteries,
but only rarely were these officially "gazetted"
through the bureaucracy, which is to say, they
were not defined in land title documents (Ward
et al. 1989; Kabaila 1995, 1996, 1998; Byrne
1998b). The result of this was that when the
reserve lands were later revoked and sold to
white farmers, as the majority of them were by
the 1960s, the cemeteries did not appear on the
title deeds of the land. Many of the cemeteries ended up in the middle of farmers' paddocks
with the graves trampled by grazing stock (Byrne
1998b:22).

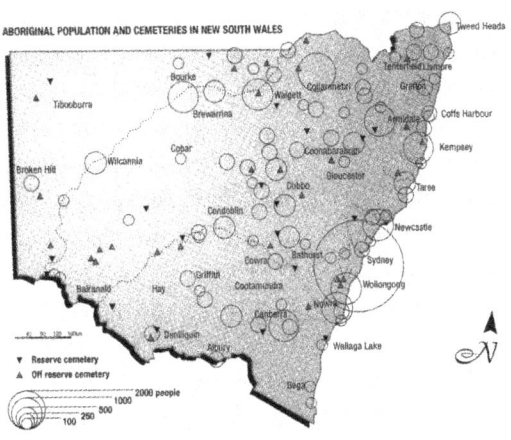

FIGURE 1. The distribution of Aboriginal population in New South Wales and the distribution of Aboriginal cemeteries of the post-1788 period.

FIGURE 2. Wooden cross with dot-painting in the Aboriginal section of the public cemetery at Bowraville, northeast New South Wales. (Photo by Denis Byrne.)

The change in government Aboriginal policy in the 1930s from segregation to assimilation put pressure on Aboriginal people to move from the reserves to nearby country towns or cities. Fay Gale's (1972) study of the situation in South Australia in the 1950s and 1960s provides a detailed account of Aboriginal urbanization during the period of the assimilation policy. This constituted a major dispersion of Aboriginal people away from local, concentrated settlements. In the present day, great efforts are made to return the bodies of the dead for burial in what people regard as their own country, whether traditional or adoptive. These returns are often made over long distances and at considerable expense. They

involve taking people home from the city to a cemetery in a country town or from a country town back to a cemetery on an old reserve, there being perhaps a dozen reserve cemeteries in NSW that continue in use. Aboriginal funerals are rites of convergence where kin and friends from different parts of the web of dispersion gather at the graveyard; the graveyard is, thus, an important geographic anchor for this web.

This homeward flow of the dead and the living, reversing the direction of dispersal, mirrors the return journey we see occurring with reburial and repatriation. If mapped, the dispersion of "local" Aboriginal communities, radiating out from the old reserve settlements like so many exploding stars, would inscribe the landscape with myriad pathways. Jeremy Beckett (1988:119) coined the term "beat" to describe the networks of movement between dispersed kin in western NSW and has written of how these beats have expanded (Beckett 1988:132). In the southwest of Western Australia, Chris Birdsall (1988) has used the words "lines" and "runs" to describe the dispersion of Nyungar extended families through particular sets of towns, the latter term evoking the continual visiting that takes place between them. These networks are, thus, more than conceptual: they are real in space, and they are alive with movement. On virtually any day of the year, somewhere in NSW, Aboriginal people will be converging at a graveside in a local cemetery and, in so doing, will be retracing their steps along the lines of their earlier dispersal.

The work of Beckett and Birdsall and others cautions us against supposing that the trajectories of dispersal represent lines of movement that have always taken people away, detaching them from local sites. It makes us aware that these trajectories are also the pathways along which contact is maintained. They are lines of communication that have, in a sense, allowed the "local" to expand. Each local landscape with its particular memory sites such as the old mission or the old cemetery now has a constituency of locals spread over several hundred kilometers. A refinement of our understanding of the local would seem to be called for (Massey 1994): one which approaches it as "a structure of feeling" (Appadurai 1996:182), which recognizes that locality is never a given but, rather, is a product of regular "work" (Appadurai 1996:

180–181) and which allows that the modern technology of communications permits and even encourages this work to be spread or stretched over very large distances.

Butterflies, Rocks, and Burials

The return of the recently deceased for burial in local cemeteries parallels the return of bones and artifacts in the repatriation context to the extent that both appear to reflect an unease or anxiety at the distancing of people and objects from local space. Others have argued that, generically, this anxiety is part of the condition of global modernity and post-modernity (Chambers 1994)—an anxiety intensified in particular ways by the condition of being an indigenous minority.

During the last two centuries, the remains of several hundred Aboriginal people from NSW went into public and private collections. The private collecting of Aboriginal skeletal remains by amateur and professional scientists, beginning at the time of white settlement and involving chance finds as well as grave openings, was superseded from the early 1900s by large-scale collecting in which hundreds of graves were systematically dug up. This phase was, in turn, superseded by the excavation of burial grounds by professional archaeologists in the 1960s and 1970s (Donlon 1994:73–74).

There is a parallel with natural history in much of the early collecting in that the graves and their contents were often treated as if they were naturally occurring phenomena. One collected skeletons much the way that one collected butterflies or rocks. Little or no regard was shown for the feelings of living Aboriginal people who were the descendants or even the immediate kin of the disinterred. As Tom Griffiths (1996) shows in his classic study of antiquarian collecting in Victoria, collectors of Aboriginal stone artifacts naturalized their quarry in the same manner as did the collectors of Aboriginal skeletons, and often the same people collected both.

> In some ways, the collectors mimicked the hunters whose artifacts many of them studied. They were themselves nomadic within defined and beloved territories; they talked of "collecting grounds," "stamping grounds," and "beats." They wrote of their "hunting" and "flinting," they boasted of "pickings," of "browsing over campsites," of "bringing back quite a useful bag," of joyfully discovering virgin sites. They moved alertly across the landscape seeking their prey (Griffiths 1996:19).

This collecting of Aboriginal skeletal remains and artifacts without reference to contemporary Aboriginal people has its context in the fact that at the time the collecting was taking place, Aboriginal people had been "emptied" from the landscape where the old burial grounds and campsites were to be found. They were emptied not just through attrition by massacre or epidemic but by the removal of the survivors from their old hunting grounds and camps to fringe camps, reserves, and institutions where, in a sense, they became invisible. The resulting history of Aborigines in Western Australia's urban space has been reviewed by Jane Jacobs (1996: 107–115). There are two aspects to the invisibility of Aboriginal people in the landscape. The first is that their visibility was low because these new places were on the outskirts of white habitation and, thus, on the periphery of white vision. The second aspect is that the specific visibility of these people as *Aboriginal* was low because so many of them had a white parent, grandparent, or great-grandparent: when whites did observe them, it was through the lens of a racism in which the darkness of skin was the measure of "real" Aboriginality. Moreover, because genetic hybridity had its cultural counterpart, they were not seen as authentically Aboriginal because their ways and their material culture were not "traditional" enough.

The offer of equality to Aboriginal people by the early British Governors on condition that they adopt "civilized" ways turned out to be false. Despite their best efforts, in the eyes of settler society they would remain, to quote Homi Bhabha (1994:86), "almost the same but not quite, almost the same but not white." They were considered to have become too similar to us to be considered "real" Aboriginals yet not similar enough to be given equal status.

Local Space and National Space

The nonurban landscape in NSW, the bush or the countryside, quickly became a space associated with the ancestors of living Aboriginal people (the "old blacks") and with white pioneer bushmen and pastoralists. But landscape was not associated with living Aboriginal people themselves. Their presence in this landscape was replaced by a population of Aboriginal "sites" (rock paintings, carved trees, coastal shell middens), which, in the minds of whites, belonged to a period well removed in time (Allen 1988; Byrne 1997). For white Australians, the "real" Aboriginals were always away on the frontier or away in the past. The challenge for Aboriginal people has thus been to re-establish their visibility in the colonized landscape. One of the ways of doing this has been to mobilize an idea of landedness in the form of an archaeological footprint.

This idea has resulted in local Aboriginal communities all over NSW emphasizing their connectedness to the thousands of Aboriginal archaeological sites present in the landscape. They have become unofficial guardians of these sites. To this extent, then, the return which reburial represents is part of a larger return—a return of Aboriginal visibility in the colonized landscape.

It is probably true of all the settler colonies that the white colonists see themselves, retrospectively, not as invaders but as inheritors of the true spirit of the land (Byrne 1998a). By the 1880s, white settlers in Australia were reinventing themselves as the "new natives." The traces of former Aboriginal occupation, along with the indigenous flora and fauna, became vectors for contacting or connecting with this "spirit of the land." Eventually, by the 1960s, these traces would be appropriated as part of the national heritage. As Benedict Anderson (1991) has argued, the very idea of the national state is tied up with the activity of collecting, whether in the context of the museum, the census, or the heritage inventory. For indigenous minorities to retain identity within the "invented community" of the settler nation, they have had to mount various localizing, decentering, "counter-collection" strategies, and it is here that the notion of a "reverse archaeology" is situated. This paper's contention is that Aboriginal people in NSW, and perhaps indigenous minorities in general, are more interested in getting things back into the ground than in getting them out of it.

"Real" Aboriginals and "Real" Conservation

It is suggested that indigenous concern about the material past is "archaeology in reverse" to the extent that it is driven by a desire to heal a rupture, one that archaeology, as practiced by whites, had a part in creating. Before going on to consider what happens to repatriated remains when they get home (the end point of the journey alluded to earlier), notice should be given to one critical dimension of the act of separation, the issue of authenticity. The physical traces of past Aboriginal presence in the landscape came to be seen by settler society as a more authentic manifestation of Aboriginality than the acculturated persons of the Aborigines themselves. Many of the white people who showed an interest in the Aboriginal rock engravings around Sydney Harbor or the ground-edged stone hatchet heads plowed up by farmers in their wheat fields associated these remains with that "timeless" culture of the "real" Aboriginals living in the remote regions in the continent's north. Any claim for continuity between the remains and the living Aborigines of NSW was likely to be met "with shock and disbelief" (Sullivan 1985:144).

One of the critical challenges Aboriginal people have faced in places like NSW over the last 30 or so years has been to stake their claim to cultural continuity, a key component of which is their ownership of and curatorial responsibility for the traces of their past. As with the rest of us in the modern world, though, the daily life of Aboriginal people in NSW requires them to be sensitive readers and manipulators of a wide spectrum of institutions, protocols, and discourses that have the power to act upon them. For example, when negotiating or remonstrating with a white developer, land owner, or town councilor over the protection of a shell midden, rock-art site, or burial ground, Aborigines must have one eye on the likelihood that this white person believes that they are not "real" Aborigines because they drive a car, use a cellular phone, and do not have dark-enough skin.

If white Australia employed the discourse of heritage in order to appropriate the Aboriginal past as part of a national patrimony, then Aboriginal people have employed this same discourse in order to get it back (Byrne 1998a: 94–101). They have had little choice but to become as conversant in the discourse of heritage as they are, say, in the discourses of land law, human rights, welfare bureaucracy, and parliamentary democracy. Inevitably, this has meant a degree of complicity with the essentialist view of culture that privileges the traditional over the contemporary, the timeless over the innovative. To some extent, Aboriginal people have to play up to white expectations and produce performative versions of traditional culture when this is what white people want to see. Gayatri Spivak (1987: 202) would term this a "strategic essentialism," and Andrew Lattas (1990, 1993) has strongly argued for the Aborigines' right to it. The only Australian archaeologist to take up the issue has been Tim Murray (1993, 1996a) who has noted that "both archaeologists and Aboriginal people trade in the currency of essentialism" (Murray 1996a:76), each for different reasons. While he has warned of the dangers this may pose to free scholarship, he also sees how there can be valid reasons for Aboriginal people to "emphasize continuity" (1993, 1996a:81).

Aboriginal use of the familiar language of heritage should not lead us to imagine they have no alternative interpretations of concepts like conservation. Indeed it seems that many indigenous people regard reburial as an act of conservation and in this they join, as it were, that alignment of other non-Western peoples who do not subscribe to the West's "conservation ethic." This would include the pious Thai Buddhists whose "restoration" of ancient stupas typically entails completely encasing them within glittering new stupas, sometimes twice the size of the original (Byrne 1995).

From the author's vantage point in a heritage agency, it is apparent that the practice of heritage by Aboriginal people in NSW is increasingly at variation with, even at odds with, archaeological practice. This practice goes beyond reburial and repatriation matters and includes the establishment by Aboriginal communities of local site registers, which may not be made available to archaeologists or the state agency. It also includes the carrying out of heritage impact assessments by people without formal archaeological credentials (Aboriginality being seen as a sufficient or superior credential) and a preparedness, in some cases, to sanction the destruction of "archaeological" sites by developers in return for jobs or the funding of community facilities.

Terra Nullius and the Issue of Visibility

The spatial or geographic dimension is obviously critical in considering reburial and repatriation. What is involved here is a return to the surface of the earth, one that retraces and reverses the journey made by artifacts and human remains to the laboratory, the showcase, or the museum vault. What makes it so important to indigenous minorities that cultural remains not stray from their resting places in the ground?

To begin with, there is the matter of spiritual integrity. Since the 1970s in Australia, large numbers of sacred ritual objects have been returned from museums and other collections to keeping places and sacred sites. These returns have been made on the grounds that they are necessary in order to restore the spiritual health of the land and, by extension, the people of that land. It is probably true to say, though, that in Australia the balance of concern among Aboriginal people in the north of the continent, where contact with white-settler culture has been least, has been with the integrity of sacred sites—mostly natural landscape features such as rock outcrops or river beds whose sacred significance is invisible to white people. In the south, the act of dispossession made it impossible for Aboriginal people to maintain the precise spiritual/ritual linkage with sacred sites, though there are significant exceptions (Creamer 1988). Here Aboriginal concern has been mostly to do with the protection of non-sacred "archaeological" sites. The proposition is that, for Aboriginal people in the south who were totally dispossessed of their land, the continued presence in the colonized landscape of precontact archaeological sites has value as a critical reminder to Australians at large that until a mere 212 years ago, Aboriginal people were in occupation of the entire landscape.

In this line of thinking, the *visibility* of these archaeological sites to white people has become a crucial part of their significance to Aboriginal people. These remains are thus fetishized in a way they undoubtedly would not have been in precontact times. The vital difference is that in precontact times, Aboriginal people did not have to contend with the doctrine of *terra nullius* (land unoccupied), "the foundational fantasy of the Australian colonies" (Jacobs 1996:105).

None of this should be taken to mean that Aboriginal people are not genuine in their desire to protect cultural remains in the landscape. The author has more than once been in the company of Aboriginal people in NSW who have been moved to tears at the sight of shell middens or stone artifact scatters torn apart by bulldozers. However, it is simply wrong to seek the meaning and motivation of this desire purely within Aboriginal culture and not in the relationship Aboriginal people have with the larger, settler culture. To do so would imply a reified understanding of their culture as something that could be quarantined, even for the purposes of discussion, from its entanglement with settler culture.

One of the methods that colonizers have employed to disempower their indigenous subjects has been to simultaneously valorize and suppress the same attributes of the latter's subjectivity. A good example is the suppression of indigenous languages by punishing children for speaking them in school or forbidding their use on reserves, while, at the same time, denigrating these people for not being "real" Aborigines partly because they could not speak their own language. Similarly, after a century and a half of delocalizing Aboriginal people by moving them away from their camps and their country to distant reserves, we, the colonizers, now privilege the attachment local people have to local sites and, through the Native Title process, effectively penalize those who cannot demonstrate continuous association with place. Nicholas Thomas has suggested that it has often been the illogicality, the internal contradictions, the very doubleness of "colonialism's culture" that made it so difficult for the colonized to fight (Thomas 1994:60, 142).

The Uneven Practice of Historical Archaeology

So far, this paper has addressed the ethos of return from the Aboriginal position, which is to say, from the author's reading of their position. The various ways in which historical archaeologists may impede or enable the project of re-establishing the historical visibility of Aborigines in the colonized landscape must also be addressed.

In enlisting archaeological remains in this project of reinscription, Aborigines in NSW have relied almost entirely on those remains that belong to the precontact period. This situation reflects the activity of archaeologists in NSW whose focus has been either on precontact

Aboriginal archaeological remains or on the archaeological record of nonindigenous settlers. The former has resulted in the recording of more than 32,000 Aboriginal precontact sites, listed on the Aboriginal Sites Register maintained by the NSW National Parks and Wildlife Service, but only some 200 postcontact sites (mostly cemeteries). The dramatic under-recording of postcontact sites is eloquent testimony to the fact that over the past 30 years, the Service has been dominated by a "culture of prehistory" in its Aboriginal heritage responsibilities. For its part, the State Heritage Inventory, maintained by the NSW Heritage Office, now has more than 17,500 sites, only 7 of which are Aboriginal postcontact sites.

Ostensibly, the reasons for recording and inventorying all these sites might be to recover scientific data and afford or facilitate legal protection, but a crucial *effect* of this work of recording is to raise the sites from being simply traces on the ground to a more elevated standing as "heritage." It is the detection, recording, investigation, and inventorying of sites that might be said to realize their potential as "cultural capital" (Bourdieu 1984). We cannot ignore or minimize the importance of archaeologists, in the role of heritage professionals, in mediating this transition. It is precisely because Aborigines, as a minority and largely disempowered group, want recognition from the larger society of their continued historical presence in the colonized landscape that they rely on heritage professionals to validate that presence. And if, among these professionals, Aboriginal postcontact archaeology is not regarded as "real" archaeology (Colley and Bickford 1996:6), then the chances of Aborigines gaining public recognition of their postcontact places as heritage are likely to be poor indeed.

Do such places, however, exist in significant numbers? Concomitant with the expansion of white settlement through the landscape after 1788 was a spatial reduction in Aboriginal settlement, a product of spatial concentration and peripheralization as well as of falling population in the face of introduced diseases and frontier violence (Reynolds 1987). But the geographically confining effect of this on the spread of the archaeological remains of the Aboriginal postcontact experience may be less than expected. Certainly the residential options for Aborigines were limited mainly to fringe camps and Aboriginal Reserves and Stations. But as Peter Read (1984, 1996) shows for the Wiradjuri people in the southwest of NSW, Aboriginal fringe camp populations were often forced by hostile townspeople and local governments to move from the edge of one country town to the edge of another. The search for work and access to schools had a similar effect at a family level. In any one region, there was also a secondary pattern of Aboriginal settlement comprised of seasonal workers (e.g., sheepshearers and fruit pickers), drovers, fencers, and domestic servants who, at differing frequencies, moved between temporary dwellings and home. All of this mobility presumably produced a considerable spread of archaeological remains and sites, analogous to that produced by the hunter-gatherer ancestors of these people, only a few generations removed. The thinness of this record in a horizontal sense (i.e., the relatively insubstantial nature of many of the sites) clearly poses a challenge to recorders but, then, the same could be said of the precontact sites.

A large and growing literature of Aboriginal autobiography tells the story from the inside. The trajectories traced by the individual lives of such people such as Bill Cohen (1987), Evelyn Crawford (1993), Kevin Gilbert (1977), and Ruby Langford Ginibi (1988, 1992), to name but a few, are rich in descriptions of the places people lived and worked, of the sites of events that marked their lives. In summary, indications are that sparsity of listed postcontact sites does not reflect a real sparsity of such places on the ground.

The issue of recognizability, to which Murray (1996b:207) has drawn attention, looms large in any consideration of the reasons for this situation. Some components of "traditional" and easily attributable Aboriginal material culture, such as stone hatchets, continued in Aboriginal use in NSW for a considerable time after 1788 (McBryde 1989a). Also easily distinguishable as Aboriginal are cutting implements made from knapped bottle glass, a case of a distinctly Aboriginal technology taking advantage of newly introduced materials. The majority of items in their postcontact material culture, however, ranging from clothing to cooking utensils, children's toys, building materials, and gardening implements were brought over in unaltered form

(though sometimes radically recontextualized) from the material culture of the European colonizers. These objects themselves are likely to be unmarked by their ownership and use by Aborigines, so that this ownership and use has no visibility on or in the objects. One could reasonably assume that these objects, discovered on or in the ground by historical archaeologists, are routinely recorded as evidence of settler, rather than Aboriginal, activity. A more rigorous investigation of a site, as Murray (1996b:207) notes, might reveal remains such as bush foods, alerting one to the Aboriginal identity of the site. Obviously, a major factor in the under-recording of Aboriginal postcontact sites by prehistorians is their lack of training, for the most part, in the recognition and analysis of European-built structures and material culture.

It is also pertinent to look at the distribution of the activity of historical archaeologists. By far the majority of historical archaeological studies in NSW are carried out in the context of environmental impact assessment (EIA) and land-use planning. The former are concentrated in the old urban core areas of cities and towns where new construction poses a threat to sites of the late-18th and the 19th centuries. It is true that Aboriginal people were present in these urban core areas during the early period of white settlement (McBryde 1989b), but their presence was far greater on the periphery of white settlement in fringe camps, pastoral station camps, and in rurally located Aboriginal Reserves. It is prehistoric archaeologists who are much more likely to be retained to participate in EIA studies in such localities (ahead of urban expansion, suburban and rural infrastructure, tourism, forestry, and mining developments). In the EIA sphere, the failure to attend to Aboriginal postcontact remains is far more the responsibility of prehistorians than historical archaeologists.

It is in the area of land-use planning that historical archaeologists are culpable. In NSW since the mid-1980s, studies of local government areas have been carried out with a view to delineating themes in local history and providing local governments with an inventory or schedule of heritage items to which it can then give protection in the course of land-use planning. That almost none of these heritage studies has taken account of Aboriginal postcontact remains is due to a complex of factors. There has been an overriding assumption by the conservation architects, historians, and historical archaeologists involved that Aboriginal postcontact remains are not to be included because they will be dealt with, via separate studies, by prehistorians. The NSW Heritage Office has tended to tolerate, if not actively encourage, this assumption. Its 1996 guidelines state:

> It is unusual for items of *Aboriginal* and *natural* significance to be included in a local or regional heritage study. While not ideal, current statutory documents, funding arrangements, and expertise usually mean that the three different categories of heritage items ... are identified and protected by separate processes and legislation (NSW Heritage Office 1996:2).

This assumption has been made continually for more than 20 years despite the absence of any evidence that prehistorians have, in fact, been attending to the excluded sites. It is symptomatic of the way this type of silencing occurs, not by edict but by a sort of blurred inattention. The overall effect or product of practitioners turning their backs on Aboriginal postcontact experiences is the construction of a version of the Australian historical landscape, which is a fictional space where races do not interrelate, a space where Aborigines do not even exist.

Social Significance Assessment and the Segregated Past

In an important recent paper on nationalism and historical archaeology, Tracy Ireland examines how in the 1970s a desire by government to construct what she terms "a unified national past, which was understood to be a national asset" (Ireland 1996:91), led to the establishment of the particular system of heritage government bureaucracy, both federal and state that we have today. What might have been an opportunity to come to terms, in a heritage context, with the entangled history of Aboriginal-European relations was passed over in favor of a heritage system that institutionalized Aboriginal and European heritage as quite separate categories. Aboriginal heritage would belong to a special category allied to the natural environment and focused on the precontact period, while white settler heritage would be developed in terms of themes (e.g., bush life, egalitarianism) that celebrated certain myths of the nation. Black and white history

belonged to different times, as if coexistence over the last two centuries had not occurred.

Particularly significant in Ireland's work is her clarification of the way the practice of historical archaeology in the heritage arena simultaneously reflects the state's view of the past, using the state-sanctioned themes and categories, and confirms it in the same way that the NSW heritage studies do: by populating the landscape with sites that seem to bear out the national(ist) myth. Populating it, for instance, with towns where interracial conflict does not exist because heritage studies have surgically removed the Aborigines from them. In an odd way, this reverts to that myth of the early colonial landscape as a frontier, a zone of racial separation and standoff—a vision that is conjured up against the historical reality of extensive and quite intimate intermingling and interdependency between white settlers and Aborigines (Griffiths 1996:108–110).

The reality of Aboriginal-settler segregation did not begin in NSW until the 1880s, lasting as government policy until the 1930s and continuing at a local level to control Aboriginal use of facilities and venues such as swimming pools, picture theaters, and hotels until the 1960s or even later (Read 1988; Goodall 1995). It is critical, from a heritage perspective, to keep in mind that much of the Aboriginal experience of segregation took place deep within settler space (e.g., in streets and within buildings that "belonged" to white people). While "segregationist" heritage management bows to the myth of the segregated frontier, it also, for the later period, removes Aboriginal people entirely from settler space. In other words, it takes the ethos of segregation far beyond anything attempted by government segregationist policies in the past.

Consider, for a moment, those components of Aboriginal lives over the last two centuries that were spent not on the mission or in the fringe camp but inside the white built environment, inside what would now, in many cases, be regarded as items of "built heritage." Consider the middle-class white homes where girls of the "stolen generation" lived and worked and, not infrequently, were assaulted and abused; the country-town police lockups where Aborigines have been incarcerated in disproportional numbers and where many have died while in custody; the segregated cinemas where Aborigines suffered the indignity of being confined to special roped-off seating (Figure 3); the hotels where liquor could only be purchased by Aborigines through an open window and consumed outside; the shearing sheds where generations of Aboriginal men labored; the rural dance halls where on occasion Aboriginal people gathered with their accordions and gum leaf bands. Consider also the verandah, that iconographic Australian heritage space, and think of the verandahs of country town hospitals where Aborigines were treated because they were not permitted into the wards, or the verandahs of farms and pastoral properties where Aboriginal workers ate their meals because they were not allowed into the kitchen or dining room to eat with the white workers.

These excursions by Aborigines into the built space of white people, however tentative or conditional, often indelibly marked the lives of people of both races and left their stamp on the histories of local communities. By contrast, one would guess that these excursions left virtually no mark on the fabric of the buildings themselves or, if they did, that such traces would only be possible to detect and interpret archaeologically with the aid of documentary evidence or, of course, with the aid of the memories of Aboriginal people themselves.

The contention here is that the meaning of the sites cannot stand apart from these memories. The events and the memory of the events may not be constitutive of the sites as items of architecture (in the sense that they were complete at the time of construction), but they are essential to them as items of heritage. In practical terms, the means for bringing this part of a site's meaning into the heritage process is through the mechanism of social significance assessment. The Burra Charter of Australia ICOMOS (Marquis-Kyle and Walker 1992), which since 1979 has been the guiding convention for Australian heritage agencies and practitioners, recognizes the equity between social and scientific value (together with aesthetic and historic value) in collectively comprising a place's cultural significance. A more recent addition (ratified in 1999) significantly enhances the social value in relation to physical evidence compared with previous editions. The methods for assessing social significance range from oral history recording at an individual level to the convening of community "workshops" (Johnston 1992). While the social significance to Aboriginal people of some mission-reserve sites in NSW has been investigated (Egloff

FIGURE 3. The formerly segregated cinema at Collarenebri, north-central New South Wales. (Photo by Denis Byrne.)

1981; Somerville 1994; Kabaila 1995, 1996, 1998), there are no cases known to the author where this has been done in an EIA context or where it has been undertaken in relation to sites or buildings that are ostensibly European.

Surely a premise of EIA in the field of cultural heritage is that the association or attachment that people have to heritage places is vulnerable. In Arjun Appadurai's (1996:179) words, "locality is an inherently fragile social achievement," an achievement that people work at maintaining against the odds. EIA recognizes that in the contemporary world the often surging economy and technology of land development can easily cut a swath through this achievement of locality, and it, hopefully, aims to balance the odds to some extent. In the time since white settlement, Aboriginal people have had to maintain their association with local places against the odds of a colonial governmentality that moved them onto reserves, and often from one reserve to another, and against the odds of fences and hostile land owners. But they have also had to contend with local history books and museum displays that frequently have not even conceded their continued presence in the landscape, let alone any attachments they might have to places in it. Rather than redressing this situation, the Australian heritage management system and, most certainly, the EIA system itself often weighs in against Aboriginal "locality."

Consequences of the Unsaid

This neglect of social significance means that the segregated cinema and the police lockup usually enter the heritage inventories only on the basis of their architectural or archaeological values. Were they to remain unrecorded and undescribed as heritage items, then the silence surrounding their Aboriginal history would be part of a more general indifference to history or heritage. Recording them without this history, however, is not a neutral act in that it actively constructs and promotes a version of history or heritage from which the Aboriginal is excluded. The term "elide" has entered the lexicon of cultural commentators in recognition of the power that what is *not said* may have in shaping public opinion. It acknowledges that in the silent space of the elision, a message is nonetheless being conveyed; thus, elision has a role in the disempowerment and exclusion of minority groups.

Part of the dramatic potential of social significance assessment lies in its ability to graphically depict Aboriginal culture not simply as being acted upon by a dominant white-colonial culture but as actively entangled with that culture. What is described here and in the previous section is the manner in which heritage practitioners in NSW have *disentangled* the two cultures, producing a segregated account of history. This has been done in conformity with the established divisions between and purviews of two administrative and disciplinary fields (prehistorical archaeology, nature conservation, Aboriginal studies on the one hand, and historical archaeology, conservation architecture, historical societies on the other). It might be said that the history of NSW over the last 200 years has been organized and nuanced to fit these two fields of practice rather than *vice versa*.

This does not necessarily reflect different attitudes to Aboriginal people and culture or to race relations. Rather, if one looks at the day-to-day work of practitioners on the two sides of the divide, one sees that what keeps it in place has more to do with the nature of their academic training, familiarity with certain established project design-and-reporting templates, experience or lack thereof in communicating with Aboriginal people and communities, and networked connections with particular funding sources, heritage bureaucracies, and their policies. The cumulative result of this, however, is a segregation of black-white heritage that has, at least, the *appearance* of continuity with much older segregationist arrangements in NSW.

Current arrangements seem to evince a discomfort with the notion of an Aboriginal postcontact heritage record that is partly *inside* white-settler heritage (the cinema, the police lockup) and, hence, an Aboriginal postcontact cultural landscape that is irrevocably entangled with the white cultural landscape. Certainly, cultural hybridity does present archaeology and heritage management with a challenge, but to avoid that challenge leaves us clinging to the fiction of pure, unalloyed, and separate cultures. Can we be comfortable with such an arrangement, one that evokes the horror of miscegnation that informed 19th-century racism (Young 1995) and the bogies of racial deterioration and cultural contamination that informed the White Australia policy?

In NSW the segregation policy of government was replaced by a policy of assimilation (1937–1968) that stressed the sameness rather than the difference of Aboriginal and white culture (Morris 1989:137). The policy seemed to be an about-face—horror of miscegenation was replaced by advocacy of miscegenation. The change actually represented a continuation of hegemonic domination in a different form, that is, by its "denial of the integrity of a separate Aboriginal identity" (Morris 1989:151). It is not difficult to see that if archaeology resiles from cultural hybridity, it is also effectively saying that cultures, when they entangle, cease to be different. From this standpoint, the remains of an Aboriginal fringe camp, for example, are functionally indistinguishable because they consist of items appropriated from settler material culture. Yet if archaeology is incapable of making such distinctions (based, for instance, on spatial patterning), one might ask whether it is capable of mapping culture at all.

Conclusion

The first half of this paper contends that Aboriginal people in NSW, and perhaps indigenous minorities in general, are more interested in getting things back into the ground than in getting them out of it. The "ethos of return" is thus "archaeology in reverse" and this ethos, particularly as manifest in the reburial campaign, is deeply contextualized within colonial-indigenous relations. Its context is not simply in a contest over who would own and possess the land—in the case of Australia, that was almost a foregone conclusion—but in a contest over who has roots in the land, who can call the land "home," and who has visibility on the land.

The neglect of Aboriginal postcontact places by heritage practitioners, including historical archaeologists, has effectively curtailed the visibility of Aboriginal people in the postcontact heritage landscape. The process of disassociation is furthered by the failure to acknowledge Aboriginal historical connections with what is seen as the white built heritage. The segregated cinema becomes a metaphor for a segregated heritage process.

What is advocated here is a dismantling of this segregationist aspect of heritage practice in NSW. The dismantling of the administrative and disciplinary borders that produced this segregation, rather than creating something new, would simply effect a return to or a reinstatement of an historical reality. But more than that, the engagement of heritage professionals in an ethos of return would, at this moment in Australian history, constitute a significant step towards Aboriginal-white reconciliation.

ACKNOWLEDGMENTS

This paper has benefited from discussions with Susan McIntyre and Cath Snelgrove. I am especially grateful to Denis Gojak, Tracy Ireland, Grace Karskens, and Susan Lawrence whose comments on an earlier draft of this paper helped considerably to improve it.

REFERENCES

ALLEN, HARRY
1988 History Matters: A Commentary on Divergent Interpretations of Australian History. *Australian Aboriginal Studies*, 2:79–89.

ANDERSON, BENEDICT
1991 *Imagined Communities*, 2nd edition. Verso, London, England.

APPADURAI, ARJUN
1996 *Modernity at Large*. University of Minneapolis Press, MN.

BECKETT, JEREMY
1988 Kinship, Mobility, and Community in Rural New South Wales. In *Being Black*, Ian Keen, editor, pp. 117–136. Aboriginal Studies Press, Canberra, ACT, Australia.

BHABHA, HOMI
1994 Of Mimicry and Man: The Ambivalence of Colonial Discourse. In *The Location of Culture*, Homi Bhabha, editor, pp. 85–92. Routledge, London, England.

BIRDSALL, CHRIS
1988 All in One Family. In *Being Black*, Ian Keen, editor, pp. 137–158. Aboriginal Studies Press, Canberra, ACT, Australia.

BOURDIEU, PIERRE
1984 *Distinction: A Social Critique of the Judgement of Taste*, Richard Nice, translator. Routledge and Kegan Paul, London, England.

BYRNE, DENIS
1995 Buddhist *Stupa* and Thai Social Practice. *World Archaeology*, 27(2):266–281.
1997 The Archaeology of Disaster. *Public History Review*, 5/6:17–29.
1998a Deep Nation: Australia's Acquisition of an Indigenous Past. *Aboriginal History*, 20 (1996):82–107.
1998b In *Sad but Loving Memory: Aboriginal Burials and Cemeteries of the Last 200 Years in New South Wales*. New South Wales National Parks and Wildlife Service, Sydney, Australia.

CHAMBERS, IAIN
1994 *Migrancy, Culture, Identity*. Routledge, London, England.

COHEN, BILL
1987 *To My Delight*. Aboriginal Studies Press, Canberra, ACT, Australia.

COLLEY, SARAH, AND ANNE BICKFORD
1996 "Real" Aborigines and "Real" Archaeology: Aboriginal Places and Australian Historical Archaeology. *World Archaeological Bulletin*, 7:5–21.

CREAMER, HOWARD
1988 Aboriginality in New South Wales: Beyond the Image of Cultureless Outcasts. In *Past and Present*, Jeremy Beckett, editor, pp. 45–62. Aboriginal Studies Press, Canberra, ACT, Australia.

CRAWFORD, EVELYN
1993 *Over My Tracks*. Penguin, Melbourne, VIC, Australia.

DONLON, DENISE
1994 Aboriginal Skeletal Collections and Research in Physical Anthropology: An Historical Perspective. *Australian Archaeology*, 39:73–82.

EGLOFF, BRIAN J.
1981 *Wreck Bay: An Aboriginal Fishing Community*. Australian Institute of Aboriginal Studies, Canberra, ACT, Australia.

GALE, FAY
1972 *Urban Aborigines*. Australian National University Press, Canberra, ACT.

GILBERT, KEVIN
1977 *Living Black*. Allen Lane, Melbourne, VIC, Australia.

GOODALL, HEATHER
 1995 New South Wales. In *Contested Ground*, Ann McGrath, editor, pp. 55–120. Allen and Unwin, Sydney, NSW, Australia.
 1996 *Invasion to Embassy: Land in Aboriginal Politics in New South Wales*, 1770–1972. Allen and Unwin, Sydney, NSW, Australia.

GRIFFITHS, TOM
 1996 *Hunters and Collectors: The Antiquarian Imagination in Australia*. Cambridge University Press, Cambridge, England.

HUBERT, JANE
 1989 A Proper Place for the Dead: A Critical Review of the "Reburial" Issue. In *Conflict in the Archaeology of Living Traditions*, Robert Layton, editor, pp. 131–166. Unwin Hyman, London, England.

IRELAND, TRACY
 1996 Excavating National Identity. In *Sites: Nailing the Debate: Archaeology and Interpretation in Museums*, pp. 85–106. Historic Houses Trust of New South Wales, Sydney, Australia.

JACOBS, JANE
 1996 *Edge of Empire*. Routledge, London, England.

JOHNSTON, CHRISTINE
 1992 *What is Social Value?* Australian Government Publishing Service, Canberra, ACT.

KABAILA, PETER
 1995 *Wiradjuri Places: The Murrumbidgee River Basin.* Black Mountain Projects, Canberra, ACT, Australia.
 1996 *Wiradjuri Places: The Lachlan River Basin.* Black Mountain Projects, Canberra, ACT, Australia.
 1998 *Wiradjuri Places: The Macquarie River Basin.* Black Mountain Projects, Canberra, ACT, Australia.

LANGFORD GINIBI, RUBY
 1988 *Don't Take Your Love to Town.* Penguin, Melbourne, VIC, Australia.
 1992 *Real Deadly.* Angus and Robertson, Sydney, NSW, Australia.

LATTAS, ANDREW
 1990 Aborigines and Contemporary Australian Nationalism: Primordiality and the Cultural Politics of Otherness. *Social Analysis,* 27:50–69.
 1993 Essentialism, Memory, and Resistance: Aboriginality and the Politics of Resistance. *Oceania,* 63:240–267. Sydney, Australia.

MARQUIS-KYLE, PETER, AND MEREDITH WALKER
 1992 *The Illustrated Burra Charter: Making Good Decisions about the Care of Important Places.* Australia ICOMOS (International Council on Monuments and Sites), Sydney, NSW.

MASSEY, DOREEN
 1994 A Place in the World. In *Displacements,* Angelica Bammer, editor, pp. 110–121. Indiana University Press, Bloomington.

McBRYDE, ISABEL
 1989a "... To Establish a Commerce of This Sort": Cross-Cultural Exchange at the Port Jackson Settlement. In *Studies from Terra Australis to Australia,* John Hardy and Alan Frost, editors, pp. 169–182. Australian Academy of the Humanities, Canberra, ACT.
 1989b *Guests of the Governor: Aboriginal Residents of the First Government House.* Friends of the First Government House Site, Sydney, NSW, Australia.

MORRIS, BARRY
 1989 *Domesticating Resistance: The Dhan-Gadi Aborigines and the Australian State.* Berg, Oxford, England.

MURRAY, TIM
 1993 Communication and the Importance of Disciplinary Communities: Who Owns the Past? In *Archaeological Theory: Who Sets the Agenda?* Norman Yoffee and Andrew Sherratt, editors, pp. 105–116. Cambridge University Press, Cambridge, England.
 1996a Creating a Post-Mabo Archaeology of Australia. In *In the Age of Mabo: History, Aborigines, and Australia,* Bain Attwood, editor, pp. 73–87. Allen and Unwin, Sydney, NSW, Australia.
 1996b Contact Archaeology: Shared Histories? Shared Identities? In *Sites: Nailing the Debate: Archaeology and Interpretation in Museums,* pp. 199–213. Historic Houses Trust of New South Wales, Sydney, Australia.

NEW SOUTH WALES HERITAGE OFFICE
 1996 Heritage Studies. Department of Urban Affairs and Planning, Sydney, NSW, Australia.

READ, PETER
 1984 "Breaking Up the Camps Entirely": The Dispersal Policy in Wiradjuri Country 1909–1929. *Aboriginal History,* 8(1):45–55.
 1988 *A Hundred Years' War: The Wiradjuri People and the State.* Australian National University and Pergamon, Canberra, ACT.
 1996 "A Rape of the Soul So Profound": Some Reflections on the Dispersal Policy in New South Wales. In *Terribly Hard Biscuits,* V. Chapman and Peter Read, editors, pp. 202–214. Allen and Unwin, Sydney, NSW, Australia.

REYNOLDS, HENRY
 1987 *Frontier.* Allen and Unwin, Sydney, NSW, Australia.

SOMERVILLE, MARGARET
 1994 *The Sun Dancin': People and Place in Coonabarabran.* Aboriginal Studies Press, Canberra, ACT, Australia.

SPIVAK, GAYATRI
 1987 Subaltern Studies. In *In Other Worlds: Essays in Cultural Politics,* Gayatri Spivak, editor, pp. 190–217. Routledge, London, England.

SULLIVAN, SHARON
 1985 The Custodianship of Aboriginal Sites in Southeastern Australia. In *Who Owns the Past?* Isabel McBryde, editor, pp. 139–156. Oxford University Press, Melbourne, VIC, Australia.

Denis Byrne

THOMAS, NICHOLAS
1994 *Colonialism's Culture*. Melbourne University Press, VIC, Australia.

WARD, GRAEME, BRIAN EGLOFF, AND LUKE GODWIN
1989 Archaeology of an Aboriginal Historic Site: Recent Research at the Collarenebri Aboriginal Cemetery. *Australian Aboriginal Studies*, 2:62–67.

YOUNG, ROBERT J. C.
1995 *Colonial Desire: Hybridity in Theory, Culture, and Race*. Routledge, London, England.

DENIS BYRNE
CULTURAL HERITAGE DIVISION
NEW SOUTH WALES NATIONAL PARKS AND WILDLIFE SERVICE
PO BOX 1967
HURSTVILLE, NSW 2220 AUSTRALIA

2003 The Ludlow Massacre: Class, Warfare, and Historical Memory in Southern California. In Remembering Landscapes of Conflict, Paul A. Shackel, editor. Thematic issue, Historical Archaeology 37(3):66-80

Mark Walker

The Ludlow Massacre: Class, Warfare, and Historical Memory in Southern Colorado

ABSTRACT

Because battlefields can be potent symbols in the construction of historical memory, they can remain sites of struggle for as long as that memory is important. History professionals, such as archaeologists, participate fully in these struggles. The commemoration of the Ludlow Massacre Site, a battlefield in the industrial wars of the early-20th century is discussed. The commemoration of Ludlow highlights the role of class interest in the construction of historical memory. Doing archaeology at Ludlow entails acknowledging these interests, both ours, as archaeologists, and those of the working class people who guard the memory of Ludlow.

Introduction

> One is not permitted to speak of one's wartime reminiscences today, nor is one under any impulse to do so. It is an area of general reticence: an unmentionable subject among younger friends, and perhaps of mild ridicule among those of radical opinions. All this is understood. And one understands also why it is so.
>
> It is so, in part, because Chapman Pincher and his like have made an uncontested take-over of all the moral assets of that period; have coined the war into Hollywood blockbusters and spooky paper-backs and television media; have attributed all the value of that moment to the mythic virtues of an authoritarian Right which is now, supposedly the proper inheritor and guardian of the present nation's interests.
>
> I walk in my garden, or stand cooking at the stove, and muse on how this came about. My memories of that war are very different (Thompson 1980).

This passage, published 35 years after World War II, illustrates the fragility of and the role of power in the construction of social memory. Although Thompson's memories remain alive, they are exiled from public airing and discussion, confined to a private realm. This is a familiar pattern. As the present becomes the past, people impose narrative structure where before there was none. Their confusing, contradictory, and disparate memories and experiences are filtered, ordered, and disciplined to create coherent and meaningful narratives. Some narratives dominate and flourish, while others are stifled, driven out of the public realm and into extinction or at least in to their proponents' homes. These latter become the property of cranks and special interest groups, at best interesting sidelights to the central "real" story, no longer quite history but memory or tradition. While exiled to the margins of mainstream memory, these alternative visions can still maintain a living presence, private and local but, nonetheless, vital. And as political-economic conditions and alliances shift, these submerged histories may re-emerge or provide the seeds for changes in the dominant histories.

Submerged histories are not static fossil forms existing in isolation from the dominant historical narratives. Like the dominant forms, they are bound up with contemporary issues and struggles (Popular Memory Group 1982). The reason they survive is that they are important, and they are useful in the present. The histories of conflict highlight this process. That "history is written by the victors" is a truism. In battles and wars, it is a given that there are going to be at least two sets of interpretations. To follow from Thompson's World War II example, the military personnel on Axis and Allied sides will have two different sets of recollections. But it is more than simply a case of victors and vanquished. Privates will have very different recollections from generals, and soldiers from civilians. Those who were civilians in Rotterdam, Dresden, or Nagasaki will not remember the war in the same way as those in New York, nor in the same way as the pilots and bombardiers in the planes that flew overhead (McGuire 1992; Linenthal and Engelhardt 1996).

Many of the papers in this volume deal with battles and how these are commemorated or remembered on the landscape, particularly through archaeology. In this article, a rather different kind of battle in a different kind of war is discussed. It was sparked by work on a multiyear archaeological project, the Colorado Coalfield War Archaeology Project, in which sites associated with a particularly brutal labor strike in Southern Colorado are being investigated

(Ludlow Collective 2000; Walker 2000). The defining moment of this strike in popular consciousness was the Ludlow Massacre, in which the Colorado National Guard killed more than 20 people in an attack on a tent colony of striking coal miners. You won't read about Ludlow in military history. In fact, you're rather unusual if you have read about it in any history. This is because the conflict was an industrial one, between corporations and a state government on one hand and striking workers and their families on the other. This article centers on the silencing of labor conflict in American public history and how workers in southern Colorado struggle to keep the memory of one such conflict alive. Archaeology can play a creative and important role in this struggle.

The Colorado Coal War and its Aftermath

The Colorado Coal Strike of 1913–1914 was one of the most violent strikes in United States history. Although they were ultimately defeated, the coal miners in this strike held out for 14 months in makeshift tent colonies on the Colorado prairie. Although the miners lost the Colorado strike, it was and still is seen as a victory in a broad sense for the union, the United Mine Workers of America (UMWA) (Foner 1980; Fox 1990). The Coal War was a shocking event, one that galvanized U.S. public opinion, turned John D. Rockefeller, Jr., into a national villain, and eventually came to symbolize the wave of industrial violence that led to the "progressive" era reforms in labor relations (Adams 1966; Gitelman 1988; Crawford 1995). Coal miners in Colorado did ultimately see some material gains.

The center of the strike was in Las Animas and Huerfano counties in the Southern Coalfield of Colorado (Figure 1). The coal seams occur in the foothills of the Sangre de Cristo Mountains. The Southern Coalfield supplied high-grade bituminous coal, primarily used for coking coal for the steel industry, which supplied rails for the expanding western rail network. Because of the interest of the railroads in maintaining a steady supply of coking coal, the southern field was heavily industrialized, dominated by a few large-scale corporate operations. The largest of these operations was the Rockefeller-owned Colorado Fuel and Iron Company (CF&I). Founded in 1880 by John Osgood, CF&I produced 75% of

Colorado's coal by 1892. CF&I was acquired by the Rockefeller and Gould interests in 1903 (Scamehorn 1992). In 1906, *The Engineering and Mining Journal* estimated that 10% of Colorado's population depended on CF&I for their livelihoods (Whiteside 1990:8–9).

Obviously, CF&I wielded formidable political clout in early 20th-century Colorado. Its control over the political life of Las Animas and Huerfano Counties was nearly total. The Colorado mines themselves were notoriously unsafe, second only to Utah as the most dangerous in the nation. Miners died in Colorado coal mines at more than twice the national average (McGovern and Guttridge 1972:66; Whiteside 1990:74–75). In 95 coal mine deaths from 1904–1914 in Huerfano County, hand-picked coroner's juries absolved the coal companies of responsibility in every case except one (Whiteside 1990:22).

The coal mines in the Southern Coalfield were located up canyons where the coal seams were exposed by erosion. Most of the miners lived in these canyons in company towns, in company

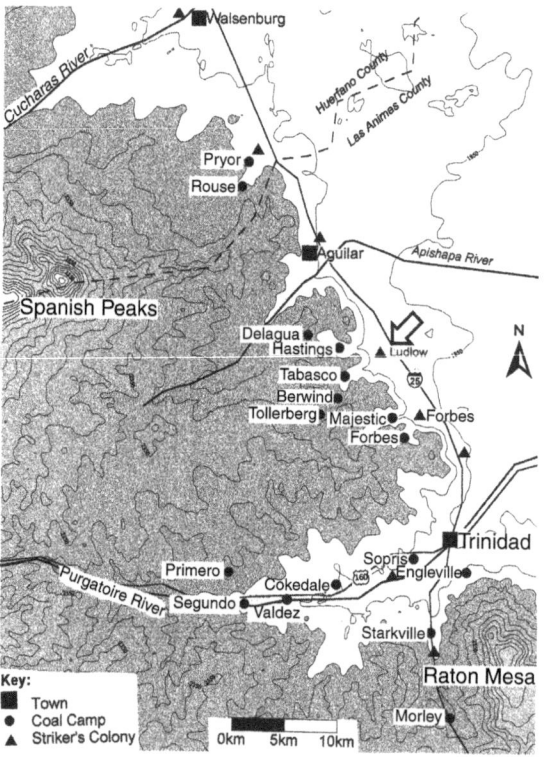

FIGURE 1. Map of the 1913–1914 strike zone showing the main coal camps and approximate location of the known strike camps.

houses, and bought food and equipment at company stores and alcohol at company saloons. The doctors, priests, schoolteachers, and law enforcement, such as it was, were all company employees. The entries to the camps were gated and guarded by deputized armed guards (Beshoar 1957:2; McGovern and Guttridge 1972:23; Foner 1980:196–198; Papanikolas 1982:39–40).

The workforce itself was largely immigrant labor from southern and eastern Europe, who had been brought in as strikebreakers in 1903 (Beshoar 1957:1; McGovern and Guttridge 1972: 50; Papanikolas 1982:40). Before the strike, the UMWA counted 24 distinct languages in the Southern Coalfield camps. In 1912, 61% of the Colorado's coal miners were of "non-Western European origin" (Whiteside 1990:48). This obviously had consequences for organizing the miners and maintaining discipline among them during the strike. It also resulted in the strike and its violence being popularly seen as a result of Greek and Balkan culture, rather than the conditions in the coalfields.

In 1903, the UMWA led a strike in the Colorado coalfields. This strike was successful in the Northern Coalfield of Colorado, but failed in the Southern. In 1910, the Northern operators refused to renew the contract, and the miners struck for the next three years. In September 1913 the UMWA, which had been secretly organizing the Southern Coalfield, announced a strike there when the operators would not meet a list of seven demands (McGovern and Guttridge 1972:102):

1. Recognition of the union.

2. A 10 percent increase in wages on the tonnage rates. Each miner was paid by the ton of coal he mined, not by the hour.

3. An eight-hour work day.

4. Payment for "dead work." Since miners were only paid for the coal they mined, work such as shoring, timbering, and laying track was not paid work.

5. The right to elect their own check-weighmen. Miners suspected, generally with good reason, that they were being cheated at the scales that weighed their coal. They wanted a miner to check the scales.

6. The right to trade in any store, to choose their own boarding places, and to choose their own doctors.

7. Enforcement of Colorado mining laws and abolition of the company guard system.

The crucial demand was recognition of the union.

Approximately 90% of the workforce struck, 10–12,000 miners plus their families (McGovern and Guttridge 1972:107). Those who lived in the camps were evicted, and on 23 September the striker families hauled their possessions through rain and snow out of the canyons to about a dozen sites rented in advance by the UMWA to house them. The UMWA supplied tents and ovens and organized the strikers into the tent colonies. The colonies were located at strategic spots covering the entrances to the canyons in order to intercept strikebreakers (Figure 1). Ludlow, with about 200 tents holding 1,200 miners and their families, was the largest of these colonies (Reed 1955:94–95; McGovern and Guttridge 1972:106; Papanikolas 1982:79–81).

The operators reacted quickly, bringing in strikebreakers. Like the strikers' tents, which were fresh from the Paint and Cabin Creek Strike in West Virginia, the operators brought in the Baldwin-Felts Detective Agency, which specialized in breaking coal-mining strikes. The detective agency and the coal operators initiated a campaign of harassment against the strikers. The harassment took the form of high-powered searchlights playing over the colonies at night, murders, beatings, and the use of the "death special," an improvised armored car that would periodically spray selected colonies with machine-gun fire. The purpose of this harassment was to goad the strikers into violent action, which would provide a pretext for the Colorado governor to call out the National Guard, thus shifting a considerable financial burden from the operators to the state. Amid steadily escalating violence in the coalfields and pressure from the operators, Governor Ammons duly called out the National Guard, which arrived in the coalfields in October 1913 (Reed 1955: 103–105; McGovern and Guttridge 1972:120–134; Papanikolas 1982:79–105).

After a brief honeymoon, the Militia commander General Chase, a Denver opthalmologist who had been involved in breaking the 1904 Cripple Creek Strike, essentially declared martial law in the strike zone. Highlights of this period of unofficial martial law included the suspension of habeas corpus, mass jailings of strikers, a cavalry charge on a demonstration by miners' wives and children, the torture and beating of prisoners, and the demolition of one of the tent colonies at Forbes. Chase also enlisted a considerable number of mine guards as militiamen (Reed 1955:107; McGovern and Guttridge 1972: 135–148; Sunsieri 1972; Papanikolas 1982: 107–123; Long 1985).

As the cost of supporting a force of 695 enlisted men and 397 officers in the field bankrupted the state, all but two of the militia companies were withdrawn after six months. The militia companies that remained were made up primarily of mine guards. At about 9:00 A.M. on 20 April, the day after the miners at Ludlow had celebrated Greek Easter, gunfire broke out at the colony. The exact circumstances are uncertain. Those miners who were armed (how many isn't known) took positions in a railroad cut and in prepared foxholes to draw fire away from the colony.

The militia sprayed the tent colony with machine-gun and rifle fire. By the end of the day, the force facing the miners consisted of 177 militia, including two machine guns. In the evening, the arrival of a train between the militia and the tent colony permitted most of the people to escape. By 7:00 P.M. the tent colony was in flames and was being looted by the militia (Figure 2). The leader of the colony, Louis Tikas, was captured by the militia and summarily executed, along with two other miners. Casualty figures vary, sometimes wildly, but a good estimate is 25 fatalities by the end of the day, including three militiamen, one uninvolved passerby, and 12 children. During the battle, 4 women and 11 children took refuge in a pit dug beneath a tent. All but two, Mary Petrucci and Alcarita Pedregone, suffocated when the tent above them was burned. The dead included Petrucci's three children and Pedregone's two children. This pit

FIGURE 2. Ludlow shortly after the massacre. The wrecked stoves on the prairie still serve as an icon of Ludlow. (Denver Public Library, Western History and Genealogy Division.)

has been preserved and is now known as the Death Pit (Reed 1955; McGovern and Guttridge 1972:210–231; Foner 1980; Papanikolas 1982: 207–237; Long 1989).

When news of Ludlow spread, the striking miners at the other colonies went to war. For 10 days they attacked and destroyed mines, fighting pitched battles with mine guards and militia along the 40 miles from Trinidad to Walsenberg. The fighting ceased when the desperate governor of Colorado asked for federal intervention. After Ludlow and the 10-Day War, the strike dragged on for another seven months, ending in defeat for the UMWA in December 1914 (McGovern and Guttridge 1972: 232–249; Papanikolas 1982:239–255).

After the strike ended, mass arrests were made of the miners, 408 in total, with 332 being indicted for murder, including the main strike leader, John Lawson. These trials dragged on until 1920. All arrests were eventually quashed with most cases never coming to trial, probably due to Rockefeller's influence, as he was anxious to see an end to the fallout from the strike. In contrast, 10 officers and 12 enlisted men were court-martialed for actions in Ludlow by the Colorado National Guard and exonerated (McGovern and Guttridge 1972:269–292).

Although it ended in the defeat of the union, the Ludlow Massacre focused national attention on the conditions in the Colorado coal camps and in labor conditions throughout the U.S. John D. Rockefeller, Jr., was singled out and excoriated in the press and in a spectacular series of public hearings before the Commission on Industrial Relations (Adams 1966; McGovern and Guttridge 1972:312–332). The strike did lead to some significant changes, including a general shift on the part of corporate managers from violent confrontation with organized labor to a policy more of co-optation. It is also generally accepted wisdom that company town conditions improved throughout the U.S. as a result of the Coal War (Gitelman 1988; Roth 1992; Crawford 1995).

For the UMWA, Ludlow came to serve as an icon of industrial conflict. It was felt to mark a turning point in the struggle for union recognition. As a result of the increasing labor violence at the turn of the century, there was a growing belief among all classes of American society that the industrial system was in need

of, if not fundamental reform, some reform to stave off class warfare (Adams 1966).

The Construction of Memory

Archaeology is an inherently political enterprise, bound up in, for example, ideologies of nationalism and colonialism (Trigger 1984, 1989; Gathercole and Lowenthal 1989; Layton 1989; Leone and Preucel 1992; Kohl and Fawcett 1995a; Schmidt and Patterson 1995; Kohl 1998), of gender (Conkey 1991; Gero and Conkey 1991; Wylie 1992; Spector 1993), race (Leone 1995; McDavid and Babson 1997), and class (Leone et al. 1987; Duke and Saitta 1998; McGuire and Walker 1999; Patterson 1999). Archaeologists, drawn largely from the middle class, have tended to draw on interpretive models that reflect the interests and concerns of that class, models that ignore conflict and contradiction within the social order, emphasizing instead its homogeneity, continuity, and the harmonious functioning of its various parts (Shanks and Tilley 1987; Paynter and McGuire 1991; McGuire 1992; Funari, this volume).

But archaeology can emancipate as well as legitimate or oppress. Through the archaeology project at Ludlow, an emancipatory and class-based archaeology was sought, "developing an archaeology of, and for, the working class" (Duke and Saitta 1998). As a goal of the Ludlow project is to create an archaeology that is relevant for the working classes, one that extends beyond the middle-class orientation of archaeology, members of the project are part of a growing movement in archaeology that seeks dialogues with groups that fall outside archaeology's traditional audience (Leone 1995; McDavid and Babson 1997; Logan 1998).

However, doing an archaeology like this is easier said than done, especially if there is mistrust or simply polite bewilderment about what you are trying to do. The Ludlow project deals with a very different audience than archaeology's traditional one. The United Archaeological Field Technicians aside, archaeology and organized labor have not often crossed paths. Those working on the Ludlow project have been confronted with the fact that many of the people who have the greatest interest in the site, for whom the memory of Ludlow is most important, are people who really don't have much use for archaeology, at least not archaeology as usual. Reaction among the mineworkers to the proposed work was at best cautious, generally ranging from polite bewilderment to outright antagonism. The antagonism is probably due to the doubt that academic professionals could contribute anything worth knowing to the story of Ludlow, although the actual expression of this reservation was somewhat earthier (Duke and Saitta 1998).

There is a very real awareness of the politics of history on the part of the miners. It is not every archaeology project where an important first step is convincing the landowner that you are not a Republican. The need for this was explained to the researchers as "History can be written a lot of ways and Ludlow is sacred ground for the mineworkers." Ludlow is sacred ground and has been ever since the massacre. The interest of the mineworkers in Ludlow is not an abstract or neutral one, for that would render Ludlow and its memory meaningless.

The important point here is that the histories of Ludlow are not simply lying in the ground waiting for archaeologists to dig them up. They precede our arrival on the scene and are rooted in different interests from ours. For the project to be at all meaningful to the local community, archaeologists must understand and engage these histories and interests (Brecher 1986; Duggan 1986; Green 1986; Leone 1986; Shopes 1986; Bishir 1989; Leone and Preucel 1992; Shanks and McGuire 1996; Potter 1998). Researchers moved from the study of history to that of memory and history making, leaving the familiar practices and attitudes of academic professionals and entering a terrain where the past is intimate, explicitly useful, and its meanings are jealously guarded (Popular Memory Group 1982; Thelen 1990; Portelli 1991; Hamilton 1994; Rosenzweig and Thelen 1998).

Unsurprisingly, discussions of memory mirror some of the debates over the nature of ideology. Much of the debate has been framed in terms of dichotomies that revolve around the opposition between dominant and submerged sets of narratives and practices—official vs. vernacular, public vs. private, national vs. local, or history vs. memory. These dichotomies do highlight the existence of real underlying processes of power and domination (Hamilton 1994:12) and are useful for some projects (Bodnar 1992). However, they are inadequate when researchers wish to look at the histories of these narratives or consider them in any detail. People do not contain within themselves different historical consciousnesses deriving from different forms of historical narrative that run along on separate but parallel tracks. Rather, these sources or narratives are pulled together, interpreted, and made coherent through preexisting understandings and experiences.

This coherent individual understanding of history, where personal experience and formal historical narratives are integrated into a practical historical consciousness, is historical memory. It is a relation constructed through the interaction of a diverse set of historical sources, narratives, and practices (Figure 3), both public and private or informal, and through political-economic interests, such as class, race, or gender.

The active negotiation of these sets of interests and narratives creates a personal but socially embedded understanding of the past that structures and provides both practical (action-oriented) understandings of identity and agency and also guidance in planning and anticipating the present and future (Rosenzweig and Thelen 1998:18). Historical memory is not an imposed dominant ideology, although dominant conceptions through the historical public sphere do play a role in constructing it. The incorporation of these different narratives is not uncritical or passive. People do absorb and retain elements and narratives from official or dominant sources and may even do so in an unquestioning manner (Frisch 1990), but they interpret these narratives and assign meaning to them through their own

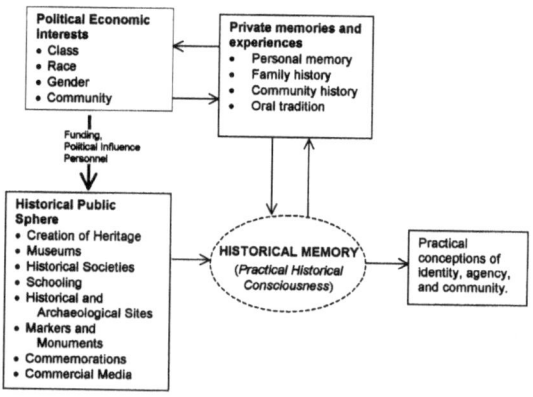

FIGURE 3. The construction of historical memory.

interests and experiences (Rosenzweig and Thelen 1998:22–32).

Archaeology is part of the historical public sphere, a constellation of media and institutions that serve to create national historical memory; institutions such as schools, historical sites, television programs, commemorative activities, and museums (Habermas 1991; Bodnar 1992:15, 19). These institutions act together, although not necessarily in concert, to create and communicate the heritage that largely defines the nation (Bommes and Wright 1982:260). This historical public sphere is an arena with a set of rules within which public historical argumentation and, thus, political and social argumentation take place through the creation of historical memory (Bommes and Wright 1982; Popular Memory Group 1982). The past becomes a theater for the enactment of dramas, presenting a primordial unity that denies social and political contradictions in the present. Within historical archaeology, for example, certain sites represent the nation, being our heritage, our history, and our past, while others represent the heritage of special interest groups within the nation.

The historical public sphere is an arena for debate but debates that are often structured by inequalities (Bodnar 1992:15–19). These structuring inequalities can be as crass as flows of money or interlocking directorates between corporate and historical boards, and as subtle as the attitudes of the middle-class professionals who largely referee the debates (Bodnar 1992: 15; Beik 1998). There are broad similarities in the narratives that tend to dominate in the end. These narratives are nationalistic and patriotic, emphasizing citizen duties over citizen rights. They emphasize social unity, the continuity of the social order, and gloss over periods of transformation and rupture (Bodnar 1992:13–19).

Public memory is still the result of negotiation and debate, albeit between opponents who are often mismatched. The domination of official histories is not total. The same historical event will be experienced, perceived, and interpreted in many ways, generating pasts as contradictory and heterogeneous as the social relations that ultimately spawned them (McGuire 1992: 816–817). Some of these pasts flourish, propagating through official commemorations and interpretations, school textbooks, and the mass media (Trouillot 1995). But the other pasts do not necessarily

disappear. The past is remembered through many means—photo albums, family conversations, and local commemorations of histories that have been excluded or marginalized within official history (Popular Memory Group 1982; Bodnar 1992; Funari 1993; Rosenzweig and Thelen 1998).

Remembering Ludlow

As early as 1916, letters, editorials, and cartoons in the *United Mine Workers Journal* were expressing the not unjustified concern that Ludlow would be erased from public memory. The memory of Ludlow became a battleground almost immediately after the massacre. In addition to Ludlow's seminal role in labor history, Rockefeller's campaign to rehabilitate his image afterwards and to control the public perception of Ludlow led to its gaining a special place in U.S. history as a birthplace of professional public relations (Gitelman 1988; Cockburn 1996; Martinson 1996). The response of the mine workers was immediate and effective. The pamphlet they put out in 1914 (Fink 1914) fixed the name as the "Ludlow Massacre," rather than the "Battle of Ludlow," or the "Ludlow Incident." At the time, defending the idea that Ludlow was an atrocity committed by people as opposed to a battle between evenly matched sides or an unfortunate accident that just happened was not a difficult argument.

The UMWA bought the 40 acres surrounding the site of the Ludlow colony before 1916 (Hayes 1916). John White, the president of the UMWA, officially proposed a memorial for the site at the 1916 UMWA convention (White 1916: 35). The convention passed the proposal. Later that year several hundred coalminers met at the site of Ludlow and joined the union (*United Mine Workers Journal* [*UMWJ*] 1916). Regular commemorations seem to have been held at the site thereafter. The monument was finally dedicated 30 May 1918 (*UMWJ* 1918b) (Figure 4). The Death Pit was also preserved and consists of a concrete-lined pit into which people can still descend.

In subsequent strikes in Southern Colorado, the memory of Ludlow was invoked in mass meetings at the site. For one thing, being owned by the UMWA made it safe ground for miners to meet during strikes. During a strike in 1921, the UMWA erected four tents on the site

FIGURE 4. The Ludlow Massacre Memorial. Dedicated 30 May 1918.

The memory of Ludlow remains an important one to working-class people and organized labor and is still annually commemorated.

But Ludlow is vulnerable to forgetting for precisely the reason that its memory is important to organized labor. It flies in the face of dominant middle-class conceptions of American society. Many of the cover illustrations and the correspondence from the *United Mine Workers Journal* after the Ludlow Massacre revolve around the contradiction between what happened at Ludlow and dominant conceptions of U.S. society.

For example, the cartoon in Figure 5 critiques the idea of the U.S. as a classless society. The heading on this cartoon, "Oh yes, we are partners," refers to one of the reforms that came out of the massacre and its aftermath. Under the influence of his advisor, Mackenzie King (who later became Prime Minister of Canada), Rockefeller argued that labor and capital were, in fact, equal partners in industrial enterprises and should cooperate, an argument that still has resonance today, even among the leadership of some unions. He established the Colorado Industrial Plan, which was one of the first company unions (Gitelman 1988). This cartoon is making the point that the partnership is, in fact,

of Ludlow in symbolic defiance of an order by the Colorado Rangers not to erect tent colonies (Pogliano 1921). The Rangers were aware of the inflammatory symbolism of the tent colony. The International Workers of the World (the IWW or Wobblies), a rival union to the UMWA, also legitimated a major strike in 1927 by holding a meeting at the site of Ludlow (Whiteside 1990:129).

In the time work has been done at Ludlow, the United Steelworkers have been participating in the UMWA annual memorial service at Ludlow. They are currently on strike at the CF&I (now Oregon Steel) plant in Pueblo. The steelworkers obviously delight in the historical parallels between the strike of 1913 and today's. In 1998 and 1999 about 400 of them marched to Ludlow carrying a banner listing all the strikers killed there. In 1999 they also held a week-long series of community educational events prior to the memorial service, with speakers, exhibits, and labor-related movies.

FIGURE 5. "Oh! Yes, We are Partners." For many middle-class Americans, Ludlow was the first hint that the rhetoric and reality of life in industrial America did not mesh (*United Mine Workers Journal*, 1 October 1914).

unequal—in living conditions, the profits from the enterprise, and the right to organize and form associations.

While the UMWA's memorialization of Ludlow was an effort to maintain a history in danger of being submerged, this effort was itself the product of power struggles and differentials within the union, which highlights the difficulty in pigeonholing dominant and submerged histories. Union politics and the residue of bitterness between the UMWA International Executive and the miners of Southern Colorado, who felt that they had been abandoned, led to two of the 1913 strike leaders, John Lawson and Ed Doyle, forming a separate and rival union in Southern Colorado (Hayes et al. 1918a, 1918b; *UMWJ* 1918a, 1918c). The dedication of the Ludlow Monument by the UMWA in 1918 (*UMWJ* 1918b) took place in the midst of this controversy. The monument and the dedication permitted the UMWA International to lay claim to the history of Ludlow and prevents its use by the dual unionists. There are submerged histories within submerged histories. This part of the history of Ludlow has, other than archival traces, all but disappeared.

Forgetting Ludlow

Labor struggle and the life of labor is prominent, if that is the word, among those events and sites that are silenced in the historical public sphere, being instead commemorated by labor unions and working people themselves (Foote 1997:296). Given the sorts of interests that tend to drive and dominate public history, the silencing of labor struggle is unsurprising. In the dominant mythology, the U.S. is a classless society—"we are all middle class." Events that bear a resemblance to class warfare or that even point to the presence of class are not easily incorporated with this mythology. A second factor for the silencing is that labor struggle lacks a resolution or, to put it another way, historical distance (Foote 1997:300). Labor struggles continue today. They cannot be effectively quarantined in the past and "antiquarianized." The problems that gave rise to them have not been resolved, and unions remain an uneasy and ambiguous presence on the fringes of middle-class consciousness.

The silencing of labor struggle can also have more obviously economic underpinnings. In

Southern Colorado, the remembered past needs to be considered in the context of deindustrialization, the decline of coal mining, and local attempts to re-create the economic base of the area through heritage tourism. The dominant history of the area is that of the Old West. Trinidad, the largest town near Ludlow, is on the Santa Fe Trail. Its history is replete with cowboys, pioneers, Indian attacks, and figures such as Kit Carson, Dick Wootten, Black Jack Ketchum, and Bat Masterson. The attraction of this history is powerful. It provides a link not only to national histories of westward expansion and growth but to a mythology that, through Hollywood, has a truly global appeal. The histories of coal mining, company towns, and labor struggle pale in comparison (Papanikolas 1995: 73–90; McGuire and Reckner 1998).

But these histories are not erased totally. They are too big a part of the past and the landscape, evident in the giant slack heaps and graveyards throughout the region. Although the last mine closed in 1996, coal mining is still a significant part of the experience of the local community, and its commemoration is increasingly prominent. In 1998 a coal miners' memorial was erected in Trinidad's historic district. The monument was erected by the Hispanic Chamber of Commerce, and the ceremony was strikingly pro-union (Bee 1997). Compared to similar such monuments, it appears to have been relatively uncontroversial. For example, a miners' memorial in Harlan County, Kentucky, was the site of considerable, although covert, political tensions (Scott 1995) and was ultimately demolished by civic authorities. This was also the case with a 1997 miners' memorial designed to commemorate those who had died in local mines in Windber, Pennsylvania (Beik 1999).

As coal mining and coal miners recede into history, it becomes likely that there will be more official interpretation of this history and a softening of this history, a trend that we can see in other deindustrializing regions of the United States, such as the coal mining and steel towns of Pennsylvania (Abrams 1994; Mondale 1994; Staub 1994; Brant 1996; Stewart 1997). As industries leave the United States for overseas plants or become economically unfeasible, their histories are often sanitized, romanticized, and redefined as "heritage" (Lowenthal 1996; Karaim 1997; Brooke 1998), a trend that one journalist aptly characterized as "Unemployment: The Theme Park" (Brant 1996). There is generally little room for labor history or the interpretation of labor struggle in this heritage of technological progress, entrepreneurs, and impressive, but, nonetheless, fetishized industrial artifacts and processes.

Archaeology and Memory

While many archaeologists may appreciate it theoretically, the political nature of the past is something that archaeologists have been dragged into in real life—generally reluctantly. Archaeologists have found themselves embroiled with communities that, rather than being passive consumers of the pasts that archaeologists produce, challenged the right of archaeologists to produce those pasts without the involvement of the community or even their right to produce these pasts at all (Condori 1989; Zimmerman 1989; McGuire 1992; Epperson 1997; LaRoche and Blakey 1997; Patten 1997).

As archaeologists, we know history matters, but it also matters to people outside the guild, people who may have different interests from ours—interests often rooted in some familiar issues such as ethnicity, race, gender, and class. Our findings and interpretations are sometimes used or rejected in unexpected ways and for unexpected reasons. Our audience is not homogeneous. There are segments of this audience that are interested in the same things professional archaeologists are interested in and are content to accept our findings. But, as we are increasingly finding, there are other segments that, while they may be vitally interested in the past, may find our research questions irrelevant or even offensive (LaRoche and Blakey 1997).

Archaeologists and their audiences are predominantly white and middle class. It doesn't take intricate or obscure textual analyses to see this orientation in a lot of historical archaeology—for example, the celebrations of consumerism, the melting pot models of acculturation, or the discomfort with the idea of class (Wurst and Fitts 1999). The issue is not whether archaeology should be made political or relevant. It already is political and relevant. The question is for whom?

In the work at Ludlow, an audience was chosen and some decisions were made. Public interpretive responsibilities at this site lie with organized labor, not only because the United Mine Workers owns the site of Ludlow and researchers work there at their pleasure but because of our own theoretical and practical concerns. Archaeology possesses considerable public appeal, although for exactly which public and why is open to investigation. We can use the appeal of archaeology to reach audiences who are largely unfamiliar with labor history and, conversely, by making ourselves useful to organized labor, broaden the awareness of archaeology.

It is by making ourselves useful, not by displaying the intrinsic "objective" worth of archaeology, that the initial suspicion has been overcome and a dialogue with organized labor has been established. Of major interest to organized labor in Southern Colorado was simply raising public awareness of the massacre. This has been done through on-site tours, newspaper articles, talks and lectures, and a traveling exhibit. Members of the project spoke and maintained an exhibit at a series of community events on the Ludlow Massacre held by the United Steelworkers of America in Pueblo who were, and at the time of writing still are, on strike against Colorado Fuel & Iron. Kim Manajek, a student in the University of Denver's Museum Studies program, designed and installed an interpretive kiosk at the site (Manajek 1999). The UMWA Local Women's Auxiliary, which was largely responsible for the maintenance of the monument, reviewed the design of the kiosk. Their suggestions centered on strengthening the connection between the Ludlow Massacre and contemporary labor struggles in the area, thus ensuring that Ludlow was not consigned to a dead past—something the very presence of archaeologists may tend to suggest. In addition, Dean Saitta designed and organized a K–12 Teachers' Institute in order to try to bring labor history into the school curriculum.

Interpreting the Ludlow Massacre to people who have little or no awareness of labor history is not an unexpected benefit of the project to organized labor. The exhibit and the archaeological work have also been a way for unions to educate their members about their history and about the sacrifices of union members. The exhibit was shown at the UMWA Ludlow Memorial Services in 1999 and 2000 and, as the project is covered in the national labor press

(Green 1999; *UMWJ* 1999), there has been recent interest in taking the exhibit to union halls.

Conclusion

Ludlow is very recent for an archaeological study, for many archaeologists shockingly so. But Ludlow does confront us with a site where archaeologists are forced to engage with audiences, audiences who will take our findings quite seriously. Ludlow highlights the political nature of history and archaeology. It is obvious that just looking at a site like this is a political statement. But what is less obvious is that it is just as much a political statement to not look at sites like this. The silencing of labor history sites and events, such as Ludlow, Blair Mountain, Lattimer, and Homestead, as well as their commemoration is bound up with historical struggles and class interests. Histories are themselves historical, changing as struggles and alliances between interest groups shift as they change and are changed by the social terrain on which their struggles take place. The erasing or trivialization of labor struggle within the historical public sphere involves a number of related processes and interests at local and national scales, from the conscious public relations campaigns of wealthy capitalists to middle-class attitudes towards labor and labor unions, from the disciplinary practices of academic professionals to the anxiousness of civic leaders anticipating tourist interests and desires.

Archaeology is an act of commemoration. It participates in the creation of historical memory, creating visions of the past that are rooted in present-day interests: not just our interests but also those of our audiences (Shanks and McGuire 1996). Engaging in dialogues with those outside the guild enriches archaeological and historical discourse by making us aware of the silences in the pasts we have been creating; thus, we open up new directions of research. This is not to deny the existence of a real past. Ludlow did happen. And as archaeologists, the skills and specialized knowledge we bring will provide important information on what happened at Ludlow. But the carefully mapped, expended bullets scattered among the charcoal staining, broken plates, toys, and buttons touch us in ways that go beyond the evidence. Knowing the importance of the past lies in knowing what

these "ways" are and why they came to be. As Michel-Rolph Trouillot notes, the authenticity of the past lies in the struggles of the present. An authentic past is one that engages us as witnesses, actors, and commentators (Trouillot 1995:150–151).

ACKNOWLEDGMENTS

This article is product of many people's work. In looking after the children, Ginette Walker worked harder on this article than I did. I wish to thank Randy McGuire, Dean Saitta, and Phil Duke for allowing me to participate in this project. I also wish to thank them, Pedro Funari, and two anonymous reviewers for their insightful comments on this article. Conversations with many others have contributed to my thoughts, prominent among them the staff and students of the University of Denver Summer Field Schools at Ludlow and Berwind. I am grateful to Paul Shackel for the opportunity to participate in the Commemoration, Conflict, and the American Landscape Conference at the University of Maryland in 1999. We work at Ludlow with the gracious permission of District 22 and Local Union 9856 of the United Mine Workers of America. They have kept the memory of Ludlow alive. The Colorado Coalfield War Archaeology Project is funded by the Colorado Historical Society, State Historical Fund.

REFERENCES

ABRAMS, JAMES F.
1994 Lost Frames of Reference: Sightings of History and Memory in Pennsylvania's Documentary Landscape. In *Conserving Culture: A New Discourse on Heritage*, Mary Hufford, editor, pp. 24–38. University of Illinois Press, Urbana.

ADAMS, GRAHAM
1966 *The Age of Industrial Violence, 1910–1915: The Activities and Findings of the U.S. Commission on Industrial Relations*. Columbia University Press, New York, NY.

BEE, TANJA
1997 Coal Miners Memorial: Five-Year Effort Culminates in Dedication of Memorial in Honor of Area Miners. *Trinidad Colorado*. <http://www.trinidadco.com/stories/features/minermem.html> 4 August [viewed August 2001].

BEIK, MILDRED A.
1998 Who Owns the Past? Windber, Pennsylvania, and the Berwind-White Coal Mining Company. Paper presented at the Oral History Association Annual Meeting, Buffalo, NY.
1999 Commemoration and Contestation: Remembering the Unsung Miners of Windber Pennsylvania. Paper presented at the North American Labor History Conference, Detroit, MI.

BESHOAR, BARRON B.
1957 *Out of the Depths: The Story of John R. Lawson, a Labor Leader*. Colorado Historical Commission & Denver Trades & Labor Assembly, Denver, CO.

BISHIR, CATHERINE
1989 Yuppies, Bubbas, and the Politics of Culture. In *Perspectives in Vernacular Architecture, III*, Thomas Carter and Bernard L. Herman, editors, pp. 8–15. University of Missouri Press, Columbia.

BODNAR, JOHN
1992 *Remaking America: Public Memory, Commemoration, and Patriotism in the Twentieth Century*. Princeton University Press, Princeton, NJ.

BOMMES, MICHAEL, AND PATRICK WRIGHT
1982 "Charms of Residence": The Public and the Past. In *Making Histories: Studies in History Writing and Politics*, Richard Johnson, Gregor McLennan, Bill Schwarz, and David Sutton, editors, pp. 253–302. University of Minnesota Press, Minneapolis.

BRANT, JOHN
1996 Unemployment: The Theme Park. *New York Times Magazine*, 28 January:46–47.

BRECHER, JEREMY
1986 A Report on Doing History from Below: The Brass Workers History Project. In *Presenting the Past: Essays on History and the Public*, Susan Porter Benson, Stephen Brier, and Roy Rosenzweig, editors, pp. 267–277. Temple University Press, Philadelphia, PA.

BROOKE, JAMES
1998 West Celebrates Mining's Past, But Not Its Future. *New York Times*, October 4.

COCKBURN, ALEXANDER
1996 Money Smoothed Troubled Oil; Public Relations in the Petroleum Industry. *The Nation*, 263(19):10.

CONDORI, CARLOS MAMANI
1989 History and Prehistory in Bolivia: What about the Indians? In *Conflict in the Archaeology of Living Traditions*, Robert Layton, editor, pp. 46–59. Unwin Hyman, Boston, MA

CONKEY, MARGARET
1991 Original Narratives: The Political Economy of Gender in Archaeology. In *Gender at the Crossroads of Knowledge: Feminist Anthropology in the Postmodern Era*, Micaela di Leonardo, editor, pp. 102–139. University of California Press, Berkeley.

CRAWFORD, MARGARET
1995 *Building the Workingman's Paradise: The Design of American Company Towns*. Verso, London.

DUGGAN, LISA
1986 History's Gay Ghetto: The Contradictions of Growth in Lesbian and Gay History. In *Presenting the Past: Essays on History and the Public*, Susan Porter Benson, Stephen Brier, and Roy Rosenzweig, editors, pp. 281–290. Temple University Press, Philadelphia, PA.

DUKE, PHILIP, AND DEAN J. SAITTA
1998 An Emancipatory Archaeology for the Working Class. Assemblage, 4 <http://www.shef.ac.uk./assem/4/4duk_sai.html> October [viewed August 2001].

EPPERSON, TERRENCE W.
1997 The Politics of "Race" and Cultural Identity at the African Burial Ground Excavations, New York City. *World Archaeological Bulletin*, 7:108–117.

FINK, WALTER H.
1914 *The Ludlow Massacre*. District No. 15, United Mine Workers of America, Denver, CO.

FONER, PHILIP S.
1980 *History of the Labor Movement in the United States, Volume V: The AFL in the Progressive Era, 1910–1915*. International Publishers, New York, NY.

FOOTE, KENNETH E.
1997 *Shadowed Ground: America's Landscape of Violence and Tragedy*. University of Texas Press, Austin.

FOX, MAIER BRYAN
1990 *United We Stand: The United Mine Workers of America, 1890–1990*. International Union, United Mine Workers of America, Washington, DC.

FRISCH, MICHAEL
1990 American History and the Structures of Collective Memory: A Modest Exercise in Empirical Iconography. In *Memory and American History*, David Thelen, editor, pp. 1–26. Indiana University Press, Bloomington.

FUNARI, PEDRO
1993 Graphic Caricature and the Ethos of Ordinary People at Pompeii. *Journal of European Archaeology*, 1(2): 133–150.

GATHERCOLE, PETER, AND DAVID LOWENTHAL (EDITORS)
1989 *The Politics of the Past*. Unwin Hyman, London.

GERO, JOAN M., AND MARGARET W. CONKEY (EDITORS)
1991 *Engendering Archaeology: Women and Prehistory*. Blackwell, London.

GITELMAN, HOWARD M.
1988 *Legacy of the Ludlow Massacre: A Chapter in American Industrial Relations*. University of Pennsylvania Press, Philadelphia.

GREEN, ARLEE
1999 UMWA Highlights Ludlow Massacre. *America@Work*, November/December:23.

Perspectives from the Society for Historical Archaeology:

GREEN, JAMES R.
1986 Engaging in People's History: The Massachusetts History Workshop. In *Presenting the Past: Essays on History and the Public*, Susan Porter Benson, Stephen Brier, and Roy Rosenzweig, editors, pp. 339–359. Temple University Press, Philadelphia, PA.

HABERMAS, JÜRGEN
1991 *The Structural Transformation of the Public Sphere: An Inquiry into a Category of Bourgeois Society*. Thomas Burger, translator. MIT Press, Cambridge, MA.

HAMILTON, PAULA
1994 The Knife Edge: Debates about *Memory and History*. In *Memory and History in Twentieth-Century Australia*, Kate Darrian-Smith and Paula Hamilton, editors, pp. 9–32. Oxford University Press, Melbourne, Australia.

HAYES, FRANK J.
1916 Report of the International Vice President Frank J. Hayes. *The United Mine Workers Journal*, 20 January: 40–42.

HAYES, FRANK J., JOHN L. LEWIS, AND AL GREEN
1918a Official Notice: To All of the United Mine Workers of America. District 15 Correspondence, D15 1918-Apr–Dec, United Mine Workers of America Archives, Pennsylvania State University, State College.
1918b Official Notice to the Colorado Mine Workers. *United Mine Workers Journal*, May 2:10.

KARAIM, REED
1997 Time out of Mine: Airstreams, Aging Hippies, and UFOs Meet the Ghosts of Miners Past in a Well-Preserved Arizona Desert Town. *Preservation*, March/April:83–86.

KOHL, PHILIP L.
1998 Nationalism and Archaeology: On the Constructions of Nations and the Reconstructions of the Remote Past. *Annual Reviews in Anthropology*, 27:2232–46.

KOHL, PHILIP L., AND CLARE FAWCETT (EDITORS)
1995a *Nationalism, Politics, and the Practice of Archaeology*. Cambridge University Press, Cambridge.

LAROCHE, CHERYL J., AND MICHAEL L. BLAKEY
1997 Seizing Intellectual Power: The Dialogue at the New York African Burial Ground. *Historical Archaeology*, 31(3):84–106.

LAYTON, ROBERT (EDITOR)
1989 *Conflict in the Archaeology of Living Traditions*. Unwin Hyman, London.

LEONE, MARK P.
1986 Symbolic, Structural, and Critical Archaeology. In *American Archaeology Past and Future: A Celebration of the Society for American Archaeology, 1935–1985*, Don P. Fowler, David J. Meltzer, and Jeremy A. Sabloff, editors, pp. 415–438. Smithsonian Institution Press, Washington, DC.
1995 A Historical Archaeology of Capitalism. *American Anthropologist*, 97(2):251–268.

LEONE, MARK P., JR., PARKER B. POTTER, AND PAUL A. SHACKEL
1987 Toward a Critical Archaeology. *Current Anthropology*, 28(3):283–302.

LEONE, MARK P., AND ROBERT PREUCEL
1992 Archaeology in a Democratic Society: A Critical Perspective. In *Quandaries and Quests: Visions of Archaeology's Future*, LuAnn Wandsnider, editor, pp. 15–135. Center for Archaeological Investigations, Southern Illinois University, Carbondale.

LINENTHAL, EDWARD T., AND TOM ENGELHARDT (EDITORS)
1996 *History Wars: The Enola Gay and Other Battles for the American Past*. Henry Holt, Metropolitan Books, New York, NY.

LOGAN, GEORGE C.
1998 Archaeologists, Residents, and Visitors: Creating a Community-Based Program in African-American Archaeology. In *Annapolis Pasts: Historical Archaeology in Annapolis, Maryland*, Paul A. Shackel, Paul R. Mullins, and Mark S. Warner, editors, pp. 69–90. University of Tennessee Press, Knoxville.

LONG, PRISCILLA
1985 The Women of the C.F.I. Strike, 1913–1914. In *Women, Work, and Protest: A Century of U.S. Women's Labor History*, Ruth Milkman, editor, pp. 62–85. Routledge & Kegan Paul, London.
1989 The Voice of the Gun: Colorado's Great Coalfield War of 1913–1914. *Labor's Heritage*, 1(4):4–23.

LOWENTHAL, DAVID
1996 *Possessed by the Past: The Heritage Crusade and the Spoils of History*. The Free Press, New York, NY.

LUDLOW COLLECTIVE
2000 Archaeology of the Colorado Coal Field War, 1913–1914. In *The Absent Present: Archaeologies of the Contemporary Past*, G. Lucas, editor. Routledge, London.

MANAJEK, KIM
1999 Ludlow Massacre Interpretive Kiosk. Master's thesis, University of Denver, Denver, CO.

MARTINSON, DAVID
1996 "Truthfulness" in Communication Is Both a Reasonable and Achievable Goal for Public Relations Practitioners. *Public Relations Quarterly*, 41(4):42.

McDAVID, CAROL, AND DAVID W. BABSON (EDITORS)
1997 *In the Realm of Politics: Prospects for Public Participation in African-American and Plantation Archaeology*. Society for Historical Archaeology, California, PA.

McGOVERN, GEORGE S., AND LEONARD F. GUTTRIDGE
1972 *The Great Coalfield War*. Houghton Mifflin Company, Boston, MA.

McGuire, Randall H.
1992 Archaeology and the First Americans. *American Anthropologist,* 94(4):816–863.

McGuire, Randall H., and Paul E. Reckner
1998 The Unromantic West: Labor, Capital and Struggle. Paper presented at the 32nd Annual Conference on Historical and Underwater Archaeology, Salt Lake City, UT.

McGuire, Randall H., and Mark Walker
1999 Class Confrontations in Archaeology. In *Confronting Class,* LouAnn Wurst and Robert K. Fitts, editors, pp. 159–183. Society for Historical Archaeology, California, PA.

Mondale, Clarence
1994 Conserving a Problematic Past. In *Conserving Culture: A New Discourse on Heritage,* Mary Hufford, editor, pp. 15–23. University of Illinois Press, Urbana.

Papanikolas, Zeece
1982 *Buried Unsung: Louis Tikas and the Ludlow Massacre.* University of Utah Press, Salt Lake City.
1995 *Trickster in the Land of Dreams.* University of Nebraska Press, Lincoln.

Patten, M. Drake
1997 Cheers of Protest? The Public, the Post, and the Parable of Learning. In *In the Realm of Politics: Prospects for Public Participation in African-American and Plantation Archaeology,* Carol McDavid and David W. Babson, editors, pp. 132–139. Society for Historical Archaeology, California, PA.

Patterson, Thomas C.
1999 The Political Economy of Archaeology in the United States. *Annual Reviews in Anthropology,* 28:155–74.

Paynter, Robert, and Randall H. McGuire
1991 The Archaeology of Inequality: Material Culture, Domination, and Resistance. In *The Archaeology of Inequality,* Randall McGuire and Robert Paynter, editors, pp. 1–27. Basil Blackwell, Oxford, England.

Pogliano, Felix
1921 Letter to Mr. Luke Brennan, International Executive Board Member, District No. 15, U.M.W. of A. District 15 Correspondence. D15-1921, Nov–Dec, United Mine Workers of America Archives, Pennsylvania State University, State College.

Popular Memory Group
1982 Popular Memory: Theory, Politics, Method. In *Making Histories: Studies in History Writing and Politics,* Richard Johnson, Gregor McLennan, Bill Schwarz, and David Sutton, editors, pp. 205–252. University of Minnesota Press, Minneapolis.

Portelli, Alessandro
1991 *The Death of Luigi Trastulli and Other Stories: Form and Meaning in Oral History.* State University of New York Press, Albany, NY.

Potter, Parker B., Jr.
1998 Ethnography in Annapolis. In *Annapolis Pasts: Historical Archaeology in Annapolis, Maryland,* Paul A. Shackel, Paul R. Mullins, and Mark S. Warner, editors, pp. 35–48. University of Tennessee Press, Knoxville.

Reed, John
1955 The Colorado War. In *The Education of John Reed,* pp. 83–121. International Publishers, New York, NY.

Rosenzweig, Roy, and David Thelen
1998 *The Presence of the Past: Popular Uses of History in American Life.* Columbia University Press, New York, NY.

Roth, Leland
1992 Company Towns in the Western United States. In *The Company Town: Architecture and Society in the Early Industrial Age,* John S. Garner, editor, pp. 173–205. Oxford University Press, New York, NY.

Scamehorn, H. Lee
1992 *Mill & Mine: The CF&I in the Twentieth Century.* University of Nebraska Press, Lincoln.

Schmidt, Peter R., and Thomas C. Patterson (editors)
1995 *Making Alternative Histories: The Practice of Archaeology and History in Non Western Settings.* School of American Research Press, Santa Fe, NM.

Scott, Shaunna
1995 *Two Sides to Everything: The Cultural Construction of Class Consciousness in Harlan County, Kentucky.* State University of New York Press, Albany.

Shanks, Michael, and Randall H. McGuire
1996 The Craft of Archaeology. *American Antiquity,* 61(1): 75–88.

Shanks, Michael, and Christopher Tilley
1987 *Reconstructing Archaeology: Theory and Practice.* Cambridge University Press, Cambridge.

Shopes, Linda
1986 Oral History and Community Involvement: The Baltimore Neighborhood Heritage Project. In *Presenting the Past: Essays on History and the Public,* Susan Porter Benson, Stephen Brier, and Roy Rosenzweig, editors, pp. 249–263. Temple University Press, Philadelphia, PA.

Spector, Janet D.
1993 *What This Awl Means: Feminist Archaeology at a Wahpeton Dakota Village.* Minnesota Historical Society Press, St. Paul.

STAUB, SHALOM
1994 Cultural Conservation and Economic Recovery Planning: The Pennsylvania Heritage Parks Program. In *Conserving Culture: A New Discourse on Heritage*, Mary Hufford, editor, pp. 229–244. University of Illinois Press, Urbana.

STEWART, DOUG
1997 Saving American Steel. *Smithsonian*, August: 86–93.

SUNSIERI, ALVIN R.
1972 *The Ludlow Massacre: A Study in the Misemployment of the National Guard*. Salvadore Books, Waterloo, IA.

THELEN, DAVID
1990 Introduction: Memory and American History. In *Memory and American History*, David Thelen, editor, pp. vii–xix. Indiana University Press, Bloomington.

THOMPSON, E. P.
1980 *Writing by Candlelight*. Merlin, London.

TRIGGER, BRUCE G.
1984 Alternative Archaeologies: Nationalist, Colonialist, and Imperialist. *Man*, 19:355–370.
1989 *A History of Archaeological Thought*. Cambridge University Press, Cambridge.

TROUILLOT, MICHEL-ROLPH
1995 *Silencing the Past: Power and the Production of History*. Beacon Press, Boston, MA.

UNITED MINE WORKERS JOURNAL (*UMWJ*)
1916 The Way of the Cave-Man. *The United Mine Workers Journal*, 2 November:7.
1918a Ingratitude Like a Serpent's Tooth! *United Mine Workers Journal*, 21 March:4–6.
1918b Memorial Day at Ludlow. *The United Mine Workers Journal*, 6:4.
1918c Stamp Out Secession. *The United Mine Workers Journal*, 13 June:4
1999 Let We Forget ... : Ludlow Project Puts Massacre in Spotlight. *United Mine Workers Journal*, March–April: 12–13.

WALKER, MARK
2000 Labor History at the Ground Level: Colorado Coalfield War Archaeology Project. *Labor's Heritage*, 11(1): 58–75.

WHITE, JOHN P.
1916 Report of the International President John P. White to the Twenty-Fifth Consecutive and Second Biennial Convention. *United Mine Workers Journal*, January 20:35.

WHITESIDE, JAMES
1990 *Regulating Danger: The Struggle for Mine Safety in the Rocky Mountain Coal Industry*. University of Nebraska Press, Lincoln.

WURST, LOUANN, AND ROBERT K. FITTS (EDITORS)
1999 *Confronting Class*. Society for Historical Archaeology, California, PA.

WYLIE, ALISON
1992 The Interplay of Evidential Constraints and Political Interests: Recent Archaeological Research on Gender. *American Antiquity*, 57(1):15–35.

ZIMMERMAN, LARRY J.
1989 Human Bones As Symbols of Power: Aboriginal American Belief Systems and "Grave-Robbing" Archaeologists. In *Conflict in the Archaeology of Living Traditions*, Robert Layton, editor, pp. 211–216. Unwin Hyman, Boston, MA.

MARK WALKER
DEPARTMENT OF ANTHROPOLOGY
UNIVERSITY OF DENVER
DENVER, CO 80208

Paul A. Shackel

Labor's Heritage: Remembering the American Industrial Landscape

ABSTRACT

Archaeology at industrial sites provides some of the greatest opportunities to tell the story of the impact of industrialization on workers and their communities. Archaeologists working on industrial sites have a long tradition of interpreting technology and industrial landscapes while issues related to labor are overlooked or glossed over. Other historical archaeologists have laid the groundwork for understanding labor relations and daily life in industrial contexts. An overview of the current state of industrial archaeology is provided, and a renewed call for addressing an archaeology of labor is issued. Work performed at industrial sites needs to address issues related to labor. The draft National Historic Landmark study by the National Park Service on labor archaeology serves as a good framework to deal with these ideas. Additional avenues of inquiry are also explored.

Introduction

Where history, archaeology, and memory meet at industrial sites is where we find the excitement of labor archaeology as well as some of the troubling aspects of how nations and communities use their past. Industrial archaeologists have a long tradition of documenting the engineering feats of the industrial age. Understanding what is studied, remembered, and interpreted at these industrial sites can show us who we are as a community and a nation. There are often inconsistencies between the official and unofficial memories of labor and capital. The memory of industry and its representation on the American landscape is like the memory of all significant events in history. There are winners and losers. In a time when American and international corporations continue to undermine the American workforce by weakening unions and extending the average workweek, we as a society need to think about labor issues and remember the long, arduous struggle of workers to secure a 40-hour workweek and other conces-

sions from capital that many take for granted today. Understanding labor as a component of industrial archaeology provides us the tool necessary to revisit the history of industrial sites, and it gives us a mechanism to think about labor in the past, present, and future. In the following, I provide a review and a plan for how archaeologists working in industrial contexts can create a more inclusive interpretation of the past by addressing issues related to laborers and their families.

Labor's Heritage

While many federally funded museums in the United States extol the glories of economic and social progress as a result of industry, some working class members view the preservation of old buildings and ruins as an attempt to save a degrading phase of human history. Robert Vogel once noted, "The dirt, noise, bad smell, hard labor and other forms of exploitation associated with these kinds of places make preservation [of industrial sites] ludicrous. 'Preserve a steel mill?' people say, 'It killed my father. Who wants to preserve that?'" (quoted in Lowenthal 1985:403). While I am not advocating the destruction or the neglect of industrial buildings, it is important to recognize individual dissenting views on the true effects of industrialization. T. E. Leary (1979: 182) suggested more than two decades ago that the restoration of 19th-century factories could be useful for interpreting and understanding work conditions that people faced several generations ago. Telling the story of labor's struggle can make the preservation of industrial complexes more acceptable to a greater portion of the working class community. Industrial archaeology has the potential to be an educational tool that provides "a sort of Rosetta Stone to decipher the language peculiar to industrial tombs" (Leary 1979:182).

Industrial archaeology can lead to a better understanding of life and work in an industrial capitalist system. While industrial archaeologists have made strides to tell the story of labor and the impact on daily life, the discipline still has a long way to go to meet Leary's expectations.

Since 1987 the America's Industrial Heritage Project, now called the Southwestern Pennsylvania Heritage Preservation Commission, began a long-term project inventorying surviving historic engineering works and industrial resources in the region. The Historic American Buildings Survey (HABS) and the Historic American Engineering Record (HAER), both part of the National Park Service, helped to record significant industrial sites in southwest Pennsylvania. The emphasis has been the recording of industrial engineering feats, the mission of HAER, while creating several important social histories. However, many of these engineering studies do not go beyond particularistic and functional inquiries, a state of the field that Leary (1979) and later George Teague (1987) cautioned us about.

There are some noteworthy museums that do describe the daily lives of workers, such as the Eckley Miners Village in Pennsylvania. The village is located near Hazleton, once the center of 19th-century anthracite mining. In 1971, a group of businessmen organized the Anthracite Historical Site Museum, Inc., and purchased the village of Eckley, with 200 residents still in the village. They deeded the land over to the state in order to create the country's only mining town museum. Today, fewer than 20 people reside in Eckley. The town has been preserved, and the museum interprets the daily living experience of mining families. Exhibits discuss the hardships of life in a mining community, such as impoverishment, illness, accidents, death, and labor discontent (Wesolowsky 1996). However, these frank discussions in public museums that highlight the workers' experiences do not dominate many of the discussions of industrial heritage on the American landscape.

There are few communities that celebrate labor while muting the voice of capital. Another community that does is the postindustrial city of Lawrence, Massachusetts. The official memory of Lawrence is presented in the Lawrence Heritage State Park, situated in the midst of the city's decaying industrial core. The museum is located in a restored boardinghouse with two floors of exhibit space devoted almost entirely to labor issues and the Bread and Roses Strike of 1912. The strike, led by young women and followed by immigrants of 30 different nationalities, closed most of the Northeast region's mills in an attempt to acquire better wages and improved work conditions. Even though the strike stimulated broader appeals for better working conditions by labor throughout the Northeast, the strike failed. Workers went back to their jobs without acquiring any concessions. Today, there are mixed reactions to remembering this strike. Some citizens believe the story should be told, while others want to forget the days of exploitation (Green 2000:57–60). "How beautiful it is to sweetly forget the clubbings of 1912, the jailings of 1919, and the clubbings again of 1931," noted one former factory worker (quoted in Green 2000:60). The city remembers this labor tradition through a museum that provides a memory of labor strife. Lawrence suffered like many other northeastern industrial cities as textile mills fled the region during the 1920s in search of cheaper, unorganized labor in the southern United States. These former textile centers lost significant capital. It was not until the 1970s that some northern industrial cities were able to retool and begin revitalization. Lawrence remains one of the poorest cities in Massachusetts, suffering from the loss of its major economic base. While the official history of the United States has a long tradition of emphasizing and glorifying industry and capitalism, Lawrence is an example of a place that remembers the struggle of labor.

The city of Lowell, Massachusetts, embraces its industrial past. Statues have been placed around the town to celebrate the efforts of industrial workers. At Lowell National Historical Park many of the exhibits present a history that includes the story of both labor and capital. One exhibit extols the material benefits of industry, but the exhibit also explains labor strife. Visitors are invited to walk through the mill with earplugs while more than 100 machines operate simultaneously. The experience is enough to make one realize the strain on the mill girls and later immigrants as they labored 10 hours per day.

The above are examples of how some stories of industry and labor are represented on the American landscape and have been made part of the national public memory. While labor and capital compete for the official memory of the past, a large proportion of the industrial archaeology performed in the United States and Great Britain has been about understanding the industrial process, often at the expense of labor.

The Story of Labor's Heritage

There are many who have gone to great lengths to document and popularize the technological side of industrial archaeology (Hudson 1971, 1978, 1979; Weitzman 1980). Other works in the United States have charted new ways to understand the development of industrial technologies (Kumar 1992; Caplinger 1997; Harshberger 2002; Miller 2003) and industrial archaeology techniques (Gordon and Malone 1994; Kemp 1996; Palmer and Neaverson 1998). A major part of industrial archaeology has explained phenomena related to technological development, the economy of industry, and the industrial revolution (Trinder 1983; Stratton and Trinder 2000; Gordon 2001). Some industrial archaeologists believe that the study of industry's physical remains and landscapes is what distinguishes industrial archaeology from other disciplines (Minchinton 1983; Clark 1987). In many of these cases, either labor is not mentioned, or it serves as a secondary thought when discussing industrial technology and landscapes at these sites (Heite 1993; Pletka 1993; Howe 1994; Butler 1999). One prominent British industrial archaeologist wrote:

> ... patterns of government, religious allegiance, domestic and foreign policy, patterns of trade (although perhaps not of consumer spending)—are better arrived at by other means. Familiarity with, or even interest in, all aspects of working life in the industrial period is not essential for the industrial archaeologist so long as he [sic] recognizes their existence and is prepared to ask for advice from other specialists whose interest they are (Palmer 1990:282).

This tradition is also prominent in the United States and is reflected in *IA: The Journal of the Society for Industrial Archeology*. The articles in it are more about industry and technology than issues related to labor (Gordon 1988; Malone 1988; Holley 2001). Some of the more recent articles do acknowledge the important role workers once played at these sites, although the authors do not explore labor issues in detail (Landon et al. 2001; Wermiel 2001). Many of the studies mentioned above are good examples of industrial archaeology that focus on machines, machine products, physical layout, and power systems, but in most cases they do not address labor issues in any significant way.

I believe archaeologists working in industrial contexts need to make labor a significant part of their studies, as many historians and anthropologists have done (Gutman 1976; Wallace 1978; Brody 1979, 1980, 1993; Montgomery 1979). Historical and anthropological perspectives on labor help to define issues related to the impact of changing technology on workers and their families. These transformations in industry not only affected work, but they also impacted domestic life and health conditions. Labor historian David Brody (1989) has also encouraged scholars to look more closely at issues related to politics and power. At the recent plenary session for the annual meeting of The Society for Historical Archaeology, there was a call for archaeologists to include social history (Martin 2003) and labor (Shackel 2003b) when examining industrial sites. Others have also made the inclusion of labor and daily life a part of their archaeology (Beaudry and Mrozowski 1989; Brashler 1991; Wegars 1991; Workman et al. 1994; Shackel 1996, 2000b; Costello 1998; Trinder and Cox 2000; Van Bueren 2002).

A. Bernard Knapp (1998:2) writes about the importance of recognizing that technology in an industrial context must also consider labor and try to understand how people could negotiate social, political, and economic relationships. Acknowledging this type of relationship allows for few generalities. Each community and region has its own distinct history, and archaeology can play a powerful role in exploring these differences while also celebrating a common labor history. An important document that provides a good starting point for understanding labor's heritage is the *Labor Archaeology National Historic Landmark Theme Study*, a draft report being developed by National Park Service (Solury 1999). This document provides a brief overview of work cultures in the United States from the colonial period until recent times. The study examines the experiences of workers and addresses issues like ethnic histories, labor mobility, community studies, worker experiences, women and minority studies, and political behavior. The study provides archaeological case studies of sites that are on the National Register of Historic Places and explores issues of labor archaeology at industrial sites. Once completed, the study will help elevate the importance of labor archaeology on the national level.

Paul A. Shackel

Housing and Communities

The rise of American industry during the late-18th and early-19th centuries was one of the most significant issues that faced the United States as a new nation. Capitalists intentionally located factories in nonurban areas because they thought they could avoid the ills of European industrial cities that were plagued with diseases, pollution, and unemployment (Marx 1964; Kasson 1979; Prude 1983:31–41; Shelton 1986:28ff). For this reason, many companies provided housing for their workers, a tradition that began in England with Arkwright's new industrial establishments at Cromford in 1771 (Burnett 1978:12; Lowe 1982). Many industrialists believed that the control of space was as important as the control of time. Therefore, while factory owners controlled workers for 10 to 12 or more hours a day in the factory or the mines, they also controlled portions of workers' domestic lives by creating regulations in town plans and housing.

Archaeological work at Lowell, Massachusetts, best summarized by Stephen Mrozowski, Grace Ziesing, and Mary Beaudry (1996), showed the effects of changing boardinghouse policies established by industrialists for a new workforce of mill girls in the first half of the 19th century. At Lowell and at other northeastern industrial cotton mill sites, women from the countryside were brought into the labor force because they were perceived as cheap and idle hands (Dublin 1979). These industrial communities contained rows of boardinghouses with standardized facades that mimicked factory architecture. The boardinghouses were always in close proximity to the factory. The interior of the boardinghouses created an atmosphere of egalitarianism as all of the rooms were of the same size. This was but one component of a strategy by corporations to exert their control to create a compliant workforce (Dublin 1979; Hareven 1982). Archaeology shows that by the end of the 19th century, the paternal philosophy for operating the boardinghouses, whereby owners influenced and to some extent controlled the domestic lives of the mill girls, had disappeared. Poor sanitation and health conditions and the degradation of the surrounding environment became the norm for northeastern industrial towns, including Lowell (Mrozowski et al. 1996).

Not all industries operated in this fashion (Shackel and Winter 1994). In the case of the United States Armory at Harpers Ferry, the federal government did not initiate any form of corporate paternalism in the early-19th century, and this lack of paternalism eventually came to haunt those who tried to manage labor in the gun factory (Smith 1977). For instance, in the early-19th century, workers built their own houses, almost anywhere in town, as long as it was outside of the industrial complex. One worker built his house in the middle of a little traveled street. Generally, workers and their families could express their own personal identity within the confines of their own homes. Each domestic site excavated shows very different house floor plans, and armory workers used a variety of construction materials. The domestic landscape of Harpers Ferry appeared eclectic, unlike the standardized boardinghouses found in the Northeast. Each armory worker family had very different ceramic forms and types (Lucas 1994; Lucas and Shackel 1994; Shackel 2000b).

The armory workers defied any attempt to unify them as a workforce and resisted the industrial process much longer than their counterparts in Springfield, Massachusetts. Supervisors made it difficult for northerners who tried to introduce new mechanized processes. The armory superintendent gave very little support to John Hall, a gun maker from Maine working in Harpers Ferry, as he perfected the process of interchangeable parts. The archaeological record shows that armorers practiced their craft in a piecework system at home until about 1841 when the military took over control of the facility and made all workers abide by a standard work discipline found in industries throughout the country. After 1841 armory work was no longer performed in a domestic context (Shackel 1996, 1999a, 1999b).

By the end of the 1840s, the Ordnance Department took control of the management of the facility's operations. Engineers imposed a grid pattern over the town, dismantling those houses that were inconveniently placed and did not follow the new plan, like the house built in a roadway. The federal government also supported a major rebuilding of the factories. The early armory managers built factory buildings on an as-needed basis, thus creating an inefficient production line. The Ordnance Department replaced the old buildings with new structures that closely followed an orderly line of production, while skilled workers became wage laborers. Both work and home spaces were reorganized in order to create a more efficient and compliant workforce (Shackel 1996).

While the federal government at Harpers Ferry chose not to implement any form of paternalist control such as was commonly found at other industrial complexes in the northeast in the first half of the 19th century, other private industrialists in the Harpers Ferry area did recognize the value of controlling workers' space and time at work and at home. An archaeological example can be found at Virginius Island, a small industrial community adjacent to Harpers Ferry. The community began as a small industrial complex with more than a dozen small crafts and industries owned by various individuals. Entrepreneurs placed their small industrial complexes at strategic points on the landscape to access waterpower, and they did not follow a development plan. One local newspaper called it a "little Pittsburgh" (Palus 2000).

By the 1850s Abraham Herr owned most of the island. Unlike the previous owners, he subscribed to the model of paternalistic oversight. Controlling workers' living space by standardizing the built environment appears to have been part of Herr's ideal for an industrial community. Herr constructed a row house for his workers that consisted of a standardized façade, much like the row houses found in northeastern industrial communities. Archaeology shows that each house had a standardized floor plan on at least the first floor. Herr built his family's dwelling on the other side of the railroad tracks from his mill and the workers' housing, keeping both places within close eyesight of the owner (Palus 2000).

Other archaeologists have examined the relationship between the built environment, town plans, and paternalistic oversight. In the American Southwest, many of the company mining towns and large labor encampments from the late-19th century usually followed a grid pattern that reflected order and rationality, while the smaller towns formed in linear strips along roadways. Such strategies allowed owners to easily account for their workforce. Donald Hardesty's work in the American West provides

considerable attention to the composition of settlements and households. He shows that hierarchy and power are explicit in town layouts (Hardesty 1988:13–14,88; 1998).

Working Conditions at Labor Sites

Factory owners often characterized unproductive workers as unreliable, careless, or lazy. Many interpret this behavior as a deliberate attempt to resist the dominance of a machine-based system of production that left operatives with little room for personal autonomy or craft pride (Prude 1983; Scott 1990). While craftsmen often owned their own means of production and were likely to treat them with care, factory workers had little loyalty to the machines that someone else owned. "Some workers abused their machinery to show that they had little traditional pride in or attachment to their machines or to the products they made" (Zonderman 1992: 48). Workers broke machinery through various acts of sabotage in an effort to reassert the primacy of human beings over machines (Paynter 1989; Paynter and McGuire 1991).

Goods were sometimes stolen even though operatives knew that they could be fired if caught. Yet pilfering was seen by operatives as a way to "even the score" and compensate for low wages. "If they were denied what they saw as the full value of their labor, they would find a way to get what they thought was due them" (Zonderman 1992:196). Operatives were also rumored to have taken revenge by setting fires to factories. While they might have lost their jobs, they could have easily found another one at another factory in a neighboring town. In one instance, suspicious fires occurred at the Springfield Armory in 1842, when the armory management was shifted from civilian to military control. Neither the armorers nor the surrounding community helped to extinguish the fires (Zonderman 1992:196).

Factory workers' search for freedom and their expression of grievances against entrepreneurs were expressed from the outset of industrialization by quitting and moving to other jobs, rather than staying and fighting for change to alleviate the boredom, tedium, and low wages of factory labor. In some ways, the workers' transient state undermined their stability and strength as they lacked the cohesiveness for social and labor change. This does not mean that protests were nonexistent. They did occur, but often they were less collective and less overt than strikes. The earliest organized strike occurred in the early 1820s. By the 1830s and 1840s, regional labor organizations became more powerful in the Northeast. The number of strikes increased dramatically thereafter (Dublin 1977, 1979; Foner 1977; Vogel 1977; Prude 1983; Stansell 1986; Zonderman 1992:197–203). The shift from craft to industry continued into the early-20th century (Fonse-Wolf 1996). When workers were not powerful enough to organize a strike, they protested by work slowdowns, working on their own projects in the factory, and theft (Scott 1990; Bruno 1998:5,11–19).

Finding labor discontent in the archaeological record often means providing a thorough contextual analysis of the labor conditions. One example is the archaeological excavation performed by Michael Nassaney and Marjorie Abel (1993) at the John Russell Cutlery Company in the Connecticut River Valley. Their study shows how discontented workers challenged the existing power structure found in the workplace. Archaeologists found a large quantity of artifacts related to interchangeable manufacturing along the riverbank near the former cutting room and trip hammer shop. These objects tended to be inferior or imperfectly manufactured parts. While it would be easy to conclude that these artifacts form a typical industrial waste pile, the archaeologists looked at the larger context of 19th-century industrial labor relations in which discontented workers often broke machinery, tools, or products. Nassaney and Abel proposed that the abundance of imperfectly manufactured parts might represent a form of defiance against the implementation of the new industrial work system. Their work shows that by understanding context, knowing that discontent existed when manufacturing shifted to the new industrial system that alienated the work process, new interpretations can be developed related to labor and working conditions at industrial sites.

The study of labor protest camps such as the Ludlow Tent Colony Site in Colorado serves as another good example of how archaeologists may explore issues related to labor concerns and living conditions for workers and their families. The Colorado coal strike ignited a yearlong cycle of violence beginning in 1913 and culminated when the militia charged the tent colony and set fire to the tents, killing 2 women and 11 children. A guerilla-style war ensued for 10 days, and the miners attacked militia encampments, mine guards, and coalmines. The United Mine Workers of America (UMWA) ran out of funds to support the workers, and the strike was soon over. The workers received few concessions for their struggle. Through the archaeology of the tent colony, the Ludlow cooperative is exploring questions about the formation of temporary communities, protest labor movements, and government and military intervention. More important, the archaeology at Ludlow, which is supported by the UMWA, raises the visibility of this bloody episode in labor relations. It is helping make this incident part of the broader public memory (Walker 2000; Ludlow Collective 2001; McGuire and Reckner 2002; Wood 2002).

Another study related to labor unrest focuses on the bottling works associated with the Harpers Ferry brewery. While monitoring some of the stabilization and rehabilitation of the building, archaeologists found more than 100 empty beer bottles stashed behind the wall lathing in the former bottling room. They also discovered more than 1,000 beer bottles in the basement of the bottling works' elevator shaft, most of them broken after falling more than two stories (Shackel 2000a:104–113). In the 19th century, the typical brewery worker labored about 14 hours a day, 6 days per week, and on Sunday for about half this time. By 1910 brewery unions had successfully fought for a 10-hour workday. Workers were exposed to radical temperature shifts and breathed air contaminated with carbonic acid and sulfuric acid. Diseases like tuberculosis were common. Brewery-related accidents were almost 30% higher than in other industrial trades because of the higher speeds of machinery (Hull-Walksi and Walski 1994). The archaeological evidence suggests that workers drank the owners' profits and concealed their subversive behavior by disposing of the otherwise reusable bottles in walls and by dropping others down the elevator shaft. Fires at the brewery in 1897, 1906, and 1909 coincided with times of labor unrest in the brewery industry, highlighting the link between labor strife and acts of sabotage. Brewing unions eventually made major strides to improve the conditions of the workers (Shackel 2000a:104–113).

In another case study, Jed Levin (1985) compared the archaeological remains of the Telco Block and Supply Company site in New York City and the Supply Mill site in Billerica, Massachusetts (from Schuyler and Mills 1976). He noted that while entrepreneurs increasingly enforced an industrial discipline in the late-19th and early-20th centuries, there was a clear pattern of alcohol use by workers on the job site. Skilled workers often resisted the transition to industrial worker. The use of alcohol at these sites may have been a form of resisting work discipline.

Other Directions for a Labor Archaeology

Race

The questions related to labor archaeology are numerous, and they need to be made part of the national public memory. I have mentioned only a few case studies, but there are many issues that a labor archaeology can and should also address. For instance, the relationship between race and industry presents a unique opportunity for those interested in labor archaeology (Dew 1994; Shackel and Larsen 2000; Shackel 2001). Industrial slave labor is understudied and this topic has the potential to reveal not only the inequalities found between labor and capital, but it can also highlight the injustices found in race relations in an industrial context.

Ann Denkler's (2001:31–32) research on race in the Shenandoah Valley shows the importance of the iron industry in relationship to an agricultural community. In particular, the Catherine Furnace and the Shenandoah Iron Works, both dating to 1836, employed enslaved and freed blacks in the furnaces along with whites. Today, the tourist literature remembers the furnaces as important because they supported the Confederacy. Iron was shipped to Richmond and Harpers Ferry. No sources in the historical society mention the laborers at the site, nor do they recognize that African Americans, freed or enslaved, participated in the industry.

Race and labor relations also become an interesting part of the post-emancipation era story. After the Civil War, northern industrialists had a chance to hire and train a newly freed workforce.

Instead, industrialists turned to a new generation of European immigrants, thus shutting out African Americans in many northern industries and keeping many tied to tenant farming in the South (Horton 2000).

From the 1890s, northern industries began their large-scale flight to the South in search of cheaper unorganized labor (Carlton 1982). But before this transition could happen, a shift in the official memory of the Civil War was necessary. Until the 1890s the struggle for emancipation served as one of the official memories of the Civil War. But after the death of Frederick Douglass and the beginning of the Jim Crow era, the emancipationist view of the war lost out to a reconciliationists' memory. Reconciliation developed between white northerners and white southerners, making African Americans and the issues of slavery and the rights of full citizenship for blacks no longer part of the Civil War story (Shackel 2003a).

Many white southerners experienced a difficult transition into industrial capitalism. They found themselves in an increasingly individualistic and competitive society, and they suffered through the economic recessions of the 1880s and the depression of the 1890s. The move to revitalize a Confederate heritage helped southerners cope with defeat and the imposition of the new industrial order in the South (McConnell 1992:213). Whites worked in the new southern industries and African Americans remained disenfranchised. An industrial archaeology in the postbellum South as well as the North needs to understand the local and regional contexts for labor, and it must look at the issue of race.

The archaeology of Buxton, Iowa, performed in the early 1980s, examines the material remains of a predominantly black coal-mining town. The place thrived as an interracial town that was mainly inhabited by African Americans in the first quarter of the 20th century. The minority of the population consisted of European-derived nationalities. One newspaper called it "the Negro Athens of the north" (quoted in Gradwohl and Osborn 1984: 192). Archaeologists demonstrated through the material remains that the residents were part of the regional, national, and international trade networks. The spatial layout is a reflection of power and separations. The superintendents' residences stood on an isolated scenic hilltop across a valley and overlooking the main part of town (Gradwohl and Osborn 1984:192).

While African Americans were disenfranchised from industrial labor in the South, other ethnic groups had to fight prejudices too. For instance, while there was a large migration of Chinese workers to America during the California Gold Rush in the 1850s, they became unwelcome competition for employment by the early 1870s. Embracing Social Darwinism, many Anglos considered the Chinese to be less than human; anthropologists placed them on the lower end of the evolutionary scale. Chinese immigrants had few legal rights and could be legally discriminated against. By 1882, the United States legally barred people of Chinese descent from migrating to the United States (Chan 1991; Choy 1995; Salyer 1995).

The National Register nomination, Chinese Mining Camp Archaeological Site – Idaho (Elliott 1994), provides evidence of Chinese workers keeping strong material and cultural ties to their heritage at the work site and on the domestic front while they faced severe discrimination. The government prohibited Chinese workers in the Warren Mining District until 1869, and only after 1870 were they allowed to lease mining operations, although they could not purchase any land. Between 1870 and 1910, five separate Chinese companies mined in the Warren District. Archaeologists found the remains of canvas and repair tools, indicating that workers constructed impermanent homes in a distinctive Chinese style. Their assemblage contained imported Asian goods such as kitchen utensils and opium bottles, and the workers built Chinese-style garden terraces. Their mining techniques and tools were also different from those of the European Americans. The archaeological record shows that the workers at this mining camp retained their strong Chinese heritage on the domestic front (Striker and Sprague 1993).

Environment, Health, and Industry

Labor archaeology should examine the health conditions at industrial sites and towns. For instance, many mining sites endangered the health and life of workers. Work sites were often unstable, machinery often malfunctioned, pollution and harmful fumes contaminated the air, and workers often put in exhaustive

work hours. These are all variables that led to accidents, chronic illnesses, and deaths. Industrialists were known for their efforts to accelerate machinery; the result was increased fatigue and an increased rate of injuries for workers (Schivelbusch 1986). Until about the mid-20th century, industrialists paid little attention to the impact that factories had on the surrounding environment until workers, scientists, and environmentalists brought these issues to the forefront of the American conscience.

One well-known example of the impact of environmental stress and pollution on the health of a working community comes from Donora, a town along the Monongahela River in Pennsylvania. Incorporated in 1901, the town contained coke ovens, coal stoves, zinc furnaces, metal works, and steel mills. The shrieking mill whistles guided the daily routines of its citizens (Davis 2002b:6). Fumes from the town's industrial plants became part of the everyday environment. The landscape stood mostly barren of vegetation because of these poisonous gasses (Davis 2002a:B9). Oral accounts attest to the extreme pollution as women reminisced about washing their curtains every week: by the time the women washed all of the windows in a house, the first one was dirty again. It was common to see elderly people in town with oxygen tanks. One person remarked, "Well, we used to say, 'That's not coal dust, that's gold dust.' As long as the mills were working, the town was in business. That's what kept your Zadde and your father employed. Nobody was going to ask if it made a few people ill. People had to eat" (Davis 2002b:8). Donora's death rate was significantly higher than that of the surrounding nonindustrial towns.

Donora became infamous on 26 October 1948 when massive blinding smog covered the town. A temperature inversion over the entire Monongahela Valley trapped the smoke and fumes of the steel mills and zinc furnace. The fumes became so thick that traffic stopped along its roads because drivers could not see in front of them. The noxious poisons killed 24 people in 24 hours. The steelworkers' union sponsored an investigative study into the sudden deaths of the workers and townspeople of Donora. Only partial and preliminary reports exist. The scanty information shows that those who died had 12 to 25 times the normal level of fluoride in their blood, a clear case of fluoride poisoning. While the investigative team never produced a final report, and the source of poison was never officially identified, the incident at Donora made the country more aware of the impact of air pollution on human health (Davis 2002b:15–25).

In a study of human osteological remains, comparing medieval urban and early industrial sites in England, Mary Lewis (2002) shows the devastating impact of industrialization on children. Children from industrial towns showed a higher rate of mortality, retarded growth, higher levels of stress, and a greater prevalence of metabolic and infectious diseases. Children from an industrial town were also more than an inch shorter than those from a contemporary urban trading town. While differences in urban and rural populations did exist in the past, Lewis (2002) argues that industrialization had the greatest impact on children's health.

Archaeology can be an important tool to examine working and living conditions at industrial towns. Archeologists have demonstrated the effectiveness of using soil samples from the area in and around factories and dwellings to search for toxins to examine general health conditions. Privy samples at workplaces may reveal the presence of parasites and other toxins, indications of poor health and resistance to paternalism (Reinhard et al. 1986; Beaudry et al. 1991; Reinhard 1994). Pollen and macrofloral samples may also supply some indication of the changing landscape and its relationship to changing ideals related to industrialization (Mrozowski et al. 1989; Cummings 1994; Rovner 1994). Exploring general sanitation landscape features (Ford 1994) and identifying the presence of medicinal and alcohol bottles may provide clues regarding workers' general health (Bond 1989; Larsen 1994). The impact of industrial pollution has had a devastating impact on human populations. It is important that these issues are made part of the story of industry and labor.

Conclusion

When we look at the historical American industrial landscape, we often see renovated buildings and stabilized ruins that tell the story of our early industrial prowess. These structures are often interpreted as a reminder of industry and stand mute when it comes to telling the story of labor practices. In 1878, Abraham J. Ryan wrote about a land of ruins in the postbellum South:

> A land without ruins is a land without memories, a land without memories is a land without liberty. A land that wears a laurel crown may be fair to see; but twine a few sad cypress leaves around the brow of any land, and, be that land barren, beautiless, and bleak, it becomes lovely in its consecrated cornet of sorrow, and it wins the sympathy of the heart and of history (quoted in Wilson 1980:59).

Industrial ruins may win the hearts of history, and they are a way to remember a prosperous economic past, but we also need to make sure that they are part of the memory of a labor archaeology.

Michael Shanks and Randall McGuire (1996) remind us that the act of archaeology is a form of commemoration. When we do archaeology, we create a memory of the past that is rooted in our present-day concerns. Therefore, labor archaeology can be a way to remember and unveil a history that has been buried all too long. The work at Lowell, Harpers Ferry, the Chinese Mining Camp, and mining sites in Nevada, the John Russell Cutlery factory, and Ludlow show that a labor archaeology may effectively address labor's heritage.

Politics will always impact the way we develop labor's history. For instance, during the Reagan and G. H.W. Bush administrations, Lynne Cheney, chair of the National Endowment for the Humanities, argued in her report to Congress that scholars were occupying themselves with issues related to gender, race, and class (Nash et al. 1998:103). She discouraged funding projects that encouraged a pluralistic view of the past. Cheney packed the Advisory Council with critics of multiculturalism and the committee rejected proposals if they questioned consensus history. NEH sharply curtailed any projects dealing with women, labor, racial groups, or any project that might conflict with the national collective memory (Nash at al. 1998:103). At about the same time columnist George Wills (1991:72) wrote that these scholars were "forces ... fighting against the conservation of the common culture that is the nation's social cement."

Recently, Secretary of the Interior Gail Norton rescinded the National Historic Landmark designation of the Fresno Sanitary Landfill because of the negative connotations associated with the site (Melosi 2002). The site was nominated for NHL status because it represents an important engineering innovation in the United States. The landfill developed because refuse could be buried and rendered inert and could not pose a health hazard or a nuisance. Landfills came into wide use after World War II because of the success of the Fresno Sanitary Landfill, and they became the primary disposal option for Americans for the second half of the 20th century. Unfortunately, the Fresno Sanitary Landfill did not have a liner, and hazardous substances were found in the adjacent groundwater. The site was closed in 1987, and it became a superfund site in 1989. The Fresno Sanitary Landfill operated for more than 50 years. Many historians consider it as the oldest "true" landfill in the United States (Melosi 2002:23–26). Unfortunately, the Bush administration, which has received increasing pressure from environmental groups (like the Sierra Club) for its environmental policies, does not want to be associated with a landfill or a landfill that is also known as a superfund site, despite its historical significance to American industrial technology.

There are always lessons and alternative views at many significant historic sites. They are places not only to celebrate our past but also to learn lessons about our history. If we look at industrial sites, there is always a counter memory to the importance of technological advancement. For instance, what about historic mills? Their history is about technological development and entrepreneurship, but it is also about exploitation of workers. And what about coal mining towns? Coal extraction was about technology and profit, but the process also destroyed landscapes and polluted water (Melosi 2002:34). These are all examples of the American past that we choose to remember and use to teach us about the past by making them part of our official history. I wonder, then, if a place that celebrates labor strife and workers' struggles for decent wages like Ludlow could receive NHL designation in today's political climate.

No matter the political climate, archaeologists should endeavor to make labor issues part of the official history of the United States. One way is to nominate these sites to the National Register of Historic Places and as National Historic Landmarks. We are all agents who have crucial moral and political choices to make. History is shaped by human intervention, and while tough choices and stances were made in the past, we need to confront what we study and how to remember our past. Designating industrial places as a prominent part of our past should also be about remembering people and their struggles. The question for all of us working at industrial sites is this: Will archaeologists working at industrial sites be courageous like the town of Lawrence, Massachusetts, and commemorate labor's heritage, or will we choose to celebrate capital and create an official history that glorifies technology at the expense of labor? That is the challenge, I believe, for any professional working in industrial contexts.

ACKNOWLEDGMENTS

A brief version of this article was presented at the plenary session at the 36th Annual Conference on Historical and Underwater Archaeology, Providence, Rhode Island. Several people were kind enough to share several sources, including Brett Burk, Bob Chidester, Terrance Martin, Randy McGuire, and Larry Zimmerman. Barbara Little and Matthew Palus provided valuable feedback on earlier drafts of this paper. I also appreciate the comments provided to me by the three journal reviewers: Thad Van Bueren, Adrian Praetzellis, and Karen Metheny.

REFERENCES

BEAUDRY, MARY C., LAUREN J. COOK, AND STEPHEN A. MROZOWSKI
1991 Artifacts as Active Voices: Material Culture as Social Discourse. In *The Archaeology of Inequality*, Randall H. McGuire and Robert Paynter, editors, pp. 150–191. Basil Blackwell, New York.

BEAUDRY, MARY C., AND STEPHEN A. MROZOWSKI
1989 The Archaeology of Work and Home Life in Lowell, Massachusetts: An Interdisciplinary Study of the Boott Cotton Mills Corporation. *IA, The Journal of the Society for Industrial Archeology*, 19(2):1–22.

BOND, K. H.
1989 The Medicine, Alcohol, and Soda Vessels from the Boott Mills. In Interdisciplinary Investigations of the Boott Mills, Lowell, Massachusetts, Vol. 3, The Boarding House System as a Way of Life, Mary C. Beaudry and Stephen A. Mrozowski, editors, pp. 121–140. *Cultural Resources Management Study*, No. 21. U.S. Department of the Interior, National Park Service. North Atlantic Regional Office, Boston, MA.

BRASHLER, JANET G.
1991 When Daddy Was a Shanty Boy: The Role of Gender in the Organization of the Logging Industry in Highland West Virginia. *Historical Archaeology,* 25(4):54–68.

BRODY, DAVID
1979 The Old Labor History and the New. *Labor History,* 20(1):111–21.
1980 Labor History in the 1980s: Toward a History of the American Worker. In *The Past before Us: Contemporary Historical Writing in the United States,* Michael Kammen, editor, pp. 252–69. Cornell University Press, Ithaca, NY.
1989 Labor History, Industrial Relations, and the Crisis of American Labor. *Industrial and Labor Relations Review,* 43(1):5–18.
1993 *In Labor's Cause: Main Themes on the History of the American Worker.* Oxford University Press, New York.

BRUNO, ROBERT
1998 Working, Playing, and Fighting for Control: Steelworkers and Shopfloor Identity. *Labor Studies Journal,* 28 (Spring):3–30.

BURNETT, JOHN
1978 *A Social History of Housing 1815–1970.* Davis and Charles, London, England.

BUTLER, WILLIAM B.
1999 The Grand Lake Lodge Sawmill, Rocky Mountain National Park, Grand County, Colorado. *Southwest Lore,* 65(1):9–42.

CAPLINGER, MICHAEL
1997 *Bridges over Time: A Technological Context for the Baltimore and Ohio Railroad Main Stem at Harpers Ferry, West Virginia.* Institute for the History of Technology and Industrial Archaeology, Morgantown, WV.

CARLTON, DAVID L.
1982 *Mill and Town in South Carolina, 1880–1920.* Louisiana State University Press, Baton Rouge.

CHAN, SUCHENG (EDITOR)
1991 *Entry Denied: Exclusion and the Chinese Community in America, 1882–1943.* Temple University Press, Philadelphia, PA.

CHOY, PHILIP P.
1995 *Coming Man: 19th-Century American Perceptions of the Chinese.* University of Washington Press, Seattle.

CLARK, C. M.
1987 Trouble at T'Mill: Industrial Archaeology in the 1980s. *Antiquity,* 61(232):169–179.

COSTELLO, JULIA G.
1998 Bread Fresh from the Oven: Memories of Italian Breadbaking in the California Mother Lode. *Historical Archaeology,* 32(1):66–73.

CUMMINGS, LINDA SCOTT
1994 Diet and Prehistoric Landscape during the Nineteenth- and Early-Twentieth Centuries at Harpers Ferry, West Virginia: A View from the Old Master Armorer's Complex. *Historical Archaeology,* 28(4):94–105.

DAVIS, DEVRA LEE
2002a The Heavy Air of Donora, Pa. *The Chronicle Review: The Chronicle of Higher Education,* Section 2:B7–B12.
2002b *When Smoke Ran Like Water: Tales of Environmental Deception and the Battle against Pollution.* Basic Books, New York.

DENKLER, ANN
2001 Sustaining Identity, Recapturing Heritage: Exploring Issues of Public History, Tourism, and Race in a Southern Rural Town. Doctoral dissertation, American Studies, University of Maryland.

DEW, CHARLES B.
1994 *Bonds of Iron: Master and Slave at Buffalo Forge.* W.W. Norton and Co., New York.

DUBLIN, THOMAS
1977 "Women, Work, and Protest in the Early Lowell Mills; 'The Oppressing Hand of Avarice Would Enslave Us.'" In *Class, Sex, and the Women Worker,* Milton Cantor and Bruce Ware, editors, pp. 43–63. Greenwood Press, Westport, CT.
1979 *Women at Work: The Transformation of Work and Community in Lowell, Massachusetts, 1826–1860.* Columbia University Press, New York.

ELLIOTT, JOHN H.
1994 Chinese Mining Camp Archaeological Site, Warren Mining District 01IH1961. National Register Nomination. U.S. Department of the Interior, National Park Service, Washington, DC.

FONER, PHILIP S. (EDITOR)
1977 *The Factory Girls.* University of Illinois Press, Urbana.

FONSE-WOLF, KEN
1996 From Craft to Industrial Unionism in the Window-Glass Industry: Clarksburg, West Virginia, 1900–1937. *Labor History,* 37(1):28–49.

FORD, BENJAMIN
1994 The Health and Sanitation of Postbellum Harpers Ferry. *Historical Archaeology,* 28(4):49–61.

GORDON, ROBERT B.
1988 Material Evidence of the Manufacturing Methods Used in "Armory Practice." *IA, The Journal of the Society for Industrial Archeology,* 14(1):23–36.
2001 *A Landscape Transformed: The Iron Making District of Salisbury, Connecticut.* Oxford University Press, New York.

GORDON, ROBERT B., AND PATRICK M. MALONE
1994   *The Texture of Industry: An Archaeological View of the Industrialization of North America.* Oxford University Press, New York.

GRADWOHL, DAVID M., AND NANCY M. OSBORN
1984   *Exploring Buried Buxton: Archaeology of an Abandoned Iowa Coal Mining Town with a Large Black Population.* The Iowa State University Press, Ames.

GREEN, JAMES
2000   *Taking History to Heart: The Power of the Past in Building Social Movements.* University of Massachusetts Press, Amherst.

GUTMAN, HERBERT
1976   *Work, Culture, and Society in Industrializing America: Essays in American Working Class and Social History.* Alfred Knopf, New York.

HARDESTY, DONALD
1988   The Archaeology of Mining and Miners: A View from the Silver State. The Society for Historical Archaeology, *Special Publication Series,* No. 6. California, PA.
1998   Power and the Industrial Mining Community in the American West. In *Social Approaches to an Industrial Past: The Archaeology and Anthropology of Mining,* A. Bernard Knapp, Vincent C. Pigott, and Eugenia W. Herbert, editors, pp. 81–96. Routledge, London.

HAREVEN, TAMARA T.
1982   *Family Tie and Industrial Time: The Relationship between the Family and Work in a New England Industrial Community.* Cambridge University Press, New York.

HARSHBERGER, P.
2002   Brooklyn: Review of the 31st Annual Conference. *Society for Industrial Archeology Newsletter,* 31(3–4): 1–2, 4–5, 7–10.

HEITE, EDWARD F.
1993   Can Sizes and Waste at the Lebanon Cannery Site: Unscrewing the Inscrutable. *Archaeological Society of Delaware Bulletin,* 30:43–48.

HOLLEY, I. B., JR.
2001   Steamrollers: Those Majestic Machines. *IA, The Journal of the Society for Industrial Archeology,* 27(2):37–48.

HORTON, JAMES
2000   Freedom Fighters: African Americans, Slavery, and the Coming Age of the Civil War. Paper presented at the National Park Service Symposium on Strengthening Interpretation of the Civil War Era. Ford's Theater National Historic Site, Washington, DC, May 9.

HOWE, DENIS E.
1994   Industrial Archaeology: A Survey of Research in New Hampshire. *New Hampshire Archeologist,* 33–34(1): 105–113.

HUDSON, KENNETH
1971   *A Guide to the Industrial Archaeology of Europe.* Fairleigh Dickinson University Press, Madison, NJ.
1978   *Food, Clothes, and Shelter: Twentieth-Century Industrial Archaeology.* J. Baker, London.
1979   *World Industrial Archaeology.* Cambridge University Press, New York.

HULL-WALSKI, DEBORAH A., AND FRANK WALSKI
1994   There's Trouble a- Brewin,: The Brewing and Bottling Industries at Harpers Ferry, West Virginia. *Historical Archaeology,* 28(4):106–121.

KASSON, JOHN F.
1979   *Civilizing the Machine: Technology and Republican Values in America, 1776–1900.* Penguin Books, New York.

KEMP, EMORY L.
1996   *Industrial Archaeology: Techniques.* Krieger Publishing Co., Malabar, FL.

KNAPP, A. BERNARD
1998   Introduction. In *Social Approaches to an Industrial Past: The Archaeology and Anthropology of Mining,* A. Bernard Knapp, Vincent C. Pigott, and Eugenia W. Herbert, editors, pp. 1–23. Routledge, London.

KUMAR, PRADEEP
1992   *A Structural Analysis of Patented Bollman Suspension Trusses.* Institute for the History of Technology and Industrial Archaeology, Morgantown, WV.

LANDON, DAVID, PATRICK MARTIN, ANDREW SEWELL, PAUL WHITE, TIMOTHY TUMBERG, AND JASON MENARD
2001   "…A Monument to Misguided Enterprise": The Carp River Bloomery Iron Forge. *IA, The Journal of the Society for Industrial Archeology,* 27(2):5–22.

LARSEN, ERIC
1994   A Boardinghouse Madonna: Beyond the Aesthetics of a Portrait Created through Medicine Bottles. *Historical Archaeology,* 28(4):68–79.

LEARY, T. E.
1979   Industrial Archeology and Industrial Ecology. *Radical History Review,* 21:171–182.

LEWIS, MARY E.
2002   Impact of Industrialization: Comparative Study of Child Health in Four Sites from Medieval and Postmedieval England (A.D. 850–1859). *American Journal of Physical Anthropology,* 119(3):211–223.

LEVIN, JED
1985   Drinking on the Job: How Effective Was Capitalist Work Discipline? *American Archaeology,* 5(3):195–201.

LOWE, JEREMY
1982   Housing as a Source for Industrial History: A Case Study of Blaenafon, A Welsh Ironworks Settlement, from 1788 to c.1845. *IA, The Journal of the Society for Industrial Archeology,* 8(1):13–36.

LOWENTHAL, DAVID
1985   *The Past Is a Foreign Country*. Cambridge University Press, Cambridge, MA.

LUCAS, MICHAEL
1994   An Armory Worker's Life: Glimpses of Industrial Life. In *An Archeology of an Armory Worker's Household: Park Building 48, Harpers Ferry National Historical Park*, Paul A. Shackel, editor, pp. 5.1–5.40. *Occasional Report*, No. 12, U.S. Department of the Interior, National Park Service, Washington, DC.

LUCAS, MICHAEL, AND PAUL A. SHACKEL
1994   Changing Social and Material Routine in Nineteenth-Century Harpers Ferry. *Historical Archaeology*, 28(4): 27–36.

LUDLOW COLLECTIVE
2001   Archaeology of the Colorado Coal Field War, 1913–1914. In *Archaeologies of the Contemporary Past*, V. Buchli and G. Lucas, editors, pp. 94–107. Routledge Press, London.

MALONE, PATRICK M.
1988   Little Kinks and Devices at Springfield Armory, 1892–1918. *IA, The Journal of the Society for Industrial Archeology*, 14(1):59–76.

MARTIN, PATRICK E.
2003   The Archaeology of Industrialization. Paper presented at the 36th Annual Conference on Historical and Underwater Archaeology, Providence, RI.

MARX, LEO
1964   *The Machine in the Garden: Technology and the Pastoral Ideal in America*. Oxford University Press, New York.

MCCONNELL, STUART
1992   *Glorious Contentment: The Grand Army of the Republic, 1865–1900*. The University of North Carolina Press, Chapel Hill.

MCGUIRE, RANDALL H., AND PAUL RECKNER
2002   The Unromantic West: Labor, Capital, and Struggle. *Historical Archaeology*, 36(3):44–58.

MELOSI, MARTIN V.
2002   National Historic Landmarks: Controversies and Definitions. The Fresno Sanitary Landfill in an American Cultural Context. *Public Historian*, 24(3): 17–35.

MILLER, CAROL POH
2003   Study Tour Takes a Close-Up Look at Sweden's Industrial Heritage. *Society for Industrial Archeology Newsletter*, 31(1):1–8,17.

MINCHINTON, WALTER
1983   World Industrial Archaeology: A Survey. *World Archaeology*, 15(2):125–136.

MONTGOMERY, DAVID
1979   *Worker's Control in America: Studies in the History of Work, Technology, and Labor Struggle*. Cambridge University Press, New York.

MROZOWSKI, STEPHEN A., GRACE H. ZEISING, AND MARY C. BEAUDRY
1996   *Living on the Boott: Historical Archaeology at the Boott Mills Boardinghouses, Lowell, Massachusetts*. University of Massachusetts Press, Amherst.

MROZOWSKI, S. A., E. L. BELL, M. C. BEAUDRY, D. B. LANDON, AND G. K. KELSO
1989   Living on the Boott: Health and Well Being in a Boardinghouse Population. *World Archaeology*, 21(2):298–319.

NASH, GARY B., CHARLOTTE CRABTREE, AND ROSS E. DUNN
1998   *History on Trial: Culture Wars and the Teaching of the Past*. Knopf, New York.

NASSANEY, MICHAEL S., AND MARJORIE R. ABEL
1993   The Political and Social Contexts of Cutlery Production in the Connecticut Valley. *Dialectical Anthropology*, 18(3–4):247–289.

PALMER, MARILYN
1990   Industrial Archaeology: A Thematic or a Period Discipline? *Antiquity*, 64(243):275–282.

PALMER, MARILYN, AND PETER NEAVERSON
1998   *Industrial Archaeology: Principles and Practice*. Routledge, New York.

PALUS, MATTHEW
2000   *"They Worked Regular": Archaeology of the Virginius Island Mill Community, Package 123 in Harpers Ferry National Historical Park, Harpers Ferry, West Virginia*. U.S. Department of the Interior, National Park Service, Harpers Ferry National Historical Park, Harpers Ferry, WV.

PAYNTER, ROBERT
1989   The Archaeology of Equality and Inequality. *Annual Review of Anthropology*, 18:369–99.

PAYNTER, ROBERT, AND RANDALL H. MCGUIRE
1991   The Archaeology of Inequality: Material Culture, Domination, and Resistance. In *The Archaeology of Inequality*, McGuire and Paynter, editors, pp. 1–27. Basil Blackwell, Cambridge, MA.

PLETKA, KARYN L.
1993   Industrial Archaeology at the Robinson-Herring Sawmill Site, Greenbush, Wisconsin. *Michigan Archaeologist*, 39(1):1–35.

PRUDE, JONATHAN
1983   *The Coming of Industrial Order: Town and Factory Life in Rural Massachusetts, 1810–1860*. Cambridge University Press, New York.

REINHARD, K. J.
1994 Sanitation and Parasitism of Postbellum Harpers Ferry. *Historical Archaeology,* 28(4):63–67.

REINHARD, K. J., S. A. MROZOWSKI, AND K. A. ORLOSKI
1986 Privies, Pollen, Parasites, and Seeds: A Biological Nexus in Historical Archaeology. *MASCA Journal,* 4(1):31–36.

ROVNER, IRWIN
1994 Floral History by the Back Door: A Test of Phytolith Analysis in Residential Yards at Harpers Ferry. *Historical Archaeology,* 28(4):37–48.

SALYER, LUCY E.
1995 *Laws Harsh as Tigers: Chinese Immigrants and the Shaping of Modern Immigration Law.* University of North Carolina Press, Chapel Hill.

SCHIVELBUSCH, WOLFGANG
1986 *The Railway Journey: The Industrialization of Time and Space in the Nineteenth Century.* University of California Press, Berkeley.

SCHUYLER, ROBERT L., AND CHRISTOPHER MILLS
1976 The Supply Mill on Content Brook in Massachusetts. *Journal of Field Archaeology,* 3(1):61–95.

SCOTT, JAMES
1990 *Hidden Transcripts: Domination and the Arts of Resistance.* Yale University Press, New Haven, CT.

SHACKEL, PAUL A.
1996 *Culture Change and the New Technology: An Archaeology of the Early American Industrial Era.* Plenum Press, New York.
1999a Public Memory and the Rebuilding the Nineteenth-Century Industrial Landscape at Harpers Ferry. *Quarterly Bulletin: Archeological Society of Virginia,* 54(3):138–144.
1999b Town Planning and Nineteenth-Century Industrial Life in Harpers Ferry. In The Archaeology of 19th-Century Virginia, Theodore R. Reinhart and John H. Sprinkle, Jr., editors, pp. 341–364. Council of Virginia Archaeologists, *Special Publication,* No. 36 of the Archeological Society of Virginia.
2000a *Archaeology and Created Memory: Public History in a National Park.* Klewer Academic/Plenum Publishing Corp., New York.
2000b Craft to Wage Labor: Agency and Resistance in American Historical Archaeology. In *Agency Theory in Archaeology,* John Robb and Marcia-Anne Dobres, editors, pp. 232–246. Routledge Press, London.
2001 Public Memory and the Search for Power in American Historical Archaeology. *American Anthropologist,* 102(3):1–16.
2003a *Memory in Black and White: Race, Commemoration, and the Post-Bellum Landscape.* AltaMira Press, Walnut Creek, CA.
2003b Remembering the American Industrial Landscape. Paper presented at the 36th Annual Conference on Historical and Underwater Archaeology, Providence, RI.

SHACKEL, PAUL A., AND DAVID L. LARSEN
2000 Labor, Racism, and the Built Environment in Early Industrial Harpers Ferry. In *Lines That Divide: Historical Archaeologies of Race, Class, and Gender,* James Delle, Robert Paynter, and Stephen Mrozowski, editors, pp. 22–39. University of Tennessee Press, Knoxville.

SHACKEL, PAUL A., AND SUSAN E. WINTER (EDITORS)
1994 An Archaeology of Harpers Ferry's Commercial and Residential District. *Historical Archaeology,* 28(4).

SHANKS, MICHAEL, AND RANDALL H. MCGUIRE
1996 The Craft of Archaeology. *American Antiquity,* 61(1996):75–88.

SHELTON, CYNTHIA
1986 *The Mills of Manayunk: Industrialization and Social Conflict in the Philadelphia Region, 1787–1837.* The Johns Hopkins University Press, Baltimore, MD.

SMITH, MERRITT ROE
1977 *Harpers Ferry Armory and the New Technology: The Challenge of Change.* Cornell University Press, Ithaca, NY.

SOLURY, THERESA E.
1999 The Labor History Theme Study: Archaeology Component. Draft version manuscript. National Register of Historic Places, National Park Service, Washington, DC.

STANSELL, CHRISTINE
1986 *City of Women: Sex and Class in New York, 1789–1860.* Alfred A. Knopf, New York.

STRATTON, MICHAEL, AND BARRIE TRINDER
2000 *Twentieth-Century Industrial Archaeology.* E&FN Spon, London.

STRIKER, MICHAEL, AND RODERICK SPRAGUE
1993 Excavations at the Warren Chinese Mining Camp Site, 1989–1992. Report to the Forest Supervisor's Office, Payette National Forest, McCall, ID.

TEAGUE, GEORGE
1987 The Archaeology of Industry in North America. Doctoral dissertation, Department of Anthropology, University of Arizona.

TRINDER, BARRIE
1983 New Course in Industrial Archaeology. *World Archaeology,* 15(2):218–223.

TRINDER, B., AND N. COX (EDITORS)
2000 *Miners and Mariners of the Severn Gorge: Probate Inventories for Benthall, Broseley, Little Wenlock, and Madeley, 1660–1764.* Phillimore & Co., Ltd., Chichester, W. Sussex, England.

VAN BUEREN, THAD M. (EDITOR)
2002 Communities Defined by Work: Life in Western Work Camps. *Historical Archaeology,* 36(3).

VOGEL, LISE
  1977 Hearts to Feel and Tongues to Speak: New England Mill Women in the Early-Nineteenth Century. In *Class, Sex, and the Woman Worker,* Milton Cantor and Bruce Ware, editors, pp. 64–82. Greenwood Press, Westport, CT.

WALKER, MARK
  2000 Labor History at the Ground Level: Colorado Coalfield War Archaeology Project. *Labor's Heritage,* 11(1): 58–75.

WALLACE, ANTHONY F. C.
  1978 *Rockdale: The Growth of an American Village in the Early Industrial Revolution.* Alfred Knopf, New York.

WEGARS, PRISCILLA
  1991 Who's Been Workin' on the Railroad? An Examination of the Construction, Distribution, and Ethnic Origins of Domes Rock Ovens on Railroad Related Sites. *Historical Archaeology,* 25(2):37–60.

WEITZMAN, DAVID L.
  1980 *Traces of the Past: A Field Guide to Industrial Archaeology.* Scribner, NY.

WERMIEL, SARA E.
  2001 America's 19th-Century British-Style Fireproof Factories. *IA, Journal of the Society for Industrial Archeology,* 27(2): 23–36.

WESOLOWSKY, TONY
  1996 A Jewel in the Crown of Old King Coal: Eckley Miners' Village. *Pennsylvania Heritage Magazine,* 22(1). <http://www.phmc.state.pa.us/ppet/eckley/> 17 July 2003.

WILLS, GEORGE F.
  1991 The Politicization of Higher Education. *Newsweek,* 22 April:72.

WILSON, CHARLES REAGAN
  1980 *Baptized by Blood: The Religion of the Lost Cause, 1865–1920.* University of Georgia Press, Athens.

WOOD, MARGARET
  2002 Fighting for Our Homes: An Archaeology of Women's Domestic Labor and Social Change in a Working Class, Coal Mining Community, 1900–1930. Doctoral dissertation, Department of Anthropology, Syracuse University.

WORKMAN, MICHAEL E., PAUL SALSTROM, AND PHILIP W. ROSS
  1994 *Northern West Virginia Coal Fields: Historical Context.* Institute for the History of Technology and Industrial Archaeology, Morgantown, WV.

ZONDERMAN, DAVID A.
  1992 *Aspirations and Anxieties: New England Workers and the Mechanized Factory System, 1815–1850.* Oxford University Press, New York.

PAUL A. SHACKEL
DEPARTMENT OF ANTHROPOLOGY
UNIVERSITY OF MARYLAND
1111 WOODS HALL
UNIVERSITY OF MARYLAND
COLLEGE PARK, MD 20742

2011 Heritage and "Those People": Representing Working-Class Interests through Hampden's Archaeology. In *Archaeologies of Engagement, Representation, and Identity*, Paul A. Shackel and David A. Gadsby, editors. Thematic issue, *Historical Archaeology* 45(1):101-113

David A. Gadsby
Robert C. Chidester

Heritage and "Those People": Representing Working-Class Interests through Hampden's Archaeology

ABSTRACT

Baltimore's historically working-class neighborhood of Hampden, like many urban neighborhoods, is contested-heritage terrain. Traditional community members worry about encroaching real-estate development, middle-class hegemony, and economic transformation. Meanwhile, area merchants, developers, and planners (ab)use representations of working-class people's history to market the area's real estate, service, and retail economies. Problematic representations of other people's pasts are often coupled with discourses on progress that simultaneously recall and dismiss workers, casting out "those people's history" in favor of an empty history of old buildings and facades. The historical archaeology project in Hampden seeks, through community-based practice and aggressive public dissemination of information, to repopulate the neighborhood's history and reassert the right of its traditional community to possess heritage. The material history of the place is used as a starting point for community engagement with the ultimate goal of countering damaging fantasy representations of the place's past with realistic ones.

Heroin Needles and Heritage: Episodes in Hampden Archaeology

"What do you think you're going to find—heroin needles?" a passerby asks of the four young people working at the screens. The kids, hot in the midday sun, roll their eyes with impatience. They have heard it before; in their weeks of summer archaeological work on Falls Road in North Baltimore several other visitors have asked the same question. While the speakers intend it as a joke, albeit a mean-spirited one, the question implies that the place's history is shallow, and that its only material remains are those discarded by the injective-drug users who sometimes frequent the block of Falls Road where the excavations are taking place (Figure 1). They further imply that the history of a place like Hampden is not really worth knowing about, an

idea that these kids—who also sometimes have trouble seeing the point of their hard work in the sweltering Chesapeake heat and humidity—have already considered.

Of course, many archaeologists assume that this type of work is worthwhile because understanding the past is an important part of constituting the present, and discourses about the past are continually adapted to contemporary conditions. The work of excavating and interpreting archaeological remains is useful and important because contemporary people continually refer to the past as a guidepost for action, and in doing so, recover and repeat old historical discourses. In these echoes of the past lie perceived connections between past people and their literal or figurative descendants. Narratives about the past inform opinion- and decision-making processes at the individual and collective levels. They are important to the construction and maintenance of contemporary power relations (Leone et al. 1987; Shanks and Tilley 1992; Smith 2004:49–50).

Heritage—history in action—tells society stories about itself. Those stories, as Lowenthal (1985) argues, possess the potential to be either emancipatory or oppressive. In other words, they can serve the common good, or they can serve one set of interests to the detriment of another. In the historic mill village of Hampden, now a neighborhood in urban Baltimore, representations of past people, particularly members of the working class, play a major role in how development decisions are made. In large measure, middle-class and business interests control the public discourse, and therefore make decisions about public spaces without considering the interests of the traditional working-class community. They do this with the aid of heritage discourses that distort or dismiss Hampden's working-class heritage and which play themselves out in everyday social settings. The Hampden Community Archaeology Project (HCAP) represents the authors' effort to present heritage that acknowledges the role of working people in Hampden's heritage.

Around the time that the authors began the HCAP, Gadsby, who lives on the outskirts of Hampden, had a conversation with a middle-class woman who had recently moved to the

FIGURE 1. Contemporary Hampden streetscape, near 18BC164, along Falls Road. (Photo by David A. Gadsby, 2004.)

neighborhood. She asked Gadsby about his research, and he answered that he was conducting historical archaeology at working-class homes in Hampden. In reply, the neighbor crinkled her nose and declared, with evident disdain, "Oh, I'm not sure I want to know the history of some of *those* people." This telling statement and statements like it are repeated and enacted daily by Hampden's middle-class residents. Such statements serve two discursive purposes. First, they split working-class people from the middle class, rendering them as "Others." Second, they deny working-class people a history. In doing so, they help to erase them from the present as well. Fabian (1983:33) describes this process of "othering" through time as the "denial of coevalness," and while his argument is focused specifically on anthropologists, the authors think it useful here to extend it to all middle-class observers. The discursive processes that deny coevalness to the working class facilitate the uncritical razing of the neighborhood's cultural, and ultimately physical, terrain for development and urban renewal. At the same time, much of the public historic preservation and restoration literature pushes the working class into the (already dismantled) past,

so that working-class families disappear from the public discourse altogether. As part of its activist approach to understanding the past, HCAP works in collaboration with community members to repopulate the working-class past.

The incidents described above point to a problem that requires further illustration. First, contemporary people often distort and misuse the historical memory of Hampden and its working class. Historical memory in Hampden often privileges wealthy and overtly powerful capitalists over other community members. Thus distorted, it becomes a powerful way to construe members of the working class as cultural and temporal Others.

In Hampden, the creation of the working-class Other is achieved through the action of public-sphere discourse, including, conspicuously, marketing and advertising campaigns. Creating historical narratives populated with working-class people can generate alternative, emancipatory discourses. Since much of the historical information available about Hampden comes from newspaper articles and middle-class industrial historians, both of which served political interests other than those of the working class, HCAP (and

380

community heritage in general) maintains the goal of reasserting the presence and power of the working class in Baltimore's history.

Hampden History and the Working Class

Hampden is a neighborhood of the city of Baltimore situated on the slopes and ridge between the two streams known as the Jones Falls and Stony Run. The area is located approximately three miles north of the city's central business district. It lies along the fall line between the coastal plain and piedmont regions of Maryland. This location has contributed to a sense that the place is isolated and insular, even after its annexation by the city in 1888 (Harvey 1988), and indeed it remains an overwhelmingly white enclave in a city that is largely African American.

Hampden's early economy relied upon its topography and particularly the ready supply of hydrologic energy available to run machinery. The "suburban factory village" of Hampden and the neighboring mill community of Woodberry (located across the Jones Falls to the west) began in the 1820s as a series of water-driven grist mills in the valley of the Jones Falls, about three miles upstream of the booming shipping town of Baltimore (Figure 2). In the early years of the 19th century, while Baltimore's waterborne commerce was booming, the *Federal Gazette* reported that farmers interested in bringing their goods to market in Baltimore suffered the perils of poor roads: "miery sloughs, dreadful precipices ... impassible streams," and other difficulties (Olson 1997).

To stimulate inland trade, Maryland's government began the construction of a series of turnpike roads. Included among these was the Falls Turnpike Road, which, after 1809, connected gristmills along the Jones Falls to the hub of international trade a few miles to the south (Olson 1997:47–48). By the 1830s, the construction of the North Central Railroad not only improved this link but also fueled real estate speculation throughout the region and spurred construction along the Falls Turnpike (Olson 1997:71–77). In 1833, Lloyd Norriss and William Tyson advertised the sale of a 238 ac. parcel on the Jones Falls. The parcel contained a mansion house, a farmhouse, a tavern, and a

FIGURE 2. The Jones Falls Valley, postcard, ca. 1910. (Photo courtesy of John McGrain.)

brick-and-stone gristmill capable of producing 120 barrels of wheat per day (*Baltimore American* 1833).

Histories of Hampden and Woodberry stretching back as far as 1872 credit Horatio Nelson Gambrill with converting gristmills into cotton-duck factories in the middle Jones Falls Valley in the late 1830s (Clendenning 1992:255). His first mill, the water-driven White Hall Cotton Factory, was destroyed by fire in 1852 and replaced with the massive, steam-driven "Clipper Mills." By this time, there were also 27 houses for mill workers erected on mill property, and the landscape was dotted with other operative housing (*Baltimore American* 1850). The paternalistic system that would characterize Hampden's socio-political structure throughout the second half of the 19th century was already taking root (*Baltimore American* 1850). These early accounts begin a long tradition of casting mill-owning capitalists, especially Gambrill and members of the Hooper family, as the main agents, and even heroes, in the story of Hampden and Woodberry.

Nineteenth-century newspaper accounts also stress the harmonious relationship between labor and capital. A *Baltimore Sun* editorialist in 1877 describes paternalistic Woodberry as having "relations ... of the best character" in a setting in which "confidence and mutual respect is encouraged." The writer credits the construction of tenements for unmarried men and women, company-owned village housing, and increasing demand for wage labor for a dramatic increase in population around the mills. At the same time, newspapers describe capitalists like Gambrill as "pioneers" in industry but seldom mention the role that mill operatives play in capitalists' successes, nor do they make note of the workers' role in controlling their own material conditions through civic and labor actions.

Often in these narratives, discourses on business success and technological advancement are paired. An 1872 report in the *Sun* lists the owner of each mill, its power supply, production statistics, and the number of hands employed. The anonymous reporter characterizes the Hooper mill as riding the cutting edge of manufacturing technology, with its own railroad switches and impressive 220 horsepower Corliss engines. The *Sun* correspondent (1872:1) describes Gambrill and Sons' Druid Mills, which not only possessed "two immense engines, supplied by 10 boilers consuming 8 tons of coal a day and giving power to over 500 different machines," but also fire escapes and a fire-extinguishing system, as "a model institution in its way." The mills' power, success, and technology extend from the mills to their owners, but not necessarily to the working people who are rendered in such accounts as passive "hands."

The few existing descriptions of workers and their living conditions contrast somewhat with those of the mills. Even though Hampden-Woodberry hosted a large foundry and the area was sufficiently populated to warrant the construction (by mill workers) of a library by 1860, the village lacked many of the amenities of Baltimore to the south (*Baltimore Sun* 1860). Simultaneously an apex of industrial development and a backward suburb lacking even paved streets, Hampden contained no less than five steam-powered cotton-duck or canvas mills and supported as many as 8,000 inhabitants (*Baltimore Sun* 1872, 1874a). Despite the fact that many of these mills were fully integrated into the regional infrastructure and were "as complete as any in the country" (*Baltimore Sun* 1872), the dwelling areas of the region lacked many of the basic amenities of 19th-century urban life:

> [T]he people on their several errands were walking up steep and unpaved streets and groping in the dark, the only light in the place being that coming down from the windows of the cottages ... [Hampden-Woodberry] has no gas, little or no supply of water, and the most meager kind of communication with the city, to which of necessity one half of the population have business every day (*Baltimore Sun* 1874b).

Throughout the 1870s and 1880s, Baltimore city politicians used the purported paucity of resources in Hampden to argue for its annexation into the city. The Knights of Labor and working-class activists generally opposed annexation on the grounds that workers would be taxed more while mill owners would get tax breaks, but annexation was eventually approved by popular vote in 1888 after the mill owners threw their support behind the ballot measure (Harvey 1988:20–21). Despite this particular defeat, organized labor gained strength over the course of the following decades, winning a series of strikes during the boom years of World War I, culminating in a successful strike in 1918. The era from the 1880s through 1920 can be viewed as the era in which organized labor was most successful in Hampden. Nevertheless, men in the picking room of Maryland cotton-duck mills in 1885 made real wages of just over $1 per day. Women and children made substantially less (Weeks 1886:167). Even as late as the 1920s, the average weekly wage of $16 was below the minimum that Beirne (1982:14) argues is necessary for survival.

The era of strident labor activism seems to have ended in Hampden in 1923. After defeating a lengthy strike in that year, mill corporations, now under the control of large trusts and holding companies, began the slow process of closing their operations and moving south. While the 20th century saw the conversion of some of the cotton mills to light industry, including a cosmetics factory, an ice-cream cone manufacturer, and a raincoat factory, even that began to dissipate by the 1970s. During that period, Hampden lost all but a few of its manufacturing jobs and much of its service sector. Up until roughly the 1930s, Hampden had been a place where goods moved freely to port, but where people were generally employed within the community and found little reason to leave. By the mid-20th century, however, many inhabitants sought employment outside the neighborhood, and community members struggled to maintain Hampden's insularity (Chidester 2009).

Under late capitalism, Hampden has gradually transformed from a community characterized by its productive economy to a site for consumption. The movement of the textile mills to the Southern piedmont has altered the neighborhood's character over the last several decades. Between the 1950s and the 1970s, the mills' decline forced many of Hampden's blue-collar residents to take jobs outside of the neighborhood. Others set up businesses in the neighborhood such as pharmacies, beauty parlors, and grocery stores to provide services for the neighborhood's residents. Since the late 1980s, antique shops, gift shops, restaurants, and artists' studios catering to visitors and tourists from other neighborhoods have begun to occupy much of the store frontage in Hampden, and many longtime residents complain that practical items, such as socks and underwear, are no longer available there.

The history of Hampden, as it is often presented to the public, lionizes the role of capitalist mill owners over workers. These "heroes," as A. F. C. Wallace (2004:156–157) casts them, thematically important to the 19th-century story

of progress, are beginning to reappear in the 20th-century narrative as well. Hampden's old history of mechanized progress is becoming a new history of development, at the expense of its working-class people.

The Representation of Heritage as a Problem in Contemporary Hampden

Despite the success of social and cultural historians in implementing their scholarly agendas in academia over the past 30 years, the general public in the United States remains woefully uninformed (or even misinformed) about the history of oppressed and marginalized groups within society. Public historical memory is shaped primarily by elementary and secondary school curricula, the popular media, and (to a lesser extent) historical museums and festivals. Unfortunately, the conservative political and social climate in the U.S. since the 1980s has carried over into these arenas.

Edward Chappell first called for historic-site museums to engage in the struggle for social justice 20 years ago, and the International Coalition of Historic Site Museums of Conscience was founded in 1999; yet, such progressive places of public-memory formation are still by far the minority, as many historic sites have retained an interpretive culture focused on the rich and powerful (and often white and male) of America's past (Chappel 1989; Stahlgren and Stottman 2007; Ševčenko and Russel-Ciardi 2008).

Paul Shackel (2001, 2004) has written about how the struggles of working-class Americans, in particular, have been written out of the dominant public narrative of American history. Industrial archaeologies have traditionally focused on the history of technology at the expense of the workers who operated the machines, while well-known social conservatives like Lynne Cheney, who promote the celebration of capitalism and the silencing of class conflict, have headed public funding agencies such as the National Endowment for the Humanities. While there are in fact a few museums and historic sites that celebrate the culture and struggles of working-class Americans, such as the Lower East Side Tenement Museum in New York City, many more historic sites ignore their history or choose to portray the working class as contented participants in the march of industrial progress (Russel-Ciardi 2008).

While Hampden has no historical museums to shape the local public consciousness of its past, its heritage has nevertheless been the subject of conflict for decades. As early as 1938, when the majority of local residents still worked in the textile mills, Hampden-Woodberry held a 50th Anniversary Golden Jubilee celebration (commemorating the area's incorporation into the city of Baltimore). The program booklet that was published for the occasion (compiled by a local publisher and a local pharmacist) emphasized themes such as education, community institutions, and consumption; any aspect of specifically working-class heritage was conspicuously absent (Hampden-Woodberry Community Association 1938). Similar booklets were published for jubilee celebrations in 1948 and 1988 (Chidester 2009).

The implied internal class conflict represented by the souvenir booklets has been replaced in recent decades by conflict between community "insiders" (longtime residents, primarily but not exclusively working-class) and recently arrived "outsiders" (primarily upper-middle-class professionals and small-business owners). As the industrial base of Hampden's economy has disappeared, it has been replaced by economic and social gentrification. Developers have renovated old mill buildings into artists' studios and offices, while expensive boutiques, restaurants, and bars have altered the look and feel of the main shopping street, locally called "The Avenue." Housing costs skyrocketed during the 1990s and early 2000s as upper-middle-class families began to move into the area.

The control and use of public space has been at the center of the current struggle in Hampden. As a result of gentrification, more traditional retail establishments such as groceries (which primarily serve a working-class clientele) have been squeezed out of the commercial core and into less-accessible areas; in a parallel development, working-class residents have slowly withdrawn from civic life in Hampden. Working-class community members see the public frontage as part of their neighborhood, while merchants and middle-class, prodevelopment reformers see the space as a place where money is to be made and find the neighborhood's more traditional community an impediment to economic "progress."

Perversely, these same merchants, developers, and reformers have embraced a new symbolic economy based on a version of the neighborhood's traditional working-class image. "HonFest," an annual street festival and beauty contest organized by local restaurateur Denise Whiting draws thousands of visitors from around the Baltimore metropolitan region. The festival lampoons an imaginary blue-collar experience by disseminating inaccurate and cartoonlike images of working-class men and women (Figure 3). Whiting's Café Hon and other shops on the Avenue capitalize on the "kitsch" of working-class lives and homes and parody the styles of working-class people in public performance. More subtly, real-estate developers are also using Hampden's working-class heritage to market expensive real estate. The Clipper Mill consists of a series of buildings on the site of the former Poole and Hunt foundry. Once a site that supported the community's production economy, it now houses retail shops, restaurants, and condominiums that working-class people from the nearby neighborhoods of Hampden and Woodberry cannot even begin to afford. Here, the developers have explicitly used the heritage of a 19th-century foundry—partially burned in 1996—as a selling point for their new luxury condominiums:

> In 1853, a modest machine plant was born on Woodberry Road, just north of a nameless branch of the Jones Falls at the foot of Tempest Hill. The new plant, coined Union Machine Shops, housed Poole & Hunt's general offices, an iron foundry, erecting and pattern shops, a melting house and stables. Instantly it became the backbone of the Woodberry/Hampden community, employing thousands of men as it grew to become the country's largest machine manufacturing plant.

> Today, Streuver Bros. Eccles & Rouse, Inc. is redeveloping Clipper Mill and the surrounding area, including the beloved Woodberry Forest. Their aim is to create a new urban corporate campus and upscale residential community (Streuver Bros. Eccles and Rouse 2005).

The new Hampden's thriving retail and real-estate economy is dependent on this use of quasi working-class images even as it strives to force the community's actual working-class residents off the streets and into the no-man's-land of Hampden-Woodberry's working past. This kind of marketing simultaneously elides the role of working people in the creation of the neighborhood and hijacks their history as a history of place over people. Longtime residents of surrounding neighborhoods—people with a stake in how redevelopment goes—are left out of the process. This commodification of local working-class heritage

FIGURE 3. The "Best Hon" contest, Honfest, 2004. (Photo by David A. Gadsby, 2004.)

is not a passive process; rather, it is actively pursued by relatively wealthier middle-class gentrifiers, and negatively impacts the ability of working people to control their own destinies and to participate fully in the political and social life of the neighborhood.

When pondering the case of contemporary Hampden, it is useful to distinguish between two kinds of heritage: that which can be marketed and that which cannot. The former, according to Erve Chambers (2006), involves attempts to preserve fading cultural practices and objects, but often "become[s] a way to separate the objects ... of heritage from their actual heirs, serving to transfer them to the marketplace as commodities." He calls this type of heritage "public heritage" and means it to encompass the kinds of heritage traditionally done by government and other heritage professionals, as well as marketers. The latter, on the other hand, which Chambers labels private heritage, "encourages us to focus on the

ways in which the past is dynamically linked to the present, with heritage values interpreted and identified by community members rather than outsiders" (Chambers 2006:5–6).

John Hartigan (2000) notes that this heritage distinction possesses a class component. He has written about the propensity of working-class whites to regard history in terms of people and events in the past, while middle-class whites tend to regard it as being related to material culture, particularly houses. In the second formulation, houses are, of course, also imbued with elevated monetary value because of their possession of (any) history. Thus, what was once particular history—the history of working-class struggle, or alternately of neighborhood unity—is transformed into a generic kind of history that is assumed to exist in old houses. Places become worth something not because they are associated with a particular person or event, but because they have "something about them," "character," or "style" that speaks to the aesthetic sensibilities of middle-class gentrifiers (Hartigan 2000).

It is important to note an additional distinction. The first kind of heritage, the marketable kind, is about forgetting. It creates separations between people and places. It sanitizes. Along with the grime of history, it washes away most (though not all) of the human beings, the subjects and agents of history, replacing them with objects that seem to remember the past, but often do not. The second kind—the more authentic kind—is about remembering the details and personages of history. It evokes a complex, living, and populated past. It also holds the potential for contributing to progressive social change, a cause that some historical archaeologists have embraced since James Deetz (1996) pointed to the democratizing potential of archaeological evidence. Artifacts, he noted, have been deposited in patterned ways as the result of human cultural behavior and have the ability to illuminate the lives of history's mutes: those who, for whatever reason, left no written records of their thoughts, feelings, or activities, but who nonetheless left behind some material remains of their lives. The activist potential for archaeology, then, in the first instance, lies in its ability to illuminate dark corners of the past. Related to this, however, is its ability to link that past with, on one hand, the material world, and on the other hand, contemporary communities (Little 1994; McGuire and Reckner 2003). This is precisely what the authors have set out to do in Hampden.

The Hampden Community Archaeology Project

The primary social goal of the Hampden Community Archaeology Project is to produce collaborative histories with Hampden-Woodberry residents as a means of empowerment in the ongoing debate over the nature and direction of the neighborhood, especially in terms of the intersection between local heritage and the economic-development process. The authors view their work in Hampden as a kind of community organizing in which the archaeologists play the role of facilitator for local stakeholders who wish to promote a more authentic representation of community heritage as one part of the struggle over the present and future of the neighborhood.

Political scientists Robert Fisher and Eric Shragge (2007) have identified two dominant models of community organizing: community development and social action. With HCAP, we have incorporated elements of both models into the agenda. On the one hand, "social action represents an engagement in the struggle for social change through organizing people to pressure government or private bodies." Social action challenges inequality and oppression by offering "an alternative politics, a critique of current conditions" (Fisher and Shragge 2007:195). Indeed, the central goal of HCAP is to use heritage to ground a local alternative discourse to the dominant paradigm of neoliberal economic progress.

At the same time, however, we have avoided the kind of actively oppositional politics that characterizes much social-action organizing, in favor of a community development model that "seeks primarily to bring together diverse community interests in a common process that contributes to the well-being of the community as a whole" (Fisher and Shragge 2007:195). What we seek is not a bitterly divided Hampden, or even a homogenous community in which the invading gentrifiers have been thrown out. Rather, HCAP's goal is to use archaeology to bring people together in a critical public dialogue, for only in such a way can it be hoped that HCAP will contribute to a more just and equitable future. While the goals of fostering a critical alternative politics and of bringing together diverse constituencies for the common good may seem to be at cross purposes, the authors believe that they are not mutually exclusive. Indeed, Fisher and Shragge demonstrate that these two models often overlap within community organizations; in many local settings such as contemporary Hampden, combining social action with community development may indeed be the most plausible and effective way of proceeding.

Methods

Over three field seasons from 2005 to 2007, HCAP personnel excavated five sites throughout Hampden, representing the residences of both working-class and middle-class families from the 1840s to the 1930s. In all, HCAP collected thousands of artifacts and recorded dozens of features left behind by past occupants of the neighborhood. Historical research on each of the five sites has revealed that their past occupants came from a variety of social classes and occupations, including mill workers and local merchants. None of this research would have been possible, however, without a carefully planned groundwork for collaborative engagement with local residents.

In order to mobilize the local community around the issues of class, heritage, representation, and community power, the HCAP was designed as a collaborative community-archaeology project in which local stakeholders would have direct and equal input into all phases of the research process. Gadsby began by organizing a series of public-history workshops during the fall of 2004. At these workshops, which were heavily attended by local residents, experts on local history gave brief presentations followed by open discussion. The topics that attendees brought up most frequently then formed the basis for HCAP's research design (Gadsby and Chidester 2004).

For a description of the workshop process and the ethical and epistemological issues involved, see Gadsby and Chidester (2007). HCAP has subsequently held periodic workshops and presented the results of its research in public talks around the neighborhood (Figure 4). The workshops are one of the main methods for disseminating the results of the project's inquiries to the community; they are a way to ask people to think critically about the past and to share their ideas and interests. A recent workshop at a local recreation center featured local historian John McGrain and drew a dozen Hampden residents, who remained in the room and attentive for about an hour while McGrain presented an exhaustive history of textile milling in the Jones Falls Valley. The ensuing discussion lasted for an additional hour. Other workshops have attracted as many as 50 attendees. The project is also currently working with the public

FIGURE 4. Hampden public-history workshop. (Photo by David A. Gadsby, 2004.)

history department at the University of Maryland Baltimore County to develop a traveling exhibit focused on working-class women's history, to be mounted at Honfest in order to present an alternative narrative about the working-class past.

HCAP has also utilized the World Wide Web to good effect in keeping the community involved. In addition to a website (Jones et al. 2008) that includes links to the research design, articles about HCAP in the popular media, and a collection of oral histories from the neighborhood, the project also maintains a blog (Gadsby et al. 2008). The blog has proven to be particularly popular: it has averaged almost 150 unique visitors and over 260 page loads per month, reaching 10,000 total hits by the end of February 2008 (within three years of being launched). The interactivity of the blog has allowed local residents to have continuing input on the focus and direction of the project.

There have been a range of responses to the blog posts, from people simply expressing interest in the project to people who remember the Hampden of 40 or 50 years ago, and even one person who is a descendant of an important individual researched by Chidester. In addition to excitement that the working-class heritage of Hampden is being uncovered, the most common tone of the comments is nostalgic. One anonymous commenter wrote in June 2007:

> My little ol' house my parents bought on Dellwood for $8000 in 1957 is now worth 1/4 million. Go figure. Hampdenfest and HonFest do nothing for Hampden except make the ORIGINAL NATIVES look stupid and uneducated. My two sisters-in-law cannot even afford a house on 34th Street ... the street they grew up on! My one sister-in-law does not have her driver's license, has never had one and never needed one. Now that Sandler's and Ponds are gone, she has nowhere affordable to shop (Gadsby et. al 2008).

These kinds of comments on the social reality of contemporary Hampden reassure the project that it is conducting research valuable to the university.

While the connections between archaeological heritage and community may be obvious to academics with an interest in heritage and archaeology, they are not as obvious to the various publics, so HCAP has sought ways to forge links not only between Hampden's past and present but between the various communities that it serves. Along with the project's ongoing series

of public-history workshops, intern Jolene Smith, from the University of Maryland, recently undertook an ambitious oral-history project with Baltimore city high school students. After a series of workshops in which she worked with students to practice conducting and evaluating oral histories, learn background history, and develop interview questions, Smith led teams of students to interview residents at local retirement communities. Students and interviewees alike came away with a sense of interest and enjoyment, and students were able to connect the archaeological work they were performing to a real and living community. Later, a public-history workshop helped to communicate the results of the oral-history project to other members of the Hampden community (Smith 2008a, 2008b).

In addition to these broader attempts to involve the community in HCAP, we have developed strong relationships with specific local stakeholders. Most importantly, HCAP has worked continuously with the Hampden Community Council and the local charter school to provide educational opportunities for local youth and to advertise HCAP to a wider audience than the project alone could manage. The project also draws student workers from the Baltimore City Youthworks Project (a city-funded program to place teenagers in summer jobs). In addition, the project has developed working relationships with the Hampden Merchants' Association, specific local businesses, and the Hampden Family Center.

Project members ensure public engagement in the research itself. In addition to hiring between 3 to 10 local youths per summer to assist in excavations, the authors also scheduled periodic public dig days each summer and welcomed volunteers at any time. The authors attended HCC meetings and submitted brief updates to the community newsletter as well, to keep members of the community informed about the project's progress. Chidester and Gadsby (2009) reflects in depth on HCAP's successes and the roadblocks faced in the area of public outreach and engagement.

Of course, not everyone has the ability or the inclination to walk around an archaeological site, even one located on an urban lot. For this reason, the authors have utilized other research methods to engage members of the community. Most prominently, during the summer of 2007, HCAP personnel conducted ethnographic and oral history interviews with about a dozen local residents. The ethnography, in particular, helped the authors to appreciate better local understandings of community heritage and of the transformations currently impacting the neighborhood. Both "outsiders" and "insiders" actually hold many of the same values, such as community stability, neighborliness, and promoting locally owned businesses. When interacting, however, they tend to talk past one another instead of to each other. Longtime residents associate newcomers with expensive condominium developments (which many newcomers also despise) and, thus, elevated property taxes, while newcomers hold a host of misperceptions about longtime residents (for example, that they blame the newcomers for driving away businesses that had been operating in the community for decades—they do not). Surprisingly, many (though not all) newer residents understand working-class residents' perception of HonFest as an insult and also dislike the event for the fact that it markets the neighborhood in a particular way that does not represent the reality of daily life in Hampden. Chidester's (2009) dissertation provides an ethnographic analysis of contemporary Hampden.

Conclusion:
Answering the Heroin-Needle Question

The "heroin-needle question" mentioned in the opening passage presents a challenge to archaeologists concerned with civic engagement and community activism. On the surface, it is a sarcastic reference to the Hampden setting, which, despite the recent gentrification, remains a gritty place where quality-of-life crimes such as injective-drug use and prostitution are widespread and often highly visible.

On another level, it is really a question about heritage, asking what an archaeologist could possibly find in a place that the asker assumes has no history. So, archaeologists have to consider the question carefully before replying. In some circumstances, a simple "no" might suffice. While Hampden's archaeological record has not yet yielded up any of its vast imagined stores of heroin needles, it has revealed one small baggie which may have contained heroin, and it contains numerous other bits of drug paraphernalia: tobacco pipes, patent medicine bottles, and liquor-, beer-, and wine-bottle fragments dating to

the 19th and 20th centuries. On the other hand, the archaeological record in Hampden reveals a great deal about the lives of individual members of the working and middle classes, and the heroin-needle question provides an opportunity to communicate some of that directly to individuals within the community.

The best answer to the question, however, is not to answer the question about heroin needles but to answer the question about heritage, and to do it in as many ways and to as many people as possible. By interpreting a little-known and even little-imagined history, archaeologists can help communities strengthen their identities and to populate an otherwise empty past. The Hampden Community Archaeology Project undertakes community outreach and consultation with the idea of changing contemporary discourses that rely on heritage. HCAP is not trying to come in as a group of outsiders to give the community the answers to all of its problems (Gadsby and Chidester 2007; Chidester and Gadsby 2009). The authors see it as their responsibility as archaeologists working in the community to forge the discursive connections between past and present through effective collaboration and community dialogue.

References

BALTIMORE AMERICAN
1833 Valuable Mill and Farm for Sale. *Baltimore American* 28 May. Baltimore, MD.
1843 No title. *Baltimore American* 24 September. Baltimore, MD.
1850 The Rockdale Factory for Sale at Public Auction. *Baltimore American* 2 March. Baltimore, MD.

BALTIMORE SUN
1860 A Library at Woodberry. *Baltimore Sun* 3 October. Baltimore, MD.
1872 Tour of Woodberry Mills. *Baltimore Sun* 8 August. Baltimore, MD.
1874a Settlement of Druid Mills Difficulties—The Operatives Return to Work. *Baltimore Sun* 2 April 1874. Baltimore, MD.
1874b Labor Meeting at Woodberry: The Ten Hour System in the Factories—Speeches by the Workingmen, etc. *Baltimore Sun* 3 April. Baltimore, MD.

BEIRNE, D. RANDALL
1982 Hampden-Woodberry: The Mill Village in an Urban Setting. *Maryland Historical Magazine* 77(1):6–26.

CHAMBERS, ERVE
2006 *Heritage Matters: Heritage, Culture, History, and Chesapeake Bay.* Maryland Sea Grant, College Park.

CHAPPEL, EDWARD A
1989   Social Responsibility and the American History Museum. *Winterthur Portfolio* 24(4):247–265.

CHIDESTER, ROBERT C.
2009   *Class, Community and Materiality in a Blue-Collar Baltimore Neighborhood: An Archaeology of Hampden-Woodberry.* Doctoral dissertation, Departments of Anthropology and History, University of Michigan. University Microfilms International, Ann Arbor, MI.

CHIDESTER, ROBERT C., AND DAVID A. GADSBY
2009   One Neighborhood, Two Communities: The Public Archaeology of Class in a Gentrifying Urban Neighborhood, Baltimore, Maryland. *International Labor and Working-Class History* 76(1):1–19.

CLENDENNING, LYNDA FULLER
1992   The Early Textile Industry in Maryland, 1810–1850. *Maryland Historical Magazine* 87(3):251–266.

DEETZ, JAMES
1996   *In Small Things Forgotten: An Archaeology of Early American Life*, expanded and revised from 1977 edition. Doubleday, New York, NY.

FABIAN, JOHANNES
1983   *Time and the Other: How Anthropology Makes Its Object.* Columbia University Press, New York, NY.

FISHER, ROBERT, AND ERIC SHRAGGE
2007   Contextualizing Community Organizing: Lessons from the Past, Tensions in the Present, Opportunities for the Future. In *Transforming the City: Community Organizing and the Challenges of Political Change*, M. Orr, editor, pp. 193–217. University Press of Kansas, Lawrence.

GADSBY, DAVID A., AND ROBERT C. CHIDESTER
2004   History from "The Bottom" Up: A Research Design for Participatory Archaeology in Hampden, Baltimore, MD. Center for Heritage Resource Studies <http://www.heritage.umd.edu/CHRSWeb/AssociatedProjects/hampden/Hampdenresearchdesign.pdf>. Accessed 11 August 2008.
2007   Heritage in Hampden: A Participatory Research Design for Public Archaeology in a Working-Class Neighborhood, Baltimore, MD. In *Archaeology as a Tool of Civic Engagement*, Barbara J. Little and Paul A. Shackel, editors pp. 223–242. AltaMira Press, Walnut Creek, CA.

GADSBY, DAVID A., ROBERT C. CHIDESTER, AND JOLENE L. U. SMITH
2008   Hampden Heritage <www.hampdenheritage.blogspot.com>. Accessed 11 August 2008.

HAMPDEN-WOODBERRY COMMUNITY ASSOCIATION
1938   *Souvenir Book of the Hampden-Woodberrry Golden Jubilee Celebration.* Privately printed, Baltimore, MD.

HARTIGAN, JOHN
2000   Remembering White Detroit: Whiteness in the Mix of History and Memory. *City and Society* 7(2):11–34.

HARVEY, BILL
1988   *"The People is Grass": A History of Hampden-Woodberry, 1802–1945.* Della Press, Baltimore, MD.

JONES, DONALD, LENA MORTENSEN, DAVID A. GADSBY, AND PAUL A. SHACKEL
2008   CHRS Web, Vol. 2008. University of Maryland Center for Heritage Resource Studies, College Park.

LEONE, MARK P., PARKER B. POTTER, PAUL A. SHACKEL, MICHAEL L. BLAKEY, RICHARD BRADLEY, BRIAN DURRANS, JOAN M. GERO, G. P. GRIGORIEV, IAN HODDER, JOSE LUIS LANATA, THOMAS E. LEVY, NEIL A. SILBERMAN, ROBERT PAYNTER, MARIO A. RIVERA, AND WYLIE ALISON
1987   Toward a Critical Archaeology [and Comments and Reply]. *Current Anthropology* 28(3):283–302.

LITTLE, BARBARA J.
1994   People with History: An Update on Historical Archaeology in the United States. *Journal of Archaeological Method and Theory* 1(1):5–40.

LOWENTHAL, DAVID
1985   *The Past is a Foreign Country.* Cambridge University Press, Cambridge, UK.

McGUIRE, RANDALL, AND PAUL RECKNER
2003   Building a Working-Class Archaeology: The Colorado Coal Field War Project. *Industrial Archaeology Review* 25(2):83–95.

OLSON, SHERRY H.
1997   *Baltimore: The Building of an American City*, Revised and expanded edition. Johns Hopkins University Press, Baltimore, MD.

RUSSEL-CIARDI, MAGGIE
2008   The Museum as a Democracy-Building Institution: Reflections on the Shared Journeys Program at the Lower East Side Tenement Museum. *Public Historian* 30(1):39–52.

ŠEVČENKO, LIZ, AND MAGGIE RUSSEL-CIARDI
2008   Foreword. *Public Historian* 30(1):9–15.

SHACKEL, PAUL A.
2001   *Myth, Memory, and the Making of the American Landscape.* University Press of Florida, Gainesville.
2004   Labor's Heritage: Remembering the American Industrial Landscape. *Historical Archaeology* 38(4):44–58.

SHANKS, MICHAEL, AND CHRISTOPHER Y. TILLEY
1992   *Re-Constructing Archaeology: Theory and Practice*, 2nd edition. Routledge, London, UK.

SMITH, JOLENE L. U.
2008a   Oral History and the Hampden Community Archaeology Project. Poster and instructional materials presented at the 41st Conference on Historical and Underwater Archaeology, Albuquerque, NM.

2008b Oral History and Community Archaeology: Developing a Program in Hampden. Paper presented at the conference, "Sharing Authority: Building Community-University Alliances through Oral History, Digital Storytelling, and Collaboration." Concordia University, Montréal, QC.

SMITH, LAURAJANE
2004 *Archaeological Theory and the Politics of Cultural Heritage.* Routledge, London, UK.

STAHLGREN, LORI C., AND M. JAY STOTTMAN
2007 Voices from the Past: Changing the Culture of Historic House Museums with Archaeology. In *Archaeology as a Tool of Civic Engagement*, edited by B. J. Little and P. A. Shackel, pp. 223–242. AltaMira Press, Lanham, MD.

STREUVER BROS. ECCLES AND ROUSE
2005 *Clipper Mill Condominiums.* Marketing pamphlet, in possession of authors, Department of Anthropology, American University, Washington, DC.

WALLACE, ANTHONY F. C.
2004 The Industrialist as Hero. In *Modernity and Mind: Essays on Culture Change, Volume 2*, Robert S. Grumet, editor, pp. 151–166. University of Nebraska Press, Lincoln.

WEEKS, THOMAS C.
1886 *First Biennial Report of the Bureau of Industrial Statistics and Information of Maryland, 1884–1885.* Guggenheimer, Weil, and Co., Baltimore, MD.

DAVID A. GADSBY
DEPARTMENT OF ANTHROPOLOGY
AMERICAN UNIVERSITY
BATTELLE TOMPKINS HALL T21
4400 MASSACHUSETTS AVENUE NW
WASHINGTON, DC 20016

ROBERT C. CHIDESTER
210 E. MAIN ST. APT. A
MILAN, MI 48160

Barbara J. Little

What Can Archaeology Do for Justice, Peace, Community, and the Earth?

The purpose of this forum is to contribute to the ongoing conversation about archaeology as it might be of service beyond its traditional roles. The observation that archaeology plays a role in society beyond its contribution to knowledge is not new; there are increasing numbers of archaeologists determined to use their expertise to make the world a better place. What I hope in this forum is that I and my colleagues make a fruitful contribution to the ongoing dialogue about potential and actual benefits of archaeology related to doing justice, making peace, building community, and restoring ecological balance.

In a recent issue of *The SAA Archaeological Record*, ethnobotanist and archaeologist Paul Minnis initiated a dialogue about "The Skeptic's Question" because he is concerned that archaeologists don't know how to make the case for what we do (Minnis et al. 2006). The skeptic, in this case, is the person who asks, essentially, why spend public money—that is, tax dollars—on archaeology instead of spending the money for more obviously important things such as schools, medical research, or reducing poverty. In addition to Minnis, six other archaeologists—five prehistorians and one historical archaeologist (me)—offered short versions of our answers to why archaeology is relevant today. Our responses ranged from ecological conservation and the diversification of crops, to the encouragement of long-term perspectives on public decision making, to tourism, to promoting heritage and identity, to battling racism.

Our responses to the "skeptic's question" assume that the archaeology that will be useful will be competent, scholarly archaeology. The need to ask the question and to "make the case" relates to increasing anxiety about public relevance throughout the sciences and humanities. Generations of archaeologists have felt strongly the need for their work to be useful, not only to justify continued funding, but also to act as responsible scholars. Archaeologists have disagreed, however, about what counts as usefulness, often ridiculing work that falls outside of one's own "camp." Archaeologists too often fight about a basic division presumed to split the discipline. One kind of archaeology is a science, which provides credible and hopefully useful knowledge. One kind of archaeology is a humanity, which provides meaning and perspective on life within the human condition over time and across space. Sometimes we integrate those two identities well, and sometimes we do not. The kinds of benefits we hope to provide depend on how we see the purpose and strengths of our field. It may be that one of the most beneficial things we could do—for ourselves, for the social sciences, for intellectual life, for policy makers, for a broad range of interested publics —is to do a better job of integrating the values of the humanities and the sciences and making the case, by example, of how to do that.

As archaeologists, we know that there are many scholars who could use archaeology to do a better job in their own research and that there are many people who could use archaeology to make their lives richer. One example contributing to research impacts outside of archeology is useful data for ecologists and environmental researchers who need a longer-term view than is often available on the ecological effects of industry and globalization.

And, for enriching lives, for example, we want teachers and students to learn archaeology, *not only* so that they'll support it, and *not only* so that they see the world is diverse in peoples and cultures, *but also* to learn about how one might make sense of a process deeply imbued with ambiguity, complexity, and uncertainty and to gain the insight that those characteristics apply to life in general no less than to the messy business of archaeology. In addition, we want communities and archaeologists to engage with each other and to use the process and results of archaeology to make sense of their community histories and to make stronger communities.

As we are more intentional about making archaeology useful and relevant, it would probably be a good idea to bring the somewhat polarized scientific and humanist aspects of archaeology together, as well as the insights of various archaeologies, including anthropological, classical, Biblical, and indigenous.

So, what's beneficial about archaeology? Are the benefits economic, cultural, spiritual, or something else? Are sites beneficial because they build patriotism or support the status quo? Are they beneficial because they challenge and subvert the deeply embedded racism and sexism of our society? If archaeology benefits one public, does another public perceive a loss? In the United States, long-running battles over history in public schools suggest that there are strong feelings about whose political agendas are served by the choice of whose history is taught. If there are losses, might the losses be appropriate, as when the lies of racist white supremacy are exposed and probed?

We have deep cultural narratives about people and also about things. We live in a bottom-line society where nothing but money seems to matter in mainstream culture, where the market rules, and where a kind of market fundamentalism is pursued with religious fervor.

Professional archaeologists resist the all-encompassing rule of the market: we contend that there is value to archaeology—artifacts, sites, knowledge, the whole archaeological process—and that value is not about the monetary value of things. That willingness to stand against the powerful cultural tide of commercialism alone makes archaeology somewhat culturally subversive in the 21st century. I believe it can be culturally subversive in a most beneficial way. And, as we insist that there is an alternative, better way to think about *value*, we are somewhat in line with others who want to work towards a society and a culture that benefit more people and support a more just and fair way of being in the world.

In November 2007 at the American Anthropological Association meetings in Washington, DC, I participated in the session that Carol McDavid and Patti Jeppson organized on "Pathways to Justice: Exploring the Intersections between the Global Justice Movement, Archeology, and Anthropology." In their invitation, McDavid and Jeppson asked the participants to consider how our work may intersect with the goals of the global justice movement which aims to find another way, a "just third way" (http://www.globaljustivemovement.org/). This "just third way" is meant to be something other than capitalism or socialism that will move humanity forward. There are growing numbers of individuals and groups with a vision of creating cultural change. There is also a group "Archaeologists for Global Justice" at the University of Sheffield in the UK (http://shef.ac.uk/archaeology/global-justice.html). I'll keep my discussion general and suggest the ways that I think archeology might intersect with the broad movement, to benefit it, and to benefit the things for which it stands.

One entry into such a big topic is to examine the mission statement. The most succinct mission statement I could find for the Global Justice Movement was a quote by Buckminster Fuller on one version of the movement's main web page, and that is, "to make the world work for 100% of humanity in the shortest possible time, through spontaneous cooperation without ecological offense or the disadvantage of anyone" (http://www.globaljusticemovement.org/mission.htm).

Interdisciplinary work (even within a discipline as amorphous as archaeology) and the intersection of movements within the overarching global justice movement, also imply that there needs to be a way to work inter-agenda. Such work means that we must in some way integrate our multiple skills, motives, cultures, and points of view. We see how difficult it is for even parts of archaeology to work together. To work together in any effective way requires connections, unity, respect, and the maintenance of individual expertise. Such work requires a whole new culture of collaboration and especially trust. It also requires expanding the kind of international cooperation we do.

The growing activist archaeology movement, including intersecting with the global justice movement, is part of the search for relevance. I do not think that there are many archeologists who would argue that archaeology is irrelevant, but opinions about what constitutes relevance, meaning, and usefulness are probably pretty widely scattered.

I suspect the same disagreements characterize the Global Justice Movement. Indeed, there are at least two major independent versions of the Movement with organized, online presence: the .org and .net versions. In general, we may be able to agree that we want the whole world to work better, both for people and for the rest of earth's inhabitants. We may be able to agree on the stated high-minded principles of "Global Justice for All," "Respect for the Earth," "Abundance and Freedom are Possible," "Creativity at Work," and "Economic Democracy." However, I am not at all sure how meeting such principles might translate into mundane details of "action plans" that we might agree upon. If, for example, various allied groups were to agree on what "respect for the earth" means, would any of us approach the achievement of that vision in similar ways? How might we agree on how to get there? Could we agree on the obstacles, or on what is actually working now, but just needs support or better understanding?

It seems to me that because Global Justice goals are out of reach in any single lifetime, the path and the process become the point. Now this sounds suspiciously like a spiritual principle: *To do good—and to do it well and faithfully—in hope, in faith, that someday the light of a better world will dawn.* It is no accident that this sounds spiritual because it is. The Global Justice Movement not only needs to be, but explicitly is, about *wholeness*. It is about the environment, justice, peace, human identity, and connections. Wholeness explicitly includes the intellectual and the emotional and the spiritual. How do we learn to accommodate the spirit in our work? How will the Global Justice Movement develop a Third Way Ecumenicalism that includes and respects all faiths, listens to all visions, and avoids becoming dangerously charismatic or apocalyptic? How will any movement avoid splitting into "camps" and falling into the familiar habit of ostracizing those outside of the camp boundaries?

Members of movements are often very jealous of membership and create dogmatic gatekeeping. I suspect that true inclusion is extraordinarily rare. *Part of the work that archaeology can do is demonstrate inclusion by including everyone in the past.*

Many questions about how archaeology might intersect with the Global Justice Movement are structural. The movement seeks to pull together across causes and across the globe. *What archaeology might add is "across time" and we become, then, an argument for the future and not for the past as we provide evidence for the continuum, for survival against the odds, and for hope.*

We also can provide alternative genealogies as we expose origin myths. I am thinking, for example, of ways in which we might explore the genealogy of market fundamentalism, by which I mean that blind idolatry of what is imagined as a free market, and reveal alternative realities that have worked, could have worked, do work, and can work. One of the ways we can do that is to engage with questions about *what the economy is for*, just as we are engaging with the question of *what archaeology is for*.

A little over a century ago the progressive politician Gifford Pinchot (two-time Governor of Pennsylvania and first Director of the U.S. Forest Service) summarized the progressive view on what the economy is for by adopting a well known idea from philosopher Jeremy Bentham (1748-1832) and John Stuart Mill (1806-1873) and adding a long-term perspective to it. In 1905 Pinchot defined his approach to the public good this way: "Where conflicting interests must be reconciled, the question shall always be answered from the standpoint of the greatest good of the greatest number in the long run" (U.S. Forest Service 2004).

"In the long run" is something that archaeologists ought to be able to relate to and, more importantly, make a contribution to understanding. As an example, I can imagine how we might be of great public benefit by taking on an investigation of modern world trends and changes in quality of life and meeting of basic needs. We will need to take 20th-century sites seriously for this. Let us take a long-term look at the way the economy serves and does not serve us. How fair are we? What do the wealth gaps look like and how are lives along that wealth spectrum experienced? What does poverty look like? How is it experienced? Those alternative realities might form the basis for new narratives that the Global Justice Movement will need to create and offer if it is to adhere to its high-minded principles.

Archaeology can examine the deep history of contemporary issues such as migration and

Barbara J. Little

treatment of foreigners; poverty, hunger, and subsistence; military power; and urban decay. Archaeologists can draw upon our discoveries and approaches to come up with new narratives to help improve present and future environmental and social conditions and to respond intelligently to climate change. As I have focused my attention on the topic of public benefits over the last ten years, I have become more convinced that archaeology offers real benefits to the wider society, but I am not sure that those benefits are what we thought they were.

I think it's true that we need a new narrative, so let me end with a story that might be inspirational to archaeologists working with issues of global justice, peace, and the well-being of communities and ecosystems.

In 2004 Wangari Maathai was awarded the Nobel Peace Prize for her work in the Green Belt Movement in Kenya (Frängsmyr 2005). That grassroots movement helps women's groups plant trees, as of now more than 30 million trees on farms, schools, and church compounds. The tree planting led to fights against land grabbing and the theft of public forests. Maathai was threatened, beaten, intimidated, eventually accommodated and finally honored. The trees became symbols of, as well as a tool for, democracy, empowerment, and human rights.

What do trees as a tool of environmental restoration have to do with archaeology? Maathai (quoted in Nagel 2005:4) has observed, "Once you start making these linkages, you can no longer do just tree planting. When you start working with the environment seriously, the whole arena comes: human rights, women's rights, environmental rights, children's rights... everybody's rights."

Trees are almost certainly a less ambiguous good than archaeology. In a parallel way, when one starts working with heritage and the meaning of the past, one must make linkages between archaeology and other activities. The lesson to be drawn is not one of ambition for its own sake—it's not about promoting one's own career or even one's own discipline—but of the real power to be found in service. It is in the genuine desire to serve that I believe we can, as individuals and maybe even as organized groups, most effectively intersect with or work within the alliances that make up the Global Justice Movement, even when not explicitly part

of any movement but simply aware of similar goals at a more local scale.

I am interested in an ongoing conversation about how archaeology figures into an imagined and created future. Can archaeology impact societies and culture so as to make a positive difference? Is it wise to make such attempts? What should our roles be if we believe that archaeology can help us do justice, make peace, build community, or restore ecosystems.

Acknowledgements

I am indebted to Sarah Bridges for providing the following sources on tools for non-market valuations: Ma and Stern (2004), Mason (2005), and Poor and Smith (2004). The Forum on Social Wealth at the University of Massachusetts, Amherst, asks the question, "what is the economy for?" in its quest to fashion a new "cognitive frame" for understanding value (de Graff et al. 2002). I delivered portions of this essay at the American Anthropological Association November 2007 and at the Society for Historical Archaeology opening plenary session in January 2008. I wish to thank: Carol McDavid and Patti Jeppson for inviting me to participate in the AAA symposium on "Pathways to Justice: Exploring the Intersections between the Global Justice Movement, Archeology, and Anthropology;" Terry Klein for inviting me to participate in the opening plenary forum on the Public Benefits of Historical Archaeology at the SHA meeting; Ronn Michael and Joe Joseph for inviting me to this Forum; my colleagues Pedro Funari, Sergiu Musteata, and Innocent Pikirayi for agreeing to participate. I am very grateful for comments and suggestions on this Forum essay by my colleagues Sarah Bridges, Martin Gallivan, Barbara Mills, Teresa Moyer, and Paul Shackel.

References Cited

ARCHAEOLOGISTS FOR GLOBAL JUSTICE
  <http://shef.ac.uk/archaeology/global-justice.html> (last accessed 30/03/08)

DE GRAFF, JOHN, DAVID WANN, AND THOMAS H. NAYLOR
  2002 *Affluenza: The All-Consuming Epidemic.* Berrett-Koehler, San Francisco.

GLOBAL JUSTICE MOVEMENT
<http://www.globaljustsicemovement.org> (last accessed 30/03/08)

FRÄNGSMYR, TORE, EDITOR
2005 *The Nobel Prizes 2004*. Nobel Foundation, Stockholm. <http://nobelprize.org/nobel_prizes/peace/laureates/2004/maathai-bio.html> (last accessed 3/30/08) Green Belt Movement <http://www.grenbeltmovemnt.org/> (last accessed 30/03/08)

MA, CHUNBO AND DAVID I. STERN
2004 *Environmental and Ecological Economics: A Citation Analysis*. Rensselaer Working Papers in Economics.

MASON, RANDALL
2005 *Economics and Historic Preservation: A Guide and Review of the Literature*. Discussion Paper prepared for The Brookings Institute Metropolitan Policy Program. The Brookings Institute, New York.

MINNIS, PAUL E., BARBARA J. LITTLE, ROBERT KELLY, SCOTT E. INGRAM, DEAN SNOW, LYNNE SEBASTIAN, AND KATHERINE A. SPIELMANN
2006 Answering the Skeptic's Question. *The SAA Archaeological Record* 6(5):17-20. <http://ww.saa.org/publications/theSAAarchRec/nov06.pdf> (last accessed 30/03/08)

NAGEL, MECHTHILD
2005 Environmental Justice and Women's Rights: A Tribute to Wangari Maathai. *Wagadu 2 :1-9*. http://wagadu.org/Volume%202/Printable/nagel.pdf (last accessed 3/30/08)

POOR, P. JOAN AND JAMIE M. SMITH
2004 Travel Cost Analysis of a Cultural Heritage Site: The Case of Historic St. Mary's City of Maryland. *Journal of Cultural Economics* 28(3):217-229.

U.S. FOREST SERVICE
2004 Pinchot and Utilitarianism. Website accompanying centennial documentary film, "The Greatest Good," released 2004. http://www.fs.fed.us/greatestgood/press/mediakit/facts/pinchot.shtml?sub3 (last accessed 30/03/08)

BARBARA J. LITTLE
ADJUNCT PROFESSOR
DEPARTMENT OF ANTHROPOLOGY
UNIVERSITY OF MARYLAND
COLLEGE PARK, MD 20742

Pedro Paulo A. Funari

Historical Archaeology and Global Justice

Archaeology has changed substantially in the last few decades. Originally, archaeology was part of imperialist and colonial practices, both within colonial powers and in their foreign enterprises. Archaeology has served in the 20th century a series of nationalist, fascist and dictatorial regimes, contributing to legitimate oppression and even to the killing of people. This is particularly clear in the case of dictatorships like the Nazi one (Legendre et al. 2007) and in other classic autocratic regimes in Europe (Galaty and Watkinson 2004). Racism has been very much associated with archaeology and oppression, particularly during the first half of the 20th century, but other restrictive measures were also grounded on archeological findings and discourses, as in the case of gender imbalances as fostered by Fascist Italy (Cavicchioli 2005). In Latin America, dictatorships during the Cold War used archaeology for their own purposes, supported by the United States, whose democratic credentials were not enough to moderate autocratic rule and abuse of archaeology (Funari and Zarankin 2006).

Since the 1980s though, archaeology has changed significantly. Social movements in several continents lead to new social realities. Gender and racial imbalances have been challenged; anti-war and environment movements gathered strength and old social models have been questioned. Interpretive models grounded on nationalist tenets (Thiesse 2001), such as social homogeneity, common roots, race, land, and language, compliance to supposedly accepted norms and rules, were all of them criticized, and they failed to survive the onslaught of social conflicts and struggle. From the 1950s but definitively from the 1980s, heterogeneity, diversity and pluralism in society lead to social theory interpretive models challenging normative tenets. Diversity as a concept has been widely applied not only to nature and the environment, but also to society, leading to the 2005 UNESCO declaration on cultural diversity (Siehr 2006).

Archaeology faced those challenges head-on and changed itself in the process, starting by accepting that the discipline cannot claim to be a neutral, objective pursuit of facts. Fact-finding was a key concept of archaeology under dictatorships everywhere and in democratic, open social contexts this claim proved impossible to keep. The discipline faced its subjective character and was thus able to acknowledge its social and public aspects. The World Archaeological Congress (WAC) is both the result of those moves and a propeller of changes in the direction of the inclusion of indigenous people, peripheral scholars, ethics and other important issues (Funari 2006). In the last decades after the setting up of WAC in 1986, archaeology has increasingly sponsored diversity and served to foster social responsibility.

In this overall context, Barbara Little argues for the overcoming of several traditional dichotomies, starting with the divide between sciences and humanities. This pledge is in tune with the common struggle for a better life for everybody, taking each person as part of a variety of communities and groups. Furthermore, this move is only possible when we acknowledge the subjectivity inherent to both scientific and humanistic knowledge, as is increasing the case, particularly as humanity faces threats to environmental and human diversity. Then, Little mentions the key concept of justice and fairness. This is also a clear move beyond traditional neutral scholarship, towards the acknowledgment of imbalances and the need to overcome asymmetry at various levels, not least through international cooperation. The discipline is still very much dominated by national disciplines with limited interaction worldwide. The English language world community contributed to a better international dialogue but this is not yet enough to overcome most barriers. The income disparities mean that most books and journals are based in rich countries and publish only a short amount of papers by peripheral scholars. Archaeologists from non-English-speaking countries are usually unable to produce papers in English, further diminishing their audience. The wealth or research in local languages is also usually ignored outside their own limited scholarly circuits. In several cases, the lack of international cooperation is still acute, such as in the Latin American archaeology. English-speakers rarely refer to papers in Spanish or Portuguese and local archaeologists seldom get their papers and books distributed beyond their own countries. The same issues are relevant in other parts of the world.

In the same vein, Little stresses the need to put the various archaeological traditional branches in closer connection. It is unreasonable to pledge for the end of the specificities of anthropological, classical, Biblical, and many other archaeologies. Within those fields, there are several other divisions, aiming at covering very specific subjects, from Rock Art to amphora studies, from petrography to gender issues, to mention just a few of them. Little reminds us that all those fields can gain a lot, if put in contact with a much wider variety of approaches and subjects. Several years ago, Little (1992) pledged for such an approach to reinvigorate historical archaeology, fostering the cooperation between archaeologists studying classical and modern contexts and others followed her lead (e.g., Funari et al. 1999). This proved a most relevant move, for several reasons, not least because it showed how useful the insights from different historical contexts could be, but also as it encouraged international contacts and cooperation.

The aim of promoting democracy, empowerment, and human rights is at the heart of the Global Justice Movement and several common people worldwide share it, including archaeologists. Those goals are not abstract, but concrete, rooted in the search for the recognition of diversity as our common key concept. It is important to pay attention to women's rights, environmental rights, but also to many other rights, such as the rights of less inequality in scholarly structures and exchanges, or the rights of sexual diversity. All those aspects of the Global Justice Movement are relevant for the common struggle for a better world.

References

CAVICCHIOLI, MARINA R.
2005 A Guerra, a Paz e o Sexo: os Discursos por Trás das Escavações de Pompéia. (The War, the Peace, and the Sex: Reflections on the Excavations of Pompei). In *XXIII Simpósio Nacional de História-História: Guerra e Paz.* Editorial Mídia, Londrina, Brazil.

FUNARI, PEDRO PAULO A., MARTIN HALL, AND SIAN JONES
1999 *Historical Archaeology, Back from the Edge.* Routledge, London.

FUNARI, PEDRO PAULO A. AND ANDRÉS ZARANKIN
2006 *Arqueología de la Represión y la Resistencia en América Latina 1960-1980.* (Archaeology of the Repression and the Resistance in Latin América, 1960-1980). Encuentro. Córdoba, Argentina.

FUNARI, PEDRO PAULO A.
2006 The World Archaeological Congress from a Critical and Personal Perspective 01/07/2006. *Archaeologies,* 2:73-79. Rowman & Littlefield Publishing Group, Blue Ridge Summit, PA.

GALATY, MICHAEL AND CHARLES WATKINSON, EDITORS
2004 *Archaeology under Dictatorship.* Springer, New York.

LEGENDRE, JEAN-PIERRE, LAURENT OLIVIER, AND BERNADETTE SCHNITLZER (EDITORS)
2007 *L'Archéologie Nazie en Europe de l'Ouest.* (The Archaeology of the Nazis in Western Europe). In Folio, Paris, France.

LITTLE, BARBARA
1992 *Text-aided Archaeology.* Telford Press, Boca Raton, FL.

SIEHR, KURT
2006 Documents: Convention on the protection and promotion of the diversity of cultural expressions, *International Journal of Cultural Property,* 13:377-391.

THIESSE, ANNE-MARIE
2001 *La Création des Identitiés Nationales.* (The Creation of National Identities). Seuil, Paris.

PEDRO PAULO A. FUNARI
STATE UNIVERSITY OF CAMPINAS
DEPARTAMENTO DE HISTÓRIA
IFCH/UNICAMP
CENTRE FOR STRATEGIC STUDIES (NEE/UNICAMP)
C. POSTAL 6110,
CAMPINAS, 13081-970, SP, BRAZIL

Sergiu Musteata

Let's Do Our Job Better and Then There Will Be No Reasons To Talk About the Relevancy of Archaeology

First of all, I would like to thank Barbara J. Little for the invitation to participate in a very actual and debated question—*why archaeology is relevant today?* Secondly, I think Barbara has excellently pointed out the most important aspects of contemporary archaeology in her paper. So, in the following lines I will try to give some comments concerning relevancy of archaeology from the Eastern European perspective.

Archaeology and Peace

I am sure that archaeologists are not sceptical about the job and perspectives of archaeology, but the rest of the people today treat the question, in most cases, from materialistic perspectives and are not interested in the fields of research and preservation of the past. A few years ago, a young political scientist from Moldova said: "historians are speaking with dead people." I considered this statement offensive, but at the same time I understood that if a University lecturer came to this conclusion, what could others say about us. As an archaeologist, I consider that we have to create a better link between the contemporary society and the past. Most of the present things have roots in the past and can be clearly understood in the light of history. Knowledge of the origins of a process, event, object, people etc. stimulates our curiosity and generates multiple questions. The questions regarding somebody's origin and identity are often raised and researched. Who if not archaeologists should make the public sensible about the past and the necessity of its preservation? Archaeology as a historical discipline has to mobilize the state bodies in order to cultivate the loyalty of its inhabitants and to build a peaceful society. History teaches the young generation about their own identity, their neighbours, about similarities and differences between cultures, traditions, and religions of the people, etc. This also means that history has the potential of teaching tolerance while it explains differences and developing analytical skills and critical thinking. Of course, in the transforming societies, we could see other priorities rather than the one of discovering the past. But, in any case, the society is built on the values established and developed within long historical periods.

Archaeology and Community

In a post-socialist country the link between archaeology and community does not always exist. The public archaeology is a good way to involve the communities in our job, but the main question still remains. How should we manage it? For the last decade I have been involved in the excavation of one of the most important archaeological sites in Moldova—the Medieval Town of Orheiul Vechi (*http://orhei. dnt.md/*). The archaeological excavations started in 1946 and were concentrated in Ancient Getic fortress and remains from Tatar's 14th century city Şehr al-Cedid. During "the soviet era" a lot of local habitants participated in the excavations, but no-one has discussed public archaeology and the role of local community for preservation of the cultural heritage. Since 1997, through the Archaeological Research Centre of the Republic of Moldova, which is a Non-Governmental Organization (NGO), we have been trying to involve the local community in our archaeological projects as much as possible. One of the positive examples that has had a real impact and has become attractive for community was a Summer School for the students of the local school. During three weeks, experienced archaeologists have organized interactive classes and excavations with about 30 young people. Other projects we fulfill are meant for University students (Summer School and International Voluntary Camp). During one month we involve young people from different universities of Moldova and abroad in such activities as excavations, excursions, discussions on policies for preservation of cultural heritage, etc. Receiving the assistance of the U.S. Ambassadors' Fund we built a new exhibition hall for the local museum and involved local community, administrators and donors in this process. But, until now the local community remains passive and unresponsive to the preservation questions. Why does it happen? The explanation is simple. The totalitarian regime is not so easy to change, the mentality of the people being the hardest part. Just through the long process of education we can get positive results. In my opinion, not only is the preservation of the archaeological heritage a moral obligation of each human being, as it is mentioned in the Article 59 of Moldovan Constitution, but it also is a public and collective responsibility, according to the *European Convention for the Protection of Archaeological Heritage* and other international conventions. So, the state bodies should pay more attention to preparing national strategies in the area of cultural preservation. For the cultural heritage of a nation encourages a sense of common belonging, this becomes an essential factor in the process of community integration and understanding.

Archaeology and Ecology

Archaeology is directly linked with ecology. Over the last decades we have been more and more involved in debates about restoring the ecological balance. For post-socialist countries, these kinds of questions are more than actual since over the last years economic reforms, land ownership, industrial intervention, etc. directly affected ecology. In the era of economic transformation and market liberalisation, the archaeology, as other sciences, is not a part of the national priorities. Actually, each archaeologist is focused on doing his job—writing projects, trying to find money for excavations and publications. In our situation we cannot speak about the possibility to outlay public money. Anyway, archaeology has a direct impact on landscape and ecology. The common problem for all archaeologists is how

to develop interdisciplinary studies and to use non-destructive techniques.

Archaeology and Justice

In the era of globalisation, of course, we could talk about some Global Justice Movement, but concerning links between archaeology and justice I think it is better to start from the local point of view. The vices of modern society (illegal traffic with antiquities, illegal excavations, etc.) minimizes the image of archaeology as science and profession. Nowadays it is more important to talk about national and international legal framework in the field of combating the mentioned vices and what could archaeologists really do for this. In 2007 I participated in archaeological excavations in Crimea, Ukraine and I was overwhelmed at the sight of the recently robbed archaeological sites. In Romania, we were witnesses of trials against people who had participated in illegal excavation and traffic of the Dacian golden bracelets from Sarmizegetusa, which, after a long process, were repatriated. In the centre of Sofia, Bulgaria we can see Greek, Thracian and Roman artefacts stolen from archaeological sites being objects of free trade. In Moldova the situation is not better. For a long time we have been talking about the necessity to create a law on archaeological heritage without getting any support from the state bodies. The one that is in function today is very general in viewing the issue of historical monuments. The illegal traffic with antiquities is also developed as a part of the European network. Recently, for instance, Dutch and German police discovered many archaeological artefacts derived from Moldova. Unfortunately, I find this treatment of the problem as a lack of responsibility on behalf of the state bodies. In this case the archaeologists have to take the initiative. This responsibility should be transformed by adopting legislation, by developing special programs, and offering guaranties of sufficient funds to programs that aim at preservation of the national heritage. From these considerations it is necessary to adopt a long-term strategy, through laws, programs, and strong attitude of the state and civil society aimed at the preservation of the national cultural heritage.

At the end, I would like to say that archaeology is a complex academic discipline and profession, which could not be learned and practiced by anyone. It is easy to judge looking from outside the field, but one can understand the gist and the real problems of archaeology only if he or she gets involved in the process of planning, researching, conservation, publications and overcoming daily bureaucratic barriers. I consider it unreasonable to open debates on efforts of each archaeologist to organise and manage excavations, analyse and publish the results, etc. which are always linked with fundraising. I think, if each of us will do his or her job in a responsible way, it will be senseless to talk about usefulness of one or another pro-fession. In the era of new communication and research technologies it is more important to talk about the future development of archaeology rather than to discuss provocative questions of relevance.

SERGIU MUSTEATA
HISTORY DEPARTMENT
"ION CREANGĂ" STATE PEDAGOGICAL UNIVERSITY
1 ION CREANGĂ STR.,
MAIN BUILDING, OFFICE 407,
MD-2069
CHIŞINĂU, REPUBLIC OF MOLDOVA

Innocent Pikirayi

What Can Archaeology Do for Society in Southern Africa?

In response to Barbara Little, I present a southern African perspective, sharing issues of mutual concern on how archaeology can be of service to society. How archaeology relates to indigenous communities, however defined, remains critical the world over, the main problem being archaeologists' treatment of cultural treasures including human remains of, or found in or among those communities. It is ironic that even here in southern Africa, South Africa in particular, archaeologists have failed to articulate the relevance of their own discipline to society, despite the region being replete with evidence for humanity's origins, and historical dynamics of social identities formed during the past half millennia. Archaeology still carries a bad image, often associated with desecration of sacred places including burials. To the majority of southern Africans, its usefulness is limited to knowledge production which only benefits archaeologists. Government authorities are distrustful of archaeologists, whose demographics are embarrassingly skewed towards the white minority. To many, archaeology in a post-colonial context is firmly grounded in a 'buried' as well as bitter past, including slavery, European colonialism, apartheid, land alienation, and other losses. The conflict arising from exhumation of human remains in Prestwich Street, Cape Town, illustrates this perception quite vividly (Shepherd 2007).

If the Prestwich Street experience represented archaeologists distancing themselves from society and culture, and leaving communities bitter, the December 2007 reburial of human remains excavated since the 1930s from the Mapungubwe Cultural Landscape brought about a sense of community building and interaction with archaeologists. This was not easy though, given the quarrels between the claimant groups, each of whom tried to authenticate their claims by proving sole ownership of the remains. In

this potentially volatile context archaeologists were not just negotiating responsible repatriation; they were also considering their role in a racially and ethnically divided present (Schoeman and Pikirayi 2008). This would fit into Barbara Little's integrative approach, where the interests of science (archaeology) have to take into account those of society (humanities). Archaeologists need to go beyond this by situating their discipline within community needs and expectations. Communities must set parameters for relevant archaeologies, and their voices must be heard (see Fontein 2006).

'Engaging Archaeologies' was one of the themes of 2008's World Archaeological Congress (WAC) in Dublin. The basis for such archaeologies lie in the advocacy for community participation in the management of archaeological and other cultural heritage. Dating from the mid 1990s, such calls did not clearly define the term 'community,' and how such participation could be achieved. Engaged archaeologies should adopt a pluralistic approach to the study of the past, as communities have rejected archaeologists' narratives of their pasts, often based on interpretations of 'layered' evidence or selected parts of sites such as garbage mounds.

The benefits of archaeology in southern Africa, particularly Zimbabwe—arguably the only country in the world named after an archaeological site—should be self evident, given its highly politicised heritage, including land restitution. Zimbabwe's archaeological past may be made to look relevant in the present, even if we do not understand what some of this past is, or represents (Pikirayi 2006). Communities still make use of such past or pasts, though. Such 'usable pasts' are a necessary public empowering tool, where those in positions of control often manipulate the public in order to project their own views of the world. In Zimbabwe, such usable pasts are driven by historical and cultural experiences such as losses experienced by communities due to European colonisation, land alienation, racial segregation, and other injustices, much of which are fixed in people's memories (see for example Holtorf

1996). Other pasts appeal to those in present in so many ways. In Zimbabwe, Mozambique and South Africa, Great Zimbabwe-style monumental architecture is used to re-create or remember the pre-European past (see for example Riegl 1996). Great Zimbabwe, Khami, Mapungubwe, and other 'monuments' symbolise a culturally rich past before European colonisation and domination. Some of the injustices of colonialism can apparently be addressed by appealing to the pre-European past as represented by these sites and places.

In articulating the relevance of archaeology, the global justice movement could not have come at a better time. The destruction of the treasures of Iraq reflected how war and those in corridors of power could violate other people's cultural heritage with impunity, all in the name of human rights and democracy, while in essence pursuing parochial national and international self-interests. I am familiar with the principles of University of Sheffield-based Archaeology for Global Justice (AGJ), through ARCH-JUSTICE, their WAC mailing list. I see them seeking to redraw or redefine the principles of archaeological practice in the post-modern world characterised by much social injustice, discrimination, social inequality, differential access to resources, poverty, violence, environmental degradation, and unsustainable development. Besides, by seeking to engage the public and re-establishing professionalism based on equality and open debate, they are advocating the kind of archaeology that southern Africa should do in a post-colonial or post-apartheid environment. While this may be seen as a way of redressing past cultural injustices committed in a violent world of European colonialism and apartheid, archaeology may address relevance in other interesting ways beyond the confines of justice. If Zimbabwean archaeologists were to team up with political scientists to probe decline or collapse in modernity and its connections, if any, with pre-colonial social formations, more answers may be found as to why we attach so much importance to Great Zimbabwe (AD 1280–1550) and associated cultural heritage.

My final point of discussion seeks to address relevance beyond communities. Relevance here is contextualised within a developing world perspective, and thus different from Western Europe and the United States. For argument sake, how can archaeology be in the service of United Nations Millennium Development Goals (MDGS)? This is where we must benchmark what society would regard as relevant to their needs, and how our discipline should situate itself to address concerns of a global nature. The UN has identified and defined eight goals: eradication of extreme poverty and hunger; achieving universal primary education; promoting gender equity and empowering women; reducing child mortality; improving maternal health; combating HIV/AIDS, malaria and other diseases; ensuring environmental sustainability; and, developing a global partnership for development (*http://www.un.org/milleniumgoals/*). These goals as outlined must be achieved by 2015! However, the goals sideline culture as a vehicle for development. A recent study by Pro Helvetia and the Swiss Agency for Development and Cooperation (SDC) in seven Eastern European countries reveals that cultural work plays a key role in the social development of transition countries (Landry 2006). According to the study, cultural work strengthens diversity of opinion and promotes debate on socially relevant topics. It also helps to create alternative structures and networks and facilitates participation in political life. Cultural work also reinforces civil society, particularly in emerging and fragile democracies. It is unfortunate that when such agendas are being conceptualized, archaeologists are nowhere to be found!

References Cited

FONTEIN, JOOST
2006 *The Silence of Great Zimbabwe: Contested Landscapes and the Power of Heritage.* UCL Press, London.

HOLTORF, CORNELIUS J.
1996 Towards a Chronology of Megaliths: Understanding Monumental and Cultural Memory. *Journal of European Archaeology* 4, 199–152.

LANDRY, CHARLES
2006 *Culture at the Heat of Transformation: The Role of Culture in Social and Economic Development, Lessons Learnt from the Swiss Cultural Programme.* Commissioned by the *Swiss Agency for Development and Cooperation (SDC)* and the *Arts Council of Switzerland Pro Helveia.* Bern, Switzerland.

PIKIRAYI, INNOCENT
2006 The Kingdom, the Power and Forevermore: Zimbabwe Culture in Contemporary Art and Architecture. *Journal of Southern African Studies* 32(4): 755-770.

RIEGL, ALOIS
1996 *The Modern Cult of Monuments: Its Character and Its Origin.* In *Historical and Philosophical Issues in the Conservation of Cultural Heritage*, ed. Nicholas Stanley Price, M. Kirby Tally, Jr., and Alessandra Melucco Vaccaro. Los Angeles: Getty Conservation Institute.

SCHOEMAN, H. MARIA AND INNOCENT PIKIRAYI
2008 Repatriating Mapungubwe: Negotiating a Shared Future out of an Artificially Divided Past. Paper presented at the 6th World Archaeological Congress, Dublin, Ireland.

SHEPHERD, NICK
2007 Archaeology Dreaming: Post-apartheid Urban Imaginaries and the Bones of the Prestwich Street Dead. *Journal of Social Archaeology* 7 (1): 3-28.

UNITED NATIONS
2008 End Poverty 2015 Millenium Development Goals, United Nations Online: (*http://www.unorg/ milleniumgoals/*). Accessed in June 2008.

INNOCENT PIKIRAYI
DEPARTMENT OF ANTHROPOLOGY AND ARCHAEOLOGY
FACULTY OF HUMANITIES, HB 8-5
UNIVERSITY OF PRETORIA
PRETORIA 0002
REPUBLIC OF SOUTH AFRICA

Barbara J. Little

What Can Archaeology Do for Justice, Peace, Community, and the Earth —Response to Comments

I would like to thank my colleagues Pedro Funari, Sergiu Musteata, and Innocent Pikirayi for participating in this forum. Each of them expresses important ideas to which I can only partially respond.

I love the title of Musteata's response because it highlights the very important question: what *is* our job? What are the purposes of archaeology in the modern world? I want to pick up just a few of the common threads I find in my colleagues' responses. The first concerns the ways in which we confront our histories, particularly as archaeologists. The second is the global nature of archaeological issues and its simultaneous community scale. Third is the issue of responsibility.

Through specific examples, my colleagues illustrate that archaeology must confront the misuses of our practice in the past and, insofar as old habits die hard, in the present and future. Archaeology has earned a reputation as a practice that is not altogether trustworthy, a judgment due more to the powers it serves than to the ambiguity of its interpretations. Archaeologists face the continuing question of whether our practice can be re-drawn as a useful tool in the re-invention of societies we describe as post-dictatorship, post-soviet or post-socialist, or post-colonialist. Regaining trust is essential if archaeology is to be a progressive force. I am encouraged by my colleagues' determined optimism. I believe that a degree of skepticism is realistic, as the challenge is serious.

Funari points out that language and the accessibility of publications are basic issues in developing a global archaeology. Considering these issues, what might the Society for Historical Archaeology (SHA) do to address the language and access needs of historical archaeologists across the globe? Can SHA encourage and facilitate translation and encourage academic departments to expand training and persuade students to develop their language skills? Individuals and professional organizations are making efforts to support global scholarship and exchange. The World Archaeological Congress (WAC) has been particularly active. Pikirayi mentions the theme on engaged archaeology at the WAC conference in 2008. As one of the co-organizers of that theme, I want to acknowledge that one of the core ideals of WAC is contemporary relevance.

As an organization, WAC continues to be a real catalyst for change in the practice of archaeology worldwide. The WAC InterCongress planned to be held in Ramallah explores the question of structural violence. The description for this meeting asks, "As anthropologists, archaeologists, cultural heritage professionals, and concerned local community members, we ask what role archaeological and cultural heritage research has in overcoming these 'in-built' obstacles. Must we engage against structural violence outside of archaeological practice, or can archaeological practice confront and impact the ravages of structural violence?" (*http://www.worldarchaeologicalcongress.org/site/ramallah.php*).

There are both Israeli and Palestinian archaeologists who have been working together toward agreements supporting the peace process, including an agreement on the disposition of archaeological collections following the future establishment of a Palestinian state. This is a remarkable achievement that lays out the principles of repatriation of artifacts and control of archaeological sites in a region where the past is an extremely volatile topic (Bohannon 2008; Sullivan and North-Hager 2008). Such work builds on earlier exchanges such as that described by Sandra Scham (2002) that began the People to People exchange programs growing out of the US-brokered Wye River Accords in 1998 (see also Scham and Yahya 2003). For further examples also see Silverman and

Ruggles (2007) and the website of Archaeologists for Global Justice to which Pikirayi refers: *http://www.sheffield.ac.uk/archaeology/global-justice.html.* I appreciate Pikirayi raising the question of how archaeology might serve the United Nation's Millennium Development Goals. I believe that archaeologists can speak to these goals, not to point out the ways that we are shaped by history, but to show that there are other possibilities for our joint future. The problem of sidelining culture is, unfortunately, a familiar shortcoming of common technologically-based approaches to solving problems. Whether as practitioners in the sciences or humanities, archaeologists as "culture workers" may be able to contribute a fresh perspective.

Musteata raises the issue of state responsibility, particularly with regard to the protection of sites and the repatriation of looted material. The need to defend against looting and the commodity driven appropriation of archaeology is immediate and dire (e.g., Renfrew 2000; Brodie et al. 2006; Greenfield 2007). Issues of protecting sites and combating the global trade in looted artifacts are connected to state and national identities and to the international community's roles in identifying and policing illegal activities. Of course, archaeologists have responsibilities at the individual level as well. Through our professional organizations we argue about and propose codes of ethics that help define those responsibilities (e.g., Zimmerman et al. 2003).

As we attempt to come to grips with diversity, pluralism, our many responsibilities, and the need for mutual trust and respect we realize how slippery our grasp is. Our degree of comfort with such ambiguity will greatly influence our future and our success at cooperation. When I emphasize relevance, I do not take a functionalist view of what archaeology is good for in the sense of "are we getting what we pay for?" The human story is deeply relevant in its own right and archaeology is relevant in that it adds to that story. In addition, it is the power of speaking to that human story that makes archaeology relevant, even essential, to current discussions about the challenges we face.

I am hopeful that archaeologists will increase our efforts toward making a positive difference. I hope that this conversation will continue among the readers of *Historical Archaeology* and in the larger archaeological community.

References Cited

BOHANNON, JOHN
2008 Team Unveils Mideast Peace Plan. *Science* 320(5874):302.

BRODIE, NEIL, MORAG M. KERSEL, CHRISTINA LUKE, AND KATHERYN WALKER TUBB (EDITORS)
2006 *Archaeology, Cultural Heritage, and the Antiquities Trade.* University Press of Florida, Gainsville, FL.

GREENFIELD, JEANETTE
2007 *The Return of Cultural Treasures.* Cambridge University Press, Cambridge, UK.

RENFREW, COLIN
2000 *Loot, Legitimacy, and Ownership: The Ethical Crisis in Archaeology.* Duckworth, London, UK.

SCHAM, SANDRA
2002 Hope Amid the Carnage. *Archaeology* 55(4):18.

SCHAM, SANDRA ARNOLD AND ADEL YAHYA
2003 Heritage and Reconciliation. *Journal of Social Archaeology* 3(3):399-416.

SILVERMAN, HELAINE AND D. FAIRCHILD RUGGLES (EDITORS)
2007 *Cultural Heritage and Human Rights.* Springer, New York, NY.

SULLIVAN, MEG AND EDWARD NORTH-HAGER
2008 Plan Brokered by Archaeologists Would Remove Roadblock to Mideast Peace. UCLA press release. Online: <*http://newsroom.ecla.edu/portal/ucla/plan-brokered-by-ucla-usc-archaeologists-477949.aspx*>. Accessed August 22, 2008.

ZIMMERMAN, LARRY J., KAREN D. VITELLI, AND JULIE HOLLOWELL-ZIMMER (EDITORS)
2003 *Ethical Issues in Archaeology.* AltaMira Press, Walnut Creek, CA.

Martin Gallivan
Danielle Moretti-Langholtz
Buck Woodard

Collaborative Archaeology and Strategic Essentialism: Native Empowerment in Tidewater Virginia

ABSTRACT

How should archaeologists respond to descendant communities whose essentialism runs counter to constructivist notions of identity? For native communities in Virginia, the 17th-century landscape described by Jamestown's colonists represents a powerful documentary basis for countering discourse that denies or ignores their existence. Strategic essentialism tied to the notion of tribes as transhistorical subjects offers a means of connecting contemporary native communities to accepted national narratives. While such strategies may be necessary in the short term, research at Werowocomoco, capital of the Powhatan chiefdom ca. 1607, highlights other modes of native social construction. Tidewater communities constructed pluralistic networks prior to contact and reconfigured social ties after 1607. They have done so by incorporating new practices while retaining connections to meaningful places and kinship ties stretching across communities. The expanding involvement of native consultants in research at Werowocomoco and elsewhere provides a point of departure for "decolonizing" discussions of this past.

Introduction

A recent critique of indigenous archaeology decries the role of an essentialist "Aboriginalism" (McGhee 2008, 2010) undergirding these practices in North America. McGhee (2008:579) argues that by adopting "the long-discarded concept of Primitive Man" indigenous archaeology has had negative consequences for scholars and natives alike. Responses to these arguments (Colwell-Chanthaphonh et al. 2010; Croes 2010; Silliman 2010; Wilcox 2010) have pointed out that, since indigenous archaeology is conducted with, for, and by indigenous peoples, its practitioners respond in diverse ways to local conditions. Unifying these approaches, though, is (1) awareness that the archaeology of the indigenous past has (until recently) largely excluded native voices and (2)

reflexivity regarding the contemporary political uses of the past. Indigenous and collaborative archaeology involving native communities almost invariably recognizes and explores cultural continuities and changes before and after the colonial era.

The following offers a discussion of related issues that have emerged in the wake of a collaborative archaeological project in Tidewater Virginia. Here, the historical processes of colonialism have been prolonged, violent, and destructive of native traditions. Partly as a result of the region's particular colonial and postcolonial history, native community agendas have, at times, differed from those in other areas of North America. In fact, an essentialist dialogue *does* play a role in conversations about native history in Tidewater Virginia, though it is most often imposed upon native communities from the outside. Native communities' adoption of essentialist discourse is typically limited, strategic, and responsive to federal Indian policies and to historical narratives promoted by a heritage industry focused squarely on the history of the Jamestown colony.

More than 400 years after Jamestown's settlement, archaeology has come to play a small but insistent role connecting Tidewater Virginia's difficult pasts with the complicated present. For residents of Virginia, heightened awareness of early colonial history became almost inescapable in 2007 as coverage of excavations at James Fort peppered the local media. Public-service announcements, local celebrations, and state-sponsored trips to the United Kingdom commemorated past relationships between the colonists who established the first enduring English settlement in the Americas and the indigenous peoples they encountered. Museum exhibits at Jamestown emphasized the blending of three cultures (English, Virginia Indian, and African) that resulted in the birth of American democracy on the shores of the James River 400 years ago. The degree to which the public's engagement with this particular narrative resulted in the nuanced historical awareness, citizen empowerment, and community building envisioned by proponents of a civically engaged archaeology remains to be seen. As others have pointed out (Horning

2006; Hantman 2008), the themes of creolization, democracy, and American origins emphasized in the Jamestown commemorations mask much of the violence, dispossession, and shifting power dynamics of the early 17th-century Chesapeake.

Recent research undertaken by a number of scholars (Moretti-Langholtz 1998; Hantman et al. 2000; Gallivan 2007; Woodard 2008) has been motivated by an effort to develop a long-term history of Virginia's native societies and to produce collaborative histories through active engagement with descendant communities. Though this work among Virginia's native peoples represents, in several respects, a counterpoise to the Jamestown commemorations, the

greater historical awareness, native empowerment, and community building sought by advocates of civic engagement are unfinished projects.

The following article discusses a set of questions (and some preliminary answers) raised by recent efforts to conduct collaborative archaeological research in the context of investigating the site of Werowocomoco—the capital of the Powhatan chiefdom ca. 1607 (Figure 1). Though the settlement's name remains obscure, early colonial events at Werowocomoco are well-known today through popular films and literature, including the 1995 animated Disney film, *Pocahontas*, and the 2005 film, *The New World*. Due to its association with figures thought of as foundational to

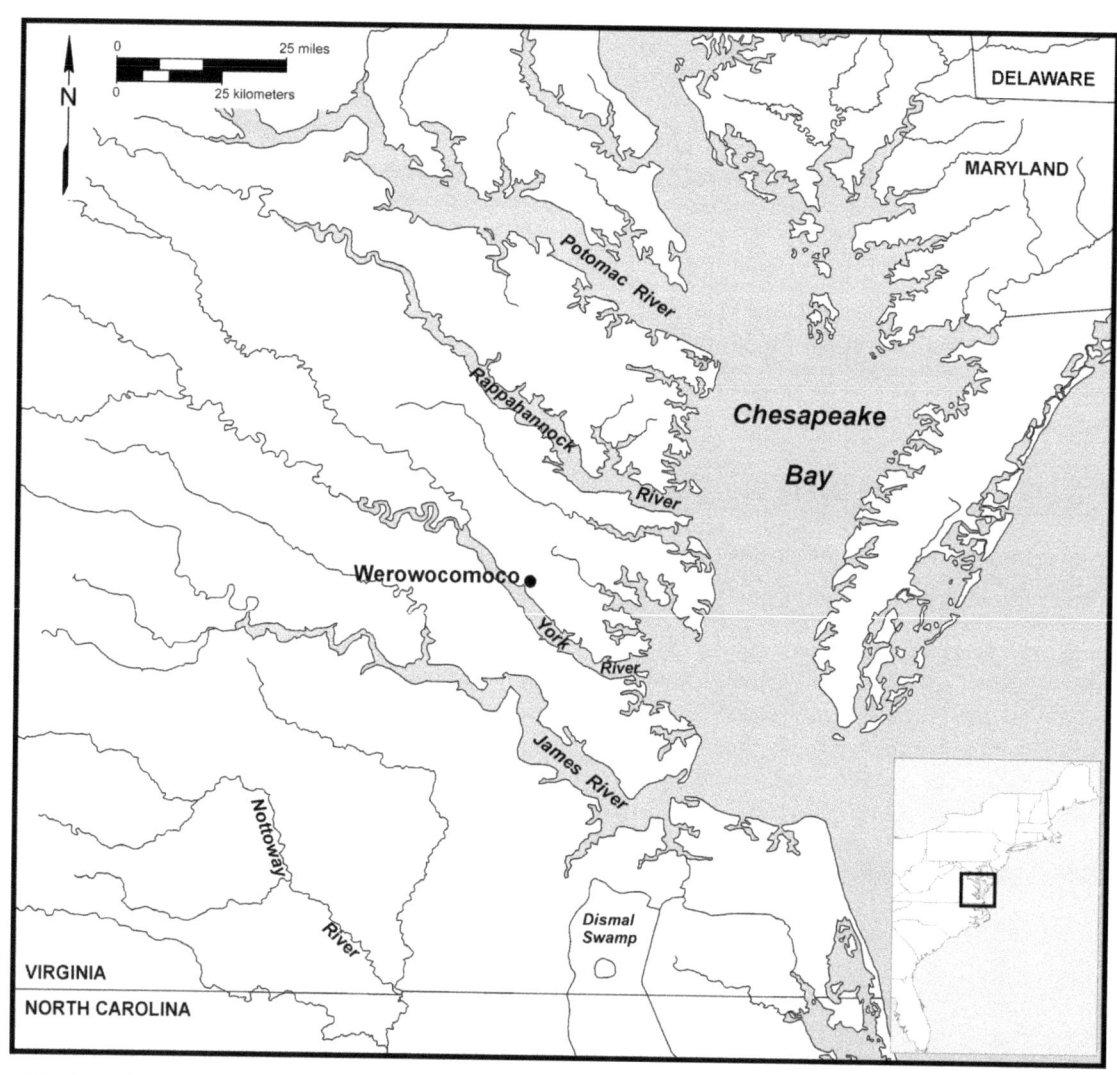

FIGURE 1. Werowocomoco site location. (Image by authors, 2010.)

American history—Pocahontas, John Smith, and Wahunsenacawh (also known as Powhatan)—the site has broad significance for those seeking to connect the past and the present in meaningful and empowering ways (Rountree and Turner 2002; Turner 2003).

Not surprisingly, several constituencies have drawn upon Tidewater Virginia's early colonial history to lend legitimacy to contemporary social and political agendas and economic goals. For example, the Jamestown-Yorktown Foundation (a Virginia governmental agency) has developed programming to commemorate Jamestown as the source and origin of American democracy and has invited tourists to experience the places where this history began. While this initiative is often portrayed as a revisionist corrective to claims that center America's origin point at Plymouth Rock, the notion that Jamestown was the birthplace of American democracy echoes themes emphasized on Jamestown's previous anniversaries (Gleach 2003; Hantman 2008).

Concurrent with this geographic adjustment to America's mythological origins are the efforts of Virginia Indian leaders to obtain recognition of the deep history and continued existence of native communities in the region. Today in Virginia there are 11 state-recognized tribes, two of which have retained reservation lands since the 17th century. None of these communities has attained federal recognition, though most are actively seeking this status.

Federal recognition represents an important priority for Virginia's tribal communities in part due to a postcolonial history marked by official efforts to deny native groups' identities and persistence (Rountree 1990; Moretti-Langholtz 1998). Virginia's tribes are persuing different paths toward recognition. For all, though, the written accounts and detailed maps produced by John Smith (1986), William Strachey (1953), and other English colonists during Jamestown's early days have become vital source materials. The guidelines created by the Department of the Interior's Bureau of Indian Affairs require that an American Indian entity petitioning for validation of government to government relations demonstrates historical and political continuity from "aboriginal" times to the present. As highlighted by Clifford (1988), this is a particularly stringent criterion for descendant communities in eastern North America whose lands were colonized more than

four centuries ago. Jamestown colonists' reports on Virginia's native inhabitants and their maps of the native political geography have become the earliest documentation of native people in the Chesapeake region, and thus a vital benchmark for contemporary communities.

The collaborative archaeological research at Werowocomoco has forced the members of the research team to confront the role that colonial documentary sources play in framing contemporary tribal agendas. The efforts to develop a collaborative archaeology at Werowocomoco raise questions of postcolonial history with implications that range far beyond Tidewater Virginia: (1) How has colonial reportage influenced the practices and identities of the colonized? (2) What are the emergent forms of native social identity and community construction after the end of the colonial era? (3) To what extent has decolonization been possible?

The remainder of this article addresses these questions through the lens of the Werowocomoco research, particularly the ways tribal members contend with expectations that their communities represent fixed, bounded, and historically continuous entities. These expectations, closely tied to the federal recognition process, shape the ways contemporary native communities in Tidewater Virginia position themselves vis-à-vis contemporary discussions of the native past. The tribes' strategic use of essentialist representations of their identities involves what may be a necessary step for communities still struggling for recognition. While documents produced during the early stages of colonial contact and related notions of essential tribal identities currently frame the relationship between contemporary Virginia Indians and the native past, opportunities to broaden these discussions are beginning to emerge. Investigations at Werowocomoco and related ethnohistoric reanalysis point toward a history of far-reaching and fluid social networks and modes of community construction that are too often masked behind colonial documentary sources. Moreover, the experience of collaborating with contemporary Virginia Indians indicates that the new social networks and forms of knowledge that have emerged from Virginia Indians' growing involvement with archaeology and heritage projects will play a role in native community construction. The discussion concludes by suggesting that the Werowocomoco Project has the potential to foster new forms of community building and new kinds of civic engagement with scholarly studies of Virginia's native past.

The Werowocomoco Project and Native Community Building, Past and Present

The Werowocomoco Research Project began in 2003 as a collaborative effort of researchers from William and Mary and the Virginia Department of Historic Resources in partnership with six tribes of Virginia Indians descended from the Powhatans. As outlined elsewhere (Gallivan et al. 2005; Gallivan 2007; Gallivan and Moretti-Langholtz 2007), the Werowocomoco Research Group has endeavored to make investigations of the site a starting point for civic engagement centered on the historical experiences of native communities in the Virginia Tidewater region. Civic engagement refers here to dialogue between researchers and various "publics" concerning the past, its contemporary consequences, and the potential for collective action that responds to these consequences. Such action is particularly important in the context of research on sites such as Werowocomoco, since native history in the region is marked by a series of ruptures separating descendant communities from their lands, their identities, and their historical narratives (Shackel 2001; Lightfoot 2005).

Particularly over the past quarter century, Virginia's tribes have taken the initiative in drawing attention to these ruptures and to their implications for contemporary political circumstances. As part of this process, native communities have become closely involved with the Werowocomoco research. This involvement grew out of a series of collaborative projects between Virginia's tribal communities and William and Mary cultural anthropologists at the American Indian Resource Center starting in 1998. Prior to initiating the project, the research group met with the Virginia Council on Indians, an intertribal advisory board to Virginia's governor and the General Assembly. The Virginia Council on Indians recommended that the Werowocomoco research include an all-native advisory board drawn from representatives from interested descendant communities. The resulting Virginia Indian Advisory Board (VIAB) meets regularly with the Werowocomoco Research Group and the owners of the Werowocomoco property, reviewing research designs, funding plans, public-outreach programs, and research reports. The VIAB consists of representatives from the two reservation tribes (Pamunkey and Mattaponi) and from four other Algonquian descendant communities: the Rappahannock, Chickahominie, Upper Mattaponi, and Nansemond. Among other guidelines, the VIAB has played a lead role in developing a policy for the discovery of human remains and for the display of artifacts and information derived from the Werowocomoco excavations. The VIAB has also facilitated regular tribal visitation to the site during the excavation season. Perhaps most importantly, the VIAB has served as a nexus of communication among various native leaders, fostering intertribal relationships built around links between the native past and present native priorities.

While efforts to share decision making with Virginia Indians in the context of the Werowocomoco research are, in many ways, unremarkable given that collaboration with descendant communities has become standard archaeological practice in much of North America, the involvement of native communities in archaeology is surprisingly unusual in Virginia. With the exception of Jeffrey Hantman et al.'s (2000) collaborative history of the Monacan Indians of central Virginia, few archaeologists have developed sustained relationships with contemporary Virginia's native communities. Until recently, investigations at native sites in the state were conducted mainly by avocationalists. The National Historic Preservation Act's cultural resource management (CRM) process frames most current investigations of native sites in the region. While openings for native consultation exist within this framework, the involvement of native representatives has been limited, in large part because most Virginia Indians have little direct experience with archaeology or with CRM.

As contemporary Virginia Indians have become more deeply involved in the Werowocomoco research, a growing number of tribal members have acquired knowledge of archaeological field methods and interpretive practices. Direct native participation in the excavations began in 2005 when the Pamunkey member of the VIAB joined the excavation crew at Werowocomoco. In 2006 two members of the Pamunkey tribe joined the excavations, and four members of Virginia's native community participated in the excavations in 2007. Since then, direct native involvement in the research has continued, and one member of the Pamunkey tribe has enrolled in the graduate anthropology program at William and Mary as a Ph.D. student. Though small in number, the archaeologists from Virginia's native communities have begun to alter the landscape of archaeological practice in Tidewater Virginia in subtle, yet important, ways.

Native archaeologists trained at Werowocomoco have begun to play roles in CRM projects as field technicians, monitors, and consultants. Tribal participation in CRM archaeology became particularly prominent in the context of the King William Reservoir, a project that saw sustained opposition from Virginia's tribal communities. The proposed reservoir would have flooded native sites near the Mattaponi and Pamunkey reservations, impacted traditional cultural properties, and harmed the region's fisheries. Tribal members from the Pamunkey, Mattaponi, and Upper Mattaponi tribes became involved in the King William Reservoir Project, developing new social networks in the process. Determined native opposition to the reservoir played an important role in its cancellation in 2009.

Strategic Essentialism and the Native Past in Virginia

Native archaeologists and leaders who have collaborated on the Werowocomoco Project generally frame the significance of Werowocomoco and other native sites differently than do cultural resource managers or academic archaeologists. They frequently discuss Werowocomoco in terms of the 2007 Jamestown quadricentenary, the native landscape depicted in colonists' accounts, and current efforts to obtain federal recognition. Some native participants in the Werowocomoco Project see the site as a bulwark against Jamestown, understood as the beachhead for English colonial expansion into native lands. Others are interested in the deep, precontact history of the site, citing their weariness of the attention paid to the English arrival at Jamestown.

Still others focus on the ways contemporary tribal identities may be linked to the native communities referenced in the early colonial accounts and on colonial-era maps depicting Virginia's social and political geography. Descriptions of the native social landscape produced by colonists

John Smith (1986) and William Strachey (1953) are typically read as reflecting the presence of over 30 tribes or districts, each with its own chiefly *werowance* residing in a central village (Turner 1976; Binford 1991; Potter 1993). Most of these tribal communities in coastal Virginia paid tribute to Wahunsenacawh as part of the Powhatan paramount chiefdom. As illustrated by John Smith in his "Map of Virginia," the Powhatan political geography was structured by a set of "king's houses" (i.e., villages with *werowances*) and "ordinary houses" (settlements lacking *werowances*), each depicted with an icon suggesting a uniform landscape of bounded polities.

In the process of joining a conversation about the past defined in large part by those living outside their communities, the native collaborators on the Werowocomoco Project engage in forms of what postcolonial theorist Gayatri Spivak has termed "strategic essentialism" (Spivak 1996) based on the fiction (often a conscious one) of tribes as "transhistorical subjects" (Hall 1996; Smith 2004) moving through time unaltered. For Spivak (1996:214), a strategic use of essentialism "in a scrupulously visible political interest" exposes how truths are created by revealing the particular historical circumstances from which they sprang. The native partners on the Werowocomoco Project have, at times, publically represented themselves and their communities in terms of tightly bounded, internally homogenous tribal identities, and a social landscape rooted in a certain moment of the past: the early 17th century as understood by English chroniclers. Privately, though, Virginia Indians also reflect upon the difficult histories of their communities after contact and upon the resilient relationships that structure native social networks in Virginia today, relationships involving important places (such as Christian churches), periodic events (such as powwows), and kinship ties (including many that transcend tribal boundaries).

As others have before (Clifford 1988, 2004; Field 1999; Fischer 1999; Meskell 2002:287), the research team has come to recognize over the course of the Werowocomoco Project that two of the primary commitments of contemporary anthropological practice can be at odds for archaeologists working toward civic engagement. The first is an obligation to collaborate closely with descendant communities that allows indigenous voices to be heard in the production of their histories (Brumfiel 2003:216). A second commitment is to studies of past social traditions guided by the principle that collective identities emerge out of political struggle and compromise rather than from fixed essences (Barth 1969; Rubertone 2001), and that the processes which maintain these identities are separate from those that created them (Comaroff and Comaroff 1992:60–61).

Archaeologists foregrounding this constructivist position have called into question previous understandings of social identity and its relationship to the archaeological record (Jones 1997; Smith 2004). These discussions start with the premise that social collectivities result when "people construct shared stories about who they are, how they are connected, and what has happened to them" (Tilly 2003:608). Objects, built environments, and meaningful places may channel and express social identities in a recursive fashion and "in relation to a specific sociocultural formation and in relation to a particular political apparatus" (Smith 2004:14). The term "identity" does not travel well across cultures, however, since people in distant times and places did not use the term in its contemporary sense. Rather, people have understood human personhood, social collectivities, and their connections in historically and culturally distinctive terms (Handler 1994:34).

Drawing from these ideas and from related efforts to throw light on the recent invention of supposedly ancient "traditions" (Hobsbawm and Ranger 1992), archaeologists have begun to call into question contemporary efforts by national, religious, and linguistic groups to claim direct and unbroken connections to ancient social entities. The archaeologists who have pursued most rigorously the implications of the social-constructivist position as it relates to contemporary identity politics often work within settings where archaeology serves an explicitly nationalist agenda (Kohl 1998), where local populations distance themselves from the archaeological past (Smith 2004), or where there are presumed links between the archaeological past and a politically powerful, historically confident, and economically dominant society (Dietler 1994).

After four centuries of colonial violence and dispossession followed by bureaucratic efforts to deny the existence of American Indians in Virginia, native communities here today are not politically powerful, historically confident, or economically dominant. As a result, scholarly deconstruction of the claimed existence of essentialized identities and transhistorical subjects runs a risk of alignment with reactionary political agendas. This is particularly true when such claims are made by disenfranchised descendants of colonized communities simply seeking a voice in discussions of the past. During the recent rise of native political activism, Werowocomoco has become an icon of Virginia Indian identity. It has been referenced in tribal agendas that reinforce boundaries and that limit discussion of continuities and discontinuities in Virginia's native history. As a result, civic engagement at Werowocomoco raises a question rarely addressed in archaeology: What should archaeologists' posture be vis-à-vis the political aspirations of descendant communities whose strategic essentialism flies in the face of constructivist notions of social identity?

Reassessing Social Construction in Tidewater Virginia

If one accepts the premise that cultures are meaningful orders and "traditions are invented in the specific terms of the people who construct them" (Sahlins 1999:409), then the Tidewater Algonquian past should offer clues to understanding contemporary social construction. The various identity claims of Virginia Indians may, in fact, be situational, strategic, and (at times) framed by today's circumstances. The ways these groups construct shared stories about who they are and how they are connected draws on older cultural structures as well as on politically expedient uses of the past, however. Understanding these structures requires knowledge of the complicated and, at times, difficult history of Tidewater Algonquian communities before and after contact. This history includes efforts by native communities to build kin-based networks that established political alliances prior to the colonial era, to maintain connections to place amidst colonial disruption of the native landscape, and to weather a postcolonial history that attempted to deny their identities as native peoples (Moretti-Langholtz 1998; Gallivan 2007; Woodard 2008).

Werowocomoco's archaeology and ethnohistory offer a starting point for considering native social construction of the past and present (Gallivan et al. 2005). Investigations at the site indicate that a horticultural village was established at the site ca. A.D. 1200. Beginning ca. 1300, residents at Werowocomoco began to construct a series of concentric ditch features within the interior of the site (Figure 2). The landscape features are roughly 2 m wide, 1 m deep, extend over 200 m, and appear to segregate the spaces behind them. A series of radiocarbon dates from the feature fill reflect construction and use of the ditches during the late 13th through early 17th centuries.

Deposits from the 13th through 16th century behind the ditches in the site interior contain pottery from several different ceramic traditions linked to communities throughout the Tidewater region. The local ceramics that occur in this portion of the site have the sizes and shapes of serving vessels (as opposed to pots for cooking or storage), possibly related to feasting events in this part of the settlement. Copper sheeting,

some of it refashioned into tubular beads, was also recovered from this portion of the site in the vicinity of a large native structure dated to the early 17th century. Testing of the copper's elemental composition indicates that the materials were trade goods coming to Werowocomoco from Jamestown.

Ethnohistorical sources note that Wahunsenacawh moved to Werowocomoco as he consolidated regional authority (Williamson 2003). By the early 17th century, Jamestown colonists wrote of visiting Werowocomoco and of meeting with paramount chief Wahunsenacawh at the village. During a series of events at the village, Wahunsenacawh proclaimed that Jamestown colonists were no longer to be considered strangers (*tassantasses*) or Paspaheghs (the Algonquian district surrounding Jamestown), but *Powhatans*. The culturally specific terms through which Wahunsenacawh framed his efforts at political and social

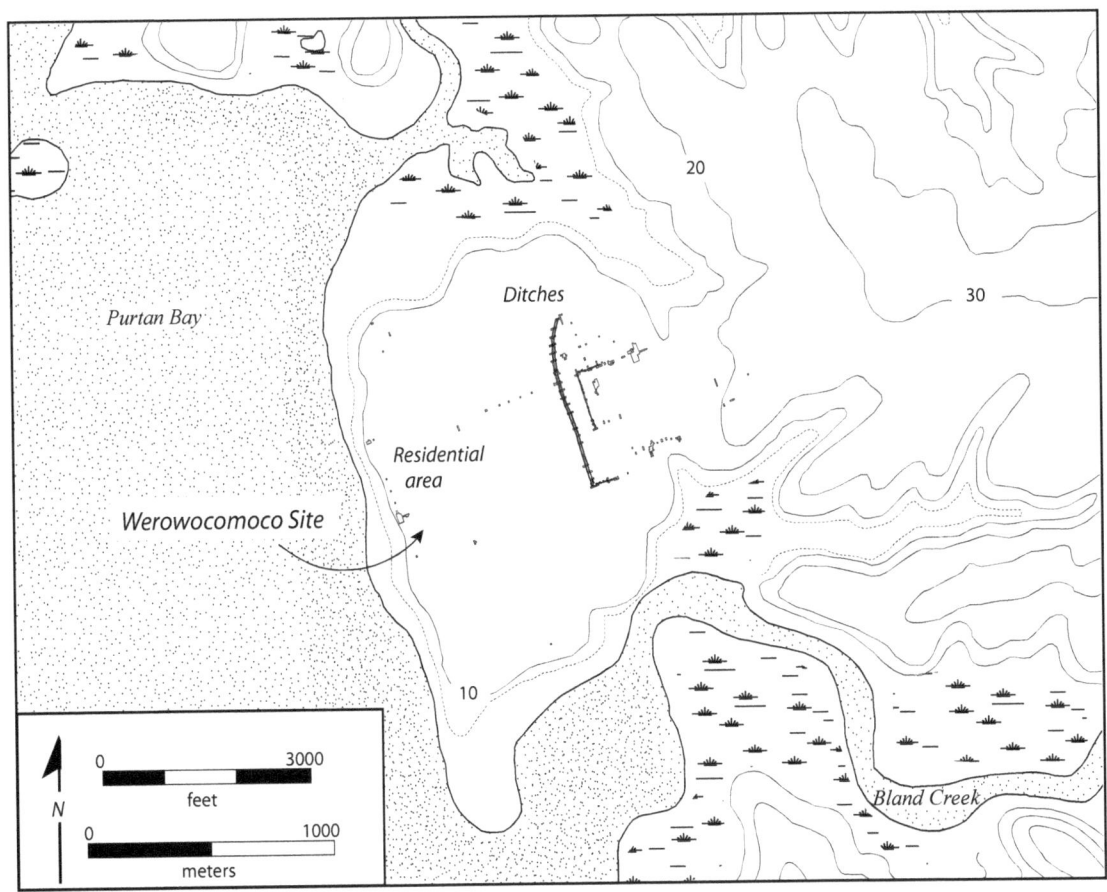

FIGURE 2. Werowocomoco site plan. (Image by authors, 2010.)

construction centered on the language of Algonquian kinship and social politics, including the ceremonial creation of fictive kin. This process involved Smith's becoming Wahunsenacawh's relative.

Werowocomoco emerges from this reading of the record as a powerful ceremonial place that existed centuries before Wahunsenacawh's rise to power. On the eve of English colonization, the site became a center for the construction of a "Powhatan" political network that stretched across communities with distinct cultural practices and alternative centers of political and sacred authority. During the contact period Wahunsenacawh took steps to ensure that Werowocomoco became a place of new social connections that briefly entangled the Jamestown colonists. Werowocomoco's history includes the construction of political networks centered on a ceremonial place, regional connections that incorporated multiple local traditions, and the instrumental use of kinship. Werowocomoco's residents incorporated "foreign" elements originating outside Werowocomoco—nonlocal pottery, Jamestown copper, the colonists, and even Wahunsenacawh himself—by redefining each in local terms. In fact, Werowocomoco's deep history highlights social networks that are difficult to recognize in colonists' depictions of the native political geography. The site's archaeological and ethnohistorical records point toward fundamental practices that structured Virginia Algonquian history before and after contact. Central places of ceremony, social networks that stretched across distinct cultural traditions, and kinship ties drawing together different communities were ordering principles of native history that continue to reverberate in Virginia Indian communities today.

Where scholars have framed the early colonial history of the "Powhatans" in the neoevolutionary terms of a chiefdom comprised of 32 tightly bounded political districts, a close reading of colonial sources indicates that Tidewater Algonquian social organization deserves to be recast in local terms. Colonists struggled to describe indigenous societies whose social structures accommodated a considerable degree of fluidity, pluralism, and transformation. The shifting native alliances detailed in the documentary record, both before and after Jamestown's settlement, indicate more sociopolitical flexibility than has been recognized. Previous interpretations of the contact-era

Tidewater saw "king's houses," villages, and estimated warrior counts as literal representations of static, bounded polities. A reassessment of the primary documents indicates that kinship relations and lineage groups' attachment to place both played fundamental roles in structuring Algonquian political strategies during the 16th and 17th centuries (Woodard 2008).

The effort to revisit previous interpretations of the primary record developed as a direct outgrowth of the Werowocomoco excavations and the recognition that the settlement represented a center of regional social networks long before Wahunsenacawh's residence there. Through collaborative efforts the research team sought to revisit and reconcile inconsistencies in colonial reports of Powhatan social organization. Equally, the researchers became interested in the ways in which native partners discussed their historical and modern relationship with the site of Werowocomoco, their past and current kinship relations with each other, and their representations of contemporary political structures. These conversations suggest that several social dynamics are key to the reassessment of Tidewater Algonquian ethnohistory. First, recent studies of Algonquian linguistics (Rudes 2003) indicate that community names were often linked to meaningful places in the region's cultural landscape (Woodard 2007). Thus, the names of settlements were often related to geography and not to the political designations that would later come to represent "tribal" names during the colonial and postcolonial periods. Secondly, the ease with which individuals moved between local communities highlights the importance of crosscutting social ties centered on matrilineages. Thirdly, the competition for elite women of distinction during the 16th and early 17th centuries parallels the importance of matrilineages and their ability to confer chiefly status. This role is evidenced by the placement of Wahunsenacawh's sons in matrilineal chiefly positions through strategic elite marriages and bride capture (Woodard 2008).

The 17th-century English colonization of the Chesapeake led to a retreat from Werowocomoco and the interruption of native social dynamics. The subsequent 18th- and 19th-century history of these communities entailed population declines, geographic dislocation, social rearrangement, loss of language, and an erosion of traditional cultural practices. With few exceptions, native communities in Tidewater Virginia faded from political power and from view after Bacon's Rebellion in 1676 and the signing of the Treaty of Middle Plantation in 1677. In time, Virginia Indians rearranged the ritual and political dimensions of Algonquian life around an outside cultural element—Christianity. During the 18th century "Indian Churches" were established throughout Virginia. These churches provided educational opportunities and a measure of political autonomy and protection for community members and leaders. The church became the primary institution around which native social relations were replicated and presented to the nonnative population. By giving Virginia Indians a cloak of respectability in the eyes of their nonnative neighbors, social ties, especially kinship structures, were retained and reconfigured. Under the auspices of a church hierarchy that supported leader-families and allowed native communities to "raise up" their own clergy, aspects of traditional decisionmaking persisted in the native communities (Moretti-Langholtz 2003).

Anthropologists have played a central role in the ways that Virginia Algonquian history was reimagined in the 20th century (Mooney 1907; Speck 1928). Both James Mooney and Frank Speck worked among Virginia's native communities in the early part of the 20th century. Speck went so far as to encourage coastal communities to reestablish the "Powhatan Confederacy." Speck's suggestion was not acted upon, and in fact from 1924 to 1968 Virginia's Indian communities kept a low profile due in large part to the Racial Integrity Law that attempted to legislate a Virginia Indian identity out of existence (Rountree 1990; Moretti-Langholtz 1998). While two of the oldest reservations in the U.S. are in Virginia, dating to 1648, these two tribes and six other state-recognized tribes only received formal state recognition between 1983 and 1989. Three additional tribes received state recognition in 2010. To date, none of the Virginia tribes has federal recognition.

There are significant gaps in the foregoing timeline, and such gaps in the historical record are problematic for tribes in the eastern part of the country who seek to be recognized as Native American (Sider 2003). The criteria for federal recognition are the principal driving force behind the creation of an "anthropologically verifiable"

account of a group with a continuous history linked by blood ties to an ancestral community that resides in a narrowly defined region. Thus, alongside such standards as enduring cultural traditions and ongoing tribal government, a geographically bounded social entity must be documented as evidence in the legal battles for state and federal recognition. The notions of sociality implicit in these criteria privilege a set of essences rarely found in the archaeological record or in ethnographic accounts. Nonetheless, anthropologists, including Mooney and Speck, have helped to create these models of Virginia Algonquian society as part of their effort to empower native communities through the strategic use of essentialism.

Such essentialism may be mobilized in defense of a group's identity or its claim to territory (Field 1999). Similar strategies have appeared with regard to the excavations at Werowocomoco such that the site has become a locus of reconnected and reordered social relations among six of the seven Powhatan-descendant tribes. The all-native advisory board to the project exemplifies this process. The two representatives from the reservation tribes have expressed a special attachment to the Werowocomoco site. The Pamunkey and Mattaponi have been particularly supportive of the research, taking pains to meet regularly with the research team and offer advice on the project. Drawing on a history that places them as the lineal descendants of Wahunsenacawh, these groups have at times publically stood against leaders of the other tribes who they perceive as exerting too great an influence over the site. The two representatives from the reservations have explained that "we used to be one ... and we are one on this project," thus asserting themselves in ways that the other tribes do not.

As the Rappahannock chief and VIAB member said, "Werowocomoco has remained hidden but it emerged at a time when the native community is in a stronger position to participate in the excavation. We know that had this excavation taken place even a few years ago no one would have asked us to participate." The collective challenge is to widen discourse about Werowocomoco's past to include new approaches to understanding the organization of native societies in the Chesapeake. This challenge is fraught with danger.

On the one hand, the Werowocomoco Project is actively building relationships with local tribes.

On the other hand, the possibility for strained relationships with these tribes exists as long as a rigid, essentialist model frames discussions of the 17th-century history and contemporary "Powhatan" society. A critique of the "nonnegotiable," essentialist model must be undertaken with sensitivity and an eye toward understanding the need for native voices to resituate themselves within the complicated relationships of the postcolonial landscape.

Conclusion

In recent years archaeologists have developed a much greater appreciation of the ways that members of descendant communities draw on the past to negotiate the present and to position themselves for the future (Zimmerman 1996; Swidler et al. 1997; Dongoske et al. 2000; Ferguson and Colwell-Chanthaphonh 2006; Kerber 2006; Little and Shackel 2007; Smith and Wobst 2007; Colwell-Chanthaphonh and Ferguson 2008; Silliman 2008). For native communities in Tidewater Virginia, the early 17th-century political landscape outlined by colonial chroniclers represents a powerful evidentiary basis from which to counter a postcolonial history that has denied their existence. Strategic essentialism offers contemporary Virginia Indians a means of reconnecting their communities to American historical narratives that resonate powerfully today.

Such strategies may be necessary in the short term, though the authors hope that the Werowocomoco research offers a point of departure for "decolonizing" the accepted models of native social construction. Werowocomoco's archaeological and ethnohistorical records indicate that the site represented a ceremonial center for the construction of social and political networks that stretched across multiple communities for centuries prior to contact. The site's deep history evidences modes of social construction that differed in important ways from the political geography of uniform settlements and tightly bounded tribes imagined by early colonial writers and cartographers. Looking beyond the colonial accounts of English settlers at Jamestown, there are indications that native communities constructed pluralistic political networks prior to the colonial era, maintained and reconfigured social ties amidst the disruptive violence of the colonial era, and successfully weathered a postcolonial history

that has, at times, denied their existence. They have done so by creatively incorporating new cultural elements including colonists, Christianity, and (most recently) archaeology, while retaining meaningful connections to place as well as kinship ties that stretch across diverse communities.

Returning briefly to the three questions posed in the introduction, it appears that archaeological sites including Werowocomoco will likely serve as a prism through which native communities negotiate the past in the present, foster decolonization, and construct new forms of postcolonial identities.

Native partners on the Werowocomoco Project have encouraged a research focus on the long-term, *precontact* history of the place, thereby shifting attention away from the post-1607 colonial narrative that centers on Jamestown. As one of the native advisory board members once said, "Let them have Jamestown, Werowocomoco is ours." In order to operationalize this perspective, the research design prioritizes investigation of Werowocomoco's Late Woodland archaeology along with its contact-period deposits. The effort to develop a long-term "biography of place" for the settlement includes an extensive regimen of radiocarbon dates and archaeobotanical analyses allowing the research team to unpack Werowocomoco's deep history (Gallivan 2007). Related efforts include public outreach that has resulted in changes to Virginia's public school curricula highlighting Werowocomoco's precolonial past. By foregrounding the precontact history, the native partners working on the project have influenced the Werowocomoco research process and resituated themselves and their communities against an overwhelmingly colonialist narrative.

For both natives and scholars who partner with them, however, it may not be possible to completely avoid a 17th-century colonialist idiom in the 21st century, particularly in the context of a federal recognition process that revolves around transhistorical tribal identities and privileges textual sources written by colonial authors. Native community members make strategic use of essentialized tribal identities drawn from 17th-century source materials, even as many are aware of the problems with these uses.

The recent study of Werowocomoco offers an opening for a respectful and public reconsideration of native social construction in the past and in the present, as well as an archaeological basis for calling into question federal recognition criteria rooted in essentialist notions of trans-historical native social organization. Despite the importance of colonial-era sources as touchstones for contemporary native communities in Virginia, social networks are emerging that offer alternative modes of community building alongside the tribal models first imagined by English colonists. Social networks that cross boundaries of community have always existed in Virginia. Often these networks have been structured by a rootedness to place, expressed through the idiom of kinship, and built on the active incorporation of new, "foreign" symbols into existing structures. The reemergence of Werowocomoco has provided a place where native advisors, archaeologists, and activists have begun to reinvent these networks for the 21st century. Virginia Indians' involvement in the Werowocomoco Project offers them a central role in the investigation of this site, the former nexus of the Powhatan chiefdom.

The results of collaborative archaeology at Werowocomoco suggest that decolonization (understood as a social reconstruction free from colonial influence) will be difficult to accomplish in Tidewater Virginia, at least in the short run. Nonetheless, the expanding involvement of native scholars in archaeological research and the growing importance of various forms of indigenous archaeology represent critical developments toward this end (Watkins 2000; Atalay 2006). Even as colonialist notions of tribal boundaries frame public discussions of the site, social links across communities are even more apparent behind the scenes of the Werowocomoco partnership. Fostering such community building around Werowocomoco will require a sustained effort to provide native descendants ready access to the site and to its history.

Acknowledgements

We thank Paul Shackel, David Gadsby, and Barbara Little for giving us the opportunity to contribute to this conversation and for their recognition that the topic deserves frank discussion. The research referenced here represents a fundamentally collaborative effort. We are deeply grateful for the opportunity to work on this project offered by our Werowocomoco Research Group colleagues Randy Turner, David Brown, and Thane Harpole who initiated investigations at the site prior to our involvement and invited us to join them. Ashley Atkins, Jeff Hantman, and Matt Liebmann reviewed drafts of this article and helped us improve our thinking and our writing. Three anonymous reviewers also offered constructive criticism of an earlier draft that was particularly valuable. Most importantly, we appreciate the support and guidance offered by our Virginia Indian partners, including Virginia Indian Advisory Board members Jeff Brown (Pamunkey), Kerry Cannaday (Chickahominy), Assistant Chief Mark Custalow (Mattaponi), Chief G. Anne Richardson (Rappahannock), Lee Lockamy (Nansemond), and Reggie Tupponce (Upper Mattaponi). Conversations with Chief Kevin Brown of the Pamunkey Tribe and Chief Carl Custalow of the Mattaponi Tribe also inform our perspectives on Werowocomoco. Finally, we thank the archaeologists from the Virginia native community, including Ashley Atkins, Jeff Brown, James Krigsvold, Ethan Brown, and Gloria Custalow, whose direct involvement in the Werowocomoco excavations and reflections on the project allowed us to see the native history of Tidewater Virginia in a different light.

References

ATALAY, SONYA
2006 Indigenous Archaeology as Decolonizing Practice. *American Indian Quarterly* 30(3&4):280–310.

BARTH, FREDRIK
1969 *Ethnic Groups and Boundaries. The Social Organization of Culture Difference.* Little, Boston, MA.

BINFORD, LEWIS R.
1991 *Cultural Diversity Among Aboriginal Cultures of Coastal Virginia and North Carolina.* Garland, New York, NY.

BRUMFIEL, ELIZABETH M.
2003 It's a Material World: History, Artifacts, and Anthropology. *Annual Review of Anthropology* 32(1):205–223.

CLIFFORD, JAMES
1988 Identity in Mashpee. In *The Predicament of Culture: Twentieth-Century Ethnography, Literature, and Art,* James Clifford, editor, pp. 277–348. Harvard University Press, Cambridge, MA.
2004 Looking Several Ways: Anthropology and Native Heritage in Alaska. *Current Anthropology* 45(26):5–30.

COLWELL-CHANTHAPHONH, CHIP, AND T. J. FERGUSON
2008 *Collaboration in Archaeological Practice: Engaging Descendant Communities.* AltaMira Press, Lanham, MD.

COLWELL-CHANTHAPHONH, CHIP, T. J. FERGUSON, DOROTHY LIPPERT, RANDALL II. McGUIRE, GEORGE P. NICHOLAS, AND JOE WATKINS
2010 The Premise and Promise of Indigenous Archaeology. *American Antiquity* 75(2):228–238.

COMAROFF, JOHN L., AND JEAN COMAROFF
1992 *Ethnography and the Historical Imagination*. Westview Press, Boulder, CO.

CROES, DALE R.
2010 Courage and Thoughtful Scholarship = Indigenous Archaeology Partnerships. *American Antiquity* 75(2):211–216.

DIETLER, MICHAEL
1994 "Our Ancestors the Gauls": Archaeology, Ethnic Nationalism, and the Manipulation of Celtic Identity in Modern Europe. *American Anthropologist* 96(3):584–605.

DONGOSKE, KURT E., MARK S. ALDENDERFER, AND KAREN DOEHNER (EDITORS)
2000 *Working Together: Native Americans and Archaeologists*. Society for American Archaeology, Washington, DC.

FERGUSON, T. J., AND CHIP COLWELL-CHANTHAPHONH
2006 *History is in the Land: Multivocal Tribal Traditions in Arizona's San Pedro Valley*. University of Arizona Press, Tucson.

FIELD, LES W.
1999 CA Forum on Anthropology in Public: Complicities and Collaborations: Anthropologists and the "Unacknowledged Tribes" of California. *Current Anthropology* 40(2):193–209.

FISCHER, EDWARD F.
1999 Cultural Logic and Maya Identity: Rethinking Constructivism and Essentialism. *Current Anthropology* 40(4):473–499.

GALLIVAN, MARTIN D.
2007 Powhatan's Werowocomoco: Constructing Place, Polity, and Personhood in the Chesapeake, C.E. 1200–C.E. 1609. *American Anthropologist* 109(1):85–100.

GALLIVAN, MARTIN D., AND DANIELLE MORETTI-LANGHOLTZ
2007 Civic Engagement at Werowocomoco: Reasserting Native Narratives from a Powhatan Place of Power. In *Archaeology as a Tool of Civic Engagement*, Barbara J. Little and Paul A. Shackel, editors, pp. 47–66. AltaMira Press, Lanham, MD.

GALLIVAN, MARTIN D., THANE HARPOLE, DAVID A. BROWN, DANIELLE MORETTI-LANGHOLTZ, AND E. RANDOLPH TURNER III
2005 *The Werowocomoco Research Project: Background and 2003 Archaeological Field Season Results*. Virginia Department of Historic Resources, Technical Report Series, 15. Richmond.

GLEACH, FREDERIC WRIGHT
2003 Pocahontas at the Fair: Crafting Identities at the 1907 Jamestown Exposition. *Ethnohistory* 50(3):419–445.

HALL, STUART
1996 New Ethnicities. In *Stuart Hall: Critical Dialogues in Cultural Studies*, David Morley and Kuan-Hsing Chen, editors, pp. 441–449. Routledge, London, UK.

HANDLER, RICHARD
1994 Is "Identity" a Useful Cross-cultural Concept? In *Commemorations: The Politics of National Identity*, J. Gillis, editor, pp. 27–40. Princeton University Press, Princeton, NJ.

HANTMAN, JEFFREY L., KARENNE WOOD, AND DIANE SHIELDS
2000 Writing Collaborative History: How the Monacan Nation and Archaeologists Worked Together to Enrich our Understanding of Virginia's Native Peoples. *Archaeology* 53(5):56–59.

HANTMAN, JEFFREY L.
2008 Jamestown's 400th Anniversary: Old Themes, New Words, New Meanings for Virginia Indians. In *Archaeologies of Placemaking: Monuments, Memories, and Engagement in Native North America*, Patricia E. Rubertone, editor, pp. 217–241. Left Coast Press, Walnut Creek, CA.

HOBSBAWM, ERIC J., AND TERENCE O. RANGER (EDITORS)
1992 *The Invention of Tradition*. Cambridge University Press, Cambridge, UK.

HORNING, AUDREY
2006 Archaeology and the Construction of America's Jamestown. *Post-Medieval Archaeology* 40(1):1–27.

JONES, SIAN
1997 *The Archaeology of Ethnicity: Constructing Identities in the Past and Present*. Routledge, London, UK.

KERBER, JORDAN E. (EDITOR)
2006 *Cross-Cultural Collaboration: Native Peoples and Archaeology in the Northeastern United States*. University of Nebraska Press, Lincoln.

KOHL, PHILIP L.
1998 Nationalism and Archaeology: On the Constructions of Nations and the Reconstructions of the Remote Past. *Annual Review of Anthropology* 27:223–246.

LIGHTFOOT, KENT G.
2005 *Indians, Missionaries, and Merchants: The Legacy of Colonial Encounters on the California Frontiers*. University of California Press, Berkeley.

LITTLE, BARBARA J., AND PAUL A. SHACKEL (EDITORS)
2007 *Archaeology as a Tool of Civic Engagement*. AltaMira Press, Lanham, MD.

McGHEE, ROBERT M.
2008 Aboriginalism and the Problem of Indigenous Archaeology. *American Antiquity* 73(4):579–597.

2010   Of Strawmen, Herrings, and Frustrated Expectations. *American Antiquity* 75(2):239–243.

MESKELL, LYNN
2002   The Intersections of Identity and Politics in Archaeology. *Annual Review of Anthropology* 31:279–301.

MOONEY, JAMES
1907   The Powhatan Confederacy, Past and Present. *American Anthropologist* 9(1):129–152.

MORETTI-LANGHOLTZ, DANIELLE
1998   *Other Names I Have Been Called: Political Resurgence Among Virginia Indians in the Twentieth Century.* Doctoral dissertation, Department of Anthropology, University of Oklahoma. University Microfilms International, Ann Arbor, MI.
2003   The Rise of Christianity Among Virginia Indians. Paper presented at the Middle Atlantic Archaeological Conference, Ocean City, MD.

POTTER, STEPHEN R.
1993   *Commoners, Tribute, and Chiefs: The Development of Algonquian Culture in the Potomac Valley.* University Press of Virginia, Charlottesville.

ROUNTREE, HELEN C.
1990   *Pocahontas's People: The Powhatan Indians of Virginia through Four Centuries.* University of Oklahoma Press, Norman.

ROUNTREE, HELEN C., AND E. RANDOLPH TURNER
2002   *Before and After Jamestown: Virginia's Powhatans and Their Predecessors.* University Press of Florida, Gainesville.

RUBERTONE, PATRICIA E.
2001   *Grave Undertakings: An Archaeology of Roger Williams and the Narragansett Indians.* Smithsonian Institution Press, Washington, DC.

RUDES, BLAIR
2005   The Evidence for Dialects of Virginia Algonquian. Paper presented at the Annual Meeting of the Society for the Study of Indigenous Languages of the Americas, Oakland, CA.

SAHLINS, MARSHALL
1999   Two or Three Things that I Know about Culture. *Journal of the Royal Anthropological Institute* 5(3):399–421.

SHACKEL, PAUL A.
2001   Public Memory and the Search for Power in American Historical Archaeology. *American Anthropologist* 103(3):655–670.

SIDER, GERALD M.
2003   *Living Indian Histories: Lumbee and Tuscarora People in North Carolina.* University of North Carolina Press, Chapel Hill.

SILLIMAN, STEPHEN W. (EDITOR)
2010   The Value and Diversity of Indigenous Archaeology: A Response to McGhee. *American Antiquity* 75(2):217–220.

2008   *Collaborating at the Trowel's Edge: Teaching and Learning in Indigenous Archaeology.* University of Arizona Press and the Amerind Foundation, Tucson.

SMITH, ADAM T.
2004   The End of the Essential Archaeological Subject. *Archaeological Dialogues* 11(1):1–20.

SMITH, JOHN
1986   A Map of Virginia. In *The Complete Works of Captain John Smith (1580–1631)*, Vol. 1, P. L. Barbour, editor, pp. 119–189. University of North Carolina Press, Chapel Hill.

SMITH, CLAIRE, AND H. MARTIN WOBST (EDITORS)
2007   *Indigenous Archaeologies: Decolonising Theory and Practice.* Routledge, New York, NY.

SPECK, FRANK G.
1928   Chapters on the Ethnology of the Powhatan Tribes of Virginia. *Indian Notes and Monographs* 1(5). Museum of the American Indian, Heye Foundation, New York, NY.

SPIVAK, GAYATRI CHAKRAVORTY
1996   *The Spivak Reader: Selected Works of Gayatri Chakravorty Spivak.* Routledge, New York, NY.

STRACHEY, WILLIAM
1953   *The Historie of Travell into Virginia Britania.* Hakluyt Society, London, UK.

SWIDLER, NINA, KURT E. DONGOSKE, ROGER ANYON, AND ALAN S. DOWNER (EDITORS)
1997   *Native Americans and Archaeologists: Stepping Stones to Common Ground.* AltaMira Press, Walnut Creek, CA.

TILLY, CHARLES
2003   Political Identities in Changing Polities. *Social Research* 70(2):605–620.

TURNER, E. RANDOLPH, III
1976   *An Archaeological and Ethnohistorical Study on the Evolution of Rank Societies in the Virginia Coastal Plain.* Doctoral dissertation, Department of Anthropology, Pennsylvania State University. University Microfilms International, Ann Arbor, MI.
2003   Werowocomoco: Ye Seate of Powhatan. *Notes on Virginia* 47:40–45.

WATKINS, JOE
2000   *Indigenous Archaeology: American Indian Values and Scientific Practice.* AltaMira Press, Walnut Creek, CA.

WILLIAMSON, MARGARET HOLMES
2003   *Powhatan Lords of Life and Death: Command and Consent in Seventeenth-Century Virginia.* University of Nebraska Press, Lincoln.

WILCOX, MICHAEL
2010   Saving Indigenous Peoples from Ourselves; Separate but Equal Archaeology Is Not Scientific Archaeology. *American Antiquity* 75(2):221–227.

Martin Gallivan, Danielle Moretti-Langhotz, and Buck Woodard

WOODARD, BUCK
  2007 Powhatan Essentialism. Paper presented at the 40th Conference on Historical and Underwater Archaeology, Williamsburg, VA.
  2008 Degrees of Relatedness: The Social Politics of Algonquian Kinship in the Contact Era Chesapeake. Master's thesis, Department of Anthropology, College of William and Mary, Williamsburg, VA.

ZIMMERMAN, LARRY J.
  1996 Epilogue: A New and Different Archaeology? *American Indian Quarterly* 20(2):297–307.

MARTIN GALLIVAN
DEPARTMENT OF ANTHROPOLOGY
COLLEGE OF WILLIAM AND MARY
WILLIAMSBURG, VA 23187-8795

DANIELLE MORETTI-LANGHOLTZ
DEPARTMENT OF ANTHROPOLOGY
COLLEGE OF WILLIAM AND MARY
WILLIAMSBURG, VA 23187-8795

BUCK WOODARD
DEPARTMENT OF ANTHROPOLOGY
COLLEGE OF WILLIAM AND MARY
WILLIAMSBURG, VA 23187-8795

2013 Reversing the Narrative of Hillbilly History: A Case Study. In *Reversing the Narrative*, Paul A. Shackel and Michael P. Roller, editors. Thematic issue, *Historical Archaeology* 47(3):36-51

Jamie C. Brandon

Reversing the Narrative of Hillbilly History: A Case Study Using Archaeology at Van Winkle's Mill in the Arkansas Ozarks

ABSTRACT

One of the most powerful and pervasive narratives at work in the Arkansas Ozark Mountains is that of the "hillbilly." This narrative emphasizes ruralness, whiteness, and an antimodern attitude that both frames how the world sees the Ozarks and how Arkansans see themselves. Since 1997, archaeological investigations have been ongoing at Van Winkle's Mill, the site of a late-19th-century sawmill community in the Arkansas Ozarks. This multidisciplinary research endeavor has provided important information about the African diaspora in the Ozarks and also aided in the understanding of the industrialization and modernization of the region. Most importantly, it provided a platform for public history that may shed light on the processes of remembering and forgetting at work in Ozark history that have led to the proliferation of myths about the Ozark past and the erasure of a rich African American heritage in the region.

Introduction

The Ozarks, like their cousins the Appalachian Mountains, hold a particular place in modern cultural memory and imagination. That "place" is uniquely American, decidedly rural, antimodern, and *white* (Brandon 2004a:78–137; Harkins 2004; Blevins 2009). This Upland South seems wholly subsumed under and conflated with what it means to be rural in America—perhaps more so than any other region of the country. Certainly, "the portrayal of southern mountain people as premodern and ignorant hillbillies is one of the most lasting and pervasive images in American popular iconography" (Harkins 2004:3).

This "hillbilly history" is not the only historical narrative at work in the Arkansas Ozarks, but it is the most powerful and pervasive one. Moreover, it is a narrative that has great currency on the local, regional, and national levels of discourse. In complex ways, this narrative frames how the world sees the region and how those who call the Ozarks home see themselves (Blevins 2009). One of the many facets of the hillbilly narrative is that it masks the diversity inherent in the region—this extends not only to class and the rural/urban dichotomy, but also to ethnicity and race. The fact that the backwoods yeomen farmer of the narrative is invariably white and of Scots Irish descent obscures the Native Americans, Germans, Mennonites, Swiss, Poles, Bohemians, Moravians, and Italians who all called the Ozarks home in the 19th century (Brandon 2004a:17–20). More importantly for this case study the hillbilly's whiteness erases any African American heritage in the Ozarks. More than that, as will be seen, removing racial diversity from Ozark history erases *racism* in the region.

While archaeological work was ongoing at the site of Van Winkle's Mill, a 19th-century sawmill community in the Arkansas Ozarks that utilized African American labor both before and after the Civil War, visitors were constantly surprised that we archaeologists were working on a site connected with the African diaspora. They were surprised that there was, in fact, *any* African American heritage in the Ozarks. This led to an in-depth study of the hillbilly trope, its history, and the social work that it does in our collective memories (Brandon 2004a). Moreover, it led to an attempt to use the archaeology at the Van Winkle's Mill site as a mechanism to "reverse the narrative" presented by hillbilly history in the Arkansas Ozarks.

While the Arkansas Ozark Mountains are not a place widely associated with the African diaspora, working on diasporic sites in such locales can materially confront the silences in the historical record and help to "reverse the narrative" that dominates cultural memory both locally and in the greater national imagination. In the Arkansas Ozarks, sites such as Van Winkle's Mill alert everyone to a deep African American heritage in the Ozark Mountains. Moreover, archaeological work on this site can become an important tool for creating a dialogue on race—a nontraditional venue to teach about race, racism, and the construction of history. This article will examine one case study that attempts to reverse one aspect of the dominant narrative in the Arkansas Ozarks.

Ozark Hillbilly History: Erasing Racial Diversity in the Ozarks

The historical narratives of the Ozarks stress their "Otherness" and rely on a series of tropes that enhance their place as a foil to an increasingly urban America—an Othering process that I think slowly began to take form in the middle of the 19th century, only to fully emerge after the turn of the 20th (Horning 2002; Brandon 2004a:78–137; Harkins 2004:13–69). Not coincidentally, this corresponds to a time when the conceptualization of whiteness was being refashioned by various contending forces in America (Roediger 1991; Ignatiev 1995; Hale 1998; Jacobson 1998:13; DuBois 1999:17).

As I have previously indicated, the trope of the Ozark hillbilly masks the diversity in the region. The whiteness of the Ozark hillbilly erases any African American heritage in the Ozarks. The hillbilly trope, however, is much more complex than that. Hillbilly history also masks racial conflict in the Ozarks. It is those conflicts that, in turn, effectively "whitened" the region and helped to reinforce the trope continuously. Finally, this recent, predominately white, state of the Ozarks becomes projected back in time, leading the Ozarks to be seen as always white and, thus, ironically, as a region with few racial conflicts.

It is important to note that in 1840, the first United States census for the state of Arkansas recorded over 20,000 inhabitants in the eight counties that made up the Arkansas Ozarks—including almost 2,000 enslaved African Americans (Blevins 2002:18) and almost 200 free persons of color (Morgan 1973:29,36). In 1850, Washington County, the second most populous county in the state, boasted 13,133 white inhabitants and almost 1,500 slaves (12% of the population, or 1 out of every 8 individuals [Catalfamo-Serio 1979:107]).

The African American population in the Ozarks peaked in 1890 when the U.S. census enumerated 7,379 blacks in the counties of the Arkansas Ozarks—with every upland Ozark county having a black population of some size

(Morgan 1973:62). The population had grown from 5,963 the previous decade, but would fall to 3,349 in 1900. This migration out of the Ozarks and nucleation within the Ozarks continued until the 1960 census recorded only 1,280 African Americans remaining in the Arkansas Ozarks—including five all-white counties.

This decline runs parallel to an overall trend in the larger Ozark population (Rafferty 2001:63); but it is a more exaggerated, precipitous drop. As the overall population of the Ozarks remained stagnant between 1900 and 1930 the region's African American population plummeted. This "whitening" of the Arkansas Ozarks is no doubt due to both economic and racial pressures.

Following the end of Reconstruction and the institution of Jim Crow, segregated black communities began to coalesce across the Arkansas Ozarks. The fact that these towns and communities became, in certain situations, the target of racial pressures and sometimes violence, played a role in the exodus of black Ozarkians.

One dramatic example from the turn of the century in Harrison, Arkansas, demonstrates how racial conflict and historical memory work hand in hand to erase African Americans from the region. For much of the 20th century Harrison, Arkansas, in Madison County, was all white (Froelich and Zimmermann 1999:131). This, however, was not always the case. Harrison's African American community numbered at least 115 in 1900. In 1905 and 1909, two separate acts of racial mob violence led to the complete depopulation of African Americans from the area (Froelich and Zimmermann 1999:132). It is an event many still have difficulty "seeing" today through the haze of historical memory.

Regional researchers later in the century were not able to find out much about Harrison's African American community due to a county courthouse fire in 1908, see, e.g., Froelich and Zimmerman (1999) and Morgan (1973:133). Ralph Rea in *Boone County and Its People* notes only that there were "several hundred blacks in the county up until just after the turn of the century" (Morgan 1973:133). Black sociologist Gordon Morgan interviewed a 98-year-old resident who remembered "vague things about several hundred Negroes," but he could not remember why they left (Morgan 1973:134). Even more suspicious were gaps

TABLE 1
AFRICAN AMERICAN POPULATION IN THE ARKANSAS OZARKS
BY CENSUS YEAR, 1840–1970

County	1840	1850	1860	1870	1880	1890	1900	1910	1920	1930	1940	1950	1960	1970
Baxter	—	—	—	—	45	18	5	7	4	1	0	0	0	144
Benton	176	202	385	182	128	92	112	110	102	88	46	20	23	290
Boone	—	—	—	74	88	91	142	7	2	3	0	0	3	49
Carroll	142	223	330	37	60	82	166	64	82	25	8	13	6	22
Cleburne	—	—	—	—	—	49	11	7	1	3	0	2	1	18
Izard	135	196	382	246	467	833	285	242	217	175	140	95	54	57
Independence*	222	840	1,137	5,158	3,614	4,543	1,483	1,264	1,075	894	801	642	527	628
Fulton	—	51	88	85	36	85	79	44	26	0	0	4	0	21
Madison	83	164	296	150	124	58	44	55	40	16	15	3	3	21
Marion	102	255	269	19	43	32	38	0	0	1	1	0	1	63
Newton	—	54	24	9	5	6	7	10	10	0	0	1	1	27
Searcy	11	29	93	30	16	28	99	104	24	1	1	1	0	18
Sharp	—	—	—	144	176	177	74	83	15	19	8	12	0	22
Stone	—	—	—	—	99	113	94	94	15	15	12	4	0	28
Van Buren	61	29	200	119	118	162	167	220	211	121	137	106	95	103
Washington	901	1,213	1,540	674	944	1,010	543	614	508	571	411	422	566	1,072
Totals	1,833	3,256	4,744	6,927	5,963	7,379	3,349	2,925	2,332	1,933	1,580	1,325	1,280	2,583

Note: After Morgan (1973:62).

in the files of Harrison's newspaper coinciding with the events of 1905 and 1909 (Froelich and Zimmerman 1999:131). Jacqueline Froelich and David Zimmerman, who finally brought the riots to light in 1999, have put together the story of the Harrison race riots by bringing together the scattered small references to the events (Froelich and Zimmermann 1999).

In 1901 Harrison was an expectant community. Track was being laid for the Missouri & North Arkansas Railroad, which, they hoped, would bring economic prosperity to the town. Local histories indicate that the white and black communities of Harrison were getting along—even coming together to raise money for a black schoolhouse (Rea 1955:122; Froelich and Zimmerman 1999:133). However, in the summer of 1905 the railroad defaulted on its bond and declared bankruptcy, leaving the town that had invested heavily in the railroad's arrival shocked and financially crippled. Moreover, a steady stream of unemployed railroad workers—mostly young, single African American men—was arriving in Harrison following the railroad's collapse (Froelich and Zimmerman 1999:136). "Their mere presence, homeless and unemployed, was no doubt perceived as threatening" in a way that the local black population had never been—a situation that "often bred racial violence in the New South" (Froelich and Zimmerman 1999:137).

Saturday night, 30 September 1905, two black men—one known as Dan, the other called Rabbit—were arrested and jailed for breaking into the residence of Dr. John J. Johnson. The following Monday, a white mob stormed the building, removed the prisoners, whipped them, and ordered them to leave town (Froelich and Zimmerman 1999:141). The rioters then turned on the residents of Dry Jordan Creek:

> [S]ome eight to ten [blacks were] tied to trees [and] whipped with five foot bull whips [while] several men and women [were] tied together and thrown into a three to four foot deep hole in Crooked Creek. Twenty or thirty well-armed men with guns, clubs, etc. burned three or four of the Negroes' homes, shot out the windows and doors of all of the other Negroes' homes ... and warned all Negroes to leave town that night (Froelich and Zimmerman 1999:141).

Much of Harrison's African American community made its way on foot that night to Eureka Springs, Springfield, or Fayetteville (Rea 1955:141–142; Froelich and Zimmerman 1999:142). It is unknown how many people were killed during the violence, but federal records suggest that the victims included at least a 14-year-old girl, her 12-year-old brother, and a 65-year-old woman (Froelich and Zimmerman 1999:143–144). For those few who stayed, random violent acts and murder against African Americans continued in Harrison for some time afterwards. It was not until 1909, however, that a second explosion of racial riots would erase Harrison's black community completely.

Charles Stinnett, unemployed son of well-respected black resident Tom Stinnett, was arrested on 18 January 1909. Emma Lovett, an elderly white woman, accused him of robbery, assault, and rape. Stinnett admitted to being at Lovett's house but denied committing any crime (Froelich and Zimmerman 1999:150–151). Two tense days passed as the jury was selected, arguments made, and the jury deliberated. The jury returned a verdict of guilty on all charges and at sentencing the following day it was clear that the punishment "specified by statute for the offense of which Stinnett was convicted was death by hanging" (Froelich and Zimmerman 1999:152).

The tension grew as news spread that Lovett, the alleged victim, was gravely ill, and a mob moved through the town headed toward the Harrison jail, but authorities had evaded the lynching of Stinnett by moving him to the jail in nearby Marshall (Froelich and Zimmerman 1999:152). The threatening presence of the mob, however, proved the last straw for the 1905 survivors. Fearing for their lives, the remainder of the black community fled the town on the night of 28 January 1909, leaving Harrison a "gray town" throughout most of the remainder of the 20th century (Froelich and Zimmerman 1999:153).

An example of how powerfully and quickly the hillbilly trope silences African American heritage in the Ozarks can be seen only 11 mi. away from Harrison and 18 years later in the small community of Kingston, Arkansas. When a Presbyterian mission was established in Kingston, Arkansas, in 1917, the Rev. Elmer J. Bouher would write copiously to his patron church in Rochester, New York, that Kingston was a "cultural seed-bed" of "Anglo-Saxon and Elizabethan culture," and that the dialect and customs of the Ozarks were "virtually unchanged from those in England in the sixteenth century" (Burnett 2000:38–39). He would write to one local that

> [y]ou and your family have maintained the British character exemplified when their ancestors first settled on the Atlantic seaboard. *There is no melting pot in these mountains.* Your people have maintained your integrity, habits and racial purity [emphasis added] (Burnett 2000:38–39).

He goes on to detail that the folks in Kingston had never even seen a black man before—highly unlikely given the aforementioned history of the region. Bouher's eugenics-influenced discourse is one of the common strains of the hillbilly trope. In this case the firm belief that the Ozarks are a "seed-bed" of whiteness—*and always had been thus*—blinds even those only briefly removed temporally and spatially from proof—not only of an African American presence in the region—but of the violence that helped diminish it.

"Hillbilly History," the powerful trope that frames the historical narrative and cultural memory of a region on both the local and national level, is a vastly interesting and complex one—see Brandon (2004a:78–91) or Harkins (2004) for a more thorough discussion. Here I have focused on only one aspect of the trope—its ability to erase the diversity historically present in the Ozark Mountains. Archaeology at places like Van Winkle's Mill can help to reverse (or at least complicate) the narrative that hillbilly history weaves.

Van Winkle's Mill

Van Winkle's Mill is situated in the extreme northwest corner of the state of Arkansas, in the Ozark Mountains (Figure 1). The project centers on the large sawmill enterprise that dominated the northwest Arkansas lumber market in late 19th century, rebuilt Fayetteville following the Civil War, and provided the lumber necessary for the establishment and expansion of regionally important towns such as Bentonville, Rogers, and Eureka Springs (Brandon 2004a:61–76). This sawmill complex is complete, with the residences of some of the workers and that of the owner and his family. Additionally, it has all of the other ancillary enterprises a mill such as this should have—a blacksmith shop, mule paddocks, and the like. This mill was founded by Peter Marselis Van Winkle, who was a seventh-generation American of Dutch descent. He had been born in New York City and had found his way to Fayetteville as a wagonmaker by the 1840s (Hicks 1990:15–18;

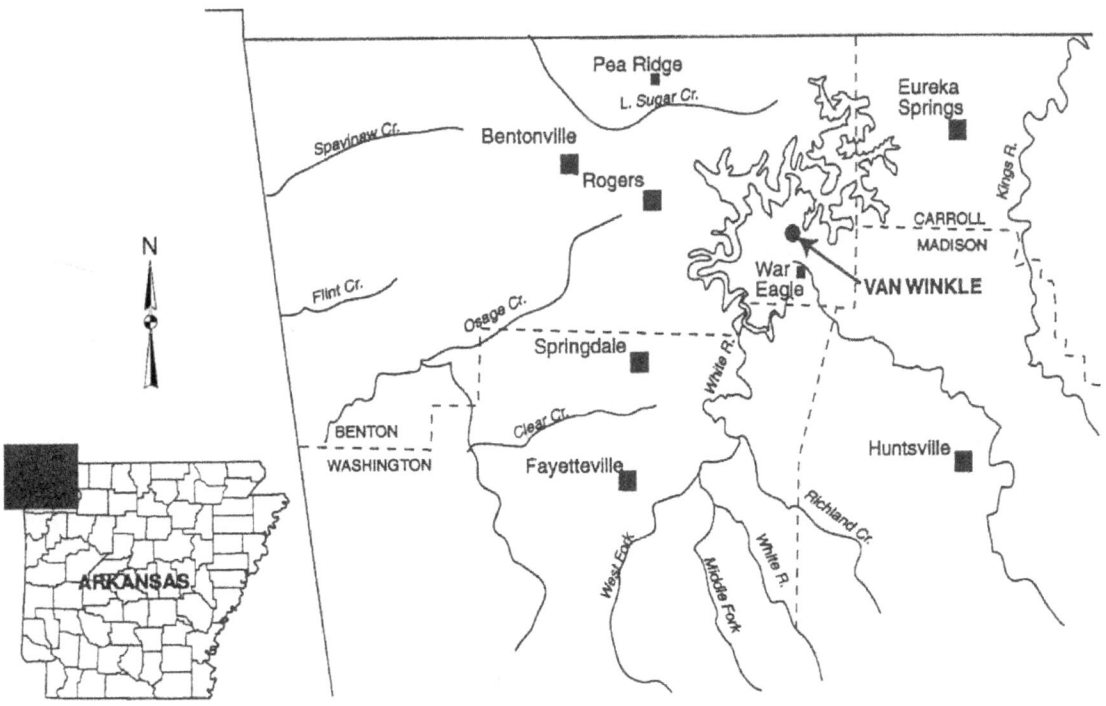

FIGURE 1. Van Winkle project area showing surrounding towns. (Map by author, 2004.)

Easley and McAnelly 1996:156; Blevins 2002:71; Brandon 2004a:54). In 1850, Van Winkle borrowed money from a local venture capitalist to buy land, equipment, and the enslaved labor to run his mill. Following emancipation some African American freedmen chose to stay on at the mill.

The site is now within the Hobbs State Park and Management Area. This project began in 1997 as an effort for Arkansas State Parks, which wanted to look at the potential for including Van Winkle's Mill in its heritage tourism program (Brandon 2004a:1–11). From that time until 2009, periodic fieldwork has been conducted in the narrow hollow that was once home to a vibrant, diverse sawmill community (Hilliard 1997; Brandon and Hilliard 1998; Brandon et al. 1999, 2000; Bowers 2003; Brandon and Davidson 2003, 2005; Brandon 2004a, 2008; Valentino 2006; Boykin 2010).

Aside from a limestone springhouse and the steps to the raised gardens, very little aboveground structural remains have been preserved. Archaeological work provided the basis for reconstructing the historical landscape of the mill community. Archaeologists have completed a thorough survey and at least five major testing programs—one at the main house belonging to Peter Van Winkle and family, one at a postbellum worker's quarters (Feature 9), one at possible antebellum slave quarters (Feature 33), one at the blacksmith shop (Feature 31), and one at the location of the sawmill boiler platform (Brandon and Hilliard 1998; Brandon et al. 1999, 2000; Bowers 2003:36–39; Brandon and Davidson 2003; Brandon 2004a:146–193; Valentino 2006; Boykin 2010).

The mapping, surveys, and testing programs have come together to give the picture of an evolving landscape—a landscape very much influenced by the structure of the cotton plantations of the Lowland South, although tailored to fit into the narrow Ozark hollow—see Brandon and Davidson (2005) and Brandon (2004a:194–223) for more discussion of this landscape.

African Diaspora Archaeology at Van Winkle's Mill across the Antebellum/Postbellum Divide

At least 18 enslaved men and women lived and labored at Van Winkle's Mill prior to emancipation. After the war, at least two freedman families returned to Van Winkle's Hollow to live and work. While African Americans worked throughout the industrial sector of the site, it is the domestic areas that provide archaeologists more discrete deposits that might be able to yield the material with which to confront the erasure of African American heritage in the region. Two archaeological contexts at Van Winkle's Mill lend themselves to such analyses—one is a potential antebellum slave quarter, the second is the home of a postbellum freedman family.

The antebellum slave quarter (Feature 33) was originally located in June of 2000 during a survey designed to assess the impact of the construction of a visitors' parking area on the south side of Highway 12. This location was subsequently tested twice; the first time in 2001 (Brandon 2004a:178–179) and the second time in 2009 (Boykin 2010). A total of 13, 1 × 2 m test excavation units revealed little in terms of solid architectural features (i.e., no in situ foundation stones or root cellars) but enough architectural artifacts (cut nails, cast-iron stove parts, etc.) and domestic artifacts (ceramics and vessel glass) to confirm the ephemeral existence of a predominantly antebellum building. Although the second testing project produced some evidence of a brief postbellum occupation (Boykin 2010:66), the vast majority of the material recovered at this location was domestic and antebellum.

The postbellum worker's quarters (Feature 9), however, provide a sharp contrast to the earlier dwelling. This building was the very substantial remains of a double-pen frame structure (perhaps a dogtrot-style building) with a continuous stone foundation and two chimney falls. This domestic structure was first discovered in 1998, and during three testing efforts (1999, 2000, and 2001) the entire footprint of the postbellum structure was uncovered via 36, 1 × 2 m excavation units (Figure 2). The materials recovered confirmed that the deposits dated between 1870 and 1910 (Brandon et al. 2000:53–55; Brandon 2004a:158–163).

The vast majority of the millworkers at Van Winkle's Mill were seasonal workers and lived on their own farms in the areas surrounding the hollow (Brandon 2004a:63). This and several other factors, including structure location, census records, artifacts recovered, and the known location of the residences of the white Van Winkle family aid in positing an identity for the family that inhabited the postbellum worker's quarters. Of the likely candidates, the

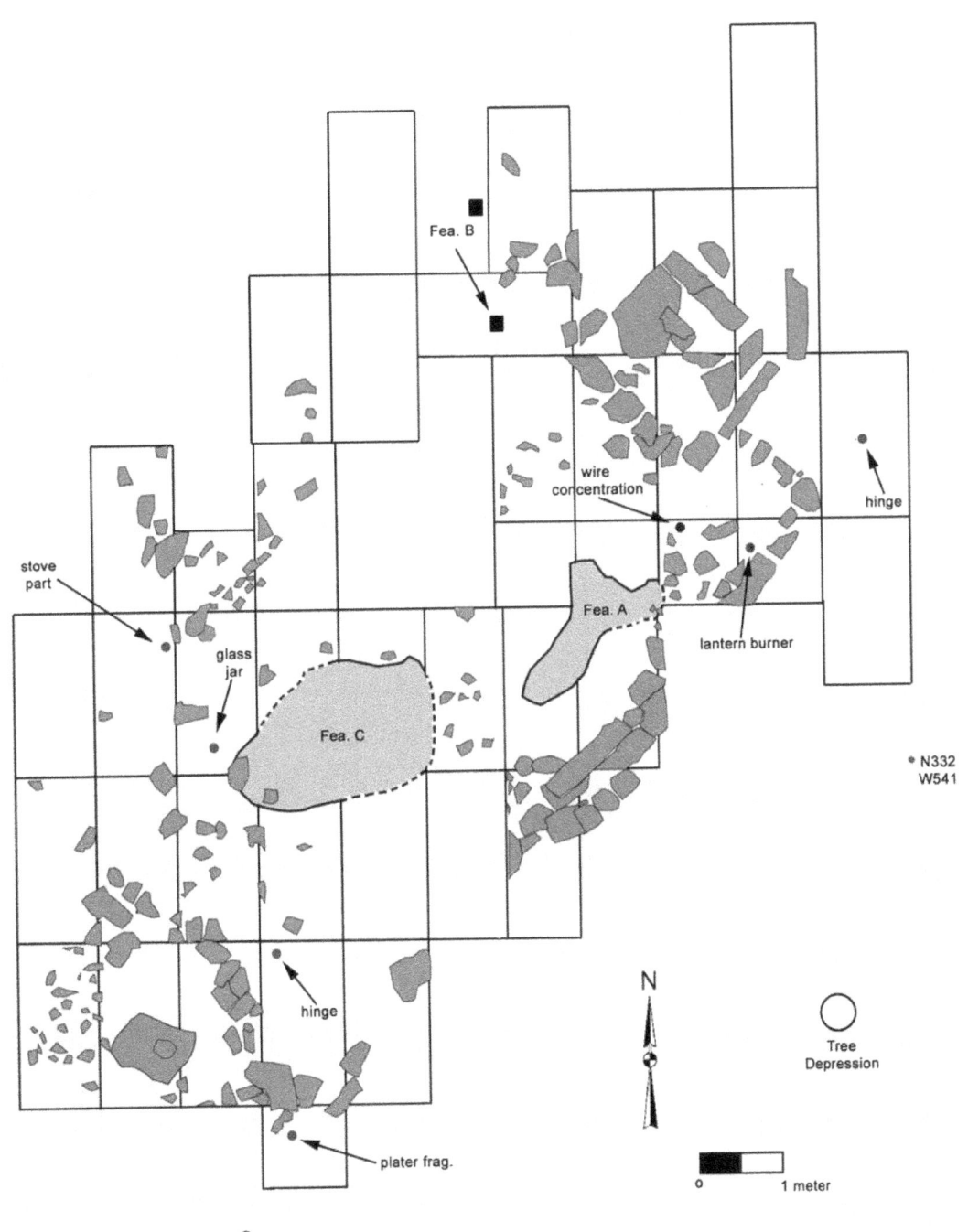

FIGURE 2. Plan view of the entire excavated footprint of Feature 9, a postbellum millworker's quarters. (Map by author, 2004.)

family of Aaron Anderson Van Winkle (Figure 3) seems to be the most compelling candidate for the residents of the postbellum house—see Brandon (2004a:133–134,162–163), Brandon et al. (2000:55), and Brandon and Davidson (2003:17) for a more detailed discussion.

At the age of 6, Aaron Anderson Van Winkle was brought in bondage from Alabama to Arkansas by Colonel Hugh Anderson (Brandon 2008:440)—also see Hilliard (1998) for a discussion of that family and slavery. It is unclear when Aaron was sold to Peter, but by

FIGURE 3. The only known photograph of Aaron Anderson Van Winkle at a Van Winkle family gathering on the front porch of the Steele home in Rogers, 1901. Temperance Van Winkle is sitting *center*, Aaron is standing behind the matriarch. (Photo courtesy of the Shiloh Museum of Ozark History.)

the end of the war he was working at the mill as an "engineer" and later "foreman" (Brandon et al. 2000:14; Brandon 2008:440). He managed to garner a great deal of respect from both the black and white communities, and when he passed away in 1904 it appears that his death was mourned across the racial divide. At least three obituaries in local white papers described his funeral at a black Bentonville church.

The artifacts recovered from these two dwellings are perfect examples of items that can materially confront the silences in the historical narratives of the Arkansas Ozarks. The documentary record says little about the lives of the black Van Winkles or many of the other 7,000 African Americans who lived in the Arkansas Ozarks in the late 19th century. The artifacts recovered from Van Winkle's Mill, however, offer tantalizing interpretive possibilities revealing not only the small aspects of daily life, but also larger issues following emancipation, equality, and identity construction (Brandon 2004a:224–245; Brandon 2008).

For instance, at the postbellum structure it is easy to see an explosion of consumer activity brought about by both emancipation and the increasing availability of consumer goods. Certain artifact classes present at the postbellum site, but absent at the antebellum slave quarters, allude to a growing engagement with consumerism and desires that the black Van Winkle family might have sought to fulfill through carefully considered, critically aware consumption (hooks 1990:3–5; Mullins 1999b:3–4; Brandon 2004a:224–245, 2008).

The archaeological assemblage of the antebellum structure is low in numbers of household items in relation to the architectural materials recovered from the site. The numbers of household items are also low in comparison to household materials from the later dwelling. Moreover, the antebellum structure's assemblage is *incredibly* low in the number of personal items recovered (restricted largely to one tobacco pipe and a few porcelain buttons).

At the postbellum dwelling, however, it is easy to see increased consumer activity. The diversity of ceramic vessel form and decoration recovered from this structure is much greater than in the ceramic assemblage recovered from the antebellum slave quarter. Additionally, the overall number of artifacts classified as "personal goods" and "small finds" is substantially larger (0.5% of the antebellum assemblage; almost 2% of the postbellum assemblage). These are the types of artifacts that can be used to tease out possible meanings that, in turn, offer potential clues to identity construction and the daily lives at Van Winkle's Mill that have been lost in cultural memory. This class of artifacts include items such as a brass pocketknife bolster embossed with a hunting scene, several harmonica reed plates, bric-a-brac fragments, and a number of children's toys (Brandon 2004a:246–253).

For the sake of brevity, I will concentrate on the large number of children's toys recovered from the postbellum worker's quarters (Figure 4). These seemingly innocuous artifacts provide a wide possibility of interpretations. Toys recovered from these excavations include 10 fragments of porcelain doll parts, 3 fragments from at least 2 alphabet plates, a cast-iron pistol fragment, 2 clay marbles, and 2 small, black, child-sized hard-rubber rings.

The presence of these artifacts in postbellum contexts can be seen as a mark of upward mobility and increased humanization through the consumption of seemingly frivolous goods. In "providing certain toys to children, adults were selling a larger ideological package. Working-class parents buying expensive dolls for their daughters may have been expressing dreams of upward mobility" (Wilkie 2000:150)—see also Brandon (2004b:197,207–208) and Mullins (1999a,1999b:155–184, 2001) for similar arguments. This large assemblage of toys does, after all, represent a considerable economic investment in the children living at Feature 9.

On the other hand, for this recently emancipated family (which was rapidly adding children

between 1870 and 1880), these purchases may be interpreted as a desire to provide certain aspects of childhood that the parents themselves had not been allowed to experience during enslavement. In the racialized atmosphere of late-19th-century Arkansas, this would have been a radical and subversive material statement. Such a statement is not without precedent, however, as children's toys have been documented as being used in dialogues on race by archaeologists in similar contexts (Wilkie 2000:151; Mullins 2001; Brandon 2004b).

Most poignant among the children's artifacts from the postbellum assemblage are the three fragments from two alphabet plates. These fragments of blue transfer-printed whiteware were from vessels typically used in Victorian America as serving dishes for children (Kwas 2009:110). The alphabet printed around the rim of the plate was meant to aid in the instruction of children in the learning of their ABC's. As literacy was socially discouraged among enslaved African Americans in Arkansas prior to emancipation (and Aaron reported to the 1870 census that he could not read or write), these plates take on an important meaning. In period discourse, education was stressed as a path to equality as often as (if not more often than) judicious consumption. The Freedmen's Bureau and African Americans throughout the South quickly moved to provide at least a rudimentary education to the newly freed masses. These plates may represent Aaron and Jane's desire to raise the first generation of literate African Americans in Arkansas and, thus, provide opportunities that they themselves had not had due to enslavement and illiteracy.

This example is just a brief glimpse of consumption among the African American community at Van Winkle's Mill. Obviously, many other such interpretations can be made using these assemblages, but it does demonstrate the way that archaeological artifacts (and their interpretations) can be used to confront the narrative of "hillbilly history." The presence of the artifacts themselves attests to an African American heritage in the Ozark Mountains, and this interpretation offers a very human story and a complex picture. Consumers such as Aaron and Jane used material culture to, in Paul Mullins's words, "imagine new social possibilities, mediate lived contradictions, and envision new personal pleasures, posing new relationships between consumers and society and portraying who we *wish* to

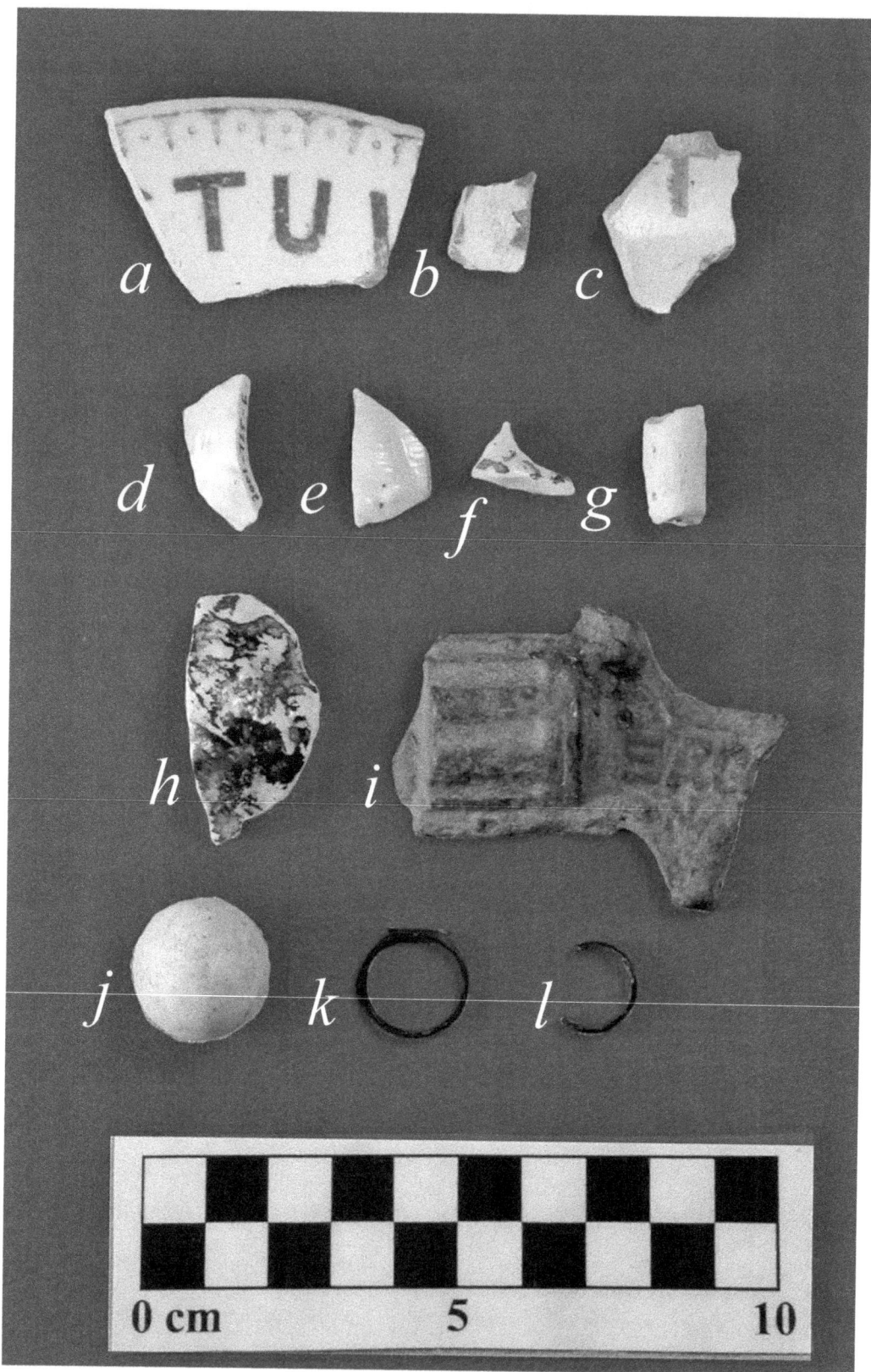

FIGURE 4. Children's toys recovered from Feature 9: (*a–c*) transfer-print alphabet plate fragments, (*d–h*) porcelain doll fragments, (*i*) cast-iron cap-pistol fragment, (*j*) porcelain marble, and (*k–l*) bakelite children's rings. (Photo by author, 2004.)

be" (Mullins 1999b:28). In order to reverse the dominant narrative of Ozark history, however, archaeologists will need to interpret these artifacts, and the stories they tell, to the public.

Historical Archaeology, Public History, and Reversing the Narrative at Van Winkle's Mill

Most archaeologists are increasingly aware of how the past is interpreted to the public and the public benefits of archaeology (Shackel et al. 1998; Little 2002; Skeates et al. 2012). As this project has grown out of the intent to interpret Van Winkle's Mill publicly for visitors to Hobbs State Park, the subject is all the more germane. Van Winkle's Mill Historical Trail is now established with developed hiking trails and signage that seek to raise public awareness of African American heritage in the Ozarks (Figure 5). Additionally, whenever archaeology is conducted in the park, we archaeologists engage in public archaeology—telling the stories of both the white and black Van Winkles that once lived and worked at the mill. These are both big steps toward attempting to challenge and complicate the dominant narrative in Ozark history.

As I have written technical reports, text for park signage, and provided State Parks with other interpretive opinions, I have always thought my job was to "encourage visitors to identify the evidence used to support historical interpretations, recognize how that data is used to interpret a research issue, and critically examine interpretations, particularly those presented as self-evident facts" (Shackel et al. 1998:3). Thus, when the Rogers Historical Museum launched its ambitious Van Winkle educational program, I saw it as an opportunity to observe the public engagement between archaeology and cultural memory, but also to understand how

FIGURE 5. Example of interpretive sign at Van Winkle's Mill. This sign, at the site of Feature 9, interprets both the archaeology and the presence of Aaron Anderson Van Winkle and his family. (Photo by author, 2006.)

public interpretation at Van Winkle's Mill can be made both more critical and accessible—especially as such "sticky and unsettling" topics as slavery, racism, capitalism, and class conflict are tackled.

From 2002 through 2009, in an attempt to tell the complex story of diversity in the 19th-century Ozarks, we archaeologists partnered with lineal descendant communities, the Rogers Historical Museum, Hobbs State Park, the Arkansas Humanities Council, and the Bentonville and Rogers school districts to launch a project as a part of their educational programs for schools. Using historical documents, archaeological information, family history, and other sources, we proposed to expose some 1,300 fifth-grade children in Benton County schools to critical history through the story of Van Winkle's Mill (Brandon 2004a:255–277; Davidson and Brandon 2012:619–622).

The curriculum was multidisciplinary and sought to introduce students to aspects of the natural environment that made the lumber mill possible; the social, political, and economic history of northwest Arkansas; the concept of industrial slavery and African American heritage in the Ozarks; the impact of the Civil War on the region; and how different types of sources (including historical archaeology) come together to reconstruct the history of a site. The program included a class visit to provide background information for (and primary documentation of) Van Winkle's Mill, and a field trip to the site where students rotated through several key interpretive locations.

The museum and educational communities in Arkansas widely considered the Van Winkle educational program an overall success. In its first year, 36 fifth-grade classes participated, and the Rogers Historical Museum won the 2004 Educational Program of the Year Award from the Arkansas Museums Association for the effort. From the archaeologists' perspective it successfully complicated the narrative of hillbilly history in the region. Exit evaluations (for both teachers and students) indicated that the majority of the teachers thought that the program led students to a better understanding of African American heritage in the Ozarks, and that the field visit to Van Winkle's Mill "to observe the architectural remains and locations of archaeological investigations" enriched

what was learned in the classroom (Brandon 2004a:260–263). Furthermore, student evaluations revealed that most of the learning objectives outlined for the Van Winkle program where met—especially in the areas of identifying archaeology as a primary resource and raising awareness of industrial and African American heritage in the region (Brandon 2004a:263).

On the surface of things, given the trails, standing signage, and yearly educational programs' impact on visitors, Van Winkle's Mill looks like a successful attempt at using archaeology to "reverse the narrative." Yet some aspects of the program were clearly more successful than others and it is believed that this is due to several factors—the resilience of cultural memory and the confusion caused by the complexity of the two historical narratives being presented (i.e., the story of the African American community at Van Winkle's Mill and the story of Peter Van Winkle and industrial heritage in the Ozarks). What follows is a cautionary tale about the difficulties inherent in attempting to engineer the reversal of a dominant narrative.

The Resilience and Complexity of Cultural Memory Challenging but Not Fully Reversing the Narrative

Student evaluations made it clear that we archaeologists were successful in challenging one of the facets of hillbilly history—the idea that the Ozarks are rural, antimodern, and nonindustrial—through the story of Peter Van Winkle and his mill. However, the students' reaction to the critical history of African American heritage was more complicated. While they were now more aware of the presence of African Americans in Ozark history, their view of racial relations in the mountains was being influenced by another narrative. For example, in a 2003 assessment a total of 673 students responded to the question: "Most African-Americans who were slaves worked on plantations. How was slavery different in Van Winkle Hollow?" Despite the direct efforts of the program designers, 281 students (41.8%) responded with an answer that depicted slavery at Van Winkle's Mill as better, more kind, or otherwise indicated that the slaves were better treated by Peter Van Winkle than they were in plantation settings (Brandon 2004a:234).

Thus, while we archaeologists have successfully challenged the erasure of African American history in the Ozarks, here students are tapping into another, secondary narrative that needs confronting in the Upland South. This is a narrative that stresses that if slavery did exist in the Upland South, it was a kinder and gentler version (Brandon 2004a:264–270; Davidson and Brandon 2012:621).

Historians have made much of the differences between upland and lowland slavery in the American South. Even in the Ozarks, researchers such as Gordon Morgan, in his study *Black Hillbillies in the Arkansas Ozarks*, have speculated that the low numbers of slaves and the degree of personal interaction between slaves and masters may have created a close social relationship between enslaver and the enslaved:

> More probably, there might have been a kind of mutual benefit relationship between some masters and their slaves, each contributing to the protection of the other in their struggle to survive in the frontier environment. Also, there is the possibility that given more of a balance between numbers of slave owners and the slaves that there was less master-servant social distance and more of a partner relationship between them (Morgan 1973:28).

According to Morgan's argument, shared living quarters, working conditions, and the frontier character of the Ozarks helped create situations where neither master nor slave preferred to break the bonds of the relationship. Echoing public impressions of slavery in the North prior to the African Burial Ground Project, the students often eventually settled on: "They must have been few; they must have been free; they must have been treated better" (Blakey 2010). None of these statements were necessarily true. Elsewhere I have argued using newspaper accounts, runaway ads, and WPA slave narratives that slavery in the Ozark uplands was far from harmonious, and that the enslaved did actively resist (Brandon 2004a:23–31).

In this case, challenging one narrative in Ozark history has triggered reliance on a secondary narrative—one that like "hillbilly history" obscures more than it explains. If researchers and educators are serious about "reversing the narrative," they must expect that they will not succeed immediately. One must be constantly thoughtful, critical, and self-reflexive

in order to engage the narratives at work in cultural memory. It should be evident that although highly flexible and contradictory, there is also a certain resilient quality to cultural memory. This can be seen in works such as Richard Handler and Eric Gable's *The New History in an Old Museum* (1997), which chronicles the complications and difficulties of the attempts of social historians to introduce critical views of colonial America (including a revised examination of slavery and the African American colonial experience) into the public interpretations at Williamsburg. The identity of Williamsburg's white citizens had been actively remade in cultural memory with the American Revolution as its focus (Handler and Gable 1997:33). This substitution of the colonial trope for the Civil War trope in both local and national cultural memory is not unlike the hillbilly trope's ascendancy in the Ozarks—focusing attention on a favored protagonist and erasing the diversity of Williamsburg from memory. This resistance to constructionist views of history and alternative historical narratives at Colonial Williamsburg strikes a resonance with some of the experiences at Van Winkle's Mill. It is difficult to complicate the cultural memory of the Ozarks with such topics as diversity, modernity, industrialism, slavery, and racism.

Conclusion

There are many powerful narratives at work in the collective historical memory. Each of these narratives focuses attention on particular topics and/or protagonists as it also obscures other facts and/or actors. In the Arkansas Ozarks—and all of the Upland South—hillbilly history focuses on a white, rural, yeoman farmer who is backward and antimodern. This obscures much diversity in the region and, more importantly, absolves the region from its history of racial conflicts.

The long-term archaeological project at the site of Van Winkle's Mill has provided a mix of documentary and artifactual evidence that can be interpreted to visitors through trail signage, museum exhibits, and educational programs. This interpretation has been aimed at reversing the work of the dominant hillbilly narrative, not only by exposing it as an oversimplification, but also carefully following its historical construction and how it works on the collective historical memory. It confronts stereotypical notions of Ozark history with a concrete landscape and artifacts that point toward not only progressive, modern technologies; industrialization; and an entrepreneurial heritage, but also to racial and ethnic diversity, and the complicated history of slavery in the region. Archaeology can help tell complicated narratives—such as stories hinted at by the artifacts and consumer patterns recovered from the possible antebellum slave quarter and the postbellum home of Aaron Anderson Van Winkle and his family.

However, these historical narratives are resilient, and while we archaeologists have had some success in reversing the narrative that completely writes African American heritage out of Ozark history, we find other narratives in its stead. These narratives convey to their audience how the present derives from the past. Moreover, they explain the present even as they shape present reality by providing the audience with a symbolic framework (i.e., the past) that enables it to make sense of the world. Historical reality is much more complicated, and one of the "public benefits" that one can derive from archaeology is the complication of these powerful, influential narratives.

Acknowledgments

The author would like to acknowledge the Arkansas Archeological Survey, the Little Rock District Corps of Engineers, and the Arkansas State Department of Parks and Tourism for their support (both monetary and professional). I would also like to thank all the educational institutions involved in the project—the University of Arkansas at Fayetteville, the University of Texas at Austin, Michigan Technological University, and the Rogers Historical Museum. In particular I would like to thank James Davidson, Jerry Hilliard, George Sabo, and Robert Mainfort for their support in time, input, and resources. Thanks to Alicia Valentino, Kristina Boykin, and Robin Bowers, who took aspects of Van Winkle's Mill as the subject of their graduate work at the University of Arkansas. Thanks also to the large number of crew, volunteers, and students who made these excavations possible from 1997 to 2009. Finally I would like to thank my two anonymous reviewers for their insightful comments, and my wife, Lydia Rees, for her unflagging help with structure and editing.

References

BLAKEY, MICHAEL
2010 New York's African Burial Ground after Nearly Two Decades of Work. Paper presented at Windows from the Present to the Past: The Archaeology of Africa and the African Diaspora Conference, Howard University, Washington, DC.

BLEVINS, BROOKS
2002 Hill Folks: A History of Arkansas Ozarkers and Their Image. University of North Carolina Press, Chapel Hill.
2009 Arkansas/Arkansaw: How Bear Hunters, Hillbillies and Good Ol' Boys Defined a State. University of Arkansas Press, Fayetteville.

BOWERS, ROBIN F.
2003 Ozark Industry: The Van Winkle Saw Mill, 1857–1890. Master's thesis, Department of Anthropology, University of Arkansas, Fayetteville.

BOYKIN, KRISTINA U.
2010 An Analysis of Feature 33 at Van Winkle's Mill: African-American Archaeology in the Ozarks. Master's thesis, Department of Anthropology, University of Arkansas, Fayetteville.

BRANDON, JAMIE C.
2004a Van Winkle's Mill: Mountain Modernity, Cultural Memory and Historical Archaeology in the Arkansas Ozarks. Doctoral dissertation, Department of Anthropology, University of Texas at Austin. University Microfilms International, Ann Arbor, MI.
2004b Segregating Households, Reconstructing Domesticity: The Intersection of Gender and Race in the Postbellum South. In Household Chores and Household Choices: Theorizing the Domestic Sphere in Historical Archaeology, Kerri S. Barrile and Jamie C. Brandon, editors, pp. 197–209. University of Alabama Press, Tuscaloosa.
2008 Van Winkle's Mill: Recovering Lost Industrial and African-American Heritages in the Ozarks. Arkansas Historical Quarterly 67(4):429–445.

BRANDON, JAMIE C., AND JAMES M. DAVIDSON
2003 Archeological Inventory and Testing of Cultural Resources at Van Winkle's Mill (3BE413) and Little Clifty Creek Shelter (3BE412), Beaver Lake, Benton County, Arkansas. Report to U.S. Army Corps of Engineers, Little Rock District, AK, from Arkansas Archeological Survey, Fayetteville.
2005 The Landscape of Van Winkle's Mill: Identity, Myth and Modernity in the Ozark Upland South. Historical Archaeology 39(3):113–131.

BRANDON, JAMIE C., JAMES M. DAVIDSON, AND JERRY E. HILLIARD
2000 Preliminary Archeological Investigations at Van Winkle's Mill (3BE413), Beaver Lake State Park, Benton County, Arkansas, 1997–1999. Report to Arkansas Department of Parks and Tourism, Little Rock, from Arkansas Archeological Survey, Fayetteville.

BRANDON, JAMIE C., AND JERRY HILLIARD
1998 The Van Winkle Mill and the Anderson Slave Cemetery: African-American Related Sites in Northwest Arkansas. *African-American Archaeology* 22:1.

BRANDON, JAMIE C., JERRY E. HILLIARD, AND JAMES M. DAVIDSON
1999 Return to Van Hollow: 1999 Excavations at a 19th Century Mill-Worker's Residence. *Field Notes* 282:10–12.

BURNETT, ABBY
2000 *When the Presbyterians Came to Kingston: Kingston Community Church, 1917–1951.* Bradshaw Mountain, Kingston, AK.

CATALFAMO-SERIO, CHRIS
1979 *The Effect of the Civil War on Ozark Culture.* Cavanaugh, Prairie Grove, AK.

DAVIDSON, JAMES M., AND JAMIE C. BRANDON
2012 Descendant Community Partnering, the Politics of Time, and the Logistics of Reality: Tales from North American, African Diaspora, Archaeology. In *The Oxford Handbook of Public Archaeology*, Robin Skeates, Carol McDavid, and John Carman, editors, pp. 605–628. Oxford University Press, Oxford, UK.

DUBOIS, W. E. B.
1999 *Darkwater: Voices from within the Veil.* Dover, Mineola, NY.

EASLEY, BARBARA PICKERING, AND VERLA PICKERING MCANELLY (EDITORS)
1996 *Obituaries of Washington County Arkansas, Volume I: 1841–1892.* Heritage, Bowie, MD.

FROELICH, JACQUELINE, AND DAVID ZIMMERMANN
1999 Total Eclipse: The Destruction of the African American Community of Harrison, Arkansas, in 1905 and 1909. *Arkansas Historical Qur terly* 58(2):131–159.

HALE, GRACE E.
1998 *Making Whiteness: The Cu tn e of 8 gregation in the South, 1890–1940.* Vintage, New York, NY.

HANDLER, RICHARD, AND ERIC GABLE
1997 *The New History in an Old Museum: Creating the Past at Colonial Williamsburg.* Duke University Press, Durham, NC.

HARKINS, ANTHONY A. R.
2004 *Hillb lly: A Cu tn al History of an American Icon.* Oxford University Press, Oxford, UK.

HICKS, MARILYN LARNER
1990 *Peter Marseilles Van Winkle (1814–1882): His Life and Times, His Ancestors Back to the 16th Century and Most of His Descendants.* Henington, Wolfe City, TX.

HILLIARD, JERRY E.
1997 A Brief Look at One of Northwest Arkansas' Largest Sawmills: The Van Winkle Site, 3BE413. *Field Notes* 279:10–12.

1998 Historical and Archaeological Account of the Anderson Slave Cemetery (3BE625), Benton County, Arkansas. Report to Scott Van Landingham, Northwest Arkansas Regional Airport Authority, Bentonville, from Arkansas Archeological Survey, Fayetteville.

HOOKS, BELL
1990 *Yearning: Race, Gender and Cultural Politics.* South End Press, Boston, MA.

HORNING, AUDREY J.
2002 Myth, Migration, and Material Culture: Archaeology and the Ulster Influence on Appalachia. *Historical Archaeology* 36(4):129–149.

IGNATIEV, NOEL
1995 *How the Irish Became White.* Routledge, New York, NY.

JACOBSON, MATTHEW FRYE
1998 *Whiteness of a Different Color. European Immigrants and the Alchemy of Race.* Harvard University Press, Cambridge, MA.

KWAS, MARY L.
2009 *Digging for History at Old Washington.* University of Arkansas Press, Fayetteville.

LITTLE, BARBARA J. (EDITOR)
2002 *Public Benefits of Archaeology.* University of Florida Press, Gainesville.

MORGAN, GORDON D.
1973 Black Hillbillies of the Arkansas Ozarks. Report from Department of Sociology, University of Arkansas, Fayetteville, to Russell Sage Foundation, New York, NY.

MULLINS, PAUL R.
1999a "A Bold and Gorgeous Front": The Contradictions of African America and Consumer Culture. In *Historical Archaeologies of Cap talism*, Mark Leone and Parker Potter, editors, pp. 169–198. Kluwer Academic Press, New York, NY.

1999b *Race and Affluence: An Archaeology of African America and Consm er Cu tn e.* Kluwer Academic Press, New York, NY.

2001 Racializing the Parlor: Race and Victorian Bric-a-Brac Consumption. In *Race and the Archaeology of Identity*, Charles Orser, editor, pp. 158–176. University of Utah Press, Salt Lake City.

RAFFERTY, MILTON D.
2001 *The Ozarks: Land and Life.* University of Arkansas Press, Fayetteville.

REA, RALPH R.
1955 *Boone County and Its People.* Press-Argus, Van Buren, AK.

ROEDIGER, DAVID R.
1991 *The Wages of Whiteness: Race and the Making of the American Working Class.* Verso Press, London, UK.

James C. Brandon

SHACKEL, PAUL A., PAUL R. MULLINS, AND MARK S.
WARNER (EDITORS)
  1998 *Annapl is Pasts: Historical Archaeology in Annapl is
        Maryland.* University of Tennessee Press, Knoxville.

SKEATES, ROBIN, CAROL McDAVID, AND JOHN CARMAN
(EDITORS)
  2012 *The Oxford Handbook of Public Archaeology,* Oxford
        University Press, Oxford, UK.

VALENTINO, ALICIA B.
  2006 *The Dynamics of Ind try as S en from Van Winkle's
        Mill, Arkansas.* Doctoral dissertation, Department of
        Anthropology, University of Arkansas, Fayetteville.
        University Microfilms International, Ann Arbor, MI.

WILLKIE, LAURIE A.
  2000 *Creating Freedom: Material Culture and African
        Identity at Oakley Plantation, 1840–1950.* Louisiana
        State University Press, Baton Rouge.

JAMIE C. BRANDON
ARKANSAS ARCHEOLOGICAL SURVEY
SOUTHERN ARKANSAS UNIVERSITY
PO BOX 9
MAGNOLIA, AR 3

2013 Reversing the Narrative from Violence to Peace. In *Reversing the Narrative*, Paul A. Shackel and Michael P. Roller, editors. Thematic issue, *Historical Archaeology* 47(3):124–129

Barbara J. Little

Reversing the Narrative from Violence to Peace: Some Thoughts from an Archaeologist[1]

ABSTRACT

Archaeologists with ambitions to be relevant, ethical, and useful can decide to confront difficult, deeply embedded current problems. We archaeologists have the power of narrative. Narratives are what drive us; they are what we teach each other. They reinforce what we believe, repeat, cite, and fund—both within the discipline and in the stories we return to the public sphere. In *Life and Death Matters*, Barbara Rose Johnston raises the crucial question: "Can we build environmentally sound and socially just solutions to our problems in ways that minimize or prevent the incidence of violent conflict?" How will archaeologists employ narrative tactics to respond?

Introduction

I believe that one of the ways we as archaeologists can "reverse the narrative" is to recognize the morals of the stories in the narratives we offer and to turn our attention to narratives to support a sustainable and wide-reaching public good. That is, one way we change the game is to start playing a new game. Our work will contribute to changing the game as we highlight the morals of our stories that can lead wider social dialogue toward sustainable peace.

Although I write from the vantage point of an archaeologist, I am ever hopeful that the walls of archaeology are truly down and that we participate in a heritage field that is turning toward fulfilling its potential to be a powerfully engaging practice with broad and self-reflexive applicability. I see us merging perspectives and expertise from the sciences, humanities, and intentional public scholarship. Individually and collectively, we have a role to play in the search for a more just and sustainable society.

Stb leP ea ea dt he Ambitionsof a E p a ded Archa oloġ cḣ P ra tice

As individual practitioners and as members of a profession, we archaeologists have the power to imagine and to co-create our heritage work as work that is conducive to a stable peace. More than a generation ago, Kenneth Boulding (1978:13) defined stable peace as "a situation in which the probability of war is so small that it does not really enter into the calculations of any of the people involved." Stable peace is defined not simply by the absence of conflict or the presence of deterrence but is a state of being where differences are expected to be resolved through dialogue and diplomacy, and violent resolutions are actually unthinkable. Boulding focused mainly on nations, but he included all kinds of social groups, which is a useful and worthy approach, as there is plenty of thinkable, actual violence within any nation, between groups, and between individuals identifying strongly with particular groups. "Stable peace" cannot be counted as the kind of truce that is enforced by mutual fear of violence, whether that violence is physical and immediate, or structural and relentlessly corrosive.

As a discipline, archaeology has come a long way toward the realization of our social and political context, and that realization has opened up our ambitions. As a discipline, we now talk about archaeologists' roles in creating justice, building peace, promoting human rights and global justice, and even mitigating the human suffering we anticipate will accompany massive ecological change. Such ambitions are grand and speak to a vision of integrating our practice with our common problems.

Larry Zimmerman and I propose that this trend reflects a quest for wisdom (Little and Zimmerman 2010). Some archaeologists have been helped in seeing the value of such a quest through working with native peoples and the cultural values curated by many indigenous societies. In his book, *Learning Native Wisdom*, Gary Holthaus (2008) characterizes the rift between sustainability and the modern worldview as a series of disconnections in a way that speaks clearly to our habits of narrative. He observes:

> For the longest-surviving cultures, the sciences, the humanities, and the arts were shot through with the

sacred. Nature and the sacred, wisdom and the sacred, were inseparably linked. ... In our time the sacred has come uncoupled from wisdom; wisdom uncoupled from knowledge; knowledge unhooked from information; information unhooked from facts; facts disconnected from data; data disassociated from firsthand observation and experience. Our culture seems to have forsaken wisdom in favor of all the latter—at a time when wisdom is our greatest need and would be its greatest asset (Holthaus 2008:29).

Indeed, wisdom appears to be our greatest need. Can we archaeologists be wise enough to give equal consideration to the needs of future generations as we do to our own? Can we be wise enough to work toward the kind of societies that future generations might appreciate inheriting? Indeed, can we even be wise enough to contribute to the kind of society that supports stable peace in the present?

I think of this article as part of an ongoing dialogue about potential and actual benefits of archaeology in our expanded ambitions. I want to recall some of the issues that I and several colleagues raised in a forum published a few years ago in *Historical Archaeology* (Funari 2009; Little 2009a, 2009b; Musteata 2009; Pikirayi 2009). Our forum grew out of both the "Public Benefits of Archaeology" plenary session at the 2008 Society for Historical Archaeology (SHA) meeting and one of two sessions on archaeology and the global-justice movement that were held at the 2007 American Anthropological Association (AAA) meetings in Washington, D.C. (McDavid and Jeppson 2007). Global-justice movements offer some examples of high-minded and integrating principles, such as "Global Justice for All," "Respect for the Earth," and "Economic Democracy." A somewhat less-abstract and more-programmatic set of global goals come from the United Nations (UN); but they are no less daunting. The UN has identified and defined eight "Millennium Development Goals"—for extensive background and information about these goals see, for example, the United Nations Millennium Project (2005) and, online, <http://www.un.org/millenniumgoals/>. In our forum discussion, Innocent Pikirayi raised the question of how archaeology might serve these goals. They are to (1) end poverty and hunger; (2) achieve universal education; (3) achieve gender equity; (4) improve child health; (5) improve maternal health; (6) combat HIV/AIDS, malaria, and other diseases;

(7) achieve environmental sustainability; and (8) develop a global partnership.

Calling archeologists to tackle such issues leaves no doubt about the expanded ambitions of archaeology and heritage. Increasing our ambitions comes with the potential cost of hubris and highlights the need for appropriate humbleness about what we think we can achieve and how right we think we might be. Our search for wisdom becomes all the more important. It is important for us to remember that lack of certainty is not an excuse for inaction; neither is silence neutral. Heritage is and heritage workers have significant roles to play.

There is no shortage of big ideas and overwhelming needs. They are not abstract problems, particularly on the local level. And they are not problems we as a society have the luxury of facing when we are ready. When we take a look around—even with the briefest of glances—it is apparent that this giant Ponzi scheme we have got going cannot last. It is, in fact, already collapsing, as we see when we look around the globe. Our reliance on incessant growth and environmental destruction cannot continue, at least not for as long as we might like, which is into the foreseeable future. We are not supporting a global society in which humans and nature exist in productive harmony. We can see that we are not fulfilling social, economic, and other requirements for much of the earth's present population, let alone for future generations.

In light of some of those big ideas and big problems, Barbara Johnston's 2011 edited volume, *Life and Death Matters: Human Rights, Environment, and Social Justice*, provides powerful detailed examples of some of the world's severe biocultural problems, such as agricultural conflicts, war, the long-term effects of radiation, climate change, and the dire circumstances surrounding water and water rights. There are many lessons to be learned if we care to learn them. And while chaos might be a necessary ingredient in crisis, we learn that it is not necessarily the endpoint for human environmental emergencies.

Johnston (2011:15) asks what she calls the crucial question of our time: "Can we build environmentally sound and socially just solutions to our problems in ways that minimize or prevent the incidence of violent conflict?" Now that is a very good question. How indeed do we attain the positive peace of justice and social stability without violence, and how do we sustain it?

What does heritage have to do with these overwhelming needs, threats, and the alternative potential for a positive future? Part of what we archaeologists offer is our contribution to—our creation of—cultural narrative. We are memory workers; we remember what has been possible, and from our remembered pasts we imagine how we ought to live and who we ought to be. The problems are big, but we are not helpless because we have tools. And we have experience upon which to draw and whole communities where there is wisdom pooling up, collecting, and informing action.

Narrative Tools

A specific definition of "narrative" is offered by the U. S. Institute of Peace (Snodderly 2011): "a people's most strongly held beliefs about the way history has unfolded" as a "separate view of reality." The institute elaborates that in

> divided societies—where there has been protracted conflict—there are often parallel narratives. The differing peoples do not agree on what occurred in the distant past and this core disagreement often causes them to dispute what has happened in recent times (Snodderly 2011).

In this context, I would call the U.S. a divided society with a long way to go toward an imagined more-perfect union. U.S. ideas about accurate and meaningful narratives about history display deep divisions in society (Linenthal and Engelhardt 1996).

The Institute of Peace recognizes that both the distant and recent past are in dispute in divided societies. Heritage practitioners know this and have come to understand the depth to which heritage can be disputed and the deeply rooted power it can have. Interestingly, though, as vital and as deeply embedded heritage is, heritage work is not often granted a seat at the big table, at least not in the U.S. However, recent work by an influential scholar of conflict and peace suggests that there may be a bit of a turn. In his 2010 book, *How Enemies Become Friends: The Sources of Stable Peace*, Charles Kupchan draws commonalities from a number of case studies where stable peace broke out and endured for variable periods of time. As a result of his research, he is far more interested

in the power of culture, narrative, and identity than the authors of many earlier influential studies. Kupchan identifies one of the key phases in developing stable peace as the generation of new narratives and identities. He emphasizes that cultural commonality is a condition for stable peace but recognizes that culture is malleable and constructed, and that seemingly intractable cultural differences can become culturally irrelevant depending on the narrative. Kupchan observes and recognizes that the unraveling of zones of peace starts with social and cultural tensions (Kupchan 2010). This kind of thinking is all very familiar to archaeologists from the anthropological tradition.

This scholarship from the international diplomacy realm strikes me as potentially helpful, as it is something upon which heritage workers might build and use to intersect with the policy and decision makers who may be in positions to influence how big goals—like the UN's Millennium Development Goals—might be achieved. As heritage workers, we create and perpetuate narratives that support imagined communities and imagined nations. We create grand narratives and mythologies about the past to sustain our faith in our current ways of life. For examples that helped to raise the consciousness of archaeologists about our social and political context, consider Conkey and Spector's (1984) analysis of archaeology's role in supporting and creating the gender bias embedded throughout our intellectual traditions, and Kohl and Fawcett's (1995) volume on archaeology's deep involvement in the creation of nationalist narratives.

When heritage is implicated in supporting unsustainable and unjust culture, we have to be vigilant about deconstructing our complicity. Because the grounding of cultural narratives in the past is one of the key places where heritage fits into the creation of those imaginaries in our society, we need to continually ask: What stories are we telling? Where are they coming from? For whom are we perpetuating them?

We in U.S. society like to say we want peace, but we commemorate and celebrate war endlessly. Parks and memorials to peacemakers are rare and remarkable; those dedicated to war are legion. In the rare times when we are not at war, we are preparing for war and using the language of war and violence to frame our approaches to social challenges.

As archaeologists, our experience and our work show us that heritage can change the game. Consider this advice from Kupchan (2010:404) concerning the increasing immigrant population of Europe, also applicable in the U.S.: "Leaders," he says, "may want to compensate for greater demographic diversity by focusing discourse on shared values and interests rather than common ancestry and history," and he adds: "If left unattended, discourses of opposition and rivalry have the potential to become a self-fulfilling prophecy." To avoid creating simple propaganda, it is necessary to keep our eyes wide open, to be aware of the power of our work, and to be very intentional and vigilant about our credibility.

We public archaeologists and those who do heritage education can actively counter the kinds of narratives that justify inequality and violence within our society. Such work is notoriously difficult, as it insists that we confront the embedded cultural biases in our language, from word choice to the conceptual frameworks supported by our common ways of thinking and talking.

A generation ago, Janet Spector and Mary Whelan (1989) identified steps necessary to develop a gendered archaeology. Similar steps are needed for any archaeology that is called to challenge embedded bias. These are (1) exposing biases, (2) defining appropriate concepts and methods, and (3) creating new interpretations. Taking these steps requires refining our narrative tools.

Social-justice activist Paul Kivel (2002:54) reminds us that "[t]hose with power have many resources for ensuring their view of reality prevails, and they have a lot at stake in maintaining the status quo." He analyzes some narrative tactics and admonishes those involved in antiracism work to challenge and counter those tactics that are used to justify violence:

> If we keep our eyes clearly on the power and the violence, we can see that these tactics are transparent attempts to prevent placing responsibility on those who commit and benefit from acts of injustice. Our strongest tools are a critical analysis of who has power and an understanding of the patterns and consequences of present actions and policies (Kivel 2002:54).

The tactics Kivel (2002:50–55) identifies are denial, minimization, blame, redefinition, "unintentionality," "it's over now," "it's only a few men," and the combined tactics of counterattack and competing victimization. He credits the battered-women's movement for identifying these tactics and expands understanding of the ways in which they are used in power dynamics surrounding gender, race, class, and sexual orientation. Archaeologists who seek to build narrative tools in support of a just and stable peace can be aware of such tactics and expose them, as in the first step identified by Spector and Whelan (1989). Examples of such tactics follow, adopted from Kivel's examples:

> *Denial*: Discrimination is a thing of the past.
> *Minimization*: There were kind slave owners.
> *Blame*: Indians had not developed the technology to compete against Europeans.
> *Redefinition*: It was mutual combat.
> *Un-intentionality*: Things got out of hand
> *It's over now*: Slavery was over a long time ago.
> *It's only a few men*: Most people do the right thing.
> *Counterattack and competing victimization*: Multiculturalism is an attack on white people.

Identifying and countering such tactics are difficult. As part of our ethical stance we archaeologists acknowledge our political context. We want to decolonize archaeology, and we make slow progress—when we make progress—because we remain unaware of the extent of our influence. Sometimes we need an impetus from outside the field's traditions to make us see how our contributions are understood and used, or misused. Analysis of Jared Diamond's work provides an example of the tactic of blame.

Diamond's intentionally far-ranging books—*Guns, Germs, and Steel: The Fates of Human Societies* (Diamond 1999) and his even more influential and provocative *Collapse: How Societies Choose to Fail or Succeed* (Diamond 2005)—have been influential bestsellers, and both draw on archaeological studies. While we cannot be responsible for the use of our work by others once we have launched it into the intellectual marketplace, we are responsible for our work, including the deeply embedded narrative constructs that structure our understanding.

Patricia McAnany and Norm Yoffee's edited volume, *Questioning Collapse: Human Resilience, Ecological Vulnerability, and the*

Aftermath of Empire, takes issue with Diamond's work. None of the contributing authors disbelieve Diamond's core *inspiration* for his work, that is, the understanding that society's current ecological behavior is untenable. They do not believe that Diamond is misguided in raising the alarm, but they object, rightly and with strong scholarship, to his assumptions, interpretations, and examples (McAnany and Yoffee 2009).

In his contribution to McAnany and Yoffee's book, Michael Wilcox confronts archaeologists' complicity in telling stories about native peoples that have not served their subject well. He writes:

> While few would agree totally with Diamond's work, North American archaeologists bear significant responsibility for many of his conclusions. Archaeological interpretations of abandonments, and a failure to integrate indigenous histories, have helped support a national mythology in which conquests are accidents and Indigenous peoples are to blame for their own problems (Wilcox 2009:122).

How do we as archaeologists move forward with new concepts and new interpretations once the tactics of bias are revealed? If we recognize and fully embrace the concept that our social science is embedded in our political and social context, then we need to recognize that our scholarship cannot stand alone or offer a disconnected authority. Archaeological expertise is unique and important, and it is a valid and valuable part of the collaboration necessary to make sense of our historical trajectories. Collaboration with other epistemologies and experiences is essential.

Applied anthropology helps to provide a way forward. Erve Chambers (2009) describes practicing anthropology as necessarily being both art and science to be both credible and useful. The same is true for any applied heritage work. He sees the science portion as a process that requires distance—the scholarly distance of observation and analysis—and the art portion as a process that requires engagement—to collaborate outside of the academic model. There is more emphasis now on our ability, as Chambers says, "to achieve a common goal out of various experiences" (Chambers 2009).

Collaboration changes what we are capable of, and it changes the narratives. If we have the ability "to achieve a common goal out of various experiences," then we have the ability to create the relationships necessary for stable peace, peace that is founded in environmental and social justice. We see good examples of how historic places are drawing people into dialogues about difficult issues. My perpetual favorite example is the Tenement Museum, <http://www. tenement.org/>, on the Lower East Side of Manhattan, with its kitchen-table dialogues about such topics as immigration and labor. The model of "dialogues for democracy" is used by member sites of the International Coalition of Sites of Conscience (2013).

As heritage workers, we have the power of narrative. Narratives are what drive us; they are what we teach each other. They reinforce what we believe, repeat, cite, and fund—both within the discipline and in the stories we return to the public sphere.

The ability to change our narratives is also a source of hope. Consider these words by Salman Rushdie (1991), as he was reflecting on living under a death sentence for the act of, one could say, committing powerful narrative: "Those who do not have the power over the story that dominates their lives, power to retell it, rethink it, deconstruct it, joke about it, and change it as times change, truly are powerless, because they cannot think new thoughts." One way that archaeologists as heritage workers can be of service is to learn to think new thoughts.

References

ANDERSON, BENEDICT
 1991 *Imagined Communities: Reflections on the Origin and Spread of Nationalism*, revised edition. Verso, London, UK.

BOULDING, KENNETH
 1978 *S ab e Peace*. University of Texas Press, Austin.

CHAMBERS, ERVE
 2009 In Both Our Possibilities: Anthropology on the Margins. *Human Organization* 68(4):374–379.

CONKEY, MARGARET W., AND JANET D. SPECTOR
 1984 Archaeology and the Study of Gender. In *Ad ances in Archaeological Method and Theory*, Vol. 7, Michael B. Schiffer, editor, pp. 1–38. Academic Press, New York, NY.

DIAMOND, JARED
 1999 *Guns, Germs, and Steel: The Fates of Human Societies*. W. W. Norton, New York, NY.
 2005 *Collap e: How Sc ieties Choose to Fail or S ceed*. Penguin, New York, NY.

FUNARI, PEDRO PAULO A.
 2009 Historical Archaeology and Global Justice. *Historical Archaeology* 43(4):120–121.

HOLTHAUS, GARY
    2008   *Learning Native Wisdom; What Traditional Cultures Teach Us about Subsistence, Sustainability, and Spirituality.* University Press of Kentucky, Lexington.

JOHNSTON, BARBARA ROSE (EDITOR)
    2011   *Life and Death Matters: Human Rights, Environment, and Social Justice,* 2nd edition. Left Coast Press, Walnut Creek, CA.

KIVEL, PAUL
    2002   *Uprooting Racism: How White People Can Work for Racial Justice,* revised edition. New Society, Gabriola Island, BC.

KOHL, PHILIP L., AND CLAIRE FAWCETT (EDITORS)
    1995   *Nationalism, Politics, and the Practice of Archaeology.* Cambridge University Press, Cambridge, UK.

KUPCHAN, CHARLES A.
    2010   *How Enemies Become Friends: The Sources of Stable Peace.* Princeton University Press, Princeton, NJ.

INTERNATIONAL COALITION OF SITES OF CONSCIENCE
    2013   International Coalition of Sites of Conscience <http://www.sitesofconscience.org/>. Accessed 14 February 2013.

LINENTHAL, EDWARD T., AND TOM ENGELHARDT (EDITORS)
    1996   *History Wars: The Enola Gay and Other Battles for the American Past.* MacMillan, New York, NY.

LITTLE, BARBARA J.
    2009a What Can Archaeology Do for Justice, Peace, Community and the Earth? *Historical Archaeology* 43(4):115–119.
    2009b What Can Archaeology Do for Justice, Peace, Community, and the Earth—Response to Comments. *Historical Archaeology* 43(4):128–129.

LITTLE, BARBARA J., AND LARRY J. ZIMMERMAN
    2010   In the Public Interest: Creating a More Activist, Civically-Engaged Archaeology. In *Voices in American Archaeology,* Wendy Ashmore, Dorothy Lippert, and Barbara Mills, editors, pp. 131–159. Society for American Archaeology, Washington, DC.

McANANY, PATRICIA A., AND NORMAN YOFFEE (EDITORS)
    2009   *Questioning Collapse: Human Resilience, Ecological Vulnerability, and the Aftermath of Empire.* Cambridge University Press, New York, NY.

McDAVID, CAROL, AND PATRICE L. JEPPSON
    2007   Pathways to Justice: Exploring the Intersections between the Global Justice Movement and Anthropological Archaeology. Symposium at the American Anthropological Association Meeting, Washington, DC.

MUSTEATA, SERGIU
    2009   Let's Do Our Job Better and Then There Will Be No Reasons to Talk about the Relevancy of Archaeology. *Historical Archaeology* 43(4):122–124.

PIKIRAYI, INNOCENT
    2009   What Can Archaeology Do for Society in Southern Africa? *Historical Archaeology* 43(4):125–127.

RUSHDIE, SALMAN
    1991   *Imaginary Homelands: Essays and Criticism, 1981–1991.* Viking and Granta, New York, NY.

SNODDERLY, DAN (EDITOR)
    2011   Peace Terms: Glossary of Terms for Conflict Management and Peacebuilding. Academy for International Conflict Management and Peacebuilding, Endowment of the United States Institute of Peace, Washington, DC. U.S. Institute for Peace <http://glossary.usip.org/>. Accessed 2 August 2013.

SPECTOR, JANET D., AND MARY K. WHELAN
    1989   Incorporating Gender in Archaeology Courses. In *Gender and Anthropology: Critical Reviews for Research and Teaching,* Sandra Morgen, editor, pp. 65–94. American Anthropological Association, Washington, DC.

UNITED NATIONS MILLENNIUM PROJECT
    2005   *Investing in Development: A Practical Plan to Achieve the Millennium Development Goals.* United Nations, New York, NY.

WILCOX, MICHAEL
    2009   Marketing Conquest and the Vanishing Indian: An Indigenous Response to Jared Diamond's Archaeology of the American Southwest. In *Questioning Collapse: Human Resilience, Ecological Vulnerability, and the Aftermath of Empire,* Patricia A. McAnany and Norman Yoffee, editors, pp. 113–141. Cambridge University Press, New York, NY.

Endnotes

[1]This article draws on several earlier works, including the Patty Jo Watson Distinguished Lecture in Archaeology, entitled "Reintegrating Archaeology in the Service of Sustainable Culture," which I delivered 4 December 2009 at the American Anthropological Association annual meetings in Philadelphia, Pennsylvania; and a plenary address, "Heritage, Resilience, and Peace," at the conference, "Why Does the Past Matter? Changing Visions, Media, and Rationales in the 21st Century," organized by the UMass Amherst Center for Heritage and Society, 6 March 2011. Readers will recognize many of my intellectual debts, including Benedict Anderson (1991), *Imagined Communities: Reflections on the Origin and Spread of Nationalism.* I presented a shorter version as a paper at the 2012 SHA conference in the session from which this issue is drawn. I thank the organizers and issue editors—Paul Shackel and Mike Roller—for inviting me to participate, and I thank Randy McGuire and an anonymous reviewer for their thoughtful, helpful comments on this article.

BARBARA J. LITTLE
DEPARTMENT OF ANTHROPOLOGY
UNIVERSITY OF MARYLAND
1W   OODS HALL
COLLEGE PARK, MD 2

Appendix A: Public Archaeology in the SHA Newsletter and Underwater Archaeology Proceedings

We did not capture post-1998 newsletter entries for our multiple keywords, so the listings here reflect that bias. In part, this is because mid-way through our search process we discovered that the SHA's online "Publications Explorer" search engine no longer included newsletter entries in its search function. As a result it was impossible to search groups of newsletters for multiple keywords (this is still possible for the journals). One must now search old newsletters by browsing individual issues and using the Adobe Acrobat "find" function to search term-by-term.

However, by the end of the 20th century public archaeology writing had become routine in the journal itself, so it became a more accurate barometer of historical archaeologists' interest in the topic.

We did not list every newsletter column for the "Public Education and Interpretation" committee because the content of these columns was largely about committee meetings, special events, etc. However, we did list individual columns in which we felt that the content reflected broader movements in the discipline.

It is worth noting that, over the years, most candidates for Board positions noted (in the "statement of qualifications" prepared for the members to read) that public archaeology is "important". This was true for almost every "Slate of Candidates" listed in all of the newsletters we scanned.

Note on Conference Programs: This listing includes a few entries gleaned from the newsletter's publication of preliminary conference schedules. However, our searches revealed that not all conference schedules appeared in the newsletter, so our coverage of conference schedules is incomplete. For example, the Preliminary Program for the 25th Annual Meetings of the Society for Historical Archaeology, held in Kingston, Jamaica in 1992, does not appear in any of the 1991 issues of the SHA Newsletter. However, there was an important session on public archaeology, chaired by Parker Potter. On the other hand, the annual underwater archaeology Proceedings volumes usually listed conference papers, so they were searchable and our coverage is more complete.

1983: Salwen, Bert

Minutes of The Board of Directors Meeting, 5 January 1983, Report by the Public Information and Action Committee. The Society for Historical Archaeology Newsletter. 16(4):6.

This posting reveals the difficulties that historical archaeology was having with respect to disciplinary recognition, while Bert Salwen was chair of what then called the "Public Information and Action Committee". There was a concern about the need to promote archaeology's interests in policy settings.

Key Quotations:

p. 6: *"Generally this has been a year for archeologists to maintain constant vigilance. Funding for cultural resources management has been questionable and the UNESCO resolution did not pass Congress. Changes in the Civil Service standards for archeologists are being developed. A draft of the Secretary of the Interior's Standards and Guidelines for the Preservation of Archeological Properties was produced. Urban archeology was not well treated and Salwen provided extensive suggestions ... The National Research Council has set up a Committee on Archaeology, including eight private and four government participants, none of which is an historical archaeologist. We have been forgotten again."*

1985/1986 Public Archaeology

Session Listed in the Preliminary Program for the 1986 SHA Annual Meetings, held in Sacramento, California. The Society for Historical Archaeology Newsletter 18(3):8.

The program listed the following presentations (no session organizers listed).

LEE, ELLEN

1986   From Prehistoric Sites and Fur Trade Posts to Warden Patrol Cabins and Lumber Camps: CRM In Canada National Parks, Prairie Region. Paper presented at the 19th Conference on Historical and Underwater Archaeology, Sacramento, CA.

LINCOLN, THOMAS, CATHERINE PEDRICK, JAMES MAXOM, AND A. E. ROGGE

1986   Theodore Roosevelt Dam: Protecting A National Historic Landmark From Itself? Paper presented at the 19th Conference on Historical and Underwater Archaeology, Sacramento, CA.

SCHROEDER, ERICH K.

1986   The Use of A Geographic Information System for Historic Site Location Modeling in Illinois. Paper presented at the 19th Conference on Historical and Underwater Archaeology, Sacramento, CA.

STASKI, EDWARD
1986   Decision-Making In Historical Archaeology: Cultural Resource Plans For Clients And The Discipline. Paper presented at the 19th Conference on Historical and Underwater Archaeology, Sacramento, CA.

AUBREY, MICHELE C.
1986   Can Federally Owned Archaeological Collections Be Regulated? Paper presented at the 19th Conference on Historical and Underwater Archaeology, Sacramento, CA.

1985/86 Captivating The Public Through The Media While Digging The Past

Session Listed in Preliminary Program for 1986 SHA Annual Meetings, held in Sacramento, California. Roger Kelly and Elizabeth Anderson Comer, Co-Chairs. The Society for Historical Archaeology Newsletter 18(3):3.

The program listed the following papers:

SCOTT, DOUGLAS D.
1986   Surviving The Second Battle Of The Little Big Horn. Paper presented at the 19th Conference on Historical and Underwater Archaeology, Sacramento, CA.

COMER, ELIZABETH AND LAURENCE BAKER
1986   Baltimore's Magnificent Media Machine. Paper presented at the 19th Conference on Historical and Underwater Archaeology, Sacramento, CA.

LEONE, MARK, AND PARKER B. POTTER, JR.
1986   Critical Theory And The Use Of Media In "Archaeology Of Annapolis". Paper presented at the 19th Conference on Historical and Underwater Archaeology, Sacramento, CA.

KELLY, ROGER E.
1986   Best Foot Forward? Relationships With Public Affairs/Media Professionals. Paper presented at the 19th Conference on Historical and Underwater Archaeology, Sacramento, CA.

ORR, DAVID
1986   Excavation And The Public Perception: A Sensible Approach To Effective Media Coverage. Paper presented at the 19th Conference on Historical and Underwater Archaeology, Sacramento, CA.

STASKI, PAULINE DARCY
1986   Exhibition Archaeology. Paper presented at the 19th Conference on Historical and Underwater Archaeology, Sacramento, CA.

HUME, IVOR NOEL
1986   After The Dig Is Done, Or, What To Do With A Used Post Hole. Paper presented at the 19th Conference on Historical and Underwater Archaeology, Sacramento, CA.

1987: Henry, Susan L.

Urban Archaeology Forum. The Society for Historical Archaeology Newsletter 20(2):30.

This illustrates how the goal of most public outreach was for archaeology's needs (to prevent looting, etc.) during this early period.

Key Quotations:
p. 30: *"One of the reasons for doing archaeology is to communicate the results of our research to the public. Non-archaeologists are intensely interested in learning about the history and prehistory of their communities, and this is as true in rural areas as it is in urban settings....A program of archaeological public outreach, either through lecture series, publications, museum exhibits, hands-on volunteer opportunities, or a combination of these approaches, not only informs the public about the results of archaeology, but It also sensitizes individuals and groups to the value of archaeology. This public awareness, with a little nurturing by archaeologists, can be transformed into public support for ongoing archaeological activities in the community".*

1988: Meniketti, Marco

Political Science For Underwater Archaeologists? Underwater Archaeology Proceedings from the Society for Historical Archaeology Conference, Reno, Nevada, James P. Delgado, editor, pp. 40-43. The Society for Historical Archaeology.

This is primarily a "call to action" paper about public relations and political action with respect to underwater looting.

Key quotations:
p.40: *"But we can do something to improve public education. We must have public support interest we so vociferously pretend to represent. If it is not for the public and their education that we work, it must be for ourselves that we labor-and the blurring of any real measure of distinction between treasure hunters and archaeologists becomes complete."*

1988/89: Historical Archaeology And The Public: Retrospective And Prospective

Session listed in Preliminary Program for the 1989 Annual Meetings, held in Baltimore, Maryland. Lu Ann De Cunzo, Organizer and Chair. The Society for Historical Archaeology Newsletter 21(3):9.

It is useful to compare this listing to 1986 papers listed above, which focused mostly on archaeology and press/media relations. The 1989 session is one of the first SHA sessions (if not the first) which dealt explicitly with public archaeology in the broader sense defined in this volume.

The program listed the following papers:

Perspectives from the Society for Historical Archaeology:

TIDLOW, EVELYN
1989   Development Of Historical Archaeology In The Public Context: Historical Overview. Paper presented at the 22nd Conference on Historical and Underwater Archaeology, Baltimore, Maryland.

KOCHAN, JAMES AND DICK PING HSU
1989   After The Digging Is Done: The Archaeologist's Role In The Interpretation And Preservation Of Historic Sites. Paper presented at the 22nd Conference on Historical and Underwater Archaeology, Baltimore, Maryland.

CREPEAU, ANDREE
1989   Public Archaeology At The Fortress Of Louisburg. Paper presented at the 22nd Conference on Historical and Underwater Archaeology, Baltimore, Maryland.

SAMFORD, PATRICIA
1989   Hey, What Are You Guys Building? The Public Interpretation Of Archaeology At Colonial Williamsburg. Paper presented at the 22nd Conference on Historical and Underwater Archaeology, Baltimore, Maryland.

GRIMES, KIMBERLY AND MARTHA ZIERDEN
1989   Archaeology And The Community In Charleston, South Carolina. Paper presented at the 22nd Conference on Historical and Underwater Archaeology, Baltimore, Maryland.

MILLER, HENRY
1989   Archaeology As Exhibit: Research And Public Interpretation In An Outdoor Museum. Paper presented at the 22nd Conference on Historical and Underwater Archaeology, Baltimore, Maryland.

PETERS, KRISTEN STEVENS
1989   Mount Clare's Public Education And Interpretation Program. Paper presented at the 22nd Conference on Historical and Underwater Archaeology, Baltimore, Maryland.

HAMMOND, MICHAEL
1989   Teaching Teachers About Archaeology And Material Culture. Paper presented at the 22nd Conference on Historical and Underwater Archaeology, Baltimore, Maryland.

1989: Zierden, Martha

Urban Archaeology And Public Significance. In Urban Archaeology Forum, edited by Susan L. Henry, The Society for Historical Archaeology Newsletter 22(2):18

Henry's regular column includes a special short article by Martha Zierden entitled "Urban Archaeology and Public Significance", which deals with outreach-related issues.

1990 (March): Sprague, Roderick

President's Corner. The Society for Historical Archaeology Newsletter 23(1):30.

The first "President's Corner" appeared in this issue, written by Roderick Sprague, who started his second term as president in 1990. This column refers to a particularly controversial topic of that period – Native American burial grounds. Sprague clearly identified a number of issues that proved to be of tremendous importance in the 1990s.

Key Quotations:
p. 2.: *"The other area of concern to me this year is the Public Education Committee. Martha Williams has agreed to chair this vital function. If we are to save sites, enact legislation, or create an awareness of historical archaeology then we need to educate the public. So far we have done a miserable job, but if we start early enough in the schools then we have a chance of accomplishing our goal in the life time of our younger members…"*

"An area of concern to some of you was my method of bringing the burial issue to the forefront of your thinking. A few of the more serious types missed the fine points of parliamentary procedure and -failed to note that I was speaking as a member of the Society and not as the new president or a member of the board. The spoken and written support for what I did in the business meeting tells me it was a correct action in spite of some shock and surprise."

"This is an important issue in much of the country and must be resolved quickly before the anti-Indian label recently given to one of our sister societies is placed on SHA. It is not just an American Indian issue but has already created severe problems with the excavation of Black cemeteries. With time we could be faced with questions about various religious, ethnic, and even fraternal cemeteries. We need a broad, positive, and ethically defensible position statement. All of us need to work on this issue because there is a special urgency to fulfill our moral obligation to the people we study and their descendents."

1991: Longenecker, Julia

Public Education And Archaeology Forum. The Society for Historical Archaeology Newsletter 24(3):8-9.

Regular column included comments by Pam Wheat on the value of archaeology education for social science, science, and art teachers.

1991: Potter, Parker B., Jr.

Opinion: Stick A Needle In My I: Whither The (Withered?) First Person? The Society for Historical Archaeology Newsletter 24(3):9-10.

This is a short satirical piece advocating the use of the first person/ active voice in academic writing. Even though it is not about public archaeology per se, without this shift in writing style (which has become more dominant across the discipline since the early 1990s, despite some journals that still discourage it) reflexive writing about collaborative "engaged" archaeological work would not have been possible.

1992: Ferguson, Leland

President's Corner: SHA: An Educational Organization. The Society for Historical Archaeology Newsletter 25(2):1-2.

> This President's column highlighted the role of public education in historical archaeology.

1992: Potter, Parker B., Jr.

Special Report: Multiculturalism In Historical Archaeology: A Request For Definition. Special Report, in The Society for Historical Archaeology Newsletter 25(2):15-16.

> In this report, Potter attempted to expand the consideration of public archaeology beyond either education or outreach. At that time, he was chair of the SHA Public Education and Information Committee.
>
> **Key Quotations:**
> p. 15: "Shortly after my appointment as chair of the Education Committee, I was approached by Leland Ferguson and Henry Miller, chair of the Government Affairs Committee, with the suggestion that the three of us think about the issue of multiculturalism as it pertains to historical archaeology."

1992: Society for Historical Archaeology

In the Minutes of the 1992 Annual Board Meeting, the Awards Committee announced that Kathleen Deagan had received the SHA's first "Award of Merit" for outstanding site interpretation and public education. The Society for Historical Archaeology Newsletter 25(2):6.

1992: Potter, Parker B., Jr.

Public Education And Archaeology Forum. The Society for Historical Archaeology Newsletter 25(3):15-16.

> We included Potter's monthly column in this listing because it amounted to an in-depth article requesting input on several questions. He was clearly attempting to use the column to do more than to report on committee events.

1994: Williams, Martha and Sue Henry

Public Education Committee Column. The Society for Historical Archaeology Newsletter 27(4):11-12.

> It is worth noting this column because it recounts the committee's accomplishments thus far (several "firsts" with respect to archaeology education efforts), but also points out how early initiatives needed to be started up again. A good overview history of the committee's work.

1994: Beasley, Thomas F.

Avocationals: Expedition Grunts Or Para-Archaeologists. Underwater Archaeology Proceedings from the Society for Historical Archaeology Conference in Vancouver, British Columbia. Robyn P. Woodward and Charles D. Moore, editors, pp. 151-156. The Society for Historical Archaeology. Presented in SHA session entitled The Role of the Avocational in Underwater Archaeology, chaired by Thomas F. Beasley.

1994: Cooper, David J.

"Come All Ye Gentlemen Volunteers": Perspectives On Avocationalists In Underwater Archaeology. Underwater Archaeology Proceedings from the Society for Historical Archaeology Conference in Vancouver, British Columbia. Robyn P. Woodward and Charles D. Moore, editors, pp. 145-149. The Society for Historical Archaeology. Presented in SHA session entitled The Role of the Avocational in Underwater Archaeology, chaired by Thomas F. Beasley.

1994: Hall, Jerome L.

Why Not Let The Public Fund Your Next Project? The Successful Integration Of Volunteers In The Monte Cristi Shipwreck Project. Underwater Archaeology Proceedings from the Society for Historical Archaeology Conference in Vancouver, British Columbia. Robyn P. Woodward and Charles D. Moore, editors, pp. 157-163. The Society for Historical Archaeology. Presented in SHA session entitled The Role of the Avocational in Underwater Archaeology, chaired by Thomas F. Beasley.

1994: Scott, Delia

Florida's Experimentation With Sport Diver Work Shops. Underwater Archaeology Proceedings from the Society for Historical Archaeology Conference in Vancouver, British Columbia. Robyn P. Woodward and Charles D. Moore, editors, pp. 164-167. The Society for Historical Archaeology. Presented in SHA session entitled The Role of the Avocational in Underwater Archaeology, chaired by Thomas F. Beasley.

1995: Majewski, Terry

Teaching Historical Archaeology. The Society for Historical Archaeology Newsletter 28(1):22-23.

> Focus was on "Teaching Archaeology" – this issue has a number of guidelines for students.

Key Quotations:
p. 23: *"Become aware of the real world issues affecting the practice of archaeology. Recognize that public archaeology is a valid and necessary part of your training and experience, and become involved in it".*

1995: Cohn, Arthur B.

Archaeology, History, And Public Policy: The Results Of The Submerged Cultural Resource Project At Lake Champlain's Fort Ticonderoga And Mount Independence, 1992-1993. Underwater Archaeology Proceedings from the Society for Historical Archaeology Conference in Washington, D.C., Paul Forsyth Johnson, editor, pp. 94-100, The Society for Historical Archaeology.

Briefly described public education activities at the site.

1995: Nobles. Connie H., Lauri T. Eddy, Marco Meniketti

Teaming Up To Teach Archaeology. Underwater Archaeology Proceedings from the Society for Historical Archaeology Conference in Washington, D.C., Paul Forsyth Johnson, editor, pp. 140-143, The Society for Historical Archaeology.

Describes coordinating with Social Studies teachers to do public education work.

1995: Tarler, David, Mara Greengrass, Richard C. Waldbauer

The National Park Service Archeological Assistance Program And Submerged Cultural Resources Protection. Underwater Archaeology Proceedings from the Society for Historical Archaeology Conference in Washington, D.C., Paul Forsyth Johnson, editor, pp. 165-175, The Society for Historical Archaeology.

Described public education activities at the site, but very briefly at the end.

1995: Edwards Ywone

Special Report: Archaeology And Public Education At Colonial Williamsburg. The Society for Historical Archaeology Newsletter 28(2):19-20.

Described the seminal and influential public interpretation work being done by the Department of African American Interpretation and Presentations at Colonial Williamsburg. Setting up that department as a separate entity was part of the wider move, in both archaeology and history, to address African American content as having its own interpretive challenges. Later, however, Colonial Williamsburg merged the Department of African American Interpretation back into the broader CW interpretive structure.

1998: Clauser, John, David Clark, and Mark Wilde-Ramsing

Special Report: Historic Archaeology In Our Big Back Yard. The Society for Historical Archaeology Newsletter 31(2):4.

A report on the public archaeology event held at SHA earlier in the year.

1998: Gibb, Jim

Public Education And Interpretation Committee Column. The Society for Historical Archaeology Newsletter 31(1):9-10.

Column included a special article entitled "Treasuring Bordellos", which was detailed description of a public education film created in California by Julia Costello and Adrian Praetzellis.

1998: Society for Historical Archaeology

1998-1999 Guide To Higher Education In Historical & Underwater Archaeology. The Society for Historical Archaeology Newsletter 31(3):33-46.

This guide listed historical archaeology programs across the globe (the Guide listed those that responded to SHA appeals for information). Of the 46 universities listed, only 4 mentioned "public archaeology" as either part of their curriculum or a specialty of one of their faculty.

Carol McDavid
Christopher Matthews

Appendix B: Public Archaeology in *Historical Archaeology*

1967-1979

1967: Landberg, Leif C.W.

Problems Of Post - Urban Sites Archaeology At Old Sacramento, California. Historical Archaeology 1:71-78.

FIRST ISSUE OF JOURNAL. There is a brief section on public relations, with a comment that shows clearly that the idea of "stakeholders" was present in 1967, even if the authors did not use that term.

Key Quotations:

p. 74: "*First, in comparison to most prehistoric sites that might be excavated in the United States, an historic sites, or one that is potentially historical, tends to be more laden with emotional content for the general public. Thus, the urban historical sites archaeologist variously has to walk a tight-rope between political factions and consider the feelings of various individuals and organizations who, although not necessarily possessing former proprietary rights in the area, have no less real sentimental attachments to the area being excavated. Second, with excavations being in the heart of an urban area the archaeologist's work, more than in rural areas, is easily accessible to mass media, including both newspapers and televisions, as well as being in full view of several sidewalk superintendents. Third, unlike the relatively simple dealing with one or a few property owners that frequently characterize the public relations of the excavation of archaeological sites in rural areas, archaeological research in an urban area most always entails coping with several persons within one or more bureaucracies*".

1969: South, Stanley

Wanted! A Historic Archaeologist. Historical Archaeology 3:75-84.

There is an entire section on the need for effective public relations, although South wrote this from the perspective of the "detached objective scientist".

Key Quotations:

p. 81: "*Therefore, although the archaeologist should never take a political stand, he may find that those in political position rely on his judgment, so it behooves him to stand firmly on the base provided for him by his archaeological, historical and scientific research, and in so doing the battle may rage around him and he will not be hit in the cross-fire*".

p. 81: "*The archaeologist should be well aware of the attitudes and concepts of the general public as well as his colleagues in regard to the development of historic sites as compared to the purely observational and descriptive aspects of his undertaking*".

He does say that archaeologists should become involved in "site development" – as an expert advisor. He does make it clear that, even in developer-funded archaeology, there are archaeological questions that may remain outside of the development interest that the archaeologist has a responsibility to investigate anyway.

1970-1979

1971: Fleming, Ronald L.

After The Report What? The Uses Of Historical Archaeology, A Planner's View. Historical Archaeology 5:49-61.

This was a special report written for the journal, but was not included in the regular journal. Very forward thinking with respect to identifying archaeology's potential public "benefit" – but, notably, written by an urban planner, not an archaeologist. Fleming discussed, in some detail, how archaeologists (and historians) should have "bolder" roles in public life. He also describes how the Weeksville project, initiated by the community, had a role in dismantling stereotypes about the Bedford-Stuyvesant community and its history. The author does not mention Bert Salwen, but does mention the community stakeholder who started the project (there are no citations).

Key Quotations:

p. 49: "*Rather, they are responsible for not being creative enough about their own roles and not being resourceful enough about the areas of public life where they could assert these roles. Like planners who make reports that are often totally divorced from implementation strategies, historians and archaeologists have sometimes preferred to maintain a scholarly detachment while producing voluminous reports and precise studies. The loss we have all suffered is not merely a loss of artifacts and buildings. It is a loss of the meaning of our society. It is a removal of the physical fabric of our culture and with it the set of associations which inform us where we are- that tell us what we have come from*".

p. 50: "*This task of restoring the significance of our environment is the very real responsibility of archaeologist, historian, and planner, and it cannot wait until all of the reports are in. This task of interpretation, of making the reports relevant to the people, demands that the scholar develop a new role. Scholarly detachment, a dubious virtue in my judgment, might be superseded by the skills of cultural impresarios who will bring the exhibits of this historical significance to the people where they live-not into the storage rooms of museums or the pages of another arcane report. Consequently I have chosen to speculate about some of the uses of historical archaeology which can make the archaeologists efforts more meaningful to the communities around them. I would suspect that these uses might well increase public support for archaeological work*".

"*I think that in order to make real progress, archaeologists and historians will have to adopt an aggressive, "What can we do for you?" role when looking for funding sources, and they will have to broaden the range of agencies to which they speak*".

p. 51: "*In the past, historians and archaeologists have often worked with such public authorities only when the bulldozers were on the street preparing to wipe out the last old house on the block. There has been much public hand wringing but little coordination*".

p. 56: Fleming outlines several key steps to achieve a greater "public benefit" from archaeology:

"1. Archaeological excavations can be employed as a tool to weld community consciousness by telling the people about their historic role in a place. Displays can clear up myths and clichés which are injurious to the pride of a community.

2. Archaeological exhibits and descriptions can enhance physical neighborhood identity and definition. Working with physical planners, archaeologists can interpret and use their skills to spark neighborhood conservation programs.

3. Archaeological work can serve as a dramatic focal point for community organization with spin offs into block clubs for-preservation efforts.

4. Archaeological projects can be utilized to encourage changes in local school curriculum. School children can be involved in exhibits and sometimes even in aspects of the project work.

5. Archaeologists can utilize work to foster environmental education programs in the community at large".

p. 58- 59: "The Weeksville urban archaeology project can be labeled a rather didactic effort to support a black sense of' identity and pride in community, and by the admission of its first director, there were many mistakes made in the actual excavation due to an abundance of volunteers and the often conflicting opinions of amateur archaeologists. Nevertheless, the project represents an interesting prototype for the uses of archaeology which I outlined above. Mr. Hurley fully utilized the resources of the local community, and he broadened the uses of his project to fit the agendas of local institutions, including schools and the community college. He acted aggressively and untiringly to affect the policy of these organizations. Coordination with governmental bodies was not accomplished without much painful effort, which perhaps, only an amateur would undertake. Mr. Hurley [this was the community person, not an archaeologist] estimated that he made some ninety phone calls, on just the proposal to utilize model cities funds, which, only now, two years after the first request, appears likely to be funded with $1000. In effect, the Weeksville project encouraged neighborhood identification, aided the preservation of surrounding buildings, generated the development of a community organization, caused funds to be spent for curriculum design, and stimulated environmental awareness in the community".

1973: Hume, Ivor Noel

Historical Archaeology: Who Needs It? Historical Archaeology 7:3-10.

This was the keynote address at the joint meetings of underwater archaeologists and SHA held in 1973, and clearly targeted towards both areas of practice. These outspoken comments included a pointed critique at the reality that National Historic Register designation offers no site protection at all.

Key Quotations:

p. 4: "I suggest, too, that while we readily see the bulldozer and the horny-handed land-developer as the architects of our crises, we are less inclined to recognize the enemy within".

p. 5: "It is now much easier to ensure the preservation of historical sites on state lands, particularly since the needs of the National Register and the establishing of state landmarks commissions have made historic preservation official business. It does not follow, however, that registered sites not on state land enjoy similar protection. As a rule they don't, nor are public funds readily available for their archaeological exploration. When we get to the local level, strictly archaeological sites must take their chances between the Scylla of the developer's bulldozers and the Charybdis of the amateur archaeologist".

p. 5: "The need for historical archaeology can be much better expressed to the people who hold the purse strings if we can show that the houses, the sites, the artifacts, have a practical and specific use. In essence, the results of what we do should be something that the public will want to see, enjoy, and learn from -if we are hoping to use public money to do it".

p. 10 : "I remain convinced that education is the best hope of gaining popular support for the study and protection of historical sites, enabling those who want to help to do so, teaching those who are going to dig anyway that there is more satisfaction in finding out than in finding, and above all making the tax-paying public and their tax-dispensing representatives believe that the dangers to our cultural environment are just as real, just as dangerous in the long run, as the destruction of the forests, the farmlands, or the rivers".

1978: Weil, Martin E.

A Canadian Perspective On Legislation And The Role Of The Private Sector In Archaeology. Historical Archaeology 12:51-57.

This is an examination of the intersection between public policy and archaeology, from a Canadian perspective. It includes a good review of legislation about public policy and archaeology – and is therefore a "public archaeology" article.

Key Quotations:

p. 55: "This is perhaps one of the most serious problems that faces the archaeological community which places great emphasis on obtaining data and retrieving objects, some emphasis on the conservation of objects but virtually no concern for the conservation of the site itself or the architectural remains so that they may be examined by future generations, developed for the education and appreciation of the public or maintained as a cultural resource.

p. 51: "In order to discuss the role of the private sector in archaeology, the paper will deal with the manner in which professional archaeologists and private industry are allowed or required to be involved either through legislation or policy by the two levels of government".

1980-1989

1980: Dickens, Roy S., Jr., and William R. Bowen

Problems And Promises In Urban Historical Archaeology: The Marta Project. Historical Archaeology 14:41-57.

There is a brief discussion of the importance of urban projects in educating the public about the goals of modem archaeology (P. 42).

Key Quotations:

p. 55: "Public archaeology often has been equated with contract (or public-funded) archaeology. Many of us working in this area would like to see the definition expanded to include public participation and education (McGimsey 1972:5-19). Some of the public's misconceptions about the goals and values of archaeological research dissolve when these activities become more visible. In the urban setting considerable visibility is insured".

1990-1999

1991: Potter, Parker B., Jr.

Research Notes And Comments: What Is The Use Of Plantation Archaeology? Historical Archaeology 25(3):94-107.

Key Quotations:

p. 94: *"The issue of meaning in particular has come to the center of archaeological discourse with the increasingly vocal and widespread debate between processualist archaeology and the many critiques of it, usually subsumed under the rubric of 'post-processual' approaches".*
p. 103: *"If an archaeologist does not take control over how her data are presented to the public at large, it is certain that control over the meaning of those data will fall to others with interests that may or may not be those of the archaeologist".*

1992: Potter, Parker B., Jr.

Critical Archaeology: In The Ground And On The Street. Historical Archaeology 26(3):117-129.

Discusses the "public performance of archaeological interpretations" (117). It was one of the first articles in Historical Archaeology to discuss the "the recursive quality of material culture: and the "capacity of objects to teach their users ways of thinking and behaving" (117). This piece was important in exploring the intersections (theoretical and practical) between "dirt" archaeology and "public archaeology". "According to Potter, public presentation is not a vehicle to present "true facts," rather the goal is to teach people to question the point of view and agenda of any presentation of history" (4). Potter others built on this through the1990s and the idea unpins much public archaeology practice today.

This paper was part of a thematic issue exploring "meaning" in historical archaeology, usually identified as part of the "post-processual approach" to archaeology. The issue was entitled Meanings and Uses of Material Culture, and was edited by Barbara J. Little and Paul A. Shackel. It derived from a session entitled "The Meanings of Consumption: Ongoing Research in Historical Archaeology,", which took place at the 1987 meetings of the Society for American Archaeology.

1992: Leone, Mark P.

Epilogue: The Productive Nature Of Material Culture And Archaeology. Historical Archaeology 26(3):130-133.

A commentary at the end of the special issue "The Meanings and Uses of Material Culture", described above.

Key Quotations:

p. 132: *"Potter and this author, and the scholars working together in "Archaeology in Annapolis," and several others as well, have argued that archaeology exhibited in virtually any public setting acts to reproduce society in its current form. Education done through museums, mass media, and most other forms is not liberating. Rather, it is replicative of and duplicative of society as it is. By pointing out the recursive nature of an archaeologist's ties to his/her society, the re-productive link may be visible".*

p. 132: *"This set of arguments depends on asserting that historical archaeology achieves little by saying it is neutral. Being engaged does not involve denying the use of standard ways of verifying knowledge. But it does involve creating a link between the archaeologist's role as producer of society, one which few are aware of, and a potential role for archaeologists as shapers of the consequences of that production".*

1992: Vrana, Kenneth J., and John R. Halsey

Shipwreck Allocation And Management In Michigan: A Review Of Theory And Practice. Historical Archaeology 26(4):81-96.

This article is about management of cultural resources in contemporary contexts, and is thus one example of public archaeology that has to do with policy planning, not public interpretation. The article considers tourism as it relates to resource management of shipwreck resources.

Key Quotations:

p. 81: *"With the passage of state legislation in 1980, shipwrecks are now formally recognized as public trust resources to be managed wisely for the benefits of present and future Michigan citizens. The values of these benefits and the costs of impacts from use should be considered in making allocation and resource management decisions".*

1992: Elia, Ricardo J.

The Ethics Of Collaboration: Archaeologists And The Whydah Project. Historical Archaeology 26(4):105-117.

The article describes the history of archaeological involvement in the salvage project and discusses the issue of collaboration from the perspective of the archaeologists who work for the treasure hunters and those in public agencies who regulate them. The authors discuss the problems of archaeological collaboration in light of ethical standards of modern archaeology.

1995: Goodwin, Conrad McCall, Karen Bescherer Metheny; Judson M. Kratzer; and Anne Yentsch

Recovering The Lost Landscapes Of The Stockton Gardens At Morven, Princeton, New Jersey. Historical Archaeology 29(1):35-61.

Key Quotations:

p. 56 (In Acknowledgements): *"Morven's strong public interpretation program built on that designed for Annapolis"*. However, there is no description of this, other than a brief mention about how some of the excavations and photographs took the needs of public interpretation into account.

1995: Cabak, Melanie A., Mark D. Groover; and Scott J. Wagers

Health Care And The Wayman A.M.E. Church. Historical Archaeology 29(2):55-76.

Other than the way the project came to be, there is no mention of the public or how the church may have participated in the work (even though that was apparently a goal of the project). There is no discussion of how they "sought to involve the congregation and community", although they mention that this was a goal. It does discuss the "use and abuse" of "functional approaches".

Key Quotations:
p. 55: *"During the summer of 1992, the Wayman African Methodist Episcopal (A.M.E.) Church congregation in Bloomington, Illinois, invited archaeologists from Illinois State University to conduct an excavation at their church. The church is one of the oldest African-American congregations in Illinois. It is also the first black congregation in the Midwest to encourage the study of their past through archaeology."*

p. 59: *"Excavation at the Wayman A.M.E. Church was initiated by the congregation, and particularly Mrs. Caribe1 Washington, the church's historian. Recognizing the historical significance of the church, the congregation sponsored archaeological research before moving to a new and larger location in Bloomington. The general research goals of the project were to recover archaeological data that could enhance the historical record affiliated with the congregation. Investigation also sought to involve the congregation and community in archaeological research related to African-American culture and history".*

1995: Jamieson, Ross W.

Material Culture And Social Death: African-American Burial Practices. Historical Archaeology 29(4):39-58.

Aside from the quote mentioned here, there was no mention of public engagement per se.

Key Quotations:
p. 39: *"Archaeologists of the African-American past have a social responsibility constantly to remind themselves of "who controlled the quality of life," and also a responsibility to ask African Americans what interests they have in their cultural heritage, and how these can be related to archaeological research".* (Citing Potter)

1995: Shackel, Paul A.

Terrible Saint: Changing Meanings Of The John Brown Fort. Historical Archaeology 29(4):11-25.

This is a good example of the use of social memory/historical memory research to understand the contemporary contexts in which archaeological research takes place.

Key Quotations:
p. 11: *"Interpretations of national icons, including John Brown, of ten present themselves as timeless, rather than as the last link in a long chain of historical revisionisms. The present analysis of the changing histories associated with John Brown and the John Brown Fort relies upon this interdisciplinary approach.*

p. 20: *"An historiography of John Brown provides an account of, first, America's changing attitudes towards John Brown by various social groups and the social and political contexts of such changes; and, second, effects of these changing attitudes on the built environment in Harpers Ferry".*

1997: McDavid, Carol, and David W. Babson (editors)

In The Realm Of Politics: Prospects For Public Participation In African American And Plantation Archaeology. Thematic issue, Historical Archaeology 31(3).

All of these articles in this thematic issue deal with public engagement in one way or another: this issue was the first in journal history that dealt specifically with the intersection between publics (in this case, African American publics) and historical archaeology.

1997: McDavid, Carol

Introduction. In In the Realm of Politics: Prospects for Public Participation in African American and Plantation Archaeology. Thematic issue, Historical Archaeology 31(3):1-4.

1997: Babson, David W.

Introduction. In In the Realm of Politics: Prospects for Public Participation in African American and Plantation Archaeology. Thematic issue, Historical Archaeology 31(3):5-6.

1997: Baker, John Jr.

The Search For My African-American Ancestry. In In the Realm of Politics: Prospects for Public Participation in African American and Plantation Archaeology. Thematic issue, Historical Archaeology 31(3):7-17.

This article is notable because it was written by a member of a descendant community about what it meant to him, personally, to be involved with an archaeology project.

1997: Derry, Linda

Pre-Emancipation Archaeology: Does It Play In Selma, Alabama? In In the Realm of Politics: Prospects for Public Participation in African American and Plantation Archaeology. Thematic issue, Historical Archaeology 31(3):18-26.

This article is often quoted because of Derry's insights regarding different African American groups, and her reflections about her preconceived assumptions about different groups and her corrective responses after learning from her constituent communities.

1997: Edwards-Ingram, Ywone

Towards "True Acts Of Inclusion" And The "Out There" Concepts In Public Archaeology. In In the Realm of Politics: Prospects for Public Participation in African American and Plantation Archaeology. Thematic issue, Historical Archaeology 31(3):27-35.

Often cited, this paper examined "true" acts of inclusion that achieve the creative and active involvement of diverse audiences. The orientation is specifically towards public education activities.

1997: Franklin, Maria

"Power To The People": Sociopolitics And The Archaeology Of Black Americans. In In the Realm of Politics: Prospects for Public Participation in African American and Plantation Archaeology. Thematic issue, Historical Archaeology 31(3):36-50

This paper was seminal in framing the problematics of white dominance in the discipline and practice of archaeology, and the resulting disconnect between this and lived realities of African American people.

1997: Gibb, James G.

Necessary But Insufficient: Archaeology Reports And Community Action. In In the Realm of Politics: Prospects for Public Participation in African American and Plantation Archaeology. Thematic issue, Historical Archaeology 31(3):51-64.

This article is about writing, and the need to publish outside the academy in order to have any true engagement with the public.

1997: Jeppson, Patrice L.

"Leveling The Playing Field" In The Contested Territory Of The South African Past: A "Public" Versus A "People's" Form Of Historical Archaeology Outreach. In In The Realm of Politics: Prospects for Public Participation in African American and Plantation Archaeology. Thematic issue, Historical Archaeology 31(3):52-65.

This article is one of the earliest that frames public archaeology as an ethnographic activity that can take place within larger archaeological projects. It is also one of the first in the journal to frame both historical archaeology and public archaeology as a postcolonial enterprise.

1997: LaRoche, Cheryl J., and Michael L. Blakey

Seizing Intellectual Power: The Dialogue at the New York African Burial Ground. In In the Realm of Politics: Prospects for Public Participation in African American and Plantation Archaeology. Thematic issue, Historical Archaeology 31(3):84-106.

This is probably the most-cited paper in the volume.

1997: Matthews, Christy S.

Where Do We Go From Here? Researching And Interpreting The African-American Experience. In In the Realm of Politics: Prospects for Public Participation in African American and Plantation Archaeology. Thematic issue, Historical Archaeology 31(3):107-113.

This paper describes Matthews' efforts to produce a public interpretation/dramatization of a slave sale at Colonial Williamsburg. She describes the process of planning it, the event itself, and the result.

1997: McDavid, Carol

Descendants, Decisions, And Power: The Public Interpretation Of The Archaeology Of The Levi Jordan Plantation. In In the Realm of Politics: Prospects for Public Participation in African American and Plantation Archaeology. Thematic issue, Historical Archaeology 31(3):114-131.

This paper is cited often, especially her comments about the need to account for differential power relationships and to insure that "true" collaboration has to be done from the beginning of a project in order to be fully effective.

1997: Patten, M. Drake

Cheers Of Protest? The Public, The Past, And The Parable Of Learning. In In the Realm of Politics: Prospects for Public Participation in African American and Plantation Archaeology. Thematic issue, Historical Archaeology 31(3):131-139.

This paper was one of Patten's last publications as an archaeologist.

1997: Blakey, Michael L.

Commentary: Past Is Present: Comments On "In The Realm Of Politics: Prospects For Public Participation In African-American Archaeology". In In the Realm of Politics: Prospects for Public Participation in African American and Plantation Archaeology. Thematic issue, Historical Archaeology 31(3):140-145.

Blakey comments on the papers in the volume. One of the most useful sections deals with the "racist power relations regime" which permeates interactions between whites and blacks with respect to decision-making.

1997: Singleton, Theresa A.

Commentary: Facing The Challenges Of A Public African-American Archaeology. In In the Realm of Politics: Prospects for Public Participation in African

American and Plantation Archaeology. Thematic issue, Historical Archaeology 31(3):146-152.

A useful overview of all of the papers, especially her comments with respect to "celebratory" interpretations of the past and the need for specialists in African American studies to be involved in archaeological projects about the African diaspora.

1998: Mary Praetzellis (editor) (Note: Adrian Praetzellis was not the co-editor; the cover of the printed version is incorrect).

Archaeologists As Storytellers. Thematic issue, Historical Archaeology 32(1).

These papers are not about the public or public archaeology per se, although the idea that archaeology can and should be interesting to multiple "publics" is embedded within all of them. These papers would be most clearly associated with interpretation, a form of public archaeology.

1998: Praetzellis, Adrian

Introduction: Why Every Archaeologist Should Tell Stories Once In A While. In Archaeologists as Storytellers. Thematic issue, Historical Archaeology 32(1):1-3.

1998: Mouer, L. Daniel

A True Story Of The Ancient Planter And Adventurer In Virginia, Captaine Thomas Harris, Gent, As Related By His Second Sonne. In Archaeologists as Storytellers. Thematic issue, Historical Archaeology 32(1):4-14.

1998: Cook, Lauren J.

"Katherine Nanny, Alias Naylor": A Life In Puritan Boston. In Archaeologists as Storytellers. Thematic issue, Historical Archaeology 32(1):15-19.

1998: Beaudry, Mary C.

Farm Journal: First Person, Four Voices. In Archaeologists as Storytellers. Thematic issue, Historical Archaeology 32(1):20-33.

1998: Ryder, Robin L.

"Why I Continue To Live Across The Tracks From Sister Sue," As Told By William Moore. In Archaeologists as Storytellers. Thematic issue, Historical Archaeology 32(1):34-41.

1998: De Cunzo, Lu Ann

A Future After Freedom. In Archaeologists as Storytellers. Thematic issue, Historical Archaeology 32(1):42-54.

1998: Praetzellis, Mary, and Adrian Praetzellis

Further Tales Of The Vasco. In Archaeologists as Storytellers. Thematic issue, Historical Archaeology 32(1):55-65.

1998: Costello, Julia G.

Bread Fresh From The Oven: Memories Of Breadbaking In The California Mother Lode. In Archaeologists as Storytellers. Thematic issue, Historical Archaeology 32(1):66-73.

Key Quotations:

p. 66: "*Occasional oral interviews also recorded the words, expressions, and feelings of those who remembered the ovens' use, stories that were not addressed by academic research. These stories told by informants may constitute, ultimately, the more valuable record of this historic oven tradition. Excerpts from five stones are presented as examples of this rich source of information*".

p. 66: "*It was in transcribing that I began to appreciate other stories about the ovens, in addition to my questions about technologies, processes, and ethnic affiliations. And, I began to learn that the I have been reporting on the bread-baking ovens of the California Mother Lode (Figure 1), stories that informants want to tell about the ovens may constitute, ultimately, more valuable records of these historical features than the information I had been asking about.* "

1998: Yamin, Rebecca

Lurid Tales And Homely Stories Of New York'S Notorious Five Points. In Archaeologists as Storytellers. Thematic issue, Historical Archaeology 32(1):74-85.

1998: Praetzellis, Adrian, and Mary Praetzellis

A Connecticut Merchant In Chinadom: A Play In One Act. In Archaeologists as Storytellers. Thematic issue, Historical Archaeology 32(1):86-93.

1998: Deetz, James

Discussion: Archaeologists As Storytellers. In Archaeologists as Storytellers. Thematic issue, Historical Archaeology 32(1):94-96.

1998: McHargue, Georgess

Great Expectations: The Public Interpretation Program For The Central Artery/Tunnel Project. Historical Archaeology 32 (3):19-23.

This is a detailed description of the public archaeology work undertaken in conjunction with the large CRM project described by Bower in the same volume. It was quite massive, and, notably, outlined in the "Scope of work" for the larger project – for that reason alone is worth noting. The article is fairly critical and somewhat reflexive, discussing the failures as well as positive aspects. The cynical but humorous tone indicates that there is likely a subtext well worth exploring (see quotations).

Key Quotations:
p. 23: *"Later, however, it developed that there was no funding for an exhibit, and no likelihood of acquiring any. This was a major disappointment, and it seems to us to be typical of the systemic problems that afflict archaeological interpretation. Regulators such as State Archaeologists may require that the artifacts be recovered, catalogued, and even conserved, but there is rarely any funding for display. Similarly, if you are lucky, there may be funds to write popular reports, but rarely any money to publish them in editions of more than 100 or 200 copies (the latter being the number of copies called for in our CA/T contract). To develop a long term interpretive plan with no funding for display or publication is akin to developing a fire-safety plan with no extinguishers or smoke alarms".*

2000-2009

2000: Gibb, James G.

Imaginary, But By No Means Unimaginable: Storytelling, Science, And Historical Archaeology. Lead Paper, Thematic Forum, Historical Archaeology 34(1):1-6.

2000: Lewis, Kenneth E.

Imagination And Archaeological Interpretations: A Methodological Tale. In Thematic Forum, Historical Archaeology 34(1):7-9.

More skeptical response to Gibb.

2000: Little, Barbara J.

Compelling Images Through Storytelling: Comment On "Imaginary, But By No Means Unimaginable: Storytelling, Science, And Historical Archaeology". In Thematic Forum, Historical Archaeology 34(1):10-13

Response to Gibb and comments on the use of storytelling as an analytical tool.

2000: McKee, Larry, and Jillian Galle

Scientific Creativity And Creative Science: Looking At The Future Of Archaeological Storytelling. In Thematic Forum, Historical Archaeology 34(1):14-16.

Key Quotations:
"What was the reason that the 1997 and 1998 storytelling sessions played to a packed audience? In my opinion it is because we as archaeologists are hungry for ways to make our work relevant to ourselves and to our colleagues as well as to the public. Interpretive archaeology is one of the most likely contexts in which this can take place".

2000: Majewski, Teresita

"We Are All Storytellers": Comments On Storytelling, Science, And Historical Archaeology. In Thematic Forum, Historical Archaeology 34(1):17-19.

2000: Gibb, James G.

Reflection, Not Truth, The Hero Of My Tale: Responding To Lewis, Little, Majewski, And Mckee And Galle. In Thematic Forum, Historical Archaeology 34(1):20-24.

This was the response article to the other papers in the forum noted here. Gibb discussed the transformative role that writing fiction (about a site for example) can have on the way both archaeologists and publics understand the site – that is, storytelling as an analytical and outreach tool.

Key Quotations:
p. 22: *"The power of this approach was made very clear to me when, during the second night's performance, D. L. Smith told me that he could no longer portray William Brown in the same way during house tours. He learned through his role in the play that this mansion-dwelling carpenter might have been a far more complex character than the scanty archival record suggested"… " Storytelling in general, and interpretive historical fiction in particular-the imaginative use of conventional archaeological, documentary, architectural, and literary data-led to an illuminating, compelling view of the past; a view not easily attainable through the analysis of any one or combination of two or three of those datasets"*

p. 23: *"….interpretive historical fiction encourages reflection, both about the past and what we, as scientists, say about the past".*

2000: Delgado, James P.

Underwater Archaeology At The Dawn Of The 21st Century. In Thematic Forum, Historical Archaeology 34(4):9-13.

Key Quotations:
p. 11: *"We have also increasingly seen, in yet another leap forward, the greater involvement of the public, a greater emphasis on education, and on all forms of outreach"…"some of us have made great strides in outreach".*

p. 12: *"The number of books that speak to a general audience about what we do, what we find, why it is relevant, and why the public needs to support us-not looters-remains low".*

A "call to action" piece for underwater archaeology.

2000: Cohn, Arthur B.

A Perspective On The Future Of Underwater Archaeology. In Thematic Forum, Historical Archaeology 34(4):18-21.

Key Quotations:

p. 19: *"Perhaps one of the most effective tools for protecting submerged cultural resources may prove to be public education, through the media and through museums, a simple process that can develop a wide network of allies, advocates, and support".*

2002: Horning, Audrey J.

Myth, Migration, And Material Culture: Archaeology And The Ulster Influence On Appalachia. Historical Archaeology 34(4):129-149.

Key Quotations:

p. 140: *"The hardships faced by this tenant family, and those elsewhere in the hollows, were seized upon by park publicists and transmuted into the portrait that was drawn of all park-area inhabitants, despite the presence of more prosperous families like that of Ambrose and Sallie Corbin".*

p. 145: *"Contemporary and historical identities linked to the same place and tied by the same trajectory of 17th- and 18th-century migration currently occupy wholly divergent universes—clear evidence of the situational character of ethnic identity as imposed on the past and acknowledged in the present. Archaeologists, with our ability to capture the public's interest and imagination, are well placed to publicly address the construction and meaning of the Appalachian myth and, by extension, other more pervasive and insidious national myths. To achieve this end, however, we must look beyond our own disciplinary boundaries".*

2003: Ireland, Tracey

The Absence Of Ghosts": Landscape And Identity In The Archaeology Of Australia's Settler Culture. Historical Archaeology 37(1):56-72.

The article has a useful section called "Historical Archaeology and Heritage" which reviews the literature with respect to landscape discourse. Another useful and interesting section is "Landscape and Identity as Discourses within Archaeological Interpretation". Overall it would qualify as a good entry in any "discourse about heritage" literature.

Key Quotations:

p. 56: *"The paper considers the ways in which this landscape discourse has operated within historical archaeological research and heritage management and discusses the implications of these discursive relationships for past and future research".*

2003: Byrne, Denis

The Ethos Of Return: Erasure And Reinstatement Of Aboriginal Visibility In The Australian Historical Landscape. Historical Archaeology 37(1):73-86

This article is about the heritage discourse (in Australia) in the "public archaeology" sense.

Key Quotations:

p. 73: *"...archaeologists have practiced a form of segregation that finds no room for Aboriginal people and their story in the historical landscape as archaeology constructs it. The case is put for archaeologists themselves to embrace an ethos of return that reverses this erasure".*

p. 77: *"If white Australia employed the discourse of heritage in order to appropriate the Aboriginal past as part of a national patrimony, then Aboriginal people have employed this same discourse in order to get it back" (Byrne 1998a: 94–101).*

p. 78: *"Aboriginal use of the familiar language of heritage should not lead us to imagine they have no alternative interpretations of concepts like conservation. Indeed it seems that many indigenous people regard reburial as an act of conservation and in this they join, as it were, that alignment of other non-Western peoples who do not subscribe to the West's 'conservation ethic.':"*

p. 78: *"From the author's vantage point in a heritage agency, it is apparent that the practice of heritage by Aboriginal people in NSW is increasingly at variation with, even at odds with, archaeological practice".*

p. 79: *"Ostensibly, the reasons for recording and inventorying all these sites might be to recover scientific data and afford or facilitate legal protection, but a crucial effect of this work of recording is to raise the sites from being simply traces on the ground to a more elevated standing as "heritage". It is the detection, recording, investigation, and inventorying of sites that might be said to realize their potential as "cultural capital" (Bourdieu 1984). We cannot ignore or minimize the importance of archaeologists, in the role of heritage professionals, in mediating this transition. It is precisely because Aborigines, as a minority and largely disempowered group, want recognition from the larger society of their continued historical presence in the colonized landscape that they rely on heritage professionals to validate that presence. And if, among these professionals, Aboriginal postcontact archaeology is not regarded as "real" archaeology (Colley and Bickford 1996:6), then the chances of Aborigines gaining public recognition of their postcontact places as heritage are likely to be poor indeed".*

2003: Armstrong, Douglas V., and LouAnn Wurst

Clay Faces In An Abolitionist Church: The Wesleyan Methodist Church In Syracuse, New York. Historical Archaeology 37(2):19-37.

One major section is entitled "Local Initiative to Protect the Sculpted Faces" (p. 33), which describes in detail the things that local community groups did to save the resource – in fact, the archaeological role was fairly minimal. A good case study of community action.

2003: Shackel, Paul A. (editor)

Remembering Landscapes Of Conflict. Thematic issue, Historical Archaeology 37(3).

2003: Shackel, Paul A.

Introduction: Archaeology, Memory, And Landscapes Of Conflict. In Thematic issue, Historical Archaeology 37(3):3-13.

Key Quotations:

p. 3: *"The authors in this volume show how various communities can use archaeology to remember a particular historical event and how groups use symbols and landscapes to reinforce particular meanings"*

p. 9: *"All of the authors in this volume show how groups create and control the collective national memory of revered sacred sites and objects. The process of archaeology helps create a particular memory of the past on several levels. First, the act of finding, locating, and documenting a site is an act of commemoration because it tells us what the archaeologist views as important (see Geier; Smith, Clement, and Wise). Second, recognizing a site has potential for nomination for the National Register of Historic Places is another level of commemoration (Geier; Smith, Clement, and Wise). Third, the actual act of performing an archaeology of a subordinate group and trying to make its history part of the official history is another level of remembering (Funari; Delle; Larsen; Scott; Reeves; Walker). Fourth, intentionally placing markers on the landscape, or setting aside lands for remembering is another form of commemoration (Shackel; Blades)".*

2003: Walker, Mark

The Ludlow Massacre: Class, Warfare, And Historical Memory In Southern California. In Thematic issue, Historical Archaeology 37(3):66-80.

There is some very good text here (in two different sections of the article) which theorizes and contextualizes the use of historical memory in archaeology, which includes a useful flow chart.

Key Quotations:

p. 66: *"While exiled to the margins of mainstream memory, these alternative visions can still maintain a living presence, private and local but, nonetheless, vital. And as political-economic conditions and alliances shift, these submerged histories may re-emerge or provide the seeds for changes in the dominant histories".*

p. 66: *"Submerged histories are not static fossil forms existing in isolation from the dominant historical narratives. Like the dominant forms, they are bound up with contemporary issues and struggles (Popular Memory Group 1982). The reason they survive is that they are important, and they are useful in the present. The histories of conflict highlight this process".*

p. 67: *"This article centers on the silencing of labor conflict in American public history and how workers in southern Colorado struggle to keep the memory of one such conflict alive. Archaeology can play a creative and important role in this struggle".*

p. 70-71: *Those working on the Ludlow project have been confronted with the fact that many of the people who have the greatest interest in the site, for whom the memory of Ludlow is most important, are people who really don't have much use for archaeology, at least not archaeology as usual. Reaction among the mineworkers to the proposed work was at best cautious, generally ranging from polite bewilderment to outright antagonism. The antagonism is probably due to the doubt that academic professionals could contribute anything*

worth knowing to the story of Ludlow, although the actual expression of this reservation was somewhat earthier

p.71: *"Researchers moved from the study of history to that of memory and history making, leaving the familiar practices and attitudes of academic professionals and entering a terrain where the past is intimate, explicitly useful, and its meanings are jealously guarded".*

2004: Franklin, Maria, and Larry McKee, editors

Transcending Boundaries, Transforming The Discipline: African Diaspora Archaeologies In The New Millenium. Thematic issue, Historical Archaeology 38(1).

Even though the articles in this volume are not specifically "about" public archaeology per se, all papers in it accept, as a taken-for-granted, that the intersections between archaeology and its diverse publics are an important part of contemporary practice. The important point for purposes here is that the articles here, and in the 2008 "Forum" listed below, make it clear that by 2004, and certainly by 2008, most archaeologists working in the field of African Diaspora historical archaeology considered public engagement "best practice".

2004: Franklin, Maria, and Larry McKee

African Diaspora Archaeologies: Present Insights And Expanding Discourses. In Transcending Boundaries, Transforming the Discipline: African Diaspora Archaeologies in the New Millenium. Thematic issue, Historical Archaeology 38(1):1-9

Like most of the other papers in the volume, this introduction foregrounds the assumption that the public is important, with this ethos integrated into the work, not added as an afterthought.

2004: Mack, Mark E., and Michael L. Blakey

The New York African Burial Ground Project: Past Biases, Current Dilemmas, And Future Research Opportunities. In Transcending Boundaries, Transforming the Discipline: African Diaspora Archaeologies in the New Millenium. Thematic issue, Historical Archaeology 38(1):10-17.

There is an entire section on "Benefits and Challenges of Public Engagement" – this project was seminal in establishing a new direction for engagement in the practice of African Diaspora archaeology.

Key Quotations:
p. 10: *"Secondly, we address the scientific value of public engagement for this particular research project. Special emphasis will be placed on the benefits and challenges of these methodological approaches".*

2004: Joseph, J. W.

Resistance And Compliance: Crm And The Archaeology Of The African Diaspora. In Transcending Boundaries, Transforming the Discipline: African Diaspora Archaeologies in the New Millenium. Thematic issue, Historical Archaeology 38(1):18-31.

This is one of the few articles that focuses specifically on CRM practice as "public archaeology" in the broader sense, so we included it in this listing.

2004: Weik, Terrance

Archaeology Of The African Diaspora In Latin America. In Transcending Boundaries, Transforming the Discipline: African Diaspora Archaeologies in the New Millenium. Thematic issue, Historical Archaeology 38(1):32-49

Although the article is not about publics or public interactions, he explicitly situates the archaeological work within contemporary contexts in a section entitled "African Diaspora Archaeology: The Past, Present and Future in Latin America".

2004: Stahl, Ann

Making History In Banda: Reflections On The Construction Of Africa's Past. In Transcending Boundaries, Transforming the Discipline: African Diaspora Archaeologies in the New Millenium. Thematic issue, Historical Archaeology 38(1):50-65

Stahl's data comes from the public as well as an analysis of documentary and archaeological sources – this is an example of what some authors refer to as archaeological ethnography, even though Stahl did not frame it in as such.

Key Quotations:
p. 50: "In this paper, I examine the tensions between what Michel-Rolph Trouillot (1995) terms "historicity 1" (the materiality of sociohistorical process) and "historicity 2" (historical narrative), arguing that it is important for archaeologists to retain a focus on how everyday practices of the past shaped the present. Yet the lived past cannot be considered in isolation from how we construct that past in the present. I examine these issues through a case study of Banda, Ghana, that draws on oral historical, archival, and archaeological sources to understand how daily life was affected by Banda's changing relationship to global trade and hegemonic polities, at the same time maintaining an eye toward how that past operates today in an area torn by a long-standing chieftaincy dispute (Stahl 2001b). In a concluding section, I reflect on implications for African American archaeology". (Emphases added).

p. 59: "I focus here on the construction of public history, the history that emerges from discussion and debate at the palace, in the context of public ceremony, or through interaction with outside researchers, foreign and national" (cf. Besteman 1993).

2004: Young, Amy L.

The Beginning And Future Of African American Archaeology In Mississippi. In Transcending Boundaries, Transforming the Discipline: African Diaspora Archaeologies in the New Millenium. Thematic issue, Historical Archaeology 38(1):66-78

Her taken for granteds are perhaps what are most important to note; see key quote below.

Key Quotations:
p. 66: "I had to align my research agenda alongside the needs and desires of the public". Her article then outlines the ways in which she applied this idea to her work".

2004: Brown, Kenneth

Ethnographic Analogy, Archaeology, And The African Diaspora: Perspectives From A Tenant Community. In Transcending Boundaries, Transforming the Discipline: African Diaspora Archaeologies in the New Millenium. Thematic issue, Historical Archaeology 38(1):79-89.

Brown does not discuss the public aspects of his work in any detail, other than to describe a process in which that he worked closely with a member of one particular descendant community to interpret the archaeology of a site in South Carolina.

2004: Barile, Kerri S.

Race, The National Register, And Cultural Resource Management: Creating An Historic Context For Postbellum Sites. In Transcending Boundaries, Transforming the Discipline: African Diaspora Archaeologies in the New Millenium. Thematic issue, Historical Archaeology 38(1):90-100.

This article is primarily concerned with archaeology as it takes place in agency-reviewed contexts, and is very relevant to scholars attempting to change CRM practice to be more sensitive to descendant/community concerns. It is therefore about public archaeology in the CRM / policy sense, not the sense of public engagement etc.

2004: Epperson, Terrence W.

Critical Race Theory And The Archaeology Of The African Diaspora. In Transcending Boundaries, Transforming the Discipline: African Diaspora Archaeologies in the New Millenium. Thematic issue, Historical Archaeology 38(1):101-108.

The author mentioned public education briefly but does suggest a theoretical perspective which has important implications for public practice.

2004: Wilkie, Laurie A.

Commentary: Considering The Future Of African American Archaeology. In Transcending Boundaries, Transforming the Discipline: African Diaspora Archaeologies in the New Millenium. Thematic issue, Historical Archaeology 38(1):109-123.

Key Quotations:

p. 116: …"*ethical client*" *and the* "*important obligations that bind archaeologists to descendants*".

Throughout the article, Wilkie reflects upon the intersections between public interests and archaeological ones, and applies this to her own practice as well, in specific terms. There is a critique of African American archaeology research, with respect to its preferred topics.

2004: Stahl, Ann, Rob Mann, and Diana DiPaolo Loren

Writing For Many: Interdisciplinary Communication, Constructionism, And The Practices Of Writing. Historical Archaeology 38(2):83-102.

One interesting aspect of this paper is that individual author voices are recognized as separate in a co-authored piece. The paper deals explicitly with how archaeologist construct narratives, for the public, for each other, and for those in other professional disciplines: "…each of us has struggled with writing about these encounters, particularly as we publish in a variety of venues serving multiple audiences of historians, anthropologists, archaeologists, and lay people. As such it foregrounds sensitivity to the "public reception" of archaeological narratives, thus is listed here (83).

Key Quotations:

p. 88: *In a section entitled* "*Audience, Power, and Local Narratives*", *one of the authors, Rob Mann, notes that* "*North American archaeologists increasingly find themselves writing for an interested lay audience because of the changing contours of cultural resource management (CRM) and public archaeology.*

p. 91: *In the section Constructing Local and Legal Histories in the Lower Mississippi Valley, Diana Loren notes that* "*In the case of popular narratives, that is poorly understood by the general public. When Native Americans are considered part of this ill-defined audience, interpretations are often structured in ways that will not incite tensions between archaeologists and indigenous groups, which are often already heightened because of recent repatriation debates. Our concern in scientific c literature centers on proposing viable interpretations of the past buttressed by archaeological evidence and authoritative citations. We feel free to expose "real" evidence in this literature, and we fall back on the position that history making in the present occurs separately from the knowledge of a lived past*".

2004: Shackel, Paul A.

Labor's Heritage: Remembering The American Industrial Landscape. Historical Archaeology 38(4):44-58.

An article about heritage and the social memory of labor movements, in the sense of public archaeology as we define it. It also works within a larger framework of industrial archaeology.

Key Quotations:

p. 52: "*use archaeology to…address labor's heritage*".

p. 53: "…*part of our past should also be about remembering people and their struggles. The question for all of us working at industrial sites is this: Will archaeologists working at industrial sites be courageous like the town of Lawrence, Massachusetts, and commemorate labor's heritage, or will we choose to celebrate capital and create an official history that glorifies technology at the expense of labor? That is the challenge, I believe, for any professional working in industrial contexts*".

2004: Russell, Matthew A., James E. Bradford, and Larry E. Murphy

E.C. Waters And Development Of A Turn-Of-The-Century Tourist Economy In Yellowstone National Park. Historical Archaeology 38(4):96-113.

In this study, the authors discuss tourism as an historical context through which they examine a local maritime system. It is not about public archaeology as "interpretation", but as part of a larger concern with tourism as an important area of anthropological research.

2005: Brandon, Jamie C., and James M. Davidson

The Landscape Of Van Winkle's Mill: Identity, Myth, And Modernity In The Ozark Upland South. Historical Archaeology 39(3):113-131.

Key Quotations:

p. 113: "*These investigations yielded information that may help clarify the changing social relations and race constructions associated with the end of the antebellum era as expressed via landscape usage. Additionally, the excavations have much to say regarding our stereotypes of both slavery (and by extension the whole African Diaspora) and the inhabitants of the American upland South*".

2005: Matthews, Christopher N.

Public Dialectics: Marxist Reflection In Archaeology. Historical Archaeology 39(4):26-44.

2007: Courtney, Paul

Interdisciplinary Approaches In Crm: Archaeology, History, And Geography. In Interdisciplinary Approaches in CRM. Special Topic Section, Historical Archaeology 41(2):8-9.

Although the papers in this "Special Topic" section all focus on CRM, the assumption embraced by most of them is that CRM is indeed "public archaeology" in the broader sense, and should therefore be concerned with the intersections between archaeology as a discipline and multiple publics. The papers are not about public interactions per se, although the authors mention public/archaeology interactions throughout the volume, and assume that they are an important component of CRM practice.

2007: Little, Barbara J.

Topical Convergence: Historical Archaeologists And Historians On Common Ground. In Interdisciplinary Approaches in CRM. Special Topic Section, Historical Archaeology 41(2):10-20.

2007: Hitch, Neal V. & Craig S. Keener

A Test Case Of Transdisciplinary Research Theory And Practice: Adena, The Home Of Thomas Worthington. In Interdisciplinary Approaches in CRM. Special Topic Section, Historical Archaeology 41(2):21-33.

2007: Courtney, Paul

Historians And Archaeologists: An English Perspective. In Interdisciplinary Approaches in CRM. Special Topic Section, Historical Archaeology 41(2):34-45.

2007: Stuart, Iain

Crossing The Great Divide. In Interdisciplinary Approaches in CRM. Special Topic Section, Historical Archaeology 41(2):46-53.

2007: Lees, William B., and Julia A. King (editors)

What Are We Really Learning Through Publicly Funded Historical Archaeology (And Is It Worth The Considerable Expense?). Forum, Historical Archaeology 41(2):54-61.

The papers in this Forum examine whether publicly funded archaeology (including CRM) should be perceived as relevant by the public and necessary with respect to society. It is "public archaeology" in the framework of this volume.

2007: Purser, Margaret

What This Place Needs Is A Few More Cats. Forum, Historical Archaeology 41(2):62-66.

2007: Noble, Vergil E.

Making Connections: Beyond The Confines Of Compliance. Forum, Historical Archaeology 41(2):67-71.

2007: Little, Barbara J.

What Are We Learning? Who Are We Serving? Publicly Funded Historical Archaeology And Public Scholarship. Forum, Historical Archaeology 41(2):2-79.

2007: Lees, William B., and Julia A. King

Response To Comments By Little, Noble, And Purser. Forum, Historical Archaeology 41(2):80-83.

2008: Staski, Edward

Living In Cities Today. Historical Archaeology 42(1):5-10.

Mention of the impact of public considerations on and from urban archaeology sites; some recommendations and general support of active public outreach, but the article is not about public archaeology, nor is it an analysis of public archaeology.

Key Quotations:
p. 6: "*Urban archaeology is highly visible. The public is ubiquitous around urban archaeological sites, creating a number of public relations and security challenges*".

p. 7: "*Public visibility is not all negative. Indeed, the conspicuousness of urban archaeology is also one of its greatest rewards. The potential to increase public awareness, education, and support is always high in a place where many people regularly live and work*".

2008: Baumann, Timothy, Andrew Hurley, and Lori Allen

Economic Stability And Social Identity: Historic Preservation In Old North St. Louis. Historical Archaeology 42(1):70-87.

Describes, in some detail, the public archaeology activities surrounding one particular site.

Key Quotations:
p. 70: "*The project advances the concept of public archaeology by demonstrating how research and interpretation can be aligned with specific urban revitalization goals*".

p. 84: "*The underlying philosophy of the project was that effective historic preservation requires broad citizen engagement. Drawing upon earlier models, historic preservation in Old North St. Louis has attempted to stimulate economic investment and reconnect people to the places where they live*".

p. 73: "*Public archaeology fell under a fourth broad category, neighborhood stabilization and historic preservation, the object of which was to conduct and publicize historical research in order to promote tourism and nurture a greater appreciation for the built environment among current residents*".

p. 83: *"In some instances, local residents have thwarted heritage tourism proposals out of fear that an influx of visitors would threaten community tranquility (Hamer 1998:95–99,105–06,122; Miller and Tucker 1998:125–137). Using history to simultaneously build community and revitalize local economies remains a major challenge for those involved in the preservation movement".*

p. 84: *"When the public is offered 'true acts of inclusion,' they can be empowered by their collective heritage, which in turn may result in tourism and urban renewal as well as change views about social relationships in the past and present"* (citing Edwards-Ingram 1997).

2008: Mullins, Paul R.

Excavating America's Metaphor: Race, Diaspora, And Vindicationist Archaeologies. Forum, Historical Archaeology

Lead paper in It is not "about" public archaeology, but in some ways is critical of how much of it is framed. It assumes that public engagement and descendant involvement are important and to be taken seriously.

2008: Armstrong, Douglas V.

Excavating African American Heritage: Towards A More Nuanced Understanding Of The African Diaspora. Forum, Historical Archaeology 123-137.

This paper is about African American heritage, but not really in the sense of interactions with or impacts on the public. Armstrong provides critique but also addresses the contemporary social issues that Mullins does in his paper in the same issue. This article is not "about" public archaeology per se, but in his response to Mullins he is clearly engaging with the arguments that Mullins is making, and doing so from the perspective of contemporary connections between Diasporan peoples and archaeology. Therefore it is listed here.

Key Quotation:
p. 123: *"Mullins's article presents a strong case highlighting the problems that archaeologists have had in translating their findings in analyses that are meaningful to contemporary descendant communities or that make strong statements regarding the underlying conditions of slavery and subjugation".*

2008: Bell, Alison

On The Politics And Possibilities For Operationalizing Vindicationist Historical Archaeologies. Forum, Historical Archaeology 138-146.

Key Quotations:
p. 138: *"I hope to build on some of Mullins's ideas in ways that might suggest avenues for their operationalization and to further situate Mullins's observations in pertinent sociopolitical and anthropological contexts. "*

p. 138: *"Showing the relevance of research to public debates and policy is not aberrant in the larger intellectual world, past or present (Franklin 2001; Meskell and Pels 2005). Frankly positioning*

scholarship in the public realm as Mullins suggests constitutes a falling into step with many anthropologists worldwide who, as a matter of course and perceived civic duty, participate as intellectuals in public life (Nader 1999)".

2008: Brandon, Jamie C.

Disparate Diasporas And Vindicationist Archaeologies: Some Comments On Excavating America's Metaphor. Forum, Historical Archaeology 147-151.

A paper about engagement. The paper includes some useful comments on the relationship of the public to African American archaeology with respect to his primary topic, in a section entitled "Disparate Diasporas, Disparate Stakeholders". The focus is not specifically on public archaeology but the assumption is that publics are and should have a stake in archaeological research.

Key Quotations:
p. 148: *"Mullins cautions archaeologists about the "rush" to "civic engagement" and the potential consequences of such, but I believe that most of us are profoundly ill equipped to fill the gap between ourselves and particular stakeholder communities".*
p. 149: *"Pyburn asserts that archaeologists need to rethink their craft with an eye towards engagement before they can go out into the world and "do good. We are still not clear about the ways we should go about our engagement with descendant communities and the broader public".*

2008: Dawdy, Shannon Lee

Excavating The Present, Vindicating The Dead. Forum, Historical Archaeology 152-156.

If anything, she is somewhat cynical about public archaeology, although her critique is very incisive and well-written.

Key Quotations:
p. 153-154: *"Perhaps an archaeology that demonstrates the chronic inter-relationship between residential patterns, transportation networks, and poverty could reveal the conditions that need to be addressed in order to improve employment opportunities for African Americans. Of the other agenda items, archaeology could perhaps address "closing the achievement gap in education" through public education efforts that make students become stakeholders in research and thus more engaged in their own educational process. A more justifiable use of resources, however, would be an educational program that provides better-remunerated job skills than archaeology does. For other goals, such as equity in health care and foreign policy, it is more difficult to imagine an archaeological contribution".*

2008: Mullins, Paul R.

The Politics Of A Global Archaeology Of Race And The Color Line: Response To Armstrong, Bell, Brandon, And Dawdy. Forum, Historical Archaeology 157-163.

Mullins' response to the preceding Forum articles.

2008: Voss, Barbara L., Rebecca Allen

Overseas Chinese Archaeology: Historical Foundations, Current Reflections, And New Directions. Historical Archaeology 42(3):5-28.

Most articles in this thematic issue present research that has developed in collaboration among archaeologists, historians, Chinese historical societies, and present-day Chinese-descendant and Chinese-immigrant communities.

Key Quotations:

p. 20: *"While collaboration between archaeologists and local heritage communities is a good beginning, it would be an insufficient ending".*

2008: Zarankin, Andrés, Melisa A. Salerno

"Looking South": Historical Archaeology In South America. Historical Archaeology 42(4):38-58.

A brief description of public archaeology in Brazil, but tacked on at the end of a larger review article.

2009: Baugher, Sherene

The John Street Methodist Church: An Archaeological Excavation With Native American Cooperation. Historical Archaeology 43(1):46-64.

This was the first time in New York City that Native Americans worked on an archaeological excavation. (p. 47). The significance of the voluntary cooperation is that the John Street Church project was carried out harmoniously during the 1980s, in the midst of the raging controversy over American Indian reburials that led to NAGPRA. Although it was not characterized as "public archaeology", the article nevertheless makes it clear that public engagement was a feature of the project itself. Interestingly, the article did not appear in print until 2009, in a special issue of HA on historical cemeteries. The article includes a brief history of the relationships between archaeology and Native Americans, particularly with respect to burials.

Key Quotations:

p. 48: *"The John Street Methodist Church project provides an early positive proactive example that still has relevance for the 21st century.*

p. 48: *"During construction work at the historic John Street Methodist Church in Lower Manhattan in New York City, workers found human bones near the foundation wall of the church. The minister and church leaders voluntarily halted the project so that archaeological work could be undertaken. Since the property had the potential to contain Native American or European American burials, the City Archaeology Program and the American Indian Community House undertook a joint excavation of the site".*

2009: Gonzalez-Tennant, Edward

Using Geodatabases To Generate "Living Documents" For Archaeology: A Case Study From The Otago Goldfields, New Zealand. Historical Archaeology 43(3):20-37.

This paper is an example of the application of GIS to public archaeology and public interpretation – frequently referred to as "PGIS", or "participatory GIS" (although the author did not use this term in the article). The idea of public engagement with the data in implicit in the article, even if not articulated as public archaeology.

Key Quotations:

p. 34: *"As important as GIS analysis is to the archaeologist, it also provides an excellent tool for the public interpretation and dissemination of data, but the sharing of data is not limited to fellow professionals. Many archaeologists have walked the thin line between attracting the public to experience heritage areas while, at the same time, discouraging private citizens from going out and digging the sites themselves (Lerner and Hoffman 2000:231). The tension between involving the public and protecting sites is increasing, especially in places where tourism has become a major industry.*

2009: Piddock, Susan, Pam Smith, F. Donald Pate

A Changed Landscape: Horticulture And Gardening In The Adelaide Hills Face Zone, South Australia, 1836-1890. Historical Archaeology 43(3):65-81.

The article is about a research project, but it is not clear that members of indigenous groups were particularly involved, not does it examine tourism as a social practice. Overall, it is a traditional article, reporting on survey results only.

Key Quotations:

p. 65: *"The project aimed to document indigenous and European cultural impacts on the landscape of the Adelaide Hills Face Zone, identify and document sites of cultural heritage significance, and recommend selected sites as cultural tourism destinations".*

2009: Jackman, Greg

From Stain To Saint: Ancestry, Archaeology, And Agendas In Tasmania's Convict Heritage--A View From Port Arthur. Historical Archaeology 43(3):101-112.

Key Quotations:

p. 102-103: *"In October 1987, the Port Arthur Historic Site Management Authority was instituted to manage the reserve. During its first three years of control, the management of archaeological values languished; archaeology was only opportunistically employed to furnish specific details or clearances for tourism-inspired interpretive reconstruction projects. Since 1997, more effort has been directed towards archaeological research, both to enable writing new stories for site interpretation and to better understand the significance and conservation parameters of archaeological resources. Interest has also emerged in the research and tourism potential of the wider cultural landscape setting".*

2009: Little, Barbara J.

Forum: What Can Archaeology Do For Justice, Peace, Community, And The Earth? Forum, Historical Archaeology 43(4):115-119.

The articles in this Forum did not aim to be specific discussions of public interactions, but rather promote the idea that archaeology can and should have relevance to modern society, in particular with respect to global justice movements and efforts to create a "better" world. Therefore, they would be situated within the more activist thread in publically-engaged archaeology, and thus would be defined as public archaeology in this volume.

2009: Funari, Pedro Paolo A.

historical archaeology and global justice. Forum, Historical Archaeology 43(4):120-121.

2009: Musteata, Sergiu

Let's Do Our Job Better And Then There Will Be No Reasons To Talk About The Relevancy Of Archaeology. Forum, Historical Archaeology 43(4):122-123.

2009: Pikirayi, Innocent

What Can Archaeology Do For Society In Southern Africa? Forum, Historical Archaeology 43(4):125-127.

2009: Little, Barbara J.

What Can Archaeology Do For Justice, Peace, Community, And The Earth—Response To Comments. Forum, Historical Archaeology 43(4):128-131 .

2010-Present

2010: Agbe-Davies, Anna

An Engaged Archaeology For Our Mutual Benefit: The Case Of New Philadelphia. Historical Archaeology 44(1):1-6.

2010: Christman, Carrie A.

Voices Of New Philadelphia: Memories And Stories Of The People And Place. Historical Archaeology 44(1):1-6.

2010: Silliman, Stephen W., Thomas A. Witt

The Complexities Of Consumption: Eastern Pequot Cultural Economics In Eighteenth-Century New England. Historical Archaeology 44(4):46-68.

Key Quotations:
p. 58: *"Excavations at the Eastern Pequot reservation have been carried out since 2003 under the direction of the senior author with the approval and collaboration of the Eastern Pequot Tribal Nation. As detailed elsewhere, this collaboration has involved Eastern Pequot tribal members inviting the field school project onto the reservation,*

engaging with the research process, helping to decide excavation locations, participating as interns and tribal historic preservation officers, offering counsel for cultural issues, sharing oral histories, reviewing manuscripts and graduate theses before finalization, and conducting smudging and offering ceremonies to ameliorate the impacts of doing archaeology on their ancestral lands (Silliman and Sebastian Dring 2008)".

2011: Shackel, Paul A. and David A. Gadsby, editors

Archaeologies Of Engagement, Representation, And Identity. Thematic Issue, Historical Archaeology 45(1).

Most of the following papers derive from a mini-plenary session on "Public Engagement" that took place in Albuquerque at SHA 2008.

2011: Shackel, Paul A.

Pursuing Heritage, Engaging Communities. In Archaeologies of Engagement, Representation, and Identity, Paul A. Shackel and David A. Gadsby, editors. Thematic issue, Historical Archaeology 45(1):1-9.

2011: Gallivan, Martin, Danielle Moretti-Langhotz, & Buck Woodard

Collaborative Archaeology And Strategic Essentialism: Native Empowerment In Tidewater Virginia. In Archaeologies of Engagement, Representation, and Identity, Paul A. Shackel and David A. Gadsby, editors. Thematic issue, Historical Archaeology 45(1):10-23.

2011: McDavid, Carol

From "Public Archaeologist" To "Public Intellectual": Seeking Engagement Opportunities Outside Traditional Archaeological Arenas. In Archaeologies of Engagement, Representation, and Identity, Paul A. Shackel and David A. Gadsby, editors. Thematic issue, Historical Archaeology 45(1):24-32.

2011: Mullins, Paul R., and Lewis C. Jones

Archaeologies Of Race And Urban Poverty: The Politics Of Slumming, Engagement, And The Color Line. In Archaeologies of Engagement, Representation, and Identity, Paul A. Shackel and David A. Gadsby, editors. Thematic issue, Historical Archaeology 45(1):33-50.

.

2011: Delle, James A., and Mary Ann Levine

Archaeology, Intangible Heritage, And The Negotiation Of Urban Identity In Lancaster, Pennsylvania. In Archaeologies of Engagement, Representation, and Identity, Paul A. Shackel and David A. Gadsby, editors. Thematic issue, Historical Archaeology 45(1):51-66.

2011: Zimmerman, Larry J., and Jessica Welch

DISPLACED AND BARELY VISIBLE: ARCHAEOLOGY AND THE MATERIAL CULTURE OF HOMELESSNESS. In Archaeologies of Engagement, Representation, and Identity, Paul A. Shackel and David A. Gadsby, editors. Thematic issue, Historical Archaeology 45(1):67-85.

2011: Praetzellis, Mary, and Adrian Praetzellis

Cultural Resource Management Archaeology And Heritage Values. In Archaeologies of Engagement, Representation, and Identity, Paul A. Shackel and David A. Gadsby, editors. Thematic issue, Historical Archaeology 45(1):86-100.

2011: Gadsby, David A., and Robert C. Chidester

Heritage And "Those People": Representing Working-Class Interests Through Hampden's Archaeology. In Archaeologies of Engagement, Representation, and Identity, Paul A. Shackel and David A. Gadsby, editors. Thematic issue, Historical Archaeology 45(1):101-113.

2011: Baumann, Timothy E.

An Historical Perspective Of Civic Engagement And Interpreting Cultural Diversity In Arrow Rock, Missouri. In Archaeologies of Engagement, Representation, and Identity, Paul A. Shackel and David A. Gadsby, editors. Thematic issue, Historical Archaeology 45(1):114-134.

2011: Nash, Stephen E., Chip Colwell-Chanthaphonh and Steven Holen

Civic Engagements In Museum Anthropology: A Prolegomenon For The Denver Museum Of Nature And Science. In Archaeologies of Engagement, Representation, and Identity, Paul A. Shackel and David A. Gadsby, editors. Thematic issue, Historical Archaeology 45(1):135-151.

2011: Silverman, Helaine

Epilogue: Perspectives On Community Archaeology In Archaeologies of Engagement, Representation, and Identity, Paul A. Shackel and David A. Gadsby, editors. Thematic issue, Historical Archaeology 45(1):152-166.

2011: Weisman, Brent R.

Florida Archaeology Confronts The Recent Past: Four Case Studies From Tampa. Historical Archaeology 45(2):16-41.

Mostly about CRM but frames the discussion of public archaeology in the broader sense. Good review of public archaeology in Florida.

Key Quotations:

p. 16: "Archaeology of the recent past can be immediately attractive to community interests seeking to develop or reinforce heritage identities, and the very act of archaeology can serve these purposes regardless of actual results. In a more traditional role, archaeology can partner with more visible historic preservation efforts to bring a community-based history to local architectural landmarks. Archaeologists (understandably) rarely devote much effort to the very recent past, and in so doing, I argue, are missing significant opportunities to truly engage with the public and to contribute to scholarly debates about the nature of modern life".

2011: Matthews, Christopher N., and Suzanne M. Spencer-Wood

Archaeologies Of Poverty. Thematic Issue, Historical Archaeology 45(3). Note: The printed version of the journal notes, in error, that Matthews was second editor. He was primary editor.

2011: Spencer-Wood, Suzanne M., and Christopher N. Matthews

Introduction: Impoverishment, Criminalization, And The Culture Of Poverty. In Archaeologies of Poverty, Christopher N. Matthews and Suzanne M. Spencer-Wood, editors. Thematic Issue, Historical Archaeology 45(3):1-10.

2011: Gadsby, David A.

"We Had It Hard. But We Enjoyed It": Class, Poverty, And Pride In Baltimore's Hampden. In Archaeologies of Poverty, Christopher N. Matthews and Suzanne M. Spencer-Wood, editors. Thematic Issue, Historical Archaeology 45(3):11-25.

Key Quotations:

p. 11: *"Understanding these strategies has implications for the contemporary community, which bases many planning decisions on its understanding of Hampden's past".*

p. 21: *Section entitled "Conclusion: Contemporary Hampden and the Power of the Past", explores the work with reference to public contexts.*

2011: Matthews, Christopher N.

Lonely Islands: Culture, Community, And Poverty In Archaeological Perspective. In Archaeologies of Poverty, Christopher N. Matthews and Suzanne M. Spencer-Wood, editors. Thematic Issue, Historical Archaeology 45(3):41-54

Key Quotations:

p. 41: *"Working in close collaboration with members of an impoverished African American community in Setauket, New York, alternative readings of poverty, culture, heritage, and archaeology are discussed. These alternatives serve as the foundations of a community-driven project informed by indigenous meanings and interests in the archaeological past in order to challenge the marginalization of this part of the broader local community".*

Data comes directly from interactions with and observations about various publics.

2011: McDavid, Carol

When Is "Gone" Gone? Archaeology, Gentrification, And Competing Narratives About Freedmen's Town, Houston. In Archaeologies of Poverty, Christopher N. Matthews and Suzanne M. Spencer-Wood, editors. Thematic Issue, Historical Archaeology 45(3):74-88.

Data comes directly from interactions with and observations about various publics.

2012: Baram, Uzi

2012 Cosmopolitan Meanings Of Old Spanish Fields: Historical Archaeology Of A Maroon Community In Southwest Florida. Historical Archaeology 46(1):108-122.

Article is clearly situated within the context of contemporary archaeology, and its attendant attention to public interests.

Key Quotations:

p. 4: *"Implicit in many, more central in others, are the heritage consequences of the arguments". Interestingly, however, the word "heritage" is discussed in only two papers (Baram's and Weik's).*

2012: Weik, Terrance

Race And The Struggle For A Cosmopolitan Archaeology: Ongoing Controversies Over The Representation And

The Exhibition Of Osceola. Historical Archaeology 46(1):123-141.

Key Quotations:

p. 123: *This too is situated within a context that takes public interest into account, and deals with issues of engagement and heritage quite directly.*

p. 125-125: ... *"archaeologists can use the root ideas of collectivist responsibility, worldwide frames of view, and inclusionary spaces of cultural preservation and engagement. If employed critically, notions such as cosmopolitanism could play significant role in promoting socially relevant archaeology and social justice".*

2012: Gijanto, Liza A., and Rachel L. Horlings

Connecting African Diaspora And West African Historical Archaeologies. Historical Archaeology 46(2):134-153.

Key Quotations:

p. 135: *"By recognizing the fluidity of past identities and the impact of interaction on them it is possible to address how contemporary African communities throughout the Atlantic basin enacted creative ways of engagement, resistance, and wealth tied to their position in the Atlantic World. Such an approach not only adds depth to African Atlantic studies but engages with discourses of memory and the meaning embedded in heritage sites".*

p. 144-145: *"In the United States, African diaspora studies have taken several forms, though two overarching branches are of interest here. The first is the focus on identity and its expression, incorporating numerous paradigms found throughout archaeological inquiry including gender, power, ritual, symbolism, Marxist interpretation, and social stratification, amongst others. The second is tied to community action, public archaeology, and heritage tourism. It is the latter that can be most directly related to the past and current state of West Africa and its place in the diaspora beyond archaeological inquiry (Gilroy 1993), although research in West Africa has tended to take different directions, favoring adaptations and change in local and regional communities. It is these multiple avenues of scholarship that necessitate yet another shift in African diaspora archaeology to an archaeology of the African Atlantic, and which necessarily takes on a truly multiregional approach to the experiences of African communities in the Atlantic basin from the 16th through the 19th centuries (Franklin and Mckee 2004:2)".*

2012: Martin, Juan G., and Beatriz Rovira

The Panamá Viejo Archaeological Project. Historical Archaeology 46(3):16-26.

Passing mention of public education and tourism

Key Quotations:

p. 18: *"The management of the archaeological site of Panamá Viejo has been conducted in an integrated manner, balancing the needs of conservation, archaeological research, tourism promotion, education, integration of the national community, and use of the site, while also resolving legal problems and land management issues".*

2013: Shackel, Paul A., and Michael P. Roller, editors

Reversing The Narrative. Thematic Issue, Historical Archaeology 47(3).

2013: Shackel, Paul A.

Changing The Past For The Present And The Future. In Reversing the Narrative, Paul A. Shackel, and Michael P. Roller, editors. Thematic issue, Historical Archaeology 47(3):1-11.

The entire issue deals directly with the intersection between contemporary public interests and heritage, memory, tourism, and education. The lens is more strictly "heritage studies" than "public archaeology", but in our broader definition we include it.

Key Quotations:
p. 1: *"The authors in this volume use historical archaeology as a form of political action to challenge the dominant narrative and develop different ways of looking at the past. These new perspectives also have an impact on the way archaeologists view the present".*

p. 6: *"One strategy that can help challenge the dominant narrative is to build coalitions and include various stakeholder participants. Civic engagement can lead to a broad societal mea¬sure of communal health with the development of social capital".*

p. 9: *"The study of heritage can bring to light some of the deeply rooted conflicts among people and regions. It can give us the tools to confront long-term embedded cultural biases. Archaeology can have a major role to play as archaeologists address some of the major issues of contemporary society".*

2013: Cipolla, Craig N.

Native American Historical Archaeology And The Trope Of Authenticity. In Reversing the Narrative, Paul A. Shackel and Michael P. Roller, editors. Thematic issue, Historical Archaeology 47(3):12-22.

Key Quotations:
p. 18: *"Through this form of public collaboration, historical archaeologists have the ability to forge new communities (Silliman 2008) as they collect data. In general, cultural heritage sites draw different types of people together, often leading to new connections between groups of people that would not otherwise interact or even encounter one another in their everyday lives".*

2013: Brandon, James C.

Reversing The Narrative Of Hillbilly History: A Case Study. In Reversing the Narrative, Paul A. Shackel and Michael P. Roller, editors. Thematic issue, Historical Archaeology 47(3):36-51.

Key Quotations:

p. 49: *"These narratives convey to their audience how the present derives from the past. Moreover, they explain the present even as they shape present reality by providing the audience with a symbolic framework (i.e., the past) that enables it to make sense of the world. Historical reality is much more complicated, and one of the "public benefits" that one can derive from archaeology is the complication of these powerful, influential narratives".*

2013: Nida, Brandon

Demystifying The Hidden Land. In Reversing the Narrative, Paul A. Shackel and Michael P. Roller, editors. Thematic issue, Historical Archaeology 47(3):52-68.

Key Quotations:
p. 64-65: *"...in addition to my work as an archaeologist, I am also involved in a grassroots-organizing project based in Blair. The purposes of the project efforts are to preserve the battlefield against encroaching permits, help revitalize the local economy in Blair based on heritage tourism, and to facilitate community-directed projects to improve the quality of life in Blair and the surrounding area".*

2013: Camp, Stacy Lynn

From Nuisance To Nostalgia: The Historical Archaeology Of Nature Tourism. In Reversing the Narrative, Paul A. Shackel and Michael P. Roller, editors. Thematic issue, Historical Archaeology 47(3):81-96.

Key Quotations:
p. 93: *"...it is critical that we historical archaeologists link past tourist experiences to the present. In the process, we can hope to expose how tourism's colonial heritage continues to influence and mask the inequality embedded in modern-day forms of tourism".*

2013: Michael P. Roller

rewriting narratives of labor violence. In Reversing the Narrative, Paul A. Shackel and Michael P. Roller, editors. Thematic issue, Historical Archaeology 47(3):109-123.

Key Quotations:
p. 117: *"Ethnographic work by members of the Lattimer Massacre Project reveals an ironic lacuna in social memory, both regional and national".*

2013: Little, Barbara J.

Reversing The Narrative From Violence To Peace. In Reversing the Narrative, Paul A. Shackel and Michael P. Roller, editors. Thematic issue, Historical Archaeology 47(3):124-129.

Key Quotations:
p. 126: *"What does heritage have to do with these overwhelming needs, threats, and the alternative potential for a positive future? Part of what we archaeologists offer is our contribution to—our creation of—cultural narrative. We are memory workers; we remember what has been possible, and from our remembered pasts we imagine how we*

ought to live and who we ought to be. The problems are big, but we are not helpless because we have tools. And we have experience upon which to draw and whole communities where there is wisdom pooling up, collecting, and informing action".

p. 128: *"Collaboration changes what we are capable of, and it changes the narratives. If we have the ability "to achieve a common goal out of various experiences," then we have the ability to create the relationships necessary for stable peace, peace that is founded in environmental and social justice".*

2013: McBride, W. Stephen

Camp Nelson And Kentucky's Civil War Memory. In Reversing the Narrative, Paul A. Shackel and Michael P. Roller, editors. Thematic issue, Historical Archaeology 47(3):69-80.

Key Quotations:

p. 78: *"And we archaeologists at the park are also attempting, along with many others, to ultimately change Kentucky and the nation's Civil War narrative and public memory from one created in support of sectional (white) reconciliation and racism, to one of Union victory and emancipation. A change in public memory is critical...".*

2013: Bailey, Megan

Beyond The Battle: New Narratives At Monocacy National Battlefield. In Reversing the Narrative, Paul A. Shackel and Michael P. Roller, editors. Thematic issue, Historical Archaeology 47(3):97-108.

Key Quotations:

p. 105: *"Archaeology projects can help disrupt these conventional or official narratives, and create something that resonates with a larger audience on a personal level. The L'Hermitage Project provides a springboard for historical interpretations that are critical of and break silences about the past, and encourage multivo¬cal narratives in the present".*

2013: Joseph, J. W.

Introduction: The Place Of History In Nagpra Determinations Of Cultural Affiliation. In Forum, Historical Archaeology 47(4):120.

Key Quotations:

p. 120

Very short – one paragraph introduction.

2013: Spude, Catherine Holder, and Douglas D. Scott

NAGPRA And Historical Research: Reevaluation Of A Multiple Burial From Fort Union National Monument, New Mexico. In Forum, Historical Archaeology 47(4):121-136.

Key Quotations:

p. 134: *"We do not dispute the need or legal requirement to rebury and/or repatriate the Apache (Native American) human remains. Our disagreement is with a flawed process that, in this case, did not require cooperators to use appropriate expertise in the fields of history and historical archaeology to reach a reasonable conclusion regarding the cultural affiliation and probable identity of the individuals in question or the manner and cause of their deaths".*

2013: McManamon, Francis P.

Comment On "NAGPRA And Historical Research" In Forum, Historical Archaeology 47(4):137-138.

Key Quotations:

p. 138: *The author's specific objective in their essay is to advocate for the broader, more informed, and common use of archival and document research when archaeologists or anthropologists are investigating historical period topics. They have selected, developed, and effectively used a cautionary tale about the limitations of investigations when the full range.*

2013: Watkins, Joe

NAGPRA Should Not Preclude Good History: A Response To Spude And Scott. In Forum, Historical Archaeology 47(4):139-141.

Key Quotations:

p. 140: *"Whether they were reburied as Native Americans through a bureaucratic situation or not, the human remains have been reburied and are no longer in a museum collection. I am not sure whether the bones themselves will know or care, and the dead truly have no rights, but respect for the people the bones represent requires the humanity of returning them to a place of rest".*

2013: Lees, William B.

Comment On Spude And Scott, NAGPRA, And History. In Forum, Historical Archaeology 47(4):142-143.

Key Quotations:

p. 14: *"Lack of time and limited resources unfortunately result in poor decisions that appear to be successes because they allow a bureaucratic process to move forward. There is typically an unfortunate difference between research conducted for bureaucratic process and that conducted to answer and academic question and not bound by strictures of time, funding, or process. The challenge is to seek ways to narrow this gap and make better decisions in all realms of bureaucratically required archaeology, whether they be the result of NAGPRA, state unmarked-burial laws, or any of a number of permutations of state, local, or federal cultural resources management.*

2014: Webster, Jane, and Louise Tolson

Introduction: Material Testimonies: Landscapes, Artifacts, And The Oral Tradition. In Archaeology and the Oral Tradition: Case Studies from Britain and Beyond, Louise Tolson and Jane Webster, editors. Thematic Issue, Historical Archaeology 48(1):1-2.

Key Quotations:

p. 1: *"This issue explores ways in which historical archaeologists based in England and Scotland engage with aspects of the rich oral tradition of the United Kingdom. It ends with some observations on this body of new work as seen from the perspective of an American scholar (Paul Mullins), who has long entwined oral history and excavation in the course of his own research".*

This was a special issue on oral history, where oral history was often discussed in as a form of outreach, collaboration, and social memory research.

2014: Tolson, Louise

Toward A Methodology For The Use Of Oral Sources In Historical Archaeology. In Archaeology and the Oral Tradition: Case Studies from Britain and Beyond, Louise Tolson and Jane Webster, editors. Thematic Issue, Historical Archaeology 48(1):3-10.

2014: Webster, Jane, Louise Tomson, and Richard Carlton

The Artifact As Interviewer: Experimenting With Oral History At The Ovenstone Miners' Cottages Site, Northumberland. In Archaeology and the Oral Tradition: Case Studies from Britain and Beyond, Louise Tolson and Jane Webster, editors. Thematic Issue, Historical Archaeology 48(1):11-29.

2014: Grant, Kevin James

"And In Every Hamlet A Poet": Gaelic Oral Tradition And Postmedieval Archaeology In Scotland. In Archaeology and the Oral Tradition: Case Studies from Britain and Beyond, Louise Tolson and Jane Webster, editors. Thematic Issue, Historical Archaeology 48(1):30-45.

Key Quotations:

p. 36: *"The limited archaeological engagement with the oral tradition presents both an opportunity and a challenge; the opportunity of exploring new ways to approach the postmedieval period for the first time..."*

p. 4: *...engagement by archaeologists with oral tradition can offer new perspectives on wider historical processes.*

2014: Carlton, Richard, and Ian Roberts

Archaeology And Oral History In Northumberland. In Archaeology and the Oral Tradition: Case Studies from Britain and Beyond, Louise Tolson and Jane

Webster, editors. Thematic Issue, Historical Archaeology 48(1):46-59.

2014: Young, Rob

"Jowel, Jowel And Listen Lad": Vernacular Song And The Industrial Archaeology Of Coal Mining In Northern England. In Archaeology and the Oral Tradition: Case Studies from Britain and Beyond, Louise Tolson and Jane Webster, editors. Thematic Issue, Historical Archaeology 48(1):60-70.

2014: Casella, Eleanor Conlin, Hannah Cobb, Oliver J. T. Harris, Héléna Gray, Phil Richardson, and Richard Tuffin

2014   From Knowing Into Telling: A Dialogue In Five Parts. In Archaeology and the Oral Tradition: Case Studies from Britain and Beyond, Louise Tolson and Jane Webster, editors. Thematic Issue, Historical Archaeology 48(1):71-86.

Key Quotations:

p. 75: *For an oral-history program, recognizing that identity production is a narrative, and ultimately a performative process, is fundamental in shaping critical engagement with the different ways of "telling the past" that are encountered, and understanding the role of the interviewer in this performance.*

2014: Allison, Penelope

Conversations And Material Memories: Insights Into Outback Household Practices At The Old Kinchega Homestead. In Archaeology and the Oral Tradition: Case Studies from Britain and Beyond, Louise Tolson and Jane Webster, editors. Thematic Issue, Historical Archaeology 48(1):87-104.

Key Quotations:

p. 95: *"Each day during fieldwork, a dozen-or-so cars, caravans, and motor homes visited the homestead. As part of their training in public archaeology and cultural heritage, stu¬dents in the field schools were posted on tourist duty, handing out project leaflets to these visi¬tors and giving them guided tours of the site".*

2014: Mullins, Paul R.

The Rhetoric Of Things: Historical Archaeology And Oral History. In Archaeology and the Oral Tradition: Case Studies from Britain and Beyond, Louise Tolson and Jane Webster, editors. Thematic Issue, Historical Archaeology 48(1):105-109.

Perspectives from the Society for Historical Archaeology: